INTELLIGENT TESTING
WITH THE WISC-III

Recent titles in the

Wiley Series on Personality Processes

Irving B. Weiner, *Editor*
University of South Florida

Intelligent Testing with the WISC-III *by Alan S. Kaufman*

Handbook of Child Behavior Therapy in the Psychiatric Setting *edited by Robert T. Ammerman and Michel Hersen*

Handbook of Play Therapy. Volume II: Advances and Innovations *edited by Kevin J. O'Connor and Charles E. Schaefer*

Handbook of Group Psychotherapy: An Empirical and Clinical Synthesis *edited by Addie Fuhriman and Gary M. Burlingame*

Psychology and the Streets: Mental Health Practice with Homeless Persons *by Thomas L. Kuhlman*

The Working Alliance: Theory, Research, and Practice *edited by Adam Horvath and Leslie S. Greenberg*

Handbook of Developmental Family Psychology and Psychopathology *by Luciano L'Abate*

A Theory of Personality Development *by Luciano L'Abate*

Anxiety and Related Disorders: A Handbook *by Benjamin B. Wolman, Editor, George Stricker, Co-Editor*

Social Origins of Mental Ability *by Gary Collier*

Symptoms of Schizophrenia *edited by Charles G. Costello*

The Rorschach: A Comprehensive System. Volume I: Basic Foundations (Third Edition) *by John E. Exner, Jr.*

Symptoms of Depression *edited by Charles G. Costello*

Handbook of Clinical Research and Practice with Adolescents *edited by Patrick H. Tolan and Bertram J. Cohler*

Internalizing Disorders in Children and Adolescents *edited by William M. Reynolds*

Assessment of Family Violence: A Clinical and Legal Sourcebook *edited by Robert T. Ammerman and Michel Hersen*

Handbook of Clinical Child Psychology (Second Edition) *edited by C. Eugene Walker and Michael C. Roberts*

Handbook of Clinical Behavior Therapy (Second Edition) *edited by Samuel M. Turner, Karen S. Calhoun, and Henry E. Adams*

Psychological Disturbance in Adolescence (Second Edition) *by Irving B. Weiner*

Prevention of Child Maltreatment: Development and Ecological Perspectives *edited by Diane J. Willis, E. Wayne Holden, and Mindy Rosenberg*

Interventions for Children of Divorce: Custody, Access, and Psychotherapy *by William F. Hodges*

The Play Therapy Primer: An Integration of Theories and Techniques *by Kevin John O'Connor*

Adult Psychopathology and Diagnosis (Second Edition) *edited by Michel Hersen and Samuel L. Turner*

The Rorschach: A Comprehensive System. Volume II: Interpretation (Second Edition) *by John E. Exner, Jr.*

Play Diagnosis and Assessment *edited by Charles E. Schaefer, Karen Gitlin, and Alice Sandgrund*

Acquaintance Rape: The Hidden Crime *edited by Andrea Parrot and Laurie Bechhofer*

The Psychological Examination of the Child *by Theodore H. Blau*

Depressive Disorders: Facts, Theories, and Treatment Methods *by Benjamin B. Wolman, Editor, and George Stricker, Co-Editor*

Social Support: An Interactional View *edited by Barbara R. Sarason, Irwin G. Sarason, and Gregory R. Pierce*

Toward a New Personology: An Evolutionary Model *by Theodore Millon*

Treatment of Family Violence: A Sourcebook *edited by Robert T. Ammerman and Michel Hersen*

Handbook of Comparative Treatments for Adult Disorders *edited by Alan S. Bellack and Michel Hersen*

Managing Attention Disorders in Children: A Guide for Practitioners *by Sam Goldstein and Michael Goldstein*

Understanding and Treating Depressed Adolescents and Their Families *by Gerald D. Oster and Janice E. Caro*

Intelligent Testing
with the WISC-III

Alan S. Kaufman
University of Alabama

A WILEY-INTERSCIENCE PUBLICATION

JOHN WILEY & SONS, INC.

New York • Chichester • Brisbane • Toronto • Singapore

This text is printed on acid-free paper.

This publication is designed to provide accurate and authoritative information in regard to the subject matter covered. It is sold with the understanding that the publisher is not engaged in rendering legal, accounting, or other professional services. If legal advice or other expert assistance is required, the services of a competent professional person should be sought.

Library of Congress Cataloging in Publication Data:

Kaufman, Alan S.
    Intelligent testing with the WISC-III / Alan S. Kaufman.
       p.   cm. — (Wiley series on personality processes)
    Includes index.
    ISBN 0-471-57845-2 (alk. paper)
    1. Wechsler Intelligence Scale for Children. I. Title.
II. Series.
BF432.5.W42K37   1994
155.4'1393—dc20   94-4257

Printed in the United States of America

10

To Nadeen,
For Everything

> What greater thing
> is there
> for two human souls
> than to feel that they
> are joined for life—
> to strengthen each other
> in all sorrow,
> to minister
> to each other
> in all pain,
> and to be
> with each other
> in silent
> unspeakable memories . . .
>
> *George Eliot*

Series Preface

This series of books is addressed to behavioral scientists interested in the nature of human personality. Its scope should prove pertinent to personality theorists and researchers as well as to clinicians concerned with applying an understanding of personality processes to the amelioration of emotional difficulties in living. To this end, the series provides a scholarly integration of theoretical formulations, empirical data, and practical recommendations.

Six major aspects of studying and learning about human personality can be designated: personality theory, personality structure and dynamics, personality development, personality assessment, personality change, and personality adjustment. In exploring these aspects of personality, the books in the series discuss a number of distinct but related subject areas: the nature and implications of various theories of personality; personality characteristics that account for consistencies and variations in human behavior; the emergence of personality processes in children and adolescents; the use of interviewing and testing procedures to evaluate individual differences in personality; efforts to modify personality styles through psychotherapy, counseling, behavior therapy, and other methods of influence; and patterns of abnormal personality functioning that impair individual competence.

IRVING B. WEINER

University of South Florida
Tampa, Florida

Preface

Instead of a conventional Preface, I have chosen to reprint an invited piece that I wrote for *The School Psychologist* (Spring 1992, Vol. 46, No. 2). This paper, which is reprinted with the permission of Dr. Stewart Ehly, Editor, and Dr. Alex Thomas, Associate Editor, chronicles the special personal and professional relationship that I shared with Dr. David Wechsler.

DR. WECHSLER REMEMBERED

It is more than a decade since David Wechsler died in May 1981 at the age of 85, and I still miss him. More than any professor or older colleague, Dr. Wechsler was my mentor. I worked closely with him between late 1970 and early 1974 to help transform the WISC into a revised and restandardized battery—a test that was known as the WISC (Rev.) until a last-minute decision changed it to the WISC-R. The recent publication of the WISC-III represents a quiet burial for its predecessor, and for an important part of my past. But the changing of the guard has also rekindled a wealth of memories and feelings regarding the great man who had the courage to challenge Terman's Binet, and the vision to triumph.

I originally entitled this informal paper "David Wechsler Remembered" but realized immediately that I never called him by his first name. He was always *Dr.* Wechsler, and not just to me, then a kid in his mid-20s, a few months past his PhD. Even the gray-haired men who were my bosses—esteemed psychologists all, whose offices lined the east wall and overlooked the United Nations Building—called him Dr. Wechsler. Behind closed doors, they referred to him smugly as "David" and liked to joke that the manuals should say "Despite David Wechsler" instead of "By David Wechsler." But to his face, no one ever complained, and no one ever called him David—unless it was after polishing off the second or third martini ("extra dry, straight up, with a twist of lemon") at the occasional, mandatory, ritualistic business lunches.

Dr. Wechsler possessed a rare blend of humility and grandeur. From the first day I met him, he treated me with kindness and with a respect I had not yet earned. He was soft-spoken, yet every word was carefully measured and carried authority. He was a man of unusual compassion and unflagging integrity. He lacked patience for the pomp and circumstance and protocol that permeated the first few corporate meetings that addressed the issue of a WISC revision. The meetings were tedious affairs, spiced with old recollections by Project Directors Past, and an incredible amount of weasel wording and bush circling by distinguished executives who couldn't quite mouth the words, "Dr. Wechsler, there are a number of black psychologists who don't much care for the WISC, and there have been some serious complaints with a lot of specific items."

At the end of the third meeting, when once more nothing was accomplished, Dr. Wechsler ended the meeting by stating simply that this was the last group meeting; from now on, he said, "Alan will come alone to my apartment, and we'll hammer out the revised WISC." And that's exactly what happened. I'd take a taxi to his East Side Manhattan apartment, and for two or three hours, week after week, we'd engage in friendly battle. He insisted that I be totally honest and tell him every thought and concern. I couldn't do that at first, but I soon realized it was the most prudent course of action. After the first meeting, he told me to put down my pen. He then talked for about 20 minutes, recounting his version of what had just transpired; he revealed every one of my "secret" feelings and perceptions, unraveling in intricate detail my attitudes and emotions about every issue we discussed and each decision we had made. I just stared at him, probably looking like retarded Benny of *LA Law,* and said nothing; how could I argue, when we both knew he was on the mark with every comment. I had always prided myself on my poker face, but I was face to face with the master clinician—the best one I would ever meet.

From that point on, I never held back anything. He would usually respond calmly, but occasionally I'd strike a raw nerve, and his grandfatherly smile would evaporate. His temples would start to pulse, and his entire face and scalp would turn crimson. I'd unconsciously move my chair back in self-protection, the way I did when I tested hard-core prisoners on the old WAIS and had to ask the question, "Why should we keep away from bad company?" I struck that exposed nerve when I urged him to eliminate the Comprehension item about walking away from a fight if someone much smaller starts to fight with you. The argument that you can't walk away from any fight in a black ghetto just added fuel to his rage. When I suggested, at a later meeting, that he just *had* to get rid of the item, "Why should women and children be saved first in a shipwreck?" or incur the wrath of the new wave of militant feminists, his response was instant. With red face and pulsing head, he stood up, leaned on his desk with extended arms, and said as if he were firing a semiautomatic, "Chivalry may be dying. Chivalry may be dead. *But it will not die on the WISC.*"

So I waited a couple of weeks before bringing up those two items again. That particular battle ended in a tie; the fight item stayed, the shipwreck item was mercifully dropped. Though it was a little like going one-on-one with Michael Jordan, I relished those meetings. He had a good sense of humor, but not when it came to eliminating items. Only once did he readily agree to dropping an item: "What should you do if you see a train approaching a broken track?" I mentioned that if a 6- or 7-year-old child sees a train coming near a broken track, waving a white flag is not the brightest thing in the world to do; a 3-point answer on a 2-1-0 scale is "Run like hell." He laughed.

One Saturday, I drove to Manhattan with my then 5-year-old daughter Jennie to deliver a manual chapter to Dr. Wechsler. For 15 minutes or so, he charmed her, played with her, and joked with her, all the while maintaining his keen clinician's eye. I still remember his nod of approval when she responded to his question "In what way are a mommy and a daddy alike?" by saying, "They're the same 'cause they're both parents—and both human beans too, y'know." He looked at me, smiled broadly, and said, "Jennie is *very* smart—'y'know.'" I took Jennie's hand and walked to the elevator. The elevator operator, who knew me quite well by then, tried to engage me in conversation, but I didn't hear a word. In fact, I didn't need the elevator, I could have flown down the eight stories. *Wechsler had just told me my daughter was very smart!* I couldn't have been more elated if Freud had told me she had a nice personality or if Bert Parks had said she was beautiful.

Dr. Wechsler liked to test me too. Whenever I arrived for our meetings, his wife Ruth always greeted me and ushered me into his study. He had one of those lamps that turned on and off by touching it—common now, but not then. I was biding my time by turning it on and off, experimenting to see how light a touch would trigger the mechanism. Out of the corner of my eye, I saw Dr. Wechsler standing in the hallway studying me, smiling, enjoying himself. I wondered how long this consummate clinician had been there, and hoped I hadn't done anything really inappropriate.

I especially enjoyed Dr. Wechsler's warm, human side, which emerged in casual moments when he didn't have to be "on." The serious and sometimes gruff side came out in business meetings, and the occasional animal rage was reserved for anyone who challenged the perfection of nearly any of his hand-picked, time-tested items, especially one that had its roots in his original Wechsler-Bellevue scales. But he displayed unabashed boylike enthusiasm when he showed off materials for the new subtests he was constantly working on (at age 75!)—his favorite was a set of three Chinese dolls that had to be tapped in the right sequence—or when he sifted through a lifetime of comic strips that he saved for new Picture Arrangement items. And his eyes twinkled when he talked about his grandchildren; or reminisced about visiting Freud in Vienna; or spoke warmly about spending a week at the home of former Israeli Defense Minister Moshe Dayan and his wife; or boasted sheepishly about being greeted at the Bucharest Airport by the

King of Romania (his birthplace in 1896); or played for over an hour with our son James, then 7 months old and called Jamie, when he and Ruth visited my family in Athens, Georgia, in April 1975.

That visit was completely unexpected. I had called him to ask if he would speak by conference phone to my Intelligence Testing class the first year I was at the University of Georgia. I was crushed when he said he didn't want to do it; I had assured my class that my friend Dr. Wechsler would say yes (they already doubted that I had even met the man). A couple of days later, he sent me a letter saying that he didn't like talking to people unless he could see them. "I would prefer, and would suggest instead, a face-to-face session at the University," he wrote. "No fee for talk, but reimbursement for travel." My school psychology students enjoyed a private question-and-answer session with him. Later in the day, I experienced high anxiety introducing him to a standing-room-only auditorium crowd of students and faculty.

That evening, Nadeen and I had dinner with the Wechslers, and we were looking forward to a bit of quiet relaxation. It was not to be. Dr. Wechsler had two things that were heavy on his mind. One was the true meaning of being an intelligent adult (he started to doubt the WAIS's effectiveness for measuring adult IQ when he realized that he had trouble solving Block Design items quickly). His other concern was the Dan Rather IQ special that was to air for the first time that night, and he absolutely didn't want to miss seeing it in his hotel room. He kept asking Nadeen and me how one could tell if an adult was smart, and no matter what we answered, he probed and challenged us until we were limp, until he was satisfied that we had covered every aspect of the issue. He confided to us that he was starting to work on a test called the Wechsler Intelligence Scale for the Elderly; had he published it, the test would have had the best acronym ever—W.I.S.E. Though the meal wasn't as relaxed as we had hoped, he was quick to praise our ideas and took a few notes on his napkin. (Years later, we would think back to that disucssion when we began developing the Kaufman Adolescent and Adult Intelligence Test, or KAIT.)

When Dr. Wechsler relented in his questioning of us, he revealed his almost desperate sadness about the Dan Rather special. Though he wouldn't see it until it aired that night, he had been tipped off by an acquaintance from the TV station that the program was blatantly anti-IQ testing. Dr. Wechsler and Ruth recalled how Rather had come to their apartment, charmed them during the interview and videotaping, and told them how much he personally valued the IQ concept and how important the Wechsler scales were to the world. Rather's demeanor led Dr. Wechsler to say things candidly and—in retrospect—a bit recklessly. He was chastising himself during the meal, but mostly he was furious at Rather's behavior. Dr. Wechsler was honest and straightforward and just couldn't fathom duplicity in someone else. The next morning, after the TV show had confirmed Dr. Wechsler's worst fears, we drove to the airport in almost total silence. When he did speak, it was clear that Dr. Wechsler's anger was under control, but he was deeply wounded by the dishonesty, the blatant abuse of trust. And he felt that the strong anti-IQ statements by "people who should know better" were a personal attack on his life's work.

The kindness that Dr. Wechsler showed me by traveling to Georgia to meet with my students was typical of how he treated me the whole time I knew him. He was aware of the steep status hierarchy that existed at The Psychological Corporation, and he made sure to praise me in the presence of the upper echelon. He consistently treated my ideas with respect and never dismissed them—even the stupid ones—without first thinking about them carefully (unless I was suggesting deleting an item). He trusted me in all aspects of test construction and deferred to my knowledge of psychometrics; when he questioned a statistical decision, he would usually give in, saying, "I'm just a clinician." It wasn't until the WISC-R was nearing publication that I found out from someone else that Dr. Wechsler had studied statistics under Charles Spearman and Karl Pearson in London after World War I.

One day, he decided that he wanted me to coauthor a book on children's intelligence with him, and he made the announcement in front of one of my bosses. It was the first I'd heard about it, and it was lucky I was sitting down when he said it. When I took the position at the University of Georgia, just after the WISC-R was published, we still planned on writing the book together. During his visit, he told me that he just didn't have the energy to participate too much in the writing of the book, and that he thought it would be hard to collaborate from a distance. But he made me promise to write a book devoted to the WISC-R, and I gave him my word. Those were the seeds for *Intelligent Testing with the WISC-R.*

The standardization of the WISC-R seemed to take forever to Dr. Wechsler, and he wanted the test to come out while he could still enjoy it. He would ask me in mock seriousness whether a standardization was even necessary. "After all," he'd say in a quiet voice while giving me a conspiratorial smile, "*we* know how well the children are going to perform on all those subtests, don't we? So why bother with all that standardization testing?" He was joking, but it was no joke that he believed firmly all he needed was 15 minutes or so of personal interview and a test item or two, and he could pinpoint a person's IQ within a few points and diagnose any pathology. He insisted that he could diagnose clinical patients by their answer to the question, "What is the population of the United States?" I never doubted that he could back up his boast. He didn't do too badly with his one-item, 15-minute assessment of my daughter Jennie's intelligence more than 20 years ago; she made Phi Beta Kappa in college, and has now almost completed her PhD in clinical psychology.

And how would Dr. Wechsler evaluate the WISC-III? Well, he'd like the artwork, but he'd insist that it wasn't necessary. The black-and-white pictures worked fine before, so why mess with them? And he'd be impressed by the immaculate standardization and supersophisticated psychometric treatment of the data, but he wouldn't admit it to anyone. Instead, he'd argue that his all-Coney Island standardization of the original Wechsler-Bellevue was pretty darned good; and he'd wonder aloud why you needed something called confirmatory factor analysis to tell the world what he knew axiomatically back in the early 1930s—that his scales primarily measured Verbal and Performance intelligence.

He wouldn't be too interested in the improved bottom and top for several subtests, most notably Arithmetic, which now gives bonus points for the six hardest items. He rejected most attempts that I made to add easy and hard items to the WISC-R, saying firmly, "My scales are meant for people with average or near-average intelligence, clinical patients who score between 70 and 130. They are *clinical* tests." When I reminded him that psychologists commonly use his scales for the extremes, and want to make distinctions within the "below 70" and "above 130" groups, he answered, "Then that is their misfortune. It's not what I tell them to do, and it's not what a good clinician ought to do. They should know better."

He wouldn't care much for the new Object Assembly item, the cut-up soccer ball. How do I know? Because when we were developing new items for the WISC-R tryout, I brought him a dozen envelopes, each with a cut-up puzzle I had made. I opened each envelope and assembled each puzzle, and he immediately said "Yes" or "No" to each one. He liked three, and hated nine. I couldn't figure out his decision rule, so he forced me to study the ones he liked and the ones he rejected, but every hypothesis I offered was wrong. Finally, with a touch of exasperation at my denseness, he said, "Don't you see. My Object Assembly items must have at least one puzzle piece that tells the person at once what the object is—like the horse's head or the front of the car. I don't want them fumbling around like one of Thorndike's cats or monkeys. I want them to know right away what they've got to put together." He also would not have permitted bonus points on the WPPSI-R for Block Design or the new Object Assembly subtest; as a clinician and grandfather he knew that even very bright young children often respond to puzzles like the fireman in the old Binet item who smoked a cigar before putting out the fire.

But the soccer ball and WPPSI-R time bonuses wouldn't have made Dr. Wechsler's temples start to pulse. That would have happened when he saw the Picture Arrangement items. He loved to expose examinees to emotion-laden situations, to watch how they solved the problems, to listen to their spontaneous comments, to study their reactions to danger, to conflict, to authority, to violence. "Where's the boxing match?" he would have stormed. "Replaced by a girl on a slide! And what happened to the burglar? And look what they did to the *fire* item! Instead of burning down his house, the kid's a damned hero!" And he would have been incensed at the emasculation of the *bench* item. In the old item, "Some poor sap gets hit by the bench and then gets clobbered in a fight. Great stuff! But now they just kiss and make up."

Dr. Wechsler also wouldn't have been too pleased with the elimination of *beer-wine* in Similarities or of *knife* and *gamble* in Vocabulary—all potent clinical stimuli. He never worried much about a person missing an item or two or three because of its clinical content. More than once, he'd chide me, until it finally sunk in, "First and foremost, the Wechsler scales are clinical tests—not psychometric tests but clinical tests." That was why he got so upset when someone complained about the unfairness of this or that item. What's a couple of items to a good clinician? He never could really accept the stupid way so many people interpreted his tests, with formulas, and cut-off points, and the like; it's not what he had ever planned for his clinical Wechsler scales.

When Nadeen and I started to develop the K-ABC back in 1978, the Wechsler influence was strong, although we differed from him in believing that tests such as Information and Vocabulary really measure achievement for schoolchildren, not IQ. (He didn't much care for my suggestion back in 1971 to pull out a few subtests from the Verbal Scale and offer the clinician a separate "Cultural Quotient.") Maybe it was because I felt a bit guilty at departing from his theory for our intelligence test, or maybe I just got too involved with too many things, but I stopped calling and writing Dr. Wechsler during the last years of his life. I didn't realize how much that hurt him until Ruth wrote to me, in response to our letter of sympathy, "I must tell you, Alan, he was very fond of you and admired you very much. I'm sorry you didn't write once in a while as he talked about you and what a pleasure it was to work with you on the WISC-R."

I can't undo it, though I wish I could, and her words still sting when I read them. But I try to focus instead on how much Dr. Wechsler taught me, both as a person and clinician. I was fortunate beyond words to have his life cross mine, to work so closely with this legend for several years, to have him as a mentor and friend. Those at The Psychological Corporation who did such a marvelous job of revising the WISC-R and assembling the WISC-III undoubtedly took for granted what I fervently wished for as a young Assistant Director two decades ago: the freedom to make objective item and subtest decisions without the interference and subjective whims of the author.

Little did I realize then that those battles with the Master would shape my own development as a test author and trainer of school psychologists, and would remain forever etched—fresh and vibrant and poignant—in my memory. The Project Directors of the "ISC-III" and the "PPSI-R" have no notion of their loss; they never knew the man behind the "W."

ALAN S. KAUFMAN

Escondido, California
August 1994

Acknowledgments

I would like to sincerely thank the following people for their important contributions to the case reports that appear throughout the book: Dr. Yossi Adir, Dr. Kristee Beres, Ms. Susan Glatz, Mr. Jose Gonzalez, Dr. Dana Grossman, Dr. Ira Grossman, Ms. Danica Katz, Ms. Jennie Kaufman, Dr. Nadeen Kaufman, Dr. Alan Lincoln, Ms. Ana Parente, Ms. Patricia Petterson, and Dr. Paul Randolph. Drs. Nadeen Kaufman and Ira Grossman merit my special thanks for permission to use the case reports from the hospital clinic that Nadeen directs and Ira supervises. Ms. Margaret Bostrom and Ms. Jennie Kaufman were extremely helpful in conducting literature searches and tracking down articles. Dr. Ed Dougherty and Ms. Karen Tuttle helped me refine the logic of the interpretive approach during several helpful discussions, and James Kaufman gave me much assistance in the preparation of the manuscript. Dr. Bruce Bracken and Dr. Steve McCallum kindly sent me manuscripts and reviews on the WISC-III prior to their publication in the *Journal of Psychoeducational Assessment,* which made my task easier. I also thank Dr. John Horn for his consultation regarding his fluid-crystallized theory of intelligence. I am grateful to Assistant Dean Dr. James McLean, Dean Rod Roth, and President E. Roger Sayers for their continued support of my research and writing in my capacity as Research Professor at the University of Alabama.

Writing a book is an arduous, time-consuming task that requires the patience and understanding of the family members who are close by, and want attention, but who cheerfully tolerate the constant tapping of the word processor keyboard. For their love and kindness, I thank Nadeen, my son James, and my granddaughter Nicole.

Nadeen has been a special source of inspiration and help to me in the project of writing this book. In addition to her patience and her generosity in contributing many illustrative reports, she graciously shared her expertise with me in clinical assessment and remediation, and served as a constant sounding board for the ideas and approaches that appear throughout the book. She has been there for me, in every way, for more than 30 years, and has made my life complete.

A.S.K.

Contents

List of Tables   xxi

1. INTELLIGENT TESTING   1

Opponents of IQ Testing in the Year 2000 ± 5   2
Basic Tenets of the Intelligent Testing Approach   6
Integration of the Basic Tenets of Intelligent Testing   14
A Response to the Critics   25
A Practical Issue: WISC-III versus WISC-R, WPPSI-R,
    WAIS-R   37

2. ABILITIES MEASURED BY THE WISC-III SUBTESTS
   AND THE CLINICAL LORE THAT SURROUNDS THEM   41

Ways of Analyzing Each WISC-III Subtest   41
Subtest-by-Subtest Analysis   63

3. SEVEN STEPS FOR INTERPRETING THE WISC-III PROFILE:
   FROM IQs TO FACTOR INDEXES TO SCALED SCORES   97

Step 1. Interpret the Full Scale IQ   98
Step 2. Determine Whether the Verbal-Performance IQ
    Discrepancy Is Statistically Significant   99
Step 3. Determine Whether the Verbal-Performance IQ
    Discrepancy Is Interpretable—Or Whether the Verbal
    Comprehension and Perceptual Organization Factor
    Indexes Should Be Interpreted Instead   102
Step 4. Determine Whether the Verbal-Performance IQ
    Discrepancy (Or VC-PO Discrepancy) Is Abnormally
    Large   115
Step 5. Interpret the Meaning of the Global Verbal and
    Nonverbal Dimensions and the Meaning of the Small
    Factors   122
Step 6. Interpret Significant Strengths and Weaknesses in
    the WISC-III Subtest Profile   122
Step 7. Generate Hypotheses about the Fluctuations in the
    WISC-III Subtest Profile   132

Overview of the Seven Steps   133
Exceptions to the Rules   133

4. INTERPRETING VERBAL-NONVERBAL DISCREPANCIES
(V-P IQ AND VC-PO INDEX)   144

Overview of Verbal-Nonverbal Differences   144
What WISC-III Verbal-Nonverbal Discrepancies
    Measure   150
Variables Associated with Input of Information   152
Variables Associated with Integration and Storage   163
Variables Pertaining to Output   188
Illustrative Case Report   201

5. THE "VALIDITY" FACTORS: FREEDOM FROM
DISTRACTIBILITY AND PROCESSING SPEED   209

The FD and PS Factors as Validity Scales   210
The WISC-R Distractibility Triad   211
Mean WISC-III Factor Indexes for Exceptional Samples   214
What about the ACID Profile?   216
The SCAD Profile   219
Interpreting the Freedom from Distractibility Factor   225
Interpreting the Processing Speed Factor   241
Illustrative Case Reports   251

6. INTERPRETING SUBTEST PROFILES   269

A Philosophy of Profile Attack   271
Tables to Aid in WISC-III Subtest Interpretation   273
The Information-Processing Model   284
A Systematic Method for Interpreting Subtest
    Fluctuations   304
Hypotheses and Recommendations   324
Illustrative Case Reports   330

7. COMPREHENSIVE CLINICAL AND
PSYCHOEDUCATIONAL CASE STUDIES   347

References   403

Author Index   431

Subject Index   439

List of Tables

Table 2.1. Proportion of the Variance of Each Subtest Attributed to Each of the Four Factors, to Other Abilities, and to Error (ages 6–16 years) 46

Table 2.2. Proportion of the Variance of Each Subtest Attributed to the Verbal and Performance Factors When Only Two Factors Are Rotated (ages 6–16 years) 48

Table 2.3. Classification of WISC-III Subtests According to the Operations and Content Dimensions of Guilford's (1967) Original SOI Model 54

Table 3.1. Size of the Difference Required for Statistical Significance When Comparing Verbal IQ with Performance IQ and VC Index with PO Index 102

Table 3.2. Size of the Difference Required for Abnormality When Comparing Verbal IQ to Performance IQ and VC Index to PO Index 114

Table 3.3. Size of the Difference Required for Significance When Comparing a Child's Subtest Score with the Average of His or Her Scores on Several Subtests 127

Table 3.4. Summary of Seven Steps for Interpreting WISC-III Profiles 134–135

Table 4.1. Factor Loadings on the WISC-III Verbal and Performance Factors When Only Two Factors Are Rotated 165

Table 4.2. Correlations of DAS Standard Scores with Verbal and Nonverbal Scores on the WISC-III and WISC-R 170

Table 4.3. Correlations of WISC-R Verbal and Performance IQs with Scores on the Seven Horn Factors Measured by the WJ-R Cognitive Ability Scales ($N = 72$) 177

Table 4.4.   Maximum Possible Scaled Score on the WISC-III Subtests That Give Bonus Points for Children Who Solve Each Item Perfectly, But Earn No Bonus Points, by Age   191

Table 5.1.   Mean Factor Indexes for Various Samples   215

Table 5.2.   Cumulative Percentages of Normal and Exceptional Children (Learning Disabled and ADHD) Who Scored Various Numbers of Points Higher on the Sum of the Four PO Subtests Than on the Sum of the Four SCAD Subtests   220

Table 5.3.   Conversion of the Sum of Scaled Scores on Arithmetic, Digit Span, Coding, and Symbol Search to a Standard Score with Mean of 100 and Standard Deviation of 15 (SCAD Index)   221

Table 5.4.   Unusually Long Forward and Backward Spans, by Age, Using Three Criteria of Unusualness   234

Table 5.5.   Unusually Short Forward and Backward Spans, by Age, Using Three Criteria of Unusualness   234

Table 6.1.   Abilities Shared by Two or More WISC-III *Verbal* Subtests   274

Table 6.2.   Abilities Shared by Two or More WISC-III *Performance* Subtests   276–277

Table 6.3.   Abilities Shared by Two or More WISC-III *Verbal* or *Performance* Subtests   278

Table 6.4.   Influences Likely to Affect Scores on Two or More WISC-III *Verbal* or *Performance* Subtests   279

Table 6.5.   Standard Errors of Measurement and Confidence Intervals for WISC-III Standard Scores Derived for Various Subtest Clusters Having Differing Degrees of Split-Half or Test-Retest Reliability   281

Table 6.6.   Size of Difference between Two WISC-III Subtest Clusters Required for Statistical Significance, Based on Their Average Split-Half or Test-Retest Reliability Coefficient   282

Table 6.7.   Specific Abilities Associated with Each WISC-III Subtest, and the Subtest Specificity of Each Subtest   314

CHAPTER 1

Intelligent Testing

This is a book about the Wechsler Intelligence Scale for Children—Third Edition (WISC-III), which, as almost any graduate student in education or psychology knows, is an IQ-yielding intelligence test. But neither the IQ nor the concept of intelligence is the focus of the chapters that follow. The focus is the child, with interpretation of the WISC-III and communication of the test results in the context of the child's particular background, behaviors, and approach to the test items as the main goals. Global scores are deemphasized, flexibility and insight on the part of the examiner are demanded, and the test is perceived as a dynamic helping agent rather than as an instrument for placement, labeling, or other types of academic oppression. In short, *intelligent testing* is the key, and the WISC-III is the vehicle.

The preceding paragraph introduced my 1979 WISC-R book, with the single change being the substitution of WISC-III for WISC-R. That paragraph summarizes my current beliefs about the value of intelligence tests, just as it did in the late 1970s. But that does not imply that I haven't changed, because I have, and it doesn't suggest that the field is static because it is as volatile as ever. I retain my beliefs about intelligence in general and the WISC-III in specific after challenging myself to think otherwise, but coming up with the same answers. The key is still intelligent testing, as opposed to the mindless testing that never quite disappears. But the context of the IQ construct, both societally and professionally, has altered with time.

The field of intelligence testing has changed profoundly since I entered it. A generation has passed since I was hired by The Psychological Corporation's Test Division in late 1968 as a young, idealistic, not-yet-dissertationed, psychologist. Sure the IQ test was at the center of heated controversy—hasn't it always been?—but the issues and the antagonists were different, and the arguments were more emotional than empirical. When I was getting my feet wet in the early 1970s as Dorothea Mc-Carthy's and David Wechsler's right-hand person (though I'm left-handed), I began to understand the depth of the feelings of the antitesting people. At that time, the opponents of the IQ, and of the tests that served this unholy purpose, were mostly individuals who were *outside* the assessment scene or on its fringe. They were social psychologists and African-American psychologists and sociologists and civic leaders. Some words were tossed around—like "biased," "unfair," "middle class," "discriminatory," and "racist"—while other words were best tossed away, like "genetic," "innate," and "Jensen."

OPPONENTS OF IQ TESTING IN THE YEAR 2000 ± 5

The IQ testing opponents are no longer primarily from outside the field. Now many reside within the field: trainers of school psychologists, developers of new approaches to intellectual assessment, cognitive theorists, psychometricians, neuropsychologists. The people who view the IQ test as an instrument of torture for minority group members are still around, but they speak with quieter voices. Sure there's a skirmish or two every time there's a new verdict or interpretation of the Larry P. case. But the biggest threats to the IQ test and its applications now come more from those who use it and research it than from those who fear its so-called lethal sting. In the 1960s and 1970s, the critics of IQ tests generally conceded that the tests were valid and appropriate for "white middle-class children," but were poison for minority groups. Now, the critics offer few concessions, and the venom applies to everyone, regardless of socioeconomic or ethnic background.

A decade and a half have passed since I wrote my 1979 WISC-R book. Then, the Wechsler Intelligence Scale for Children—Revised (WISC-R; Wechsler, 1974) was virtually the only well-normed, psychometrically sound IQ test for children; now there are several. Then, clinicians interpreted small differences between scaled scores as meaningful and tended to interpret "high" and "low" scores in isolation: A scaled score of 8 on Picture Completion meant that the child had trouble distinguishing essential from nonessential details, an 11 on Comprehension meant good social maturity. A major purpose of *Intelligent Testing with the WISC-R* was to impose some empirical order on profile interpretation, to make sensible inferences from the data with full awareness of errors of measurement.

Now, some researchers and clinicians have gone full swing in the opposite direction and argue that using any type of subtest or profile interpretation is like taking illegal drugs: "Such approaches essentially violate primary principles guiding valid test interpretation" (McDermott, Fantuzzo, Glutting, Watkins, & Baggaley, 1992, p. 522); "we are compelled to advise that psychologists just say 'no' to subtest analysis" (McDermott, Fantuzzo, & Glutting, 1990, p. 299). These psychologists base their conclusions on a variety of psychometric analyses that they believe "prove" their points beyond dispute. They represent the new breed of anti-IQ testing professionals that I spoke of, but despite their strong words, they are perhaps the mildest of the species. They want to kick out subtest interpretation (a practice that Wechsler was devoted to and that the so-called Kaufman method endorses), but they'll keep the IQ test and even Wechsler's three IQs.

You do not, however, need to look too far to find stronger opposition. Macmann and Barnett (in press) share the same psychometric tree as the

McDermott-Glutting team, but they've gone farther out on the limb. They use exploratory and confirmatory factor analysis to conclude that the Wechsler scales measure little more than *g*, or general intelligence. They aren't content to toss out subtest profile interpretation; Macmann and Barnett (in press) also want to discard the Verbal and Performance IQs, because the separate factors that underlie these IQs are really nothing more than "truncated or degraded versions of the general factor." They then ride the steam of their empirical argument a little further and decide to chunk the Full Scale IQ as well. They seek alternative types of assessment, "but see no constructive role for the assessment of general IQ within this system" (Macmann & Barnett, in press).

McDermott and his colleagues shun subtest analysis in favor of the global IQs. Macmann and Barnett first flush the Verbal and Performance IQs and then toss Full Scale IQ into the bowl for good measure. Yet at the same time that these statistics-oriented psychologists are traveling the global path, neuropsychologist Muriel Lezak (1988) takes her own potshots at IQ tests ("IQ: R. I. P."). But she argues the *opposite* perspective: "When the many and various neuropsychological observations elicited by so-called 'intelligence' tests are lumped and leveled into a single IQ score—or even three—the product of this unholy conversion is a number that, in referring to everything, represents nothing. . . . [W]e need to conceptualize [mental abilities] in all their multivariate complexity and report our examination findings in a profile of test scores" (pp. 352, 358).

If we depart the field of neuropsychology and turn to cognitive psychology, the news still isn't so good. John Carroll (1993b), an authority on factor analysis, reviewed the WISC-III and rejected it on empirical grounds. Carroll resurrected Frank's (1983) diatribe against "the Wechsler enterprise" and did not dispute Frank's proclamation that it is time for Wechsler's scales "to become extinct." Carroll (1993b) concluded, "One can raise the question of whether the revisions and improvements introduced in the WISC-III justify a more favorable judgment of the validity and usefulness of this test" (p. 142). But Carroll was not condemning just the WISC-III; like many cognitive psychologists, he'd vote for extinction of all conventional intelligence tests.

Sternberg (1993) is kinder in his WISC-III review, stating, "I do not share the view of some contemporary theorists that the conventional tests are worthless or worse" (p. 163). But he criticizes the WISC-III for remaining too static ("Recycling is no longer the exclusive province of environmentalists," p. 162). And, in his analogy of the WISC to *Rocky*, Sternberg (1993) says, "Eventually, we hope, Hollywood will stop recycling material and instead will retire Rocky in favor of a new shining light. Let's also hope the same happens with the WISC series" (p. 164).

But it doesn't just take statistics-minded or theory-based educational and cognitive psychologists, or clinical neuropsychologists like Lezak, to demean IQ tests. School psychology trainers, speaking from a different perspective, can be just as vitriolic. In their review of the WISC-R, Witt and Gresham (1985) spoke metaphorically:

> The WISC-R is an anachronistic albatross which hangs gamely around the necks of applied psychologists. . . . Using the WISC-R to assess intelligence in light of the surge of information in [the fields of cognitive psychology and neuroscience] is analogous to applying Newtonian formulae to modern physics problems. . . . The WISC-R lacks treatment validity in that its use does not enhance remedial interventions for children who show specific academic skill deficiencies. In this sense, the WISC-R is biased for all children and for this reason should be replaced with assessment procedures which have greater treatment validity. (pp. 1716–1717)

Edwards and Edwards (1993) end their very favorable WISC-III review by extending the metaphor: "Individuals who viewed the WISC-R as burdening our profession (Witt & Gresham, 1985) will probably see the WISC-III as nothing more than an albatross that has molted and grown a few new feathers" (p. 149).

Other school psychology trainers have echoed the Witt-Gresham push for a switch from conventional assessment to a focus on intervention and the substitution of alternate forms of assessment such as curriculum-based measurement and natural observation (Batsche, 1992; Reschly, 1988, 1993; Reschly & Tilly, 1993). Still others within the field have developed alternative assessment approaches to measure intelligence and would like to see psychologists abandon the Wechsler system in favor of theirs, such as the Luria-based PASS model (Planning-Attention-Simultaneous-Successive) that forms the foundation of Das and Naglieri's (in press) new intelligence test: "[S]chool psychology in particular, and psychology in general, has relied too much on the Wechsler series and techniques that encourage overinterpretation of scale and subtest variation[;] . . . traditional IQ measures will need to be replaced by more modern ones" (Naglieri, 1993b, pp. 14–15). "I suggest that to move the state of the art of assessment forward, professionals will need to consider the PASS model as an alternative (Naglieri, 1992, p. 140). The seriousness of these rumblings within the field of school psychology prompted Shaw, Swerdlik, and Laurent (1993) to warn that "the WISC-III could be rendered irrelevant in the schools in a short time" (p. 158).

Strong sentiments and strong words, coming from multiple directions, but with a singleness of purpose: Dump the intelligence test. Or, if you must use it, be a psychometrician and forget your clinical training.

I treat the death threats leveled at IQ tests with respect, and I don't dismiss any of the theoretical rantings or empirical ravings without careful thought and scrutiny. When Joe Glutting first mailed me copies of three of his articles, I read them carefully and did some soul-searching. Was I advocating rampant test abuse by encouraging subtest profile interpretation? That team of researchers certainly thought so (McDermott et al., 1992).

First they put my method securely under the blade of the guillotine:

Perhaps most popular among contemporary practices is the method of ipsative ability assessment advocated by Kaufman (1979b). . . . He cautioned
practitioners not to overvalue IQ scores. . . . A major aspect of this interpretation process is the discovery of children's intellectual strengths and
weaknesses by studying the magnitude and direction of each subtest score's
deviation from a child's average subtest score. (p. 506)

Then they damned my method with faint praise:

The Kaufman method is presently a common element in university curricula
for preparing professional psychologists, with the ipsative procedure now
generalized to many other ability tests. (p. 506)

And, finally, they interpreted their data with no mercy, letting the blade
drop:

Thus we cannot recommend either ipsative or normative approaches for
subtest interpretation. Such approaches essentially violate primary principles guiding valid test interpretation. (p. 522)

After a few days of incubation and mild depression, I came to the ines-
capable conclusion that my method of Wechsler test interpretation is sound
and defensible, and that those researchers simply do not (or do not choose
to) understand it. They have extracted from the system the few empirical
steps that were imposed primarily to keep clinicians "honest"—the practice
had long existed within the field of clinical assessment to interpret as meaningful small differences between subtests or IQs. But they missed the crux
of the book, the part that outlined a method of intelligent assessment that
encourages examiners *not* to interpret subtest profiles or IQ discrepancies in
isolation. To prove their point that the ipsative approach should be punished
painfully, they stripped the method of all dignity. They gutted it of its heart
and soul, and lopped off the skull of a skeleton.

So I will put forth, once more, the basic principles of the intelligent testing
approach. Some points that may have been implicit in the original text are
now made explicit. But the method of ipsative interpretation of the WISC-III
outlined in the next section represents the substance of the method that has
been butchered by McDermott-Glutting, Macmann-Barnett, and others. After I spell out the postulates of the intelligent testing approach, and a philosophy of test interpretation, I'll address specifically the most pertinent
criticisms of this method by some of the ardent empiricists. I'll try to over-
turn the 10-to-20-year sentence handed down by the McDermott-Macmann
judge for advocating ipsative test interpretation, and the concurrent 25-
years-to-life sentence delivered by the jury of school psychology trainers for
suggesting that intelligence tests are valuable.

BASIC TENETS OF THE INTELLIGENT TESTING APPROACH

The ability to individualize test interpretation is complex and subtle, suggesting that intelligence tests should be administered by examiners who are sufficiently knowledgeable to interpret them intelligently. The burden is on test users to be "better" than the tests they use. Training in psychological theory must be put to good advantage when interpreting a profile of scores on an intelligence test. Like the WISC-R (Wechsler, 1974) and other Wechsler scales, the WISC-III (Wechsler, 1991) yields three IQs and about a dozen scaled scores on the separate subtests. But in addition, the WISC-III yields four Factor Indexes (each with mean of 100 and standard deviation of 15) that further define the global abilities measured by the battery.

The three IQs, four Factor indexes, and bucketload of scaled scores should be the raw materials for understanding an individual's cognitive functioning. By regrouping the subtests in specified or novel ways and by carefully analyzing "wrong" responses from different vantage points, the examiner can apply knowledge of Piaget, Guilford, Luria, Sternberg, Horn-Cattell, Sperry, and so on to produce a theoretically relevant WISC-III profile interpretation. This type of psychological sophistication and flexibility of profile analysis, coupled with awareness of the tests' limitations, is essential for breaking an examiner's overdependency on the obtained scores. Psychologists, learning disabilities specialists, or counselors who routinely call on their theoretical knowledge of development and learning to interpret WISC-III profiles set up a hierarchy where they are at a considerably higher level than the intelligence tests they use.

The approach to WISC-III interpretation outlined in this book rests on five premises that are discussed in the following sections.

1. The WISC-III Subtests Measure What the Individual Has Learned

This is a point stated simply, but elaborated cogently, by Wesman (1968) in his article on intelligent testing. From this vantage point, the WISC-III is really a kind of achievement test; not the same type of achievement test as reading or science, but a measure of past accomplishments that is predictive of success in traditional school subjects. When intelligence tests are regarded as measures of prior learning, the issue of heredity versus environment becomes irrelevant. Since learning occurs within a culture, intelligence tests obviously must be considered to be culture loaded—a concept that is different from culture biased. Treating the WISC-III as an achievement test may actually have vital social implications. Flaugher (1978, p. 672) notes that poor performance on a test viewed as an index of *achievement* pressures society to apply additional educational resources to improve the children's achievement; in contrast, poor performance on a test interpreted as a measure of *aptitude* "may be seen as a justification of the *withdrawal* of educational resources."

Intelligence tests, as a measure of achievement, consistently prove to be good predictors of conventional school achievement. That is an expected outcome, and provides one justification for using them in academic settings. Correlations galore between WISC-III IQs or Factor Indexes and diverse measures of achievement were provided in the WISC-III manual (Wechsler, 1991, pp. 206–209) and in Bracken and McCallum's (1993a) compilation of WISC-III articles. Coefficients, mostly substantial in magnitude, were presented for large samples of normal children (including separate groups of whites, African-Americans, Hispanics) and for language-disordered, learning-disabled, "at risk," deaf, and emotionally disturbed samples of exceptional children. Similar concurrent and predictive coefficients will continue to dot the professional literature for the next decade or so, and that's fine. There's nothing wrong with objective evidence of a test's validity, especially its differential validity for diverse ethnic groups (Weiss, Prifitera, & Roid, 1993).

However, intelligence test scores should result ultimately in *killing the prediction.* The fact that most children who score very poorly on the WISC-III will also do poorly in school should not be accepted as a statement of destiny. Judicious test interpretation and translation of test findings to action can alter what is sometimes treated as inevitable; when cast in this role, the intelligence test can justifiably be termed a "helping agent."

2. The WISC-III Subtests Are Samples of Behavior and Are Not Exhaustive

As samples of behavior, one must be cautious about generalizing the results to other behaviors or to performance under different circumstances. The other implications of this assumption regarding behavior sampling are (a) the Full Scale IQ should not be interpreted as an estimate of a child's global or total intellectual functioning; and (b) the WISC-III should be administered along with other measures, and the IQs interpreted in the context of the other test scores.

Careful, insightful WISC-III interpretation by well-trained and appropriately experienced examiners helps reduce test abuse, such as treating Full Scale IQ as a necessarily valid indicator of the child's total intelligence. But from both a legal and practical standpoint, much more is needed. To fully comprehend a child's ability spectrum and learning potential, the IQs, Factor Indexes, and scaled scores should be interpreted in the context of (and in conjunction with) scores from other measures. In neuropsychological batteries, examiners supplement intelligence tests with perceptual—motor, speech, language, memory, and motor tests; projective measures make suitable adjuncts when emotional disturbance or maladjustment is suspected. Adaptive behavior scales are necessary supplements whenever a diagnosis of mental retardation is in question, as are individual achievement tests for children referred for possible learning disabilities. Measures of creativity help in the identification of gifted children.

The WISC-III, when administered alone, should never form the basis for decisions such as diagnosis or placement. These types of decisions require the administration of several measures in addition to an intelligence test and should reflect the consensus of a multidisciplinary team that includes the child's parents (as directed by PL 94-142). But the precise IQs obtained by an individual should not be given too much stress, even when supplementary tests are administered. It is of greater interest and potential benefit to know what children can do well, relative to their own level of ability, than to know how well they did. Finding out that a girl with a Full Scale IQ of 63 did poorly, compared with other children her age, in all abilities tapped by the WISC-III leads to a dead end. Discovering that she has strengths in nonverbal reasoning and short-term memory, relative to her own level of functioning, provides information that can be used to help write her individualized education program.

3. The WISC-III Assesses Mental Functioning under Fixed Experimental Conditions

The standardized procedures for administration and scoring of the WISC-III help ensure objectivity in evaluating a child, but they sacrifice the in-depth understanding of a youngster's cognitive processing that may be obtained from a technique such as Piaget's probing *methode clinique,* Feuerstein's (1979) test-teach-test dynamic assessment approach, or Sternberg's (1977) componential analysis. The rigidity of test instructions, the use of materials such as a stopwatch, and the recording of most words spoken by a child add to the artificial nature of the situation and make the standardized intelligence test scores comparable to data obtained in a psychological experiment. Do *not* deviate from required administration procedures or add nonpermissible probes to elicit a correct response from the child (except when testing the limits). Strict adherence to standardized procedures is essential, for otherwise the obtained scores—derived from normative data collected painstakingly—are utterly meaningless. But interpretation is another matter, one that demands flexibility and awareness of the limitations of the standardized procedures so as to make the most sense out of the numerical scores.

Thus the finding by Hardy, Welcher, Mellits, and Kagen (1976) that urban children really "know" the answers to some WISC questions they get wrong, based on a testing-the-limits procedure, is of considerable interest. However, their conclusion that "a standardized test, in this instance the WISC, may not be a valid estimate of the intellectual capabilities of inner-city children" (Hardy et al., 1976, p. 50) follows logically only if the intelligence test is viewed as a criterion-referenced measure rather than as a sampling of abilities assessed under carefully specified conditions. Realization of the experimental nature of the testing process will prevent an examiner or researcher from interpreting a child's IQs as evidence of maximum performance or capacity.

When an examiner is able to relate observations of the child's behaviors in the testing situation to the profile of obtained scores (e.g., by noting that the child's anxiety disrupted test performance on all timed tasks), two things occur: (a) The examiner learns important information about the child that can be translated to practical educational suggestions, thereby enhancing the value of the intelligence test; and (b) the actual IQs earned by the child may become gross underestimates of his or her real intellectual abilities. In general, the actual IQs are valuable because they provide evidence of a child's mental functioning under a known set of conditions and permit comparison with youngsters of a comparable age. The value of the scores increases when the examiner functions as a true experimenter and tries to determine *why* the child earned the particular profile revealed on the record form; the IQs become harmful when they are unquestioningly interpreted as valid indicators of intellectual functioning and are misconstrued as evidence of the child's maximum or even typical performance.

Examiners will be helped by using objective aids to categorize children's behavior during a WISC-III administration, and two good ones are available that are based specifically on administrations of the WISC-III: the Guide to the Assessment of Test Session Behavior (GATSB; Glutting & Oakland, 1993), and the Kaufman WISC-III Integrated Interpretive System Checklist for Behaviors Observed During Administration of WISC-III Subtests (Kaufman, Kaufman, Dougherty, & Tuttle, 1994b). The Glutting and Oakland Guide assesses general test behaviors and is unique in that it was normed during WISC-III administrations, provides standard scores on factor-based scales, and has clearly articulated psychometric properties. Kaufman et al.'s Checklist includes both general behaviors (e.g., distractibility, anxiety) and subtest-specific behaviors (e.g., obsessiveness when aligning puzzles in Object Assembly), and is used to interpret the child's WISC-III score profile and help generate an individualized case report using the interpretive method presented in this book. For observing and categorizing children's adaptive and problematic behaviors in school, a particularly valuable tool is the Behavior Assessment System for Children (BASC; Reynolds & Kamphaus, 1992) Student Observation Scale (see illustrative case reports of Lucy O. at the end of Chapter 5 and Tony G. at the end of Chapter 6).

The wisdom of interpreting test scores in the context of observed behaviors is based neither on clinical whimsy nor on impractical idealism. Empirical studies have supported significant relationships between certain observed behaviors and children's test scores. Task attentiveness, task confidence, and cooperative disposition, as observed by clinicians during WISC-R administrations, correlated mostly in the .40s and .50s with the WISC-R Verbal and Performance IQs they obtained during those same administrations (Glutting, Oakland, & McDermott, 1989). A subsequent study found coefficients of a similar magnitude between the same three behavioral dimensions and the three WISC-R IQs; further, the values were comparable by gender and socioeconomic status, and for white, African-American, and Hispanic children (Oakland & Glutting, 1990). "Together these findings help to confirm the value of formally evaluating children's test behaviors and suggest that white clinicians are keen observers of children's test behaviors" (Oakland & Glutting, 1990, p. 88).

Using the GATSB with the WISC-III produced statistically significant correlations between the instrument's three factors of behavior (avoidance, inattentiveness, and uncooperative mood) and WISC-III IQs. Although the obtained coefficients were lower in magnitude than the ones obtained in the earlier investigations, this time mostly .20s and .30s (Glutting & Oakland, 1993), the conclusions are still the same: Clinicians are able to serve as good observers of children's test behaviors, and these behaviors relate meaningfully to the children's performance on Wechsler's scales.

4. The WISC-III Is Optimally Useful When It Is Interpreted from an Information-Processing Model

The field of learning disabilities has benefited by evaluating learning tasks in terms of a cybernetics or information-processing model (Silver, 1993). Such models identify the processes involved in solving any learning task, which facilitates the examiner's job of identifying the specific area or areas of dysfunction for a learning-disabled individual. Because the information-processing model applies to the learning process in general, and to any given cognitive task, the applicability of this model extends beyond the field of learning disabilities or the investigation of education-based referral issues. The basic model has four components (Silver, 1993):

1. *Input.* How information from the sense organs enters the brain.
2. *Integration.* Interpreting and processing the information.
3. *Storage.* Storing the information for later retrieval.
4. *Output.* Expressing information via language or muscle activity.

The use of this model provides examiners with a conceptual framework for interpreting IQs, Factor Indexes, and scaled scores that extends beyond the specific scores obtained. The model enables examiners to organize the test data in a meaningful way that can help translate significantly high and low scores to pragmatic, fundamental areas of asset and deficit.

Regarding input, the WISC-III Verbal subtests tend to be auditory and the Performance tasks visual, although the auditory, understanding-of-directions, component of most Wechsler "nonverbal" subtests can present difficulty for children with weak auditory reception skills. The input aspect of WISC-III tasks is more subtle than a simple auditory-visual dichotomy, however. Verbal subtests present different auditory challenges for children. Some tasks like Information and Comprehension demand understanding of long questions, whereas Vocabulary and Similarities require the ability to interpret single words in isolation. The former types of tests are difficult for children who can't make sense of long strings of words (perhaps because of a memory, sequential, or auditory-perceptual deficit); the latter can become trouble spots for children who need context clues, maybe because of an auditory discrimination problem or hearing impairment. Performance subtests, too, present different types of intake challenges. Picture Completion and Picture Arrangement, for example, depend on visual perception of meaningful stimuli, as opposed to the abstract stimuli that must be interpreted for Block Design, Coding, and the new Symbol Search.

The integration component of the information-processing model addresses the fact that different mental tasks often demand different cognitive processes for success. Similarities, Comprehension, Arithmetic, Picture Arrangement, and Object Assembly call on reasoning and problem solving; Block Design, Digit Span, and Coding require imitation of a model. Similarly, the storage requirements differ from task to task. Digit Span, Coding, and Symbol Search measure the ability to store information for a brief time, whereas Information and Vocabulary require children to retrieve facts and concepts from long-term store. Arithmetic, for example, demands both skills. Children must retrieve knowledge of number facts from long-term storage while using their short-term storage capacities to remember the precise question and work out the problem in their head. Indeed, all problem-solving tasks on the WISC-III involve what cognitive psychologists refer to as working memory (Kolligan & Sternberg, 1987; Vernon & Jensen, 1984), which reflects the reciprocal nature of storage and mental processing: Information that is taken in or encoded must be recoded long enough to allow the person to identify the strategies needed to solve the problem; to some extent, retention and processing must occur simultaneously.

The output mode is basically vocal for Verbal subtests and motor for Performance subtests, although Picture Completion is commonly a vocal task as most children opt to name the missing part instead of pointing to it. The tasks differ in terms of the amount of output required. Children who point to the missing part in Picture Completion barely tax their motor abilities, quite a contrast to the psychomotor speed that is needed to score well on Coding. Likewise, children with verbal expression problems can often handle the one-word responses required for most Information items, but crumble when they have to use their own words to answer Comprehension items.

Even the four factors that define the new structure of the WISC-III seem to correspond to different aspects of the information processing model. Verbal Comprehension and Perceptual Organization refer to cognitive processes and are best interpreted as measures of integration. The new Processing Speed factor is intended as an output factor. And the Freedom from Distractibility factor can fill several slots, depending on how it is interpreted. If an examiner interprets the factor literally, then it is a measure of input, because poor attention and distractibility impair the intake of information. However, if the examiner interprets it as assessing number ability or sequential processing, then it is best thought of as an integration factor; if it is looked at as measuring memory, then it is a storage factor.

Although intelligence is typically evaluated in terms of the integration or processing component (Lohman, 1989, 1993), the importance of considering the input and output when interpreting a child's cognitive assets and deficits is illustrated by data for African-American children on the Kaufman Assessment Battery for Children (K-ABC; Kaufman & Kaufman, 1983) Achievement Scale. The K-ABC's Faces & Places is the most culture-loaded task on the battery, the kind of task that produces large African-American/white discrepancies on Wechsler's Scales (Jensen & Reynolds, 1982; Kaufman, 1990a, Chapter 6). This subtest assesses general information in visual format instead of the auditory format used for Wechsler's Information subtest. Faces & Places is just a turn of the kaleidoscope from Information. Yet, unlike Information, Faces & Places produced very small race differences; African-American children averaged about 96, close to the normative mean of 100 (Kaufman & Kaufman, 1983, Table 4.35). In Naglieri and Jensen's (1987) comparison of blacks and whites on the K-ABC and WISC-R, the differences on K-ABC Faces & Places (blacks averaged 96.1, whites averaged 99.6) were about half the magnitude of race differences on WISC-R Information.

Similarly, a simple change in the type of output required to demonstrate reading ability may pertain to the relatively good performance by African-American children on Reading Understanding (Kaufman & Kaufman, 1983, Table 4.35; Naglieri & Jensen, 1987). This K-ABC subtest requires children to read a statement silently and then act out with movements or gestures what the statement means. African-American children averaged 93 to 94 on this subtest, whereas they have typically performed at a more deficient level on conventional tests of school achievement (Minton & Schneider, 1980; Oakland, 1983). This finding is consistent with the claims of several African-American psychologists who have stressed the central role attributed to nonverbal and gestural communication within the African-American community (Abrahams, 1973; Carter, 1977). According to Carter (1977, p. 24), nonverbal communication among African-Americans "is a way of expressing love, contempt, admiration, strength, sadness, and many other emotions which only people of equivalent experiences understand." Torrance (1977, 1982) provides additional evidence of African-American children's skills in nonverbal and gestural communication by citing their strengths in activities such as music, visual arts, and creative movement and dance.

The roles of input and output on understanding children's ability spectrum is potentially as important as the roles of integrative, mediating processes and storage of material. Throughout this book, different groupings of subtests will be organized from the vantage point of the complete information-processing model to facilitate a meaningful and potentially translatable interpretation of fluctuations within the subtest profile. For learning-disabled children and adolescents, this approach is especially beneficial for helping to hypothesize functional areas of strength and dysfunction.

5. Hypotheses Generated from WISC-III Profiles Should Be Supported with Data from Multiple Sources

As samples of behavior obtained under conditions that resemble psychological experiments, test scores can mislead just as easily as they can lead. An investigation of peaks and valleys in WISC-III profiles can, for example, lead to hypotheses of good number ability and poor visual-motor coordination based on plausible interpretations suggested for different groupings of subtests. But such designations must be thought of as hypotheses, nothing more. How should one best interpret a particular grouping of subtests? Is the supposed strength or weakness repeatable, or a one-time phenomenon? Both of these questions can be answered, with varying degrees of confidence, by using multiple sources of information and diverse pieces of data. Some of these bits of evidence come from diligent observation during the WISC-III administration and careful scrutiny of response patterns; others come from the background information provided by referral sources, including previous test data, and from the administration of additional subtests and tests.

Consider the child with WISC-inspired hypotheses of weak visual-motor coordination and strong number ability. The coordination hypothesis is based on a WISC-III grouping of subtests that includes all Performance subtests except the two "Picture" tasks. The low scores on Block Design, Object Assembly, Symbol Search, and Coding might be due to poor visual-motor coordination. However, they also might be due to poor visual-spatial ability, processing speed, or fluid ability; or to low motivation, reflectiveness, or obsessiveness; and so forth. What was the child like during the evaluation? Did he or she handle the pencil, blocks, and puzzle pieces awkwardly and appear uncoordinated? Was the child unusually reflective or unmotivated? What picture was painted of the child by parents or teachers? Did the child score low on other tests of visual-motor coordination given sometime in the past, or administered as part of the present evaluation; for example, Design Reproduction on the Detroit Tests of Learning Aptitude–Third Edition (Detroit-3; Hammill, 1991), Hand Movements from the K-ABC, or Cross Out on the Woodcock-Johnson—Revised Tests of Cognitive Ability (WJ-R; Woodcock & Johnson, 1989)?

Similarly, good number ability might be hypothesized from high scores on Arithmetic and Digit Span. To check out this hypothesis, examiners need to evaluate performance on Coding B (for children ages 8 and above) because that task also involves numbers. They might also examine the child's scores on the first 12 items of Information: Half require numerical answers or knowledge of number concepts, and half do not—did the child do better on the number items than on the nonnumber items? Children with good number ability also might have unusually good backward spans, perhaps relative to their forward spans, because the ability to repeat numbers *backward*—unlike the more mindless task of mimicking a forward span—is aided by a child's facility in handling numbers. The WISC-III manual is helpful in this regard, providing tables to determine the unusualness of various lengths of forward and backward spans, by age, and to compare the length of a child's forward versus backward span (Wechsler, 1991, Tables B.6 and B.7).

Other checks on hypotheses of good number ability might come from scores on Mathematics achievement subtests in group or individual batteries that were included on the child's record or administered as part of the evaluation; report card grades in arithmetic; statements by a referral source, or by the child, that he or she is good at math; performance on cognitive subtests from other batteries that demand number ability, such as Logical Steps in the Kaufman Adolescent and Adult Intelligence Test (KAIT; Kaufman & Kaufman, 1993), Equation Building on the Stanford-Binet Fourth Edition (Binet-4; Thorndike, Hagen, & Sattler, 1986), and Sequential and Quantitative Reasoning on the Differential Ability Scales (DAS; Elliot, 1990a). Some examiners may wish to pit the child's hypothesized strength and weakness against each other, to determine which one is more potent, by administering tasks that require *both* skills for success. Examples of tasks that demand both visual-motor coordination and number ability are the Matching Numbers and Planned Connections subtests included in the Das-Naglieri Cognitive Assessment System (Das & Naglieri, in press).

Because of the importance attached to the examiner's need to verify hypotheses with multiple sources of data, I will continually feature throughout the chapters that follow the integration of WISC-III profiles with background information, clinical observations of behaviors, subtleties of differences hidden within the WISC-III profile (such as forward versus backward span), and other test scores. This integration will also be reflected in the illustrative case reports that are provided, just as it is reflected in the software that we developed to produce interactive, computer-generated WISC-III case reports (Kaufman, Kaufman, & Dougherty, 1994a). Throughout this book, subtests and scales from the following comprehensive cognitive test batteries will be included in discussions of hypothesized areas of strength and weakness on the WISC-III: Binet-4, DAS, Das-Naglieri, Detroit-3, K-ABC, KAIT, and WJ-R.

INTEGRATION OF THE BASIC TENETS OF INTELLIGENT TESTING

The five basic principles outlined in the preceding section converge on a single focus—WISC-III assessment is of the individual, by the individual, and for the individual. The aim is to urge examiners to be less dependent on the specific scores and to come to the interpretive task armed with research knowledge, theoretical sophistication, and clinical acumen. Examiners who are weak in any of these areas are not supposed to *give* the WISC-III, much less interpret it. The WISC-III IQs and Factor Indexes, a total of seven standard scores, may all prove to be irrelevant or inaccurate information for understanding some children's functioning. The examiner's main role is to generate hypotheses that pertain mostly to assets and deficits within the information-processing model, and then confirm or deny these hypotheses by exploring multiple sources of evidence.

Finding the hypotheses that explain the pattern of scores obtained for each new child evaluated is the crux of individualized WISC-III interpretation. Evaluating the validity of these hypotheses with multiple sources of information, before accepting them as gospel, is the goal of meaningful psychoeducational, neuropsychological, and clinical assessment. Translating well-validated hypotheses into practical, implementable recommendations is the end-goal of the process.

The hypotheses explaining the scores, rather than the scores themselves, form the basis for making recommendations. For some individuals, the Verbal and Performance IQs of the WISC-III may provide great insight into their mental functioning. For others, the best explanations may come from clinical interpretation of the child's behavior and its impact on the obtained scores, from the four factors yielded by factor analysis, from Bannatyne's (1971, 1974), Meeker's (1969, 1975), or Horn's (1989, 1991) alternate cognitive interpretations of Wechsler's subtests, from Silver's (1993) information-processing approach, from developmental or neuropsychological theory, from knowledge of Black English and its impact on test performance, or from a novel set of hypotheses that is applicable only to one specific child.

These considerations are addressed in the following sections.

Clinical and Psychometric Considerations

The WISC-III provides the astute examiner with an excellent set of stimuli for generating hypotheses. Auditory-vocal and visual-motor items include socially relevant as well as abstract content, and the subtests range from school-related achievement to the kinds of skills (such as short-term memory or psychomotor speed) that are usually not formally trained. The nature of the child's verbalizations to some items, such as the socially relevant Comprehension questions or the *cash* item in Picture Arrangement, permit the examiner to obtain clinical information about the child's attitudes and emotional makeup that cannot be revealed by the profile of scores. In addition, some of the tasks are known to be especially vulnerable to the effects of distractibility, anxiety, concentration problems, or impulsivity, thereby enhancing their potential for providing the examiner with useful information.

When the WISC-III is used as part of a decision-making process, the IQs and Factor Indexes, therefore, should not be used rigidly. Precise cutoff points, formulas, or minimum IQ requirements distort the meaning of what is measured and prevent intelligent test interpretation. An instrument as reliable as the WISC-III still has standard errors of measurement of about 3 to 5 points for the Verbal, Performance, and Full Scale IQ, and about 4 to 6 points for the four Factor Indexes. A child whose IQ is near the cutoff point, even 6 or 8 points away, may be labeled or placed because of the chance error surrounding his or her true IQ.

Apart from errors of measurement, another strong argument for avoiding rigid cutoff points is that IQs or Indexes may not be valid assessors of a child's real functioning because of mitigating factors (e.g., behavioral or subcultural variables). A clerk can interpret an intelligence test when only the precise magnitude of the IQ is considered. A thoroughly trained professional, knowledgeable in testing and psychology, is needed when intelligence tests are used appropriately, as tools for helping to understand the child's strong and weak areas of functioning so that appropriate decisions can be made. It is important to be a good clerk when scoring the WISC-III and computing scaled scores, Factor Indexes, and IQs, but the examiner's role as clerk ends when the final computation is made. The 10 illustrative case reports included in this book (one at the end of Chapter 4; two at the end of Chapters 5 and 6; five in Chapter 7) demonstrate what good clinicians can do with test data; they show how *unimportant* global scores can be for understanding a child's cognitive functioning and making meaningful recommendations, and they highlight the notion that measures of cognition and achievement often go hand in hand with measures of personality functions for a more complete unveiling of the child's total behavior.

It is important to remember that David Wechsler viewed intelligence as a component of personality, as something inseparable from a person's affect. Drawing from Aristotle's perception of mental faculties, popularized by Kant, Lohman (1989) states:

> By this account, a complete theory of mind must explain not only the cognitive dimension but also the emotional and intentional dimensions as well. Attempts to simplify the task of understanding intelligence by ignoring emotion and intention may prove as ineffective as early attempts to ignore knowledge in AI [artificial intelligence]. . . . Thus, one direction research on intelligence seems to be taking is to expand its horizons to include affective dimensions long recognized as central to intelligence (e.g., Wechsler, 1939) but rarely combined with the systematic study of the cognitive dimensions. (p. 360)

Theoretical Considerations

To understand the "why's" of test performance examiners need to be more than just good clinicians; they must also have a good grasp of research findings within the pertinent psychological literature, and they must come equipped with a sound theoretical framework. Interpretation of WISC-III scores from a well-researched theory of intelligence or learning can make sense of an otherwise uninterpretable set of fluctuations, although Wechsler developed his scales from a practical and clinical foundation, not a theoretical one.

In my 1979 WISC-R book, I targeted test publishers, a conservative lot by nature, for refusing to spend the money necessary to build better tests and take the risk of challenging the Wechsler-Binet monopoly. I also took aim at test authors for failing to incorporate modern cognitive and neuro-psychological theories into the test construction process, a precursor to some of the arguments put forth by Witt and Gresham (1985) in their WISC-R review. These criticisms now must be tempered by the burgeoning number of theory-based tests put out by diverse publishers and authors.

The K-ABC is rooted in a blend of cerebral specialization theory and Luria's neurological theory, with a focus on sequential versus simultaneous information processing. The Das-Naglieri test stems from a different perspective on Luria's theory, summarized by the Planning-Attention-Successive-Simultaneous (PASS) model (Naglieri & Das, 1988; Naglieri, Das, Stevens, & Ledbetter, 1991). The Horn-Cattell theory of fluid and crystallized intelligence has also been influential in the development of new tests, notably the Binet-4, KAIT, and WJ-R. The WJ-R provides scores on seven separate factors of intelligence, conforming to Horn's (1989, 1991) extension and expansion of the Horn-Cattell dichotomy; the KAIT used a blend of Piaget's and Luria's theories in task selection.

Edward Thorndike (1926) bemoaned the fact that the then-available intelligence tests did not measure directly an individual's ability to learn more things, or the same things more quickly, than another individual. A half-century later, Estes (1974) complained that Thorndike's words were still true, and more recently, Lohman (1989) still identifies a gap between existing instruments for measuring intelligence and the advances within cognitive science. Nonetheless, several of the newer breed of intelligence tests include true "learning" tasks among their subtests, an important inclusion in view of the common use of the IQ to predict school learning, and have as their foundations aspects of cognitive theory and research. Examples of learning tasks are KAIT Mystery Codes and Rebus Learning, WJ-R Analysis-Synthesis and Memory for Names, Das-Naglieri Planned Search, and DAS Sequential and Quantitative Reasoning. The only item types that may be thought of as actual "learning" tasks in the Wechsler scales are Animal House/Coding/Digit Symbol and the WISC-III's new Symbol Search, but these tasks do not require the high-level mental processing needed to solve the learning tasks on the new intelligence tests.

The Binet-4, Das-Naglieri, K-ABC, KAIT, and WJ-R have their roots in cognitive science. Whereas Symbol Search resembles tasks found in the experimental psychology and cognitive processing literature, neither the

WISC-III's new task nor its new four-factor organization conforms to a theoretical framework. Even the common crystallized-fluid interpretation of V-P IQ discrepancies has come under attack in recent times by Horn and his colleagues (Horn & Hofer, 1992), and by other researchers (Kaufman & Kaufman, 1993; Stone, 1992a; Woodcock, 1990). Also, the once axiomatic assumption of the Verbal Scale's correspondence with left-hemisphere mental functioning and the Performance Scale's linkup with the right cerebral hemisphere has not been validated by the results of many studies with brain-damaged patients (Kaufman, 1990a, Chapter 9).

The items in the WISC-III Verbal Scale are essentially the tasks that were developed by Binet and his collaborators Henri and Simon in France near the turn of the century. Some of the WISC-III Performance subtests also resemble the old Binet items, and all of them have their roots in the nonverbal test batteries in use about a half-century ago (especially the ones based on the World War I Army Beta and Army Individual Performance Scale). This historical perspective is not intended to demean the genius of Alfred Binet or the innovative contributions of David Wechsler, a man before his time who saw the desirability of administering nonverbal tests to clients even if they spoke English well. But the fact remains that the impressive findings in the areas of cognitive development, learning theory, and neuropsychology during the past 50 to 75 years have not invaded the domain of the Wechsler test. WISC-III stimulus materials have been improved and modernized (and like many old movies they've been color-enhanced); new test items and pictures have been constructed with keen awareness of the needs and feelings of both minority-group members and women, and with the direct input of minority experts; and advances in psychometric theory have been rigorously applied to various aspects of test construction, norming, and validation. However, both the item content and the structure of the WISC-III have remained basically unchanged from its Wechsler-Bellevue ancestor.

And yet, the lack of a clear-cut theoretical base is not debilitating and does not justify turning the WISC-III into a historical relic. The WISC-III has state-of-the-art psychometric properties (see Bracken & McCallum, 1993a; Kaufman, 1992, 1993b; and Little, 1992), and it rests on more than a half-century of research findings based on thousands of studies with IQs and scaled scores yielded by its forefathers. It has the appeal of familiarity to a legion of practitioners to whom it remains King WISC the Third. And even though the numbers yielded by the WISC-III do not correspond to known developmental or neuropsychological constructs, the tasks that constitute the test battery align closely with a variety of theoretical approaches. One key to intelligent WISC-III interpretation rests on the examiner's ability to apply these theories to the Factor Index and scaled-score profiles. A second key is to know when to supplement the WISC-III with subtests from other well-constructed intelligence tests, both as a means of following up hypotheses from the WISC-III and to provide measurement in areas (such as learning ability) in which the WISC-III is notably weak.

As noted, the correspondence with Horn and Cattell's (1966) Crystal-lized (Verbal) versus Fluid (Performance) dichotomy is not as direct as once believed (even by Horn, 1985), but the WISC-III nonetheless lends itself to meaningful analysis from Horn's (1989, 1991) extension and refinement of that theory. The Verbal Comprehension factor reflects Crystallized Intelli-gence (Gc); the Freedom from Distractibility factor and the Processing Speed factors correspond to Short-Term Acquisition and Retrieval (SAR or Gsm), and Broad Speediness (Gs), respectively; and the Perceptual Organi-zation factor seems to reflect a blend of Fluid Intelligence (Gf) and Broad Visual Intelligence (Gv).

The coordination with Piaget's experimental tasks is evident in areas such as judgment and reasoning (Comprehension), logical classification (Similar-ities), space (Object Assembly), and number (Arithmetic). Also, three of the four WISC-III factors are definable from the perspective of Guilford's Structure of Intellect (SOI) *content* dimension (Meeker, 1969, 1975): (a) Verbal Comprehension (semantic); (b) Perceptual Organization (figural); (c) Freedom from Distractibility (symbolic).

Sternberg (1993) offers his own interpretation of the WISC-III from the vantage point of his triarchic theory (Sternberg, 1985) and Gardner's (1983) multiple intelligence theories. From the Gardner perspective, the WISC-III measures linguistic intelligence (Verbal Comprehension factor), Arithmetic assesses aspects of logical-mathematical intelligence, and the Performance Scale measures spatial intelligence; but the WISC-III falls short on the other four intelligences, such as bodily-kinesthetic and inter-personal. And, as Sternberg (1993) notes, the WISC-III subtests would be unsatisfying to Gardner because they are too testlike and not reality based.

Regarding his own triarchic theory, Sternberg (1993) points out several ways that the WISC-III can be interpreted from his model:

> The WISC-III is a decent measure of memory-analytical abilities. For ex-ample, Digit Span (especially 'backwards'), visual memory, and Arithmetic provide fairly direct measures of working memory capacity, and other sub-tests as well (especially the Performance ones) also require substantial working memory capacity. Information and Vocabulary measure the prod-ucts, although not the processes, of long-term memory. Analytic processing is required for similarities and comprehension. But the scale provides only a poor measure of synthetic-creative and practical-contextual abilities, as is true of virtually all conventional intelligence tests. (p. 162)

Although one can easily focus on the ways that the WISC-III or other in-telligence tests fall short of measuring all pertinent components of cogni-tive theories such as Gardner's and Sternberg's, my preference is to stress the similarities and to take advantage of the theoretical overlaps whenever possible.

In addition to theories developed in cognitive laboratories, the field of clinical neuropsychology also provides fruitful conceptual frameworks for interpreting the WISC-III. For example, some Wechsler subtests are classifiable in terms of Sperry's (1968) cerebral specialization theory. Certain tasks seem to require so-called right-hemisphere processing (Picture Completion, Object Assembly), left-hemisphere processing (Vocabulary, Arithmetic, Digit Span), or an integration of the two (Picture Arrangement, Block Design). From Luria's (1966, 1973, 1980) neuropsychological theory, WISC-III subtests can be assigned to each of the three Blocks or functional units that are postulated in Luria's theory, and that form the basis of the Das-Naglieri PASS model. Picture Completion, often associated with alertness and concentration, has elements in common with Block 1 tasks, which measure attention. Luria's Block 2 is responsible for coding functions, that is, the processing of stimuli via successive (Digit Span) and simultaneous (Object Assembly) processing. Block 3 subsumes planning and decision-making functions, abilities associated with Picture Arrangement and Symbol Search.

Practical and Cultural Considerations

There is no limit to the types of theoretical interpretations that can be applied to WISC-III profiles. Examiners are encouraged to select those theories that are most meaningful to their view of the world, or that seem most applicable to a particular child being evaluated, when investigating peaks and valleys within a child's set of scores. But neither clinical perceptiveness, awareness of research findings, nor data-based theories can substitute for hands-on experience with, and firsthand knowledge of, the children who are likely to be referred to a particular examiner.

Matching the type of interpretation given to a WISC-III profile with the nature and background of the child tested is applicable to all children, regardless of their racial group or exceptionality, and shifts the focus from the group to the individual. Although group differences in obtained scores, per se, are not meaningful for individualized test interpretation, the examiner's complete familiarity with characteristics of the pertinent group is essential. Thus the fact that hearing-impaired children, as a group, score below average on intelligence tests is of some importance. More valuable, however, is the examiner's understanding of the impact on test scores of variables such as living in an institution or of the role of auditory feedback in the learning process. Also necessary for effective test interpretation is the ability to communicate directions to deaf or partially deaf youngsters and to comprehend their efforts at responding to test items.

Similarly, examiners who test cerebral-palsied children and others with physical handicaps need much experience interacting with these youngsters to develop the clinical ability to estimate the degree to which failure on a test item is a function of mental ability versus physical impairment. Emotionally disturbed children sometimes perform very poorly on mental tasks because their disorder interferes with and disrupts their cognitive processing; it takes an exceptionally perceptive and experienced examiner to distinguish between valid and invalid estimates of an emotionally disturbed child's intellectual functioning. Gross underestimates of the intelligence of normal preschool youngsters are also quite frequent when examiners are inexperienced in deciphering immature speech or in gaining rapport with individuals who are uninterested in their performance and tend to be impulsive.

To individualize WISC-III interpretation of an African-American school-age child, examiners must understand the rules of Black English, respect this dialect as being different but not deficient (Garner & Rubin, 1986; Hoover, 1990; Washington & Miller-Jones, 1989; Williams, 1970), and view language as an interaction between content, form, and use (Lewnau, 1986). They should strive to be familiar with the child's subculture and home life, but not in the stereotypical sense, and internalize the role that oral language plays within African-American families as an integral part of family and community life (Heath, 1989). Experienced examiners must learn to determine the relationship of language and culture to the profile of scores of African-American children at all ability levels. They should realize that interpreting standardized test performance of African-American students is a complex task that has to take into account interacting or mediating variables such as cultural and physiological factors (Asbury, Knuckle, & Adderly-Kelly, 1987; Asbury, Stokes, Adderly-Kelly, & Knuckle, 1989) plus various cross-cultural, educational, methodological, racial, and gender-based factors (Butler-Omololu, Doster, & Lahey, 1984).

Analogous approaches are vital for interpreting the test scores of Hispanic children (McShane & Cook, 1985), Native American children (McShane & Plas, 1984a), and bilingual children in general (Hakuta & Garcia, 1989), especially in an age when the United States has become increasingly multicultural and multilingual. And the diverse groups extend well beyond Spanish-speaking, Hispanic populations, as the need to assess children who communicate primarily in Tagalog, Vietnamese, Japanese, Russian, and so forth has increased geometrically in the past generation.

Regarding the assessment of minorities, it is instructive to realize that the knee-jerk reaction of some IQ test critics—that intelligence tests are irrelevant to nonwhite subcultures and therefore minority children will not be motivated to do their best—is not supported by research. In a comprehensive investigation of children's behaviors during a WISC-R administration, white examiners generally observed more cooperation, attention, and self-confidence among African-American and Hispanic children ages 7 to 14 years old, than among their white counterparts, and lower-class children displayed these behaviors more so than middle-class children (Oakland & Glutting, 1990).

Test Bias

The assessment of African-American and bilingual children invariably raises issues of test bias and culture fairness, issues that are argued with regularity in professional journals, popular magazines, local newspapers, and TV talk shows. Once again, group data are used to make inferences about individual assessment. In this case, group data are used both to support bias, based on group differences in IQs, and nonbias, based on varied empirical definitions. The "mean difference" definition is unreasonable and oversimplified (Thorndike, 1971), but the sophisticated statistical definitions that stress predictive, content, or construct validity (Cleary, Humphreys, Kendrick, & Wesman, 1975; Reynolds & Kaiser, 1990) are not necessarily more potent in their implications. Numerous studies of the differential validity of various ability tests, including the WISC-R, for whites versus minority groups have generally found that the tests are not unfair for minority group members (Reynolds & Kaiser, 1990).

A recent WISC-III study likewise found the Full Scale IQ to be equally good as a predictor of academic achievement for white, African-American, and Hispanic children (Weiss, Prifitera, & Roid, 1993). But the WISC-III contains a finite set of subtests that represents just a sampling of the infinite tasks that might be administered. Change the tasks, and the results are likely to change. This fact was pointed out previously when it was noted that when the type of input or output is changed—even if the process remains the same—the magnitude of differences between African-Americans and whites on achievement tasks can drop substantially. And when less verbal-loaded and culture-steeped subtests are used to assess mental processes, white-African-American, white-Hispanic, and white-Native American discrepancies are sometimes found to be substantially smaller than conventional IQ differences (Kaufman & Kaufman, 1983, Table 4.35).

Therefore, the fact that WISC-III Full Scale IQ was found to be nonbiased for African-Americans and Hispanics is of little solace to individuals whose strengths may lie outside the set of Wechsler subtests, or whose language and cultural differences make the Verbal Scale unfair (via common sense if not a statistical sense). For all children, in fact, the global Wechsler IQ is just not "full" enough when evaluated from an intelligent testing viewpoint. The Full Scale IQ's so-called empirical fairness does not impel me to accept it as valid for certain bilingual groups for whom I advise not to interpret it (see Chapter 4), and it should not be taken at face value for any individual. Treat a given set of tasks as samples of behavior, obtained under fixed conditions, nothing more. Modify a task, even slightly, and it is likely to become easier for some children and harder for others. Supplement the WISC-III with additional tasks from a variety of sources, such as creativity tests, to measure abilities that are not within the WISC-III's domain. Also, supplement the WISC-III with subtests that are within its domain but that switch the task demands a bit (such as K-ABC Faces & Places), to help confirm or deny hypotheses developed from the WISC-III profile.

The items constituting the WISC-III and most other intelligence tests may not be unfair or biased, but potential unfairness stems from areas and items that are *not* included in the computation of a person's IQ. Biased assessment does not result from the use of an intelligence test per se, but it may easily be the product of educational decisions made by test users who pay homage to global IQs, perceive these IQs to be immutable reflections of the magical *g* factor, and pay nothing more than lip service to the need for supplementary tests.

Effortful Test Interpretation

There's no question, individualizing WISC-III interpretation requires effort. It is fairly easy to look at the three IQs, four Factor Indexes, and those scaled scores that are extremely high or low, and come up with some predictable statements about the child's general intellectual functioning and specific strengths and weaknesses. This type of cookbook interpretation is not compatible with the intelligent testing approach or intent of federal legislation, and has led to the insistence on accountability (in the form of treatment validity) by school psychology trainers. Individualization demands a flexible examiner, who is not wedded to just one approach that is applied indiscriminately to all children assessed. If an interpretive approach relies strictly on one view of the world, no matter how theoretically or psychometrically defensible that view may be, it is doomed to fail for some children. Strict adherence to the three IQs, or the set of four Factor Indexes, or a fluid–crystallized interpretation of the subtests, or a psychodynamic explanation of profile fluctuations, should give way to an eclectic approach. Thorough knowledge of many techniques for interpreting the WISC-III is important, as is mastery of the core areas of psychology, since these are the inputs necessary for interpreting a child's test profile.

With experience, a well-trained examiner will be able to shift from one approach to another to find the best explanations for the observed fluctuations in a child's profile and to infer cause-effect relationships between behaviors and test performance. But experience and good intentions are sometimes not enough in the real world. The approach to interpretation advocated in this book may be impractical for some practitioners in the field. School psychologists and psychometrists, faced with long waiting lists and inordinate numbers of cases that must be tested each week, cannot usually administer very many tests as supplements to the WISC-III or conduct dynamic assessment from either a Feuerstein or Budoff model. Psychologists or learning disabilities specialists in a clinic have to assess an urban bilingual Korean child referred for evaluation whether or not they speak Korean or have any knowledge whatsoever of the child's subculture. These realities force evaluations of school-age children to be less than ideal in some instances, but they should not be used as excuses for fostering inadequate test interpretation or other types of test abuse.

Regardless of case loads, there is much the conscientious examiner can do to facilitate intelligent testing:

1. Try to enlighten school administrators, teachers, and other professional colleagues about the pros and cons of intelligence tests and their proper use.

2. Treat the tasks in intelligence tests as samples of behavior that measure, under fixed experimental conditions, what the individual has learned.

3. Interpret test results from an information-processing model and in the context of multiple data sources.

4. Don't overvalue the IQs or treat them as a magical manifestation of a child's inborn potential.

5. Learn and truly internalize a method of interpretation, such as the one presented in this book, that promotes flexibility, provides a systematic method of attacking profiles, and encourages going beyond the scores to understand the individual's functioning.

6. Spend time interacting in the neighborhoods that are serviced by the examiner's school or clinic as a firsthand means of learning local pronunciations and dialects and of gaining insight into the backgrounds and subcultural customs of the children who will be referred for evaluation.

7. Become closely involved with teachers by observing their classrooms, working with them to follow up and modify recommendations made in psychological reports.

8. Be alert to the potential benefits of existing and new tests in a variety of assessment areas, particularly short-to-administer measures of skills such as creativity that are barely tapped by the WISC-III, as well as well-normed, comprehensive, cognitive batteries such as the DAS, KAIT, and WJ-R.

9. Be constantly aware of the limitations of standardized tests and, especially, of the examiner's ability to interpret the test for certain individuals because of limited exposure to them and their environments.

10. Keep abreast of new research and theories in psychology and related areas, since they may provide novel insights into profile interpretation.

11. Become familiar with curriculum-based assessment, dynamic assessment, and other supposed alternatives to standardized intelligence tests, and learn how to use these techniques to supplement the data obtained from the WISC-III and other well-normed instruments.

12. Learn what curriculum materials and educational approaches are used in local schools and keep current about new materials and procedures, and then use this knowledge by writing specific, crisp educational recommendations based on the results of an assessment.

An examiner who follows these suggestions (several of which are stated in the federal guidelines on nondiscriminatory evaluation) will be an intelligent tester despite a crowded schedule, rigidities in the policies of school administrators or state officials, and the claims of researchers and school psychology trainers who spout empirical dogma that is meant either to squelch the use of intelligence tests or to bind the hands of the clinicians who interpret them.

A RESPONSE TO THE CRITICS

Those who have criticized the WISC-III, other intelligence tests, or the "Kaufman method" on empirical grounds have continually stressed the child's *obtained* scores, not an intelligent interpretation of them. They have focused on the specific theory a test was designed to measure, not on the multiplicity of theories that might offer alternate views of the scores, and they have usually argued their positions from the vantage point of *group* data. In short, they have abandoned the fundamental principles that were set forth to make IQ testing intelligent.

This myopic view extends from the McDermott-Glutting antiprofile stance, to the Macmann-Barnett position on the meaninglessness of V-P discrepancies, to the Witt-Gresham insistence on treatment validity or bust, to the cognitive psychologists' rejection of conventional tests because of their theoretical poverty, to a variety of other arguments against intelligence tests. I've dealt with some of these controversies elsewhere (Kaufman, 1990a, pp. 52–62; in press-a), and I'll deal with others later in this section. Some of my arguments are clinical and from the gut, and others are empirical and from the brain. But all have their basis in my view of what intelligence tests are supposed to be. And fundamental to that view is Dr. Wechsler's credo, spoken to me with various degrees of exasperation when he had to deal with my psychometric tendencies: "The Wechsler scales are, first and foremost, *clinical* instruments."

A Right-Brained Intuitive View

Well, we can't behave as clinicians with our hands tied behind our backs. If we ignore V-P IQ differences and subtest profile fluctuations in our attempts to be psychometric purists, we are throwing away our license to be clinicians and are a short stone's throw from the Dark Ages. And if we abandon IQ tests altogether, while waiting for the promised Holy Grail from respected cognitive scientists and "wanna-be" test developers such as Robert Sternberg or Howard Gardner, then we face a Black Hole in the interim. To paraphrase novelist Evan Hunter, you shouldn't toss something into the trash until you've got something of value to replace it.

Times have changed since my 1979 WISC-R book, as I've noted repeatedly, but many things remain the same. The number of available children's intelligence tests of high quality has grown geometrically, but the WISC-III is still the main test of choice for the school-age population.

Controversy reigned in the late 1970s and it's no stranger today. The "malpractice" of subtest interpretation is not new (Hirshoren & Kavale, 1976). Larry P. never quite goes away. School psychologists want to do less IQ testing, *much* less IQ testing, and more of something else, anything else (Reschly & Tilly, 1993). Proponents of curriculum-based assessment continue to have little use for IQ tests.

Cries of racial bias reverberate across the United States, as they did in the heyday of Robert Williams in the 1970s, even if words like genocide are now more likely to be found in Rap songs than professional journals. Some state government and local school-district officials still commonly demand the use of rigid cutoff points for diagnosis and placement, not understanding that errors of measurement are a built-in part of the package. Examiners haven't stopped giving tests of questionable psychometric properties, such as "that infamous rodent of the psychoeducational assessment world, the WRAT-R" (Reschly & Tilly, 1993, p. 4). Computerized, depersonalized case reports continue to proliferate, with software for personal computers as plentiful as beer ads at a ballpark.

I've ingested the changes, even been a part of it by developing IQ tests (Kaufman & Kaufman, 1983, 1993) and interactive software (Kaufman, Kaufman, Dougherty, & Tuttle, 1994a) with Nadeen. I see what's new and what's old, and I still fall back on one basic notion: Children who are referred for evaluation have problems, and we can help solve those problems by interpreting IQ tests intelligently. I've seen so much stupid testing—then and now—and I remain a strong advocate of intelligent testing.

The child referred for evaluation must remain the focus of assessment, and as clinician-scientists we must come well equipped; our judgment, knowledge of psychology, and clinical training are more important than the obtained IQs. Each person we assess is an *individual* who comes from a unique background and attacks test items in his or her own characteristic way. That person cannot be summarized by a few numbers, laser-printed into those computerized reports that fail to consider a child's uniqueness, or be abandoned by those who heed the results of anti-IQ testing studies that rest solely on group data.

I believe in profile interpretation, with all of its clinical implications and practical ramifications. I stick, naively some would argue, to the ideal that IQ tests should be a dynamic helping agent. I despise cutoff scores and blind reliance on reliable, global IQs. And I have faith in the judgment of well-trained psychologists. If I didn't, I would get out of the test-making business, and I'd have let the 1979 WISC-R book die a quiet death.

I've come to accept some facts of life. Intelligence tests will always reside at the center of heated controversies, both public and professional, and will continue to be the focus of litigation and legislation. As authors of the K-ABC, Nadeen and I have felt the intense heat that permeates the core of controversy. Polarization about IQ testing will remain rampant. Some worship the IQ and treat it like a number that is immutably and indelibly etched in DNA; others would squelch all attempts to measure anyone's so-called intelligence. Some accept Wechsler's approach to IQ measurement and oppose any attempt to refine or replace it; others find no value in any aspect of Wechsler's life's work, and would replace his tests in a heartbeat with a test from this or that theoretical position.

Extremists on both sides of each emotional issue are not likely to be appealed to by rational arguments. In this WISC-III book, as in the 1979 WISC-R book, I have sought a middle ground between the extreme positions. Clinicians must be allowed to do what they do best. Throwing out IQ tests, and with them more than a half-century of research findings and clinical acumen, is not sensible. At least not now, when applications of cognitive and neuroscience theory to the practical world of testing have yet to make significant inroads in the field of *clinical* assessment. Preaching psychometric dogma that turns clinicians into glorified clerks by permitting interpretation only of the bottom-line IQs is likewise not a good solution. Clinical assessment is part art, part science. Neither part can be ignored; not when a good clinician, using a good test and mindful of psychometric procedures, can make a difference regarding the diagnosis and treatment of individual children. And the WISC-III *is* a good test.

The potential benefits of well-standardized and carefully developed intelligence tests, with their rich research heritage and clinical/neurological applications, demand to be preserved. At the same time, rampant test abuse, in the form of deification of the test itself, overvaluation of global IQs, equation of test scores with genetic potential, and interpretation of low IQs as a call to passive placement rather than active intervention, must be squelched. The flaws of intelligence tests need to be understood by all test users—not to impel examiners to reject the tests or to ignore fluctuations among subscores, but to facilitate a more incisive interpretation of what the scores mean. Examiners must not be subservient to the tests they use or to the scores that their instruments yield.

The method of attack proposed in this chapter and operationalized throughout this book stresses that the WISC-III is an *individual* intelligence test. If administration is individual, so too should be the interpretation of the profile of scores for each child tested. The focus of the WISC-III interpretation presented here is one of personalization, an approach that I trace to the clinical methods of David Wechsler and the mandate for individualization that was advanced in the late 1960s and early 1970s by professionals on the cutting edge of the learning disabilities movement (e.g., Bannatyne, 1971; Kirk & Kirk, 1971). On a personal level, this integrated approach had several important sources. I benefited greatly from the training I received in psychometrics at Columbia University under Robert L. Thorndike, Fred Davis, and Marvin Sontag and at The Psychological Corporation under the tutelage of Alexander Wesman and Jerome Doppelt. But that empirical orientation would not have given birth to the intelligent testing approach without cross-fertilization from serendipitous clinical sources: working closely with David Wechsler and Dorothea McCarthy in an informal clinical apprenticeship; and learning firsthand about intraindividual test interpretation from Nadeen, courtesy of her Learning Disabilities training at Columbia under Margaret Jo Shepherd and Jeannette Fleischner.

A Left-Brained Scientific View

The attacks on Wechsler's scales and other intelligence tests during the early 1990s have been ostensibly empirical, but the arguments have an emotional bite that lies just beneath the statistical surface. In this section, I will address three of the main thrusts for turning back the clock on Wechsler interpretation: Macmann and Barnett's insistence that Wechsler's scales measure *g*, not separate verbal and performance constructs of any substance; the McDermott-Glutting team's unrelenting stance against profile interpretation; and Witt and Gresham's soapbox proclamations about treatment validity. I will try to blend rationality with the findings of pertinent investigations to demonstrate the importance of not taking at face value the seemingly ironclad, data-based conclusions of some researchers.

Macmann and Barnett: There's Nothing but g

Empirical "facts" can be illusory, and that is the case with the Macmann-Barnett "psychometric proof" that Verbal-Performance differences on a Wechsler scale are almost worthless. They insist that nothing meaningful comes from a Wechsler test administration except, perhaps, for Full Scale IQ; by the end of their long article, they are advising professionals not to administer conventional intelligence tests, because *g* is all you get, and *g* is not enough.

Macmann and Barnett (in press) used sound statistics to reach their conclusion, but as I analogized in my invited commentary on their article (Kaufman, in press-a), they are like two blind men trying to describe an elephant. They are standing with their feet planted firmly in one spot and are giving a good description of the elephant's tail, but like the blind men in the apocryphal story, they are unaware that the elephant has a trunk, tusks, thick hide, and massive body. If one relies solely on the empirical techniques applied by Macmann and Barnett to data obtained on normal people, it's easy to agree with their conclusions about V-P IQ discrepancies. But if one examines other kinds of data, pores over dozens of research studies, and considers the use of intelligence tests in clinical practice, their quick dismissal of Wechsler's two separate IQ scales becomes an exercise in foolishness.

From an ivory tower, insisting that examiners interpret only the Full Scale IQ may have a kind of simplistic appeal. Within the real world, though, such an approach ignores clinical issues and findings. A *g* orientation prevents the sound clinical use of intelligence tests with brain-damaged, delinquent, psychotic, and other abnormal samples; it prevents the fair use of these tests with bilingual and Native American samples; it ignores "base rate" data on V-P IQ discrepancies within the normal population; and it prevents in-depth understanding of the differential effects of aging on Verbal versus Performance IQ.

For example:

- The results of 40 Wechsler studies involving more than 1,100 patients with right-hemisphere damage indicate that the average patient had High Verbal-Low Performance to the tune of 8 to 10 IQ points (Kaufman, 1990a, Table 9.7). Furthermore, the size of these $V > P$ profiles was related to gender, race, type of lesion (stroke versus tumor), location of lesion, and the acuteness of the brain injury (Kaufman, 1990a, Chapter 10).
- Numerous investigations of Hispanic children indicate that they earn Performance IQs that are typically 10 to 15 points higher than their Verbal IQs. Navajo children tend to have $P > V$ by about 30 points (McShane & Cook, 1985; McShane & Plas, 1984a; see Chapter 4 for more details).
- It is common for *normal* individuals to display statistically significant differences between their V-IQ and P-IQ. About 2 out of 5 normal children, adolescents, and adults have significant discrepancies on the WISC-III (Wechsler, 1991, Table B.2; see Chapter 3) or WAIS-R (Kaufman, 1990a, Table 9.3).
- When education level is controlled and a common norms group is used, life-span changes on the WAIS-R Verbal and Performance Scales differ dramatically: Mean V-IQ remains basically constant across the 10–74-year range; mean P-IQ plunges more than 20 points between ages 20–24 and 70–74. These results conform to predictions from the Horn-Cattell theory of fluid and crystallized intelligence (Horn, 1985, 1989; see Kaufman, 1990a, Chapter 7).

Would Macmann and Barnett (in press), I wonder, really argue that "the factor measured by the Performance scale subtests . . . might be just as readily defined in terms of verbal skills" for Hispanics, Native Americans, patients with right-brain damage, and normal elderly adults? Or is it time for them to unplant their feet, walk away from the tail, and shift to a different part of the empirical elephant? As I once stated in response to O'Grady's (1983) similar insistence that the WAIS-R is best thought of as a one-factor test: "But where do such conclusions lead? Not very far, at least in the real world, and not towards the future. A one-factor interpretation of the WAIS-R is as progressive as a return to Spearman's *g* theory and to the original Binet scale, and is as clinically relevant as the rigid use of cut-off scores" (Kaufman, 1990a, p. 237).

McDermott-Glutting and Profile "Malpractice"

The anti-IQ testing school of thought makes some assumptions that I find indefensible or illogical. The series of articles by McDermott and his colleagues attacks the approach I have advocated of ipsative assessment of Wechsler subtest profiles. That method requires the interpretation of strengths and weaknesses relative to the child's own level of ability. A normative approach would compare all subtest scores to the mean of 10 that applies to children in general; an ipsative approach uses the child's own mean score, whether that value is 5, 8, 10, 12, or 15. As I stated, the ipsative method makes it more likely that both assets and deficits will be identified for a child. Even though such deviations are relative and not absolute, how valuable are a string of just strengths for a gifted child or a string of just weaknesses for a mentally retarded child? The use of ipsative interpretation in my approach is a practical convenience, nothing more. It's not built on a theoretical foundation and is intended only to paint a more balanced picture of a child's cognitive patterns. It's never been proposed as an alternate to normative interpretation; but I've always felt that the use of IQs (and now Factor Indexes) handles the normative end of interpretation quite nicely.

Yet the antiprofile interpretation folks have built a sand castle out of untenable assumptions. They've coined terms such as "person-relative metrics" (McDermott et al., 1992, p. 504), and have insisted that sets of ipsative scores be evaluated against the kinds of psychometric parameters that are used to evaluate norms-based scores (e.g., reliability, predictive validity, construct validity). They offer the postulate that "the ultimate purpose of any psychological measure rests on its ability to improve prediction" (McDermott et al., 1990, p. 293) and then proceed to show that ipsatization fails to do this; they argue that the procedure "automatically removes from a person's scores all common variance, as associated with Spearman's g . . . [which] means the loss of nearly 60% of the test's reliable variance" (p. 293).

What? No one is changing a single scaled score from the profile. When g is truly partialed out of a set of scores, then the order of a child's subtest scores (from high to low) will conceivably change as a function of each subtest's correlation with global IQ. But that's not what is done. The examiner simply shifts the midpoint from the normative average of 10 to the child's own mean score. The scores themselves are not altered; the profile remains static. The psychometric arguments, based on group data, are bogus and are irrelevant for individualized profile interpretation. In the real world, who would ever combine ipsative data from child to child, using as the "score units" positive and negative deviations from the child's own mean? That's simply absurd. They should not ordinarily be combined, and it's inappropriate to subject the ipsative scores for each individual child to procedures meant for group data. The midpoint for each child is simply shifted, up or down, to allow the generation of a more balanced set of hypotheses. That's it. No big deal, worthy of the development of a new psychometric system for the ultimate purpose of trashing it. Ipsative assessment on the WISC-III is a clinical convenience. It's also a starting point to see if there's multiple support for various strengths and weaknesses in the subtest profile. If there is additional support, then the finding becomes reliable by virtue of its cross-validation. If there isn't, then the hypothesized asset or deficit is of no consequence. The McDermott team is making its vociferous claims and fostering a new science of the psychometrization of ipsativity based on a clinical, practical convenience that is meant as an informal starting point for hypothesis generation.

They did ask one pertinent question: Do strengths and weaknesses identified on one testing remain stable over time? They used WISC-R test-retest data obtained over a short term (1 month) and long term (3 years) to determine whether significant discrepancies above and below the mean continue to exist. Their answer was, in a nutshell, "No." They did ask the right question, but they didn't use the right method. There's such a thing as practice effects on any test, and these effects are profound on Wechsler's Performance Scale. On the WISC-R, the average child or adolescent gains 10 Performance IQ points from test to retest over a 1-month interval (Wechsler, 1974, Table 11); on the WISC-III, the practice effect on the Performance Scale is an even larger 12 points (Wechsler, 1991, Tables 5.3, 5.4, and 5.5). In contrast, gains on Verbal IQ are about 2 to 3 points.

Performance subtests are generally novel tasks, not like the familiar arithmetic, general information, and vocabulary items on the Verbal Scale. After a child has taken a Wechsler scale once, the novelty is gone. The initial evaluation assessed the quickness of the child's ability to generate strategies for solving new problems. The next time, especially just a few months later, the tests are no longer novel; the strategies for solving the problems are remembered to some extent. Some children will remember them better than other children, and each child will remember strategies for some subtests better than other subtests. The retest Wechsler profile, especially on the Performance Scale, therefore, has additional types of error thrown in, not just the expected kinds of error that are present on the first administration of a subtest. Robert DeNiro said to Christopher Walken, in *The Deer Hunter,* that you just get "one shot." What applies to deer hunting applies to Wechsler profiles. You get one shot.

The average 6- to 7-year-old child earned a mean scaled score of 10.4 on the first administration of WISC-III Picture Arrangement and a mean of 13.7 (more than one standard deviation higher!) on the second testing, 3 weeks later (Wechsler, 1991, Table 5.3). The children weren't told the answers, but they did much better, on the average, when this no-longer-novel task was administered again. What could one possibly say about the stability of a strength or weakness on Picture Arrangement for a given child, given the confounding due to the practice effect? How can one possibly interpret the stability of Verbal versus Performance strengths and weaknesses when the practice effect is so different for these scales? And how can data that specifically investigate the stability of single subtest scores *in isolation*—not merged with other subtests to form hypothesized *areas* of asset and deficit, and not enriched with support from clinical observations, background information, and additional test data—be used to refute an interpretive approach that is, by definition, integrative and complex?

One might argue that the practice effect would not be a factor in the long-term stability study reported by the McDermott team. That's only partially true. There is a progressive error that occurs when a person is tested several times on Wechsler's Performance Scale, even when the tests are administered years apart (Kaufman, 1990a, pp. 204–206). But forget the progressive practice effect when evaluating the long-term data used to analyze the stability of significant subtest deviations. Three years is a long time; real change takes place in cognitive abilities, and you can't be sure what portion of the variance is due to instability of the subtests versus reliable changes in ability. When profiles are investigated to identify strengths and weaknesses, the obtained hypotheses, if cross-validated with observations and other data, are useful at that time—not 3 years later. Besides, maybe the subjects in the long-term study were evaluated by intelligent testers who were able to apply the initial test results to create meaningful (not random) change.

McDermott and Glutting use their statistical arguments to damn normative as well as ipsative profile interpretation. They also have investigated standardization samples through cluster analysis (Q methodology) to identify "core" profiles on intelligence tests (Glutting, McDermott, Prifitera, & McGrath, in press; McDermott, Glutting, Jones, Watkins, & Kush, 1989), and have used the results of core profiles as an additional argument against interpretation of subtest profiles (Glutting, McGrath, Kamphaus, & McDermott, 1992). Once more, the approach of these investigators, however empirically sophisticated, uses group data to make judgments about individual assessment. Once more, the conclusions about profile interpretation are based on the test scores in isolation, ignoring any type of cross-validation with multiple data sources.

The bottom line: Individual assessment with the WISC-III or other tests is unique to each person evaluated and has a meaning beyond the simple obtained scaled-score profile; the McDermott-Glutting team, though well-intentioned and armed with complex statistics, has continually rebutted the intricate intelligent testing model by operationally defining it in simple-minded, one-dimensional terms. Many of the illustrative case reports in this book, all based on actual clinical cases, make it clear that in the real world of referred children, the global scores often mean less than nothing and true understanding of cognitive and perceptual dynamics frequently comes from insightful subtest interpretation (see, for example, the case of Dana Christine, age 8½, in Chapter 7).

I don't mean to imply that the McDermott-Glutting group hasn't made important contributions to the field. The core profile approach, when it's not being used to curtail clinical ingenuity, represents a provocative new line of inquiry. The McDermott group has established a base line of typical subtest profiles for evaluating the abnormality of any given profile for a referred child and their recent work with the WISC-III includes a stepwise procedure for determining whether a profile is common or uncommon (Glutting et al., in press). They urge extreme caution in using the WISC-III for diagnosis, particularly when the child's subtest profile may be completely normal. In this regard, by using sophisticated statistical techniques and a good bit of cleverness, they are echoing policies I've advocated for the WISC-R (Kaufman, 1976a, 1976b, 1979b) and other tests (Kaufman, 1990a; Kaufman & Kaufman, 1983).

The Witt-Gresham Cry for Treatment Validity

A portion of the school psychological community decries the lack of treatment validity for Wechsler's scales (Witt & Gresham, 1985) and other intelligence tests such as the K-ABC (Good, Vollmer, Creek, Katz, & Chowdhri, 1993). Witt and Gresham (1985) boldly state, "The WISC-R lacks treatment validity in that its use does not enhance remedial interventions for children who show specific academic skill deficiencies" (p. 1717). *But they provide not one reference citation to support their statement.* The clear implication is that the WISC-R's treatment validity has been evaluated and found wanting. Where is the evidence? Reschly and Tilly (1993) "agree with [Witt and Gresham's] Buros review of the WISC-R" [p. 4], regarding its lack of treatment validity. They cite a host of references that damn modality or process training and claim that "matching processing strengths to intervention methodology (teaching strategies) . . . ought to work. But it doesn't according to research findings for at least two decades" (p. 5). The list of references at the end of their article is long, but studies specific to Wechsler's scales are lacking. The most comprehensive reviews included among their citations (e.g., Arter & Jenkins, 1979; Kavale, 1990) focus mainly on modality studies of visual versus auditory learners that mostly used the outdated-and-no-longer-in-vogue Illinois Test of Psycholinguistic Abilities (ITPA; Kirk, McCarthy, & Kirk, 1968).

The WISC-R, and by inference the WISC-III, have been hanged for lack of treatment validity without a fair trial, or really any trial at all. Not that the results of the kinds of studies likely to have been conducted on Wechsler's scales would have been positive. Negative results are almost built in to the design for pragmatic reasons. Modality or process groups are selected exclusively based on a child's obtained scores, a practice that ignores clinical observations of how they actually did solve problems on various tasks, or whether a behavior such as anxiety contributed substantially to a low score on Wechsler's Freedom from Distractibility factor or the K-ABC's Sequential Processing Scale. The criteria used to evaluate the different treatments are often not validated as being clearly associated with the constructs under study, a problem with the two learning tasks developed by Ayres and Cooley (1986) to evaluate the treatment validity of the K-ABC. Samples are often very small, such as the total N of 6 children used by Good et al. (1993);

these authors admitted, "The difficulties inherent in researching the K-ABC instructional model are formidable" (p. 20).

In fact, if the difficulties in evaluating the K-ABC model are a land mine, the difficulties in researching WISC-III profile fluctuations are even more overwhelming. The K-ABC offers a clear set of educational procedures for teaching with different processing styles and offers a blueprint for how the evaluation study should be set up. Wechsler's scales have no intuitive link between test profile and educational treatment. The most intuitive would be to assign high Verbal and high Performance subsamples to methodologies that emphasize verbal and nonverbal strategies, respectively. Unquestionably, if previous research serves as a guide, the subgroups would be formed exclusively on the basis of obtained Verbal and Performance IQs. Perhaps a more insightful investigator would rely on the "purer" Verbal Comprehension and Perceptual Organization Factor indexes, but the decision would be number-based in true "scientific" fashion.

However, groups with high verbal and low nonverbal skills, even with identical IQ or Factor Index discrepancies, may display that pattern for an infinite number of reasons. The assumption that all members of a group have the same learning style because they obtained the same pattern of scores on an intelligence test violates the basic principles of the intelligent testing approach. The untenability of the one-to-one correspondence between obtained discrepancies and processing preference also applies to children who display high Sequential-low Simultaneous on the K-ABC or Das-Naglieri; high Fluid-low Crystallized on the KAIT or WJ-R; or high Nonverbal-low Verbal on the DAS, Detroit-3, or Binet 4.

Proceeding with the WISC-III illustration, a significantly higher Verbal than Performance IQ may be due to a plethora of factors other than good verbal ability and poor nonverbal ability. Low Performance IQs could be caused by an inability to understand the *verbal* directions to the subtests, by obsessive concern with detail, anxiety on highly speeded tasks, a reflective or field-dependent cognitive style, poor fine-motor coordination, and so forth (see Chapter 4, as well as the case reports of James C. and Greg T. in Chapter 7). Examinees who are obsessive or reflective, in fact, might enhance their Verbal subtest scores (by offering a string of responses to some items and giving extensive elaborations to queries) at the same time that they are unwittingly sabotaging their Performance subtest scores (by earning few bonus points on Perceptual Organization subtests and performing slowly on Processing Speed tasks). When behavioral and motor factors contribute to the magnitude of the V-P IQ difference, even striking discrepancies may not truly indicate differences in the child's verbal versus nonverbal learning.

Yet any groups formed during the evaluation of a Wechsler scale's treatment validity would invariably be identified by attending simply to the size of the V-P difference, not its clinical explanation. And, if history is used as a guide, the groups would probably not be distinct even from a strictly empirical perspective. In a review of modality training studies (visual, auditory, kinesthetic), Kavale (1990) found that once measurement errors were accounted for, "Only 7 out of 10 subjects actually demonstrated a modality preference score different enough to warrant placement in a particular modality preference group" (pp. 880–881).

Witt and Gresham (1985) state, "Many professionals are beginning to question the desirability of spending an hour and a half administering and scoring the WISC-R and ending up with only an IQ score. School psychologists, for example, find that teachers want to know specifically what to do for and with children. The WISC-R provides no such information" (p. 1717). Reschly and Tilly (1993) offer a number of useful suggestions for alternate types of assessment, mostly behavioral, curriculum-based, and outcome-oriented in nature. Like Witt and Gresham's position, there seems to be little room in the Reschly-Tilly system reforms approach for the WISC-III or other conventional intelligence tests.

The goals of these school psychology leaders are upbeat and sensible. One of my qualms concerns their condemnation of the WISC-III for lack of treatment validity when such evidence specific to the Wechsler scales is no more available than evidence that the Wechsler approach does have treatment validity. That doesn't mean that I believe studies should be conducted in abundance on the WISC-III. If they are conducted, the results probably will be negative because of the multiplicity of reasons already mentioned. Also, I object to the notion that conventional intelligence tests yield just a score, and I disagree that it is the instrument's responsibility to provide direct treatment information. It is the *examiner's* responsibility, not the *test's,* to provide recommendations for intervention. It is the examiner's responsibility to ensure that a series of clinically relevant, cross-validated statements about the child's strengths and weaknesses is the outcome of an administration of a standardized intelligence test, not just a few bottom-line IQs or standard scores.

If the WISC-III is interpreted from the information-processing model described previously, then assets and deficits within the learning process are likely to be identified. It's a short step from understanding possible gaps in the child's learning process to making educational recommendations regarding the teaching process. The treatment validity of each *Individualized* Education Program (IEP) can't easily be evaluated via research conducted on groups and it's hard to do $N = 1$ research. But that doesn't mean carefully thought out suggestions for intervention are doomed to automatic failure and there is some evidence that different types of instructional strategies are effective for good versus poor planners (Andrews & Naglieri, 1994). Advocates of the total abandonment of standardized intelligence tests in favor of curriculum-based assessment and criterion-referenced tests want to identify *what* must be taught—a good goal—but they are content to teach it without too much emphasis on *why* or *how* for each unique individual. The "what" is obviously important. But clinically astute examiners will usually be able to understand the "why" and recommend the "how" based on a Wechsler profile. They've been doing that for years.

I don't dispute that criterion-referenced tests (Hambleton, 1990) and curriculum-based assessment (Shapiro & Derr, 1990) make important contributions to the complete understanding of a child's functioning in school. So do testing methods that are intended to uncover children's learning potential by assessing their ability to profit from teaching, such as Feuerstein's (1979) dynamic assessment and Budoff's (1987) test-train-retest paradigm. But proponents of criterion-referenced measurement, curriculum-based assessment, and test-train-retest paradigms often see these approaches as *alternatives* to intelligence tests, and that I do not buy. I seem them as useful *supplements* to the data yielded by conventional standardized instruments, especially for the assessment of minority group children (Hausman, 1988; Haywood, 1988; Jones, 1988).

Although Naglieri (1992, 1993b) would like to see psychologists abandon traditional IQ tests in favor of his Das-Naglieri test, and reorient themselves toward the PASS model (Andrews & Naglieri, 1994; Das & Naglieri, in press; Das, Naglieri, & Kirby, 1994; Naglieri & Das, 1988), he supports norms-based assessment. And Fagan and Bracken (1993), both trainers of school psychologists, make some cogent points regarding those who would throw away intelligence tests because of the treatment validity issue:

> In contrast to some assertions, intelligence and achievement measures are highly reliable, have experienced a long history of validity support, and they are appropriately sensitive to student progress. . . . Intelligence tests are designed to identify social or academic symptoms (e.g., intellectual deficiency) much as a thermometer is designed to identify a symptom of an illness (i.e., fever). The thermometer is not intended to translate directly into treatment; nor are intelligence tests. Intelligence tests are valid for their intended diagnostic and classification purposes. The fact that some wish to hold them accountable for other purposes (e.g., treatment validity or social utility) is neither appropriate nor diminishes how well they do what they were intended to do. (p. 6)

A common theme of the Macmann-Barnett, Glutting-McDermott, and Witt-Gresham camps is to rely almost exclusively on *group* data to support their claims. I have no qualm with the use of group data to make a point; that's exactly what I did when I cited studies of Native Americans, normal elderly, and right-damaged adults to refute the Macmann-Barnett notion that g is the sum total of what's measured by Wechsler's scales. Strong artillery to combat strong artillery. But when you use the WISC-III and related tests, you're dealing with *individuals*. I believe that the failure to ingest that fact is a pitfall of most of the strong anti-IQ testing critics.

It may be, as Matarazzo (1992) argues, that the future of intelligence testing during the 21st century is to "record individual differences in brain functions at the neuromolecular, neurophysiologic, and neurochemical levels" (p. 1007). If that time does come during my lifetime, then I will undoubtedly revise my approach to intelligent testing and may need to find a new vocation. But that time is not here yet.

A PRACTICAL ISSUE: WISC-III VERSUS WISC-R, WPPSI-R, WAIS-R

Whenever a new version of a test is published, some clinicians cling to the old instrument and are reluctant to try the revised edition. A survey of test use for adolescent and adult assessment indicated that the WAIS was still commonly used several years after the WAIS-R was published (Harrison, Kaufman, Hickman, & Kaufman, 1988), and the half-century-old Wechsler-Bellevue remains the test of choice for some clinicians and researchers in neuropsychology (e.g., Herring & Reitan, 1986). Chapter 1 concludes with a practical question: Should the WISC-R ever be used in preference to the WISC-III, and which Wechsler scale is preferred at the ages at which they overlap?

WISC-III versus WISC-R

When the WISC-R came out in 1974, I didn't realize there would be a hard-core group of WISC-ophiles who would resist the switch to the revised edition. Some tried the WISC-R and went back to the 1949 battery. "The WISC-R gives IQs that are too low by 5 or 10 points," they'd argue. Then they'd ask, "What'd you do wrong?" And that resistance to change seems at least as prevalent now, in the 1990s, with the publication of the WISC-III.

John Flynn's extensive research within North America and Australia, and across a variety of Eurasian countries, has uncovered an uncontestable truth: People in technologically advanced nations do better on intelligence tests as time goes by; when compared with other people of the same age who were tested 5, 10, 20, or 30 years previously, today's children and adults answer more verbal questions right and solve more nonverbal problems correctly (Flynn, 1984, 1987; Kaufman, 1990a, pp. 46–52). In the United States, people increase at the rate of 3 IQ points per decade—an impressive feat, until you compare that gain to the even greater gains displayed by most other developed nations (Flynn, 1987). Gains averaged 10 points per decade in Germany, and were 6 to 8 points per decade in Japan, Austria, France, The Netherlands, and Belgium (Kaufman, 1990a, Figure 2.2).

But forget about the other nations. Three points per decade is a huge amount of gain, and it has remained a steady increment whether the data are based on tests for children or adults, and whether the decade in question is 1940 to 1950, 1965 to 1975, or 1983 to 1993. The result for test users is that norms continually get steeper. As time goes by, norms get out of date in the United States at the rate of 3 points every 10 years. Old norms get "soft."

The WISC-R yielded average IQs of 100 when it was first normed in the early 1970s. By the early 1980s (unbeknownst to most test users), the average shifted to about 103, and it had risen to about 107 when this book went to press. The WISC-III was standardized in 1990, 18 years after the 1972 norming of the WISC-R, so the prediction from Flynn's research is that the WISC-R should yield higher IQs than the WISC-III by 5.4 points (1.8 decades × 3 points per decade). That's just about what happened. The counterbalanced WISC-R/WISC-III study reported in the WISC-III manual (Wechsler, 1991, Table 6.8) reveals a discrepancy of 5.3 Full Scale IQ points on the WISC-R (108.2) versus the WISC-III (102.9) for normal children. Similar findings have been observed for exceptional samples (Doll & Boren, 1993; Newby, Recht, Caldwell, & Schaefer, 1993), although there is an indication that the differences may be a bit larger for some exceptional groups (Dumont & Faro, 1993; Post, 1992) which would have a substantial impact on special education placement decisions (Post & Mitchell, 1993).

Scientists don't know exactly why there has been a steady worldwide gain in performance on intelligence tests. Lynn (1990) makes a provocative argument for improved nutrition as a causative factor. Spitz (1989), relying on WAIS and WAIS-R data, refined Flynn's conclusions by determining that the 3-point gains are true for people with average IQs, but the gains dwindle gradually as you stray from the average range, and the direction reverses for retarded individuals. Regardless of causal factors and the subtleties of the pattern, the end-result stays the same: The WISC-R gives the good news (just as the old WISC did back in the 1970s), but the WISC-III gives the more accurate news. The WISC-III norms are predictably steeper, tend to yield the lower IQs, and are likely to impact placement decisions and reevaluations. Those are just the facts of life. Plain and simple, if you haven't already switched to the WISC-III, do so now.

Since you're reading this book, you've undoubtedly made the switch; but you might want to persuade your colleagues to do the same. Even if you prefer the old black-and-white figures on WISC-R Picture Completion and Picture Arrangement, or if you don't want to lose the clinical items that were deleted from the WISC-III (e.g., *fight* in Picture Arrangement), it doesn't matter. Norms are the main name of the game, and the WISC-III's norms are excellent and modern (Kaufman, 1993b), far better than the outdated norms of the WISC-R. Use the WISC-III.

I've stated, in the Preface, my personal misgivings about the elimination of clinically rich items from the WISC-III, and how upset Dr. Wechsler would have been by their deletion. (Of course, had he been alive, those items would still be there.) Other clinicians have responded even more strongly. Scarbaugh (1992) complained:

> When I was asked to present a program on the projective and personality aspects of the WISC-III, I discovered to my shock and dismay that it has been pretty thoroughly ruined in terms of its clinical aspects. The WISC

was developed as a clinical measure. But can anyone think that the similarity between milk and water is clinically the same as that between beer and wine? One of the distressed members of my audience said she was heavily tempted not to use the WISC-III. . . . Almost all the items that provide information about antisocial behavior have been removed. . . . As a Quaker, I should be glad of less emphasis on violence, but as a clinician I could only mourn. (p. 11)

There's no need to mourn the clinical items, or to decide to give the WISC-R instead of the WISC-III because they've departed. The solution is really simple. Test the limits. Take a few extra seconds or minutes after *completing* the administration of certain WISC-III subtests and ask the child to define *knife*, to tell how *beer* and *wine* are alike, or to arrange the pictures for *fight, burglar,* or the old *fire* item. The child's scores won't count—you don't even need to score them—but the clinical information will be there for the taking.

Now a different question: What about the choice of Wechsler test at the ages where the WISC-III overlaps with the WPPSI-R (6-0 to 7-3) and WAIS-R (16-0 to 16-11)? In each case, the answer is simple: Choose the WISC-III. I'll explain why.

WISC-III versus WPPSI-R

The WPPSI-R leaves much to be desired as a preschool and primary-grade test, in part because of its heavy emphasis on speed (Kaufman, 1990b). Unlike its predecessor, WPPSI-R gives bonus points for quick, perfect performance on Block Design, and bonus points are an essential aspect of the new Object Assembly subtest that was added to the battery. Test a 6½ or 7-year-old child on the WPPSI-R, and that child cannot earn a scaled score above 7 on Object Assembly or 10 on Block Design without earning at least one bonus point for quick, perfect performance. Young school-age children can solve every item perfectly and still not score higher than the 50th percentile—unless they are quick. And many 6- or 7-year-olds just don't know enough to hurry. On the WISC-III, it's a different story: A child of 6½ or 7 who gets every Block Design item right, but earns no bonus points for speed, earns the maximum scaled score of 19; on Object Assembly, the slow-but-steady child earns a scaled score in the 16–19 range.

The WISC-III also has a much better "top" than the WPPSI-R for 6- and 7-year-olds, a definite plus when testing bright and gifted children (Kaufman, 1992). All WISC-III subtests yield scaled scores of 19 at ages 6 and 7 years; only Vocabulary, among the 10 regular WPPSI-R subtests, consistently yields the maximum scaled score of 19. By age 7, the peak score on six of the 10 subtests is just 16 or 17. Even more of a problem is the reliability of the WPPSI-R at age 7. Coefficients for Verbal IQ (.86) and Performance IQ (.85) were lower than the .90+ values for other ages, and the subtest reliabilities were downright poor (uncharacteristically so for a Wechsler scale):

They ranged from .54 on Object Assembly and Similarities to .86 on Block Design, with a median value of .66. There's really no contest between the WPPSI-R and the WISC-III when the examiner faces that choice for a 6- or 7-year-old.

WISC-III versus WAIS-R

And the same goes for the WISC-III versus the WAIS-R at age 16. For one thing, the WAIS-R was normed in 1976 to 1980, about 12 years before the WISC-III, so its norms are outdated by about 3½ points relative to the WISC-III norms. This fact was once again illustrated in the WISC-III manual (Wechsler, 1991, Table 6.10) in the counterbalanced study of 16-year-olds tested on the WISC-III and WAIS-R. The group scored 3.9 Full Scale IQ points higher on the WAIS-R (105.3) than the WISC-III (101.4). But the problem with the WAIS-R adolescent norms goes well beyond their datedness. There's something wrong with them (Kaufman, 1990a, pp. 83–85).

For some reason, probably related to unknown biases in sample selection, the 16–19-year-olds in the WAIS-R norms group performed quite poorly on the Verbal and Performance subtests compared with adults ages 20–24 years. Enter the mean sums of scaled scores earned by 16–17-year-olds in the norms table for 20–24-year-olds, and the adolescent group winds up with average IQs of 91–92. For the WAIS, those averages were 96–98. Even more peculiar, is that the 18–19-year-olds didn't do any better on the WAIS-R—not a jot—than the 16–17-year-olds. All of which makes no sense at all because of the higher level of education achieved by the older adolescent sample (60% of the 18–19-year-olds in the WAIS-R sample had 12 or more years of schooling compared with 3% of the 16–17-year-olds). On the WAIS, the age changes were lawful, with the 18–19-year sample performing midway between those aged 16–17 and 20–24.

The WAIS-R norms for ages 16–19 years suggest that the test be used cautiously, if at all, for individuals below 20 years of age. At age 16, if it's a question of which Wechsler scale to use, then choose the WISC-III. Even apart from the norms, the Performance Scale is more reliable for the WISC-III (.92) than WAIS-R (.88) at age 16.

CHAPTER 2

Abilities Measured by the WISC-III Subtests and the Clinical Lore That Surrounds Them

This chapter focuses on the separate subtests to provide a foundation for the integrative interpretation that is featured in the chapters that follow. The empirical and clinical material for each subtest is intended to serve as a source of raw materials for the generation and testing of hypotheses that characterize the method of profile interpretation operationalized in step-by-step fashion in Chapter 3 and conceptualized in Chapters 4 through 7. Learn what is special about each subtest and understand each task's unique contribution to the WISC-III, cognitively, behaviorally, and clinically. But pay particular attention to the diversity of abilities assessed by several subtests and try to internalize an understanding of these "shared" abilities.

Overlapping abilities, not unique skills tapped by a single subtest, remain in the forefront of this chapter despite the sequential treatment of the individual subtests. The WISC-III is maximally useful when tasks are grouped and regrouped to uncover a child's strong and weak areas of functioning, so long as these hypothesized assets and deficits are verified by multiple sources of information. Whereas the detective work outlined in Chapters 4 and 5 (IQs and Factor Indexes) and Chapter 6 (subtest profile) may lead to the ultimate conclusion that a child has a strong or weak ability only in the skill assessed by a single subtest, such a finding should be the last resort of a good detective and is usually of limited practical value.

WAYS OF ANALYZING EACH WISC-III SUBTEST

Each subtest is first analyzed empirically: reliability (split-half and test-retest); g loading, or the degree to which it measures general intelligence; subtest specificity, or its amount of reliable, unique variance; intercorrelations with other subtests, highlighting the tasks with which it correlates best and worst; the proportion of variance for each subtest that is attributed to each of the four factors, Verbal Comprehension, Perceptual Organization, Freedom from Distractibility, and Processing Speed; and variance proportions just for the Verbal and Performance factors when two-factor solutions are studied.

Following the empirical summary are lists of (a) cognitive abilities that each subtest is presumed to measure, organized in terms of the learning disabilities model discussed in Chapter 1–Input, Integration, Storage, Output; (b) influences from a child's background or behavioral repertoire that are presumed to most affect performance on each subtest; and (c) clinical considerations about each subtest that have emerged from more than a half-century of clinical application of Wechsler's scales and thousands of research studies with these tests.

The next sections provide the foundation for understanding some of the empirical techniques applied to each subtest, and a few of the more pertinent theory-based models for reorganizing the WISC-III into alternate groupings. The chapter ends with a practical discussion of the three subtests that are supplements (Digit Span, Symbol Search, and Mazes), and one that should have been (Coding).

Empirical Considerations

In the psychometric analyses for each test, data are provided for the total standardization sample of 2,200 children ages 6 to 16 years, unless otherwise noted. Age trends were relatively minor for the statistics reported for each subtest. When occasional differences did occur for certain ages, such differences seemed more arbitrary than systematic, and more likely due to chance fluctuations than to meaningful developmental changes. The large normative sample provides a far more stable database than the 200 children per age group, and is utilized throughout. Split-half and test-retest reliability data, intercorrelational data, and proportions of variance associated with different factors were obtained from the WISC-III manual (Wechsler, 1991, Tables 5.1, 5.5, 6.2–6.6, C.12). General factor loadings and subtest specificity proportions were provided by Kamphaus (1993, Chapter 6).

Loadings on the General Factor

There are several methods of determining the degree to which a subtest measures g or general intelligence, and all give highly similar results. Kamphaus (1993) used the loadings on the unrotated first factor in principal components analysis, and those will do just fine. By convention, factor loadings of .70 or greater define tasks that are "good" measures of g, whereas loadings of .50 to .69 define "fair" g loadings. Loadings below .50 on the general factor are usually considered poor. These guidelines were used to categorize g loadings for the WISC-III subtests, using data for the entire normative group. Extremely similar results were obtained in a large-scale cross-validation of the WISC-III's factor structure for 1,118 children ages 6–16 years (Roid, Prifitera, & Weiss, 1993) who were tested in conjunction with the standardization of the Wechsler Individual Achievement Test (WIAT; Psychological Corporation, 1992). WISC-III subtests are classified as shown (*g* loading in parentheses):

Good Measures of *g*	Fair Measures of *g*	Poor Measures of *g*
Vocabulary (.80)	Comprehension (.68)	Digit Span (.47)
Information (.78)	Object Assembly (.61)	Coding (.41)
Similarities (.77)	Picture Completion (.60)	
Arithmetic (.76)	Symbol Search (.56)	
Block Design (.71)	Picture Arrangement (.53)	

In general, the good measures of general ability are on the Verbal Scale and the fair measures are on the Performance Scale. Block Design joins the Verbal subtests as a good measure, and is easily the best nonverbal measure of *g*. The only two poor measures of *g* are associated with the smaller WISC-III factors, although Digit Span squeaked into the fair category with a .50 loading in Roid et al.'s (1993) cross-validation study; no other subtest changed classifications. Mazes is excluded from the above groupings, and from the interpretive system in this book, for reasons explained later in the chapter. Had it been included, a new category would have been needed to accommodate Mazes' *g* loading of .30: Terrible.

One should not overvalue the notion of *g*. As expressed in Chapter 1 and elaborated by Carroll (1993a, 1993b), the WISC-III Full Scale IQ does not adequately reflect the diversity of cognitive capabilities that have been identified in many studies of children's thinking. Consequently, the notion of *g* must be thought of as the global ability underlying a conventional intelligence test such as the WISC-III, K-ABC, DAS, or Binet-4, but not as a theoretical construct underlying human intellect. As such, the so-called *g* factor still has relevance in a practical sense, but it should be stripped of the almost magical powers that are sometimes attributed to it.

Practically, knowledge of the magnitude of each subtest's loadings on the unrotated general factor facilitates profile interpretation. The loadings foster an anticipation of which subtests are most likely to be deviant from a child's overall level of functioning. Coding, as a very poor measure of global ability, will frequently deviate from children's scores on other WISC-III subtests; the good measures of *g* will not. This point is evident in Table 3.3, which is based on abnormal deviations and is used to determine which subtests deviate significantly from a child's own mean score.

When individuals score very high or low on tasks that ordinarily reflect very closely their Full Scale IQ, it is reasonable to anticipate noncognitive explanations for the discrepancies. For example, relatively poor performance on Information and Vocabulary may be a direct function of an impoverished cultural environment at home, whereas uncharacteristically high scores on the same two subtests may be indicative of an enriched home environment and perhaps a strong parental push for achievement. Unusually low scores on Similarities and Block Design may be related to a difficulty in handling abstractions, a problem sometimes considered to have neurological implications. Certainly, discrepant scores on the "high *g*" subtests are insufficient evidence for any noncognitive interpretation of the fluctuations unless there is strong additional background, behavioral, and test data to corroborate the hypothesis. However, knowledge of the *g* loadings for the WISC-III subtests can provide examiners with a sense of anticipation of what to expect in a profile, thereby enhancing their ability to lend meaningful interpretation to peaks and valleys in a scaled-score pattern.

Subtest Specificity

Highly related to the concept of a general factor, and to some extent an inverse of *g*, is the notion of subtest specificity. Just as a subtest has reliable variance that is shared with other subtests, so does it have a portion of its reliable variance that is unique to it. To determine the feasibility of interpreting the unique abilities or traits attributed to a subtest, one must first calculate the amount of its reliable variance that is not shared with any other WISC-III subtests. If this unique variance for a given subtest is sufficient in magnitude (arbitrarily, about 25% or more of the total variance), and if it exceeds the error variance, it is reasonable and justifiable to interpret that subtest's unique contributions to the test battery.

The statistical technique for computing a subtest's unique variance or specificity is objective and straightforward. First, an estimate of the common or shared variance for each subtest has to be obtained, often the squared multiple correlation, which is what Kamphaus (1993) used for his computations. The common variance is then subtracted from the subtest's reliability coefficient (which equals the total reliable variance for the subtest), yielding the reliable unique variance or subtest specificity. When the specificity is compared with the error variance for the subtest (equal to 1 minus the reliability), the examiner can determine whether it is sensible to interpret that task's uniqueness.

WISC-III subtests are classified here as having "ample," "adequate," or "inadequate" specificity based on Kamphaus's (1993) computations and classifications. The values shown in parentheses indicate the subtest specificity (reliable unique variance) followed by the subtest's error variance. These classifications, based on the total sample, are applicable to children of all ages. Examiners who feel compelled to use data for separate age groups should consult articles that provide such data (Bracken, McCallum, & Crain, 1993; Kamphaus & Platt, 1992). Note, however, that Kamphaus and Platt indicate that age trends are minor, and Kamphaus features the overall values in his text.

Ample Specificity	Adequate Specificity	Inadequate Specificity
Digit Span (.63/.15)	Symbol Search (.34/.26)	Object Assembly (.26/.31)
Coding (.49/.23)	Arithmetic (.30/.22)	
Picture Arrangement (.48/.24)	Comprehension (.30/.23)	
Picture Completion (.39/.23)	Information (.25/.16)	
Block Design (.34/.13)	Vocabulary (.24/.13)	
	Similarities (.23/.19)	

In general, Digit Span and Performance subtests have ample specificity and Verbal subtests have adequate specificity. Only Object Assembly has an inadequate amount of reliable specific variance (in large part because it doesn't have that much reliable variance of any type). How does the subtest specificity information translate to action? First, it gives examiners the right to make subtest-specific interpretations for all subtests, *except* Object Assembly. The data do not, however, elevate unique interpretations of subtests into the foreground. Because examiners *can* make specific inferences about subtests does not mean they necessarily *should* make such inferences. The proposed rules for applying the subtest specificity data to profile interpretation are outlined in Chapter 6 (see Guideline 5 of the method for generating hypotheses).

Intercorrelations

The degree to which each WISC-III subtest correlates with other subtests provides examiners with another practical aid for anticipating the shape of children's scaled-score profiles. The subtests with which each task correlates best and worst help in understanding which pairs of tasks are most likely and least likely to vary together. Overall for the 12 subtests, correlations for the total normative sample range from a low of .18 for Picture Completion/Coding to a high of .70 for Information/Vocabulary (excluding Mazes which correlated in the teens with half the subtests).

Study the best and worst correlates listed for each subtest. Some will surprise you. For example, Coding is one of the two worst correlates of Picture Arrangement, even though both measure visual sequencing skills, are highly speeded, and measure convergent-production according to Guilford's system (described later in this chapter). Arithmetic, though included on the FD factor, correlates best (mid-.50s) with Information, Similarities, and Vocabulary (it correlates .43 with Digit Span).

Proportions of Variance Associated with Different Factors

The four-factor solution of the WISC-III, as demonstrated with standardization data and verified with a totally independent sample of over 1,000 children, established the construct validity of the instrument and showed that each subtest legitimately belonged to its designated factor. The final outcome of the analyses, however, does not address the issue of how closely each subtest is associated with its own factor or the degree to which it measures the other factors.

Table 2.1 provides data to address these issues. This table indicates the proportion of a test's variance (which altogether sums to 100) that is associated with its assigned factor; the proportion associated with the other three factors; the proportion that is reliable but not associated with any of the four factors; and the proportion that is a function of measurement error. This table features the proportions obtained from factor analysis of the total standardization sample, but also indicates the proportions obtained for the separate sample tested by Roid et al. (1993).

As indicated, each subtest is associated more with its own factor than with any other factor. For the Verbal Comprehension (VC) subtests, the association is powerful, as each is barely associated with the other dimensions. The factor analysis with the separate sample agrees with that finding. The degree of robustness for VC does not characterize the other three factors. Block Design and Object Assembly are very strong measures of the Perceptual Organization (PO) factor, but Picture Completion is just adequate and Picture Arrangement is marginal at best. The latter two subtests

TABLE 2.1.   Proportion of the Variance of Each Subtest Attributed to Each of the Four Factors, to Other Abilities, and to Error (ages 6–16 years)

WISC-III Subtest	1. VC	2. PO	3. FD	4. PS	Other	Error
Verbal Comprehension (VC)						
Information	**52 (52)**	8 (6)	6 (5)	1 (4)	17 (17)	16
Similarities	**52 (56)**	8 (7)	5 (2)	1 (4)	15 (12)	19
Vocabulary	**62 (66)**	5 (6)	3 (2)	3 (3)	14 (10)	13
Comprehension	**42 (46)**	4 (5)	3 (2)	4 (4)	24 (20)	23
Perceptual Organization (PO)						
Picture Completion	14 (16)	**28 (25)**	1 (0)	1 (1)	33 (35)	23
Picture Arrangement	11 (11)	**14 (18)**	1 (0)	6 (7)	44 (40)	24
Block Design	8 (8)	**49 (45)**	6 (5)	3 (6)	21 (23)	13
Object Assembly	7 (4)	**48 (52)**	1 (0)	2 (2)	11 (11)	31
Freedom from Distractibility (FD)						
Arithmetic	16 (24)	7 (8)	**53 (28)**	2 (4)	0 (14)	22
Digit Span	7 (8)	4 (2)	**12 (12)**	3 (11)	59 (52)	15
Processing Speed (PS)						
Coding	1 (3)	2 (3)	1 (0)	**62 (31)**	11 (40)	23
Symbol Search	4 (2)	12 (6)	4 (3)	**31 (50)**	23 (13)	26

Note: The first values shown for each subtest are for the total standardization sample, based on factor analyses reported in the manual (Wechsler, 1991, Tables 6.3 to 6.6). The values in parentheses are based on data for 1,118 children tested in the cross-validation study of the WISC-III factor analysis (Roid et al., 1993, Table 3). Values for the subtest's designated factor are in bold print. Decimal points are omitted. "Other" refers to reliable variance associated with abilities other than the four factors. "Error" refers to error variance, computed from reliability coefficients reported in the WISC-III manual (split-half for most subtests, test-retest for Coding and Symbol Search).

are associated more with abilities other than the four factors than they are with their designated factor.

Arithmetic is much more closely associated with the Freedom from Distractibility (FD) factor than any other factor for the normative sample, but for the large cross-validation group it is related almost as much to VC as to FD. Digit Span is a barely adequate measure of FD in both analyses, and a majority of its variance is related to other abilities. The Processing Speed (PS) factor is primarily a Coding factor for the standardization sample, but that flip-flops in the analysis with the independent sample for whom Symbol Search defines the PS factor.

The results of the partitioning of each subtest's variance indicate that VC subtests are more likely to hang together for a particular child than are the subtests composing any of the other three factors. Picture Arrangement and Digit Span, especially, are likely to fractionate from the PO and FD factors, respectively. Each is primarily associated with abilities other than the four factors, and, concomitantly, each has a great deal of subtest specificity. Expect these subtests to be mavericks.

Table 2.2 looks at two-factor solutions of the WISC-III (Wechsler, 1991, Table 6.2) which conform fairly closely to Wechsler's division of subtests on the basis of item content (verbal, nonverbal). These data offer construct validity evidence for Wechsler's V-IQ and P-IQ. Symbol Search is a good measure of general Performance ability. Arithmetic, Digit Span, Picture Arrangement, and Coding—two Verbal and two Performance subtests—are marginally associated with their respective scales. But only Digit Span falls below my imaginary cutoff point for "belonging" to a factor. It does not measure general verbal ability by any reasonable standard.

In the subtest-by-subtest analysis, the data presented in Tables 2.1 and 2.2 are listed for each task. Only the data for the standardization sample, not the cross-validation group, are included for the two-factor solution.

Abilities Shared with Other Subtests

Following the psychometric analysis, each of the 12 WISC-R subtests is analyzed in terms of the abilities it presumably assesses and the influences (e.g., richness of early environment, anxiety) to which it is believed to be vulnerable. The abilities are organized within each subtest in accordance with the information processing described in Chapter 1 (Silver, 1993), a model that relates closely to psycholinguistic communication models (Osgood & Miron, 1963). Abilities are grouped under the heading "Input" if they involve the type of stimuli to be handled (e.g., perception of abstract visual stimuli) or under the heading "Output" if the mode of response is of primary importance (e.g., verbal expression, visual-motor coordination). The "Integration" and "Storage" aspects of the model are merged for the ability analysis because it is difficult to tease out the processing and memory components from many of the abilities that are assessed by the subtests. As an illustration,

TABLE 2.2.   Proportion of the Variance of Each Subtest
Attributed to the Verbal and Performance Factors When Only
Two Factors Are Rotated (ages 6–16 years)

WISC-III Subtest	Verbal	Performance (Nonverbal)
Verbal		
Information	**58**	9
Similarities	**56**	8
Arithmetic	**31**	18
Vocabulary	**66**	7
Comprehension	**46**	6
Digit Span	**12**	9
Performance		
Picture Completion	15	**25**
Coding	3	**15**
Picture Arrangement	12	**18**
Block Design	12	**52**
Object Assembly	8	**44**
Symbol Search	7	**29**

Note: The values shown for each subtest are for the total standardization sample, based on factor analyses reported in the manual in which only two factors were rotated (Wechsler, 1991, Table 6.2). Values for the subtest's designated scale are in bold print. Decimal points are omitted.

consider numerical reasoning, an ability measured by Arithmetic. One cannot easily separate the long-term memory and retrieval requirements for performing the computations, the short-term requirements needed to maintain the question in working memory, and the reasoning skills necessary for identifying the correct numerical operation.

This section serves as a road map and foundation for understanding the terminology used in the subtest-by-subtest analysis. Most of the abilities and influences were first advanced by clinical and empirical interpretive pioneers such as Wechsler, Rapaport, and Cohen (Cohen, 1952, 1957, 1959; Mayman, Schafer, & Rapaport, 1951; Rapaport, Gill, & Schafer, 1945–1946; Wechsler, 1939). During the previous generation, they were refined by leaders such as Matarazzo (1972) and Glasser and Zimmerman (1967), and during the past 10 or 15 years they have been amended to incorporate advances in neuropsychology. The theories of cerebral specialization researchers such as Sperry (1968) and his students and colleagues (Bever, 1975; Levy & Trevarthen, 1976) have enhanced our understanding of the different processing styles believed to be associated with the two hemispheres. The left hemisphere specializes in analytic, linear, sequential information processing in contrast to the holistic/simultaneous processing of the right hemisphere (Kaufman, 1979a; Springer & Deutsch, 1981). From Luria's (1966, 1973, 1980) alternate neuropsychological perspective, the successive and simultaneous processes are considered Block 2 coding functions in contrast to the attentional functions of Block 1 and the planning abilities of Block 3.

Syntheses of these various old and new perspectives have been cycled and recycled and now appear in a variety of alternate forms (Kamphaus, 1993; Kaufman, 1990a; Sattler, 1988, 1992; Zimmerman & Woo-Sam, 1985), all fairly similar but diverging in accordance with each author's personal orientation. In addition to neuropsychological orientations, most analyses of Wechsler's scales include the cognitive theories of Horn and Cattell (Horn & Cattell, 1966, 1967; Horn, 1989) and Guilford (1967), and Bannatyne's (1971, 1974) reorganization of Wechsler's subtests stemming from his initial research with dyslexic children.

All the abilities listed for each WISC-III subtest are considered to be required for successful performance on that task, although poor performance may be due to a deficiency in an isolated skill. The lists are necessarily not exhaustive. Psychologists from different orientations would compile somewhat different lists of abilities, and any given child tested on the WISC-III may succeed or fail on some subtests due to skills and variables that are unique to him or her. Consequently, the lists of abilities shared by two or more subtests should be a starting point to be used flexibly by examiners, with additional skills added to the lists based on their clinical experiences and theoretical beliefs.

Following the enumeration of shared abilities for each subtest is a list of the influences that are considered to affect an individual's performance on that task. Although these influences are basically derived from the same sources as the conventional abilities and are sometimes not treated separately from the abilities by various authors, they are grouped separately here. Distractibility, anxiety, cultural opportunities at home, attention span, and other factors play an important role in a person's Wechsler profile. However, it is difficult to conceive mental tasks as being primarily a measure of concentration or attention, as Rapaport and his colleagues claim for Arithmetic and Digit Span, respectively. By keeping the abilities and influences in discrete groupings, examiners will have a constant reminder of whether their hypotheses are in the cognitive or the behavioral-background domain. As explained in Chapter 5 regarding the FD and PS factors, hypotheses of low scores due to a behavioral or background variable (i.e., due to an "influence") do *not* imply that the child is deficient in the abilities measured by the Factor Index.

Even more so than the lists of abilities for the subtests, the lists of influences affecting subtest scores can always be increased and modified based on the particular testing conditions, the child's unique background and approach to each new task, the examiner's clinical acumen and range of experiences, and so forth. Keen observational skills, coupled with the social intelligence to interpret the observed behaviors (these two skills don't always go together), are important ingredients for relating behaviors to test scores.

The unique ability or abilities probably tapped by each WISC-III subtest are indicated in the lists of abilities with asterisks. These so-called unique abilities are essentially those skills that seem to be associated primarily with one and only one subtest. Thus, for example, Similarities is often considered to measure verbal concept formation, degree of abstract thinking, distinguishing essential from nonessential details, and logical abstractive (categorical) thinking. The first two abilities are also assessed by Vocabulary, and distinguishing essential from nonessential details is measured as well by Picture Completion and Picture Arrangement. Only logical abstractive (categorical) thinking is associated just with Similarities, so it is asterisked as the unique ability.

The next sections go into depth on three of the models mentioned previously to facilitate the examiner's understanding of pertinent constructs and categories: Horn-Cattell, Guilford, and Bannatyne.

Horn and Cattell's Fluid-Crystallized Theory

Horn and Cattell (1966, 1967) distinguished between two broad constructs, Crystallized Intelligence (Gc) and Fluid Intelligence (Gf). Gc reflects problem solving and factual learning that is dependent on formal schooling and acculturation, whereas Gf refers to the ability to solve new problems where neither formal schooling nor acculturation facilitate task performance to any meaningful extent (Cattell & Horn, 1978). The original theory focused on these two constructs, and Matarazzo (1972) was among the first, according to Horn (personal communication, 1993), to interpret the Wechsler scales according to this dichotomy: Verbal = Gc, and Performance = Gf. That association has an intuitive validity and has remained a pervasive interpretation of V-IQ and P-IQ (Kaufman, 1990a), although recent research coupled with Horn's (1985, 1989, 1991) extension of the theory has challenged the relationship (see Kaufman & Kaufman, 1993; Woodcock, 1990; and the discussion of Gf–Gc theory in Chapter 4).

Horn identified "purer" cognitive measures of intelligence, and now focuses on eight or so abilities rather than the original two. His well-respected theory (Lohman, 1989, 1993) is still called Gf-Gc theory, but these abilities are included among more than a half dozen rather than standing alone. Gf tasks that place too much emphasis on visual-spatial ability, long-term memory, or speed of performance are too multifaceted to provide good measures of fluid ability. Horn's current definition of Gf demands that reasoning be the key cognitive ability measured without contamination of variables such as visualization or speed. Similarly, Gc tasks should focus on knowledge and comprehension and not include other factors such as short-term memory or fluid reasoning. The intervening variables, when defined unidimensionally and converted into mental tasks, join Gc and Gf as measures of cognitive capabilities in Horn's expanded theory. Some of these additional abilities include Short-Term Acquisition and Retrieval (SAR or Gsm), Broad Speediness (Gs), Broad Visualization (Gv), Quantitative Thinking (Gq), and Auditory Intelligence (Ga).

The influence of the Horn-Cattell theory has been strong in shaping recent tests. Broad definitions of Gf and Gc form the foundation of the Binet-4 and the KAIT, and Horn's expanded model provides the theoretical framework for the seven ability factors assessed by the Revised (not the original) Woodcock-Johnson cognitive scale. In addition, other recent tests such as the Detroit-3, K-ABC, and DAS have the unmistakable imprint of Horn-Cattell theory. The DAS, for example, organizes its Core subtests into scales that are easily interpretable as Gf (Nonverbal Reasoning), Gc (Verbal), and Gv (Spatial); and it includes Diagnostic subtests that are measures of SAR, Gs, and Long-Term Storage and Retrieval (TSR).

I have grouped WISC-III subtests into Horn factors based on Woodcock's (1990) suggestions, Horn's recent writings (Horn, 1989, 1991; Horn & Hofer, 1992), and my collaboration with Horn on a KAIT article (Kaufman & Horn, 1994). These groupings differ from my Horn-Cattell groupings of WAIS-R subtests (Kaufman, 1990a) because of the research published after I wrote that book and, especially, based on personal communication with John Horn during our collaboration. Although Woodcock (1990) based his classifications on extensive data analyses, I have deviated in some cases from his conclusions because some of his labels for factors are occasionally at odds with Horn's perspective. For example, Woodcock defines Arithmetic as measuring Gq even though Horn (1989) insists that to distinguish Gq from Gf, tests of Gq "should involve problems that are most readily solved only by application of previously worked methods and principles of mathematics, rather than by application of general skills of reasoning" (p. 87). By that definition, WISC-III Arithmetic is clearly not Gq.

Classification of WISC-III subtests as Gc and Gf are shown here, followed by groupings of subtests into other Horn factors.

Crystallized Intelligence (Gc)	Fluid Intelligence (Gf)
Information	Picture Arrangement
Similarities	Block Design
Vocabulary	Object Assembly
Comprehension	Similarities
Picture Arrangement	Arithmetic

Broad Visualization (Gv) include "tasks that call for fluent visual scanning, Gestalt closure, mind's-eye rotations of figures, and ability to see reversals" (Horn, 1989, p. 80):

Picture Completion
Block Design
Object Assembly

Short-Term Acquisition and Retrieval (SAR) are similar to sequential processing of information. SAR or Gsm "involves processes of becoming aware of information, discriminating between different bits of information, retaining such awarenesses and discriminations for short periods of time, and using these awarenesses and discriminations . . . in performing various kinds of tasks" (Horn & Hofer, 1992, p. 62).

Arithmetic
Digit Span

Broad Speediness (Gs) "Speediness in intellectual tasks relates to carefulness, strategies (or metacognition), mood (such as depression), and persistence" (Horn, 1989, p. 84).

Coding
Symbol Search
Object Assembly

The Horn system provides a theoretical interpretation of the four WISC-III factors: VC is Gc, PO is Gv, FD is SAR, and PS is Gs. Object Assembly joins the two PS subtests because analyses of the contribution of time bonuses to a child's score on WISC-R Object Assembly is considerable, more than the role played by time bonuses on Block Design and Picture Arrangement scores (Kaufman, 1979c; see Chapter 4).

The Fluid Intelligence factor cuts across the Verbal and Performance Scales. The Gc and Gf components of Picture Arrangement may account for its associations with both the VC and PO factors. The Gf aspect of Similarities and Arithmetic may explain why these subtests sometimes have secondary loadings on Perceptual Organization factors (Kaufman, 1990a, Chapter 8).

In addition to providing a theoretical rationale for the new WISC-III structure, the Horn system also helps identify specific abilities that the WISC-III does not measure: Gq, TSR (e.g., retention of learning after several minutes or hours), and Ga (chunking streams of sounds, such as blending phonemes into a word). More importantly, the Horn analysis permits easy integration of scores obtained on the WISC-III with scores earned on the KAIT, WJ-R, K-ABC, Binet-4, Detroit-3, and DAS. These relationships are explored in greater depth in the section on the Horn-Cattell model in Chapter 4. Several illustrative case reports integrate the WISC-III with subtests or scales from the WJ-R, KAIT, and DAS, thereby providing an interpretation of the child's fluid versus crystallized abilities that is not evident from the global scores yielded by the WISC-III (see the comprehensive reports for James C., Ira G., and Greg T. in Chapter 7).

Guilford's Structure of Intellect Model

Guilford's (1967) three-dimensional theoretical model of intelligence has provided a convenient technique for labeling the abilities measured by various cognitive tasks. Meeker (1969, 1975) has used Guilford's method to define structure-of-intellect (SOI) factors for the Wechsler batteries and other tests, and has developed a comprehensive technique for interpreting these tests. Her method involves the use of cardboard templates placed over the pages of a record form to facilitate obtaining scores on each SOI factor measured by the intelligence test. Meeker's approach is fine for a devotee of Guilford's theory, but it is generally too time-consuming for the type of eclectic interpretation advocated in this book. Although the model has three dimensions, the products dimension (the way the stimuli are organized) seems less important for WISC-III interpretation than the other two dimensions, which are defined as follows:

Operations—Intellectual Processes

Cognition (C): Immediate awareness, recognition, or comprehension of stimuli.

Memory (M): Retention of information in the same form in which it was stored.

Evaluation (E): Making judgments about information in terms of a known standard.

Convergent production (N): Responding to stimuli with the unique or "best" answer.

Divergent production (D): Responding to stimuli where the emphasis is on variety or quality of response (associated with creativity).

Contents—Nature of the Stimuli

Figural (F): Shapes or concrete objects.

Symbolic (S): Numerals, single letters, or any coded symbol.

Semantic (M): Words and ideas that convey meaning.

Behavioral (B): Primarily nonverbal, involving human interactions with a stress on attitudes, needs, thoughts, and so on.

Guilford (1977, 1988) modified his model, replacing Figural content with Auditory and Visual contents, and dividing the Memory operation into Memory Recording (long-term) and Memory Retention (short-term). I have elected to define WISC-III subtests from Guilford's original model, the one that remains more popular and is probably more readily understood by clinicians, especially those who have applied SOI theory to Wechsler's scales in the past. For those who are interested in his revised model, all of the WISC-III subtests with Figural content would be classified as having Visual content. Of the subtests that assess the Memory operation, Arithmetic and Information measure Memory Recording and Digit Span measures Memory Retention. Note that Arithmetic is seen as a short-term memory test from Horn's system (SAR), but as a long-term memory test from the Meeker-Guilford approach. In actuality, this subtest measures *both* aspects of the

Memory operation, requiring the ability to retain the question in working memory while trying to solve the problem (Retention) and the prior acquisition of number facts (Recording).

Table 2.3 provides a brief Guilford analysis of the WISC-III. Neither the Divergent-production operation nor the Behavioral content is assessed by any Wechsler subtest. It is evident that the Verbal subtests are predominantly of semantic content with the Performance subtests composed primarily of figural content. As discussed in Chapter 4, another distinction between the two scales is that virtually all Performance subtests involve the operation of evaluation, as opposed to only a single Verbal subtest (Comprehension).

Although factor analysis no longer supports a three-subtest distractibility factor when Symbol Search is included in the matrix, the Guilford SOI model provides a theoretical rationale for continuing to interpret the Arithmetic-Digit Span-Coding B triad: All include symbolic content. Thus the first three WISC-III factors might easily be defined in terms of the content dimension of Guilford's model: Semantic, Figural, Symbolic. Arithmetic's association with both the FD and VC factors follows from its measurement of both symbolic and semantic content.

Despite its name, Symbol Search has figural content (as does Coding A) because its stimuli are shapes, not coded symbols. And despite the drawings used for Picture Arrangement items, they involve semantic content, according to Meeker, because it is the *semantic* meaning of the pictures that is

TABLE 2.3. Classification of WISC-III Subtests According to the Operations and Content Dimensions of Guilford's (1967) Original SOI Model

WISC-III Subtest	Cognition	Memory	Evaluation	Convergent-Production
·Verbal Comprehension				
Information		Semantic		
Similarities	Semantic			
Vocabulary	Semantic			
Comprehension			Semantic	
Perceptual Organization				
Picture Completion	Figural		Figural	
Picture Arrangement			Semantic	Semantic
Block Design	Figural		Figural	
Object Assembly	Figural		Figural	
Freedom from Distractibility				
Arithmetic	Semantic	Symbolic		
Digit Span		Symbolic		
Processing Speed				
Coding A			Figural	Figural
Coding B			Symbolic	Symbolic
Symbol Search A & B			Figural	Figural

manipulated mentally. Interestingly, Picture Arrangement and Comprehension are the only two WISC-III subtests that involve semantic evaluation. Individuals who score high or low on both subtests may have a strength or weakness on that SOI ability rather than the more conventional interpretations in terms of social understanding or common sense. In fact, two prime assets of including the SOI system in this chapter are that it provides alternate, less conventional, ways of viewing a child's cognitive capabilities, and it is sometimes the only way to make sense out of a perplexing Wechsler subtest profile. For example, when a child's score on Comprehension is more similar to his or her scores on Performance than Verbal subtests, the child may have a strength or weakness in the Guilford operation of Evaluation.

Bannatyne's Recategorization System

The well-known reorganization of WISC subtests that Bannatyne (1971, pp. 591–592) found useful for diagnosing dyslexic children, including the slight modification he made to it (Bannatyne, 1974), are shown here. Unlike most other labels for abilities from diverse systems, the names given by Bannatyne for his categories communicate directly and need no explanation:

Verbal Conceptualization Ability	Acquired Knowledge
Similarities	Information
Vocabulary	Arithmetic
Comprehension	Vocabulary

Spatial Ability	Sequencing Ability
Picture Completion	Arithmetic
Block Design	Digit Span
Object Assembly	Coding

Picture Arrangement (and the new Symbol Search subtest) are excluded from this recategorization system, whereas Arithmetic and Vocabulary appear twice. Picture Arrangement was originally classified as a Sequencing task, but Bannatyne (1974) reconsidered and replaced it with Arithmetic based on the results of factor analysis. The Bannatyne approach was developed from clinical application of Wechsler's scales and has a quasi-empirical foundation, but it does not enjoy the theoretical foundation and broad-based construct validation of the Guilford and Horn cognitive theories. Nonetheless, it is easily the most popular alternative interpretive approach for Wechsler's scales, appearing with regularity throughout the voluminous Wechsler literature (Kaufman, 1990a; Kaufman, Harrison, & Ittenbach, 1990), including early WISC-III studies (e.g., Prifitera & Dersh, 1993). The four-category system offers the best explanation of some children's WISC-III profiles such as the set of scaled scores for Tony G., whose case report appears at the end of Chapter 6.

Rugel's (1974) landmark application of the Bannatyne approach to the WISC profiles of reading- and learning-disabled children, using an informal meta-analysis procedure, began the popularization of the recategorization system and generated dozens of studies with diverse exceptional populations. Initial investigations frequently explored the existence of the Spatial > Verbal Conceptualization > Sequential profile among reading- and learning-disabled children. Though this pattern was identified for many *groups* of children with learning problems, it has not been found to characterize very many *individual* children or adolescents or to achieve success at differentially diagnosing learning-disabled children from those in other special education classifications (Berk, 1983; Clarizio & Bernard, 1981; Kavale & Forness, 1984).

Differential diagnosis, however, is not a prerequisite for the Bannatyne system's usefulness. Its main function should be to describe the cognitive functioning of individuals who are assessed on Wechsler's scales to obtain a better understanding of their cognitive functioning. Like any approach at reorganization, it should provide the clinician or researcher with information not readily apparent from the IQs or standard scores yielded by the instrument to offer better understanding of the cognitive capabilities of individual children or well-defined groups. That is precisely how the Bannatyne groupings have begun to be used; for example, they are commonly applied to the Wechsler profiles of minority children (including normal samples) such as Hispanics (McShane & Cook, 1985), African-Americans (Asbury, Stokes, Adderly-Kelly, & Knuckle, 1989), and American Indians (Connelly, 1983).

Most Bannatyne investigations in the 1970s omitted the Acquired Knowledge category from consideration, although subsequent studies included this category, and for good reason: It bears an obvious relationship to school learning problems. Children who perform poorly on the Acquired Knowledge triad may be reflecting their limited academic success such that their V-IQ grossly underestimates their intellectual potential. The Acquired Knowledge grouping has specifically been criticized because it does not emerge as a separate dimension in WISC-R factor analyses (Matheson, Mueller, & Short, 1984), but the authors' arguments strike me as another instance of putting rigid empirical findings above clinical utility. In fact, I consider the Acquired Knowledge category to be the most valuable of Bannatyne's groupings because of the frequency with which his model is applied to children with learning problems. The Acquired Knowledge category, when compared with the Verbal Conceptualization category, effectively dichotomizes the Verbal Scale into two components: school achievement versus verbal reasoning and concept formation. Including Vocabulary in both categories shouldn't prevent conscientious examiners from interpreting the pattern of scores on these two groupings in an intelligent manner by integrating the test data with other information about the child.

The other Bannatyne category of special clinical value is Sequential. On the WISC-R, this category was identical in composition to the distractibility triad. Its primary interpretive value was in providing a cognitive explanation for high or low performance on Arithmetic, Digit Span, and Coding, namely sequential ability or sequential processing. For the WISC-R, Bannatyne's interpretation was nothing more than a cognitive hypothesis to check out with multiple sources of data, like Guilford's symbolic or number ability interpretation of the FD factor, but it was an important new hypothesis for WISC-R clinicians. For one thing, it related closely to the findings of cerebral specialization researchers regarding left-hemisphere functions (Springer & Deutsch, 1981) and to Luria's (1966, 1980) explication of Block 2 successive coding functions. Plus, many examiners previously interpreted the distractibility factor either as a memory dimension or as a behavioral measure of attention-concentration, freedom from distractibility, or freedom from disruptive anxiety.

With the WISC-III, it offers these same benefits along with an important additional one: The new FD factor includes only two-thirds of the previous FD dimension. Routine investigation of Bannatyne's Sequential category, therefore, ensures that examiners will at least consider the possible grouping of Coding with Arithmetic and Digit Span, something that does not pop out automatically with the four-factor WISC-III solution. That same benefit is afforded to examiners who routinely evaluate the old FD triad from the content dimension of Guilford model.

Reynolds and Ford (in press) factor analyzed the WISC-III standardization data *without* Symbol Search to see if the old FD factor would emerge. The authors concluded that it did emerge, and that it was reasonably congruent with the FD factors identified for the WISC-R (Kaufman, 1975). I don't interpret their data in quite the same way. For the WISC-R, the FD factor was defined by the three subtests for *seven* of the eleven age groups, using a criterion of a factor loading of at least .40. For the WISC-III, in great contrast, the three subtests defined the FD factor for only *two* ages, 13½ and 16½ years (Reynolds & Ford, in press). If the criterion is dropped to a factor loading of .30, then a total of four WISC-III age levels show the old triad pattern (ages 11½ and 12½ climb aboard), half the number for the WISC-R.

These data indicate that even without Symbol Search, Coding would have been summarily dismissed from the FD factor. In practical terms, the three scaled scores are less likely to cluster together on the WISC-III than the WISC-R. That doesn't diminish the importance of Bannatyne's Sequential category for any given individual assessed, but it does suggest that the number of children for whom this interpretation is applicable will be considerably fewer than for the WISC-R.

Note that Bannatyne's Spatial category includes the same subtests as Horn's Gv grouping, and they really measure the same ability, visual-spatial thinking or simultaneous processing of information. The three subtests are also the ones that have continually had the highest loadings on the PO factor for any Wechsler scale for children, adolescents, and adults, suggesting that spatial ability, visualization, or simultaneous processing might be better names for that ever-present Wechsler nonverbal factor.

Clinical Considerations

The final section in the subtest-by-subtest analysis details a variety of clinical suggestions and observations for each subtest. Many of these points come from the same accumulated Wechsler lore that has been passed down from one generation of clinicians to the next. Some come from research findings, others come from my personal experience as a trainer of school and clinical psychologists and vicariously through Nadeen's direct services and supervision of interns and practicum students. Within the literature, my main sources for the clinical considerations are the following: Kamphaus (1993), Kaufman (1990a), Reitan and Wolfson (1992), Sattler (1988, 1992), and Zimmerman and Woo-Sam (1985).

The inferences and clinical suggestions attempt to explore each task's specific clinical potential without going overboard into the realm of psychoanalytic or projective interpretations (e.g., Allison, Blatt, & Zimet, 1968). The points listed should be treated as hypotheses to consider (and to reject if they don't fit your personal schema), not as factual or conclusive. They are presented to be consistent with Wechsler's intended use for his tests, and in the belief that there is much more to be gained from an individual evaluation of a person's intelligence than a cold profile of scores. As Lohman (1989) points out, even "theorists are once again beginning to argue that affect must be included in accounts of learning and cognition (Snow & Farr, 1987)" (p. 360).

Be advised, however, that most empirical research has not supported the clinical hypotheses about Wechsler profiles initially proposed by Rapaport and other clinical pioneers (Lipsitz, Dworkin, & Erlenmeyer-Kimling, 1993; Piedmont, Sokolve, & Fleming, 1989). Lipsitz et al.'s (1993) words are echoed throughout this book: "It is impossible to replicate the inferential process of an astute clinician, and hypotheses based on subtest patterns are typically applied in the context of other pieces of information, such as qualitative aspects of test responses, information from other tests, and interpersonal observations" (p. 436).

Practical Considerations: Symbol Search, Coding, Mazes, and Digit Span

The WISC-III includes two supplementary subtests, Symbol Search and Mazes, and the publisher made a mistake with both of them. Symbol Search is an excellent task that should have been included among the five regular Performance subtests instead of Coding. Mazes is an awful task that should have been dropped completely from the WISC-III.

Symbol Search versus Coding

The WISC-R manual stated clearly that the examiner had the option of choosing either Coding or Mazes as the fifth regular Performance subtest. The WISC-III manual is less clear about substitutes. It states that Digit Span and Mazes are supplementary subtests for the Verbal and Performance Scales, respectively; each one can substitute for a regular subtest on its scale, "if one of the standard subtests is invalidated or cannot be given" (Wechsler, 1991, p. 5). That's pretty clear. But for Symbol Search, we are told simply, "Symbol Search can substitute only for Coding in the determination of IQ scores" (Wechsler, 1991, p. 7). The manual doesn't say when; it doesn't say why; it doesn't say if we need a good reason or not. But what's a good reason? It can't be because you forgot your pencils or broke their points or you forgot a pencil sharpener; both subtests need pencils. It can't be because you've forgotten your Coding booklets; Coding no longer comes in a separate booklet, but it is now right in the record form. Symbol Search, in fact, is the one with a separate booklet. I can't figure out what the publisher had in mind for the acceptable substitution. So I've come up with a Letterman-like 10 situations when Symbol Search should be given instead of Coding:

10. The child or adolescent is left-handed.
 9. The child or adolescent is right-handed . . . or compulsively switches hands during nonverbal tasks.
 8. The examinee looks nervous when you open up the WISC-III manual and say, "I am going to show you some pictures. In each picture there is a part missing."
 7. The examinee sneers when you say, "I am going to ask you some questions, and I would like you to tell me the answers."
 6. Rapport is easy to establish.
 5. Rapport is damn near impossible to establish, much less maintain.
 4. The examinee rolls his or her eyes when you take out the Picture Completion booklet, and says, "Oh no! Not another WISC!"
 3. The adolescent stops halfway through the Information subtest and says in a smug voice, "This stuff is just bull, and IQ tests aren't valid anyhow!"
 2. The examinee gives you the impression that he or she would rather be anywhere—even the dentist or proctologist—than with you at this moment.
 1. You're assessing the child or adolescent on a weekday.

In short, there's no rational reason for the publisher to have rigidly clung to Coding as a regular part of the WISC-III when the new Symbol Search task is so clearly a better choice for the following (serious) psychometric reasons (based on data for the total standardization sample):

	Symbol Search	Coding
Correlation with Performance Scale	.58	.32
Correlation with Full Scale	.56	.33
Loading on Perceptual Organization Factor in Two-Factor Varimax Solutions	.54	.39
g Loading	.56	.41

In addition, Symbol Search measures primarily speed of *mental* processing, whereas Coding is mostly a fine-motor measure of psycho*motor* speed; there's already enough of an emphasis on visual-motor speed and coordination, thanks to the heavy emphasis on bonus points on the Block Design and Object Assembly subtests.

Therefore, I recommend strongly that WISC-III examiners routinely substitute Symbol Search for Coding as part of the regular battery, and use Symbol Search to compute Performance IQ and Full Scale IQ. The manual doesn't tell you to do this, but neither does it prohibit it. Psychologically, clinically, and psychometrically, this routine substitution makes a whole lot of sense. Also administer Coding, but only to get a Processing Speed Factor Index. This score offers examiners a reliable score (mid-.80s) of speed of mental and motor processing, an ability akin to Naglieri and Das's (1988) planning ability from Luria's neuropsychological model. Each subtest alone has reliability coefficients that average in the mid to high .70s, so the factor score offers a more stable alternative to either speed score in isolation.

The main negative to the proposed substitution is that the norms for Performance IQ and Full Scale IQ were computed using Coding, not Symbol Search, as the fifth regular Performance subtest. How much of a problem is this? Probably not too much. Silverstein (1989) investigated the use of the two WISC-R supplementary subtests (Digit Span and Mazes) as alternates for a regular subtest, and Boyd and Hooper (1987) conducted a similar study, but just with Digit Span. The impact on reliability, validity, and obtained IQs was relatively slight when Digit Span or Mazes was used as an alternate, and the differences are likely to be even slighter when Symbol Search is substituted for Coding. Unlike Digit Span, which bears virtually no association to the Verbal Comprehension subtests it is likely to replace, Symbol Search loads on the same factor as Coding, and correlates fairly well with it (.53). And whereas Mazes correlates poorly with the five regular Performance subtests (mean of .34 on the WISC-R and .24 on the WISC-III), Symbol Search correlates nearly as well with the four Perceptual Organization subtests (mean of .41) as they correlate with each other (mean of .46).

In short, the arguments for following the letter of the law and administering Coding as a regular subtest are meager; the arguments for substituting Symbol Search are strong. I urge you to make this modification in the regular WISC-III battery for any child or adolescent you test. The substitution will not lower the reliability of the Performance IQ or Full Scale IQ because the subtests have similar stability coefficients (the only type of reliability that is suitable for highly speeded subtests): .77 for Coding, .74 for Symbol Search. And since Symbol Search correlates substantially higher with the other Performance subtests than does Coding, that fact will offset its slightly lower reliability (reliability of an IQ scale is a function of both the reliability of its component subtests and the magnitude of the intercorrelations among them).

If you decide to follow my suggestion of substituting Symbol Search for Coding, *it is imperative that you make that decision prior to administering the battery and stick with it even if the examinee earns a higher scaled score on Coding than Symbol Search.* It is never reasonable to base such a decision on the child's obtained scores. And since examiners are strongly advised to give Coding (in its regular sequence, as the third subtest given) in addition to Symbol Search, to permit computation of the Processing Speed Factor Index, that temptation to choose the higher score will be there. Resist it.

Mazes

WISC-III Mazes is hopeless, a poor excuse for a subtest on a major intelligence test. Its correlations with the Performance Scale (.35) and Full Scale (.31) are weak. Its correlations with the other 12 WISC-III subtests are pathetic, ranging, for the total sample, from .14 with Digit Span to .31 with Block Design (mean = .21). Though the subtest was barely changed from the WISC-R to WISC-III (one hard item was added), the correlations inexplicably plunged; with the WISC-R, Mazes correlated in the mid-.40s with Performance and Full Scales, and had a mean correlation of .30 with the remaining subtests. And Mazes isn't just of questionable validity: It is also relatively unreliable (.78 for ages 6–8 years, .67 for ages 9–16), and totally unstable (.60 for ages 6–7, .56 for ages 10–11, and .54 for ages 14–15). It doesn't load too well on the Performance factor in the two-factor solutions of the WISC-III (.40, lower even than the loading for Arithmetic, and outranking only Coding's .39 among Performance subtests; Wechsler, 1991, Table 6.2), and Mazes isn't anywhere to be seen in the WISC-III's spanking-new four-factor solution. Of the three supplementary subtests, Digit Span and Symbol Search are included in the factor structure; of the 13 WISC-III subtests, 12 are included. Only Mazes stands alone, left out. Do you think the publisher is trying to tell us something? Yes, and we ought to listen.

I've left Mazes out of the tables of shared abilities in Chapter 6. Mazes supposedly measures planning ability, spatial ability, and nonverbal reasoning, but how good a job can it be doing with correlations in the low to mid .30s with Performance Scale and Full Scale, and a *g* loading of .30 (Kamphaus, 1993)? I don't have confidence in Mazes' internal consistency and stability, or in the validity of what it measures. Maybe its validity as an intelligence task has been compromised by the prevalence, and easy availability, of game books filled with mazes that are just like the items in the

Mazes subtests. Mazes may be more a measure of specific experience with maze books than of perceptual organization, planning, or visual-spatial ability. Puzzles are also readily available and popular, but they invariably involve interlocking pieces or formboards, not pieces like Object Assembly's that fit adjacent to each other without the benefit of an outline of the whole puzzle. So Object Assembly would not be as negatively affected as Mazes by children's toys and games; neither would Block Design, because the children's games that use analogs of Wechsler's Block Design cubes (e.g., Trac 4) don't seem to be very popular.

Really, I don't know why Mazes is such a poor task, and why it has gotten noticeably worse from WISC-R to WISC-III. But I feel confident that it shouldn't be included in any type of WISC-III profile analysis. Better yet, don't give it. To anyone. For any reason. If a regular Performance subtest is invalidated or cannot be given, prorate from four subtests. Don't substitute Mazes. Since the publisher does not want examiners to include both measures of Processing Speed (Coding and Symbol Search) in the computation of Performance IQ, simply prorate if a regular Perceptual Organization subtest is spoiled or not given. In Silverstein's (1989) study with the WISC-R, he compared substitution of an alternate subtest to proration. He found that substitution yielded slightly higher reliabilities than proration, but that proration actually produced higher validities. That is to say, prorated Performance and Full Scale IQs correlated higher with the actual IQs than did the IQs obtained when Mazes was used as a substitute for a regular subtest—more proof that you're better off not messing with Mazes at all.

Just a random thought: Do you know anyone who gave Mazes routinely, or even occasionally, on the WISC-R? I had to twist my students' arms just to administer it during my introductory course in intelligence testing.

Digit Span

Digit Span isn't a problem like Mazes, but the same suggestion applies about proration versus substitution. If a Verbal Comprehension subtest is spoiled or cannot be given, prorate Verbal IQ from the four remaining subtests; don't follow the publisher's suggestion of substituting Digit Span for the regular subtest. Digit Span loads a meager .34 on the Verbal Comprehension factor in the two-factor varimax solutions of the WISC-III (Wechsler, 1991, Table 6.2); even Arithmetic loads a respectable .56. Digit Span's correlations with Verbal subtests range from .29 with Comprehension to .43 with Arithmetic (mean = .35), much lower than the average intercorrelation among the five regular subtests (.60).

And the same research result held true for Digit Span that was found for Mazes: Substitution of Digit Span for a regular Verbal subtest yielded slightly higher reliabilities (Silverstein, 1989) than simple proration from four subtests, but proration produced a more valid set of Verbal and Full Scale IQs than did substitution for both normal (Silverstein, 1989) and clinical (Boyd & Hooper, 1987) samples. The only area of ambiguity concerns the instance in which Arithmetic is the spoiled or omitted subtest in question. Then examiners can legitimately choose to substitute Digit Span for Arithmetic in the computation of IQs; the choice is yours, because at least these two subtests are measures of the same factor, FD.

But, unlike Mazes, I don't suggest that you abandon Digit Span. It makes a unique contribution to the scale as a measure of auditory short-term memory, and is a necessary ingredient for obtaining a profile of Indexes on the four factors. Give Digit Span. In fact, administer it routinely. Just don't substitute it for a regular Verbal subtest—except, perhaps, for Arithmetic.

SUBTEST-BY-SUBTEST ANALYSIS

This analysis presents the six Verbal subtests first, followed by the six Performance subtests. Mazes is excluded.

Information

Empirical Analysis
Reliability:

Split-half	.84
Test-retest	.85

g loading	.78 (Good)

Subtest specificity vs. error variance	25% vs. 16% (Adequate)

Most related to:

Vocabulary	.70
Similarities	.66

Least related to:

Coding	.21
Digit Span	.34
Symbol Search	.35

Proportion of Variance Attributed to:

Factor 1. Verbal Comprehension	52%
Factor 2. Perceptual Organization	8%
Factor 3. Freedom from Distractibility	6%
Factor 4. Processing Speed	1%
Abilities other than the 4 factors	17%
Error	16%

Proportion of Variance When 2 Factors Are Rotated:

Factor 1. General Verbal Ability	58%
Factor 2. General Nonverbal Ability	9%

Abilities Shared with Other Subtests (Unique abilities are asterisked)

INPUT

Auditory perception of complex verbal stimuli (understanding questions)

INTEGRATION/STORAGE

Verbal Comprehension (Factor Analysis: 4-Factor and 2-Factor)

Gc—Crystallized Intelligence (Horn)

Memory (primarily), mostly of semantic stimuli (Guilford)

Acquired Knowledge (Bannatyne)

Culture-loaded knowledge

Fund of information

Long-term memory

*Range of general factual knowledge

OUTPUT

Simple vocal

Subject to Influence of:

Alertness to the environment

Cultural opportunities at home

Foreign language background

Intellectual curiosity and striving

Interests

Outside reading

Richness of early environment

School learning

Clinical Considerations

- Items are generally nonthreatening and emotionally neutral, but may produce anxiety in children referred for school learning problems. Even for children with learning problems, however, success is likely on the first few items, which demand simple, overlearned responses. Because of the minimal verbal expressive demands (many items have one-word answers), children with language problems or who are excessively shy will not be too threatened or penalized.

- This subtest elicits rationalizations and excuses ("I wasn't taught that yet" "That's not important").

- Children who can respond effortlessly and automatically improve their chances for success.

- Early failures, followed by successes on harder items, suggests several hypotheses to check out: retrieval difficulties, anxiety, poor motivation, boredom.
- Alertness to the environment is the likely source of most of the factual knowledge needed for the first dozen or so items, but formal schooling seems to be the primary source for most of the remaining items.
- Problems with numbers may lower scores substantially for younger and lower functioning children, but are not a factor for older, brighter children (because numbers or number concepts are measured by 6 of the first 11 items, but by only 21 and 29 among the remaining Items 12–30).
- Unnecessarily long responses, filled with trivial detail, suggest obsessiveness.
- High scores relative to other Verbal subtests, sometimes in tandem with Vocabulary, can reflect intellectual ambitiousness or parental stress for the child's achievement.
- Low scores relative to other Verbal Comprehension subtests can reflect hostility to a "schoolish" task.
- Test the limits with children who have suffered a head injury or are otherwise suspected of neurological impairment to help determine if failures reflect ignorance, loss of facts learned previously, or retrieval difficulties.
- The pattern of a child's failures may be related to the child's cultural background; for example, children from other cultures who now live in the United States and speak English adequately are likely to have more difficulty with items like "Columbus" than "stomach."
- Wrong responses can give insight into the child's general mental functioning; the same score can be obtained by a child whose wrong answers are wild or bizarre ("Water is made of soup," "Iron rusts because it gets lonely," "London is 3 million miles from New York) as by a child who is unable to elaborate answers that are almost right ("Darwin was a scientist" or "Brazil is in Latin America").

Similarities

Empirical Analysis
Reliability:

Split-half	.81
Test-retest	.81
g loading	.77 (Good)
Subtest specificity vs. error variance	23% vs. 19% (Adequate)

Most related to:

Vocabulary	.69
Information	.66

Least related to:

Coding	.20
Digit Span	.34
Symbol Search	.35

Proportion of Variance Attributed to:

Factor 1. Verbal Comprehension	52%
Factor 2. Perceptual Organization	8%
Factor 3. Freedom from Distractibility	5%
Factor 4. Processing Speed	1%
Abilities other than the 4 factors	15%
Error	19%

Proportion of Variance When 2 Factors Are Rotated:

Factor 1. General Verbal Ability	56%
Factor 2. General Nonverbal Ability	8%

Abilities Shared with Other Subtests (Unique abilities are asterisked)

INPUT

Auditory perception of simple verbal stimuli (understanding single words)

INTEGRATION/STORAGE

Verbal Comprehension (Factor Analysis: 4-Factor and 2-Factor)

Gc—Crystallized Intelligence (Horn)

Gf—Fluid Intelligence (Horn)

Cognition of semantic stimuli (Guilford)

Verbal Conceptualization (Bannatyne)

Degree of abstract thinking

Distinguishing essential from nonessential details

Reasoning (verbal)

Verbal concept formation

*Logical abstractive (categorical) thinking

OUTPUT

Verbal expression

Subject to Influence of:

Flexibility

Interests

Negativism ("They're not alike")
Overly concrete thinking
Outside reading

Clinical Considerations

- Evaluate responses for their degree of abstractness; they may be *abstract* (*piano* and *guitar* "both are musical instruments"), *concrete* (*apple* and *banana* have "a peel"), or *functional* (*mountain* and *lake* are "for camping").
- Children's verbal responses provide clinically rich information: long strings of responses, or single responses filled with unnecessary detail (*overelaboration*), suggest obsessiveness; some responses are too general or *overinclusive* (*milk* and *water* "contain cells and molecules," *shirt* and *shoe* "are both words and they both start with S-H"); other responses may demonstrate *ellipsis* (omitting words, such as "both trees" for *rubber* and *paper*), or include *self-references* ("A *candle* and *lamp* are hot, very hot, and they can burn me if I'm not careful"). Overinclusive responses may suggest a thought disorder, and several self-references are noteworthy because personal preoccupations are uncommon during Similarities.
- Obsessive children may earn unusually high scores when their strings of answers vary in quality; as long as no response "spoils" the answer, a child will earn a score of 2 even if a single abstract response is embedded among 1-point and even 0-point responses.
- Two children who earn the same scaled score may differ substantially in potential if their patterns of responses differ: A child who accumulates points by giving virtually all 1-point responses may have concretistic thinking and relatively limited potential; a child who mixes 2's and 0's probably has a greater capacity for excellent performance.
- Unlike the other four regular Verbal subtests, Similarities depends relatively little on facts learned in school, but has a clear-cut "fluid" or "new problem-solving" component; the child's task is to relate two verbal concepts (preferably with an abstract category), but the separate concepts are fairly easy (the hardest item uses the concepts of *salt* and *water*).
- Children who give abstract responses to easy items (e.g., "clothing," "fruits"), but not to harder items, may reflect overlearned associations rather than high-level abstract thought.
- Examiners have the opportunity to observe the child's ability to benefit from feedback on the first two items and Items 6 and 7. For Items 1 and 2, the examiner gives examples of correct answers if children fail them. And if the child gives a 1-point response to item 6 or 7, the examiner demonstrates a 2-point response to try to steer the child in the right (abstract) direction. Children who catch on quickly to these

prompts demonstrate adaptability and flexibility. In contrast, some children display rigidity and cannot benefit from the feedback. Rigidity may also be shown by insisting that certain pairs of concepts "are not alike," a negative, oppositional response to frustration.

- As children search for the relationship between pairs of concepts, they sometimes invoke creative thinking and visual imagery; unlike Comprehension or Picture Arrangement, the creativity does not invariably mean a failure.
- "Same" and "alike" are sometimes difficult concepts for young or disadvantaged children. The WISC-III (unlike the WISC-R) includes a Sample Item to teach this concept; do not read the Sample in a quick, perfunctory manner, because the brief teaching about *red* and *blue* being "colors" may help unlock the key to the entire subtest for a child who is weak on basic concepts.

Arithmetic

Empirical Analysis

Reliability:

Split-half	.78
Test-retest	.74

g loading	.76 (Good)

Subtest specificity vs. error variance	30% vs. 22% (Adequate)

Most related to:

Information	.57
Similarities	.55
Vocabulary	.54

Least related to:

Coding	.27
Picture Arrangement	.35

Proportion of Variance Attributed to:

Factor 1. Verbal Comprehension	16%
Factor 2. Perceptual Organization	7%
Factor 3. Freedom from Distractibility	53%
Factor 4. Processing Speed	2%
Abilities other than the 4 factors	0%
Error	22%

Proportion of Variance When 2 Factors Are Rotated:

Factor 1. General Verbal Ability	31%
Factor 2. General Nonverbal Ability	18%

Abilities Shared with Other Subtests (Unique abilities are asterisked)

INPUT

Auditory perception of complex verbal stimuli (understanding questions

Freedom from Distractibility (Factor Analysis: 4-Factor)

Mental alertness

INTEGRATION/STORAGE

Verbal Comprehension (Factor Analysis: 2-Factor)

Gf—Fluid Intelligence (Horn)

SAR—Short-Term Acquisition and Retrieval (Horn)

Cognition of semantic stimuli (Guilford)

Memory of symbolic stimuli (Guilford)

Acquired Knowledge (Bannatyne)

Sequential (Bannatyne)

Sequential processing

Facility with numbers

Short-term memory (auditory)

Long-term memory

Reasoning (numerical)

Speed of mental processing (especially for adolescents who must earn bonus points to achieve high scores)

*Computational skill

OUTPUT

Simple vocal

Subject to Influence of:

Attention span

Anxiety

Concentration

Distractibility

Learning disabilities/ADHD

School learning

Working under time pressure

Clinical Considerations

- Analyze incorrect responses to infer whether the error was in computation, reasoning (selection of the wrong operation), or failure to attend to the question or understand its meaning. For example, consider different responses to the item about the cost of 3 T-shirts at $8 apiece: an answer of 26 suggests a computation error; an answer of 11 suggests a reasoning error; and an answer of $2,000 is bizarre, suggesting possible inattention, lack of comprehension, or a thought disorder. Bizarre responses on Arithmetic are unusual and require exploration.

- There is a shift in what is required for success on the earlier versus later items: The first 11 items utilize skills that are closely aligned to counting, and the remaining items require good computational skills and arithmetic problem-solving ability.

- Test the limits whenever possible by removing the stopwatch, allowing paper and pencil, writing out the numbers that are read as part of the question, asking children how they solved particular problems, and so forth, to help assess the roles of memory problems, carelessness, anxiety, distractibility, and concentration on subtest performance. These hypotheses must first be ruled out, and corroborating evidence from multiple sources is needed, before inferring that a low score on Arithmetic reflects a math problem.

- For older retarded children, Arithmetic measures an aspect of adaptive behavior or social intelligence because items involve counting, handling money, and other real-life, functional abilities.

- Children referred for school learning problems may become anxious when asked school-like Arithmetic questions. Their response to the anxiety and possible frustration is noteworthy and clinically interesting: Do they reject the test? Compose themselves and perform well? Act distressed, agitated, or hostile?

- The addition of bonus points to the six hardest Arithmetic items makes the WISC-III comparable to the WAIS-R, but different from its predecessors, the WISC-R and WISC. These bonus points make the role of speed especially important for success, which may affect children with good math skills who are reflective, obsessive, neurologically impaired, anxious, or insecure. (The highest possible scaled score for a 15- or 16-year-old who solves every Arithmetic item correctly, but earns 0 bonus points, is only 12.)

- This subtest is different from conventional arithmetic subtests on Achievement batteries because it makes no attempt to measure mathematics curriculum in a systematic, content-valid way, and deliberately avoids specialized types of skills such as estimation or graphing; consequently, Arithmetic does not measure Horn's (1989, 1991) Gq ability, Quantitative Thinking, and should not be interpreted as a test of mathematics achievement. Arithmetic scores may be very different from school performance in math (in either direction), especially for adolescents, because of content differences, the need to work very fast, and the inability to use paper and pencil or a calculator. Wechsler intended the test to be a clinically relevant measure of general intelligence that depends on basic computational skills and reasoning ability.

- Be alert for evidence during the administration of this subtest of the child's insecurity or fear regarding arithmetic (spontaneous comments like "I stink at math" or "That's not fair. I didn't learn that yet"), and of behavioral evidence of a possible number problem (counting on fingers, using "finger writing" to solve some items, asking to use pencil and paper, or complaining that it's not fair without a calculator).

Vocabulary

Empirical Analysis
Reliability:

Split-half	.87
Test-retest	.89

g loading	.80 (Good; best in WISC-III)

Subtest specificity vs. error variance	24% vs. 13% (Adequate)

Most related to:

Information	.70
Similarities	.69

Least related to:

Coding	.26
Digit Span	.35
Symbol Search	.35

Proportion of Variance Attributed to:

Factor 1. Verbal Comprehension	62%
Factor 2. Perceptual Organization	5%
Factor 3. Freedom from Distractibility	3%
Factor 4. Processing Speed	3%
Abilities other than the 4 factors	14%
Error	13%

Proportion of Variance When 2 Factors Are Rotated:

Factor 1. General Verbal Ability	66%
Factor 2. General Nonverbal Ability	7%

Abilities Shared with Other Subtests (Unique abilities are asterisked)

INPUT
   Auditory perception of simple verbal stimuli (understanding single words)

INTEGRATION/STORAGE

Verbal Comprehension (Factor Analysis: 4-Factor and 2-Factor)

Gc-Crystallized Intelligence (Horn)

Cognition of semantic stimuli (Guilford)

Verbal Conceptualization (Bannatyne)

Acquired Knowledge (Bannatyne)

Degree of abstract thinking

Fund of information

Learning ability

Long-term memory

Verbal concept formation

*Language development

*Word knowledge

OUTPUT

Verbal expression

Subject to Influence of:

Cultural opportunities at home

Foreign language background

Intellectual curiosity and striving

Interests

Outside reading

Richness of early environment

School learning

Clinical Considerations

- Repression may push from conscious awareness any word meanings that are even mildly conflict-laden, and impairs both the acquisition of new word meanings as well as recall of specific words on the Vocabulary subtest.
- As is true for Information, high scores relative to other Verbal subtests can reflect intellectual ambitiousness or parental stress for the child's achievement.
- Children's responses to items, whether correct or incorrect, lend themselves to clinical analysis of fears, guilt, preoccupations, feelings, interests, background, cultural milieu, bizarre thought processes, perseveration, and clang associations (*hat-fat, fable-table*). Recurring themes in Vocabulary responses are of greatest clinical interest, especially if observed in the child's responses to Similarities or Comprehension items, comments during Picture Arrangement items, and

comments made spontaneously throughout the evaluation. Perseveration is sometimes noted when individuals begin each answer the same way ("Now *brave* is a word that I can easily define as . . .")

- As for Similarities, children's verbal responses may reveal overelaboration, overinclusiveness, ellipsis, or self-references.

- Obsessive children who give overinclusive responses may earn unusually high scores by finally hitting on concepts or examples that turn 0's into 1's or 1's into 2's. Watch for the tendency to assign credit to responses that are verbose by unconsciously equating quantity of words with quality.

- Defining words is not usually affected by impulsive behavior. In an investigation of the cognitive tempo of 188 fourth-grade boys, Vocabulary was the only WISC-R subtest on which reflective children failed to outperform impulsive children (Walker, 1985).

- Note the efficiency of a child's verbal expression. Are words that easily lend themselves to one-word synonyms (*seclude*—hide, *boast*—brag, *compel*—force) answered concisely or with roundabout, excessive verbiage (even if these responses earn 2 points)? The open-ended nature of children's responses to single-word stimuli make Vocabulary a measure of verbal fluency, not just word knowledge.

- Distinguish between children who give overlearned, almost rote, bookish responses, and those who approach the task with intellectual vigor and personalization of the responses to their current experiences.

- Hearing difficulties are sometimes more evident on this subtest than any other because the words are administered without a context of any sort. Similarly, auditory discrimination problems are sometimes detected when the child defines *grave* instead of *brave* or *boats* instead of *boast.*

- As for Similarities items, evaluate responses for the degree of abstract thinking. Do responses tend to be abstract (*affliction* is a "handicap"), concrete (*seclude* is "locking yourself in a closet"), or functional (a *donkey* "carries stuff on its back").

Comprehension

Empirical Analysis
Reliability:

Split-half	.77
Test-retest	.73
g loading	.68 (Fair to Good)
Subtest specificity vs. error variance	30% vs. 23% (Adequate)

Most related to:

Vocabulary	.64
Similarities	.59
Information	.56

Least related to:

Coding	.25
Digit Span	.29

Proportion of Variance Attributed to:

Factor 1. Verbal Comprehension	42%
Factor 2. Perceptual Organization	4%
Factor 3. Freedom from Distractibility	3%
Factor 4. Processing Speed	4%
Abilities other than the 4 factors	24%
Error	23%

Proportion of Variance When 2 Factors Are Rotated:

Factor 1. General Verbal Ability	46%
Factor 2. General Nonverbal Ability	6%

Abilities Shared with Other Subtests (Unique abilities are asterisked)

INPUT

Auditory perception of simple verbal stimuli (understanding single words)

INTEGRATION/STORAGE

Verbal Comprehension (Factor Analysis: 4-Factor and 2-Factor)

Gc—Crystallized Intelligence (Horn)

Evaluation of semantic stimuli (Guilford)

Verbal Conceptualization (Bannatyne)

Common sense (cause-effect relationships)

Culture-loaded knowledge

Reasoning (verbal)

Social judgment (social intelligence)

*Demonstration of practical information

*Evaluation and use of past experiences

*Knowledge of conventional standards of behavior

OUTPUT

Verbal expression

Subject to Influence of:

Cultural opportunities at home

Development of conscience or moral sense

Negativism ("You shouldn't turn off lights" "Paperbacks aren't better")

Overly concrete thinking

Clinical Considerations

- Selecting the pertinent information needed to respond to the social reasoning items with appropriate evaluation demands an emotionally stable, balanced attitude and orientation; any type of maladjustment lowers scores. Comprehension, more than other WISC-III subtests (including the socially relevant Picture Arrangement) straddles the emotional and cognitive arenas.

- Do not interpret high or low Comprehension scores as evidence of social adjustment without corroborating evidence from clinical observations, background information, or data from adaptive behavior inventories. Research with children and adolescents who are at risk for psychopathology, and who are normal, offers only mild empirical support for Comprehension's social sensitivity (Lipsitz, Dworkin, & Erlenmeyer-Kimling, 1993).

- Items tend to fall into two distinct categories: those that have moral implications and call on some type of social judgment (finding a wallet, keeping a promise) versus those that are more objective and detached from emotion (turning off lights, advantages of paperback books). Moral-emotional items are 1, 2, 4, 5, 8, 16, and 18. Therefore, most of the socially interesting and provocative items are among the easiest in the test, suggesting that the clinical value of Comprehension is at a peak for younger and lower functioning children. Children ages 9 and above of approximately average intelligence are likely to give automatic, socially appropriate, correct responses to the first half-dozen items, including those with emotional, personal stimuli, and may not even get to Items 16 and 18. Consequently, for many children assessed on the WISC-III, Comprehension is likely to be more of a verbal reasoning "can-you-explain-this" subtest than an emotional, morally challenging task.

- Responses offer clues about a disturbed child's social-adaptive functioning in practical, social situations (washing a cut, finding a purse), but be cautious about generalizing from single-issue questions to the complexities of the real world. And, as noted, most of the pertinent items are too easy even for disturbed children, unless they are young or low functioning.

- Test the limits routinely when children give overlearned, stereotypical, seemingly "parroted" responses, to check for real understanding and reasoning ability. This procedure is especially important for children suspected of retardation or emotional disturbance.

- For all items, creativity is not rewarded; high scores go to the conventional thinkers.

- Children born in foreign countries, or raised in the United States in subcultures that are not mainstream, are handicapped by a number of Comprehension items, especially the ones identified previously as moral-emotional items.
- The content of responses, especially to the moral-emotional items, is extremely valuable for denoting children's current areas of conflict, concern, fear, or preoccupation, and for inferring their acceptance or rejection of societal conventions. The following illustrative types of themes may be observed in children's responses:

  Passive, dependent. "Tell my mother" about the lost wallet or purse; "Ask my teacher to look" for the lost ball.

  Oppositional. "Paperback books *aren't* better than hard-cover books"; "You want me to say 'give the wallet back,' but personally I'd keep it."

  Impulsive. "Yell fire" if you see thick smoke.

  Hostile/aggressive. "Punch" the little child that starts a fight; "A person who keeps a promise is a jerk."

  Guilt. "Give the purse back and make it clear I didn't steal it."

  Denial. "I'd never lose a ball, I'm always careful about things like that."

  Alogical. Cars have license plates "because some cars get 50 miles to a gallon."

  Sociopathic. "Take the money out of the wallet and then return it."

  Coping ability. "Don't do nothing about the fire, just get out of there!"

  Phobic. "The meat must be inspected because it might have germs, lots of germs, that could kill people. Or maybe they won't die, but they could get typhus or AIDS or hepatitis or God knows what."

  Obsessive. "If a girl, a really tiny girl, started to beat me up, I'd just walk away, at least that's what I ought to do because she might not even be in school yet. But some kids just look small—like Jana in Mrs. Grissom's class who is almost 8 but looks like 3—and then maybe I ought to fight back or they'd think I'm afraid of a nobody."

- Some obsessive children (not the one in the previous illustration) can substantially improve their Comprehension scores by giving examples and details, especially on items that require two separate ideas for 2 points. But as with Vocabulary items, distinguish between quantity and quality on Comprehension items. Assess the relevance of the details and elaborations that are maintained in a long response as an indicator of the child's coping skills. Avoid the tendency to give 2 points on the "two-ideas-for-full-credit" items to a child who seems to elaborate forever; sometimes all their words amount to just one distinct idea.

- Because of the built-in need to query children for a second reason on half of the Comprehension items, and because ambiguous or incomplete responses need follow-up questioning, this subtest (even more so than Vocabulary) typically offers examiners numerous chances to observe children's emotional responses to "Tell me more" or "Tell me a second reason." Do they usually elaborate or give no further answer? Do their elaborations raise their scores or are they too inflexible to shift gears? Do they feel threatened by the frequent requests to say more? The child's score does not reflect the spontaneity of responses versus the need for excessive questioning, but there is quite a difference between the child who confidently gives a short abstract response or two concise "reasons" and the child who needs constant structure and prodding.

- Like responses to Similarities and Vocabulary, responses vary in their degree of abstractedness. Some children are able to think in abstract terms (*seatbelts* are "for safety"; *a promise should be kept* "because it's your word of honor" or "because our social system is built on trust"; *paperback books are better than hard-cover books* "because they're flexible and more compact"). Others give concrete answers to most items (*seatbelts* "keep you from breaking your neck"; *the government inspects meat* "so people don't sell rotten meat"; *paperback books are better than hard-cover books* "because you can put them in your pocket").

Digit Span

Empirical Analysis
Reliability:

Split-half	.85
Test-retest	.73
g loading	.47 (Poor)
Subtest specificity vs. error variance	63% vs. 15% (Ample)

Most related to:

Arithmetic	.43
Vocabulary	.35
Similarities	.34
Information	.34

Least related to:

Picture Arrangement	.20
Coding	.23

Proportion of Variance Attributed to:

Factor 1. Verbal Comprehension	7%
Factor 2. Perceptual Organization	4%
Factor 3. Freedom from Distractibility	12%
Factor 4. Processing Speed	3%
Abilities other than the 4 factors	59%
Error	15%

Proportion of Variance When 2 Factors Are Rotated:

Factor 1. General Verbal Ability	12%
Factor 2. General Nonverbal Ability	9%

Abilities Shared with Other Subtests (Unique abilities are asterisked)

INPUT

Auditory perception of simple verbal stimuli (understanding single words)

Freedom from Distractibility (Factor Analysis: 4-Factor)

Mental alertness

INTEGRATION/STORAGE

SAR—Short-Term Acquisition and Retrieval (Horn)

Memory of symbolic stimuli (Guilford)

Sequential (Bannatyne)

Sequential processing

Encoding information for further cognitive processing (Digits Backward)

Facility with numbers

Short-term memory (auditory)

*Immediate rote recall

OUTPUT

Simple vocal

Subject to Influence of:

Ability to receive stimuli passively

Attention span

Anxiety

Distractibility

Flexibility (when switching from forward to backward span)

Learning disabilities/ADHD

Negativism (refusal to try to reverse digits, to exert effort until the more challenging Backward Series, or to take a "meaningless" task)

Clinical Considerations

- Record children's errors to determine if the problem is sequential (the right numbers in the wrong order), probably due to poor rote memory (forgetting one digit, but otherwise getting the series correct), or probably due to inattention, distractibility, or anxiety (giving responses that bear little relationship to the stimuli).
- Test the limits to further help identify whether poor performance is likely due to forgetting, sequencing problems, anxiety, distractibility, inattention (possibly caused by anxiety), negativism, low motivation, poor strategy generation (e.g., chunking), or low intelligence in general.
- Number ability is more likely to affect performance on Digits Backward (which requires mental manipulation or visualization of the numbers) than Digits Forward (which can be answered in a simple, rote, mindless way). Children with good number ability may have longer backward than forward spans, or demonstrate unusually long backward spans for their age; those with poor number ability may perform very poorly on Digits Backward, or not be able to reverse digits at all (see discussion in Chapter 5). Make use of the tables provided in the WISC-III manual (Wechsler, 1991, Tables B.6 and B.7) on forward and backward spans, or of the summary tables presented in Chapter 5 (Tables 5.4 and 5.5).
- Number ability is one of several explanations for children who have better backward than forward spans. Other possibilities include perceiving the digit reversal task as more challenging and worthy of sustaining effort, and having better skill at representational (high-level) tasks such as Digits Backward than at automatic (overlearned) tasks such as Digits Forward. The latter explanation relates to Osgood's theory of communication (Osgood & Miron, 1963). Longer backward than forward spans occur relatively rarely within the normal population of children and are therefore noteworthy: less than 3% of the time at ages 6–11 years, about 5% at ages 12–14, and about 10% at ages 15–16 (Wechsler, 1991, Table B.7).
- The average Forward span stays remarkably constant across the WISC-III age range, averaging about 5 digits for ages 6–8, and about 6 digits for ages 9–16. Backward spans show a bit more of a developmental trend, averaging about 3 digits for ages 6–8, 4 digits for ages 9–12, and 5 digits for ages 13–16. In general, the average child has a forward span that is 2 digits longer than his or her backward span.
- Test performance is unusually susceptible to testing conditions that are less than ideal (e.g., sporadic noise outside the testing room), and is vulnerable to hearing impairment.
- Digit repetition is impaired more by state or test anxiety than by chronic anxiety.

- Impulsive children are likely to begin responding before the examiner has completed the series of digits, and may tend to repeat the digits very rapidly.
- Children who fail the first trial of items, and then pass the second trial, may be demonstrating good learning ability; such children may also proceed more rapidly on Coding and Symbol Search near the end of the time limit than at the beginning, and may catch on to Block Design after experiencing some early failures. This pattern, however, may indicate the need for warm-up rather than true learning ability.

Picture Completion

Empirical Analysis
Reliability:

Split-half	.77
Test-retest	.81

g loading	.60 (Fair)

Subtest specificity vs. error variance	39% vs. 23% (Ample)

Most related to:

Block Design	.52
Object Assembly	.49

Least related to:

Coding	.18
Digit Span	.25

Proportion of Variance Attributed to:

Factor 1. Verbal Comprehension	14%
Factor 2. Perceptual Organization	28%
Factor 3. Freedom from Distractibility	1%
Factor 4. Processing Speed	1%
Abilities other than the 4 factors	33%
Error	23%

Proportion of Variance When 2 Factors Are Rotated:

Factor 1. General Verbal Ability	15%
Factor 2. General Nonverbal Ability	25%

Abilities Shared with Other Subtests (Unique abilities are asterisked)

INPUT
   Visual perception of meaningful stimuli (people—things)

INTEGRATION/STORAGE
   Perceptual Organization (Factor Analysis: 4-Factor and 2-Factor)
   Gv—Broad Visual Intelligence (Horn)
   Holistic (right-brain) processing
   Cognition and Evaluation of figural stimuli (Guilford)
   Spatial (Bannatyne)
   Simultaneous processing
   Distinguishing essential from nonessential details
   Visual organization without essential motor activity
  *Visual recognition and identification (long-term memory)

OUTPUT
   Simple motor (pointing) or vocal

Subject to Influence of:
   Ability to respond when uncertain
   Alertness to the environment
   Cognitive style (field dependence—field independence)
   Concentration
   Negativism ("Nothing's missing")
   Working under time pressure

Clinical Considerations

- This subtest, the first one administered, is a good choice to serve as an icebreaker. The task of finding what's missing in common pictures is basically simple, easily understood with minimal verbalization by the examiner, and is usually considered enjoyable and nonthreatening.

- The subtest is timed, but the 20-second limit is ample for most children who are neither mentally retarded nor neurologically impaired. Extremely quick, incorrect responses indicate impulsivity, but even reflective children should be able to respond within the time limit.

- Children who keep on insisting that nothing is missing may be hostile, oppositional, inflexible, or immature (failing to understand the nature of the task).

- Although this is a Performance task, and pointing to the correct place is acceptable, note that the directions to the child specifically say, "*Tell* me what is missing." Therefore, verbal responses to most items are far more common than nonverbal responses. Children who point to most missing parts may have word retrieval problems. Similar problems may be evidenced by children who respond vocally, but frequently must be told "Show me where you mean." Illustrating with the drawer missing its knob, some responses are imprecise ("the opener"), vague ("the wood thing"), or roundabout ("the thing you grab and pull when you want to open the drawer").

- This subtest is not a consistent or reliable indicator of right cerebral damage, perhaps because of the verbal responding by most subjects, and "it is entirely possible that the nature of the task is not as heavily demanding of adequate brain functions as are some of the other subtests" (Reitan & Wolfson, 1992, p. 107).

- Children who say that a trivial part of the picture is missing (the "number 2" on the pencil, "a design" on the belt) may be demonstrating obsessiveness or a concentration problem. Similarly, confabulatory responses (indicating that something not in the picture is missing (e.g., legs of the man who is missing a watchband, the pants that go with the belt) are of clinical interest. Giving trivial or confabulatory responses several times during the subtest is of potential diagnostic interest, especially because examiners are instructed to redirect children the first time they give a trivial response ("Yes, but what is the *most important* part that is missing?") or a confabulatory response ("A part is missing *in* the picture. What is it that is missing?").

- Perseveration is sometimes observed on this subtest. For example, a child who identifies the missing fingernail in Item 4 may say that the elephant in Item 5 is missing a toenail, and the people in Items 6 and 7 are missing fingernails.

Coding

Empirical Analysis
Reliability:

Split-half	—
Test-retest	.77 (.70 for Coding A; .79 for Coding B)
g loading	.41 (Poor)
Subtest specificity vs. error variance	49% vs. 23% (Ample)
Most related to:	
Symbol Search	.53 (next highest is .28)
Least related to:	
Picture Completion	.18
Similarities	.20
Information	.21
Proportion of Variance Attributed to:	
Factor 1. Verbal Comprehension	1%
Factor 2. Perceptual Organization	2%

Factor 3. Freedom from Distractibility	1%
Factor 4. Processing Speed	62%
Abilities other than the 4 factors	11%
Error	23%

Proportion of Variance When 2 Factors Are Rotated:

Factor 1. General Verbal Ability	3%
Factor 2. General Nonverbal Ability	15%

Abilities Shared with Other Subtests (Unique abilities are asterisked)

INPUT
   Visual perception of abstract stimuli (designs—symbols)
   Auditory perception of complex verbal stimuli (following directions)

INTEGRATION/STORAGE
   Perceptual Organization (Factor Analysis: 2-Factor)
   Coding A—Convergent-production and Evaluation of figural stimuli (Guilford)
   Coding B—Convergent-production and Evaluation of symbolic stimuli (Guilford)
   Integrated brain functioning (verbal-sequential and visual-spatial)
   Sequential (Bannatyne)
   Sequential processing
   Encoding information for further cognitive processing
   Facility with numbers (Coding B only)
   Learning ability
   Reproduction of models
   Short-term memory (visual)
   Visual sequencing

OUTPUT
   Processing Speed (Factor Analysis: 4-Factor)
   Gs—Broad Speediness (Horn)
   Paper-and-pencil skill
   Visual-motor coordination
   Clerical speed and accuracy
   *Psychomotor speed

Subject to Influence of:
   Anxiety
   Distractibility
   Learning disabilities/ADHD

Motivation level
Obsessive concern with accuracy and detail
Persistence
Visual-perceptual problems
Working under time pressure

Clinical Considerations

- Visual impairment must be ruled out before interpreting a low Coding score.
- Children who are known to be obsessive or perfectionistic, or who display these characteristics during the first two subtests, should be told *during the administration of the Sample items* that they need to copy the symbols legibly but not perfectly.
- It is a good idea to note the number of symbols copied during each of the four 30-second periods within the 120-second interval. Differences in response rate may relate to motivation, learning ability, distractibility, adjustment to the task, fatigue, boredom, visual short-term memory, and so forth.
- Be a good observer during the administration of Coding and take notes. A low or high scaled score can mean many things, and it is fairly easy to note a child's coordination (grip on the pencil, ease or difficulty in copying the symbols), attention/concentration, distractibility, motivation level, visual-perceptual problems (rotating or distorting symbols), perfectionistic tendencies, perseveration (copying the same symbol for a whole line), immaturity (not understanding the need to work fast, having to be reminded to continue after coming to the end of a line), or anxiety. Sometimes a child will demonstrate a sequential problem by not grasping that numbers follow a sequence; during Coding B, such children may search for each number in the row of stimulus pairs without awareness, for example, that the "5" is always in between the "4" and "6." Though these behaviors are easily observed during the test administration, they are quickly forgotten after testing a few more children on the WISC-III.
- In addition to observing behaviors, astute examiners can infer the quality of a child's visual short-term memory by carefully observing the child's eye movements during the task. Children who keep referring back to the "key" before copying symbols are likely to have a poor visual memory (or to be very insecure); those who copy some symbols without having to look at the key, because they memorized pairs of stimuli, have a good visual memory—as long as they made no copying errors.
- Reitan and Wolfson (1992) state: "Coding requires adequacy of brain-behavior relationships generally[;] . . . the complex nature of the

subtest could limit the performance of the individual brain-damaged subject regardless of the specificity of the impairment" (p. 123).

- Testing the limits to determine how many symbol pairs were memorized is an additional way to learn about the child's incidental memory and spontaneous application of an efficient problem-solving strategy. Sometimes children verbally encode the symbols to facilitate the paired associate learning of the symbol-symbol or number-symbol pairs. During limit testing, if the child demonstrates that several symbols were committed to memory, ask the child how he or she remembered which symbol went with which number. Although testing the limits should ordinarily be conducted after the entire WISC-III is administered, these suggestions are an exception; limit testing on Coding should be conducted before proceeding with subtest 4 because too much forgetting is likely to occur between the third subtest and the end of the battery. Consult Imm, Foster, Belter, and Finch (1991) for an interesting research investigation of recall on Coding (and the Bender-Gestalt). Their technique for assessing a child's short-term visual memory on Coding B is simple: Place a blank, opaque sheet of paper over the symbols, exposing only the numbers; then have the child write as many symbols as can be remembered on the blank sheet below the corresponding number in the key.

Picture Arrangement

Empirical Analysis

Reliability:

Split-half	.76
Test-retest	.64
g loading	.53 (Fair to Poor)
Subtest specificity vs. error variance	48% vs. 24% (Ample)

Most related to:

Block Design	.41
Information	.40
Vocabulary	.40

Least related to:

Digit Span	.20
Coding	.28

Proportion of Variance Attributed to:

Factor 1. Verbal Comprehension	11%
Factor 2. Perceptual Organization	14%

Factor 3. Freedom from Distractibility	1%
Factor 4. Processing Speed	6%
Abilities other than the 4 factors	44%
Error	24%

Proportion of Variance When 2 Factors Are Rotated:

| Factor 1. General Verbal Ability | 12% |
| Factor 2. General Nonverbal Ability | 18% |

Abilities Shared with Other Subtests (Unique abilities are asterisked)

INPUT
   Visual perception of meaningful stimuli (people—things)
   Auditory perception of complex verbal stimuli (following directions)

INTEGRATION/STORAGE
   Perceptual Organization (Factor Analysis: 4-Factor and 2-Factor)
   Gc—Crystallized Intelligence (Horn)
   Gf—Fluid Intelligence (Horn)
   Integrated brain functioning (verbal-sequential and visual-spatial/synthetic)
   Convergent-production and Evaluation of semantic stimuli (Guilford)
   Simultaneous processing
   Planning
   Common sense (cause-effect relationships)
   Distinguishing essential from nonessential details
   Reasoning (nonverbal)
   Social judgment (social intelligence)
   Speed of mental processing
   Synthesis (part-whole relationships)
   Visual organization without essential motor activity
   Visual sequencing
  *Anticipation of consequences
  *Temporal sequencing and time concepts

OUTPUT
   Simple motor

Subject to Influence of:
   Creativity
   Cultural opportunities at home
   Exposure to comic strips
   Working under time pressure

Clinical Considerations

- As I indicated in the Preface, Dr. Wechsler's favorite clinical items from the WISC-R were eliminated (*fight, burglar*) or altered (*smoke, bench*) in an attempt by the publisher to minimize emotional content, violence, and personal conflict. In *smoke,* the boy becomes a hero instead of a villain, and in *bench* the men shake hands instead of slug it out. With the elimination or modification of these items, some of the clinical value of the subtest is lost. Picture Arrangement is still a good source of clinical information because of its social content, but children are much less likely to verbalize their conflicts, fears, or preoccupations while arranging pictures of a girl playing on a slide than while demonstrating a story of a boxing match. As Scarbaugh (1983) notes about WISC-R Picture Arrangement, "*Fight* can cause feelings of being bad, of doing something wrong, of a dangerous activity, one likely to result in personal injury. It also very clearly involves the win-lose syndrome" (p. 8). But items that were retained (though redrawn) can elicit important clinical themes as well: "*Picnic* often seems to trigger delicious feelings of wickedness, of getting away with something . . . It's of interest [when testing the limits] that some [children] identify with the dog, others with the people" (Scarbaugh, 1983, p. 8).

- Do not interpret high or low Picture Arrangement scores as evidence of social adjustment without corroborating evidence from a similar level of performance on Comprehension *and* from clinical observations, background information, or data from adaptive behavior inventories. Research with children and adolescents who are at risk for psychopathology, and who are normal, offers mild empirical support for Comprehension's social sensitivity, but no support for Picture Arrangement's sensitivity (Lipsitz, Dworkin, & Erlenmeyer-Kimling, 1993).

- Observing children handling the cards tells much about their problem-solving approach and impulsive-reflective cognitive style. Reflective children are likely to study the pictures for at least 5 seconds on most items before moving any pictures, to make good use of visual feedback when they make an error, and to carefully check their arrangements before saying they're done. Impulsive children are faced with a set of stimuli that often invites impulsivity (an array of several visual stimuli that are fairly similar to each other) and are likely to begin moving pictures around before the examiner has finished the directions, and to arrange them carelessly. Trial-and-error versus insightful problem solving are also easy to observe: Does the child put pairs of pictures together, seemingly at random, until they make sense, or does the child select the picture that goes first in the story, then second, and so on, until the item is solved? That is to say, do the child's hands or brain seem to be calling the shots?

- Test the limits, *after* completing the subtest, by putting out pictures in the same order that they were arranged by the child (some items that were gotten right, some wrong), and asking the child to verbalize the stories. These verbalizations are valuable for clinical understanding and for gaining insight into the child's thought processes (precise, confused, socially- or self-oriented, reality based or bizarre, conventional or creative). Some children don't know what some stories are about that they solved *correctly.* Resist the temptation to ask for verbalizations during the subtest because such a procedure violates the norms and may give the child verbal mediation strategies for solving subsequent items. For some children, it may be better to test the limits on this subtest after the entire WISC-III is administered to avoid tiring the child before a valid profile has been secured.

- Check out visual acuity and visual perception before concluding that low scores reflect a cognitive deficit or some type of social-emotional problem.

- Failure on some items may occasionally be related to the child's cultural or subcultural background, which may teach different interpretations of situations that depict social interactions.

- Performance on the logical, time-dependent, sequential Picture Arrangement task is often impaired for children with thought disorders.

- Be alert to behaviors shown during this subtest, and record them systematically. Children with good verbal ability are likely to verbalize the stories aloud while arranging the pictures. Those with problems involving part-whole relationships will group pairs of pictures for some items, but not get the "whole," and others with visual-spatial difficulties may arrange at least one series of pictures backward, from right to left. Manipulative children may want to look at the numbers and letters on the back of the pictures, and complain when you say no. Antisocial children may make clinically meaningful comments, especially during the *cash* or *smoke* items.

- The WISC-III has two items that help teach the task to children: the first one has the examiner demonstrate the correct response to the child, and then the child is given a second trial; the second allows the examiner to show the first picture in the story and the child completes the arrangement during the second trial. These items provide a good opportunity to observe children's learning ability and the degree to which they can benefit from feedback, and are especially valuable for low-functioning children and 6- or 7-year-olds in general. With the WISC-R, there were four such items. I urged Dr. Wechsler to have a gradual shaping process for this task because, from Piaget's research, the time concept is known to be quite difficult, even for children ages 8 and 9 years. Consequently, the WISC-III subtest may be more difficult than its WISC-R counterpart for some children. This variable may be related to the fact that a group of severely language-impaired students earned a mean scaled score of 6.4 on WISC-III Picture Arrangement, nearly 3 points below their WISC-R scaled score of 9.2—the largest difference by far among Performance subtests (Doll & Boren, 1993).

- This subtest offers 3 bonus points for speed for most items, one more than was allotted on the WISC-R; the WAIS-R gives no bonus points for quick, perfect performance, where the emphasis is more on problem-solving ability than speed. WISC-III Picture Arrangement, therefore, differs substantially from other Wechsler subtests of the same name. It correlated only .42 with WISC-R Picture Arrangement and .35 with WAIS-R Picture Arrangement, both of which are easily the lowest for "same-name" Wechsler subtests (Wechsler, 1991, Tables 6.8 and 6.10). Speed is so important in determining a child's Picture Arrangement scaled score that children of age 12 who solve every single item right but earn no bonus points for speed will earn a scaled score of 8; at age 16, the maximum score with no bonus points is 6. The speed component may account for the fact that Picture Arrangement was the only WISC-III subtest not to load on its designated factor in a factor analysis of 78 special education students (Hishinuma & Yamakawa, 1993); instead it joined Coding and Symbol Search on Processing Speed.

Block Design

Empirical Analysis
Reliability:

Split-half	.87
Test-retest	.77
g loading	.71 (Good; best on Performance Scale)
Subtest specificity vs. error variance	34% vs. 13% (Ample)

Most related to:

Object Assembly	.61
Picture Completion	.52
Arithmetic	.52

Least related to:

Coding	.27
Digit Span	.32

Proportion of Variance Attributed to:

Factor 1. Verbal Comprehension	8%
Factor 2. Perceptual Organization	49%

Factor 3. Freedom from Distractibility	6%
Factor 4. Processing Speed	3%
Abilities other than the 4 factors	21%
Error	13%

Proportion of Variance When 2 Factors Are Rotated:

Factor 1. General Verbal Ability	12%
Factor 2. General Nonverbal Ability	52%

Abilities Shared with Other Subtests (Unique abilities are asterisked)

INPUT

Visual perception of abstract stimuli (designs—symbols)

Auditory perception of complex verbal stimuli (following directions)

INTEGRATION/STORAGE

Perceptual Organization (Factor Analysis: 4-Factor and 2-Factor)

Gv—Broad Visual Intelligence (Horn)

Gf—Fluid Intelligence (Horn)

Integrated brain functioning (analytic and synthetic)

Cognition and Evaluation of figural stimuli (Guilford)

Spatial (Bannatyne)

Simultaneous processing

Trial-and-error learning

Reproduction of models

Spatial visualization

Speed of mental processing

Synthesis (part-whole relationships)

*Analysis of whole into component parts (analytic strategies)

*Nonverbal concept formation

OUTPUT

Visual-motor coordination

Subject to Influence of:

Cognitive style (field dependence—field independence)

Visual-perceptual problems

Working under time pressure

Clinical Considerations

• Reflectivity or obsessive concern with detail (e.g., aligning the blocks precisely, complaining that the blocks are not exactly identical) can lower scores substantially, especially for individuals ages 12 and above, because a total of 27 bonus points can be earned for quick, perfect performance. Whereas this subtest primarily measures problem-solving ability for children ages 6 to 8 or 9 years, it is decidedly a test of problem-solving speed for older children. A child of 8 who solves every single item right but earns no bonus points for speed will earn a scaled score of 16; but, the maximum score with no bonus points drops to 9 at age 12 and to 7 at age 16.

- According to Reitan and Wolfson (1992), this task is "an excellent indicator of right cerebral damage, particularly in subjects with lesions in the posterior part of the hemisphere[;] . . . it appears that Block Design depends heavily upon the specialized visual-spatial functions of the right cerebral hemisphere as well as the general functions of abstraction, reasoning and logical analysis" (p. 124).

- Observing children manipulate the blocks tells much about their problem-solving approach, behaviors, and emotional attitudes: trial-and-error problem-solving versus a systematic and insightful attack, ability to establish and implement a learning set, persistence, motor coordination, hand preference, concentration, distractibility, anxiety (hand tremor, negative response to stopwatch, excessive fumbling of the blocks, failing to check the pattern constructed against the model), impulsive-reflective cognitive style, ability to tolerate frustration, rigidity, perseveration, speed of mental processing, carelessness, work habits, self-concept, cautiousness, and ability to benefit from feedback.

- Some children refuse to try and give up easily, whereas others persist and suddenly catch on to the task. The basic principles of pairing up blocks, especially the split (half-red, half-white) blocks, that are learned on easy items can be applied on harder items. Because of the 2-failure discontinue rule, it is not uncommon for a child to figure out the "trick" to constructing the designs just as he or she discontinues the subtest. Be alert to this belated learning, and test the limits right then by continuing to test beyond that point. The child may pass several items that don't count in the score, but are of clinical value and help interpret the child's possible significant weakness in Block Design.

- Visual-perceptual difficulties are sometimes observed during this subtest when children have figure-ground problems, lose the square shape for some designs, fail to recognize differences between their production and the model, rotate designs more than 30 degrees, twist their body or rotate the model in the card book to improve their perspective, or be unable to solve any problem past Item 5 (the last one that retains "guidelines"). Even without these observations, some children's low scores may be due to perceptual problems (input) rather than problem-solving ability (integration) or coordination (output). Testing the limits is useful to distinguish between visual-perceptual and other problems. Have the child recognize (rather than construct) designs that are the same as a model.

Object Assembly

Empirical Analysis
Reliability:

Split-half	.69
Test-retest	.66

g loading	.61 (Fair)

Subtest specificity vs. error variance	26% vs. 31% (Inadequate)

Most related to:

Block Design	.61
Picture Completion	.49

Least related to:

Coding	.24
Digit Span	.26

Proportion of Variance Attributed to:

Factor 1. Verbal Comprehension	7%
Factor 2. Perceptual Organization	48%
Factor 3. Freedom from Distractibility	1%
Factor 4. Processing Speed	2%
Abilities other than the 4 factors	11%
Error	31%

Proportion of Variance When 2 Factors Are Rotated:

Factor 1. General Verbal Ability	8%
Factor 2. General Nonverbal Ability	44%

Abilities Shared with Other Subtests (Unique abilities are asterisked)

INPUT
Visual perception of meaningful stimuli (people—things)

INTEGRATION/STORAGE
Perceptual Organization (Factor Analysis: 4-Factor and 2-Factor)
Gv—Broad Visual Intelligence (Horn)
Gf—Fluid Intelligence (Horn)
Holistic (right-brain) processing
Cognition and Evaluation of figural stimuli (Guilford)
Spatial (Bannatyne)
Simultaneous processing

Reasoning (nonverbal)
Speed of mental processing
Synthesis (part-whole relationships)
Trial-and-error learning
*Ability to benefit from sensory-motor feedback
*Anticipation of relationships among parts

OUTPUT
Gs—Broad Speediness (Horn)
Visual-motor coordination

Subject to Influence of:
Ability to respond when uncertain
Cognitive style (field dependence—field independence)
Experience with puzzles
Flexibility
Persistence
Visual-perceptual problems
Working under time pressure

Clinical Considerations

- Reflectivity or obsessive concern with detail (e.g., aligning the puzzle pieces precisely) can lower scores substantially, even for 9- or 10-year-olds, because four of the five items allot 3 bonus points for quick, perfect performance. A child of 10 who solves every single item right but earns no bonus points for speed will earn a scaled score of 11, and the maximum scaled scores with no bonus points at ages 12 and 16 are 9 and 7, respectively. Even earning 1 bonus point per item will yield a below-average scaled score of 9 for a 16-year-old who solves every puzzle correctly.
- As on Block Design, observing children manipulate the puzzle pieces tells much about their problem-solving approach, behaviors, and emotional attitudes: trial-and-error problem-solving versus a systematic and insightful attack, persistence, motor coordination, hand preference, concentration, distractibility, anxiety, impulsive-reflective cognitive style, ability to tolerate frustration, rigidity (trying, over and over, to put the same puzzle piece in the same wrong place), perseveration, speed of mental processing, carelessness, work habits, self-concept, cautiousness, and ability to benefit from feedback. Also of interest is *when* during the solving of the last three items the child realizes what object is being assembled; some children never figure it out. (For Items 1 and 2, the child is told the name of the object.) Because the entire

subtest comprises only five items, it is important to observe carefully if a behavior, rather than lack of ability, caused a low score. Carelessness on a single puzzle can sabotage an entire subtest score, especially if the child would have earned 2 or 3 bonus points if not for a single careless error.

- Children who cannot figure out what they are assembling may have visual-perceptual difficulties. Such input problems are also evidenced by children who construct the puzzles at an angle or upside down, are upset that the *horse* puzzle has no lines, or who are unaware that some of the puzzle pieces they have connected are not even close to being correct. Integration problems are demonstrated when a child assembles separate groups of pieces for some items, but can't get the "whole," or insists that a piece is missing from at least one puzzle. And output or coordination problems are seen when the child aligns the puzzle pieces correctly, but too far apart, or inadvertently misaligns a piece or two while adding pieces to complete the puzzle.
- Children who try to "peek" behind the setup screen while the examiner is arranging the puzzle pieces may be insecure, impulsive, or low in moral development.

Symbol Search

Empirical Analysis
Reliability:
    Split-half   —
    Test-retest   .74 (.70 for Symbol Search A;
                                  .76 for Symbol Search B)

g loading   .56 (Fair)

Subtest specificity   34% vs. 26%
   vs. error variance   (Adequate)

Most related to:
    Coding   .53
    Block Design   .45
Least related to:
    Digit Span   .28
    Picture Completion   .33

Proportion of Variance Attributed to:
    Factor 1. Verbal Comprehension   4%
    Factor 2. Perceptual Organization   12%
    Factor 3. Freedom from Distractibility   4%

Factor 4. Processing Speed	31%
Abilities other than the 4 factors	23%
Error	26%

Proportion of Variance When 2 Factors Are Rotated:

| Factor 1. General Verbal Ability | 7% |
| Factor 2. General Nonverbal Ability | 29% |

Abilities Shared with Other Subtests (Unique abilities are asterisked)

INPUT

Visual perception of abstract stimuli (designs-symbols)
Auditory perception of complex verbal stimuli (following directions)

INTEGRATION/STORAGE

Perceptual Organization (Factor Analysis: 2-Factor)
Convergent-production and Evaluation of figural stimuli (Guilford)
Integrated brain functioning (verbal-sequential and visual-spatial)
Planning
Encoding information for further cognitive processing
Learning ability
Short-term memory (visual)
Spatial visualization
Speed of mental processing
*Speed of visual search

OUTPUT

Processing Speed (Factor Analysis: 4-Factor)
Gs—Broad Speediness (Horn)
Paper-and-pencil skill
Visual-motor coordination
Clerical speed and accuracy

Subject to Influence of:

Anxiety
Distractibility
Learning disabilities/ADHD
Motivation level
Obsessive concern with accuracy and detail
Persistence
Visual-perceptual problems
Working under time pressure

Clinical Considerations

- Be careful when scoring Symbol Search. *Total raw score equals the number right minus the number wrong.* The manual mentions this rule, but the record form does not reinforce the rule by telling the examiner to subtract wrong responses from right responses to obtain the total score. I have come across numerous WISC-III record forms with Symbol Search total raw score incorrectly computed as the number of correct responses, ignoring the number of mistakes.

- As for Coding, visual impairment must be ruled out before interpreting a low Symbol Search score.

- As was suggested for Coding, it is a good idea to note the number of items answered during each of the four 30-second periods within the 120-second interval. Differences in response rate may relate to motivation, learning ability, distractibility, adjustment to the task, fatigue, boredom, visual short-term memory, and so forth. Since Symbol Search is the 11th subtest administered, the response rate may be different from Coding; fatigue and boredom are more feasible near the end than the beginning of the test administration.

- Also, as for Coding, carefully observe and record the child's behaviors during the paper-and-pencil Symbol Search subtest to help explain low or high scaled scores. It is fairly easy to note a child's coordination, attention/concentration, distractibility, obsessive concern with detail, impulsivity versus reflectivity, motivation level, visual-perceptual problems (making errors on several items), immaturity, or anxiety.

- In addition to observing behaviors, astute examiners can—as with Coding—infer the quality of a child's visual short-term memory by carefully observing the child's eye movements during the task. Children who go back and forth several times between the Target and Search Groups before marking "yes" or "no" are likely to have a poor visual memory (or to be very insecure); those who respond to most items by looking at the Target Group once, scanning the Search Group efficiently, and marking "yes" or "no"—without referring back to the Target Group or marking mistakes—have a good visual memory.

- Test the limits (after first administering Digit Span, the last WISC-III subtest) for children who make 3 or more errors. Point to some items answered correctly and to some gotten wrong, and ask the child to explain the answer, why he or she marked "yes" or "no."

CHAPTER 3

Seven Steps for Interpreting the WISC-III Profile: From IQs to Factor Indexes to Scaled Scores

Interpretation of any Wechsler profile requires a systematic method of attack, and the WISC-III, in particular, demands an organized approach rather than diving in blindly. Unlike other Wechsler scales, the WISC-III provides examiners with a set of four Factor Indexes alongside the traditional set of three IQs. Each Index, like each IQ, is a standard score with a mean set at 100 and a standard deviation set at 15. The front page of the WISC-III record form lists the seven standard scores in a box on the top-right, and provides a graph for these standard scores just below. The left half of the front page lists the subtest-by-subtest scaled scores on top, each with a mean of 10 and standard deviation of 3, and provides graphing space in the bottom left.

Stare at the top half of the record form, and you are faced with an array of up to 20 scores; stare at the bottom half, and you'll get a quick snapshot of the nearly two dozen scores. A sequential processor may focus on the numbers, and a simultaneous processor may feel at home with the graphs, but neither one of Luria's "Block 2" processes will do much good without a systematic "Block 3" plan.

One sensible approach is to begin with the most global score and work from the general to the specific until all meaningful hypotheses about the child's abilities are unveiled. This technique, which also provides a useful logic for writing the Test Results and Interpretation section of WISC-III reports, corresponds to the organization of this chapter, and to the sequencing of information in Chapters 4 through 7 as well.

This chapter provides seven steps for interpreting WISC-III profiles, from statistical treatment of the Full Scale IQ (Step 1) to the identification of significant strengths and weaknesses within the subtest profile (Step 7). Along the way, the statistical significance and practical meaningfulness of the Verbal-Performance IQ discrepancy is determined, with the four Factor Indexes figuring prominently in these computations. At all times, however, examiners must function as clinicians, and know when to reject empirical rules in favor of alternate interpretations of the data. At the end of this chapter are several instances of exceptions to the rules, all of which relate to a clinical and incisive understanding of the complexities that surround any administration of an intelligence test.

Chapter 3 is designed to offer an *empirical* framework for profile attack. Interpretations of the fluctuations requires much conceptual and clinical understanding, and that type of in-depth treatment of the profile's peaks and valleys is within the domain of the rest of the book: interpretation of the meaning of V-P discrepancies, whether measured by IQs or Factor Indexes (Chapter 4), interpretation of the two small factors, Freedom from Distractibility and Processing Speed (Chapter 5), and generating hypotheses to explain subtest fluctuations that are not governed by the four WISC-III factors (Chapter 6). Illustrative case reports, which appear at the end of Chapters 4 through 6 and comprise all of Chapter 7, offer dynamic applications of the seven interpretive steps to actual clinical cases.

STEP 1. INTERPRET THE FULL SCALE IQ

As the most global and reliable score yielded by the WISC-III (mean split-half coefficient = .96), the Full Scale IQ merits the examiner's immediate attention. The norms tables for converting sums of scaled scores to IQs (Wechsler, 1991, Tables A.2 to A.4) conveniently list the percentile rank and confidence interval (90% and 95%) for each IQ, and another table (Wechsler 1991, Table 2.8) gives the ability level associated with different IQ ranges; for example, IQs of 110–119 are labeled "High Average" and IQs of 69 and below are called "Intellectually Deficient."

By converting Full Scale IQ to an ability level and percentile rank and bounding it by a band of error, examiners will put the IQ in better perspective and enhance its meaning to the reader of their case reports. Confidence intervals for the Full Scale IQ, based on data for all children in the standardization sample, are about ± 5 points for 90% confidence and about ± 6 points for 95% confidence. The bands of error, as reported in the WISC-III norms table, take into account the statistical phenomenon of regression to the mean. This appropriate statistical correction assumes that people who score high on an intelligence test have benefited a bit from good luck (positive chance error) and those with low scores suffered from a dose of negative chance error (rotten luck). As a result, their "true" IQs are a little closer to the designated mean of 100 than are their actual, obtained IQs (hence, regression to the mean).

The bottom line of what seems like statistical witchcraft is to produce confidence intervals that often are not symmetrical. When the IQs are close to 100, regression effects are minimal, and the confidence bands are symmetrical. For example, a Full Scale IQ of 105 has a 90% confidence interval of 100–110. But the more you depart from the mean of 100, the more asymmetrical the intervals become. A Full Scale IQ of 80 has a 90% band of 76–86, and a Full Scale IQ of 155 has a 90% band of 148–158. I've been illustrating with 90% confidence because I consider 90% to be an appropriate confidence level for most testing purposes.

Beginning test interpretation with the Full Scale IQ does not elevate this global score into a position of primacy. Rather, the Full Scale IQ serves as a target at which the examiner will take careful aim. In fact, as examiners explore peaks and valleys in the WISC-III profile while attempting to reveal the underlying dynamics of a child's ability spectrum, they are, in effect, trying to declare the Full Scale IQ ineffectual as an explanation of the child's mental functioning. Large V-P IQ differences, notable fluctuations in the Factor Index or scaled-score profile, or inferred relationships between test scores and extraneous variables (e.g., fatigue, anxiety, subcultural background) greatly diminish the importance of the Full Scale IQ as an index of the child's level of intelligence. This point is made clear by most of the illustrative case reports in this book, most notably the five comprehensive reports that appear in Chapter 7.

Even if children or adolescents obtain Verbal, Performance, and Full Scale IQs that are fairly similar and display only a few unremarkable fluctuations in their Factor Indexes and scaled scores, it would be inappropriate to attribute too much value to the Full Scale IQ. For such individuals, the global IQ is surely a good summary score of his or her performance in about a dozen samples of behavior and reflects relative level of ability under the standardized conditions prescribed by the WISC-III Manual (Wechsler, 1991). As elaborated in Chapter 1, the Full Scale IQ is an incomplete measure of the various mental capacities of the human brain and must be supplemented by additional measures. For example, when assessing black children, tests of memory, creativity, and adaptive behavior are valuable supplements. Although these aspects of intelligence are not assessed very well by the WISC-III Full Scale IQ, research studies have shown that black children, including those from disadvantaged backgrounds, tend to perform quite well on measures of short-term memory (Kaufman & Kaufman, 1983), creative thinking (Torrance, 1982), and social-adaptive behavior (Ittenbach, 1989; Sparrow, Balla, & Cicchetti, 1984, Table 3.32).

A first step in deemphasizing the Full Scale IQ is to establish a rationale for inferring a child's level of functioning in separate skill areas. Wechsler provides one type of rationale by his grouping of the WISC-III subtests into the Verbal and Performance Scales; the V and P IQs are next to capture our attention.

STEP 2. DETERMINE WHETHER THE VERBAL-PERFORMANCE IQ DISCREPANCY IS STATISTICALLY SIGNIFICANT

As noted, the WISC-III offers a potpourri of standard scores with a mean of 100 and standard deviation of 15, some called Factor Index Scores, others the more familiar IQs; all are potentially befuddling. The WISC-III record form doesn't make the examiner's task any easier. A box on the front page lists the IQs and Indexes in single file. The seven standard scores are dwarfed in one of three identical looking columns. Below this box, the seven scores reappear in a row to enable examiners to graph them more easily. Nothing is highlighted in a meaningful way. The immediate response of many examiners who are used to dealing with three IQs, but are now confronted with an array of the magical number of seven standard scores, is "*help!*"

And help is needed. As Dumont and Faro (1993) noted: "An overriding issue with the WISC-III test and its manual is the paucity of interpretative direction provided to the examiner" (p. 12). But the publishers of the WISC-III are to be thanked, nonetheless, for providing the additional four Index scores; they make the examiner's job of profile interpretation easier, not harder. Easier, that is, as long as the examiner is given a clear road map for navigation. And any Wechsler road map ought to begin with the Verbal and Performance IQs.

Some Empirical and Historical Considerations

We know from more than a half-century of factor analysis research that the main dimensions that underlie various Wechsler scales resemble the Verbal and Performance scales, but they're not usually identical to Wechsler's subtest dichotomy. The association has been pretty close for young children on the WPPSI and WPPSI-R, but as people become more complex, so does the factor structure. Arithmetic and Digit Span on the Verbal Scale, and Coding/Digit Symbol and Picture Arrangement on the Performance Scale, sometimes stubbornly refuse to join the right factor. Frequently, two or more of these subtests form their own factor. And now with Symbol Search on board, there's a fourth factor to contend with on the WISC-III.

On any Wechsler test, the factors are "purer" than the IQ scales they resemble (whether Verbal or Performance), and psychometric "purists," naturally, tend to push interpretation of factor scores instead of IQs. But the same half-century that witnessed more factor analyses of Wechsler's tests than there were psychologists when Wechsler first conceived the Wechsler-Bellevue has remained populated with a bastion of traditionalist clinicians. And these psychologists continue to interpret V-P IQ discrepancies, often without regard to whether the IQs correspond to unitary dimensions.

So the next step in WISC-III interpretation, Factor Indexes or no Factor Indexes, is to compute the size of the V-P IQ difference. Regardless of the direction of the discrepancy, determine whether the difference is statistically significant. If you don't provide the Verbal and Performance IQs in a case report, and interpret whether the difference between them is significant, many readers won't forgive you; they'll think you are ignorant, even if you can personally perform Kaiser normalizations and iterations without using software.

Calculating Significance

The WISC-III norms tables include 90% and 95% confidence intervals for all IQs and Factor Indexes, so by the time examiners have completed the task of converting sums of scaled scores to global scores having a mean of 100 and *SD* of 15, they have already banded these scores with a suitable band of error as an aid in communicating the notion that all obtained scores include a certain amount of built-in error. As with the Full Scale IQ, I consider 90% to be an appropriate confidence band, in most testing situations, for V-IQ, P-IQ, and all four Factor Indexes.

Verbal IQ is more reliable than Performance IQ (.95 versus .91, on the average), so its band of error is smaller to denote its greater accuracy. For V-IQ, the 90% error band is about ± 5; and for P-IQ, it is about ± 7. As noted for the Full Scale IQ, however, the WISC-III reports asymmetrical confidence intervals for most values of IQs and Factor Indexes to account for regression effects.

After banding the separate IQs with a 90% error band, the next step is to determine if the V-P IQ discrepancy is significant. The manual (Wechsler, 1991, Table B.1) gives values for statistical significance at the .05 and .15 levels, although the latter level is too liberal for any testing purpose that I can think of (15% is just too much built-in error). Naglieri (1993a) provides values for the .05 and .01 levels, but his values are too large. He corrected them for seven simultaneous comparisons using the Bonferroni procedure, but why would anyone want to make all of those comparisons at once? Examining the V-P IQ discrepancy alongside all possible pairs of Factor Indexes is a shotgun approach that ignores the logical planned-comparison method described later in Step 3.

Table 3.1 presents age-by-age values for statistical significance at the .05 and .01 levels when making the single comparison between V-IQ and P-IQ. (It also presents comparable values for VC vs. PO Factor Indexes, but more on that later. Values in Table 3.1 for .05 are from the WISC-III manual, rounded to the nearest whole number; I computed the values for .01.)

The overall values for V-P IQ discrepancies are 11 points at the .05 level and 15 points at the .01 level. Examiners may choose to use the specific values for each age level, but the overall values are quite acceptable for all children and adolescents within the WISC-III age range. They provide a close approximation for each age except age 15, and that age seems like an aberration more than anything else.

For most testing purposes, the .05 level represents an appropriate degree of confidence for V-P comparisons. Although 90% confidence is usually ample when banding an IQ with error, difference scores are notoriously unreliable; hence 95% confidence is sensible for V-P IQ discrepancies. Insisting on a 15-point V-P IQ discrepancy before inferring a meaningful difference between a child's verbal and nonverbal abilities seems extreme. The name of the WISC-III interpretation game is to generate useful hypotheses

TABLE 3.1.   Size of the Difference Required for Statistical Significance When Comparing Verbal IQ with Performance IQ and VC Index with PO Index

Verbal-Performance IQ Discrepancy			Verbal Comprehension-Perceptual Organization Factor Index Discrepancy		
Age	p < .05	p < .01	Age	p < .05	p < .01
6	12–15	16+	6	12–15	16+
7	12–15	16+	7	13–16	17+
8	11–13	14+	8	12–15	16+
9	12–15	16+	9	12–15	16+
10	11–13	14+	10	12–15	16+
11	11–14	15+	11	12–15	16+
12	11–13	14+	12	11–13	14+
13	12–15	16+	13	12–15	16+
14	12–15	16+	14	12–15	16+
15	9–11	12+	15	10–12	13+
16	11–13	14+	16	12–15	16+
All Ages	11–14	15+	All Ages	12–15	16+

via flexibility; 99% confidence is too conservative to permit flexible interpretation. *Therefore, whenever interpretation of V-P IQ discrepancies is warranted, any difference of 11 or more points should be treated as statistically significant.*

STEP 3. DETERMINE WHETHER THE VERBAL-PERFORMANCE IQ DISCREPANCY IS INTERPRETABLE—OR WHETHER THE VERBAL COMPREHENSION AND PERCEPTUAL ORGANIZATION FACTOR INDEXES SHOULD BE INTERPRETED INSTEAD

Step 2 identified the significance of a child's V-P IQ discrepancy, but that doesn't automatically give examiners the go-ahead to start interpreting these differences. Maybe the IQ discrepancies aren't interpretable because the IQs don't correspond to unitary abilities. The WISC-III includes purer versions of the verbal and nonverbal dimensions, namely the Verbal Comprehension and Perceptual Organization Factor Indexes, and it's possible that these factorially pure standard scores give a better picture of a child's verbal versus nonverbal skills than is provided by a gross discrepancy between the global IQ scales. That is what Step 3 is all about—determining whether the V-P IQ discrepancy is interpretable in a clinical or practical sense.

To determine the interpretability of the V-IQ and the P-IQ, Wechsler's armchair dichotomy must give way to the results of the empirical technique of factor analysis. We now turn to the four WISC-III factors to help formulate a rationale and approach for interpreting the WISC-III beyond the IQ level.

The Four WISC-III Factors

In factor-analytic studies of data from the WISC-III standardization sample of 2,200 children and adolescents at four age levels between 6–7 and 14–16 years, the WISC-III manual (Wechsler, 1991, pp. 187–196) identifies four factors, as discussed in Chapter 2: Verbal Comprehension, Perceptual Organization, Freedom from Distractibility, and Processing Speed. These same four factors emerged in analyses conducted with a large cross-validation sample of 1,118 individuals ages 6–16 years (Roid, Prifitera, & Weiss, 1993), a group that was tested in conjunction with the Wechsler Individual Achievement Test (WIAT; Psychological Corporation, 1992) standardization.

By way of review, the subtest composition of the factors follows (factor loadings appear in parentheses—first for the total norm sample, then for the WIAT sample):

Factor 1. Verbal Comprehension
Information (.72/.72)
Similarities (.72/.75)
Vocabulary (.79/.81)
Comprehension (.65/.68)

Factor 2. Perceptual Organization
Picture Completion (.53/.50)
Picture Arrangement (.37/.43)
Block Design (.70/.67)
Object Assembly (.69/.72)

Factor 3. Freedom from Distractibility
Arithmetic (.73/.53)
Digit Span (.34/.35)

Factor 4. Processing Speed
Coding (.79/.56)
Symbol Search (.56/.71)

These four factors were supported by confirmatory factor analysis for the two large samples, as well as by the exploratory factor analyses reported here. Confirmatory factor analysis also supported these four factors for a clinical sample of 167 children (mostly males) with learning disabilities, reading disorders, or attention-deficit disorders; for a high-ability sample of 157 that combined gifted children from validity studies with standardization cases with Full Scale IQs ≥ 125; and for a low-ability sample of 141 that combined mentally retarded children from validity studies with standardization cases with Full Scale IQs ≤ 75 (Wechsler, 1991, p. 196). Exploratory analysis also identified the same four factors for 78 special education and "at risk" children (Hishinuma & Yamakawa, 1993).

The only mild exception to the factor pattern concerned Picture Arrangement, which split its loading for the clinical sample, defined a weak fifth factor for the high-ability sample, and loaded on the Perceptual Speed factor for the special education/at risk group. In fact, Picture Arrangement is only marginally associated with the Perceptual Organization factor for the total standardization sample, and is more associated with Factor 3 than Factor 1 for ages 6–7 years. But the slight glitch involving Picture Arrangement (a maverick subtest for the WAIS-R as well; Kaufman, 1990a, Chapter 8) does not detract from an otherwise strong and meaningful four-factor solution for the WISC-III.

Sattler (1992) and Thorndike (1992) have argued against interpreting the Freedom from Distractability factor based on their reanalysis and reinterpretation of WISC-III data, but I disagree with their conclusions. Rather, I find the psychometric arguments made by Roid et al. (1993) in support of the distractibility factor to be compelling, and agree with these authors that the Sattler/Thorndike position is "contradicted by certain fundamental considerations of factor-analytic methodology" (p. 7).

The first three WISC-III factors resemble closely the three "same-name" factors consistently identified for the WISC-R with a wide variety of ethnically diverse and clinical samples (Kaufman, Harrison, & Ittenbach, 1990). The only difference is the Coding subtest, which usually joined Arithmetic and Digit Span as part of the WISC-R distractibility triad but is excluded from WISC-III Factor 3. The addition of the highly speeded Symbol Search subtest to the WISC-III attracted Coding like a magnet, forming a robust fourth factor, Processing Speed.

The Verbal Comprehension and Perceptual Organization factors bear a clear resemblance to Wechsler's Verbal and Performance Scales, respectively. Although the correspondence between the factors and scales is not identical, it is close enough to provide construct validity support for Wechsler's Verbal and Performance Scales, and to justify assigning a primary role in WISC-III interpretation to their respective IQs. These empirical results suggest that the Verbal and Performance IQs reflect a child's performance on real and meaningful dimensions of mental ability.

Thus the discrepancy between these IQs and Indexes may well suggest important differences in the child's learning style and ability to handle different types of stimuli. If the factor structure of the WISC-III, or the WISC-R before it, had produced a factor pattern that was totally at variance with Wechsler's dichotomous division of subtests, the Verbal and Performance IQs (and the difference between them) would have been of little psychological value. Even with the 1949 WISC, the V-P IQ discrepancy was not as meaningful as it is for its successors. Unlike the WISC-R and WISC-III analyses, factor analyses of the 1949 WISC (Cohen, 1959) usually found the Verbal Comprehension factor to split in two and the Perceptual Organization factor to contain high loadings primarily by the Block Design and Object Assembly subtests.

As presently defined, the first two WISC-III factors are in the cognitive domain, whereas the distractibility dimension is in the behavioral or affective domain. The fourth factor seems to bridge the two domains;

"processing" implies cognition, but "speed" has behavioral as well as cognitive components. A thorough treatment of the third and fourth factors, including a discussion of what they each seem to measure within both the cognitive and behavioral domains, appears in Chapter 5. For now, the focus is on the Verbal and Performance IQs, and on the Verbal Comprehension and Perceptual Organization factors—which capture the essence of what Wechsler intended to measure with these separate scales.

Pairing Up the Factor Indexes

Think of the Factor Indexes in pairs. Two factors are entirely composed of Verbal subtests, and two of Performance subtests. Verbal Comprehension (VC) and Freedom from Distractibility (FD) are the Verbal duo; Perceptual Organization (PO) and Processing Speed (PS) are the Performance pair.

The Verbal Scale of Wechsler's tests measures two major abilities, the first associated with the VC factor, and the second with FD:

1. *Verbal Conceptualization, Knowledge, and Expression.* Answering oral questions that measure factual knowledge, word meanings, reasoning, and the ability to express ideas in words.
2. *Number Ability and Sequential Processing.* Responding to oral stimuli that involve the handling of numbers in a step-by-step, sequential fashion and require a good nondistractible attention span for success.

Likewise, Wechsler's various Performance Scales measure two major abilities, with PO corresponding to the first ability, and PS to the second:

1. *Nonverbal Thinking and Visual-Motor Coordination.* Integrating visual stimuli, reasoning nonverbally, and applying visual-spatial and visual-motor skills to solve the kinds of problems that are not school taught.
2. *Response Speed.* Demonstrating extreme speed in solving an assortment of nonverbal problems (speed of thinking as well as motor speed).

The parallelism of the factors aids the interpretive process. Wechsler's true intent in developing the Verbal Scale was to measure verbal conceptualization, knowledge, and expression with all subtests, and for Verbal IQ to depict the person's so-called verbal intelligence. But dozens of factor-analytic studies with a handful of Wechsler scales, stretching back to the 1939 Wechsler-Bellevue, have indicated a split in the Verbal Scale. An extra factor, sometimes referred to in behavioral terms such as attention-concentration or distractibility, and sometimes given cognitive labels such as memory or sequencing ability, has persistently emerged alongside a dimension of global verbal intelligence. Sometimes the factor includes Coding or Digit Symbol and sometimes it doesn't. For the present purpose, it makes no difference. In straight language, Arithmetic and Digit Span commonly split apart from the VC quartet of Information-Similarities-Vocabulary-Comprehension. When the split is large, then Verbal IQ doesn't mean very much. It's not a unitary construct.

The creation of Symbol Search and the emergence of the fourth factor, PS, provide a Performance analog to the Verbal split. Examiners have known for years that both problem solving and speed are the essential ingredients for earning a high Performance IQ. But before the WISC-III's four-factor structure, there was no easy way to tease out the difference in these two aspects of nonverbal functioning. The PS Factor Index reflects both psychomotor speed and mental speed. Coding places the emphasis on motor activity; Symbol Search features mental processing. Together, they provide an estimate of the person's speed of solving nonverbal problems. Wechsler intended the Performance Scale to measure nonverbal intelligence (the ability to reason with visual-spatial stimuli and solve new problems). Sometimes, however, a person will earn low scaled scores because of noncognitive variables such as poor motor coordination, reflectiveness, or compulsiveness. The PS Index often gives insight into the impact of such variables on nonverbal test performance. When Coding and Symbol Search split off from the rest of the Performance Scale, the Picture Completion-Picture Arrangement-Block Design-Object Assembly tetrad that comprises the PO factor, then the Performance IQ does not correspond to a single construct. It should not be interpreted.

When Should the Verbal-Performance IQ Discrepancy Be Interpreted?

The Verbal-Performance IQ discrepancy gave the early Wechsler scales an interpretive advantage over the old, original one-score Stanford-Binet, and it has provided a buffet of thought for countless Wechsler clinicians and researchers over the past half-century. But for any given individual, this discrepancy may not truly be interpretable. Determining its interpretability should be the first order of business for any clinician. For the WISC-III, the four Factor Indexes offer a convenient method of determining empirically whether or not to interpret the V-P IQ discrepancy. To these Indexes, I will add one other simple statistic to help determine whether each IQ is measuring a unitary construct: the scaled-score range, an indicator of subtest scatter within the Verbal and Performance Scales. The range is easy to compute. For the Verbal scaled-score range, subtract the person's lowest Verbal scaled score from his or her highest Verbal scaled score. Use an analogous procedure for the Performance subtests. *For these computations, use only the five subtests per scale that were used to compute the IQ.*

Some have suggested that the scaled-score range is too simplistic, not sophisticated enough to be an index of anything. After all, it only deals with the two extreme scores in an array, ignoring the fluctuations in the rest of the profile (e.g., Plake, Reynolds, & Gutkin, 1981). Plake et al. (1981) offered an alternative to the scaled-score range, the profile variability index, which accounts for all fluctuations in the subtest profile by providing the standard deviation of the subtest deviations. Burgess (1991) even suggested a new index for subtest scatter that goes by the name "Mahalanobis distance, D-sup-2" and requires a computer program to compute!

The relationship between the simple range procedure and the more complex Plake-Reynolds standard deviation approach was put to the empirical test for the WAIS-R (Matarazzo, Daniel, Prifitera, & Herman, 1988). The surprising finding was that the simple (easy-to-compute) stat correlated nearly perfectly with the complex (harder-to-compute) stat to the tune of .97 for the Verbal Scale and .98 for the Performance Scale. So the scaled-score range, a deceptively easy index to compute, serves my purposes quite well for deciding whether to interpret V-P IQ differences.

Why does scatter within the Verbal or Performance Scales imply that the IQs they yield may not be interpretable? Scatter among the Verbal subtest scores means that the child's so-called verbal intelligence was not primarily responsible for his or her scaled scores on the Verbal subtests, but that other variables loomed more important; hence the Verbal IQ represents an overview of a few diverse abilities or traits and does not correspond to a unitary entity. The same logic applies to scatter on the Performance Scale. If either of the scales does not reflect a reasonably unitary ability, the V-P IQ discrepancy for the youngster may not be a very meaningful or interpretable concept.

Sometimes scatter characterizes groups, not just individuals. Keogh and Hall (1974), for example, pointed out that the lack of significant V-P differences in the WISC profiles of the mentally retarded children they studied masked the significantly higher scores these youngsters obtained on the Analytic Field Approach factor (composed of the field-independent subtests of Picture Completion, Block Design, and Object Assembly) than on Verbal Comprehension. For individual assessment, however, the subtest scatter concept has come under attack as a vestige that has no clinical value for diagnosis, remediation, or prediction (Kramer, Ullman, & Schellenberg, 1987; Ribner & Kahn, 1981), and that has virtually no incremental validity—over and above a child's mean scaled score—in predicting achievement (Kline, Snyder, Guilmette, & Castellanos, 1992). But, as Ribner and Kahn (1981) state, subtest scatter indexes do "describe present uneven abilities" (p. 41). That is precisely how I am using these indexes: to identify children whose skill areas are so unevenly developed that the Verbal or Performance IQ is challenged as a meaningful summary score.

Whenever the examiner speculates that the V-P dichotomy is inefficient for understanding a given child's profile, some reorganization of the subtests is needed. One type of regrouping involves the four WISC-III factors, and that is the first order of business because these factors have solid empirical support (see Chapters 4 and 5). If that approach fails, then a variety of other regroupings stemming from theory, research, and clinical practice should be explored (see Chapters 6 and 7). Most of these potential explanations come from a thorough understanding of what each subtest measures (Chapter 2), coupled with systematic and energetic detective work (Chapters 3 through 7).

For now, though, we attempt to understand the child's profile from the vantage point of Wechsler's Verbal-Performance model. That model forms the foundation of all of Wechsler's intelligence scales, and must be respected.

Ask Four Questions about the Verbal and Performance Scales

For each WISC-III profile, ask the following four questions, two pertaining to the Verbal Scale and two pertaining to the Performance Scale:

Verbal Scale

1. Is there a significant difference ($p < .05$) between the child's standard scores on Verbal Comprehension (VC) versus Freedom from Distractibility (FD)?

   Size Needed for Significance (VC-FD) = 13 or more points

2. Is there abnormal scatter among the five Verbal subtests used to compute Verbal IQ: Is the Verbal scaled-score range (highest scaled score minus lowest scaled score) so large that it occurs only in the extreme 15% of the children in the normal standardization sample?

   Size Needed for Abnormal Verbal Scatter = 7 or more points

Performance Scale

3. Is there a significant difference ($p < .05$) between the child's standard scores on Perceptual Organization (PO) versus Processing Speed (PS)?

   Size Needed for Significance (PO-PS) = 15 or more points

4. Is there abnormal scatter among the five Performance subtests used to compute Performance IQ: Is the Performance scaled-score range (highest scaled score minus lowest scaled score) so large that it occurs only in the extreme 15% of the children in the normal standardization sample?

   Size Needed for Abnormal Performance Scatter = 9 or more points

The values given for significance and abnormality are for the total age range of 6–16 years. Statistical significance at the .05 level for VC/FD and PO/PS are derived from values provided in Appendix B of the WISC-III manual (Wechsler, 1991, Table B.1) for the total sample. The values presented here are *not* corrected by the Bonferroni procedure, even though two comparisons are made simultaneously, because the application of that procedure for profile analysis has been challenged by both rational and statistical arguments (Krauskopf, 1991; Silverstein, 1993; see Step 6). The values for significance are smaller than the ones offered by Naglieri (1993a, Table 1), who applied the Bonferroni correction for seven simultaneous comparisons (V-IQ vs. P-IQ and all possible contrasts among the four Factor Indexes).

The manual gives data for 11 age groups between 6 and 16 years, but the values for the total sample are rather close to the separate values, and should be used for all children and adolescents. For examiners who prefer to make their lives more difficult, the values shown in Table B.1 of the WISC-III manual can be used for each separate age. And if you believe that the .05 level is too liberal, preferring the .01 level for more conservative analysis, then use the following values for $p < .01$: VC versus FD (17 points) and PO versus PS (19 points). But I advise simplicity, and a liberal approach to hypothesis generation. The easiest method is to use the overall $p < .05$ value of 13 points for VC versus FD, and 15 points for PO versus PS. Why make things hard?

The values for abnormal subtest scatter are taken from the WISC-III manual (Wechsler, 1991, Table B.5) for the total sample. No values are available for the separate age groups, so data for the entire sample will have to suffice for everyone.

If you didn't administer all 12 subtests needed to compute the four Factor Indexes, then answer as many of the four questions as you can. If you only administered 10 subtests, then answer questions 2 and 4 regarding subtest scatter. If you administered 11 subtests, then answer both questions for one scale, and just the scatter question for the other scale. The method proposed here is optimal when all 12 subtests are given, but it is still valuable (and applicable) for 10 or 11 tasks.

Answer the Questions

Compare the VC and FD Indexes, and you discover if the child performed at about the same level, or very differently, on the two major abilities assessed by the Verbal Scale—verbal conceptualization and expression versus immediate memory/sequential ability/number ability/attention-concentration. Examine subtests scatter within the Verbal Scale, and you determine whether the child performed consistently or inconsistently on the diverse tasks that constitute the Verbal IQ.

If the answer to *either* question is yes, then the Verbal IQ does not reflect a unitary construct for that person, and *V-IQ probably should not be interpreted.* It makes no difference whether VC is higher than FD or vice versa; if they differ significantly, the Verbal IQ is not unitary in what it measures.

Likewise, compare the PO and PS Indexes, and you determine whether the child performed at about the same level on the two major abilities assessed by the Performance Scale—nonverbal thinking versus speed of problem solving. Examine subtest scatter within the Performance Scale, and you discover whether or not the child performed consistently on the diverse tasks that comprise the Performance IQ.

If the answer to *either* question is yes, then the Performance IQ does not reflect a unitary construct for that person, and *P-IQ probably should not be interpreted.* Again, it doesn't matter if PO is significantly higher or lower than PS, as long as the two Indexes differ significantly.

In short, if the answers to all four questions are no, then the V-P IQ difference provides a meaningful way to denote whether a child differs in verbal versus nonverbal intelligence. If the V-P IQ difference is statistically significant (see Table 3.1), then the child truly differs in his or her verbal and nonverbal intelligence. If the V-P IQ discrepancy falls short of significance, then the child probably has verbal skills that are about as well (or poorly) developed as his or her nonverbal skills. If the separate scales are unitary, then the Verbal and Performance IQs merit interpretation. The VC and PO Factor Indexes are probably best ignored.

If, however, the answer to at least one *of the four questions is* yes, *the Verbal-Performance IQ discrepancy is probably not interpretable, and the difference between V-IQ and P-IQ (whether statistically significant or not) should usually not be interpreted.* As noted previously, ask as many of the four questions as possible. If you gave only the 10 regular subtests, then only the two scatter questions can be answered; if you administered 11, then three of the four questions can be answered. As in the 12-subtest case, all no answers imply that it's okay to interpret the V-P IQ discrepancy; a single yes answer suggests that VC and PO should be evaluated.

The next step is to examine the discrepancy between the VC and PO Factor Indexes.

Examine the Verbal Comprehension-Perceptual Organization Factor Index Discrepancy

The WISC-III offers the examiner two ways to compare verbal and nonverbal intelligence, so if the V-P IQ discrepancy doesn't work, try the VC-PO Factor Index discrepancy. With or without interpretable IQs, Wechsler's goal in dividing tasks by the nature of their content and type of response (verbal/nonverbal) was to compare people on these two fundamentally different ways of expressing intelligence. If the IQs aren't unitary constructs for a given child, then examine the "purer" Factor Indexes.

The VC factor is composed of the four subtests that measure conceptual thought and verbal expression and that seem to capture the essence of verbal intelligence. The PO factor, also composed of four subtests, excludes the tests of unbridled speed and measures the kind of nonverbal thinking abilities that Wechsler probably had in mind when he first sought to use alternate modes of assessment for people who were unable to display their intellect verbally. The VC and PO Factor Indexes are only slightly less reliable than the global IQ scales they represent: VC has an average split-half coefficient of .94 compared to .95 for V-IQ; PO averages .90 compared to .91 for P-IQ.

The right half of Table 3.1 gives the size of the differences needed for significance at the .05 and .01 levels between the VC and PO Factor Indexes. The overall values for the total sample of 12 and 16 points, respectively, provide a good approximation of the values required for each age group except the maverick sample of 15-year-olds. I recommend that these overall values be used for all children, and that the 12 points required for $p < .05$ be used in most circumstances.

Like the V-P IQ comparison, after evaluating statistical significance of the VC-PO difference, determine whether each factor is unitary, and, therefore, meaningful in a practical, clinical sense. Ask these two questions to find out if either factor is compromised by too much scatter (Wechsler, 1991, Table B.5):

1. Is there abnormal scatter among the four Verbal subtests that make up the VC factor: Is the VC scaled-score range (highest scaled score minus lowest scaled score) so large that it occurs only in the extreme 15% of the children in the normal standardization sample?

   Size Needed for Abnormal VC Scatter = 7 or more points

2. Is there abnormal scatter among the four Performance subtests that make up the PO factor: Is the PO scaled-score range (highest scaled score minus lowest scaled score) so large that it occurs in the extreme 15% of the children in the normal standardization sample?

   Size Needed for Abnormal PO Scatter = 8 or more points

If the answer to either question is yes, then you probably shouldn't interpret the VC-PO Index discrepancy—unless the discrepancy is just too big to ignore. As we'll discover in Step 4, some V-P IQ or VC-PO discrepancies are unusually large, too large to declare "uninterpretable," even if the IQs and Factor Indexes are scatter-filled and break into pieces.

But before moving on to Step 4, here are two illustrations of how to apply the question-and-answer method to WISC-III interpretation.

Illustrations of the Question-and-Answer Approach

Here are two examples to demonstrate how to apply the question-and-answer approach to the interpretation of Verbal/Performance differences. Ultimately, both examples show instances in which the V-P IQ discrepancy is misleading.

Harvey A.

IQs		Factor Indexes	
Verbal	93	Verbal Comprehension	96
Performance	106	Perceptual Organization	96
Full Scale	99	Freedom from Distractibility	101
P-IQ > V-IQ($p < .05$)		Processing Speed	134

Verbal	Scaled Score	Performance	Scaled Score
Information	7	Picture Completion	11
Similarities	10	(Coding)	(16)
Arithmetic	7	Picture Arrangement	7
Vocabulary	11	Block Design	10
Comprehension	9	Object Assembly	9
(Digit Span)	(13)	*Symbol Search	17

* Symbol Search was used in IQ computations

In the example of Harvey A., simple examination of the V-P IQ difference indicates a significant discrepancy of 13 points in favor of Performance IQ, but responses to the four questions suggest that the difference may not be interpretable.

1. *No,* the VC and FD Factor Indexes (96 and 101) do *not* differ significantly.
2. *No,* the Verbal scaled-score range of 4 points (11 minus 7) does *not* reflect abnormal Verbal scatter.
3. *Yes,* the PO and PS Factor Indexes (96 and 134) *do* differ significantly.
4. *Yes,* the Performance scaled-score range of 10 points (17 on Symbol Search minus 7 on Picture Arrangement) *does* reflect abnormal Performance scatter. (Note that the 16 on Coding does not enter into the computation because it was not used to compute Harvey's P-IQ.)

With two yes responses (or even one), the V-P IQ discrepancy is probably not meaningful, so the VC-PO difference should be examined. In contrast to the significant V-P IQ difference, Harvey earned equal standard scores of 96 on VC and PO. Neither the VC scaled-score range of 4 points nor the PO range of 4 points approaches abnormality, indicating that the VC and PO factors are unitary and should be interpreted as the best estimate of Harvey's verbal-nonverbal difference (or lack of it).

The example of Harvey A. shows how a significant V-P difference of 13 points may exist even though the child actually has no difference between his or her Verbal Comprehension and Perceptual Organization skills. In this example, Symbol Search has inflated the Performance IQ (Coding would have done the same if it had been used to compute IQs), thereby overestimating Harvey's nonverbal thinking ability. When only the four Perceptual Organization and four Verbal Comprehension subtests are considered, the apparently significant V-P IQ discrepancy vanishes. The example of Melinda B. demonstrates the opposite phenomenon:

Melinda B.

IQs		Factor Indexes	
Verbal	108	Verbal Comprehension	100
Performance	108	Perceptual Organization	119
Full Scale	109	Freedom from Distractibility	142
V-IQ = P-IQ		Processing Speed	67

Verbal	Scaled Score	Performance	Scaled Score
Information	9	Picture Completion	14
Similarities	8	(Coding)	(3)
Arithmetic	17.	Picture Arrangement	12
Vocabulary	13	Block Design	15
Comprehension	10	Object Assembly	11
(Digit Span)	(18)	*Symbol Search	4

*Symbol Search was used in IQ computations

In the example of Melinda B., the V-P IQ difference is 0 which would lead many examiners to the simple conclusion that the child has no meaningful difference between verbal and nonverbal intelligence. They'd be dead wrong. The four questions:

1. *Yes,* the VC and FD Factor Indexes (100 and 142) sure *do* differ significantly.
2. *Yes,* the Verbal scaled-score range of 9 points (17 on Arithmetic minus 8 on Similarities) *does* reflect abnormal Verbal scatter. (The 18 on Digit Span doesn't count; it's not used to compute V-IQ.)
3. *Yes,* the PO and PS Factor Indexes (119 and 67) *do* differ significantly, to say the least.
4. *Yes,* the Performance scaled-score range of 11 points (15 on Block Design minus 4 on Symbol Search) *does* reflect abnormal Performance scatter.

With four yes responses, forget the V-P IQ discrepancy and examine the discrepancy between VC (100) and PO (119). The 19 points is significant at the .01 level (see Table 3.1), and it is abnormal since discrepancies of 19 or more points between the VC and PO Indexes occur in the Extreme 15% of children (see Table 3.2). There's no scatter to speak of within either the VC Scale (range of 5 points) or the PO Scale (range of 4 points), so the difference between the Indexes can be interpreted meaningfully.

TABLE 3.2.   Size of the Difference Required for Abnormality When
Comparing Verbal IQ to Performance IQ and VC Index to PO Index

Percentage of Normal Children Showing Discrepancy	V-P IQ Discrepancy	VC-PO Index Discrepancy
Extreme 15%	19–21	19–21
Extreme 10%	22–24	22–25
Extreme 5%	25–29	26–29
Extreme 2%	30–31	30–32
Extreme 1%	32 & above	33 & above

In the example of Melinda B., the Verbal IQ and Performance IQ are the same, suggesting equal functioning in the verbal and nonverbal spheres. However, Arithmetic elevates Verbal IQ while Symbol Search depresses Performance IQ, creating the illusion of similar intellectual behavior. When Factor Indexes are examined, a significant and unusually large PO > VC discrepancy of 19 points is obtained—a strikingly different picture from the one portrayed by the original IQ comparison.

Harvey A. demonstrated a significant V-P IQ discrepancy that dissolved to 0 points when the VC and PO Factor Indexes are used, and Melinda B. had a 0-point V-P IQ difference that exploded to 19 points when the results of factor analysis are applied. Are these examples a bit contrived? Sure. But they do happen, and even if the changes aren't as dramatic as the illustrations that I chose for instructive purposes, it is common for V-P IQ discrepancies that are on either side of the significance threshold to flip to the other side after using the suggested question-and-answer method.

Arithmetic and Symbol Search correlate moderately, .41 for the total WISC-III standardization sample, as both require good attention-concentration for success and measure the ability to handle symbols. Whereas *extremely* different performance on the two subtests is not an everyday occurrence, it does happen. And if Coding is used instead of Symbol Search to compute Performance IQ, then situations such as Example B won't be all that unusual: Arithmetic and Coding don't correlate too well (.27, on the average, less than a 10% variance overlap). At ages 6 and 7, when Coding A is given, they hardly correlate at all (.18, a mere 3% overlap).

It should be noted that the procedure described here for inferring real verbal-nonverbal differences despite nonsignificant V-P IQ discrepancies (Melinda B.) or a meaningless verbal-nonverbal difference even when the V-P IQ discrepancy is statistically significant (Harvey A.) cannot be applied indiscriminately or arbitrarily. The VC and PO Factor Indexes only become appropriate substitutes for the Verbal and Performance IQs when the "pure" factors really are fairly pure and are not replete with scatter. That is why it is so essential to evaluate whether the scaled-score ranges for VC and PO are abnormally large. If the factors aren't unitary, then the verbal-nonverbal split just may not apply for a given child.

But the question-and-answer procedure is not infallible. Sometimes it must yield to other considerations, as discussed in Step 4.

Naglieri's Alternate Interpretive Approach

Naglieri (1993a) offers an alternate approach to the interpretation of the four Factor Indexes. His approach, like the preceding methodology, is contingent on the assumption that the four WISC-III factors reflect construct valid, meaningful dimensions of ability. However, when using his procedure, examiners would ordinarily bypass the IQs and go directly to the four Factor Indexes.

Naglieri (1993a, Table 2) offers a table that permits examiners to interpret significant strengths and weaknesses within the Factor Index profile. First compute the average of the child's four Factor Indexes. Then determine whether each of the four Indexes differ significantly from the child's mean standard score. The Bonferroni-corrected values for the total standardization sample (.05 level) are as follows: VC (±9), PO (±10), FD (±11), and PS (±12). Although the advisability of applying the Bonferroni technique to profile interpretation has been questioned (Krauskopf, 1991), Naglieri's technique is statistically sound because there is no clear-cut answer to the technical issues raised by Krauskopf (Silverstein, 1993).

My personal preference is to use the Factor Indexes in the ways suggested in Step 3. With that procedure, both the IQs and Factor Indexes are considered in the interpretation of WISC-III profiles, and both are used to address the question that was of primary importance to Wechsler: Does the child differ in his or her verbal versus nonverbal abilities? My main objections to Naglieri's approach are (a) it equates the major (four-subtest) factors with the minor ones, and (b) it doesn't allow for a direct verbal-nonverbal comparison of VC with PO. However, Naglieri's method does represent an alternative to a portion of the approach presented in this chapter. Examiners who opt for his procedure should perform Step 1 of my suggested method; then substitute Naglieri's approach for Steps 2, 3, and 4; and continue with Steps 5 through 7 to interpret the factors and subtests.

STEP 4. DETERMINE WHETHER THE VERBAL-PERFORMANCE IQ DISCREPANCY (OR VC-PO DISCREPANCY) IS ABNORMALLY LARGE

In Step 2, we determined whether the V-P IQ discrepancy is large enough to be statistically significant. In Step 3 we asked a few questions to decide whether the V-IQs and P-IQs should be interpreted, or whether it is more sensible to interpret the VC and PO Indexes instead. In the latter instance, we determined, in Step 3, whether the VC-PO discrepancy is statistically significant. Now we turn to a different issue, but one that relates to every possible outcome of the preceding three steps: Is the size of the verbal-nonverbal discrepancy (V-P IQ or VC-PO Index) large enough to be considered abnormal or rare among the normal population? We asked similar questions before regarding subtest, or *intra*scale, scatter. The verbal-nonverbal issue concerns *inter*scale scatter.

We commonly apply statistical criteria, as in Table 3.1, to determine the statistical significance of a difference. Such criteria are based on the standard error of measurement of the difference between IQs on the Verbal and Performance Scales (or Indexes on the VC and PO Factors) and help identify meaningful discrepancies. When examiners use values for the $p < .05$ level or the $p < .01$ level, they determine whether any particular discrepancy is "real," as opposed to purely a function of chance error. The level of significance chosen merely translates to the amount of confidence that can be placed in the conclusion that a child's Verbal and Performance IQs are really different from each other—that the discrepancy between them is significantly different from zero points ($p < .05$ means 95% confidence in that conclusion; $p < .01$ means 99% confidence), but significance doesn't mean abnormally or unusually large.

The issue of significance says nothing about the *frequency* with which discrepancies of various magnitudes occur within the normal population. Yet the degree to which an individual's discrepancy is common or rare (abnormal) has important interpretive significance. The mean V-P IQ discrepancy for the WISC-III standardization sample is 10.0 points, ignoring the direction of the difference, and the mean VC-PO difference is a very similar 10.3 points (Wechsler, 1991, Table B.2). Values of about 9 to 10 points for V-P IQ discrepancies (with a whopping standard deviation of 7 to 8 points) have been virtual constants for Wechsler's scales—from preschool to adult levels—for tests normed a half-century ago or a few years ago.

It is, therefore, common for children and adults to differ in their verbal and nonverbal abilities. The average difference falls just short of the value of 11 points between V and P IQs needed for statistical significance at the .05 level for the WISC-III (12 points for VC vs. PO). The table of discrepancies between V-IQ and P-IQ provided in the WISC-III manual (Wechsler, 1991, Table B.2) reveals that about 2 out of 5 normal children have significant V-P IQ differences at the .05 level (11 points or greater) and about 1 out of 4 have significant differences at the .01 level (15 + points). As noted, these results generalize to other Wechsler scales, to the VC and PO Factor Indexes, and to preschoolers and adults. Thus about 25% of *normal* children and adults have V-P discrepancies of a magnitude that Wechsler (1974, p. 34) stated, right in the WISC-R manual, "is important and calls for further investigation," and that some researchers (e.g., Black, 1974, 1976) once considered predictive of neurological dysfunction.

Verbal-Performance discrepancies on the 1949 WISC (Seashore, 1951) were virtually identical to the findings for the WISC-R (Kaufman, 1976a) and WISC-III (Wechsler, 1991). The WISC results were published by Seashore shortly after the test was available for clinical use, yet it seems that the findings were not internalized by very many clinicians or researchers. Not until the WISC-R data became common knowledge in the late 1970s did a slew of researchers begin to investigate the V-P IQ discrepancies in a variety of clinical samples and compare the magnitude of these discrepancies to the "base rates" that characterize normal populations (Kaufman, 1982). Prior to that time, it was common to view differences of 15 or more points as suggestive of brain dysfunction, and to use a significant V-P discrepancy as an important piece of evidence for diagnosing an individual as learning disabled. There had been a basic unawareness among test users regarding the frequency of significant V-P discrepancies within the normal population.

But how can a difference of 15 points, which is "normal" in the sense that one out of four individuals displays a difference at least that large, be used to help confirm an "abnormal" diagnosis? Significant discrepancies certainly imply different functioning on the two scales and thus are valuable for helping the examiner make meaningful recommendations for the child's educational planning. But V-P differences that are fairly common in the normal population should *not* be used to diagnose abnormality. Furthermore, research data indicate that groups of exceptional children such as learning disabled do *not* tend to have larger V-P IQ discrepancies than a typical stratified sample of normal children (Kaufman, Harrison, & Ittenbach, 1990).

The bottom line is that examiners should always determine whether a significant difference is also an abnormal difference. If the discrepancy is statistically significant, then it is meaningful, it is real. But it may not be unusual. Typically, a child is administered the WISC-III because of a suspected abnormality—whether it is emotional, behavioral, cognitive, developmental, or otherwise. Normal profiles are rarely seen or studied, and thus it is easy for a clinician or researcher to assume that observed fluctuations and patterns are in some way characteristic of a suspected or confirmed diagnosis. But even exceptional samples have, on the average, a normal amount of V-P scatter, so there's clearly no one-to-one relationship between abnormal scatter and a diagnosis of an abnormality.

Primarily to help test users keep a proper perspective when interpreting the WISC-III of a child referred for evaluation, Table 3.2 is presented. This table provides a base rate of V-P IQ discrepancies (plus VC-PO Index discrepancies), thereby enabling examiners to determine how unusual or abnormal any particular V-P IQ discrepancy or VC-PO difference may be. When a verbal-nonverbal difference is significant, examiners have a basis for making remedial suggestions; when it is both significant *and* abnormal (occurring infrequently in the normal population), they also may have a basis for interpreting this test information in the context of other test scores and clinical evidence to reach a diagnostic hypothesis. However, *any* such linkup between abnormality and clinical diagnosis still remains a clinical decision, largely devoid of research documentation. And even very large V-P IQ discrepancies, when evaluated in isolation, may not relate significantly to neurological and related variables (Moffitt & Silva, 1987).

Table 3.2 was developed from data provided in the WISC-III manual (Wechsler, 1991, Table B.2). It allows examiners to enter with the size of the child's V-P IQ discrepancy (or VC-PO Index discrepancy) and determine whether differences of that magnitude or greater occurred infrequently within the normal standardization sample. Five different levels of abnormality are provided: the extreme 15% of the normal population (which corresponds approximately to one standard deviation above the mean), along with the extreme 10%, 5%, 2%, and 1%.

Although a V-P IQ difference of 15 points is significant at the .01 level, it is evident from Table 3.2 that a V-P IQ discrepancy must be at least 19 points to be considered abnormal, using the most liberal (Extreme 15%) criterion of abnormality. If a V-P IQ discrepancy is 32 or more points, then that difference is unambiguously abnormal, occurring in 1 child per 100 among the normal population of children and adolescents ages 6 to 16 years. Values for VC-PO Index discrepancies required to denote abnormality are very similar in magnitude to the V-P IQ values. Table 3.2 is intended for all children tested on the WISC-III, regardless of age, ability level, or direction of the difference between V-IQ and P-IQ or between VC Index and PO Index.

In my 1979 WISC-R book, a table was presented of abnormal WISC-R V-P IQ discrepancies separately by socioeconomic background, defined as parental occupation. Children of unskilled laborers averaged a discrepancy of about 9 points between their WISC-R Verbal and Performance IQs, as contrasted with a discrepancy of almost 11 points for children of professionals. Separate socioeconomic data are not available for the WISC-III, so Table 3.2 has to be used for all children assessed. That's no real problem, though, because the mean V-P IQ discrepancies observed for different parental occupations on the WISC-R did not differ dramatically, and differences due to gender, race, and age were nonsignificant (Kaufman, 1976b). Also, for most subgroups studied on the WISC-R, significant V > P discrepancies were as common as P > V discrepancies. Again, the only exception concerned parental occupation where children of unskilled workers tended to be more "performance minded," whereas the reverse was true for children of professionals. It is not known whether this relationship holds true for the WISC-III. We do know, however, that children whose parents completed 0–8 years of schooling had P > V by 4 points (Granier & O'Donnell, 1991).

The decision as to how rare constitutes "abnormal" rests with the individual examiner, who also has to interpret the frequency of occurrence in the context of what the V-P or VC-PO discrepancy means for a given child. It is not important exactly how Table 3.2 is used, just that it *is* used as a kind of "norm table" for establishing a base line of normal interscale scatter. It is also a helpful tool for deciding when to interpret verbal-nonverbal differences even if the question-and-answer method suggests that such differences are not interpretable. The rules for using the abnormality table follow.

Determining Abnormality in Verbal versus Nonverbal Ability

- If Step 3 indicates that the Verbal and Performance IQs are unitary dimensions and, therefore, interpretable, then use Table 3.2 to determine if the V-P IQ discrepancy is abnormally large. Enter the *left* half of the table with the size of the V-P IQ difference (ignoring the direction of the difference) and see if it is so large that it occurs infrequently among normal children. For most purposes, I consider the Extreme 15% to be sufficiently rare to denote an abnormally large V-P IQ discrepancy. But examiners ought to use Table 3.2 discriptively, as a means of communicating the degree of interscale scatter to the reader of a case report. Thus, a V-P IQ discrepancy of 17 points would be described as statistically significant ($p < .01$), but as occurring fairly frequently within the normal population; a difference of 23 points would be described as abnormal, occurring in the Extreme 10% of the normal population (it is not large enough to be classified as "Extreme 5%"; 25 points is needed); a difference of 30 points would be described as occurring in the Extreme 2% of the population; and so forth. Obviously, nonsignificant V-P IQ discrepancies won't be abnormally large, so there's no need to bother with Table 3.2 if an interpretable V-P difference is found (in Step 2) to be too small to be real.
- If Step 3 indicates that the Verbal and Performance IQs are *not* unitary dimensions, but the VC and PO Indexes *are* unitary (and, hence, interpretable), then use Table 3.2 to determine if the VC-PO Index discrepancy is abnormally large. Enter the *right* half of the table with the size of the VC-PO Index difference (ignoring the direction of the difference) and see if it occurs rarely among normal children. Use the same interpretive procedures described for the V-P IQ difference; again, there's no sense entering Table 3.2 if the VC versus PO difference fails to reach statistical significance.
- If Step 3 indicates that *neither* the V-P IQ discrepancy *nor* the VC-PO Index discrepancy is interpretable because of too much variability among subtest scores, then use Table 3.2 anyway. Why? Because some verbal-nonverbal differences are just too big to ignore, even if, technically, the IQs or Indexes aren't measuring unitary dimensions.

First, decide whether you want to enter Table 3.2 with the IQ or the Index discrepancy. Ordinarily, enter with the V-P IQ difference since IQs are more readily understood. If the Factor Indexes don't correspond to unitary factors, then they lose much of their practical appeal. However, if you have a compelling reason for using the VC-PO Index difference in this instance, then do so; it doesn't really matter. The main point is that if the child's verbal-nonverbal difference is unusually large, then it needs to be addressed. Regardless of what else is going on in the profile, the child's difference between verbal and nonverbal skill has at least something to do with the observed fluctuations.

So enter Table 3.2 with the V-P IQ discrepancy or the VC-PO Index difference. If either one is at least 19 points in size, then the difference is abnormal, corresponding to the Extreme 15% of the population. Interpret the child's verbal-nonverbal difference as meaningful even if you obtained one or more yes answers in the question-and-answer approach in Step 3. If, however, the discrepancy is 18 points or less, do not interpret verbal-nonverbal differences whenever Step 3 produced at least one yes answer. There just may not be an easy way to contrast such a child's verbal and nonverbal abilities; probably you should abandon Wechsler's basic two-pronged model for the WISC-III in favor of alternate models. In such instances, skip over Chapter 4 on verbal-nonverbal differences, examine the FD and PS factors in Chapter 5, and then hop to the later chapters to try to make sense out of the fluctuations in the child's subtest profile.

But if the verbal-nonverbal difference is huge, then interpret the child's discrepancy on Wechsler's favorite dichotomy despite the peaks and valleys within the subtest profile. The example of Nathan S. illustrates this circumstance.

Illustration of a Large Verbal-Performance IQ Discrepancy plus Subtest Scatter

Consider the case of Nathan S., an African-American male age 9 years 9 months, who was tested on the WISC-III to determine his eligibility for a gifted program.

Nathan obtained the following WISC-III profile:

Nathan S.

IQs		Factor Indexes	
Verbal	122	Verbal Comprehension	118
Performance	95	Perceptual Organization	91
Full Scale	109	Freedom from Distractibility	124
V-IQ > P-IQ ($p < .01$)		Processing Speed	117

Verbal	Scaled Score	Performance	Scaled Score
Information	9	Picture Completion	11
Similarities	14	(Coding)	(14)
Arithmetic	15	Picture Arrangement	8
Vocabulary	17	Block Design	9
Comprehension	13	Object Assembly	6
(Digit Span)	(13)	*Symbol Search	12

* Symbol Search was used in IQ computations

When we ask the four questions we discover:

1. *No,* Nathan's VC and FD Factor Indexes (118 and 124) do *not* differ significantly.
2. *Yes,* his Verbal scaled-score range of 8 points (17 on Vocabulary minus 9 on Information) *does* reflect abnormal Verbal scatter.
3. *Yes,* his PO and PS Factor Indexes (91 and 117) *do* differ significantly.
4. *No,* his Performance scaled-score range of 6 points (12 on Symbol Search minus 6 on Object Assembly) does *not* reflect abnormal Performance scatter. (Note that the 14 on Coding does not enter into the computation because it was not used to compute P-IQ.)

Two of the four questions are answered *"yes,"* which ordinarily means that the V-P IQ discrepancy should not be interpreted. The next step is to see if the difference between the VC and PO Factor Indexes is interpretable. The answer is *"no,"* because of abnormal scatter within the VC Factor (Nathan's extreme scores on the Verbal Scale are on subtests that are both included on the VC factor).

If Step 3 is followed rigidly, then neither the V-P IQ discrepancy nor the VC-PO Index discrepancy should be interpreted. But that's ridiculous for a child who obviously differs in his verbal and nonverbal skills. That's why Step 4 prevents rigid application of the "yes-and-no" method for inferring whether a verbal-nonverbal difference is interpretable. Whether Nathan's IQs or Factor Indexes are used, he has much better verbal than nonverbal skills. He scored 27 points higher in both instances, too large a difference to ignore. You can use the IQs or the Indexes in this case—take your pick—but don't ignore Nathan's verbal-nonverbal discrepancy when interpreting his profile. The Verbal scatter is due to a low score on Information, a subtest of questionable fairness for an African-American child in the first place. The Performance scatter is due to a large difference between Nathan's PO and PS Indexes. He does differ in these two components of nonverbal intelligence, but that discrepancy does not alter the fact that his range of ability on nonverbal measures (scaled scores of 6 to 14) barely overlaps with his 13 to 17 range (excluding Information) on Verbal measures.

Ignoring that obvious verbal-nonverbal difference would be counterproductive. But so would it be inappropriate to ignore the split in the Performance Scale or the fluctuations in the subtest profile. These additional considerations are treated in Steps 6 and 7 when Nathan's profile is used to illustrate empirical and rational methods of subtest interpretation.

One aspect of Step 4 is to permit examiners to bypass the outcome of the question-and-answer method when there is reason to interpret a verbal-nonverbal discrepancy despite the fact that one or both constructs are multidimensional. There are also other, more subtle, reasons for going against the systematic guidelines spelled out in Step 3, or even the empirical rules for identifying statistically significant V-P or VC-PO differences in Step 2. Illustrations of when to violate the rules are given at the end of this chapter in the section "Exceptions to the Rules." As a general approach, bypass the rules whenever the outcome of the questions and answers is not sensible.

STEP 5. INTERPRET THE MEANING OF THE GLOBAL VERBAL AND NONVERBAL DIMENSIONS AND THE MEANING OF THE SMALL FACTORS

The preceding four steps are mostly empirical. Step 5 is conceptual and requires the application of clinical observations and inferences, theoretical perspective, and test scores on other instruments to obtain maximal understanding of the child's scores on the global scores yielded by the WISC-III. Steps 2 through 4 identify significant and unusual fluctuations within the IQ and Factor Index profile. Step 5 concerns interpretation of these significant differences and inferring when it's wisest to minimize the specific statistical findings. Consult Chapter 4 for a variety of theoretical, clinical, and research-based interpretations of a child's verbal-nonverbal differences. Consult Chapter 5 for a similar eclectic approach to the interpretation of Factor 3, Freedom from Distractibility, and Factor 4, Processing Speed.

STEP 6. INTERPRET SIGNIFICANT STRENGTHS AND WEAKNESSES IN THE WISC-III SUBTEST PROFILE

After the global scores have been taken about as far as they can go in the preceding interpretive steps, the next topic is to try to make sense out of the subtest profile. Although any inferences drawn from analysis of subtest fluctuations have been analogized to punishable felonies, or worse, by some, that's not my perspective, as I spelled out in Chapter 1. Consequently, I'll plunge ahead with ipsative interpretation of a child's subtest profile in the belief that the best use of a test that was originally developed as a clinical tool is to take full advantage of the clinical raw materials that David Wechsler so carefully assembled. But that doesn't mean that the clinical horse pulls the empirical cart. It doesn't. Here are the empirical guidelines that define Step 6.

I think of profile interpretation as an experiment with $N = 1$, and I like to start off—as in an experiment of any sort—with null hypotheses. With the WISC-R, I used the results of factor analysis to generate the null hypotheses. I believed that the strong factorial support for the Verbal Comprehension and Perceptual Organization factors offered a rationale for investigating subtest fluctuations separately for the Verbal and Performance Scales, and the null hypotheses were tied in to that rationale.

With the WISC-III, the situation is more complicated. Evidence for the four-factor solution is strong, but so is the support for the placement of all subtests (except Digit Span) on their designated scale, whether Verbal or Performance, when only two factors are interpreted. Also, the *g* loadings give empirical support for the Full Scale IQ construct. Ultimately, the issue of two factors (IQs) versus four factors (Indexes) makes it difficult to support any one set of null hypotheses as a framework for subtest interpretation. So the best solution is probably the simplest one, as Kamphaus (1993) suggests: to interpret subtest fluctuations relative to the child's mean of all subtests administered. At least that solution works well when the child's verbal and nonverbal abilities are not very discrepant. When these abilities differ substantially, however, the overall mean of the 12 subtests is fairly "mean"-ingless. Instead, it makes more sense to evaluate Verbal and Performance subtests separately for children with substantial V-P IQ discrepancies.

Three null hypotheses are proposed: one for a child whose V-P IQ discrepancy is of normal magnitude (even if it is statistically significant), and two for a child whose V-P IQ discrepancy is unusually large (19 or more points based on empirical criteria in Table 3.2). For the purposes of subtest profile interpretation, select the appropriate null hypotheses based on the simple V-P IQ discrepancy. For this determination, forget whether the VC-PO Index difference makes more sense for a given child. Keep it simple. If the V-P IQ discrepancy is smaller than 19 points, use the first null hypothesis for evaluating that child's subtest profile. If the V-P difference is 19 points or more, use the second set of null hypotheses.

The null hypotheses for the experiment that is conducted each time a child's profile is evaluated are as follows:

For Children with Verbal-Performance IQ Discrepancies of 0 to 18 Points

Null Hypothesis: Children's global General ability determines their scores on all WISC-III subtests; therefore, all fluctuations in their scaled scores are due to *chance error.*

Working from this experimental perspective, determining the meaningfulness of fluctuations in a child's WISC-III profile becomes an easy and straightforward clerical exercise. The examiner's task is to discover whether each Verbal or Performance scaled score differs significantly from the mean of the child's scaled scores on all subtests administered. Use the mean of all 12 subtests (excluding Mazes) if the complete battery was administered. Use the mean of the 10 regular subtests if one or both supplements were excluded.

The mean scaled score serves as a convenient estimate of the child's level of General ability. Each time a significant deviation between a Verbal or Performance scaled score and the grand mean is obtained, a "subhypothesis" is rejected. These significant fluctuations represent relative strengths and weaknesses for the individual and serve as starting points for developing alternative hypotheses for interpreting the WISC-III profile. Two or more significantly deviating subtest scores are usually sufficient grounds for rejecting the null hypothesis and for beginning the detective work necessary to generate new hypotheses (see Step 7). When only one WISC-III scaled score deviates significantly from its mean, the null hypothesis cannot be rejected. The global scores, interpreted in Steps 1 through 5, should be featured in the Test Interpretation section of the case report. Fluctuations within the subtest profile should be minimized.

For Children with Verbal-Performance IQ Discrepancies of 19 or More Points

Null Hypothesis 1: Children's global Verbal ability determines their scores on all Verbal subtests; therefore, all fluctuations in their scaled scores are due to *chance error.*

Null Hypothesis 2: Children's global Performance ability determines their scores on all Performance subtests; therefore, all fluctuations in their Performance scaled scores are due to *chance error.*

In this case, the examiner's task is to discover whether each Verbal scaled score differs significantly from the mean of the child's Verbal scaled scores, and whether each Performance scaled score differs significantly from his or her Performance mean. Use the mean of all 6 Verbal or Performance subtests (excluding Mazes) if the complete battery was administered. Use the mean of the 5 regular subtests if the supplements were excluded.

The mean Verbal scaled score and the mean Performance scaled score serve as convenient estimates of the child's Verbal and Performance ability, respectively. As indicated previously, each time a significant deviation between a Verbal or Performance scaled score and the appropriate mean is obtained, a "subhypothesis" is rejected. And, as before, these significant fluctuations represent relative strengths and weaknesses for the individual and serve as starting points for making sense out of the profile fluctuations (Step 7). At least one significantly deviating Verbal subtest score is usually sufficient grounds for rejecting the first null hypothesis; a similar rule of thumb applies to the Performance Scale regarding the rejection of the second null hypothesis. When no Verbal or Performance scaled score deviates significantly from its mean, the null hypotheses cannot be rejected. The sizable split between the two IQs probably represents the primary thrust of profile interpretation for children with few subtest fluctuations. Steps 1 through 5 will be instrumental in interpreting the WISC-III for such children. Either the Verbal and Performance IQs, or perhaps the four Factor Indexes, will be featured, depending on the question-and-answer approach and the results of the kind of exploration recommended in Chapters 4 and 5. But Step 7 in the WISC-III interpretive process will probably not be needed.

The Empirical Method

Davis (1959) developed a valuable set of formulas regarding differences between averages and individual test scores. One of these formulas, which Sattler (1974) revived, is particularly useful for testing the null hypotheses: It permits computation of the size of the difference required for statistical significance when comparing a single scaled score to the child's average scaled score on several subtests. Silverstein (1982) pointed out that the simple application of Davis's formulas failed to account for the errors that creep in whenever several comparisons are made simultaneously. In analysis of variance research, for example, statistical control is routinely built into the statistical procedure when many pairs of means are compared at once.

Silverstein (1982) offered a solution to the problem, thereby making "Bonferroni" a household word to school and clinical psychologists. Applying the Bonferroni procedure to the Wechsler interpretive process became commonplace (Kaufman, 1990a; Wechsler, 1991). For the WISC-R, I had recommended using a constant ±3 points from a child's mean to determine significant strengths and weaknesses for each subtest (Kaufman, 1979b). With the Bonferroni correction, the value of 3 points was no longer a good generalization for all subtests; instead, ±4 was necessary for all Performance subtests, except Block Design (Kaufman, 1990a, p. 426). In the WISC-III manual, Bonferroni-corrected values are presented for each subtest, permitting comparison of each Verbal subtest with the mean of 5 or 6 subtests; of each Performance subtest with the mean of 5, 6, or 7 subtests; and of each Verbal or Performance subtests with the mean of 10, 12, or 13 subtests (Wechsler, 1991, Table B.3).

As with everything else involving Wechsler subtest interpretation, even the Bonferroni correction has come under attack. Krauskopf (1991) notes that Silverstein's plea for the Bonferroni correction addresses the problem of Type I errors, but ignores Type II errors and the notion of statistical power. He argues that instead of increasing the size of the differences needed for significance, it's wiser to reduce the size to about 1.5 to 2 points (Krauskopf, 1991, Table 1). In his response to Krauskopf's arguments, Silverstein (1993) commends Krauskopf for alerting clinicians to the multiple statistical issues involved in profile analysis, but he also points out that if you follow Krauskopf's logic and use his statistical values, then the original problem identified by Silverstein becomes exacerbated; the new values make it conceivable that a clinician will make errors when interpreting the strengths and weaknesses of four out of five children.

Silverstein (1993) concedes that continuing to apply the Bonferroni correction is not a good idea, and he offers a few suggestions for dealing with the problem. The one that makes the most sense to me, and the method that he ultimately advocates, is to avoid conventional statistical significance and to use the concepts associated with subtest scatter. That is, instead of using any formulas at all to determine significance, use the notion of abnormality. Examine the actual frequency distributions of scores and treat as meaningful only those differences that occurred infrequently within the normal population. Fortunately, the WISC-III manual provides data on the abnormality of the differences between a child's subtest score and the child's mean of several subtest scores (Wechsler, 1991, Table B.3). From this table, for example, it is possible to look at differences between a child's scaled score on Information and his or her average scaled score on the six Verbal subtests. From pure statistical significance, the Bonferroni-corrected value for the .05 level is 3.0 points. From the vantage point of abnormality, the WISC-III table tells us that 1% of the total standardization sample had discrepancies 5.0 points or more from their own mean Verbal score; 2% of the sample had discrepancies of 4.3 points or more; 5% of the sample had discrepancies of 3.7 points or more; 10% of the sample had discrepancies of 3.2 points or more; and 25% of the sample had discrepancies of 2.2 points or more.

Of the values offered in the WISC-III manual, I think that the extreme 10% makes the most sense. (I would have preferred the extreme 15% to be consistent with the value used in Steps 3 and 4, but 10% is fine.) As Silverstein (1993) indicates, when you deal with statistical abnormality instead of statistical significance, the various problems associated with making multiple comparisons become irrelevant. Consequently, I suggest abandoning the conventional significance approach in favor of an abnormality approach. I've constructed Table 3.3 from the values provided in the WISC-III manual that denote the size of the difference for each subtest that occurred in the extreme 10% of the total standardization sample. The magnitude of these differences is similar to the size of the discrepancies that have typically been used for evaluating Wechsler profiles.

The differences required for interpreting a significant strength or weakness, regardless of the number of subtests used to compute the child's average, may be meaningfully summarized as follows:

±3 Points	±4 Points	±5 Points
Information	Comprehension	Coding
Similarities	Digit Span	
Arithmetic	Picture Completion	
Vocabulary	Picture Arrangement	
	Block Design	
	Object Assembly	
	Symbol Search	

There are slight exceptions to the preceding overview. The values for Arithmetic round to 3 when compared with the 5 or 6 Verbal subtests, but round to 4 when compared with the 10 or 12 subtests. The value for Comprehension rounds to 3, not 4, when compared to the 5 Verbal subtests. But these deviations are trivial. The preceding overview for each subtest is suitable regardless of the number of subtests on which the average scaled score

TABLE 3.3.   Size of the Difference Required for Significance When Comparing a Child's Subtest Score with the Average of His or Her Scores on Several Subtests

WISC-III Subtest	Average of		Average of	
	5 Subtests	6 Subtests	10 Subtests	12 Subtests
Verbal				
Information	±2.8	±3.2	±3.3	±3.4
Similarities	±2.8	±3.0	±3.2	±3.3
Arithmetic	±3.4	±3.2	±3.6	±3.5
Vocabulary	±2.8	±3.0	±3.2	±3.4
Comprehension	±3.4	±3.7	±3.9	±3.9
Digit Span		±4.2		±4.4
Performance				
Picture Completion	±3.8	±3.8	±3.9	±3.9
Coding	±4.6	±4.3	±4.9	±4.8
Picture Arrangement	±4.0	±4.2	±4.3	±4.4
Block Design	±3.6	±3.8	±4.0	±4.0
Object Assembly	±3.6	±3.8	±4.0	±4.1
Symbol Search		±3.8		±4.2

Note: The size of the differences in this table correspond to the values that denote the extreme 10% of the standardization sample (Wechsler, 1991, Table B.3); they do not correspond to values computed from formulas for conventional statistical significance. For example, when comparing Picture Completion with the mean of all 12 subtests, the value of 3.9 indicates that 10% of the children in the total WISC-III standardization sample had Picture Completion scaled scores that deviated by 3.9 points or more from their average scaled score on all 12 subtests.

is computed. Examiners may use the overview or the values in Table 3.3. Or they may commit to memory a simpler rule: Use ±3 for all Verbal subtests and ±4 for all Performance subtests. That rule is less exact than the overview or Table 3.2, but it still fits the data fairly well; it will ensure that examiners are not likely to interpret as meaningful deviations from the mean that are trivial or due to chance.

I like rules of thumb because they make examiners less dependent on tables. They impose some statistical order on a set of data without making the examiner's job onerous. Such rules are especially useful for examiners who are not altogether comfortable with numbers. Others will disagree (e.g., Campbell & Wilson, 1986), but I find it silly to stress precision to the nearest 10th of a point when the scaled scores are just not that accurate in the first place. Conscientious examiners will often differ on the scoring of several Vocabulary and Comprehension items; some children have mastered the knack of giving clear-cut ½ or 1½ point responses. And more often than not, even experienced examiners will make unabashed errors on test protocols—due to administration errors, mathematical mistakes, ambiguity of scoring rules, and general carelessness—causing substantial differences between the scores on the record form and the scores the child truly earned (Slate & Chick, 1989; Slate & Hunnicutt, 1988; Slate & Jones, 1990; Slate, Jones, Coulter, & Covert, 1992). These errors do not even figure into the known standard error of measurement for each subtest, because during the standardization of a test such as the WISC-III every record form is scored and checked for accuracy; any differences of opinion are settled systematically and objectively.

Therefore, it is more important to use some statistical guideline than to get hung up on rigidity or detailed analyses. I will use Table 3.3 for the following set of steps for determining significant deviations from the child's mean, but feel free to use the previous grouping of subtests into ±3, ±4, or ±5 classifications, or any rule of thumb that can be easily committed to memory.

Make the following computations to identify significant strengths and weaknesses:

1. Determine whether the V-P IQ discrepancy is 19 or more points.

If the discrepancy is 0–18 points, compute the mean of all 12 subtests. If only 10 or 11 subtests were given, compute the mean of the 10 subtests used to contain IQs. Round the mean to the nearest whole number.

If the discrepancy is 19 or more points, compute the mean scaled score of all Verbal subtests administered (five or six), and then do the same for all Performance subtests administered. Round each mean to the nearest whole number.

2. Compare each scaled score to the child's relevant mean score.

Use the values in Table 3.3 (rounded to the nearest whole number), or the summary of these values presented earlier, to identify subtests that deviate significantly from the relevant mean. All Verbal or Performance scaled scores that are the designated number of points above the mean are significant *strengths* for the child and should be labeled with an "S." All values that are the designated number of points below the mean should be labeled with a "W" to signify *weaknesses*.

Examiners who prefer *not* to round the mean to the nearest whole number, and to use the exact values to the nearest 10th presented in Table 3.3, may certainly do so. That's why I included the precise deviation values in Table 3.3. But it's not necessary.

3. Treat all scaled scores that do not deviate significantly from the appropriate mean as chance fluctuations.

They should not be interpreted as strengths or weaknesses per se but may be used to support hypotheses (see Step 7).

The method described here for WISC-III profile interpretation has several advantages to recommend it, as long as you don't fall prey to the anti-profile and anti-ipsative empiricism of McDermott-Glutting et al. (see Chapter 1). It permits the examiner to obtain an overview of the child's abilities. It does not depend on haphazard decisions about apparent peaks and valleys in the profile or on arbitrary comparisons of extreme scaled scores; rather, each scaled score is systematically compared with the child's own midpoint, with abnormally large differences used to determine meaningful fluctuations. Using the midpoint as the frame of reference also serves the function of assuring that strengths and weaknesses will be relative to the child's own level of ability on each scale. This type of ipsative measurement forces the examiner out of a normative mold and paves the way for a more insightful understanding of whatever scatter might define the child's cognitive structure.

The fairly common practice of using the *group* mean of 10 and the *group* standard deviation of 3 as the statistical bases for determining significant strengths and weaknesses is antagonistic to individualized profile interpretation. Group parameters are useful when dealing with group data; individual mean scores serve better for individual profile interpretation. Besides, the normative means have already been applied extensively in Steps 1 through 5 of the WISC-III interpretive process for evaluating the child's performance on the IQs and Factor Indexes. The use of 10 ± 3 to determine strengths and weaknesses leads to particularly one-sided views of the abilities of high-IQ and low-IQ children, with the former individuals emerging with few weaknesses and the latter with only an occasional strength. Yet a balanced spectrum of relatively good and poor skills is especially conducive to translation of test scores to educational suggestions. A normative referent is fine for computing the scaled scores, Factor Indexes and IQs and for interpreting some aspects of the global IQs and Indexes; however, an ipsative referent, which employs each child as his or her own private norm, is ordinarily preferable for analyzing subtest fluctuations.

I also find little value in methods of interpretation that depend on tables showing significant differences between pairs of subtest scores, such as the ones presented in the WISC-III manual (Wechsler, 1991, Table B.4). Pairwise comparisons are sometimes made between the several extreme values that are evident in a profile rather than systematically or between predetermined pairs. Selecting the extremely high and low scores takes fortuitous advantage of chance errors, thereby distorting the meaning of the values required for significance that are reported in the tables.

Apart from this statistical consideration, evaluating the significance of the difference between pairs of scaled scores fails to give the kind of crisp overview that is obtained by using the child's own mean as the yardstick of comparison. Rather, the pairwise method yields a series of separate statements about the child's abilities that are not integrated and sometimes require a competent logician to convert to a meaningful overview of the profile. Furthermore, focusing on the separate subtest scores as important entities by themselves does not take advantage of the empirical results of factor analysis that emphasize the primacy of the global verbal and nonverbal abilities and the smaller third and fourth factors in profile interpretation. Hypotheses about the unique abilities presumably measured by each subtest should be secondary to global hypotheses involving the IQs and Factor Indexes. The use of the pairwise comparisons usually puts the uniqueness of each subtest in the foreground and, in effect puts the cart before the horse. Thus, even through the computation of significant differences between various pairs of scaled scores provides an ipsative view of the child's strengths and weaknesses, this technique may not offer the most insight into a child's WISC-III profile.

Nonetheless, I would prefer to see examiners systematically generate hypotheses from a series of pairwise comparisons than to see them avoid subtest interpretation like the plague because of the cautionary tales told from a purely empirical perspective by a group of anti-profile researchers of the McDermott-Glutting and Macman-Barnett ilk (see discussion in Chapter 1).

Illustrations

Two profiles presented earlier in this chapter (Harvey A. and Nathan S.) are used to demonstrate the mechanics of the empirical method for identifying significant subtest strengths and weaknesses in the WISC-III profile. The detective work required to make interpretive sense out of the relative strengths and weaknesses constitutes the final step of the interpretive process.

WISC-III Profile of Harvey A.

Verbal	Scaled Score	Performance	Scaled Score
Information	7-W	Picture Completion	11
Similarities	10	(Coding)	(16)-S
Arithmetic	7-W	Picture Arrangement	7-W
Vocabulary	11	Block Design	10
Comprehension	9	Object Assembly	9
(Digit Span)	(13)	Symbol Search	17-S

V-IQ = 93   P-IQ = 106

1. **Determine whether the V-P IQ discrepancy is 19 or more points.** Harvey's V-P IQ discrepancy is 13 points, a statistically significant difference. However, the discrepancy is less than 19 points, and therefore not unusually large. Consequently, the overall mean of his scaled scores on the 12 subtests administered constitutes the midpoint for computing his strengths and weaknesses. The mean of the 12 scaled scores equals 10.6, which rounds to 11.

2. **Compare each scaled score with the child's relevant mean score.** Using the values in Table 3.3, rounded to the nearest whole number, reveals significant strengths in Coding and Symbol Search. Coding has to be at least 5 points above the mean, and Harvey's scaled score of 16 is exactly 5 points above his mean of 11. Symbol Search, which is 6 points above the mean, easily qualifies as a significant strength (4 points is required). These strengths are indicated with an "S."

Three significant weaknesses are evident in the profile, the three 7's earned on Information, Arithmetic, and Picture Arrangement. All are four points below Harvey's mean of 11. From Table 3.2, Arithmetic and Picture Arrangement require 4 points for significance, whereas Information requires 3 points. The weaknesses are denoted with a "W" in Harvey's WISC-III subtest profile.

3. **Treat all scaled scores that do not deviate significantly from the appropriate mean as chance fluctuations.** Although Harvey's scaled score of 13 on Digit Span is significantly greater than his scaled score of 9 on both Comprehension and Object Assembly (Wechsler, 1991, Table B.4), those findings are treated as artifacts. Based on the technique presented here, the values of 13 and 9 merely represent chance deviations from the overall mean; individual subtest interpretation is discouraged. In fact, Object Assembly shouldn't be interpreted in isolation in any case because it has an inadequate amount of subtest specificity (see Chapter 2). However, his below-the-mean scores on Object Assembly and Comprehension might offer insight into the explanation for his significant weakness in Picture Arrangement, just as his above-the-mean score on Digit Span might relate to his significant Coding and Symbol Search strengths.

WISC-III Profile of Nathan S.

Verbal	Scaled Score	Performance	Scaled Score
Information	9-W	Picture Completion	11
Similarities	14	(Coding)	(14)
Arithmetic	15	Picture Arrangement	8
Vocabulary	17-S	Block Design	9
Comprehension	13	Object Assembly	6-W
(Digit Span)	(13)	Symbol Search	12

V-IQ = 122   P-IQ = 95

1. **Determine whether the V-P IQ discrepancy is 19 or more points.** Nathan's V-P IQ discrepancy is 27 points, an unusually large difference that is well above the 19-point cutoff. Therefore, the mean of his six Verbal scaled scores serves as the midpoint for all Verbal subtests, and the Performance mean is likewise used for each Performance subtest.

The mean of the six Verbal scaled scores equals 13.5. Rounding to the nearest whole number yields a Verbal mean of 14. The Performance mean is exactly 10.

2. **Compare each scaled score to the child's relevant mean score.** Based on Table 3.3, Nathan demonstrates one strength (Vocabulary) and one weakness (Information) relative to his Verbal mean, and a single deviating subtest relative to the Performance mean: the 6 in

Object Assembly. Each of these subtests is denoted by an "S" or "W" in Nathan's profile.

3. **Treat all scaled scores that do not deviate significantly from the appropriate mean as chance fluctuations.** Coding yielded a scaled score of 14, which is 4 points above his Performance mean; that difference is statistically significant at the .05 level (Wechsler, 1991, Table B.3). However, it does not meet the requirements for significance set forth in this interpretive procedure, namely unusual differences that occur less than 10% of the time in the normal population. For Coding, ±5 points is needed for significance by the abnormality criterion, so the apparent peak on Coding should be treated as a chance fluctuation that should not be interpreted in isolation. (Coding is the only subtest that requires such a large deviation for significance. That means it is common for children to have substantial differences between their Coding scaled score and their own midpoints. That finding stems from Coding's low g loading and its concomitant low correlations with other WISC-III subtests.)

But that doesn't mean Coding is unimportant for understanding Nathan's profile. As we saw previously, when it is paired with Symbol Search (its factor-analytic Siamese twin), Nathan's Processing Speed standard score of 116 is significantly and substantially higher than his Perceptual Organization standard score of 91. Coding just doesn't merit any type of interpretation in isolation.

STEP 7. GENERATE HYPOTHESES ABOUT THE FLUCTUATIONS IN THE WISC-III SUBTEST PROFILE

The last step, ultimately, represents the crux of WISC-III profile interpretation and is treated comprehensively in Chapter 6; it is also illustrated by the 10 sample case reports in this book, one appearing at the end of Chapter 4, two each appearing at the end of Chapters 5 and 6, and five composing Chapter 7. Careful detective work is needed to group and regroup subtests by the abilities that they share; to integrate the WISC-III test profile with background information, clinical observations of the child's behaviors, and scores obtained on other tests and subtests; to interpret the WISC-III profile in the context of theory and research results; and to attempt to translate the cross-validated interpretation of the child's profile to sensible behavioral and educational intervention.

Without additional information, it is impossible to interpret the subtest fluctuations displayed by Harvey and Nathan. Harvey's weaknesses in Information and Arithmetic suggest a school-related hypothesis or a memory hypothesis to explain them. His significant weakness in Picture Arrangement—when paired with a below-the-mean score in Comprehension—implies a weakness in social understanding. But when paired with his scores on Object Assembly and Block Design (both below his mean of 11), there is a suggestion of a poor ability to synthesize parts into a whole. All of these subtest groupings are hypotheses that can only have meaning if they are given support from other sources about Harvey. The WISC-III cannot be interpreted in an empirical vacuum.

Similarly, the only things we know about Nathan is that he is African-American and was referred to a gifted program. Perhaps his weakness on the culturally loaded Information subtest is related to his African-American background. We can't tell without knowing more about his specific environment and subculture. His relatively low Performance IQ may be due to a spatial reasoning deficit, a field dependent cognitive style, or any number of cognitive or behavioral variables. Without knowing pertinent test behaviors, background information, and scores on other tests, no meaningful interpretation of his WISC-III IQ, Index, or subtest profile is feasible.

In Chapter 6, various splits of the Verbal and Performance Scales are considered and interpreted to enable examiners to anticipate some common, meaningful divisions of WISC-III subtests that usually do not conform very well to the four-way factorial division. That chapter also provides a systematic, step-by-step approach to hypothesis generation to arm examiners with an organized plan of attack for making clinical and psychological sense out of peaks and valleys in the subtest profiles. The illustrative case reports at the end of Chapter 6, and the five comprehensive reports that compose Chapter 7, demonstrate the integration of WISC-III subtest fluctuations with background information, test behaviors, and scores on other tests. Both chapters are needed to understand the nuances of Step 7 in the WISC-III interpretive process.

OVERVIEW OF THE SEVEN STEPS

Table 3.4 was developed to provide an overview of the seven interpretive steps for WISC-III profiles. Use it after first reading this entire chapter thoroughly to understand the rationale behind the methodology and guidelines.

EXCEPTIONS TO THE RULES

Within the set of rules described in this chapter are two main circumstances in which V-P IQ discrepancies are not interpretable (both described in Step 3)—when the two factors that compose either scale differ significantly, and when either scale has a significant amount of subtest scatter. In Step 4, examiners are told to interpret verbal-nonverbal discrepancies even when the scales have scatter if the IQ or Index discrepancies are unusually large. These are all rule-governed, systematic ways of knowing when to interpret

TABLE 3.4.   Summary of Seven Steps for Interpreting WISC-III Profiles

Step 1. Interpret the Full Scale IQ

Convert it to an ability level and percentile rank and band it with error, preferably a 90% confidence interval (about ±5 points).

Step 2. Determine if the Verbal-Performance IQ Discrepancy Is Statistically Significant

Values are presented in Table 3.1. Overall values for V-P IQ discrepancies are *11 points* at the .05 level and *15 points* at the .01 level. For most testing purposes, the .05 level is adequate.

Step 3. Determine if the V-P IQ Discrepancy Is Interpretable—Or if the VC and PO Factor Indexes Should Be Interpreted Instead

Ask four questions about the Verbal and Performance Scales

Verbal Scale

1. Is there a significant difference ($p < .05$) between the child's standard scores on VC versus FD?

Size Needed for Significance (VC-FD) = 13+ points

2. Is there abnormal scatter (highest minus lowest scaled score) among the five Verbal subtests used to compute V-IQ?

Size Needed for Abnormal Verbal Scatter = 7+ points

Performance Scale

3. Is there a significant difference ($p < .05$) between the child's standard scores on PO versus PS?

Size Needed for Significance (PO-PS) = 15+ points

4. Is there abnormal scatter (highest minus lowest scaled score) among the five Performance subtests used to compute P-IQ?

Size Needed for Abnormal Performance Scatter = 9+ points

If all answers are no, the V-P IQ discrepancy is interpretable. If the answer to one or more questions is yes, the V-P IQ discrepancy may not be interpretable. Examine the VC-PO discrepancy. Values are presented in Table 3.1. Overall values for VC-PO discrepancies are *12 points* at the .05 level and *16 points* at the .01 level.

Determine if the VC and PO Indexes are unitary dimensions:

1. Is there abnormal scatter among the four VC subtests?

Size Needed for Abnormal VC Scatter = 7+ points

2. Is there abnormal scatter among the four PO subtests?

Size Needed for Abnormal PO Scatter = 8+ points

If the answer to either question is yes, then you probably shouldn't interpret the VC-PO Index discrepancy—unless the discrepancy is too big to ignore (see Step 4). If both answers are no, interpret the VC-PO difference as meaningful.

Step 4. Determine if the V-P IQ Discrepancy (Or VC-PO Discrepancy) Is Abnormally Large

Values for determining unusually large V-P and VC-PO discrepancies are given in Table 3.2. Differences of at least *19 points* are unusually large for both the V-P and VC-PO discrepancies. Enter the table with the IQs or Indexes, whichever was identified by the questions and answers in Step 3.

If neither set of scores was found to be interpretable in Step 3, they may be interpreted anyway if the magnitude of the discrepancy is unusually large (19+ points).

TABLE 3.4. *(Continued)*

Step 5. Interpret the Meaning of the Global Verbal and Nonverbal Dimensions and the Meaning of the Small Factors

Study the information and procedures presented in Chapter 4 (verbal/nonverbal) and Chapter 5 (FD and PS factors). Chapter 5 provides the following rules regarding when the FD and PS factors have too much scatter to permit meaningful interpretation of their respective Indexes:

1. Do not interpret the FD Index if the Arithmetic and Digit Span scaled scores differ by *4 or more points.*
2. Do not interpret the PS Index if the Symbol Search and Coding scaled scores differ by *4 or more points.*

Step 6. Interpret Significant Strengths and Weaknesses in the WISC-III Subtest Profile

If the V-P IQ discrepancy is less than 19 points, use the child's mean of all WISC-III subtests administered as the child's midpoint.

If the V-P IQ discrepancy is 19 or more points, use the child's mean of all Verbal subtests as the midpoint for determining strengths and weaknesses on Verbal subtests, and use the Performance mean for determining significant deviations on Performance subtests.

Values are presented in Table 3.3 for determining if a subtest deviates significantly from the child's own mean. Use either the specific values in the table (rounded to the nearest whole number) or the following summary information for determining significant deviations:

± 3 points: Information, Similarities, Arithmetic, Vocabulary

± 4 points: Comprehension, Digit Span, Picture Completion, Picture Arrangement, Block Design, Object Assembly, Symbol Search

± 5 points: Coding

Step 7. Generate Hypotheses about the Fluctuations in the WISC-III Subtest Profile

Study the information and procedures presented in Chapter 6, which deal with the systematic reorganization of subtest profiles to generate hypotheses about strengths and weaknesses.

---

the V-P IQ discrepancy, the VC-PO index discrepancy, or neither. But sometimes rules don't work for a specific child or a specific circumstance.

Be guided by common sense more so than by particular rules. Bypass the guidelines whenever your clinical and rational judgment tells you that Wechsler's dichotomy is indeed meaningful for a particular child or adolescent, despite the outcome of the questions and answers in Step 3. The first and most basic rule of an intelligent testing approach is *not* to interpret any rule too rigidly. Sometimes a V-P IQ discrepancy will be meaningful even if one or more of the four questions is answered yes. The same is true for the VC-PO difference, even if one or both factors have substantial scatter. Occasionally, a seemingly nonsignificant verbal-nonverbal difference will be meaningful. What follows are three general situations in which interpretation of verbal-nonverbal differences requires clinical acumen and knowledge of pertinent research findings, not strict adherence to a set of rules.

These exceptions are the need to compute prorated IQs, verbal compensation of performance deficit, and the effects of retesting.

The Need to Compute Prorated IQs

If a child has a very deviant score in Arithmetic, then the V-IQ may miscommunicate the child's real abilities because of what we know about the four-factor structure of the WISC-III. The same holds for a deviant score on Symbol Search or Coding (whichever one is used to compute P-IQ). But if, say, a deviantly high Similarities scaled score elevates V-IQ, or an uncharacteristically low Block Design score depresses P-IQ, the examiner shouldn't automatically abandon the separate IQs and jump on the Factor Index bandwagon. Neither the IQs nor Indexes may be very useful for a given child. As in the case of children like Nathan S., who have very large verbal-nonverbal discrepancies, the empirical considerations stemming from the questions and answers must be juxtaposed with logic and clinical sensitivity.

Occasionally, the examiner may find good reason for eliminating from the child's V-IQ or P-IQ subtests other than those associated with the third or fourth factor. For example, an African-American child may score very low on Comprehension and the examiner may infer from the child's responses and from knowledge of his or her background that subcultural differences largely accounted for the depressed scaled score. Or some children may score uncharacteristically high on Object Assembly and subsequently explain to the examiner that their hobby is putting together puzzles, of which they have a collection of over 100. Analogously, a schizophrenic child may perform unusually low on Picture Arrangement because of tangential thinking in the interpretation of the social situations depicted in the pictures; or an extremely distractible child may become preoccupied with a noise in the environment and not concentrate on a subtest that is not ordinarily associated with anxiety/distractibility, such as Similarities.

In all of these instances, the uncharacteristically low or high scaled score does not measure the particular ability it was intended to measure and is not assessing the child's verbal or nonverbal intelligence, depending on the subtest's scale placement. The examiner would have justification for eliminating the subtest in question when computing the best estimate of the child's verbal or nonverbal ability. As when applying the VC or PO Factor Indexes in place of their respective IQs, the goal is to identify the child's "real" verbal or nonverbal ability, underlying skills that transcend any particular task on the WISC-III and generalize to other verbal and nonverbal arenas at home or in school.

Identification of a maverick subtest in the Verbal or Performance Scale supports the prorating of IQs from four subtests (see Wechsler, 1991, Table A.8). As discussed in Chapter 2, prorating is a better alternative than substituting a supplementary subtest for estimating IQs. However, don't prorate without a well-supported rational justification for doing so. Examiners would be just as wrong to eliminate a deviant subtest from the child's global verbal or nonverbal scores—simply because it is deviant—as they would be to call a 10-point V-P difference meaningful merely because "it's so close to being significant."

When examiners prorate IQs to get a better estimate of the child's "real" verbal and nonverbal intelligence, they are advised *not* to mention these prorated IQ equivalents in a case report because they will confuse rather than clarify. (There are already an ample number of standard scores with a mean of 100 with which to confuse the reader.) But examiners are obligated to point out that an individual really does have meaningful differences in his or her verbal and nonverbal abilities, despite a nonsignificant V-P IQ discrepancy that suggests otherwise; percentile ranks corresponding to the prorated IQs can effectively communicate such a meaningful difference.

The one time that it's appropriate to report prorated IQs is when the administration of a Verbal or Performance subtest is truly spoiled. In that case, the prorated IQs should be provided *instead* of the actual IQs. In the preceding examples, there surely was no spoilage in the low Comprehension score for the African-American child or the high Object Assembly score for the puzzle fanatic, and probably not for the schizophrenic who exhibited tangential thinking during Picture Arrangement (if you eliminate that type of thinking from a psychotic's cognitive profile, you will be left with an artificially high estimate of his or her intellectual functioning). Only the low Similarities score for the distractible child may have legitimately been spoiled. That decision rests on whether the interfering noise was an uncharacteristic interruption in the test procedures (such as a loud argument between two students just outside the testing room), one that would likely have impaired the test performance of a nondistractible child as well. In that case, though, the examiner ought to have stopped the test administration until the disturbance ended (or was stopped by the examiner). Even a readministration of Similarities would have been preferable to proration because Similarities has a relatively small practice effect (Wechsler, 1991, Tables 5.3–5.5).

Verbal Compensation of Performance Deficit

Children with exceptionally well-developed verbal skills can sometimes use their strength to compensate for relatively deficient nonverbal ability. Picture Completion and Picture Arrangement are two Performance subtests that frequently are influenced by good verbal skills; indeed, both have secondary loadings in the .30s on the Verbal Comprehension factor, even when four factors are extracted (Wechsler, 1991, Table 6.3). Active use of verbal mediation facilitates the arrangement of pictures to tell a sensible story, and the use of verbal responses for Picture Completion can classify this task in the visual-vocal rather than visual-motor modality. Highly verbal children are sometimes observed to vocalize their problem-solving strategies and even to direct their hands to perform a series of movements during Block Design and Object Assembly. Such mediating processes may improve scaled scores on these subtests, although undue emphasis on verbalization can be costly in view of the speed component inherent in the tasks. Coding and Symbol Search are less likely to be helped very much by compensatory efforts on the part of the verbally bright youngster.

A sample profile illustrative of verbal compensation follows for Aliza G., a white girl age 12 years, 2 months.

Aliza G.

IQs		Factor Indexes	
Verbal	123	Verbal Comprehension	124
Performance	113	Perceptual Organization	116
Full Scale	121	Freedom from Distractibility	118
V-IQ = P-IQ *(n. s.)*		Processing Speed	101

Verbal	Scaled Score	Performance	Scaled Score
Information	15	Picture Completion	14
Similarities	12	(Coding)	(10)
Arithmetic	12	Picture Arrangement	17-S
Vocabulary	13	Block Design	9-W
Comprehension	17-S	Object Assembly	10
(Digit Span)	(14)	*Symbol Search	10

*Symbol Search was used in IQ computations

When we ask the four questions from Step 3 of the WISC-III interpretive process we discover:

1. *No,* Aliza's VC and FD Factor Indexes (124 and 118) do *not* differ significantly.
2. *No,* her Verbal scaled-score range of 5 points (17 on Comprehension minus 12 on Arithmetic) does *not* reflect abnormal Verbal scatter.
3. *No,* her PO and PS Factor Indexes (116 and 101) do *not* differ significantly.
4. *No,* her Performance scaled-score range of 8 points (17 on Picture Arrangement minus 9 on Block Design) does *not* reflect abnormal Performance scatter.

With four no responses, the V-P IQ discrepancy is supposed to be interpretable. The 10-point difference is not statistically significant, so one might infer no meaningful difference in the child's verbal and nonverbal abilities. But that's not the case here. Even though a nonsignificant V-P discrepancy of 10 points is observed, the magnitude of the difference grossly underestimates the degree of verbal superiority that probably characterizes this child. She scored highest on the two subtests that are known to have a verbal component, and—importantly—was observed to talk her way through the Object Assembly puzzles and most Picture Arrangement items. She spontaneously told the story after completing several picture sequences in the latter subtest.

Despite the inability to quantify Aliza's true verbal-nonverbal discrepancy, the hypothesis of spontaneous verbal compensation should be featured in the case report, and tied in to educational plans that will take full advantage of this strength. As in the example of Aliza, there must be behavioral support to the hypothesis, before inferring that verbal compensation has occurred. The mere existence of relatively high scores on the two "Picture" subtests cannot stand alone without clinical support.

It would be most advisable for the examiner to test the limits after completing the WISC-III by administering nonverbal items under modified conditions to better understand the apparent strength. For example, the examiner can instruct the child to verbalize aloud when solving Block Design items if the child did not seem to make use of his or her verbal skills for that task, or the examiner can prohibit the child from vocalizing on Picture Arrangement items if he or she seemed too dependent on that compensatory technique. Any marked changes in problem-solving ability during the testing-the-limits session would give support to the verbal compensation hypothesis and would enhance the examiner's ability to make educational recommendations.

Also desirable would be the administration of supplementary nonverbal tasks under standard and adapted conditions to determine the facilitating effect of verbal ability on visual-motor performance. Illustrative tasks that are especially facilitated by application of verbal skills are Arthur's (1947) Stencil Design, Raven's Matrices Test (Raven, Court, & Raven, 1983), Binet-4 Paper Folding and Cutting, DAS Recall of Designs, WJ-R Spatial Relations, K-ABC Photo Series, KAIT Mystery Codes, Das-Naglieri Planned Codes, and Detroit-3 Design Sequences. The Arthur test is old and outdated, but the Stencil Design subtest—which requires individuals to put abstract, cut-out stencils one on top of another to match an abstract design—remains a gem. One needn't give Raven's matrices to assess that important ability; other similar tasks are available such as Naglieri's (1985) Matrix Analogies Test, the abstract items on the Test of Nonverbal Intelligence (TONI; Brown, Sherbenou, & Johnsen, 1990), and subtests on multiscore batteries such as the K-ABC; DAS, Detroit-3, and Binet-4. The Matrices subtest on the Kaufman Brief Intelligence Test (Kaufman & Kaufman, 1991) also includes easy "prematrices" visual association items using pictures that especially lend themselves to verbalization.

Tests that emphasize visual-motor coordination, such as Coding and Symbol Search, are usually less amendable to verbal compensation. For example, Binet-4 Copying, DAS Speed of Information Processing, the two WJ-R subtests that compose its Gs (Processing Speed) factor, and Das-Naglieri Planned Connections are also worthy supplements. Since the typical kind of profile for a child using verbal compensation during the Performance Scale may be identical to the profile of a youngster with motor coordination problems (see Chapter 4), it is essential that behavioral observations made during the WISC-III, along with scores and observations based on supplementary measures, be used as corroborating evidence.

Effects of Retesting

It is not uncommon for a child to be tested on the WISC-III and then to be retested within a few months. Second testing sessions are arranged when the child scores lower than the examiner might have anticipated, when mitigating circumstances are subsequently discovered (such as the recent divorce of his or her parents) that may have influenced the child's test performance, when the initial scores are challenged by a parent or teacher, and so forth. In clinics, a child is occasionally tested on the WISC-III, despite being given the same test fairly recently. The child referred to the clinic may have been tested by a school psychologist, but the results may not be available or complete. To benefit from clinical observations of the child's test performance, the psychologist in the clinic may wish to retest a child even if the first record form is available, or the psychologists may discover, to their surprise, that the child was recently given the WISC-III based on the innocent statement during Object Assembly, "I can't wait until we get to the car puzzle."

Whenever children are retested on the WISC-III after one or several months, their V-P discrepancy and Full Scale IQ obtained on the second administration are suspect. All children within the entire age range covered by the WISC-III may be expected to gain about 8 points in their Full Scale IQ on a retest after three weeks have elapsed (Wechsler, 1991, Tables 5.3–5.5). However, this gain—which occurs despite the lack of feedback regarding correct responses—is not divided evenly across the Verbal and Performance Scales. Rather, the gain is 2 to 2.5 points in Verbal IQ and a striking 12 to 12.5 points in Performance IQ. Thus a child may be expected to achieve a relative gain of 10 points on the Performance Scale, compared with the Verbal Scale, merely by taking the WISC-III for a second time. A gain of this magnitude can convert a trivial discrepancy in favor of Performance IQ into a significant difference or a barely significant P > V discrepancy into a substantial one, and it can totally mask a legitimate V > P discrepancy. And the 10-point relative gain in Performance IQ, compared with Verbal IQ, occurred for all three age groups tested twice (each with a substantial sample greater than 100): ages 6–7, 10–11, and 14–15.

The notion of a relative gain on Performance IQ has been well known for years (Zimmerman & Woo-Sam, 1973), but the magnitude of the relative 10-point gain for the WISC-III is larger than the magnitude for the WISC-R (6 points), WPPSI-R (3.5 points), or WAIS-R (5 points) (see Kaufman, in press-b, for a thorough treatment of practice effects). The gain for the WISC-III is, therefore, striking even when using its predecessor or other

Wechsler scales as points of comparison, and the impact for the WISC-III clinician is potentially dramatic.

Probably the larger gain in Performance IQ relates to the relative familiarity of the tasks. School-age children are quite used to a barrage of questions closely similar to Verbal items, but they are not usually asked to assemble blocks rapidly to match a design or to tell a story with pictures. The experience gained with the use of the concrete test materials probably leads to the increase in scores of Performance subtests, rather than recall of specific items; the only exception to this generalization may involve the Object Assembly puzzles. As soon as the Performance subtests are administered, they cease being novel. The child may develop effective strategies for solving different kinds of problems that carry over from test to retest. And even if they don't solve many more items correctly on the retest, they are likely to respond more quickly to the items the second item around. On the WISC-III Performance Scale, especially, speed is unduly rewarded with bonus points (see discussion in Chapter 4). The speed variable alone may explain the larger P > V retest gain on the WISC-III than on the WISC-R or on other Wechsler and non-Wechsler tests that offer verbal-nonverbal splits.

It is difficult to interpret V-P discrepancies, as well as Full Scale IQ, when a retest is given a few months after the initial battery. An average gain of 8 points on the Full Scale may mean 2 points or 14 points when a reasonable amount of error is considered, and similar bands of error surround the gain of + 10 in P-IQ relative to V-IQ. The availability of a variety of school-age and adolescent intelligence tests with excellent psychometric properties, such as the K-ABC, DAS, KAIT, and WJ-R, makes it almost a mandate to use a different retest instrument when the WISC-III has been administered within the previous year.

If the WISC-III is given for a second time, the best solution to the practice-effect problem is cautious interpretation, highlighted by not placing undue stress on the specific Full Scale IQ obtained on the retest or on the precise magnitude of the V-P discrepancy. A WISC-III V > P discrepancy on a retest that is almost significant should be considered as probably reflecting a meaningful difference in the face of the relative 10-point boost that is given, on the average, to Performance IQ. Any P > V discrepancy that is barely significant should be ignored. When large P > V discrepancies are found, the hypothesis that the magnitude is partly due to retesting must remain viable. Supplementary administration of other well-normed nonverbal tests that differ in content from Wechsler's subtests is advised.

When determining the child's overall level of performance on the WISC-III, both the original and new set of scores should be examined (if the old scores are available). If the current scores are higher than the first scores by the expected margin (up to about 14 points on the Full Scale), the gains are probably due primarily to the retest factor, and the original scores should be interpreted as the valid estimates of mental functioning. If the latest scores are substantially higher than the previous values, it might be wise to take the *average* of corresponding IQs and scaled scores on the two administrations for the most accurate guess as to the child's true performance. The main exception to the latter rule is when the examiner feels reasonably certain that the first set of scores is predominantly invalid. In such cases, which may occur when the examiner is aware of an important external variable that interfered with performance or when the second set of scores is very much (say, 30 IQ points) higher than the first set, the examiner should simply ignore the first testing.

A word of warning applies to the situation where a child is retested because of surprisingly low scores the first time. In that instance, the retest effect along with the statistical phenomenon of regression to the mean will jointly serve to inflate the second profile of scores; under such circumstances, extreme caution in interpreting gains is needed.

In any retest situation, the four questions that are asked to determine whether the Verbal and Performance IQs are unitary are not sufficient to evaluate the meaningfulness of the V-P IQ discrepancy. Even four no answers will not attest to the interpretability of the discrepancy on a retest. The likelihood that P > V is inflated by an average of 10 points on a WISC-III retest supersedes everything when it comes to interpreting verbal-nonverbal differences. A 9-point P > V profile becomes 19 points just due to predictable practice effects. A trivial 3 points in favor of P-IQ becomes a significant, and misleading, 13 points. And a significant V > P difference of 15 points ($p < .01$) can dwindle to almost nothing just because of the child's previous exposure to the "unfamiliar" visual-spatial problem-solving subtests on the Performance Scale.

Children and adults gain more on nonverbal and fluid tasks than on verbal and crystallized tasks, but the striking 10-point relative gain on the WISC-III Performance Scale is not matched on other tests (Kaufman, in press-b). As noted, the relative gains on other Wechsler scales, including the WISC-R, are substantially less than 10 points. The same holds true for other tests that include a verbal-nonverbal split. The K-ABC Simultaneous Processing Scale resembles the visual-spatial, nonverbal Performance Scale, while its Achievement Scale has tasks similar to the Verbal Scale. Gains on Simultaneous Processing averaged about 4 points higher than on Achievement. The Binet-4's analogs are the Abstract/Visual Reasoning and Verbal Reasoning Scales; gains on the former scale were about 3 points higher than gains on the latter scale. Similarly, retest gains on the DAS Special Nonverbal Scale were 3 points higher than Verbal Ability gains for school-age children, and about 2.5 points higher at the preschool level. On the KAIT, gains in Fluid IQ were about 2.5 points greater than gains on Crystallized IQ. (See Chapter 4 for a discussion of how verbal-nonverbal differences on the WISC-III relate to comparable discrepancies on other intelligence tests.)

In short, nothing can match the WISC-III for practice effects; the retest gain of nearly a standard deviation on Performance IQ is so large that it makes a child's "real" nonverbal intelligence (and, hence, V-P difference) an unsolvable mystery on a WISC-III retest. If you know that the WISC-III was given within the past year to a child referred for evaluation, do yourself an interpretive favor and give a different intelligence test this time.

We don't know for sure how long the practice effect lasts, but a multiple regression analysis based on data from 34 separate test-retest studies indicates that age at initial testing and interval between tests were the only significant predictors of test-retest reliability (Schuerger & Witt, 1989): The younger the individual and the longer the interval, the lower the stability coefficient. Research with the WAIS that explored different retest intervals indicates that a relative P > V gain of ½ of a standard deviation occurred after 4 months (Catron, 1978; Catron & Thompson, 1979). And it's also true that the mandatory 2-year or 3-year reevaluations dictated by state departments of education for special education placement fall prey to practice effects. Test someone two, three, or four times on a Wechsler scale—any Wechsler scale—and the Performance subtests soon stop being a novel set of tasks. They become as familiar as tests of vocabulary or oral arithmetic, such that scores obtained on the Performance Scale during reevalutions are extremely suspect. Such scores are inflated to an unknown degree, as are Full Scale IQs, making a mockery of the reevaluation process. Similar practice effects, known as progressive error, occur during longitudinal aging research, often obscuring the developmental implications of such studies (Kaufman, 1990a, pp. 204–206).

In the excellent study by Moffitt and Silva (1987), which showed that unusually large V-P IQ differences were not related to neurological and other pertinent variables (discussed previously), these authors also investigated the stability of the V-P discrepancies. Children were tested three times, at ages 7, 9, and 11 years. As in the investigation of developmental change in the aging studies, progressive error due to practice effects wreaks havoc with any understanding of the stability of V-P IQ differences over time. The authors found that the discrepancy scores correlated significantly at ages 7 and 9 years ($r = .52$), 9 and 11 years ($r = .62$), and 7 and 11 years ($r = .50$), but noted substantial differences in the magnitude of the discrepancy for many children. Moffitt and Silva (1987) concluded, "On the whole, VIQ–PIQ discrepancies did not remain a stable characteristic across childhood" (p. 772). However, the authors did not consider the differential practice effect in their results, which would elevate P-IQ substantially more than V-IQ on retests. That progressive error in their study made the so-called instability of the discrepancy predictable from their experimental design and, therefore, conceivably was an artifact of the practice effect.

So if you conduct the actual assessments for mandatory reevaluations, or are involved in the decision-making process, don't use the WISC-III to reevaluate children who were initially identified with the WISC-R or WISC-III. Use a different test.

CHAPTER 4

Interpreting Verbal-Nonverbal Discrepancies (V-P IQ and VC-PO Index)

Chapter 3 provided examiners with a seven-step method for interpreting WISC-III profiles that proceeds from global (Full Scale IQ) to specific (the 12 separate subtests). But it is the intermediary steps involving verbal-nonverbal differences that serve as the fulcrum of the interpretive approach: Is the Verbal-Performance IQ discrepancy statistically significant (Step 2)? Can the V-P IQ discrepancy be meaningfully interpreted, or should examiners interpret the Verbal Comprehension-Perceptual Organization Index discrepancy instead (Step 3)? Is the V-P or VC-PO difference unusually large (Step 4)? How should examiners interpret the meaning of the verbal and nonverbal dimensions (and the meaning of the small factors as well) (Step 5)?

The goal of Chapter 4 is to answer the portion of Step 5 that concerns verbal-nonverbal differences; Chapter 5 addresses the aspect of Step 5 concerned with the two small factors, Freedom from Distractibility (FD) and Processing Speed (PS). The present chapter is titled Interpreting Verbal-Nonverbal Discrepancies, *not* Interpreting Verbal-Performance IQ Discrepancies, because its aim is to understand a child's different performance on the constructs that underlie the WISC-III. For some children, the separate V and P IQs provide the best estimates of those constructs, and for other children the VC and PO Indexes offer the most meaningful interpretation of their verbal versus nonverbal abilities. This chapter is intended for all children who display significant differences in their verbal versus nonverbal functioning, regardless of whether the IQs or Indexes assume primacy.

OVERVIEW OF VERBAL-NONVERBAL DIFFERENCES

The clinical and neuropsychological history of Wechsler's scales is rich with various interpretations of discrepancies between a person's Verbal and Performance IQs. Such interpretations sometimes have psychoanalytic overtones or are filled with inferences about brain damage, and they usually produce debate and controversy among researchers and clinicians. Psychoanalytic claims (e.g., Allison, Blatt, & Zimet, 1968) have little or no research documentation, and brain damage studies with children (Aram & Ekelman, 1986; Bortner, Hertzig, & Birch, 1972; Dennis, 1985a, 1985b; Donders, 1992; Holroyd & Wright, 1965; Lewandowski & DeRienzo, 1985; Morris & Bigler, 1987) are filled with unanswered questions and inconsistencies.

Children with Unilateral Brain Lesions

Problems arise in interpreting V-P IQ differences in patients with unilateral brain damage even when samples are adult patients with well-defined lesions (Kaufman, 1990a, Chapters 9–11). Simplistic notions that left-hemisphere damage leads to depressed Verbal IQs, and right-hemisphere damage leads to depressed Performance IQs, have given way to the realization that a one-to-one relationship does not exist between Wechsler's V-P dichotomy and the two cerebral hemispheres. For example, whereas lowered P-IQ, relative to V-IQ, is frequently associated with damage to the right hemisphere, adults with left-hemisphere damage show no tendency to display P > V patterns (Kaufman, 1990a).

The brain-behavior relationships are complex. With samples of brain-damaged children, the complexity is compounded by the difficulty in finding children with well-localized brain lesions and in obtaining refined neurological criterion information (Reed, 1976), and by the fact that there is greater plasticity in younger than older brains (Smith, 1983). Also, sizable V-P differences can be traced to a variety of causative factors other than neurological impairment (Simensen & Sutherland, 1974).

Researchers continue to investigate brain damage in children, and their experimental designs are aided by modern technological and neuropsychological advances that help pinpoint the location of lesions with accuracy that was not possible in studies conducted a generation ago. But these studies continue to yield equivocal information. For example, Lewandowski and DeRienzo (1985), in their WISC-R investigation of left- and right-hemiplegic children ages 6 to 12 years, found a significant association between right-hemisphere damage and depressed P-IQ, but not between left damage and depressed V-IQ. Morris and Bigler (1987), also investigating neurologically impaired children ages 6 to 12 years on the WISC-R, obtained the reverse finding: The relationship of left damage to V-IQ was more substantial than the relationship of right damage to P-IQ. And Shapiro and Dotan (1986) found no meaningful relationships between location of focal lesion and depressed scores on either WISC-R scale for their sample of brain-damaged children.

Each of the preceding sets of investigators administered the K-ABC along with the WISC-R to explore predicted hypotheses of low Sequential for left-damaged children and low Simultaneous for right-damaged children. Again, the results were equivocal. Right-hemisphere damage was associated with low Simultaneous Processing in all three studies, but the relationship between low Sequential and left-damage was observed only in the Shapiro and Dotan (1986) investigation.

The best conclusion from the diverse brain damage studies with children as well as adults is *not* to interpret Wechsler's V-P IQ or VC-PO Index discrepancies as measures of the lateralization of the cerebral hemispheres and, especially, to limit neurological inferences from global standard scores on any children's test. There are too many intervening variables that affect children's test performance. From the perspective of cerebral specialization theory (Sperry, 1968; Springer & Deutsch, 1981), the hemispheres differ primarily in the way they process information, not in the content of the problems to be solved. That research finding alone implies that Wechsler's content distinction should not be expected to elicit predictable verbal-nonverbal patterns on the WISC-III. But even the K-ABC, with its process-oriented scales, has not been successful in distinguishing clearly between children with left-versus-right-hemisphere damage. Examiners should avoid expectations of characteristic patterns for children (and adolescents and adults) on conventional intelligence tests regardless of the presence of focal lesions believed to be confined to a single hemisphere.

The Search for Characteristic Profiles

The abundance of research studies on V-P IQ discrepancies through the years has extended well beyond the studies of brain-damaged individuals. Literally thousands of investigators have searched for characteristic differences in the Wechsler profiles of a wide variety of exceptional and minority-group populations with the fervor and dedication of Jason in his quest for the Golden Fleece. Occasionally a consistent finding emerges, such as the P > V IQ discrepancy noted for numerous populations of delinquents on the WISC and WISC-R (Andrew, 1974; Culbertson, Feral, & Gabby, 1989; Eaves & Cutchen, 1990; Grace & Sweeney, 1986; Meinhardt, Hibbett, Koller, & Busch, 1993; Rosso, Falasco, & Koller, 1984; Zimmerman & Woo-Sam, 1972). That asymmetry on Wechsler's children scales characterized behaviorally diverse samples such as psychopathic delinquents and subcultural delinquents (Hubble & Groff, 1982). The P > V difference was significantly larger for recidivists (repeat offenders) than nonrecidivists in studies of both female delinquents (Haynes & Bensch, 1983) and male delinquents (Bleker, 1983).

The pervasiveness and generalizability of the P > V profile was given a further boost by Cornell and Wilson's (1992) investigation of 149 juvenile delinquents, all but 4 of whom were male. They identified WISC-R P > V patterns of 7 to 10 points for separate samples of white and African-American delinquents, and found that the pattern held for those who committed violent crimes (homicide, serious assault) or nonviolent crimes (larceny, breaking and entering).

WISC-III data for 26 children, aged 11–15 years, with severe conduct disorders was basically consistent with WISC and WISC-R results, revealing

P > V of 4.3 points and PO > VC of 6.3 points (Wechsler, 1991, p. 214). But other studies suggest that the P > V finding does not generalize to delinquents tested on the WAIS or WAIS-R (Grace, 1986) or to prison inmates and other samples of "adult delinquents" (Kaufman, 1990a, pp. 286–288; Kender, Greenwood, & Conard, 1985). Cornell and Wilson's (1992) claim that the P > V pattern was observed on both the WISC-R and WAIS-R is given only weak empirical support.

Virtually the entire V-P literature—not just the studies pertaining to brain dysfunction and delinquency—is beset by contradictions and a lack of success in identifying characteristic patterns for various groups; clear-cut findings are few and far between. Even novelist-psychologist Jonathan Kellerman joined the V-P discrepancy controversy (Kellerman, Moss, & Siegel, 1982), arguing against earlier contentions that pediatric cancer patients had a high rate of verbal-nonverbal differences.

Poorly defined samples or samples that fail to control for essential variables are probably partially responsible for some of the study-to-study inconsistencies. However, another likely source of the problem is that a V-P discrepancy may signify quite different things for different individuals. Within the delinquency literature, for example, one adolescent may have a P > V WISC-III profile because poor school achievement lowered V-IQ, especially the subtests in Bannatyne's Acquired Knowledge grouping. A different delinquent may have the identical pattern because of the influence of socioeconomic factors; P > V profiles are associated with adults having limited education (Kaufman, 1990a, Table 10.16) and with children whose parents have 0–8 years of schooling (Granier & O'Donnell, 1991; see later section of this chapter). Or, as Quay (1987) suggests, an interaction between low verbal ability and variables such as poor parenting may lead to the behavioral acting out seen in delinquency.

Verbal-Nonverbal Differences and the Information-Processing Model

Similar to the delinquency illustration, a half-dozen children may have identical V-P or VC-PO discrepancies of 15 points in the same direction, and yet each may have an entirely different reason for manifesting this discrepancy in his or her ability spectrum. For example, a child with a previously undetected visual or hearing problem may score very poorly on the Performance or Verbal Scale, respectively, merely because of the sensory loss. No judgment about that child's relative verbal and nonverbal abilities can be made until a retest is arranged after the child has been examined by a physician and given the appropriate corrective devices. In addition to "Input" explanations of a significant verbal-nonverbal discrepancy, such as sensory loss, there are also reasons associated with other aspects of the information processing model (Silver, 1993). Integration or processing differences might relate to the child's ability to solve reasonably new, non-school-related problems (Performance Scale) versus items that tap knowledge and comprehension (Verbal Scale), a distinction that pertains to the Horn-Cattell theory (see Chapter 2 and later sections of this chapter).

Storage and retrieval might relate to V-P or VC-PO discrepancies when children are especially strong or weak in their long-term or tertiary memory. Exceptionally good long-term storage capacities are likely to elevate V-IQ because of the need to retrieve information from the long-term store to answer Information and Vocabulary items, solve Arithmetic problems, and demonstrate verbal reasoning during Similarities and Comprehension. Poor long-term memory will often lead to depressed V-IQ or VC Index, but it has minimal impact on P-IQ or PO Index. Output strengths and weaknesses can also explain large verbal-nonverbal differences for some children: Poor verbal expression can lead to P > V, whereas problems with fine motor coordination can produce V > P. A main goal of this chapter is to identify a variety of other plausible explanations for significant differences in the Verbal and Performance IQs (or VC and PO Indexes), although the hypotheses discussed will not come close to exhausting the possibilities.

The Meaning of Very Large Discrepancies

Since the mid-1970s researchers have commonly reported the mean absolute value of the discrepancy between V-IQ and P-IQ for a given sample. This index, which ignores the direction of the V-P IQ difference, serves as a measure of interscale scatter on a Wechsler test. A summary table of mean V-P IQ discrepancies for numerous normal and exceptional samples (Kaufman, Harrison, & Ittenbach, 1990) indicates that the largest discrepancies, by far, are for samples of Native Americans (Navajos) classified as educationally disadvantaged (34 points), normal (30 points), and learning disabled (29 points). Those findings are associated with the subcultural background of Native Americans, and not with exceptionality, and are discussed later in this chapter. When excluding Native Americans, and limiting the discussion to exceptional samples classified as learning disabled, referrals for reading or learning disabilities, minimally brain injured, mentally retarded, emotionally disturbed, and the like, one thing becomes apparent. Very few of the 18 exceptional samples that reported the magnitude of the V-P IQ discrepancy had mean values that differed very much from the mean value for normal individuals. Most had average discrepancies within the 8- to 12-point range. Only two samples had means above 13, and one of those samples, a group of 20 learning-disabled children tested by Naglieri (1979), did not differ significantly from its own normal control group.

Only a single exceptional sample (excluding the learning-disabled Native American sample) had a V-P IQ discrepancy that was notably above the values for the other groups: the mean of 18.6 points for the "gifted learning disabled" sample tested by Schiff, Kaufman, and Kaufman (1981), a group of very high-functioning children with school learning difficulties and concomitant emotional problems.

Moffitt and Silva (1987) turned the table in their ambitious study of large V-P IQ discrepancies. Instead of identifying a sample of exceptional children and evaluating the magnitude of their verbal-nonverbal differences, they tested normal children (from New Zealand) and studied those individuals who displayed unusually large V-P IQ differences. Starting with a sample of over 1,000 children who were assessed at age 3, they continued to assess these children through age 11. The WISC-R was administered to over 900 children at ages 7, 9, and 11. Moffitt and Silva identified those children at each age who had unusually large V-P IQ discrepancies of about 22 IQ points or more (the extreme 10%). Sample sizes for these extreme individuals among the normal population were about 90 per age group.

When Moffitt and Silva (1987) compared the sample that had large V-P discrepancies with the remaining 850 or so children at each age on a variety of neurological and health variables, they found almost no significant differences on these etiological factors. In comparison with the control sample, the high V-P group did not have significantly more perinatal problems, neurological abnormalities in early childhood, neurologically significant health problems, or concussion. In a comparison of behavioral problems (rated by parent or teacher), motor problems, and academic problems, again the high V-P group did not differ significantly from the control group in virtually any comparison.

The only significant difference was at age 11, when the V-P sample had lower oral reading vocabulary scores than the control group. However, V-P differences on a Wechsler scale are not very meaningful the third time the test is administered, or even the second time, because of the potent practice effect on P-IQ (this topic was discussed in Chapter 3 in the section "Effects of Retesting"). Consequently, only the results of Moffitt and Silva's 7-year-old sample truly address the association between large V-P IQ discrepancies and the diverse factors studied by the authors. Generalizations from their findings are also limited by the all New Zealand sample and by the use of prorated IQs (Picture Arrangement and Comprehension were eliminated because of time constraints).

Nonetheless, the complete lack of significant differences between children who display large V-P differences and those who do not on a wide array of variables for which one would logically anticipate differences makes a compelling statement. V-P IQ discrepancies, when interpreted in isolation, do not seem to be very meaningful in and of themselves. Some similar investigations have found that large V-P IQ discrepancies do relate significantly to neuropsychological variables (Gilger & Geary, 1985), developmental factors (Bloom, Topinka, Goulet, Reese, & Podruch, 1986), and aphasia and achievement deficits (Lueger, Albott, Hilgendorf, & Gill, 1985), but these and other studies lack the scope, sample sizes, and experimental design of the Moffitt and Silva (1987) investigation.

One conclusion is warranted from the child and adult clinical and neuropsychological literature: V-P IQ or VC-PO Index discrepancies should not be used to infer neurological dysfunction or psychopathology. They may be used as additional support for such hypotheses in the presence of convincing evidence from supplementary test data, psychiatric and clinical observations, neurological and neuropsychological evaluation, and consideration of base-rate tables of verbal-nonverbal differences (Table 3.3). Interpretations assigned to differences between verbal and nonverbal IQs or Indexes need to be considered in the context of each person's unique background, behaviors, and pattern of test scores on the WISC-III and other instruments.

WHAT WISC-III VERBAL-NONVERBAL DISCREPANCIES MEASURE

Wechsler's original goal in distinguishing between verbal and nonverbal ability was to measure a person's general intelligence in two different ways: through verbal stimuli and through nonverbal, performance materials. He assembled his cast of Verbal subtests systematically, ensuring that every subtest included items requiring the verbal comprehension of spoken questions and at least a minimal amount of verbal expression to convey correct responses. In contrast, all Performance subtests rely on visual stimuli and some sort of motor response, whether pointing or constructing a design with blocks. Picture Completion permits vocal responses, but pointing to the missing part is always acceptable. A mute child can earn a scaled score of 19 on Picture Completion. Only WISC-III Arithmetic uses visual stimuli. but these are limited to the five easiest counting items.

Wechsler's scales, therefore, differ primarily in their input and output. The Verbal Scale measures auditory-vocal intelligence and the Performance Scale measure visual-motor ability. The mental processes and storage requirements for the two scales overlap to a far greater extent than do the input or output. Consider the following illustrative abilities that are measured by both the V and P Scales of the WISC-III (only one subtest per scale is listed for simplicity):

Abilities	Verbal	Performance
Reasoning	Arithmetic	Object Assembly
Short-Term Memory	Digit Span	Coding
Long-Term Memory	Information	Picture Completion
Social Understanding	Comprehension	Picture Arrangement
Concept Formation	Vocabulary	Block Design
Verbal Mediation	Similarities	Picture Arrangement
Speed of Processing	Arithmetic	Symbol Search

The WISC-III Verbal Scale places great emphasis on facility of verbal expression, as Vocabulary and Comprehension (and, to a lesser extent, Similarities) require children to spontaneously put words together to convey mature thought processes and distinguish between subtle differences in verbal concepts. On the Performance Scale, the great emphasis is on responding to problems quickly. Bonus points are awarded in abundance (3 for most items on Block Design, Picture Arrangement, and Object Assembly), and the two PS subtests reward children on the basis of how many easy items they can complete in a 2-minute span. When a child earns a large V-P or VC-PO discrepancy on the WISC-III, it reflects some specific assets and deficits. Children who score much higher on V-IQ or VC Index than on their nonverbal counterparts operate with facility within the auditory-vocal channel and are usually able to express their ideas in words with precision. In contrast, P > V or PO > VC children are at ease in the visual-motor channel and those who are at least 10 or 11 years of age (when bonus points really count, as discussed later in this chapter) not only solve nonverbal problems well— they solve them quickly.

The rest of this chapter is designed to facilitate understanding of a child's verbal-nonverbal differences, especially unusually large discrepancies. The topics explore just what the WISC-III V-P IQ discrepancy or VC-PO Index difference measures; how this difference relates to the information-processing model; and which kinds of samples are particularly impaired primarily because of the Input, Integration/Storage, or Output aspects of the model. For example, autistic and other severely language-disordered groups, hearing-impaired children, and American Indian and Hispanic children have P > V patterns primarily because of Input problems; learning-disabled children usually display P > V and PO > VC patterns primarily because of difficulties with the Integration and Storage components of the information-processing/learning model; and gifted and reflective children tend to have V > P profiles because of Output (visual-motor speed) problems.

An important question addressed in the section devoted to Integration/ Storage variables is, Do the V and P IQs, or the VC and PO Indexes, measure crystallized and fluid intelligence as these constructs were originally defined by Horn and Cattell (1966, 1967) and later expanded and refined by Horn (1989, 1991)? In that section, WISC-III verbal-nonverbal discrepancies are related to fluid-crystallized differences on scales that are based on the Horn-Cattell model either explicitly (KAIT, Binet-4, WJ-R) or implicitly (DAS, K-ABC).

Although topics are discussed under the main headings of "Input," "Integration/Storage," and "Output," that does not imply that each topic is unidimensional or otherwise categorizable as pertaining to only one aspect of the information-processing model. Each aspect of the model affects other aspects. Children with hearing problems have receptive difficulties regarding the input of sensory stimuli, but those sensory problems affect expression and are likely to have an impact on both integration (learning ability) and storage (exposure to information learned visually rather than aurally) as well. Similarly, the language difficulties of autistic children involve verbal expression as well as comprehension, and the integration and storage problems of learning-disabled children may be related to impaired communication abilities (reception or expression) due to minimal brain dysfunction. Consequently, the topics have been organized by what I perceive to be their *primary* relationship to the information-processing model, but each topic is complex, as are the deficiencies or differences associated with each exceptional or ethnic group that is discussed.

VARIABLES ASSOCIATED WITH INPUT OF INFORMATION

From the vantage point of Osgood's communication theory (Osgood & Miron, 1963) and the information-processing model (Silver, 1993) all Verbal subtests, including the alternate Digit Span task, are within the auditory-vocal modality (channel of communication) and all Performance subtests, including the pair that define the PS factor, are in the visual-motor channel of communication. When children have problems associated with interpretation of the input stimuli, then they are not able even to attempt to integrate or process the information. When they cannot respond appropriately, they are not able to communicate their efforts at problem solving, even if they possess high levels of conceptual thought and reasoning ability.

Hearing-impaired children illustrate quite well the difficulties associated with both the intake and output components of the auditory-vocal channel, and they earn characteristic P > V profiles primarily because of these communication difficulties. Typically, hearing-impaired and deaf individuals score close to the normative mean of 100 on the Performance Scale but earn IQs of about 85 on the Verbal Scale (Braden, 1985, 1992). On the WISC-III, 30 deaf children earned a mean P-IQ of 106 and a mean V-IQ of 81 (Maller & Braden, 1993). In a WISC-R investigation of 368 hearing-impaired children (Sullivan & Schulte, 1992), P > V discrepancies were larger for severely hearing-impaired children than for those classified as hard-of-hearing (34 vs. 17 points), but were comparable for children with deaf versus hearing parents (31 and 30 points, respectively).

Hearing-impaired individuals, who suffer from documentable sensory loss, are obvious examples of a group that is unfairly penalized by the intake and output demands of an entire WISC-III scale, and whose large V-P discrepancy is largely explainable either by the sensory loss or concomitants of the loss. Other aspects of the intake components of the WISC-III sometimes have more subtle impact on test performance, but can nonetheless affect verbal-nonverbal differences. Additional topics on this theme are discussed in the following sections.

Psycholinguistic Deficiency

A child who has a learning disability may well be deficient in one or more aspects of psycholinguistic functioning (Kirk & Kirk, 1971) despite intact sensory abilities. Such deficiencies may be fairly global and involve an entire channel of communication or level of organization (automatic processing versus representational, high-level processing), or they may be specific and affect a single psycholinguistic process. When these communication problems occur in children, intelligence test scores will undoubtedly suffer. For example, a child with a deficiency in the auditory-vocal channel of communication will probably perform quite poorly on most verbal subtests and may have difficulty with the nonverbal subtests that demand comprehension of lengthy instructions spoken by the examiner. Similarly, a child with a psycholinguistic deficiency within the visual-motor modality, such as poor visual reception (interpretation of visual stimuli), is likely to have considerable difficulty with most tasks on the Performance Scale (see case report of Greg T. in Chapter 7).

From the perspectives of research and the experience of clinicians, children with serious psycholinguistic problems in one or the other major channel of communication may evidence V-P discrepancies of substantial magnitude. When this type of causality can be inferred (by supplementary testing with instruments designed to assess psycholinguistic ability and by clinical observations), the V-P IQ difference does not necessarily reflect a discrepancy in the child's verbal versus nonverbal intelligence. Children with receptive problems do not have the opportunity to demonstrate their intelligence in the affected channel, whereas children with expressive problems are unable to communicate their thought processes. In both cases, the children's intelligence on the scale with the depressed IQ must remain a question mark, pending a more subtle type of mental or neuropsychological assessment by the experienced clinician who can select cognitive tasks that circumvent the psycholinguistic deficiency.

For example, children who are found to have serious intake problems with auditory stimuli, but are otherwise able to reason verbally and express their ideas in words should be administered the Binet-4 Absurdities subtest, which requires children to state what is incongruous or absurd about pictures, and the Detroit-3 Story Construction task, which involves making up a story about a picture. By removing auditory stimuli and using visual stimuli instead, the Absurdities and Story Construction subtests permit the evaluation of the verbal, conceptual, reasoning, and expressive abilities of a child who cannot interpret spoken words.

The case of Ryan A., an 8-year-old white male tested by Dr. Kristee Beres, demonstrates how visual-perceptual and visual-motor problems can render a child's P-IQ and PO Index meaningless as estimates of his or her nonverbal reasoning ability. Ryan's WISC-III IQs and Factor Indexes are presented here. His scaled scores on the five regular Verbal subtests ranged from 13 to 16; his 11 on Digit Span was not a significant weakness. Performance scaled scores ranged from 5 to 12 with only his 5 on Object Assembly deviating significantly from his Performance mean.

Ryan A.

IQs		Factor Indexes	
Verbal	126	Verbal Comprehension	124
Performance	89	Perceptual Organization	93
Full Scale	109	Freedom from Distractibility	118
V-IQ > P-IQ ($p < .01$)		Processing Speed	96

Ryan's profile indicates no significant differences between the two Verbal Factor Indexes (VC, FD) or between the two Performance Factor Indexes (PO, FD). The best summary of his intellectual profile is therefore provided by his Superior V-IQ and Low Average to Average P-IQ. The 37-point difference in favor of V-IQ is huge, suggesting that he is far more intelligent verbally than nonverbally.

However, in her case report on Ryan, Dr. Beres noted: "When Ryan was only a few weeks old, his mother noticed that his eyes would sometimes drift and cross. At the age of 11 months, he was diagnosed with Strabismus. He had surgery at age 3, but still has to patch his right eye every day for 45 minutes to strengthen the muscles in his left eye. . . . At the age of 4½, Ryan was diagnosed with a perceptual deficit and visual-motor integration impairment, and has since received recreational, occupational, and educational therapy. . . . Ryan has difficulty playing team sports because of his visual-motor impairment and perceptual deficits. . . . His teacher reports that he is doing well in school both socially and academically."

Observation of his test behaviors indicated that Ryan has mixed hand dominance, scanned visual stimuli from right to left, made numerous errors on Coding and Symbol Search, held the pencil awkwardly, and did not always know what object he was constructing in Object Assembly. Ryan's P-IQ seemed to underestimate his nonverbal thinking ability because of his visual-perceptual and visual-motor problems. To check out this hypothesis, Dr. Beres administered K-BIT Matrices, DAS Sequential & Quantitative Reasoning (included in the Nonverbal Reasoning Composite), and the WJ-R Fluid Reasoning Scale. On these measures he scored in the High Average to Superior range, indicating that his nonverbal reasoning ability is more commensurate with his verbal ability and school achievement than with his so-called level of intelligence indicated by his obtained WISC-III Performance IQ.

For a similar instance of a misleading P-IQ due to a visual processing problem, see the complete case report of Greg T. in Chapter 7. Also, consult the cases of Ira G., who has both visual and auditory processing problems, and Dana Christine T., who has auditory processing difficulties, also in Chapter 7.

Children with Severe Language Disorders

Data from a group of 40 severely language-disordered children illustrate the degree to which a psycholinguistic deficiency can impact an entire test profile (Phelps, Leguori, Nisewaner, & Parker, 1993). The group evidenced only a modest P > V pattern (P-IQ = 77, V-IQ = 70), despite the severity of the language impairment. They likely had difficulty with some Performance tasks because of the verbal comprehension required to understand the lengthy directions to several subtests and the verbal mediation needed for Picture Arrangement. The sample also had special difficulty with the speeded nonverbal tasks (PS Index = 74); slow response times have previously been found to characterize language-impaired children (Sininger, Klatzky, & Kirchner, 1989). The group performed closer to the average range on the K-ABC Simultaneous Processing Scale (mean = 85), a nonverbal scale that limits both the demands for verbal comprehension and for quick responding. Notably, on the WISC-III, the language-handicapped sample displayed deficits on both segments of the Verbal Scale, earning mean standard scores of 72 and 69 on the VC and FD Indexes, respectively.

One cannot, however, conclude that the deficits displayed on the WISC-III and K-ABC are simply due to a defective auditory-vocal channel. As Phelps et al. (1993) point out, the severity of the children's language impairment makes it likely that they have other, concurrent neurological dysfunction. For similar reasons, undoubtedly, another group of children with severe language handicaps ($N = 25$) evidenced a P > V profile on the WISC-III, but also scored well below the normative mean on both IQ scales (P-IQ = 85, V-IQ = 74) (Doll & Boren, 1993). That sample, too, was consistently weak within the auditory-vocal modality (scaled-score range of 4.6 to 6.1), performing equally poorly on FD and VC subtests. And like the Phelps et al. (1993) sample, Doll and Boren's (1993) group of language-impaired children scored as low on PS tasks as they did on Verbal tasks.

Children with Autism

Autism, a pervasive developmental disorder characterized by severe social, language, and adaptive functioning deficits, and accompanied by mental retardation in three out of four cases, also produces P > V profiles (Asarnow, Tanguay, Bott, & Freeman, 1987; Lincoln, J. Kaufman, & A. Kaufman, in press). (See the case report of Jennie L., an adolescent diagnosed with both mental retardation and autism, that appears at the end of this chapter.)

Autistic children demonstrate poor receptive and expressive language skills on all Wechsler verbal tasks, although some samples perform relatively higher on Digit Span (Lincoln, Allen, & Piacentini, in press). A review of studies with the WISC-R and WAIS-R (Lincoln, Allen, et al., in press) indicates that autistic individuals are weakest in the tasks that place the heaviest emphasis on verbal expression (Vocabulary and Comprehension) and do best—sometimes averaging 10 or higher—on the two visual-constructive subtests (Block Design, Object Assembly). In Asarnow et al.'s (1987) investigation of 23 nonretarded autistic children, for example, the group averaged about 6 on the two tests of verbal expression compared with means of about 13 on Block Design and Object Assembly.

Autistic children's scores on the two Performance subtests with the most pervasive verbal component (the two "Picture" subtests), and their Coding score, are usually commensurate with the Verbal Scale (Lincoln, Allen, et al., in press), and their subtest scatter is sometimes extreme. Twenty non-retarded autistic children had mean WISC-R scaled scores that ranged from 1.3 on Comprehension to 11.2 on Block Design, and mean K-ABC Mental Processing scaled scores that ranged from 4.4 on Hand Movements to 11.4 on Triangles (Allen, Lincoln, & Kaufman, 1991). In the latter study, autistic children had substantially larger V-P IQ differences (P = 85, V = 57) than did a matched control group of language-impaired children (P = 97, V = 82). However, the discrepancies for both samples were inflated by imposing minimum P-IQs of 80 and 85, respectively, to eliminate retarded children from the study.

Psycholinguistic Clues from the WISC-III Profile

Thorough cognitive, linguistic, and neuropsychological evaluation is needed to identify specific deficit areas for children with psycholinguistic impairments within either the auditory-vocal or visual-motor channel of communication. But just as the very low scores on Vocabulary and Comprehension are suggestive of weak verbal expression, so too are other WISC-III subtests suggestive of weaknesses in other aspects of psycholinguistic functioning. Blending the Osgood communication model and the information-processing model with the major psycholinguistic demands of selected WISC-III subtests yields the following hypothesized relationships:

Channel	Input (Reception)	Integration (Processing)	Storage (Memory)	Output (Expression)
Auditory	Information	Similarities	Digit Span	Vocabulary
Visual	Picture Completion	Picture Arrangement	Symbol Search	Coding

Information mainly measures intake of auditory stimuli: Does the child understand the question? The integration is minimal, and although the child must retrieve the answer from long-term storage, many of the items, especially the first dozen or so, are overlearned facts that are unrelated to schooling. Responses are usually one word, so expression is minimal. Except for children from culturally different or disadvantaged backgrounds, Information provides a good measure of auditory reception. And Picture Completion is an excellent measure of visual reception, the intake of visual stimuli. Again, some retrieval is necessary from long-term store, but both the processing demands and the expressive demands are minor.

Similarities and Picture Arrangement are good measures of integration and processing of information. Success on each is primarily a function of reasoning and problem-solving ability. For Similarities, the stimuli are easy verbal concepts and from a psycholinguistic perspective require the intake of just two words; facility of verbal expression is unnecessary for a good conceptual thinker, since most items can be answered at a 2-point level with one well-chosen word. Whereas Picture Arrangement places heavy demands on the intake of visual stimuli, the coordination requirements are small. Speed is important, but a child's quickness at integration and processing is the primary determinant of whether bonus points are earned, not the child's fine motor skill.

The storage components for each modality are adequately measured by Digit Span (auditory short-term memory) and Symbol Search (visual short-term memory). Both subtests utilize stimuli of limited complexity, require minimal integrative skills, and are not taxing in terms of output. Putting a slash through a Yes or No during Symbol Search requires far less motor coordination than copying symbols precisely during the Coding task. Children with good visual short-term memories will earn high scores by looking once at the Target Group, scanning the Search Group, and marking their answer; those with poor visual memories will go back and forth between the Target and Search Groups and complete relatively few items within the 2-minute period.

Vocabulary and Coding do a good job of measuring expression within their respective modalities. Both place demands on storage, either long-term (Vocabulary) or short-term (Coding), but the key to success on both is expression. Neither one demands much problem solving. For Vocabulary, children earn points by putting words together coherently; for Coding, an exercise in clerical speed and accuracy, motor speed and coordination lead to high scaled scores.

Examiners who are alert to the role that each subtest plays within the broader information-processing spectrum can interpret peaks and valleys from that perspective, especially for children with suspected learning disabilities, speech or language impairments, or other deficits related to neurological functioning. When input or output is believed to be the area of deficiency, then all obtained scores may grossly underestimate the child's true intelligence. But do not rely on the possible relationships between WISC-III performance and psycholinguistic functioning without support from multiple sources, including observations during the testing session and other WISC-III scores. If Vocabulary is unusually low, what about Comprehension? How well did the child express him- or herself during spontaneous talk? If Picture Completion is low when Picture Arrangement is high, visual reception cannot be the explanation because the pictures in the latter task are more complex than the stimuli in Picture Completion and require perception of subtle differences between similar pictures. If a visual input problem is suspected, then examiners need corroborating evidence from the child's behaviors such as constructing block designs that bear no relationship to the model or being oblivious to errors in Object Assembly.

Good WISC-III supplements for following up psycholinguistic hypotheses are subtests from other tests that alter the modalities from the common auditory-vocal and visual-motor combinations that dominate the WISC-III. When a child demonstrates a problem in a specific area within a particular channel on the WISC-III (such as a possible deficit in verbal expression or visual integration) or demonstrates a pervasive modality weakness, check out those findings with subtests that require visual-vocal or auditory-motor channels of communication. The following illustrative list excludes visual-vocal subtests that credit motor responses or that have a substantial auditory as well as visual component:

Visual-Vocal	Auditory-Motor
Detroit-3 Story Construction	Detroit-3 Reversed Letters
Detroit-3 Picture Fragments	K-ABC Word Order
K-ABC Gestalt Closure[a]	Das-Naglieri Simultaneous Verbal
K-ABC Faces & Places	Das-Naglieri Auditory Selective Attention
Binet-4 Absurdities	
Binet-4 Paper Folding and Cutting	
WJ-R Picture Vocabulary	
WJ-R Visual Closure	
WJ-R Concept Formation	

[a] For adolescents, administer the Gestalt Closure subtest in the Kaufman Short Neuropsychological Assessment Procedure (K-SNAP; Kaufman & Kaufman, 1994b).

The auditory-motor tests measure key aspects of input (Auditory Selective Attention), integration (Simultaneous Verbal), and short-term storage (Word Order, Reversed Letters). Several visual-vocal tests are primarily measures of a single information processing component: input (Gestalt Closure and related subtests), Integration (Concept Formation and Paper Folding and Cutting), retrieval from long-term storage (Picture Vocabulary and Faces & Places) or output (Story Construction). Absurdities measures integration (verbal reasoning) and output (verbal expression).

Interpret the WISC-III subtests as sources of hypotheses about a child's psycholinguistic deficits, nothing more. Confirm or deny the hypotheses based on clinical observations and fluctuations within the child's overall cognitive profile, but reach conclusions only if appropriate neuropsychological tests are administered.

Hispanics and American Indians

Spanish-speaking children who learn English as their second language or who learn two languages simultaneously during their childhood are likely to score significantly higher on Wechsler's Performance than on the Verbal Scale (McShane & Cook, 1985), about 75% of Hispanic children earn higher Performance than Verbal IQs (Taylor, Ziegler, & Partenio, 1984). (Consult the case report for Lourdes I., a Mexican-American girl with Tourette's syndrome and obsessive-compulsive disorder, at the end of Chapter 5.) American Indians from diverse tribes also have a characteristic High nonverbal-Low verbal profile (McShane, & Berry, 1989; McShane & Plas, 1984a). Many studies of American Indians, and of Hispanics living in the United States (from Puerto Rico, Mexico, and other Spanish-speaking countries), using various Wechsler scales, have found fairly consistent P > V patterns of about 10 to 15 IQ points; these studies have been reviewed and interpreted by McShane and his colleagues. Some American Indian tribes have remarkably large differences of about 30 points in favor of Performance IQ, notably the Navajo (Kaufman & Kaufman, 1983, Table 4.19; Teeter, Moore, & Petersen, 1982), and occasional Hispanic samples evidence huge mean differences on a Wechsler Scale, such as the 20-point differences found in three WPPSI studies (McShane & Cook, 1985). Most differences, however, are between ½ and 1 standard deviation. A WISC-III normative study of the Tohono O'odham Indians, using 10 children at each year of age from 6 to 16, yielded a mean P > V pattern of 7.4 points (Tanner-Halverson, Burden, & Sabers, 1993).

In the Tanner-Halverson et al. study, the American Indian sample earned a mean P-IQ of 92, but not infrequently American Indian and Spanish-speaking children and adolescents score very close to the normative mean on nonverbal measures of intelligence; in contrast, they score at about a Low Average level of functioning on the verbal portions of the same test batteries. These findings apply to Wechsler's scales and to other tests as well (Cummings, & Merrell, 1993; Kaufman & Kaufman, 1983; Kaufman & Wang, 1992; McCullough, Walker, & Diessner; 1985; Shellenberger & Lachterman 1979). An overall score such as the Full Scale IQ is totally meaningless in such instances and should never be used for categorization or labeling.

The low Verbal scores by many Spanish-speaking and American Indian children should not be considered as reflecting an intellectual deficit because of the obvious interaction of scores on crystallized tasks with variables such as language ability, culture, and cognitive style. Nevertheless, the P > V for these children does not merely reflect a difficulty in understanding the meaning of the test items or instructions spoken by the examiner. Bilingual children who speak English quite adequately often show a marked superiority on nonverbal tasks relative to verbal tasks even when the tests are administered in Spanish (McShane & Cook, 1985; Shellenberger, 1977).

Nor is the nonverbal-verbal discrepancy likely to be solely a function of cultural differences. Different cultural experiences cannot account for the much larger P > V profiles found for Navajos than for other tribes such as the Tohono O'odham, Cree, Sioux, and Tlingit. Also, Shellenberger and Lachterman (1979) found that bilingual Puerto Rican children who spoke English adequately were no more deficient in highly culture-loaded tasks (WISC-R or WPPSI Information and Comprehension subtests) than in tests of verbal memory and verbal concept formation. Similarly, a sample of 65 Hispanic children referred for a gifted program (Ortiz & Volloff, 1987) displayed the characteristic pattern (P-IQ = 126, V-IQ = 116), but earned their highest Performance scaled score (15.0) on Picture Arrangement and their highest Verbal scaled score (13.4) on Comprehension—the two Wechsler subtests with the greatest sociocultural component. And the Tohono

O'odham Indian children and adolescents did better on Picture Arrangement than on Object Assembly or the Processing Speed subtests (Tanner-Halverson et al., 1993, Table 2).

These research results are not meant to minimize the importance of language and cultural differences, or to imply that the relatively low V-IQs of Hispanic and American Indian children are due to an integration problem rather than the nature of the input. Too much research, and common sense, indicates otherwise (McShane & Berry, 1989; McShane & Cook, 1985; McShane & Plas, 1984a). Rather, they show that simple answers are not satisfactory for the complex questions regarding V-P discrepancies in Hispanics, American Indians, and other bilingual groups such as Asian Americans (Stone, 1992b). Additional research is needed to help clarify the psychological, sociological, and educational meaning of the two disparate indexes of intellectual functioning for the various bilingual-bicultural groups. Shellenberger (1977) speculated that the strength in nonverbal skills for Spanish-speaking children may reflect a variety of factors, one of which is that verbal test performance suffers in both languages when two languages are learned simultaneously. A study of 497 preschool children (mean age = 5–9) from Alsace, France, reinforces that speculation (Chevrie-Muller, Bouyer, le Normand, & Stirne, 1987). The group who spoke both French and Alsacian at home performed more poorly on verbal tests than monolingual children who spoke only French, even when controlling for factors such as parents' education.

McShane and his colleagues identified numerous variables that require further study regarding the nonverbal superiority of Hispanics and American Indians (McShane, & Berry, 1989; McShane & Cook, 1985; McShane & Plas, 1984a). For example, both groups are known to have high incidences of otitis media (middle ear disease), resulting in possible mild to moderate conductive hearing loss—a different type of input problem that might pertain to $P > V$ profiles. In addition to hearing loss, otitis media is known to have other consequences, either short- and long-term, such as difficulties with auditory sequential memory, sound blending, auditory closure and other auditory perceptual skills, and language delay (Katz, 1978). In one study of Native American Eskimos, WISC Verbal scores correlated negatively with the number of episodes of otitis media (Kaplan, Fleshman, & Bender, 1973). A study of Ojibwa Indians that used the WPPSI and WISC-R revealed that greater verbal deficits were displayed by children with more than four episodes of otitis media than by children having one to four episodes (McShane & Plas, 1984a).

Other variables that might relate to the low Verbal scores of American Indians are fetal alcohol syndrome, sociocultural factors that place an emphasis on nonverbal communication, and neurological factors associated with brain lateralization (McShane & Plas, 1984a). Although these topics are controversial (Brandt, 1984; McShane & Plas, 1984b), they remain viable topics in need of systematic research. So do issues such as experience with working under time pressure, the degree that children understand test directions and test-taking formats, and social desirability, which may pertain to test profiles observed for Hispanic children and others (such as American Indians) from bicultural and bilingual backgrounds (McShane & Cook, 1985).

Regardless of why Hispanic, American Indian, and other bilingual children obtain relatively low Verbal scores, it is quite clear that Verbal IQs or other indexes of verbal ability—although they may be meaningful for understanding the children better—do not reflect their intellectual potential. When the WISC-III is deemed an appropriate instrument for use with a bilingual-bicultural child based on federal, state, and local guidelines, *the examiner is advised not to interpret the Full Scale IQ*. The fact that all three WISC-III IQs, including Full Scale IQ, have been found to have adequate psychometric properties, as documented in the reviews conducted by McShane and his colleagues, does not alter the inadvisability of interpreting an overall IQ for bilingual and bicultural children. Similarly, an investigation of the differential predictive validity of the WISC-III Full Scale IQ for whites, African-Americans, and Hispanics indicated that bias was not present in the prediction of achievement on standardized tests and in their school grades (Weiss, Prifitera, & Roid, 1993). But that does not change my recommendation, because the problem with V-IQ and FS-IQ is a rational and conceptual one, not just an empirical one. And even some of the data in the Weiss et al. (1993) investigation should make clinicians take notice regarding the applicability of Full Scale IQ for Hispanics: The mean correlation of WISC-III Full Scale IQ with teachers' grades in math, reading, and English averaged .40 for whites and .38 for African-Americans, but only .20 for Hispanics.

The P-IQ or PO Index should be stressed for estimating the intellectual functioning and school-related potential of American Indians, Hispanics, and other bilingual children. Whereas a verbal deficit cannot be ignored for educational planning, it should never penalize an American Indian, Spanish-speaking, or other bilingual child during the diagnostic process. Hence V-P IQ discrepancies require sensitive interpretation for bilingual children; supplementary tests have to be given to facilitate profile analysis. Bilingual-bicultural children who evidence school learning problems need a remedial program that capitalizes on the nonverbal strengths they have developed, both for teaching specific academic skills and for improving verbal areas of functioning.

African-American Children and Black English

Psychologists and educators have not dealt very well with the assessment and placement of Hispanic and American Indian children, but at least they recognize that the children may be taught a different language at home and be exposed to different cultural values. A similar type of awareness has been slow to emerge regarding the language development and unique subculture of African-American children, as discussed briefly in Chapter 1.

Too frequently, the pronunciations, grammatical structure, or vocabulary of the African-American child is considered deficient or inferior and in need of substantial improvement (Hoover, 1990). In fact, "Ebonics" or "Negro Nonstandard English" or "Black Dialect" or "Black English" is complex (Hoover, 1990), a fact made clear by the careful research and cogent arguments of linguists, psycholinguists, and philosophers. Baratz (1970), for example, cites numerous studies showing that Black English is a rule-governed linguistic system that is different from standard English but decidedly *not* deficient.

Linguists assume that any verbal system used by a community is a language if it is well ordered with a predictable sound pattern, grammatical structure, and vocabulary, and that no language is structurally superior to any other language (Baratz, 1970, pp. 13–14). The internal consistency of Black English and the predictability of its phonological and grammatical rules have been supported empirically (Marwit, Marwit, & Boswell, 1972) and also by the results of ethnographic investigation (Bauman, 1971). Whereas a group of African-American professionals acquired proficiency in standard English in order to fit into the mainstream culture, they assigned positive value to Black English as a form of linguistic behavior and perceived it as a way of maintaining their minority cultural identification (Garner & Rubin, 1986).

Black English should gain the respect that it rightfully deserves, and the language-deficiency stigma must be removed from children who use this systematic language. Furthermore, the differences between standard English and Black English should be understood well by teachers and psychologists. Since these differences span grammar, phonology, syntax, semantics, and "soul" (Carter, 1977), and have their roots in traditions associated with *community* interactions rather than *school* use (Heath, 1989), the necessary task of learning the African-American student's language demands conscientious effort.

Even when the examiner is familiar with African-American language and culture, the impact of Black English on WISC-III IQs is likely to be felt. The words to be spoken are in standard English, which may lead to comprehension problems. Whereas Performance IQ as well as Verbal IQ may be depressed because of the lengthy verbal instructions for some Performance subtests, Verbal IQ is the most vulnerable. The Performance tasks involve concrete visual stimuli, and the tasks include demonstration items, so that African-American children typically understand the aim of each subtest despite the highly verbal instructions. When examiners do not know Black English, the influence of language differences on Verbal IQ may be profound. Because of pronunciation differences, the African-American child may have special difficulty with words that are not in context, such as the stimuli for Vocabulary and Similarities. Also, the child may use subcultural slang words and concepts that are specific to African-American culture when answering verbal items. An unaware examiner may regard these responses as wrong or fail to query them appropriately, even though the answers are partially or completely correct.

The lack of verbosity that often characterizes African-Americans (Labov, 1970) may also penalize their scores on the more subjectively scored verbal items; white children who tend to give longer (although not necessarily more correct) responses are more likely to be given the benefit of the doubt in questionable cases. Thus when an African-American child scores much higher on the Performance than on the Verbal Scale, the possibility that the Verbal score was depressed due to a linguistic difference must be considered. Although discrepancies of this sort are not typical for African-American children (Cole & Hunter, 1971; Lowe, Anderson, Williams, & Currie, 1987; Naglieri & Jensen, 1987), as they are for American Indian and Hispanic children, the implication is the same. In other words when a $P > V$ discrepancy for an African-American child can reasonably be traced to a language difference, the Verbal Scale (and hence the Full Scale) is not an adequate measure of the intellectual functioning of that individual.

The finding by some researchers that African-American children show little improvement on standardized ability tests (Quay, 1971, 1972) or achievement tests (Marwit & Neumann, 1974) that have been translated into Black English merely points out that a simple solution to a complex problem will not usually work. The fact that translating a test into Black English facilitates the performance of a few individual children on standardized tests, despite nonsignificant differences in group means, is still an important finding. Furthermore, a few studies involving nonstandardized measures have shown that Black English does significantly affect a child's performance. Baratz (1970), for example, showed that although whites were superior to African-Americans when repeating sentences in standard English, African-Americans far exceeded the performance of whites when repeating sentences spoken in Black English.

Crowl and MacGinitie (1974) found that experienced white teachers assigned significantly higher grades to the responses given by white boys to typical school questions than to the responses given by African-American boys, even though they gave answers with identical wording. In an investigation of how teachers' knowledge of the linguistic features of Black English relates to their sensitivity to students' reading development, there was some evidence that greater knowledge was associated with supportive behavior and limited knowledge led to more negative teacher response to African-American children's mistakes (Washington & Miller-Jones, 1989).

VARIABLES ASSOCIATED WITH INTEGRATION AND STORAGE

What mental abilities are measured by the Verbal and Performance Scales? What processing and storage requirements distinguish one scale from another? Long-term retrieval from storage is an obvious difference since this tertiary memory ability is essential for success on all regular Verbal subtests but is of limited importance on the Performance Scale, especially the two PS subtests and Block Design, which involve nonmeaningful stimuli. Another clear difference is the ability to process verbal visual-spatial stimuli, the basic two-pronged distinction that Wechsler had in mind when he made the armchair decision to group the dozen or so tasks into a verbal and nonverbal scale.

During the 1950s and 1960s, when the field of neuropsychology emerged and began to flourish (Reitan, 1955, 1959, 1966) the simple dichotomy was believed to correspond to the primary functions of the left and right hemispheres of the brain. But the theoretical position of Sperry (1968) and other cerebral specialization researchers modified the relationship between brain functioning and test behavior to stress process differences between the hemispheres (linear-sequential vs. holistic-simultaneous) rather than content differences (verbal vs. nonverbal). Decades of research showed that verbal-nonverbal discrepancies among patients with lesions to the left or right hemisphere did not conform to the predictions of the early neuropsychologists (Kaufman, 1990a, Chapters 9–11).

As leaders in the field of neuropsychology developed their own tests and had access to refined technology for assessing brain dysfunction, it became clear that brain-behavior relationships were far more complex and specific than simple verbal-left hemisphere and performance-right hemisphere relationships (Reitan & Wolfson, 1985, 1992). Many of the controversies regarding the Wechsler scales and brain functioning occurred because the tests were devised for normal individuals, were related to brain lesions only secondarily, and do not meet fully the criteria for a neuropsychological test battery (Reitan, 1988). So any speculation about how the global scales differ in what they measure should remain separate from inferences about brain functioning.

Verbal versus Nonverbal Intelligence

For some individuals, the V-P discrepancy may mean what it is supposed to convey according to Wechsler's original logic: They may simply have a significantly different facility in expressing their intelligence with words, in response to verbal stimuli, than manipulatively in response to visual-concrete stimuli. Such individuals are not likely to have wide scatter on either the Verbal or Performance Scale; their VC and FD Indexes won't differ significantly, and neither will their PO and PS Indexes. Their consistent functioning in dealing with verbal versus nonverbal stimuli will be suggestive of a split in accordance with Wechsler's framework. If one subtest per scale differs significantly from others in its scale, it is likely to be Digit Span or Coding, which often relate weakly to their designated scales.

Wechsler's verbal-nonverbal distinction has empirical support from the two-factor WISC-III solutions. Although a structure with four factors has

TABLE 4.1.   Factor Loadings on the WISC-III Verbal and
Performance Factors When Only Two Factors Are Rotated

Subtest	Verbal	Performance
Information	**.76**	.30
Similarities	**.75**	.29
Arithmetic	**.56**	.42
Vocabulary	**.81**	.26
Comprehension	**.68**	.24
Digit Span	**.34**	.30
Picture Completion	.39	**.50**
Coding	.17	**.39**
Picture Arrangement	.34	**.43**
Block Design	.35	**.72**
Object Assembly	.28	**.66**
Symbol Search	.26	**.54**

Note: Data are maximum-likelihood factor loadings for the total
standardization sample, taken from the WISC-III manual
(Wechsler, 1991, Table 6.2). Each subtest's highest factor loading is in bold print.

support as the best solution for the grouping of WISC-III subtests (Roid, Prifitera, & Weiss, 1993), there is no universally accepted criterion for the
"right" number of factors. When two factors are accepted as the best interpretation of the dimensions that underlie the WISC-III, the pattern of factor
loadings (shown in Table 4.1) supports the verbal-nonverbal nature of the dichotomy. As indicated in Chapter 2, only Digit Span shows neither a preference for one scale over the other nor a meaningful overlap with either scale.

Two-factor solutions for the WPPSI-R and WAIS-R also conform closely
to Wechsler's division of subtests into Verbal and Performance Scales. For
WPPSI-R, two factors is the appropriate number to interpret (Wechsler,
1989); and for WAIS-R, either a two- or three-factor solution is defensible
(Kaufman, 1990a, Chapter 8). Of interest for clinicians is whether the two
factors that underlie the WISC-III are essentially the same as the verbal and
nonverbal factors that define alternate forms of the WISC-III, including its
predecessor, the WISC-R. The correlations between V-IQs on the various
Wechsler scales, and between P-IQs, are shown here (*Source:* Wechsler,
1991, Tables 6.8, 6.10, 6.12):

	WISC-R (Ages 6–16) (N = 206)		WPPSI-R (Age 6) (N = 188)		WAIS-R (Age 16) (N = 189)	
WISC-III	V-IQ	P-IQ	V-IQ	P-IQ	V-IQ	P-IQ
V-IQ	.90	—	.85	—	.90	—
P-IQ	—	.81	—	.73	—	.80

The three Verbal constructs are quite similar, and the WISC-III P-IQ
correlates substantially with its namesake on the WISC-R and WAIS-R.

The correlation between WISC-III and WPPSI-R P-IQs is statistically significant, but nonetheless reflects an overlap of only about 50% suggesting that each nonverbal dimension has ample uniqueness. As discussed in the section "WISC-III versus WPPSI-R" in Chapter 1, speed of performance plays a much more important role in determining a 6-year-old's P-IQ on the WPPSI-R than on the WISC-III. That variable alone might explain the relatively modest overlap between the P-IQs. The WISC-III V-IQ also correlates a bit lower with WPPSI-R V-IQ than with the other two V-IQs. That may be a function of the numerous visual stimuli included in the WPPSI-R Verbal Scale: Arithmetic uses pictures or blocks for the first half of the subtest; and the first six items of Information and Similarities use pictures, as do the first three Vocabulary items. Many of the visual items on the Verbal scale are too easy for most 6-year-olds, but the fact that the WPPSI-R Verbal subtests are not exclusively within the auditory-vocal modality may lower its correlations with the WISC-III Verbal Scale.

The preceding discussion suggests that variables involving input affected correlations between WISC-III and WPPSI-R V-IQs and that an output variable (response speed) lowered P-IQ coefficients. However, the integration component of the information-processing model offers other plausible explanations. The WPPSI-R Performance Scale excludes Picture Arrangement, and the one subtest that measures speed of processing (Animal Pegs) is an alternate; instead, Mazes and Geometric Design contribute to WPPSI-R P-IQ. On the Verbal Scale, the first half of the WPPSI-R Similarities subtest uses item styles (visual classification and sentence completion) that differ from the WISC-III item style.

Apart from Wechsler's own scales, only the Detroit-3 claims to follow the Wechsler verbal-nonverbal model in grouping its subtests. In fact, Hammill (1991) organizes the 11 subtests in seven different ways, four of which are intended to conform to theoretical models including Wechsler's. Hammill does not, however, provide any empirical support for the accordance of his rational division of subtests with IQs or factor scores derived from a Wechsler scale. In an investigation of 78 special education students, WISC-III V-IQ correlated .66 with the Detroit-3 Verbal composite and P-IQ correlated .54 with the Performance composite (Hishinuma & Yamakawa, 1993). The magnitude of those coefficients does *not* suggest that the Detroit-3 scales measure the same constructs as Wechsler's scales. One problem may be the inclusion of Picture Fragments on the Detroit-3 Verbal composite. Similar tests of Gestalt or visual closure, despite requiring vocal responses, are associated with visual-spatial as opposed to verbal factors (Kaufman & Kamphaus, 1984; Woodcock & Mather, 1989).

The latter contention is supported by a joint factor analysis of the Detroit-3 and other tests (none of which were Wechsler scales), as Picture Fragments loaded on a visual-spatial factor that was defined primarily by the WJ-R Gv subtests and DAS Pattern Construction (McGhee, 1993). In fact, only three of the seven presumed Detroit-3 Verbal subtests—Word Opposites, Story

Construction, and Basic Information—were consistently associated with verbal/crystallized factors in McGhee's study; the others loaded on memory factors.

Selected subtests from the Detroit-3 were used as WISC-III supplements in the assessment of Lourdes I., whose report appears at the end of Chapter 5.

Fluid versus Crystallized Intelligence

Differences in Verbal and Performance IQs may be indicative of discrepancies in fluid and crystallized ability rather than in verbal and nonverbal thinking, as discussed in Chapter 2, and illustrated in the case of Ira G., a 15-year-old with a learning disability in writing, whose case report appears in Chapter 7. The comprehensive Cattell-Horn theory of fluid and crystallized intelligence relates to Hebb's (1949) theoretical distinction between Intelligence A and Intelligence B and involves aspects that pertain to the heredity-environment issue, differential rates of development, and the effects of brain damage (Cattell, 1968, 1971; Horn, 1968, 1970, 1985, 1989; Horn & Cattell, 1966, 1967). Fluid ability (Gf) involves problem solving and reasoning where the key is adaptation and flexibility when faced with unfamiliar stimuli; crystallized ability (Gc) refers to intellectual functioning on tasks calling on previous training, education, and acculturation. The theory has been well validated for children, adolescents, and adults (Horn, 1985, 1991).

Tests of oral vocabulary and matrices are prototypes of crystallized and fluid ability tests, respectively. Globally, the WISC-III Verbal IQ reflects skills on tests that seem to relate closely to the theoretical construct of Gc, and the Performance IQ apparently denotes Gf abilities. In that sense, a child from a very advantaged background whose parents place great stress on school achievement may demonstrate V > P, as may any child who achieves school success through excessive effort. For these children, V > P may well reflect high intelligence in the crystallized, specifically trained skill areas but a poor ability to solve fluid tasks. In contrast, children from disadvantaged backgrounds who have had limited opportunities for cultural enrichment and acculturation to mainstream American society may lack the knowledge base to solve problems saturated with Gc. Such individuals may have P > V patterns, reflecting strengths on Gf subtests, the type of tasks that Cronbach (1977, p. 287) terms "intellectual surprises" or that demand the ability to cope with novelty (Sternberg, 1987).

In the first example, the examiner cannot discount the possibility that the exceptional school achievement (reflected in the high Verbal IQ and VC index) has been accomplished by intensive, mostly rote, learning in the absence of the development of a flexible understanding of pertinent underlying concepts. In the second example, the examiner must deal with the possibility that the low V-IQ or VC Index denotes lack of opportunity rather than lack of intelligence. Similarly, low WISC-III verbal scores for learning-disabled children (a topic discussed later in the chapter) may reflect nothing more than their poor school achievement.

The match between the V-P and fluid-crystallized dichotomies is not perfect, a fact that has been known for some time. Digit Span has been recognized as being misplaced on a Gc scale; Coding was seen as measuring Broad Speediness (Gs), not Gf; and Similarities was conceded to have a Gf component because of the fluid abilities needed to identify the relationship between common verbal concepts (Horn, 1985). And Performance subtests were also interpreted as measuring Broad Visualization (Gv), a factor within the Horn-Cattell system associated with spatial ability (Horn, 1985). But despite the slight exceptions to a perfect model, the Verbal and Performance scales and the IQs they yield were almost universally interpreted as corresponding closely to the Gc (Verbal) and Gf (Performance) constructs (Horn, 1985; Kaufman, 1990a, Chapter 7; Matarazzo, 1972).

More recently, however, that almost axiomatic correspondence has been seriously challenged, as indicated in the section on Horn-Cattell in Chapter 2. Horn (1989, 1991) has provided ample research documentation for the existence and construct validity of eight or so ability factors of which Gf and Gc are only two. In the original Horn-Cattell system (Cattell & Horn, 1978; Horn & Cattell, 1966, 1967), most cognitive tasks were classified as measuring one or the other of these broad constructs of general intelligence. As Horn revised and expanded the Gf-Gc system, he strived for greater purity in these dimensions. Gf should stress the reasoning component of a novel task; test performance should not be clouded by other intelligence factors such as visual-spatial ability or speed, or be dependent on motor coordination. Gc tasks should emphasize comprehension and knowledge, and not measure short-term memory, called Short-Term Acquisition and Retrieval (SAR) by Horn, or require too much Gf for solving the acculturation-saturated problems. Therefore, although Block Design was commonly seen as being a prototype of fluid reasoning (Kaufman, 1979b; Matarazzo, 1972), more recent elaboration of the theory stresses the confounding variables of spatial visualization, response speed, and coordination rather than its presumed Gf component.

From the expanded Gf-Gc theory, the Freedom from Distractibility factor measures SAR, and the Processing Speed factor measures Gs (see Chapter 2). So the real questions from the perspective of current Horn-Cattell theory are (a) Is the Verbal Comprehension factor a legitimate measure of Gc? and (b) Does the Perceptual Organization factor adequately assess Gf? Woodcock (1990) conducted joint factor analyses of the WJ, WJ-R, and various cognitive test batteries and concluded that the WAIS-R and WISC-R VC factor does measure Gc, but PO does *not* measure Gf. Instead, Woodcock interprets the PO factor as simply a measure of Gv.

Horn (1989) has identified a broad spectrum of spatial visualization abilities that form a factor (Gv) that is distinct from Gf and Gc and yet appears to be an important form of intelligence. From the outset of research on Gf-Gc theory, it has been recognized that this Gv factor is difficult to distinguish from Gf (Horn, 1968; Horn & Stankov, 1982; Humphreys, 1967). Tests designed to require a minimum of verbal abilities often are presented in terms of figures, diagrams, and drawings and require, therefore, spatial visualization abilities; these abilities are the core of Gv. They may also require reasoning, and it is reasoning at the extremes of complexity that is the essence of Gf (Horn, 1989, 1991).

Despite the apparent Gv component of most Performance subtests, Horn continued to interpret Wechsler's nonverbal subtests as primarily measures of Gf (Horn, 1985; Horn & McArdle, 1980). Not until his recent writings has he hedged on interpreting the Performance subtests as indicating mainly the fluid abilities Horn (1989, 1991; Horn & Hofer, 1992). Responding to the findings of Woodcock (1990), McArdle (1988), and others, Horn states that Wechsler's Perceptual Organization factor "involves visualization to a very considerable extent. . . . Further research is needed to clarify the extent to which it indicates the *Gf* or *Gv* factor" (Horn & Hofer, p. 72).

Horn (personal communication, 1993) believes that Woodcock has done an excellent job of translating Gf-Gc theory and research to an assessment tool, but he also believes that Woodcock (1990) used a highly constrained structural equation model analysis in his research, casting some doubt on Woodcock's conclusions. The sections that follow address the same questions Woodcock tried to answer regarding which of Horn's factors are assessed by Wechsler's verbal and nonverbal subtests. These questions are explored by studying relationships between WISC-III and WISC-R and other cognitive batteries that follow the Horn-Cattell model either explicitly (Binet-4, KAIT, WJ-R) or implicitly (DAS, K-ABC).

The analyses cited have mostly been limited to normal samples to permit generalizations to children in general. In addition to helping examiners understand the cognitive abilities measured by the WISC-III, by viewing them in the context of different measures of Gc and Gf factors, the next few sections will facilitate joint interpretation of verbal-nonverbal discrepancies on the WISC-III with similar discrepancies on other cognitive batteries.

WISC-III and DAS

The DAS, for ages 2½–17, provides three separate scales for school-age children: Verbal, Spatial, and Nonverbal Reasoning. Each scale is composed of two subtests. These six subtests constitute the Core subtests, and the DAS cognitive battery also includes two immediate memory subtests and a processing speed test. The Verbal Scale, composed of analogs of WISC-III Vocabulary and Similarities subtests, is a clear-cut VC clone. Spatial and Nonverbal Reasoning seem to be measures of Gv and Gf, respectively (Keith, 1990). Joint factor analysis of the DAS, WJ-R, and Detroit-3 for 100 normal children in grades 3–5 supported the predicted correspondence between the three DAS scales and the WJ-R Gc, Gv, and Gf clusters, especially in the three-factor solution (McGhee, 1993). The DAS, therefore, presents a good testing ground for determining whether Wechsler's PO factor measures Gf, Gv, or some combination of the two.

Stone (1992a) performed confirmatory factor analysis on data obtained on 115 normal children tested on both the DAS and WISC-R. The best-fitting model produced five factors. As expected, the four WISC-R VC subtests loaded on a factor with the two DAS Verbal subtests. The two Gf subtests on the DAS (Matrices, Sequential & Quantitative Reasoning) formed their own factor, but the two Gv subtests (Pattern Construction, Recall of Designs) loaded on the same factor as all four PO subtests. If the DAS Spatial factor truly measures Horn's Gv, then these results suggest that Wechsler's Performance Scale may be primarily a measure of Broad Visualization, not fluid reasoning.

Table 4.2 presents correlations of V-IQ and P-IQ on the WISC-III and WISC-R with scores on the three DAS scales for normal samples. Correlations with the VC and PO Indexes are also shown for the WISC-III sample. All three studies reveal a close relationship between the DAS and Wechsler Verbal scales (correlations in the mid-.80s). The WISC-III study suggests that P-IQ and the PO Index correlate about .80 with *both* the Gf and the Gv scales on the DAS. The WISC-R data for two age groups indicate that P-IQ relates more closely to the DAS measure of Gv than Gf; the Gf scale, in fact, correlated higher with V-IQ than P-IQ for ages 8–10 years, and correlated equally with the two IQs for ages 14–15. The WISC-R results agree

TABLE 4.2. Correlations of DAS Standard Scores with Verbal and Nonverbal Scores on the WISC-III and WISC-R

| Test and Sample | Differential Ability Scales (DAS) | | |
	Verbal	Nonverbal Reasoning (Gf)	Spatial (Gv)
WISC-III			
Ages 7–14 (N = 27)			
V-IQ	.87	.58	.66
P-IQ	.31	.78	.82
VC-Index	.85	.54	.66
PO-Index	.30	.75	.82
WISC-R			
Ages 8–10 (N = 66)			
V-IQ	.84	.77	.55
P-IQ	.42	.57	.69
WISC-R			
Ages 14–15 (N = 60)			
V-IQ	.84	.68	.27
P-IQ	.47	.69	.77

Note: Data on the WISC-III are from the WISC-III manual (Wechsler, 1991, Table 6.15). Data on the WISC-R are from the DAS handbook (Elliott, 1990b, Tables 9.26, 9.28).

with Stone's (1992a) factor analysis, but that's no surprise since Stone used essentially the same samples shown in Table 4.2 for his analyses. The WISC-III findings suggest that P-IQ and PO Index measure both Gf and Gv, although that study is limited by a very small sample.

Regardless of what the WISC-III Performance Scale measures, the DAS Nonverbal Reasoning Scale is an excellent supplement to the WISC-III, and is used in that manner for Jennie L., whose case report appears at the end of this chapter, and Greg T., whose report is included in Chapter 7. The DAS's two subtests are quite different from the subtests that compose the WISC-III, and they measure nonverbal reasoning without using time limits or requiring visual-motor coordination. In that sense, they provide a good measure of the kind of uncontaminated tests of Gf that Horn prefers.

WISC-III and KAIT

The KAIT, normed for ages 11–85 and older, was developed from Horn-Cattell theory and yields a Crystallized IQ and a Fluid IQ. Each IQ scale includes three subtests; the six subtests compose the Core Battery. The Expanded Battery includes four additional subtests, a fourth Gc and Gf subtest (alternates for each scale) and two measures of delayed recall. Piaget's concept of formal operational thought and Luria's notion of planning ability were used to develop most KAIT subtests to ensure that the cognitive tasks were adult-oriented and measured decision-making capacities. Visual-motor coordination was deemphasized. The Gf subtests emphasize reasoning abilities; only the alternate Fluid subtest (Memory for Block Designs) has a decided visual-spatial and visual-motor component, but that subtest does not contribute to Fluid IQ. Tests of verbal as well as nonverbal reasoning are included on the Fluid Scale. Factor analyses provide construct validity evidence for the KAIT scales (Kaufman & Kaufman, 1993), and the aging patterns across the life span indicate that Fluid IQ follows age-related patterns associated with Gf, not Gv (Kaufman & Horn, 1994).

As was true for the DAS, joint factor analyses for individuals tested on both the KAIT and a Wechsler scale address the questions of whether P-IQ and PO Index measure Gf or Gv, and if V-IQ and VC Index are measures of Gc. Factor analyses for 118 adolescents tested on the KAIT and the WISC-R resulted in three distinct factors (Kaufman & Kaufman, 1993, Table 8.9). The first factor was defined by eight subtests with loadings of .40 and above: the four Gc subtests from the KAIT and the four VC subtests from the WISC-R. The five highest loading subtests on the second factor included the four PO subtests plus KAIT Memory for Block Designs. Factor 3 included five subtests with loadings above .50, the four KAIT Gf subtests, and WISC-R Arithmetic (a task that measures Gf and SAR according to Horn). Memory for Block Designs loaded a bit higher on the Gf than the PO factor.

The results of a joint factor analysis of the KAIT and WAIS-R with 338 adolescents and adults also produced three factors, and the results were virtually identical to the KAIT/WISC-R factors (Kaufman & Kaufman, 1993,

Table 8.10). These findings support the notion that Wechsler's VC factor reflects Horn's Gc ability, and they indicate that the PO factor does not seem to measure Gf. Whether or not the PO factor identified in these analyses reflects Gv or some amalgam of Gf, Gv, and perhaps Gs (because of the importance of visual-motor response speed) is speculative.

Correlational analyses between the WISC-R and KAIT IQs for the same 118 children and adolescents used for the factor analysis are as follows (Kaufman & Kaufman, 1993, Table 8.19):

WISC-R	Crystallized	Fluid
V-IQ	.79	.74
P-IQ	.67	.67

These correlations show the substantial relationship between V-IQ and KAIT Crystallized IQ, but they also indicate that V-IQ correlates a bit higher with KAIT Fluid IQ than does P-IQ. Like the DAS Nonverbal Reasoning Scale, the KAIT three-subtest Core Fluid Scale is an excellent supplement to the WISC-III. It measures fluid reasoning and learning ability, skills that are not tapped very well by the WISC-III Performance Scale. The Mystery Codes and Logical Steps subtests provide assessment of planning ability and formal operational thought. In addition, Logical Steps measures new problem solving through verbal comprehension and verbal reasoning, and Rebus Learning demands vocal responding. All these aspects of the Fluid subtests enhance the examiner's understanding of how well a child of 11 or older can solve new problems. Several of the KAIT Gc subtests also reflect good supplements to the WISC-III Verbal Scale. Auditory Comprehension assesses memory and understanding of a mock news broadcast, a real-life cognitive task. Double Meanings assesses formal operational thought within the crystallized domain. And Famous Faces, a variant of Information, uses pictorial stimuli that are integrated with verbal clues about the famous people. The comprehensive case report for Ira G. in Chapter 7 integrates data from the complete KAIT and WISC-III (along with selected WJ-R subtests).

WISC-III and Binet-4

The Binet-4 offers four Area scores, Verbal, Abstract-Visual, Quantitative, and Short-Term Memory. The Horn-Cattell theory forms a foundation of the test, as Verbal and Quantitative are supposedly measures of Gc, and Abstract-Visual is intended as a Gf scale. Short-Term Memory seems to blend Horn's SAR and Gv factors. Factor-analytic support for the four area scores is weak at best, and controversial for sure (Kamphaus, 1993; Thorndike, 1990). Examination of factor loadings indicates that Gc and Gf factors are interpretable from the analyses, but the component subtests do not conform to the test authors' assignment of Areas to the Horn-Cattell model. For ages 7–11 years, the Gc factor is defined by two Wechsler-like

Verbal subtests (Vocabulary and Comprehension) and Memory for Sentences, but no Quantitative tasks (Thorndike, 1990). Gf includes substantial loadings by Pattern Analysis (a Block Design analog), Matrices, Copying, Number Series, Bead Memory, and Absurdities. From Horn's (1989, 1991) definition of Gf subtests, Matrices and Number Series are clearly fluid reasoning tasks; the other subtests seem to measure primarily Gv (Copying, Bead Memory) or a blend of Gf and either Gv (Pattern Analysis) or Gc (Absurdities). From the Binet-4 perspective, the Gf factor cuts across the entire battery and includes subtests from all four areas.

At ages 12–23, the Gc factor includes the same three subtests mentioned previously plus a Verbal subtest that is intended for older children (Verbal Relations). The Gf factor is defined by all age-appropriate subtests from both the Abstract-Visual and Quantitative Areas, plus Bead Memory (Thorndike, 1990).

From a Gf-Gc perspective, the Binet-4 authors made two mistakes: Quantitative measures Gf, not Gc; and the assignment of subtests to the four Areas does not conform to Gf-Gc theory or to any apparent theory. Therefore, one would not expect any clear-cut relationships between Wechsler's Verbal and Performance IQs and the Binet-4 Area scores. And that's precisely the outcome of correlational analysis involving the WISC-R and Binet-4 for 205 normal children with a mean age of $9\frac{1}{2}$ (Thorndike, Hagen, & Sattler, 1986, Table 6.7), as shown:

WISC-R	Achievement	Abstract-Visual	Short-term Memory	Quantitative
V-IQ	.72	.68	.64	.64
P-IQ	.60	.67	.63	.63

The two Verbal Scales relate substantially to each other, but the Binet-4 Absurdities subtest probably lowers the relationship with V-IQ and raises the correlation with P-IQ because it uses visual stimuli and has a Gf component. Correlational analyses with the WISC-R, therefore, do not aid our understanding of what Wechsler's verbal and nonverbal scales measure. In Woodcock's (1990) factor analyses of the WJ and WJ-R subtests with Binet-4, WISC-R, and WAIS-R subtests, Binet-4 Matrices is the only subtest on the Binet-4 or Wechsler's scales to have a substantial loading on the Gf factor. The other three Binet-4 Abstract-Visual subtests joined most Wechsler PO subtests on the Gv factor. The Binet-4 Quantitative subtests loaded on a separate Quantitative factor (Gq) that included Wechsler Arithmetic and WJ-R math achievement subtests. The Binet-4 Verbal subtests (including Absurdities) joined Wechsler VC subtests and Picture Arrangement on the Gc factor.

When using the Binet-4 to supplement the WISC-III, the tasks that will help examiners most in understanding a child's V-P or VC-PO discrepancy are Absurdities and Verbal Relations from the Verbal Scale; Matrices and

Paper Folding and Cutting from the Abstract-Visual Scale; and Number Series and Equation Building from the Quantitative Scale. The two Binet-4 Verbal supplements are good conceptual subtests that permit examiners to assess the generalizability of the child's Gc abilities measured by the WISC-III, and Absurdities, especially, allows measurement of Gc abilities without requiring verbal comprehension skills. The two Abstract-Visual subtests measure nonverbal intelligence without the imposition of coordination or rapid responding; the harder Matrices items that are included on the record form (involving letters as stimuli) are especially clever items that measure high levels of Gf ability without resorting to visual-spatial skills. The two Binet-4 Quantitative subtests enable examiners to determine whether the child's fluid reasoning strength or weakness generalizes to number manipulation activities.

Binet-4 subtests were used as WISC-III supplements in the case reports of Jennie L. (end of this chapter) and Lourdes I. (end of Chapter 5).

WISC-III and K-ABC

The K-ABC intelligence scales were developed from cerebral specialization and Luria-Das notions of sequential and simultaneous processing, but the entire K-ABC had its roots in the broad fluid–crystallized dichotomy (Kaufman & Kaufman, 1983): "The Achievement Scale resembles closely the crystallized abilities, and the two Mental Processing Scales together resemble the fluid abilities, that characterize the Cattell-Horn theory of intelligence" (p. 2). It is clear that the K-ABC Sequential Processing Scale measures SAR, not Gf, in the expanded Horn model, but the distinction between Simultaneous Processing and Achievement may pertain directly to Gf and Gc, respectively. Like Wechsler's Performance scale, however, the K-ABC Simultaneous Processing Scale is believed to be primarily a measure of Gv (Horn, 1991; Woodcock, 1990).

In fact, whatever construct Wechsler's PO factor measures, the K-ABC Simultaneous Processing Scale undoubtedly assesses the same construct. Ample factor-analytic evidence from joint K-ABC/WISC-R analyses has accumulated to show that PO and Simultaneous subtests load together on a single, robust factor. This finding holds for normal children (Kaufman & McLean, 1987), including separate groups of African-American and white children (Naglieri & Jensen, 1987), and for children with school learning problems (Kaufman & McLean, 1986; Keith & Novak, 1987). Woodcock (1990) also found the PO and Simultaneous subtests to load together, on the factor he labeled Gv. Two K-ABC Simultaneous subtests, the ones with the largest reasoning component (Matrix Analogies and Photo Series), split their loadings between Woodcock's Gv and Gf factors.

Regarding the matchup between VC and K-ABC Achievement, the same joint factor-analytic studies cited previously indicated that the WISC-R and K-ABC verbal-factual subtests loaded together on a robust factor that presumably measures Gc. For children with reading and other learning problems, the two K-ABC reading subtests split off to form their own factor (Kaufman & McLean, 1986; Keith & Novak, 1987), but that is an expected result for children who have already been identified as having reading difficulties.

Correlations between the separate K-ABC and WISC-R scales (including K-ABC nonverbal) reveal the following relationships for 182 children, ages 6–12 years (Kaufman & Kaufman, 1983, Table 4.19); this sample was included in the sample factor analyzed by Kaufman and McLean (1987):

WISC-R	Achievement	Sequential	Simultaneous	Nonverbal
V-IQ	.78	.49	.51	.54
P-IQ	.51	.30	.68	.63

These data affirm the V-IQ/Achievement and P-IQ/Simultaneous correspondence. The Nonverbal Scale does not do as good a job as the Simultaneous scale in discriminating P-IQ from V-IQ. When using the K-ABC to supplement the WISC-III, the entire Simultaneous Processing Scale serves as a good addition for children with motor and/or speed problems, because the K-ABC scale minimizes both of these variables. Among Achievement subtests, Faces & Places and Riddles are the best WISC-III supplements for measuring Gc. The former task uses visual stimuli to measure range of general knowledge, and the latter requires the child to use verbal reasoning to demonstrate word knowledge rather than just the ability to retrieve word definitions from long-term storage (an ability demanded for WISC-III Vocabulary and its clones on the Binet-4 and DAS).

Three case reports illustrate the integration of the K-ABC and WISC-III: Lucy O. (end of Chapter 5), Nicole A. (Chapter 7), and Dana Christine T. (Chapter 7). These reports feature the interface between the sequential-simultaneous processing model and subtest patterns on the WISC-III as well as the relationship of Faces & Places and Riddles to the Gc subtests on the WISC-III.

WISC-III and WJ-R

The WJ-R Tests of Cognitive Ability provide standard scores that correspond to seven Horn factors, reflecting the greater purity in intellectual assessment that Horn (1989,1991) has strived for in his empirical research and theoretical writings (see Bracken & McCallum, 1993b). The WJ-R standard battery includes one subtest per Horn factor, and the complete 21-subtest cognitive battery measures each factor with two to four subtests; two tasks are included on two factors apiece. Woodcock (1990) provides ample documentation of the construct validity of the WJ-R, making analyses with his scales probably the best test of what Wechsler's verbal and nonverbal scales measure.

In Woodcock's (1990) joint analyses with other instruments, the VC subtests on the WISC-R and WAIS-R load on a broad Gc factor, joining a variety of language and factual subtests from the WJ-R, WJ, K-ABC, and Binet-4. Knowledge in the areas of Science, Social Studies, and Humanities (subtests from the achievement portion of the WJ and WJ-R) also load on the Gc factor. As mentioned earlier, the Wechsler PO subtests load with K-ABC Simultaneous Processing subtests and most Binet-4 Abstract-Visual subtests on the Gv factor, joining Woodcock's own measures of Gv (Visual Closure and Picture Recognition).

Is Woodcock (1990) correct in labeling the factor Gv? His measures of Gv assess simple perception and memory. Visual Closure is an analog of K-ABC Gestalt Closure and Detroit-3 Picture Fragments, and Picture Recognition assesses visual memory (the examinee is shown pictures and has to recognize them in an array). These subtests measure Gv according to Horn's (1989, 1991) definition of the construct, which stresses perceptual closure, visual memory, and the kind of visualization abilities needed for the Binet-4 Paper Folding and Cutting subtest. Pure measures of Gv deemphasize reasoning. However, except for the PO Picture Completion subtest and two K-ABC Simultaneous subtests (Gestalt Closure and Spatial Memory), the Wechsler and K-ABC nonverbal subtests have a healthy dose of reasoning and conceptual ability. According to Horn (1989), "It is difficult to distinguish *Gv* from *Gf* if visual tests can be performed by reasoning" (p. 81).

Woodcock's (1990) factor might be a pure Gv factor, or it might be a factor composed primarily of subtests that measure *both* Gf and Gv, (tests that require visual-spatial ability *and* reasoning such as Block Design or Matrix Analogies). To determine the best name for the factor that Woodcock called Gv, let's examine the pattern of factor loadings of the subtests that define it, based on Woodcock's (1990, Table 5) summary table of many factor analyses. Measures that minimize reasoning and provide fairly pure measures of Gv, based on Horn's definition, are the following (factor loadings are in parentheses): WJ-R Visual Closure (.47) and Picture Recognition (.38); K-ABC Gestalt Closure (.32); WISC-R/WAIS-R Picture Completion (.45); and Binet-4 Copying (.47) and Paper Folding and Cutting (.51). Those six subtests had an average loading of .43. But the subtests with the highest loadings on the so-called Gv factor were K-ABC Triangles (.67), Wechsler Object Assembly (.62), Wechsler Block Design (.58), and Binet-4 Pattern Analysis (.57). Three visual reasoning subtests with loadings below .30 on the Gv factor split their loadings with either the Gc factor (Picture Arrangement) or the Gf factor (Photo Series, Matrix Analogies).

I believe that Woodcock was wrong to label his factor Gv in view of the pattern of factor loadings. A more supportable name would have been Gf/Gv, indicating the dual nature of the dimension. Evidence for a Gv factor that is separate from Gf and Gf/Gv dimensions comes from a joint factor analysis that I conducted on 121 children, ages 11 to 12 years, tested on both the KAIT and K-ABC (Kaufman, 1993a). The joint analysis yielded six meaningful factors. Among them were a Gf factor that was defined by the three Core Fluid subtests on the KAIT; a factor reflecting an amalgam of Gf and

Gv that was composed of all Simultaneous Processing subtests except Gestalt Closure; and a Gv factor that was defined by four subtests, three of which are measures of Horn's Broad Visualization—Gestalt Closure, Hand Movements, Memory for Block Designs.

Table 4.3 presents correlations of WISC-R Verbal and Performance IQs with the seven WJ-R Horn factors for 72 children age 9 (Woodcock & Mather, 1989, Table 7.10). The WJ-R factors are grouped in accordance with their hypothesized relationship with either Wechsler's Verbal or Performance Scale. The Gc and V-IQ correlation of .80, coupled with the low correlation of Gc with P-IQ (.29) suggests that Wechsler's Verbal Scale is a good measure of Gc. The WJ-R Ga and Gsm scales also relate much more closely to V-IQ than P-IQ, but the moderate correlations with V-IQ make it clear that it is the Gc construct that primarily defines Wechsler's Verbal Scale (excluding Digit Span).

None of the WJ-R factors that use visual stimuli, and measure abilities that seem more associated with Wechsler's Performance than Verbal construct, correlate substantially with P-IQ. The highest correlation for P-IQ is with Gf, but the value of .45 represents only a 20% overlap in the constructs, not even as large as the overlap of about 40% between Gf and V-IQ. P-IQ correlated higher than did V-IQ with both Gv and Gs, but the meager 9% overlap between P-IQ and Gv indicates that Wechsler's nonverbal dimension cannot be summarized in simple fashion as a measure of Gv.

Teeter and Smith (1993) tested 60 children on the WISC-III and the WJ-R Gf scale, 30 with severe emotional disturbance and 30 control children. They presented correlations between Gf and the WISC-III Factor Indexes

TABLE 4.3.   Correlations of WISC-R Verbal and Performance IQs with Scores on the Seven Horn Factors Measured by the WJ-R Cognitive Ability Scales ($N = 72$)

WISC-R	Woodcock-Johnson-Revised Tests of Cognitive Ability Scales Associated with Wechsler's Verbal Scale		
	Crystallized Intelligence (Gc)	Auditory Intelligence (Ga)	Short-Term Memory (Gsm)
V-IQ	.80	.39	.46
P-IQ	.29	.04	.18

WISC-R	Woodcock-Johnson-Revised Tests of Cognitive Ability Scales Associated with Wechsler's Performance Scale			
	Fluid Intelligence (Gf)	Broad Visualization (Gv)	Broad Speediness (Gs)	Long-Term Retrieval (Glr)
V-IQ	.64	−.03	.31	.26
P-IQ	.45	.30	.40	.10

Note: Data are from the WJ-R Cognitive Tests of Ability Manual (Woodcock & Mather, 1989, Table 7.10). Gsm is an alternate name for Horn's SAR factor.

for both samples. Within the emotionally disturbed sample, Gf correlated higher with PO (.71) than with VC (.57); for the control sample, Gf correlated about equally with PO (.66) and VC (.70). These results, though obtained with small samples, reaffirm that PO is not a clear-cut measure of Gf. Similar conclusions apply to the results of a WISC-R/ WJ-R investigation of 52 incarcerated adolescent delinquents (Meinhardt, Hibbett, Koller, & Busch, 1993): Gf correlated .66 with P-IQ and .55 with V-IQ. Also, the latter study reveals a small correlation (.34) between P-IQ and Gv.

I believe that the WJ-R, as a factorially pure test, lacks some of the complexity that might be desired in a clinical instrument. But its pure factors make the WJ-R an ideal supplement for other clinical tests of intelligence. The four WJ-R factors with visual stimuli each fit into one aspect of the information-processing model: Input (Gv), Integration (Gf), Storage (Glr), and Output (Gs). Whenever a child earns a significantly low or high P-IQ or PO Index, examiners should attempt to derive hypotheses that explain the aspect or aspects of the learning process that represent the child's weakness or strength within the visual-motor modality (see discussion earlier in this chapter on psycholinguistic deficiencies and the case report of James C. in Chapter 7). The WJ-R provides an excellent way of verifying or denying those hypotheses. Administer the two-subtest version of each of the four pertinent WJ-R factors to help identify the child's specific area of strength or weakness on Wechsler's Performance Scale.

The three WJ-R factors associated with the Verbal Scale can serve an analogous function for strengths or weaknesses within the auditory-vocal channel: Input (Ga), Integration (Gc), and Storage (Gsm). The Ga scale, which is composed of auditory perceptual tasks that assess whether a child can perceive words (via sound blending or filling in gaps) measures one aspect of the intake of stimuli, but it is more on the "molecular" level—the ability to interpret isolated words. Children who demonstrated auditory processing problems of this sort on the WJ-R include Ira G. and Dana Christine C., whose comprehensive reports appear in Chapter 7. Sometimes children have no trouble taking in single words, as on the WJ-R Ga tasks but have difficulty understanding phrases or the long questions in Information, Comprehension, or Arithmetic. To identify children with the latter type of information processing deficit, also administer a subtest such as ITPA Auditory Reception (Do babies cry? Do carpenters kneel? Do barometers congratulate?) or the Das-Naglieri Simultaneous Verbal subtest (Which picture shows the boy wearing the man's hat? Which picture shows the triangle above the circle?).

Portions of the WJ-R Tests of Cognitive Ability were administered to 6 of the 10 cases whose reports appear throughout this book. Examiners administered 8 to 14 of the subtests in the Extended Battery to James C., Nicole A., and Ira G., all of whose case reports appear in Chapter 7; these reports provide the best illustrations of the integration of the scores yielded by the WJ-R and WISC-III.

Overview: Does the Verbal Scale Measure Gc?

The available evidence indicates that Wechsler's V-IQ and VC Index correspond to the construct that Horn defines as Gc. The FD Index denotes SAR, but since Digit Span does not enter into the computation of V-IQ, that global score still serves as a good estimate of a child's Gc ability. The particular subtests that compose the WISC-III VC factor resemble closely the kinds of Gc tasks that Horn and his colleagues have used for decades in their research. But the VC subtests are confined to the auditory-vocal channel, stress long-term retrieval of facts, and depend on well-developed verbal expressive abilities. It is a good idea to administer Gc supplements that include visual stimuli such as Binet-4 Absurdities, K-ABC Faces & Places, Detroit-3 Story Construction, KAIT Famous Faces, WJ-R Picture Vocabulary, and the PPVT-R (Dunn & Dunn, 1981). Gc supplements that assess verbal *reasoning* ability but minimize verbalization by requiring only a one-word response are also advised. K-ABC Riddles, WJ-R Verbal Analogies, and KAIT Double Meanings fit that category. In addition, tests of verbal *conceptual* ability that demand only a one-word answer are good VC supplements: WJ-R Oral Vocabulary (called Antonyms-Synonyms in the WJ), Detroit-3 Word Opposites, and KAIT or K-BIT Definitions.

Overview: Does the Performance Scale Measure Gf or Gv?

The bulk of evidence suggests that P-IQ and the PO Index measure *both* Gf and Gv, as well as a bit of Gs. Woodcock's (1990) argument that the Performance Scale is nothing but a measure of Gv has some holes in it. His model has no room in it for factors that might blend two or more of Horn's "intelligences," so he chooses to interpret as a Gv factor a dimension that is defined primarily by tests that have *both* a visual-spatial and a reasoning component.

That is not to deny the Gv aspect of Wechsler's nonverbal subtests. Research on the Gv construct "suggests that it relates to laterality in brain function, field independence, and differences in the developments of males and females" (Horn & Hofer, 1992, p. 65). Those findings pertain as well to the Wechsler P-IQ and PO factor. Patients with right-hemisphere damage perform poorly on the WAIS and WAIS-R Performance Scale (Kaufman, 1990a, Chapters 9–11; Turkheimer & Farace, 1992); field-independent Individuals score high on the PO factor (see discussion later in this chapter); and males tend to outperform females on spatial subtests, especially Block Design (Kaufman, 1990a, Chapter 6; Jensen & Reynolds, 1983). But a Gv component does not preclude a Gf dimension as well.

I have to admit that I was at first persuaded by Woodcock's (1990) claim that Performance subtests measured Gv and not Gf, especially when joint factor analyses of Wechsler's scales with the DAS (Stone, 1992a) and KAIT (Kaufman & Kaufman, 1993) showed no tendency for the PO subtests to load on the same factor as face-valid and construct-valid measures of Gf such as DAS Sequential & Quantitative Reasoning and KAIT Mystery Codes. In the KAIT manual, Nadeen and I strongly suggest that the emergence of separate PO factors and Gf factors implies that PO is a Gv factor. However, collaboration with John Horn on an article that explored age changes on KAIT subtests and scales across the life span (Kaufman & Horn, 1994) taught me otherwise. He made it quite clear to me that *he* didn't buy the notion that Wechsler's nonverbal subtests were measures of Gv. Maybe they had a Gv component, but so what. Horn (personal communication, 1993) wrote, "I am quite prepared to believe that what [Woodcock] calls Gv would align with the Gf of my studies, as would, I suspect, his Gf—that is, both are components of broad Gf." If John Horn believes that the PO subtests are primarily measures of Gf, who am I to argue with the model builder?

In Chapter 2, I grouped the Performance subtests by probable Horn factor. The PS subtests are measures of Gs. Object Assembly measures Gf, Gv, and Gs (because of the important role of bonus points in determining a child's score, as demonstrated later in this chapter). Block Design measures Gf and Gv, whereas Picture Completion is the only Performance subtest considered to measure just Gv. Picture Arrangement demands little visualization, so it does not have a Gv component. It measures Gf and Gc, based on information gained from acculturation rather than formal schooling.

The fact that the PO factor is seen as partly a measure of Gf does not mean that the WISC-III provides thorough measurement of fluid reasoning. With large and varied sets of reasoning tasks, Horn and his colleagues have found that Gf involves verbal and auditory content as well as spatial content (Horn, 1968; Horn & Cattell, 1982; Horn & Stankov, 1982). Similarities and Arithmetic are classified as tests with a Gf component, broadening the scope of the Gf assessment, but those subtests are, respectively, primarily measures of Gc and SAR. It is therefore important for examiners to supplement the WISC-III with Gf subtests that include verbal comprehension and reasoning as an integral part of the problem-solving process. KAIT Logical Steps and WJ-R Analysis-Synthesis do this well. And in view of the coordination, spatial, and speeded aspects of PO subtests, it is essential to administer supplements that measure reasoning without these interfering variables: for example, DAS Sequential & Quantitative Reasoning, WJ-R Concept Formation, KAIT Rebus Learning, Binet-4 Equation Building and Number Series, and the diversity of Raven-like matrices tests. All these Gf tests obtain difficulty through the complexity of the problem solving and have no need for bonus points for speed to achieve age differentiation above age 11.

Gf-Gc Theory and Learning Disabilities

The associations between the Horn-Cattell Gf and Gc constructs and Wechsler's verbal-nonverbal dichotomy suggest certain predictions regarding the test profiles of children with reading and learning disabilities. First, one would hypothesize characteristic P > V and PO > VC patterns for groups of children with school learning problems. Their difficulty in performing well in school implies difficulty in solving school-related problems, or a deficiency in Gc. In that sense, poor Gc might be seen as a causative factor in the learning problem. But the causality could work in the opposite way: Low Gc, and hence low V-IQ and VC Index, may result from the learning problem itself. Learning-disabled children may perform low on the Verbal Scale because their lack of school achievement is likely to impair performance on fact-oriented items in Information and Vocabulary, and their limited knowledge base may penalize them on the verbal reasoning items in Similarities and Comprehension.

A second prediction from Gf-Gc theory relating to the previous line of thought is that children with school difficulties should perform especially poorly on the subtests that Bannatyne groups together as measuring Acquired Knowledge (Information, Arithmetic, and Vocabulary), because these tasks are academic-oriented and may reflect the child's learning problems directly. And the third theoretical prediction is that the Verbal deficit for learning-disabled children should be cumulative, such that verbal ability should decrease over time when these children are tested throughout their school careers. If learning problems persist, preventing the acquisition of facts and the skills to broaden one's knowledge base, then learning-disabled children should fall farther and farther behind their peers.

All three predictions have been borne out in the bulk of research investigations using Wechsler's scales for the evaluation of children with school-related deficiencies that appear in every nook and cranny of the assessment literature. Groups of children with learning or reading problems have typically obtained P > V profiles on the WISC, WISC-R, and WISC-III (Kaufman, Harrison, & Ittenbach, 1990; Prifitera & Dersh, 1993; Rugel, 1974; Slate, Jones, Graham, & Bower, in press). Two initial studies with the WISC-III, totalling 163 learning-disabled children, each yielded with the same results: P > V of 4 points and PO > VC of 5 points (Prifitera & Dersh, 1993; Slate et al., in press). P > V differences of approximately 8 to 9 points on the WISC-R characterized one large sample of 1,024 children with school learning difficulties (Strom, Mason, Williams, Dean, & Fischer, 1988), and P > V differences ranging from 3 to 10 points (weighted mean = 7) were identified for samples of at least 100 children (total $N = 874$) included in a summary table of LD samples tested on the WISC-R (Kaufman et al., 1990, Table 7).

It is especially important to administer supplementary measures to children with school learning problems who display P > V or PO > VC patterns on the WISC-III. The nature of the verbal deficit must be understood in terms of the processing model: Is the problem on the auditory-perceptual level (input)? Does it reflect processing difficulties that may have led to the learning disability (integration)? Is the low score possibly a result of the learning problem, leading to a deficient knowledge base, or is a memory and retrieval problem at the root of the learning difficulties (storage)? Does the child have difficulty expressing his or her ideas in words (output)? Similarly, does the high P-IQ or PO Index seem to reflect Gf, Gv, coordination, or some other ability? Answers to all these questions pertain to the remedial approach that might be most effective for a given child. It is also essential to realize that many learning-disabled children, based on their specific perceptual or cognitive deficits, may have the opposite pattern of V > P. Such children may be more likely to experience memory difficulties, especially in retrieval within either the auditory or visual modality, than learning-disabled children with the more common P > V profile (Silver & Tipps, 1993).

The second prediction of low Acquired Knowledge scores for learning-disabled children was found for the WISC-III (Prifitera & Dersh, 1993) and for numerous samples tested on the WISC-R (Decker & Corley, 1984; Fischer, Wenck, Schurr, & Ellen, 1985; Kaufman et al., 1990). A summary table of WISC-R scaled scores for 18 learning-disabled samples (total $N = 1,536$) indicated that a rank-ordering from high to low of the 10 regular WISC-R subtests across samples placed Information 10th, Arithmetic 9th, and Vocabulary 7th (Kaufman et al., 1990, Table 7). In Strom et al.'s (1988) sample of more than 1,000 children referred for school learning problems, a comparable analysis of the 10 regular subtests indicated that the 3 Acquired Knowledge subtests yielded the three lowest mean scaled scores. An investigation of 813 children with learning disabilities indicated that Information and Arithmetic yielded the lowest scaled scores among regular subtests for girls and were among the three lowest for boys; Vocabulary, however, was not a weakness for either gender (Nichols, Inglis, Lawson, & MacKay, 1988).

And the third prediction is borne out as well. Verbal IQs for learning-disabled samples decrease over time (e.g., Anderson, Cronin, & Kazmierski, 1989; Haddad, Juliano, & Vaughan, 1994; Nichols et al., 1988; Truscott, Narrett, & Smith, 1994; Weltner-Brunton, Serafica, & Friedt, 1988). But the support for the three hypotheses generated from Gf-Gc theory does not imply that those two broad constructs provide the best insight into the learning-disabled child's deficits. When the supplementary Digit Span subtest is included in rank orderings of Wechsler subtests, then Digit Span typically yields the lowest scaled score of all (e.g., Nichols et al., 1988; Strom et al., 1988). And Coding is usually found near the bottom of the heap as well, leading to the hypothesized ACID profile of deficit areas for learning-disabled children—low scores on *A*rithmetic, *C*oding, *I*nformation, and *D*igit Span.

Ample evidence indicates that neither subtest scatter nor possible characteristic profiles have value for differential diagnosis of learning disabilities (Kavale & Forness, 1984). However, it is of interest that the deficit areas of children with school learning problems are on subtests associated primarily with the WISC-R Freedom from Distractibility factor, and recent evidence suggests weakness on WISC-III Symbol Search as well (Prifitera & Dersh, 1993). Despite the likelihood that differential diagnosis is not possible with the WISC-III, the patterns of scores for learning-disabled children on the four factors, especially FD and PS, are of considerable clinical interest for practitioners, as is an understanding of ACID profiles on the WISC-III. These topics are addressed in Chapter 5.

Gf-Gc Theory and Socioeconomic Influences

Part of the reason for a V-P discrepancy may stem from a child's socioeconomic background. From Gf-Gc theory, one might predict high Gc for children with extensive opportunities for cultural experiences, and low Gc for children from disadvantaged backgrounds who lack the requisite knowledge base to score well on either the fact-oriented or reasoning subtests within the Verbal domain. Research has shown that children from professional families tend to score higher on the Verbal Scale, with the reverse holding true for the children of unskilled workers; this finding was observed both for the 1949 WISC (Seashore, 1951) and the WISC-R (Kaufman, 1976b).

Data based on parents' occupation is unavailable for the WISC-III, but data for parents' education has been provided (Granier & O'Donnell, 1991), and is summarized here. Overall, WISC-III Full Scale IQ is directly proportional to amount of parental education, averaging 106 for college graduates, 101 for parents with some college experience, 98 for high school graduates, 92 for those with a 9th to 11th grade education, and 86 for parents with less than a 9th grade education. Subtracting P-IQ from V-IQ yields the following set of differences:

Parental Education	V-IQ Minus P-IQ
College graduate	+0.9
Some college	−0.1
High school graduate	−0.5
9th to 11th grade	−2.4
Less than 9th grade	−4.2

Although there is considerable variability within each socioeconomic category in all such studies, the trend is worthy of note since it suggests that a child's background experiences can help shape his or her relative skills in the verbal and nonverbal spheres. For the WISC-III, there is a slight P > V profile for children from low socioeconomic backgrounds; the corresponding verbal superiority for children from high socioeconomic backgrounds, which emerged in WISC and WISC-R studies that investigated parental occupation, was not observed on the WISC-III.

P > V scores for culturally disadvantaged children may suggest true intellectual ability ("potential") despite inadequate learning experiences. The poor school achievement that often accompanies cultural deprivation is, almost by definition, consistent with the low Verbal IQ (reflecting a deficiency in crystallized thinking). However, the significantly higher Performance IQ suggests that the child may have an adaptive, flexible problem-solving approach that can lead to successful school achievement in learning environments that actively encourage and utilize these skills. Illustrations of these environments are Montessori's (1964) approach to education; Piaget-based methods and curriculums (Wadsworth, 1978); and programs that stress creative problem solving for the gifted (Stanley, George, & Solano, 1977) and for children from all types of backgrounds (Torrance, 1982). Again, it is important to administer a variety of Gf tests to children from low socioeconomic backgrounds to determine whether a strength on P-IQ or PO Index denotes good fluid reasoning or is just indicative of well-developed visual-spatial skills.

Guilford's Operation of Evaluation

Wechsler's Verbal and Performance Scales differ on another cognitive dimension that reflects neither verbal versus nonverbal abilities nor the Gf-Gc distinction—the degree to which they assess Guilford's (1967, 1988) operation of *evaluation,* the ability to make judgments in terms of a known standard (see Table 2.3). This mental process is required for success on all six Performance subtests, but only on one Verbal subtest (Comprehension). Therefore, it is possible that some children obtain significant V-P discrepancies because of either very good or very poor evaluation ability, rather than because of differences between their Verbal Comprehension and Perceptual Organization or Gc-Gf skills. This hypothesis becomes a viable explanation of a significant verbal-nonverbal difference when two conditions are met: (a) the P-IQ is interpretable, based on the empirical criteria delineated in Step 3 of the WISC-III interpretive process (see Chapter 3), and (b) the Comprehension scaled score is more consistent with the child's Performance than Verbal scaled scores.

Since most of the evidence for the strength or weakness in evaluation comes from nonverbal subtests that emphasize coordination and visual-motor speed, supplementary testing should include assessment of the ability to evaluate hypotheses generated in tasks that do not demand these abilities, such as KAIT Logical Steps, WJ-R Analysis-Synthesis, Das-Naglieri Planned Search, and the various matrices tests.

Interestingly, the results of many research investigations may be explainable from the Guilford model. In summaries of WISC-R studies of learning-disabled children and mentally retarded children, the mean Comprehension scaled scores for both types of exceptionality were more in line with the Performance than Verbal scores (Kaufman et al., 1990, Tables 7 and 9). These findings are conceivably related to the Guilford operation of evaluation, although any such inference must remain purely speculative pending the outcome of systematic empirical investigation.

Field Dependence/Field Independence

It is quite possible that a V-P IQ or VC-PO Index discrepancy, in either direction, may reflect a dimension of behavior that is far more pervasive than a cognitive distinction between verbal and nonverbal intelligence or fluid and crystallized thinking. A substantial body of research has accumulated regarding the cognitive style of field dependence versus field independence (Witkin, Dyk, Faterson, Goodenough & Karp, 1974), with several studies directly pinpointing the relationship of this bipolar cognitive style to nonverbal scaled scores on various Wechsler batteries (Coates, 1975; Goodenough & Karp, 1961; Karp, 1963; Swyter & Michael, 1982).

Like other cognitive styles, field dependence-field independence deals with the process or form of a cognitive activity (e.g., *how* we perceive, learn, relate to people), rather than the content; it is pervasive, spanning the intellective and personal-social domains, and is stable over time; and unlike extremes of intelligence, each pole has adaptive, positive value in specified circumstances (Witkin, Moore, Goodenough, & Cox, 1977). The tools for measuring individuals on this bipolar cognitive style continuum are two laboratory tasks involving spatial orientation (Rod-and-Frame test and Body-Adjustment test, described by Witkin et al., 1977), and the nonverbal, perceptual Embedded Figures Test or Children's Embedded Figures Test (Witkin, Oltman, Raskin, & Karp, 1971). Success on all tasks depends on "the extent to which the person perceives part of a field as discrete from the surrounding field as a whole, rather than embedded in the field" (Witkin et al., 1977, pp. 6–7). People who can adjust a rod to an upright position regardless of the tilt of the frame surrounding it, adjust their own body to an upright position when placed in a disoriented environment, and locate a simple figure that has been embedded in a complex geometric design are said to be *field independent.* Inability to perform well on these tasks, presumably because of the power the field exerts on an individual's perception of its components, characterizes *field-dependent* people.

Based on summaries and discussions of numerous research investigations, Witkin et al. (1977) paint the following picture of individuals at the two poles of the cognitive style continuum. Field-independent people are flexible in problem-solving situations, impose structure where it is lacking when dealing with perceptual and verbal materials, have an impersonal orientation, are interested in the abstract and theoretical, and use specialized defense mechanisms such as intellectualization. In contrast, field-dependent individuals are well attuned to the social aspects of their environment, make use of prevailing social frameworks, do not spontaneously structure stimuli but leave them "as is," are drawn to people and like being with them, are better liked, have a global (rather than a distinct) body concept, and use nonspecific defenses such as repression.

The analytic mode of perceiving that characterizes field-independent people facilitates performance on the Wechsler Picture Completion, Block

Design, and Object Assembly subtests, and these tasks have been shown to load substantially on the same factor as the field-independent measures, namely, the Rod-and-Frame test, Body-Adjustment test, and Embedded Figures Test or Children's Embedded Figures Test (Goodenough & Karp, 1961; Karp, 1963; Swyter & Michael, 1982). Consequently, it is possible that sizable V > P or VC > PO discrepancies on the WISC-III may indicate a more pervasive field-dependent cognitive style, with P > V or PO > VC differences signifying field independence.

Hypotheses regarding this cognitive style may be checked out in a number of ways. First, the child's subtest profile should be scrutinized; the Picture Completion, Block Design, and Object Assembly scaled scores should cluster together and be substantially different (either higher or lower) than the mean of his or her other scaled scores, both nonverbal and verbal. Next, the Children's Embedded Figures Test might be administered to get an independent measure of field independence, and other supplementary measures such as the Rorschach test also relate to this cognitive style (Witkin et al., 1974; Witkin et al., 1977). Finally background information and behavioral observations pertaining to cognitive, social, and personal aspects of the child's functioning should be integrated and studied carefully to determine whether his or her pattern of behavior aligns closely with the "typical" pattern of field-dependent or field-independent individuals (Witkin et al., 1977; Witkin & Goodenough 1977).

If a hypothesis relating to this cognitive style can be supported, examiners may have far more important information at their disposal than mere knowledge of a V-P or VC-PO discrepancy on the WISC-III. It is of interest to note that mentally retarded children have consistently scored higher on the three field-independent Wechsler subtests than on Verbal Comprehension tasks (Kaufman, Harrison, & Ittenbach, 1990; Kaufman & Van Hagen, 1977; Keogh & Hall 1974; Silverstein, 1968), as have children with reading and learning disabilities (Kaufman et al., 1990; Nichols, Inglis, Lawson, & MacKay, 1988; Prifitera & Dersh, 1993; Rugel 1974) and Attention-Deficit Hyperactivity Disorder (ADHD) (Prifitera & Dersh, 1993). Since several of these studies were specifically investigating Bannatyne's (1971) Spatial grouping of Wechsler subtests—composed of the same three subtests as the field-independence triad—or were not tied to any theoretical framework, the relationship of these exceptionalities to Witkin's field dependent/field independent framework remains speculative. These research results raise the possibility that numerous children from these exceptional populations may have field-*independent* cognitive styles, although studies with the Children's Embedded Figures Test suggest that ADHD children (Stoner & Glynn, 1987) and mildly retarded black children and white children (Bice, Halpin, & Halpin, 1986) may have field-*dependent* cognitive styles.

In addition, assessment of field dependence/field independence for different cultural groups is a fruitful avenue of research (Oakland, De Mesquita, & Buckley, 1988; Ramirez & Price-Williams, 1974; Swyter &

Michael, 1982). Evidence exists to support the notion that groups that emphasize respect for family and group identification (e.g., Mexican-Americans) are more likely to be field dependent than groups that foster individuality and the challenging of conventions (Ramirez & Price-Williams, 1974). However, the initial belief that the relative school failure of Mexican-American students can be explained by their field-dependent cognitive style (Ramirez, 1972) has not been supported by systematic research (Oakland et al., 1988). Buriel (1978) found the relationship between cognitive style and achievement to be dependent on the instrument used to measure field independence and on the type of achievement (coefficients were generally significant for mathematics, but not for reading), and he interpreted these data as a challenge to the well-accepted notion that Mexican-Americans are more field dependent than Anglo-Americans.

Inferred relationships between Witkin's cognitive style and school achievement have been based on both rational and empirical considerations. Witkin et al. (1977) have enumerated educational implications and suggestions pertaining to field dependence that should aid the examiner in making practical recommendations for a child who is judged to fall near either extreme of the bipolar cognitive style. Logically, the analytic requirements for learning to read and to compute are quite similar to the requisite skills for success on the field-independence tasks (Cohen, 1969). As Buriel (1978) explains, children who are beginning readers must identify vowels and syllables within the context of a more complex word, and analytic procedures are needed as well to carry out computations in mathematics.

According to Cohen (1969), the amount of field independence and analytic thinking required for successful achievement in verbal and quantitative areas actually becomes greater with increasing grade level. Empirically, various measures of Witkin's cognitive style have been shown to correlate significantly with school achievement in reading and mathematics, with field-independent children outperforming field-dependent students (Kagan & Zahn, 1975; Oakland et al., 1988; Watson, 1969). Field independence among female college students was associated with better detection of letters in reading, and with the use of visual strategies rather than phonological strategies (Davies, 1988). One important caution regarding the application of Witkin's cognitive style to intellectual assessment and educational applications concerns the possibility that the so-called cognitive style may be nothing more than cognitive ability. McKenna (1990) argues that the assumption that measures of the so-called field independent/field dependent cognitive style truly assess that cognitive style is false. He maintains that the various measures, especially the Embedded Figures Test, are no more and no less than cognitive ability tests; he cites the failure of "cognitive style matching" experiments as providing additional support for his contention. The possibilities for positive contributions of cognitive style theory and research to clinical and school psychology remain viable, but the conflicting and negative research findings must be weighed against the initial enthusiasm and claims of its developers and proponents.

VARIABLES PERTAINING TO OUTPUT

The topic of output problems has already been addressed to some extent because it is so inextricably bound to input, especially within the auditory-vocal channel. Of particular interest regarding verbal-nonverbal discrepancies are those individuals who earn low P-IQs or PO Indexes because of difficulties with the output demands of the tasks. Most Performance subtests have considerable coordination and response speed requirements, making it feasible that some children will show nonverbal decrements because of motor or personality variables rather than cognitive factors. Poor motor coordination or a reflective approach to problem solving can depress nonverbal scores for children who have good nonverbal reasoning.

Coordination Problems

Children who are unable to respond appropriately to most WISC-III Performance subtests because of their heavy visual-motor demands are likely to earn P-IQs and PO Indexes that do not adequately reflect their nonverbal reasoning ability as discussed and illustrated earlier in this chapter in the section titled Psycholinguistic Deficiency. Whether the problem is due to poor coordination stemming from cerebral palsy or other types of neurological dysfunction, or to a more subtle deficiency regarding visual-motor expressive skills, examiners must first identify coordination deficits as a primary cause of low Performance scores.

Hints about possible subtle motor deficits are readily available from an integration of clinical observations of the child's motor behavior with the child's profile of scaled scores on Performance tests. Such children commonly score highest on the two "Picture" subtests that have the fewest motor requirements. Picture Completion requires virtually no coordination, and its items may even be answered vocally. Picture Arrangement demands some motor coordination to organize the pictures, but the emphasis is on discovering the correct sequence; the straightness of the line formed by the picture cards and the proximity of the cards to each other are both irrelevant. Block Design, Object Assembly, and Symbol Search require good coordination to rapidly align the blocks or pieces to form the correct product, or place a slash through a word. However, the role of nonverbal thinking for all these tasks is sufficiently important to take precedence over motor coordination in determining the scaled scores of most children. Nevertheless, poor coordination is especially penalizing to adolescents on Block Design and Object Assembly (particularly the latter subtest) because of the increasingly important role played by time bonuses in determining the scaled scores of older children (see discussion of time bonuses in the next section). In contrast, as noted previously, Coding is more of a clerical than an intellectual task, thereby elevating motor coordination as a primary element for successful performance at all ages. A child cannot use quick nonverbal thinking to compensate or partially compensate for poor coordination when responding to Coding items.

Whenever the examiner notices that the child's pattern of scaled scores on the Performance subtests is consistent with a hypothesis of motor deficits, the possibility of a coordination problem should be considered. If no coordination difficulty was apparent during the examination, particularly during the Performance subtests, the hypothesis probably requires quick rejection. Similarly, a hypothesized motor problem would be rejected if the examiner had different explanations for the relatively good performance on the two Picture tasks and poor performance on Coding. For example, the scores on Picture Completion and Picture Arrangement may have been elevated by the child's good verbal ability (see section on verbal compensation of performance deficit in Chapter 3), and the low Coding score may have been due to factors such as extreme distractibility, obvious fatigue, or low motivation (see Chapter 5).

When coordination difficulties are believed to explain low PO Index or P-IQ scores, assess the child's Perceptual Organization abilities using tasks that do not demand a motor response. Picture Completion can be administered validly to such children, but it does not measure a high-level reasoning ability. Supplement the WISC-III with K-ABC Photo Series, in which the examiner moves the photos; WJ-R Spatial Relations and Binet-4 Paper Folding and Cutting, which measure spatial visualization without demanding a motor response; and DAS Matrices, K-BIT Matrices, Detroit-3 Symbolic Relations, Das-Naglieri Matrices, or the Matrix Analogies Test (Naglieri, 1985), which use multiple choice formats to assess this Raven-like skill. All these tasks measure abstract and visual-spatial reasoning abilities without requiring a motor response. The examiner can effectively bypass the child's motoric deficit and still measure nonverbal intelligence. For children with motor problems, the WISC-III P-IQ and PO index do not adequately reflect intellectual functioning. But don't just administer supplementary tests that tap nonverbal reasoning without demanding coordination as a means of estimating the child's nonverbal mental ability. Also administer a test of fine and gross motor abilities such as the Bruininks-Oseretsky Test of Motor Proficiency (Bruininks, 1978) to identify the degree and nature of the motor impairment.

The WISC-III assesses verbal and nonverbal intelligence through the auditory—vocal and visual—motor channels of communication. When one of these vehicles is damaged, some or most of the battery is no longer measuring intelligence for that individual. Thus for a child whose V-P or VC-PO discrepancy can be traced to, or assumed to result from, a psycholinguistic deficiency, the Full Scale IQ becomes a totally meaningless statistic. Since some psycholinguistic problems (e.g., auditory reception) can affect scores on both the Verbal and Performance Scales, even the higher of the Verbal and Performance IQs, or of the VC and PO Indexes, may be an underestimate of the child's level of intellectual functioning. Primarily for this reason, rules stipulating that a learning-disabled child must have "normal" intelligence (based on scores on conventional intelligence tests) are unfair.

Greg T., whose report is included in Chapter 7, and Lourdes I., whose report appears at the end of Chapter 5, both had problems associated with output. Greg had visual-perceptual and visual-motor problems. Lourdes had output problems within both channels: expressing her ideas in words, and coordination difficulties using paper and pencil.

Speed of Nonverbal Problem Solving

Speedy performance in solving nonverbal problems on Wechsler's scales has been heavily rewarded since the Wechsler-Bellevue's debut in 1939. Bonus points for quick, perfect solutions to items on Picture Arrangement, Block Design, and Object Assembly have been given in abundance—partly to improve reliability and partly to ensure that mean scores on these subtests improve throughout the entire childhood-to-adolescent age span covered by Wechsler's children's scales. Without the bonus points, mean numbers of items solved correctly tend to plateau at about age 11 or 12, the precise time that children are moving into Piaget's stage of formal operational thought. With the stress on no-nonsense, respond-as-quickly-as-possible problem solving, the output required for solving nonverbal items assumes great importance.

And that emphasis on speedy output has grown as part of the WISC-R revision process. The role of speed was considerable on the WISC-R, and it is even more pervasive on the WISC-III, as I've pointed out in my otherwise very favorable test review, "King WISC the Third Assumes the Throne" (Kaufman, 1993b). When Dr. Wechsler revised the WISC and WAIS, he reduced the role of speed on Picture Arrangement, preferring the task to stress the reasoning aspect. Picture Arrangement bonus points per item were reduced from 3 on the WISC to 2 on the WISC-R, and were eliminated altogether on the WAIS-R. Now, WISC-III Picture Arrangement offers three bonus points per item, not two. As on the WAIS-R, bonus points have even invaded the Verbal Scale; one bonus point for each of the six hardest items is given for quick, perfect solutions on WISC-III Arithmetic problems. And the downside of adding the clinically important Symbol Search subtest and the Processing Speed factor to the WISC-III is that speed assumes more importance than ever before during a Wechsler administration.

A child will earn 28 points for solving every WISC-III Picture Arrangement item correctly but can earn even more points (as many as 36) for speed of responding. On the WISC-R, the ratio of points earned by solving the items *correctly* versus solving the items *quickly* was 32 to 16. The increased emphasis on speed in the WISC-III may account for the relatively low correlations between scores on WISC-III Picture Arrangement and scores on the subtest of the same name on the WISC-R (.42) and the WAIS-R (.35) (Wechsler, 1991). Across the four subtests that allot time bonuses, the number of possible bonus points has grown from 51 on the WISC-R to 83 on the WISC-III.

It is hard to do well on the WISC-III if you don't solve problems very quickly or respond well to time pressure, factors that are likely to produce V > P profiles for children who work slowly because of coordination problems, cognitive style (reflectivity), personality variables (anxiety, insecurity, compulsiveness), or whatever reason. Children who have difficulty working within time limits, or who become extremely anxious when face to face with a stopwatch, will be extremely penalized on the Performance Scale and may well score significantly higher on the Verbal Scale, even if their nonverbal intelligence per se is on a par with or possibly superior to their verbal intelligence.

All five comprehensive case reports in Chapter 7 depict children who had difficulty with speeded tasks, although the reason for the difficulty varied from child to child. James was reflective and indecisive, Nicole had perfectionistic tendencies, Ira and Greg were impaired on problems that had heavy visual-perceptual demands, and Dana Christine was slowed on problem-solving tasks because of reflectivity and verbal mediation difficulties.

Speed of Performance and Chronological Age

Table 4.4 indicates what happens to the scaled scores of children who solve problems quite well, but slowly. This table indicates, for each age between 6 and 16 years, the maximum scaled score a child can earn by solving every single item in a subtest correctly, but without earning a single bonus point for quick, perfect performance.

As shown, children ages 12 and older won't even score at the normative mean of 10 on the three Performance subtests if they earn zero bonus points, and 15- to 16-year-olds peak out at a score of 12 on Arithmetic, and a score of a mere 7 on the nonverbal subtests. The average scaled score on the three WISC-III Performance subtests for 12-year-old children who are

TABLE 4.4. Maximum Possible Scaled Score on the WISC-III Subtests That Give Bonus Points for Children Who Solve Each Item Perfectly, But Earn No Bonus Points, by Age

WISC-III Subtest	Maximum Scaled Score by Age										
	6	7	8	9	10	11	12	13	14	15	16
Arithmetic	19	19	19	19	18	17	16	14	13	12	12
Picture Arrangement	19	17	14	12	10	9	8	7	7	7	6
Block Design	19	19	16	14	12	11	9	9	8	7	7
Object Assembly	19	16	14	12	11	10	9	9	8	7	7

Note: The number or raw score points earned for correctly solving all items on each subtest are as follows (the number of bonus points that one can earn for speed are shown in parentheses): Arithmetic—24 (6); Picture Arrangement—28 (36); Block Design—42 (27); Object Assembly—30 (14). Adapted from Kaufman (1993b).

perfect but slow equals 8.7; by way of comparison, the corresponding average for the WISC-R is 10.3, with the biggest change occurring for Picture Arrangement (8 vs. 11).

A relationship of considerable magnitude was observed between chronological age and speed of problem solving on the WISC-R Performance Scale (Kaufman, 1979c); a similar relationship was observed for the WISC (Woo-Sam & Zimmerman, 1972). In these studies, older children were found to be far quicker (and therefore to earn many more bonus points) than younger children in solving Picture Arrangement, Block Design, and Object Assembly items. Consequently, speed of performance plays a more important role in the Performance IQs (and hence the Full Scale IQs) earned by older children than by younger ones, a point made abundantly clear in Table 4.2. Thus the meaning of the Perceptual Organization factor for both the WISC (Cohen, 1959) and WISC-R (Kaufman, 1975) changes across the age range, with speed of responding constituting a more integral aspect of this nonverbal dimension for adolescents than for primary-grade children. Unfortunately, data on time bonuses on the WISC-III are not available for systematic study, but the WISC-R data are likely to generalize to the WISC-III. If anything, the relationships observed for the WISC-R are likely to underestimate the WISC-III relationships, especially for Picture Arrangement, because of the increased emphasis now placed on speed of performance.

To dramatize the decrease in performance time with increasing age, consider the following results of statistical analyses of the WISC-R standardization data (Kaufman, 1979c); all item numbers refer to the WISC-R, not the WISC-III, subtests.

1. *Average performance times of children solving WISC-R Picture Arrangement, Block Design, and Object Assembly items correctly decreased steadily across the 6½–16½-year range.* For example, 6½-year-olds solved Picture Arrangement item No. 8 (Lasso) correctly in an average of 28 seconds, compared with an average of 18 seconds at age 11½, and 14 seconds at age 16½. Average performance times for children solving Block Design item No. 7 correctly were 43 seconds at age 6½, 28 seconds at age 11½, and only 19 seconds at age 16½. Similarly, performance times for Object Assembly item No. 3 (Car) decreased from 83 seconds for 6½-year-olds to 41 seconds by age 16½.

2. *Bonus points for quick perfect performance on the WISC-R were rarely earned by children below age 8, but were plentiful for adolescents.* The average child of 6½ or 7½ earned a *total* of only 1–2 bonus points on Picture Arrangement, Block Design, and Object Assembly. By age 8½, the average child earned 4–5 bonus points, with the number of bonus points earned increasing steadily to 9 at age 10½, 18 at age 13½, and 23–24 at age 16½. Thus the average adolescent of 16½ earned over 20 raw score points due to quickness of response, obtaining about 7 bonus points on Picture Arrangement, 11–12 on Block Design, and 5 on Object Assembly.

Further analysis of data revealed that 6½ and 7½-year-olds earned 96% of their raw score points on the three subtests under investigation due to the accuracy of their solutions and only 4% of their points due to time bonuses. By age 11½, the ratio of points obtained due to accuracy versus speed shifted to 85:15, and by age 16½, nearly 25% of an individual's raw scores on Picture Arrangement, Block Design, and Object Assembly were earned via time bonuses (Kaufman, 1979c). In addition, about 75%–80% of all correct responses given by 16½-year-olds on Picture Arrangement, Block Design, and Object Assembly were quick enough to merit at least one bonus point. It was thus *unusual* for an older teenager to solve a nonverbal problem and *not* earn a bonus point! At age 11½, about 55%–60% of the correct responses merited bonus points, which was substantially higher than the value of about 20%–25% for 6½-year-olds (Kaufman, 1979c).

3. *The amount of variance in children's WISC-R scores due to speed of performance increased rapidly with age,* as borne out by additional data analyses (Kaufman, 1979c). For Picture Arrangement and Block Design, the ratio of the test score variances for accuracy versus speed is a sizable 35:1 at age 6½, reducing to 3:1 at age 11½, and to a mere 1.5:1 at age 16½. For Object Assembly, the descent is even more dramatic, plunging from 70:1 at age 6½ to 1.5:1 by age 11½. At ages 13½ and above, the variance due to speed *exceeds* the variance due to accuracy for Object Assembly, with the ratio reaching 3:1 at age 16½. In a very real sense, Object Assembly is a measure of speed of problem-solving ability for teenagers. As suggested earlier, there is every likelihood that these results generalize to the WISC-III.

Data analyses on time bonuses with the WISC-R, when interpreted in the context of the WISC-III data in Table 4.4, affirm the essential part played by performance time in determining an older child's Performance IQ. Table 4.4 and the WISC-R results also indicate that even though the *average* primary-grade student does not earn too many bonus points, even at age 7 or 8, very high scaled scores are reserved for the children who solve at least some problems quickly.

Speed of Performance and Ability Level

The key role played by speed of responding to nonverbal problems, especially for teenagers and very bright preadolescents, raises some interpretive questions. For example, does performance time belong in the intellectual domain, or does it fit in better with noncognitive variables? It is obvious that nonintellective factors can greatly influence an individual's rate of responding to a nonverbal problem. Children with a reflective cognitive style (Kagan, 1966) are not likely to earn too many bonus points for speed on the WISC-III, whereas impulsive youngsters will tend to respond more quickly and make more errors. For children at both ends of the reflective-impulsive spectrum, rate of responding to certain types of problems is probably more a function of a pervasive and characteristic cognitive style than of intellect.

Other children may solve problems slowly due to a variety of nonintellectual variables such as anxiety, perseveration, distractibility, compulsiveness, or poor motor coordination.

The basic issue, however, is not whether "irrelevant" variables may be related to a slow response time, but whether children who solve a problem quickly are brighter, in some way, than children who solve the same problem more slowly. The study cited earlier (Kaufman, 1979c) explored this question for the WISC-R. The answer was clear-cut: Children who solved Picture Arrangement, Block Design, and Object Assembly items quickly performed better on other similar problems than did those solving the items slowly. In other words, children who responded correctly to a Picture Arrangement item in a brief time scored higher on other picture arrangements than did those responding correctly in a longer time, and analogous relationships were obtained for Block Design and Object Assembly items. Indeed, systematic linear relationships were obtained for most items, as individuals solving an item in 1–5 seconds were better problem solvers in general than those solving the item in 6–10 seconds; the children getting the item right in 6–10 seconds were better at solving similar problems than those getting it correct in 11–15 seconds, and so forth. Evidence for the linearity came from rank-order correlations between speed of responding to an item and total score on other similar items. Median coefficients of 0.87, 0.94, and 0.89 were obtained for Picture Arrangement, Block Design, and Object Assembly items, respectively (Kaufman, 1979c).

The impressive relationships obtained in the study of speed of performance suggest that an individual's quickness to respond to a nonverbal problem is, at least in part, an intellectual attribute. Despite the variety of nonintellective factors that can affect speed of performance, the study provided empirical justification for Wechsler's practice of assigning bonus points for quick perfect performance, and for the contribution these points make to an individual's Performance IQ and Full Scale IQ. Had nonsignificant correlations been obtained between performance time and problem-solving ability, or if response time had not decreased steadily with chronological age (Anastasi, 1988, pp. 153–154), the role of bonus points in determining a child's IQs would have been open to challenge.

Rattan (1992) investigated speed of responding on the WISC-R Picture Arrangement, Block Design, and Object Assembly subtests and discovered that response times to these three subtests formed their own factor, separate from the verbal and nonverbal dimensions. Further, response times for Rattan's sample of 131 referred children correlated about .00 with all WISC-R subtests, including the three that yield bonus points. However, no inference can be made from Rattan's (1992) results about the degree to which response speed relates to intelligence on the WISC-R because of the researcher's decision (an unfortunate one, I believe) to merge incorrect responses with correct ones in obtaining a child's score on each response speed measure. A response time of 10 seconds means one thing if the child gets the item right, but quite another thing (or two, or three) if the child's answer is wrong.

Although ability level was positively correlated with quicker performance times on the WISC-R in my 1979 study, there was *considerable* variability in the abilities of children who solved a given problem at different rates (Kaufman, 1979c). That variability indicates that factors other than mental ability also affect speed, most notably nonintellective factors, and the children most affected will be the ones with visual-motor coordination problems, reflective cognitive tempos, or perfectionistic tendencies. But other, less obvious groups will be affected as well. As mentioned earlier, children with severe *language* disorders have been shown to respond unusually slowly to problem-solving tasks (Phelps et al., 1993; Sininger et al., 1989), and samples of learning disabled, dyslexic, Attention-Deficit Hyperactivity Disordered, and gifted children have all scored relatively low on the Processing Speed Index (Bracken & McCallum, 1993a; Wechsler, 1991). Consequently, gifted children may score below the cutoff needed to qualify for an enrichment program when given the WISC-III if they tend to be reflective or have even a mild coordination problem. Similarly, learning-disabled children may score below the average range of intelligence, even if they have normal mental functioning, because of the speed factor.

Behavioral Variables and Problem-Solving Speed

Some of the major causes of poor performance on timed items (other than poor motor coordination) are immaturity, anxiety, distractibility, reflectiveness, and compulsiveness. An immature child often pays no attention to the watch, or, if aware of it, either does not understand its implications or does not care. Irrelevant comments during a timed task are frequent for immature children, and examiners may have to redirect children who have interrupted their performance with a story or lengthy discourse. Immature physical behavior and silliness are often noted throughout the test, but the impact of these actions on untimed verbal tasks is usually less pronounced. An anxious or distractible child is likely to evidence the pertinent behaviors from time to time during the testing session. The perceptive clinician who notes these behaviors should scrutinize carefully the child's profile of scaled scores. Depressed scores on highly speeded tasks, on Digit Span, and on any other subtest during which the distractible or anxious behaviors were specifically observed, would help corroborate a cause-effect relationship between those behavioral variables and a child's low Performance IQ.

Reflective children, who may respond deliberately because of their characteristic style of approaching ambiguous problems (Kagan, 1966), may fail Performance items because they do not solve them correctly within the allowable time limit. Many cross-sectional and longitudinal studies have shown that children typically become more reflective with age (Messer, 1976). Whereas older reflective children may have no difficulty completing items before the time limit expires and indeed may be very accurate problem solvers, they may still obtain depressed Performance IQs because of their failure to earn bonus points for quick perfect performance. Interestingly, the polar opposite of reflectivity may also lead to a lowered Performance IQ.

Like the highly reflective child, the compulsive or perfectionistic child—who may be observed copying the Coding symbols in painstaking fashion or aligning the Block Design cubes and Object Assembly pieces until the fit is "perfect"—commonly gets items right on overtime. Although credit is never given for these belated correct responses, this behavioral observation can be crucial for test interpretation, and it has obvious implications for the type of nonpressured learning environment that may be optimum for such a child. Ironically, reflective or compulsive behavior on the Verbal Scale may have an effect opposite to that observed on the Performance Scale. Scores on Verbal Comprehension subtests may be elevated substantially by children who give a string of responses of varying quality (Similarities) and who respond to probing with a variety of ideas (Comprehension) or with much elaboration (Vocabulary). The combined effect of the child's reflective cognitive style or compulsive tendencies on the WISC-III profile may thus be to inflate V > P discrepancies or to produce no V-P difference for the child who really has a nonverbal superiority.

Giftedness and Speed of Performance

Speed of performance on the WISC-R subtests that give bonus points was shown to be positively related to ability level (Kaufman, 1979c). That conclusion is consistent with a growing body of research on the relationship of IQ to reaction time (Jensen, 1985; Vernon, 1987) and with the findings of cognitive psychologists who have been investigating the components of mental tasks (Dover & Shore, 1991; Lajoie & Shore, 1986; Sternberg, 1977). But despite the positive relationship between speed of problem solving and IQ, the application of intelligent strategies often demands reflectiveness, thereby penalizing intelligent problem solvers on intelligence tasks that overly reward speed of performance (Sternberg, 1982). Also, there are likely to be individual differences in children's preference for solving problems quickly (Marr & Sternberg, 1987; Reams, Chamrad, & Robinson, 1990; Siegler, 1989).

When problems had alternate solutions in the metacognitive study conducted by Dover and Shore (1991), significant differences in response speed that had favored gifted over control children disappeared. Further, the flexibility-rigidity dimension interacted with response speed and metacognitive knowledge (awareness of different strategies for solving problems) for gifted and average children, indicating that speed of problem solving is a complex, multifaceted variable (Dover & Shore, 1991). In an investigation of 52 children (mean Primary Mental Abilities IQ = 120) that used a variety of measures of speed (including WAIS Digit Symbol) and of accuracy to predict PMA IQ, Lajoie and Shore (1986) determined that the speed measures were able to account for a substantial 67% of the PMA variance when they were entered first in the regression equation; speed and accuracy together accounted for 89%. However, when the accuracy measures were entered first, the speed measures did not add significantly to the prediction obtained from accuracy alone. Lajoie and Shore (1986) concluded that being quick relates to intelligence, but not always, and that children who score high on ability tests "have different learning styles and speeds" (p. 101), and "superior performance might best be achieved by attention to accuracy at whatever speed the subject is comfortable working" (p. 85).

Speed, per se, in the absence of the application of high-level problem solving, is not a specific strength of gifted individuals. Coding has typically emerged as a relative weakness for gifted children on the WISC-R (Brown & Yakimowski, 1987; Macmann, Plasket, Barnett, & Siler, 1991; Reams et al., 1990), and the sample of 38 gifted children reported in the WISC-III manual obtained a mean Processing Speed Index of 110 compared with IQs and other Indexes in the mid- to high-120s (Wechsler, 1991, Table 6.20). And even when speed of response to high-level problem-solving tasks is studied, gifted children do not particularly excel. Reams et al. (1990) compared 66 high-scoring children (FS-IQ = 131) with a control group of 36 average-scoring children (FS-IQ = 112) on the three WISC-R Performance subtests that award bonus points. The groups were compared on the number of items solved correctly and the number of bonus points earned for speed. The High-IQ group solved significantly more items correctly on all three subtests, but only on Block Design did they earn significantly more bonus points. The authors interpreted their results "as casting serious doubt on the utility of including speed bonuses in tests of general intelligence" (Reams et al., 1990, p. 110).

Perhaps the results of other investigations (e.g., Kaufman, 1979c) might dispute that conclusion, particularly because of the small sample size in the Reams study, but that does not minimize the problem of interpreting the WISC-III Performance IQ for gifted children, especially those who use reflective strategies, have mild visual-motor deficits, or are insecure or compulsive. From group data, V > P patterns for samples of identified gifted children and gifted referrals are modest. The gifted sample reported in the WISC-III manual had V > P of 3.4 points, a group of 29 gifted referrals had a WISC-III V > P difference of 4.8 points (Levinson & Folino, 1994), and various WISC-R gifted samples had similar differences of about 4 to 7 points in favor of Verbal IQ (Brown & Yakimowski, 1987; Clark, McCallum, Edwards, & Hildman, 1987; Karnes, Whorton, Currie, & Cantrall, 1986; Phelps, 1989; Robinson & Nagle, 1992; Saccuzzo, Johnson, & Russell, 1992). An occasional gifted population (e.g., Macmann et al., 1991) displayed no V-P IQ discrepancy at all, while others had differences in favor of V-IQ by as much as 10 points (Sapp, Chissom, & Graham, 1985). However, we're not talking about groups of gifted children; we're concerned with the particular gifted or potentially gifted child you happen to be testing whose P-IQ and PO Index may grossly underestimate his or her nonverbal intelligence because that child didn't work fast enough to earn many bonus points.

A way to reduce the influence of performance speed is to focus more on the Factor Indexes than the IQs for gifted or potentially gifted children. The VC factor excludes Arithmetic, the one Verbal subtest that allots bonus points, and the PO factor excludes subtests that are primarily measures of response speed. The verbal-nonverbal discrepancy for the gifted sample included in the WISC-III manual dropped from about 3½ points to 1 point when the VC and PO Indexes were used instead of the IQs. Again, however, there are individual differences to consider. Some reflective gifted children will earn low P-IQs even if Coding or Symbol Search is excluded from consideration because they earn few bonus points for quick perfect performance on the PO subtests.

Understanding the Impact of Time

Inferring that a relatively low Performance IQ may be largely explained by factors related to time—regardless for the reason for the slow response speed—is contingent on the examiner's perceptiveness and his or her ability to integrate background information and behavioral observations with test scores. From the WISC-III profile, one would expect a child to score relatively low on the Arithmetic subtest, in addition to obtaining a depressed Performance IQ; otherwise, hypotheses concerning the importance of time factors are conceivably not correct. If the examiner is aware of cultural or subcultural influences that may impel a child to work slowly due to caution or noncompetitiveness, such background knowledge can certainly support a hypothesis regarding the role of time. More typically, however, support comes from the child's behavior. Some children will make obvious negative gestural responses to the stopwatch or make an anxious comment about it. Others, as mentioned previously, may be totally oblivious to the watch or to the importance of working fast.

Testing the limits after the entire WISC-III is administered provides a method of estimating a child's nonverbal problem-solving ability in the absence of time pressure. With the stopwatch removed, the examiner can again present items the child failed or present the more difficult items that may not have been reached and observe the child's performance. Since correct responses obtained during the testing-the-limits procedure do not "count" and do not affect the IQs, the examiner can modify the instructions if need be ("Now take as much time as you need to put these pictures in the right order to tell a story; there's no hurry") or use other means to calm an anxious child. Children who far surpass their previous nonverbal or arithmetic performance in the more informal setting were probably unduly penalized by the influence of the clock on the timed WISC-III subtests.

Supplementing the WISC-III with Other Measures

Another method of trying to estimate the nonverbal intelligence of a child believed to be overly bothered by the stopwatch is to administer supplementary tests. The various subtests mentioned in the section on coordination problems are good supplements because they assess nonverbal reasoning without imposing time limits on the child. Of these tasks, the K-ABC Photo Series permits evaluation of temporal sequencing skills similar to the ones measured by Picture Arrangement; WJ-R Spatial Relations and Binet-4 Paper Folding and Cutting assess spatial visualization, as does Block Design; and the various derivatives of Raven's matrices test provide measures of nonverbal reasoning.

However, by using supplementary tasks that reduce or eliminate *both* the coordination and speeded aspects of the subtests, examiners will not know whether a child's low P-IQ or PO Index was a function primarily of poor coordination or of difficulties dealing with the speeded aspects of the WISC-III tasks. It is therefore a good idea also to administer supplementary subtests that have a decided coordination component but that place minimal demands on speeded performance. Possibilities include Binet-4 Copying; K-ABC Triangles and Hand Movements; DAS Recall of Designs and Pattern Construction (using the alternative, unspeeded administration and scoring procedure); Detroit-3 Design Reproduction; Das-Naglieri Planned Codes, Planned Connections, and Figure Memory; and KAIT Memory for Block Designs.

The subtests that come closest to measuring the combination of coordination and conceptual skills assessed by the WISC-III Performance Scale are the DAS alternate administration of Pattern Construction, K-ABC Triangles, and KAIT Memory for Block Designs. The first two measure design construction with blocks, allotting two minutes to complete each item; the KAIT subtest allows 45 seconds for a response, but gives examinees who are working productively toward a correct solution an additional 45 seconds without penalty. Tests to avoid as supplements for children who have difficulty with the highly speeded aspects of WISC-III Performance subtests are Binet-4 Pattern Analysis (a Block Design analog) and Detroit-3 Story Sequences (a Picture Arrangement clone). Pattern analysis "can be dramatically affected by speed of performance" (Kamphaus, 1993, p. 282), and Story Completion smashes all existing records for time bonuses held by Wechsler's Perceptual Organization subtests by allotting one point for a correct solution and *four* points for speed of responding.

The entire K-ABC Simultaneous Processing Scale serves as a good Wechsler supplement for children with coordination problems, speed problems, or a combination of the two. That scale deemphasizes both speed and coordination, yet its subtests measure the same cognitive dimension as Wechsler's PO factor (Kaufman & McLean, 1986, 1987; Naglieri & Jensen, 1987). The K-ABC scale, however, should not be used as a WISC-III supplement for gifted children older than 10 years of age because of its limited "top."

One word of caution: The examiner should not be too surprised if testing the limits and administering supplementary tests fail to result in improved performance. It is important to remember that quick performance is not just related to behavior or personality, but also bears a clear relationship to problem-solving ability, as indicated earlier.

Testing Children with Orthopedic Handicaps

In light of the considerable coordination and speed demands of Performance subtests, questions regarding the administration of the WISC-III Performance Scale to children with orthopedic handicaps must be answered from the dual vantage points of the degree of the handicap and the child's age. All Performance subtests are timed, not just the three that allot bonus points for speed. If the orthopedic handicap is so severe that the child is unable to respond within the reasonably generous time limits, then certainly the WISC-III Performance Scale is inappropriate at any age as a measure of the child's nonverbal intelligence. If the handicap definitely impedes performance (making bonus points unlikely) but is not debilitating, the Performance Scale should provide a reasonable estimate of ability for young children. Certainly below age 9, Picture Arrangement, Block Design, and Object Assembly more closely resemble power than speed tests. Accuracy of performance contributed 90% or more of the points earned on all three subtests on the WISC-R by the average child of 6½ years, 7½ years, and 8½ years (Kaufman, 1979c). In addition, the variances for accuracy are far greater than the variances for speed at the young ages, indicating that individual differences in test scores are more a function of accuracy than speed of problem solving for 6½–8½-year-olds. The ratio in variances (accuracy: speed) averaged about 11:1 for the three subtests at age 8½; by 9½ years of age, the ratio dropped to about 6:1, and by 10½ the ratio was 4:1.

For 9- and 10-year-old children with orthopedic handicaps, the administration of the WISC-III Performance Scale becomes risky and requires the thoughtful clinical judgment of the examiner. The role of speed looms more important for success at these ages, and even a child with a mild orthopedic problem will be penalized, perhaps substantially. A 10-year-old who solves every nonverbal problem perfectly but earns no bonus points will only earn scaled scores of 10 to 12 on the three subtests in question (see Table 4.4). At ages 11 and above, the prominent role of speed renders the Performance IQ inadequate as an index of the orthopedically handicapped child's nonverbal ability; consequently, the WISC-III Performance Scale should not be administered in such cases. Woo-Sam and Zimmerman (1972) reached similar conclusions regarding the ages at which it is appropriate to administer the WISC Performance Scale to orthopedically handicapped children. The K-ABC Simultaneous Processing Scale is probably the best alternative to the WISC-III Performance Scale for such children.

As a final note, whenever an examiner deems the WISC-III Performance Scale suitable for a child with a mild orthopedic handicap, it is probably a good idea to exclude *both* of the Processing Speed subtests from the scale, and interpret only the PO Index. Coding and Symbol Search are inappropriate as contributors to the IQs of orthopedically handicapped youngsters. Examiners who choose to administer the PS subtests in these instances should do so for clinical reasons but should not use the Factor Index as an estimate of cognitive ability. Examiners would also be wise to administer some of the subtests indicated in the previous section as supplements, especially the tasks that minimize or eliminate both coordination and speed.

ILLUSTRATIVE CASE REPORT

An illustrative case report follows for Jennie, an adolescent of 16 diagnosed with autism and mental retardation, who displayed better nonverbal than verbal ability. Jennie was administered the WISC-III, and supplementary subtests from the DAS, WJ-R, Binet-4, and K-ABC. The client's name and pertinent identifying information have been changed to ensure anonymity.

Percentiles are ordinarily used in preference to age equivalents to communicate ability level in case reports, but age equivalents are sometimes useful to help distinguish among different abilities that are well below average for low-functioning individuals. For that reason, both percentiles and age equivalents are used in Jennie L.'s report. Age equivalents for the WISC-III were obtained from the manual (Wechsler, 1991, Table 1.9).

Jennie L., Age 16-9, Autism and Mental Retardation

WISC-III Profile

IQs		(90% conf.)	Factor Indexes		(90% conf.)
Verbal	55	(52–62)	Verbal Comprehension	54	(51–62)
Performance	69	(65–79)	Perceptual Organization	73	(69–83)
Full Scale	58	(55–64)	Freedom from Distractibility	72	(68–83)
P-IQ > V-IQ ($p < .05$)			Processing Speed	67	(64–80)

Verbal	Scaled Score	Age Equiv.	Performance	Scaled Score	Age Equiv.
Information	3	8-10	Picture Completion	6	10-2
Similarities	1-W	6-6	(Coding)	(4)	11-2
Arithmetic	4	9-2	Picture Arrangement	3	7-6
Vocabulary	1-W	6-2	Block Design	5	10-6
Comprehension	1	< 6-2	Object Assembly	7	11-6
(Digit Span)	(6)	8-10	*Symbol Search	3	9-2

* Symbol Search was used in IQ computations

Mean of 12 subtests = 4; median age equivalent = 9-0

Supplementary Subtests	Percentile	Age Equiv.
Differential Ability Scales (DAS)		
Recall of Objects (immediate)	8th	9-9
Recall of Designs	12th	10-3
Sequential and Quantitative Reasoning	< 1st	6-7
Woodcock-Johnson Psycho-Educational Battery (WJ-R) Tests of Cognitive Ability		
Oral Vocabulary	< 1st	6-6
Verbal Analogies	< 1st	5-0
Stanford-Binet—Fourth Edition (Binet-4)		
Memory for Sentences	4th	8-5
Kaufman Assessment Battery for Children (K-ABC)		
Riddles (percentile based on norms for age 12½)	< 1st	5-9

Referral and Background Information

Mr. and Mrs. L. requested the evaluation of 16½-year-old Jennie at this time because of their concern over the most appropriate educational placement for their daughter. She currently attends a private program for educable mentally retarded adolescents, and Mr. and Mrs. L. wonder if a more academically oriented facility (like a regular high school) would serve Jennie's needs better. Her very long history of psychological, neurological, educational, and medical examinations are all duly recorded and are available to the various institutions involved with Jennie. She has repeatedly been diagnosed as autistic and has had special services of one type or another since early childhood. One year ago, she returned from 7 years at a well-known residential treatment center specializing in autism. She currently lives at home with both parents and an older brother, Chuck, age 21. Her 28-year-old sister, Veronica, returns home on weekends; there is friction noted between both Veronica and Jennie, and between Veronica and Mrs. L, Jennie is in good physical health.

Previous test scores of note (all within the past year) include Kaufman Brief Intelligence Test (K-BIT) Composite standard score of 53 (Vocabulary = 54, Matrices = 59), PPVT-R (Form L) standard score of 45 (age equivalent = 6-10), and PIAT-R achievement scores all hovering at the first-grade level. Based on an administration of the AAMD Adaptive Behavior Scale to Jennie's teacher, Jennie was noted to have the following weaknesses: rebellious behavior, stereotyped behavior and odd mannerisms, unacceptable vocal habits, unacceptable or eccentric habits, and hyperactive tendencies. Strengths on the AAMD Scale were listed as physical development, language development, numbers and time, domestic and vocational activity, responsibility, and socialization skills. These adaptive behaviors are based on 19–29-year-old retarded institutionalized subjects as a reference group.

Jennie's mother reports that she spends at least two hours each day tutoring Jennie, and that Jennie displays some age-appropriate behaviors regarding kitchen chores and self-help skills. Administrators at the residential treatment center continually emphasized the notion that Jennie could be totally normal, cognitively and behaviorally, if the family followed the center's detailed treatment guidelines. Despite little change in Jennie after 7 years at the center and the family's ultimate decision to take Jennie out of the facility, the parents (especially Mr. L.) still cling to the hope that someday Jennie will be completely normal. This issue seems at the root of the family conflicts.

Appearance and Behavioral Characteristics

Jennie appeared older than her 16½ years, with a matronly figure characterized by a full bosom and broad hips. The blouse that she wore at the first session was snug and gaped open at each button. Whereas she was dressed up for each testing session in a style fitting a young woman (medium-high heels, skirt), she walked with her feet awkwardly apart, one step at a time, and closed her eyes as she felt her way down the corridor to the examiner's office. She carried a small black purse, but it seemed more like a little girl's accessory or toy than something of practical use. Jennie's straight black hair was chin length, framing a face whose blank affect took away from otherwise pleasant features.

Jennie was seen during three separate sessions. The first one was to establish initial rapport and to structure the sessions to follow in such a way as to facilitate an anxiety-free setting for the standardized tests administered. Jennie was quite agitated on this first meeting as she sat in the examiner's office with her mother present. She exhibited many socially inappropriate behaviors, such as lying face down on the cement hall floor when she wanted to rest and sitting with her skirt up. Conversation initiated by the examiner was rejected with loud screams and repeated ritualistic phrases. This negative and oppositional attitude became especially strong when Jennie was requested to answer a question or perform any simple task (e.g., drawing a circle during an unstructured rapport-making activity). Nevertheless, she was able to function despite this resistance when tasks were very subtly introduced. When Jennie genuinely did not know an answer, she tended to whisper "don't know" if she was in a cooperative mood (as opposed to screaming "No way!" when agitated). Frequently she rejected tasks because they frustrated her. Jennie stared off into space and lost her attention intermittently.

The next two testing sessions (each limited to about 45 minutes, Jennie's tolerance level) presented a much calmer, relaxed Jennie. She appeared far more appropriate, and worked hard with good concentration. She closed her eyes when walking (as before), but she attended well visually to most of the tasks presented to her. Jennie often talked to herself as if she were an observer (e.g., "No cheating," "Good girl," "Jennie, no!"). Her articulation is excellent, but her receptive vocabulary appears no better than her expressive abilities. When she was asked for much verbal expression, she became more anxious and shouted, "Talk to Mama!" She was unable to string together more than two or three words in coherent fashion.

There were many signs of poor impulse control, yet Jennie often said, "I'm sorry Mama" in a way that appears to indicate some level of awareness of inappropriate behavior. Jennie occasionally left her purse behind when she moved from room to room for various reasons.

Overall, Jennie was able to cooperate on the standardized evaluation procedures and exhibited true desire to perform well on many of the tasks presented. She worked especially hard when solving cut-up puzzles, which she enjoyed very much. Some ritualistic behaviors were observed; for example, after arranging pictures to tell a story, Jennie needed to stroke each card with her finger, in reverse sequence, before she could proceed with the next item. These behaviors did not impair her response production, however. To be as certain as possible that Jennie performed at an optimal on the WISC-III during session two, three subtests were readministered by the examiner at session three; she performed virtually identically on all three subtests. Mrs. L. was present for all testing sessions, remaining quiet and noncommittal at all times. On occasion, when the examiner was not certain if Jennie was refusing to answer or if she truly did not know the answer, Mrs. L. was requested to try to elicit a response from Jennie.

Based on all behaviors observed, this examiner believes the test results are valid and wholly representative of Jennie's current state of functioning.

Tests Administered

Wechsler Intelligence scale for Children—Third Edition (WISC-III)

Selected subtests from the Woodcock-Johnson Psycho-Educational Battery (WJ-R) Tests of Cognitive Ability, Differential Ability Scales (DAS), Stanford-Binet—Fourth Edition (Binet-4) and Kaufman Assessment Battery for Children (K-ABC)

Test Results and Interpretation

On the WISC-III Jennie earned a Verbal IQ of 55, a Performance IQ of 69, and a Full Scale IQ of 58. These IQs classify her ability in the Intellectually Deficient category, consistent with previous assessments of her ability and adaptive behavior. Her Performance IQ is significantly higher than her Verbal IQ, although a clearer picture of her better skill on tests of nonverbal thinking and visual-motor coordination than verbal comprehension and expression is provided by her Perceptual Organization (PO) and Verbal Comprehension (VC) Factor Indexes of 73 and 54 respectively. She surpassed 4% of adolescents her age on the PO factor, but scored higher than only 1 out of 1,000 on the VC factor. The 19-point discrepancy in favor of her non-verbal abilities is unusually large, occurring in the extreme 15% of the normal population.

Within the Verbal Scale, Jennie scored significantly higher on tests of short-term and long-term memory than on tests of reasoning and conceptual ability. That is to say, she performed at 9-year level on tasks of oral arithmetic, digit repetition, and knowledge of facts, but scored at about a 6–6½-year level on tests requiring her to define words, relate pairs of verbal concepts, and answer socially relevant questions. Her weakness in social maturity, so evident in her behaviors and the previous report of her adaptive functioning, was also observed on a nonverbal test that involves understanding of social interactions. She performed at a 7½ year level on that subtest, which required the rearrangement of pictures to tell a story; that level of functioning is about 2 to 4 years lower than her age level on the other nonverbal subtests. Her relative strength in immediate memory was found to be consistent regardless of the stimuli to recall, based on the administration of three supplementary subtests: The 9th percentile that she achieved on the WISC-III Digit Span subtest was consistent with her scores on the DAS Recall of Objects and Recall of Designs subtests (8th and 12th percentiles, respectively) and on the Binet-4 Memory for Sentences subtest (4th percentile).

The verbal reasoning tasks on which Jennie performed so poorly involve considerable verbal expression as well as conceptualization. Her expressive problems were obvious, as she had difficulty combining more than two words at a time either in spontaneous conversation or in response to verbal test items. To determine whether her conceptual ability is as weak as her expressive ability, three subtests were administered that tap verbal problem solving with minimal (one-word) responses: WJ-R Oral Vocabulary (giving antonyms and synonyms) and Verbal Analogies, and K-ABC Riddles. The latter task is normed only through age 12½, but it was suitable for Jennie's ability level, which averages out to age 9. Jennie performed at the 5–6½-year level on all three tests of verbal reasoning and conceptualization, which is consistent with her performance on the three WISC-III subtests and also with the PPVT-R age equivalent of 6-10 that she achieved about 9 months ago. Thus, she is weak in her verbal problem-solving skills as well as in her verbal expressive abilities.

Jennie's best performance on the WISC-III was on three tests of spatial ability (7th percentile), indicating a Borderline to Low Average ability level in the nonverbal tasks of assembling cut-up puzzles, copying abstract designs with blocks, and finding the missing part of incomplete pictures. Her spatial reasoning and ability to process information simultaneously in integrated fashion, however, does not extend to nonverbal problem solving in general. As noted, she performed poorly on the WISC-III picture-arranging subtest, and scored in the Intellectually Deficient range (standard score = 59, well below the 1st percentile) on the K-BIT Matrices subtest, administered 3 months ago. During the present evaluation, she was given the DAS Sequential and Quantitative Reasoning subtest (included on the DAS Nonverbal Reasoning Scale). Her *T* score of 20 (1st percentile) is well below the mean of 50, and indicates that she was not able to apply nonverbal reasoning to relationships involving numbers.

Her cognitive strengths are in memory and visual-spatial ability, specifically in visual perceptual functioning and seeing spatial relationships when concrete materials are provided. Her weaknesses are in verbal conceptualization and expression, social intelligence, and abstract reasoning ability. Jennie's weaknesses reflect deficiencies in early language development, poor verbal comprehension and expression, and an apparent inability to apply verbal mediational strategies to solve nonverbal problems. Her pattern of abilities is quite consistent with the patterns observed on the WISC-R for children diagnosed with autism, and seems to categorize groups of autistic children who are high functioning as well as those who, like Jennie, have concomitant mental retardation.

It is apparent that Jennie, with distinctly defined autistic behaviors, is functioning at a mild-to-moderate mentally deficient level (based on present and previous cognitive and adaptive behavior evaluations), and is multiply handicapped. The present findings confirm Jennie's lengthy history of cognitive and behavioral difficulties. Her spatial strengths pertain to the holistic, gestaltlike functioning associated with the right cerebral hemisphere and her verbal and analytic weaknesses are associated with left hemispheric functioning.

Summary and Recommendations

Jennie, age 16½ years, is functioning academically and intellectually in a manner expected of a young child. Her WISC-III IQs categorize her mental ability as Intellectually Deficient, although she scored substantially higher on nonverbal than verbal tasks. Overall, she performed as well as the average child of about 9 years, although her verbal and reasoning abilities are at about a 6-year level. Her social skills are inconsistently developed; she can reportedly perform certain kitchen chores and demonstrate other age-appropriate adaptive behaviors at the same time that she reveals great deficiencies in her social and personal behaviors. Jennie has not progressed academically beyond first- to second-grade skills, and these have been drilled in her at home with her mother's frequent tutoring. Brief observation of Jennie's reading abilities indicates that she has beginning knowledge of phonics and depends mostly on memorized sight vocabulary with pictures necessary to reinforce her skills. However, given her level of mental functioning in verbal and problem-solving tasks, her academic performance is commensurate with her measured abilities.

Jennie is both moderately to mildly mentally retarded and autistic. As she grows older, the discrepancy between her actual skills and those expected for a young woman her age will continually widen. In this manner, she will appear to become more and more "different" from other adults as expectations for independent living and job acquisition become prerequisites for acceptance into the normal community. It is highly unlikely that Jennie will change dramatically in her mental functioning as the years go by. She is capable, however, of learning specific skills under a specific set of circumstances. She appears somewhat receptive to learning and academic work, despite the interference of low frustration tolerance and a short attention span. Jennie has cognitive strengths in her memory and spatial abilities, and she may learn best if these assets are capitalized on when teaching her academic skills in reading, arithmetic, and spelling. Suggested strategies for teaching and remediation that focus on a child's simultaneous processing abilities (akin to spatial), sequential processing abilities (akin to memory), and a blending of the two have been xeroxed from the *K-ABC Interpretive Manual* and mailed to Jennie's parents and teacher. Jennie's academic progress using these new approaches should be monitored to determine whether they work better than previous methods; if they do not, then alternative teaching strategies should be explored as part of an ongoing process to identify the best approaches for Jennie.

Another important asset that Jennie has is a devoted and supportive family. Therefore, the following recommendations are made at this time:

1. Research has indicated that exceptional people benefit from contact with less handicapped peers, who serve as models. Since Jennie does possess certain socialization skills, it is likely that she will do better having opportunities to see and interact with more age-appropriate young adults. An article has been mailed to Mr. and Mrs. L. that reports a program that employed normal children as peer-tutors for autistic children with success. Whereas Jennie is a young adult, not a child, it is definitely advisable for her to gain social and personal skills by interaction with more normal agemates. She does qualify for the EMH program at the local high school, although contact with that program indicates that no other autistic children are presently enrolled. It is recommended that Jennie should attend that program on a trial basis to assess whether her peculiar behaviors will be too disturbing to others in the special class. It is also suggested that Mr. and Mrs. L. seek out an after-school community program for the mentally retarded, as well as attempt to provide Jennie with the opportunity to be integrated with more normal age-appropriate peers whenever possible.

2. To make the fullest use of all Jennie's potential intellectual skills, the simultaneous and sequential approaches to learning new material should be attempted, as suggested previously. In addition, the Feuerstein Instrumental Enrichment Program should be started to help facilitate maximum performance in both academic and life situations. Two sources of information have been mailed to Mr. and Mrs. L., including a description of this program designed for retarded adolescents and adults with the ability to be taught cognitive skills. Feuerstein developed a structured tutoring system to help students shift from the role of passive recipient and reproducer of

information to the role of active generator of new information. This transition will help Jennie function at her optimal level. An experienced teacher can be employed to conduct these training sessions (3 to 5 hours weekly, at spaced intervals, is the desired framework). References within the articles provide the names of local universities that teach and research this approach. If no trained professionals are available, the text on which this program is based can be self-trained; any interested adult could assume this role, as no other formal academic prerequisites are essential beyond training in Feuerstein's text and program materials.

3. Mr. and Mrs. L. are to be deeply encouraged to resist promises of "cures" or obtaining "normal functioning" for Jennie if certain procedures are followed, exercises performed, diets ingested, or any other developments pursued in the long tradition of nonvalidated, unresearched methods that prey on people's hopes. It is this examiner's fullest professional belief that Jennie has a form of organic brain damage, and whatever advances she may achieve will not translate to normal behavioral or cognitive functioning. In light of the difficulties the L.'s have endured with Jennie, and now especially as new sources of family friction may be developing between Jennie and her sister Veronica, it is extremely important for family counseling to take place on a regular basis. For one thing, Mrs. L. needs to be guided to release the intense guilt and defensiveness she has built up over the years. Both Mr. and Mrs. L. have not received adequate feedback with explanation about Jennie's functioning despite the many evaluations they have undergone. Now more than ever, they need to accept Jennie's mentally retarded level of functioning as well as her interpersonal and social difficulties concerning her assimilation into normal society. Helping the L. family members to each assume a less "Jennie dominant" lifestyle will be important for a more gratifying future for all through counseling and other supportive services.

4. Plans need to be made for Jennie's future as an adult. There are independent-living group homes available for autistic adults (one is opening in the immediate area next year), and complete information may be gotten by speaking to Dr. M. (whose telephone number was communicated to the L.'s). She is an experienced clinician who has completed her doctorate in the area of autism. She is fully aware of conditions at the well-known treatment center Jennie attended and should be considered a valuable local resource person.

5. The L.'s might find joining the Council for Exceptional Children (CEC) another source of information and support. The International Autism Hotline may answer more questions (an edition of CEC's newspaper with relevant information has been mailed to Mr. and Mrs. L.).

Examiner:
Dr. Nadeen L. Kaufman

CHAPTER 5

The "Validity" Factors: Freedom from Distractibility and Processing Speed

The third and fourth factors are small, composed of just two subtests apiece. The Freedom from Distractibility (FD) factor is controversial, the occasional subject of philosophical debates about its existence and its meaning. And neither factor fits into Wechsler's tidy two-pronged approach to the measurement of intelligence.

Yet these two factors are important. The introduction of the fourth factor in the WISC-III is the most critical innovation in a Wechsler scale since the mid-1940s when Dr. Wechsler decided that he ought to have a test just for children. What's so valuable about the four-factor approach? One aspect of the vital role played by Factors 3 and 4 has already been documented in Chapter 2: They permit systematic evaluation of a child's verbal and nonverbal abilities by allowing the examiner to subdivide each scale into two meaningful components. With the WISC-R, examiners had to interpret the two global IQ scales with awareness of the impurities inherent in each construct, but without a clear-cut rationale for reorganizing the verbal and nonverbal profiles. The four factors provide a psychometric rationale for test interpretation and offer a simple solution to a complex task.

But that is not even the key perk of the addition of Symbol Search to the WISC-III. The main plus is the clinical flavor of the subtests that compose Factors 3 and 4.

As the name of Factor 3 implies, and as research has shown, performance on the subtests that define the distractibility factor is greatly facilitated by attention and concentration, whereas it is impaired by distractibility and anxiety (Beck & Spruill, 1987; Lufi & Cohen, 1985; Lutey, 1977; Wielkiewicz, 1990), and is related to motivational problems in school (Holcomb, Hardesty, Adams, & Ponder, 1987) and to somatic complaints (Dollinger, Goh, & Cody, 1984). And the two highly speeded subtests that compose Factor 4 seem to be just as related to clinical, personality, behavioral, and neurological variables.

If the fourth factor were given a name to parallel Factor 3, it would have been called Freedom from Bad Attitude. Because if a child or adolescent comes into a testing session with minimal motivation to perform well and put out optimal effort, which tasks are likely to be most affected by a negative attitude? The ones that ask you to go at breakneck speed to get high scores. Sure, speed is awfully important for Object Assembly, and bonus points rear their ugly little heads on Block Design and Picture Arrangement as well. But at least puzzles, blocks, and cartoonlike photos have some intrinsic interest value and may present a mild motivational challenge to a passive aggressive child or one who would rather be at the dentist than with you.

With Coding and Symbol Search, there's no saving grace. Copying symbols is about as interesting in standing on a long movie line, and scanning symbols is almost as mindless. If a child comes in with a bad attitude and you can't make a dent during the evaluation, that child is likely to walk out with a low Processing Speed (PS) Index. And that's all right because it serves as a validity scale.

THE FD AND PS FACTORS AS VALIDITY SCALES

Indeed, both two-subtest factors may be thought of as WISC-III validity scales. Examiners sometimes complete a psychological evaluation of a child and are convinced that the obtained scores are underestimates of the child's elusive "true" intellectual functioning. But they have no specific proof of that belief, and their clinical observations of the child's behavior are sketchy and inconclusive. That's when the child's Indexes on the FD and PS factors come in handy. If a child is distractible and inattentive or bored and unmotivated, then it's extremely unlikely that the child will earn very high scores on any of the four subtests that compose Factors 3 and 4. If the FD Index is significantly higher than the Verbal Comprehension (VC) Index, then the likelihood is that the VC Index reflects a fairly accurate depiction of the child's verbal intelligence. Similarly, a significantly higher PS than Perceptual Organization (PO) Index indicates that the PO Index is probably a valid reflection of the child's nonverbal problem-solving ability. If the child was truly having difficulty concentrating during the evaluation or seemed to be apathetic, it is extremely unlikely that he or she would have performed best on the very tasks that are so vulnerable to these aspects of behavior.

If children score about equally well on VC and FD (and on PO and PS), the conclusion is similar but less emphatic. The odds are that attentional problems would have depressed scores to a greater extent on the FD and PS subtests than on the WISC-III tasks that are generally more resilient to such behaviors. The fact that deficits on FD and PS were not observed limits an examiner's justification for declaring the IQs clear-cut underestimates of the child's true ability—unless behavioral support for that contention is apparent and easily documentable.

If the examiner detects attentional or motivational problems during the administration of several of the six Verbal subtests, and the child scores significantly lower on FD than VC, then the argument for declaring the child's IQs and Scale Indexes as probable underestimates of verbal intelligence is well supported. If scores on tests known to be greatly influenced by attentional and motivational factors are relatively low for a child who displayed pertinent validity-threatening behaviors, then that deficit is conceivably a function of those negative behaviors. And if the behaviors were noted during VC subtests as well, then the validity of the whole Verbal Scale is suspect. The VC Index is undoubtedly a better indicator than V-IQ of the child's verbal ability, but both scores are suspect. The same logic applies to the Performance Scale. If the examiner detects attentional or motivational problems during the administration of several of the six Performance subtests, and the child scores significantly lower on PS than PO, then the invalidity of all nonverbal estimates of mental functioning must be strongly considered.

Incidentally, the Symbol Search and Digit Span scaled scores are especially important in any subjective evaluation of WISC-III validity because they are the 11th and 12th subtests administered, and are the most likely victims of attentional-motivational variables; even willing participants in the assessment process may be tired or bored after 90 or so minutes of scrutiny. Nonetheless, the *Indexes* should be featured in any analysis of test validity. The reliability of the FD and PS Indexes (average values of .87 and .85, respectively) makes their interpretation far more meaningful than inferences drawn from the four separate subtests that compose these factors, three of which have average reliability coefficients in the .70s.

No hard-and-fast rules can be applied for assessing the validity of test scores obtained under standard conditions. Children can obtain low scores on any or all of the Factor 3 and 4 subtests for a variety of cognitive reasons, and these must always be weighed carefully before inferring behavioral or personality-based causation. But the validity component of the two small factors should be internalized by examiners because of its enormous clinical utility. When interpreted in the context of observed behaviors, indexes on FD and PS serve an important validity function: As indicated, they may suggest that the obtained profile of scores is valid, despite apparently poor attention and motivation, or they may suggest that the entire set of WISC-III scores is not to be trusted.

THE WISC-R DISTRACTIBILITY TRIAD

The Arithmetic-Digit Span-Coding triad that formed the WISC-R FD factor was subjected to many research investigations and has been assigned diverse interpretations such as attention-concentration, freedom from disruptive anxiety or distractibility, sequencing ability or sequential processing, memory, number ability, automatic processing, and executive processing or planning ability (Kaufman, 1979b; Wielkiewicz, 1990). I labeled the third factor Freedom from Distractibility (Kaufman, 1975) for historical reasons involving factor analyses of the Wechsler-Bellevue, WAIS, and 1949 WISC

(Cohen, 1952, 1957, 1959) because of research (Wender, 1971, pp. 88–93) showing that drug therapy with minimally brain-impaired children typically resulted in decreased distractibility coupled with a corresponding increase in their scores on memory and arithmetic tests, and because in the early to mid-1970s I was a practicing and devout coward. Jacob Cohen and Irla Lee Zimmerman called the factor by the mouthful label of Freedom from Distractibility, and I lacked the courage to split with tradition. In truth, that label should have been trashed years ago. I cringe whenever I read "Kaufman's Freedom from Distractibility factor." It's not mine, and I don't want it.

Sure, distractible children earn low scores on the triad, as I've just discussed in the previous section on the use of the FD and PS factors as validity scales. But that doesn't mean that distractibility or any behavioral trait is the primary explanation of the dimension. It is easy to see how children may score very poorly on the three WISC-R subtests constituting the third factor because of distractible behavior, but it is more difficult to visualize children scoring very well on the three subtests merely or primarily because of close attention to the tasks. Wechsler's scales are cognitive tests, and the great likelihood is that any factor that consistently emerges for school-age children and adults from various ethnic backgrounds and diagnoses (Kaufman, 1990a, Chapter 8; Wechsler, 1991, pp. 181–182; Wielkiewicz, 1990) is best assigned a cognitive name. That conclusion is punctuated by the fact that no distractibility factor has been found in factor analyses of the WPPSI or WPPSI-R (Stone, Gridley, & Gyurke, 1991; Wechsler, 1989, Chapter 6). Distractibility (or perhaps impulsivity) is the middle name of many preschool children, who represent the biggest administrative challenge to any examiner. If a third factor fails to emerge for that age group, how can anyone truly believe it's mainly a behavioral dimension? Further, the cognitive complexity of the WISC-R FD factor was supported by research analyses with normal fifth graders involving a variety of cognitive and behavioral measures (Stewart & Moely, 1983). The Psychological Corporation should have taken a risk and called Factor 3 by a proper cognitive name.

Regardless of the FD triad's interpretation and whether it is best classified within the behavioral or cognitive domain, a multiplicity of investigations with the WISC-R indicated that clinical group after clinical group earned relatively low scores on the FD factor. Results from the literature are summarized in the following partial list of samples of children with depressed scores on the FD triad; documentation is illustrative, not exhaustive:

- Reading- and learning-disabled children (Joschko & Rourke, 1985; Kaufman, Harrison, & Ittenbach, 1990; Nichols, Inglis, Lawson, & MacKay, 1988).
- Children with leukemia who have received cranial irradiation therapy (Cousens, Ungerer, Crawford, & Stevens, 1991; Said, Waters, Cousens, & Stevens, 1989).
- Children with Attention-Deficit Hyperactivity Disorder (Lufi, Cohen, & Parish-Plass, 1990; Sutter, Bishop, & Battin, 1987).

- Children referred for school learning problems (Grossman & Galvin, 1989).
- Children with unilateral lesions in *either* the left or right hemisphere (Aram & Ekelman, 1986).
- Children with emotional problems categorized *either* as internalizers (withdrawn, anxious) or externalizers (impulsive, distractible) (Matson & Fischer, 1991).
- Children with epilepsy, both with and without mental retardation (Forceville, Dekker, Aldenkamp, Alpherts, & Schelvis, 1992).
- Heterogeneous clinical samples (Wielkiewicz & Daood, 1993).
- Psychiatric patients (Greenblatt, Mattis, & Trad, 1991; Hodges, Horwitz, Kline, & Brandt, 1982).
- Nonretarded children with autism (Allen, Lincoln, & Kaufman, 1991; Freeman, Lucas, Forness, & Ritvo, 1985).
- Children with developmental receptive language disorder (Allen et al., 1991).
- Children with schizophrenia (Asarnow, Tanguay, Bott, & Freeman, 1987).
- Children with conduct disorders (Paget, 1982).
- Children with Duchenne muscular dystrophy (Anderson, Routh, & Ionasescu, 1988).
- And—believe it or not—normal children, especially girls, living in the Western part of the United States (Silver & Clampit, 1988)!

Researchers have criticized the WISC-R for its poor differential diagnostic ability, for example for the inability of the FD factor, with or without the Information subtest, to discriminate effectively between learning-disabled and other exceptional children (Barkley, DuPaul, & McMurray, 1991; Berk, 1983; Kavale & Forness, 1984; McDermott, Fantuzzo, & Glutting, 1990). More important than differential diagnosis, it seems to me, are the questions of normal versus abnormal and the pinpointing of deficient cognitive processes; the WISC-R FD factor has been quite effective at identifying exceptional groups from normal ones, and in suggesting the possible attentional, sequential, memory, or numerical problems that have contributed to the abnormality. The FD subtests are like a land mine that explodes on a diversity of abnormal populations but leaves most normal samples unscathed. Group data, of course, do not translate to each individual in that group, and low FD scores do not at all characterize all members of a sample or LD subtype (Joschko & Rourke, 1985), no matter how homogeneously that sample is defined. Variability in test performance is axiomatic, and the need to treat each referral as a separate individual is the crux of intelligent testing. But the fact that so many samples with medical, educational, and psychiatric-behavioral problems have difficulty with Arithmetic, Digit Span, and Coding has made the FD factor a small but potent bit of diagnostic information to consider when evaluating the presence of an abnormal condition in any child referred for evaluation.

With the WISC-III, Symbol Search is added to that triad, and the early returns indicate that the new tetrad is a potent land mine for clinicians to continue to exploit when searching the WISC-III subtest profile, as well as other pertinent information, observations, and data, for diagnostic clues. The results won't identify the type of exceptionality, but they are likely to be valuable for making a presence-absence decision and helping to pinpoint specific areas of deficiency.

MEAN WISC-III FACTOR INDEXES FOR EXCEPTIONAL SAMPLES

Table 5.1 presents mean Factor Indexes on the four WISC-III factors for a variety of samples. The groups are limited to the samples reported in the WISC-III manual and the special monograph devoted to the WISC-III (Bracken & McCallum, 1993a). Many exceptionalities (LD) are included, ranging from gifted and mentally retarded to learning disabled and language disordered; a normal sample of 353 children from the test-retest study is included for comparison purposes. The sample sizes for the exceptional groups are small (25 to 65), but the pattern is clear: Most groups scored relatively low on one or both of the small FD and PS Factor Indexes. Many exceptional samples have disorders that involve impaired school learning or language development, either directly or indirectly, which hinders performance on the VC factor. Consequently, the VC Index does not reflect the intellectual capabilities of most of these samples. Instead, the PO Index serves as the best estimate of cognitive potential for most of the exceptional groups in Table 5.1 and was therefore used as the point of comparison for evaluating depressions on the FD and PS indexes. The rightmost column of Table 5.1 shows the difference for each sample between its mean PO Index and the average of its FD and PS indexes.

Mentally retarded children performed 7 points higher on the small WISC-III factors, but every other sample scored at least 5 points (one-third of a standard deviation) lower on the FD-PS combination than on the PO Index. Several groups showed discrepancies of 10 or more points, namely samples of children with reading and learning disorders, Attention-Deficit Hyperactivity Disorder (ADHD), and hearing impairment. And each of the samples with school learning problems or ADHD earned remarkably similar Indexes on the FD and PS factors—within 2 points of each other—suggesting possible deficiencies in the abilities measured by *both* of these factors. The relatively low VC Indexes for these groups conceivably reflect the direct impact of the children's learning difficulties, just as the low mean VC Indexes for the language-impaired and hearing-impaired samples denotes their language difficulties. But low scores on the FD Index, PS Index,

TABLE 5.1.   Mean Factor Indexes for Various Samples

Nature of Sample	N	VC	PO	FD	PS	PO Minus FD-PS
Normal (6–15 years)[a]	353	100.3	100.9	100.8	100.7	+0.1
Gifted (7–14 years)[b]	38	126.9	125.8	123.0	110.2	+9.2
Mentally Retarded (6–16 years)[b]	43	61.3	59.4	62.5	70.2	−7.0
Learning Disabled (6–14 years)[b]	65	93.8	100.5	87.1	89.1	+12.4
Reading Disordered (9–14 years)[b]	34	100.4	104.7	93.2	95.4	+10.4
Dyslexic (9–13 years)[c]	26	101.2	104.9	94.6	94.7	+10.3
Attention-Deficit Hyperactivity Disordered (ADHD) (7–16 years)[b]	68	98.8	105.0	93.4	92.0	+12.3
(8–11 years)[d]	45	97.0	105.1	93.0	92.6	+12.3
Hearing Impaired (11–16 years)[b]	30	80.9	106.0	87.1	101.4	+11.8
Severely Language Impaired (6–12 years)[e]	40	72.3	80.6	68.8	73.8	+9.3
(8–13 years)[f]	25	75.7	87.3	75.4	80.4	+9.4
Remedial (age not given)[g]	40	101.3	105.6	97.7	101.0	+6.2
Severely Emotionally Disturbed (11–16 years)[h]	29	79.3	86.1	82.0	80.2	+5.0

Note: PO Minus FD-PS equals the difference between the mean PO Index and the average of the FD and PS Indexes.

[a]Data are weighted means from the first testing of 353 children (ages 6–7, 10–11, and 14–15) included in the test-retest study of the WISC-III (Wechsler, 1991, Tables 5.3–5.5).

[b]Data are from WISC-III manual (Wechsler, 1991, pp. 210–216).

[c]Data are from Newby, Recht, Caldwell, and Schaefer (1993). Mean Indexes were computed by weighting the means provided for separate groups of phonological ($N = 19$) orthographic ($N = 7$) dyslexics.

[d]Data are from Schwean, Saklofske, Yackulic, and Quinn (1993).

[e]Data are from Phelps, Leguori, Nisewaner, and Parker (1993).

[f]Data are from Doll and Boren (1993). Mean Indexes were computed by entering the sum of pertinent subtest means into the Factor Index conversion tables in the manual.

[g]Data are from Hishinuma and Yamakawa (1993). Mean Indexes were computed by weighting the means provided for separate groups of high potential/remedial (e.g., gifted/learning disabled; $N = 9$) and remedial (e.g., learning disabled; $N = 31$) subsamples. Other subsamples (e.g., gifted) were excluded.

[h]Data are from Teeter and Smith (1993).

or both, are less enmeshed with the known referral problem and are more indicative of behavioral or process deficiencies. An exception to that generalization is the profile for hearing-impaired children, who displayed average Processing Speed and who undoubtedly scored low on the FD Index because of the component subtests' use of auditory stimuli.

Processing Speed (*not* the abilities measured by the FD factor) emerged as an area of relative strength for mentally retarded children (mean = 70) and of relative weakness for gifted children (mean = 110). The retarded sample scored about 60 on the other three Indexes, and the gifted sample scored in the mid-120s on VC, PO, and FD.

WHAT ABOUT THE ACID PROFILE?

The WISC-R literature was invaded by the ACID profile during the 1970s and 1980s when researchers began to notice substantially lower mean scaled scores for reading- and learning-disabled children on four WISC-R subtests: *A*rithmetic, *C*oding, *I*nformation, and *D*igit Span. The name ACID began to appear in the titles of articles (e.g., Greenblatt et al., 1991) and mean standard scores on the ACID quartet for children with school learning problems or ADHD even sneaked into a table in no less an authoritative source than the WISC-III manual (Wechsler, 1991, Table 6.21). Three-fourths of the ACID profile is the WISC-R distractibility triad, and the remaining fourth is a test of general factual knowledge that has all the earmarks of being a measure of school achievement. Like the WISC-R FD factor, the ACID profile flunked the differential diagnosis test (Kavale & Forness, 1984), indicating that it reflected pitfalls for a series of exceptional populations, not just those with diagnosed learning disabilities. But the ACID profile did represent a variant of the WISC-R FD snare that was likely to entrap a slew of abnormal samples (Kaufman et al., 1990).

Does the ACID profile work for the WISC-III? In a statistical sense, the answer is yes. Children with school problems or ADHD earned standard scores on the ACID grouping that were about 1 to 3 points lower than their Indexes on either FD or PS (Wechsler, 1991, Table 6.21). And the ACID profile on the WISC-III was found to be significantly more common in learning-disabled and ADHD children than in the normative population (Prifitera & Dersh, 1993). Only 1% of the standardization sample earned their lowest four scaled scores on the ACID subtests compared with 5% of LD and 12% of ADHD children. Similarly, and more dramatically, three of the four ACID subtests were the very lowest for 6% of normal children compared with 21% of LD and 29% of ADHD children.

In a practical sense, however, I don't think the ACID profile will be of much use for WISC-III evaluations. Its apparent success in the aforementioned analyses is primarily because of the A-C-D subtests, not Information. Heterogeneous samples of reading- and learning-disabled children invariably earned low mean scaled scores on all four ACID subtests on the WISC-R (even if many individual LD children failed to display the complete profile or if the profile did not discriminate among exceptionalities). On the WISC-III, the 99 learning-disabled children studied by Prifitera and Dersh (1993)—a merger of the two samples with school-related problems included in Table 5.1—earned their lowest mean scores (7.9 to 8.5) on the four subtests that compose the FD and PS factors. Their mean of 9.5 on Information was similar to their means on other VC subtests (9.1 to 9.8) and was not a notable weakness for the group. Nor was Information a particular weakness for a group of 40 children described as remedial (Hishinuma & Yamakawa, 1993; see Table 5.1, note *g*), or for the sample of 65 ADHD children included in Table 5.1. The latter group earned its lowest four means (7.8 to 9.3) on the FD and PS subtests, and scored 9.8 on Information (VC means ranged from 9.5 to 10.6). Among LD and ADHD samples, only the group of 45 ADHD children tested by Schwean et al. (1993) included Information among its lowest four WISC-III scaled scores.

I don't know if the WISC-III results for the relatively small groups totaling about 250 children will generalize to other learning-disabled and ADHD groups or not, but there are some additional indications that the Information subtest behaved a bit differently on the WISC-R than it does on the WISC-III. The WISC-R factor analysis produced an FD factor that was really composed of the ACID profile, not the well-known FD triad. In that age-by-age analysis (Kaufman, 1975), Information had a median factor loading of .41, nearly identical to the .42 loading for Coding. However, Information's primary loading (.63) was on VC. For the sake of simplicity, I recommended that each WISC-R subtest be assigned to one and only one factor, but the truth is the WISC-R FD factor was an ACID factor. That's not so for the WISC-III. When Symbol Search is eliminated from consideration, the so-called FD factor includes median loadings above .40 only for Arithmetic and Digit Span; Coding and Block Design have median loadings in the mid-.30s, but Information loads a trivial .18 (Reynolds & Ford, in press).

Why might the Information subtest behave differently on the WISC-R and WISC-III? Perhaps more than other subtests, it is item-dependent. The switch in the specific facts that must be learned may impact greatly the test performance of learning-disabled children or the subtest's factor loading. Of the 30 WISC-R Information items, 9 are new or substantially modified (Wechsler, 1991, Table 2.1). One change in item content, for example, concerns items that demand a specific numerical answer. Two moderately difficult items of that type were dropped from the WISC-R Information subtest (pounds in a ton, height of average American man). Perhaps the so-called WISC-R distractibility factor was really a number ability dimension, and the elimination of those two items influenced the loading of the whole subtest. Perhaps the WISC-R ACID profile denoted a number achievement problem for some learning-disabled samples. Or maybe the change in research findings has nothing to do with number ability. The fact that the

WISC-III Information subtest has 30% new or highly modified items still renders the modified content a possible culprit. A couple of WISC-R Information items that may have discriminated significantly between learning-disabled and normal children may have been inadvertently replaced by items that do not discriminate between these samples. I'm not talking about the pros or cons of such a modification; my point is that small, unknown changes in the item content of any test of acquired knowledge can turn that test from a weak area for learning-disabled children to just another test of verbal ability.

Alternately, as suggested to me by Ms. Jo Jenkins, a Mississippi school psychologist, the different results for WISC-R and WISC-III Information may pertain to the flip-flop of Information and Picture Completion in the administration sequence. Information is no longer the first subtest administered. Relatively low scores on WISC-R Information may have resulted from a warmup effect or a gradual establishment of rapport with the examiner that affects test performance of school-referred children more than normal children.

But let's suppose that the preliminary findings regarding Information are flukes, and that future LD and ADHD samples have full-blown ACID attacks. It still doesn't mean much. If the ACID grouping on the WISC-R was arguably the best interpretation of the third factor, that is no longer the case on the WISC-III, with or without Symbol Search. Table 5.1 suggests that diverse clinical samples of children earn relatively low Indexes on the FD and PS Indexes. When separate subtest scores are provided, the four subtests that constitute these two small WISC-III factors emerged as the four lowest for the sample of 99 children with reading and learning disabilities and the 65 children with ADHD (Prifitera & Dersh, 1993), and four of the six lowest for the sample of 45 children with ADHD (Schwean et al., 1993). The sample of 40 children described as remedial (Hishinuma & Yamakawa, 1993) earned its lowest scaled scores on Coding, Arithmetic, Digit Span, and Vocabulary.

The WISC-III provides standard scores on the FD and PS Indexes, and these scores may be entered and graphed on the front page of the record form. Computing standard scores, or summary scores of any kind, on the ACID profile has never been easy. Also, the FD and PS indexes correspond to validated constructs and have known (and good) psychometric properties. My suggestion to clinicians and researchers who have found value in the ACID profile is to abandon it for the WISC-III and to focus instead on the two small factors. In addition to the aforementioned advantages, the FD and PS Indexes are based on subtests that mostly measure process without contamination of content (Arithmetic is an exception). Information, in contrast, may often be measuring the outcome of a learning disability or of poor school achievement due to an emotional or behavior disorder. For many referred children, it is probably best thought of as a measure of school learning and not as a test of intelligence. In that regard, it is better to replace Information with Symbol Search, which is decidedly a measure of process and not product, when trying to understand the cognitive deficiencies of a child referred for evaluation. Standardized achievement tests that are developed from curriculum blueprints and assess academic skills systematically are far more effective at detecting school-related weaknesses than is a test of general factual knowledge that includes a haphazard array of items and topics.

So I'm advocating the replacement of the ACID profile with the SCAD profile (Symbol Search-Coding-Arithmetic-Digit Span). The sections that follow include some empirical hints and guidelines for interpreting the two indexes either separately or as a unit.

THE SCAD PROFILE

The SCAD profile requires a merger of the four subtests that compose the FD and PS factors. This merger was studied by Prifitera and Dersh (1993) who compared children's sum of scaled scores on the VC and PO subtests with their sum of scaled scores on Arithmetic + Digit Span + Coding + Symbol Search. They only investigated *positive* differences, ignoring children who scored higher on the four SCAD subtests than on either VC or PO. As I indicated previously, the VC Index is a shaky measure of the cognitive abilities of most exceptional samples because of their known academic and/or language deficiencies. Therefore, I have developed Table 5.2 from data provided by Prifitera and Dersh (1993, Table 6) which permits comparison of PO performance to SCAD performance.

Table 5.2 shows the percentages of normal and exceptional children who earned higher sums of scaled scores on the four PO subtests than on the four SCAD subtests. Prifitera and Dersh (1993) provided percentages of normal, learning-disabled, and ADHD children who scored different numbers of points higher on PO than SCAD. Their normal sample ($N = 2,158$) includes all standardization cases except those earning Full Scale IQs below 70 (since children scoring in the intellectually deficient range were excluded from the LD and ADHD samples). The data they presented for the separate LD and ADHD samples have been merged in Table 5.2 to increase the size of the exceptional sample; also, the cumulative distributions of percentages for the two groups appeared to be quite similar.

As explained in the note to the table, subtract the sum of the SCAD subtest scaled scores from the sum of the PO subtest scaled scores. These sums are readily obtained from the front of the WISC-III record form. The PO, FD, and PS sums appear in two places in the top half of the record form. Obtain the SCAD sum of scaled scores by adding together the FD and PS sums. If the PO sum exceeds the SCAD sum, then enter the value of the difference into the right-hand column of Table 5.2. Read across to determine the percentage of normal and LD/ADHD children who displayed that

TABLE 5.2.   Cumulative Percentages of Normal and
Exceptional Children (Learning Disabled and ADHD) Who
Scored Various Numbers of Points Higher on the Sum of the
Four PO Subtests Than on the Sum of the Four SCAD Subtests

Difference (PO Minus SCAD)	Normal ($N = 2,158$)	LD and ADHD ($N = 164$)
18	2	17
17	3	21
16	4	23
15	4	26
14	6	29
13	7	33
12	9	37
11	11	43
10	14	49
9	16	54
8	19	58
7	23	63
6	26	65
5	30	68
4	34	74
3	39	80
2	44	82
1	48	84

Note: To use this table, sum the four PO subtests and sum the four SCAD subtests (the tasks composing the FD and PS factors). Subtract the SCAD sum from the PO sum. If the difference is greater than zero, enter the left-hand column with the precise difference. Then read across that row to determine the percentage of normal children and the percentage of LD and ADHD children who have discrepancies that high or higher. Differences of 9 points are needed for significance at the .05 level, and differences of 12 points are needed at the .01 level.

Of the exceptional sample, 54% displayed significant differences at the .05 level (9 or more points) versus 16% of normal children. At the .01 level, the corresponding percentages are 37 and 9. Data are from Prifitera and Dersh (1993, Table 6).

difference or greater. Significant differences are as follows: 9 points ($p < .05$) and 12 points ($p < .01$). Entering Table 5.2 with 10 points, for example, indicates that about half of the exceptional sample (49%) had differences in favor of PO of 10 points or greater, compared with only 14% of normal children. Nearly 85% of the LD/ADHD children in the exceptional sample had higher PO than SCAD sums versus 48% of the standardization cases.

These differences won't diagnose the presence or absence of an exceptionality, and they certainly won't differentially diagnose learning-disabled children from other exceptional children. But groups of LD and ADHD children differ significantly from normal children in the magnitude of the discrepancy between PO and SCAD subtests (Prifitera & Dersh, 1993), and that research finding indicates that large PO/SCAD differences are more likely to occur for abnormal than normal samples. Less than 5% of normal

TABLE 5.3. Conversion of the Sum of Scaled Scores on Arithmetic, Digit Span, Coding, and Symbol Search to a Standard Score with Mean of 100 and Standard Deviation of 15 (SCAD Index)

Sum of Scaled Scores	SCAD Index	SCAD Percentile	Sum of Scaled Scores	SCAD Index	SCAD Percentile
69–76	150	> 99.9	39	99	47
68	149	> 99.9	38	97	42
67	147	99.9	37	95	37
66	145	99.9	36	93	32
65	144	99.8	35	91	27
64	142	99.7	34	90	25
63	140	99.6	33	88	21
62	138	99	32	86	18
61	137	99	31	84	14
60	135	99	30	83	13
59	133	99	29	81	10
58	131	98	28	79	8
57	130	98	27	77	6
56	128	97	26	76	5
55	126	96	25	74	4
54	124	95	24	72	3
53	123	94	23	70	2
52	121	92	22	69	2
51	119	90	21	67	1
50	117	87	20	65	1
49	116	86	19	63	1
48	114	82	18	62	1
47	112	79	17	60	0.5
46	110	75	16	58	0.3
45	109	73	15	56	0.2
44	107	68	14	55	0.1
43	105	63	13	53	0.1
42	103	58	12	51	< 0.1
41	102	55	11	50	< 0.1
40	100	50	4–10	Less than 50	< 0.1

children have discrepancies of at least 15 points compared to about 1 out of 4 (26%) of the LD/ADHD children. This difference, when interpreted in the context of other relevant information and test data, becomes an important piece of evidence for diagnosing a possible abnormality.

I have developed another table to permit examiners to compute a standard score (mean = 100, standard deviation = 15) to correspond to the sum of the four scaled scores that constitute the SCAD pattern. Table 5.3 converts sums of scaled scores on the SCAD subtests to a standard score and a percentile rank. It was developed by a formula based on the intercorrelations among the four subtests for the total sample (Wechsler, 1991, Table C.12), using a linear equating procedure (Tellegen & Briggs, 1967). The formula for the SCAD standard score equals 1.74 times the sum of the four SCAD scaled scores plus 30.4.

Table 5.3 is applicable for all children within the WISC-III age range. Enter with the SCAD sum, and read off the standard score, referred to as the SCAD Index, and the corresponding percentile rank. This Index has an average split-half reliability of .90 and an average test-retest reliability of .88, which I computed by entering the average coefficients for the FD and PS Indexes reported in the manual, along with the .41 correlation between the Indexes, into Tellegen and Briggs' (1967) pertinent formula. The SCAD Index has a standard error of measurement of about 4.7 points—the same as the PO Index. To determine the best estimates of 90% and 95% confidence intervals for the SCAD Index, enter Table A.6 in the WISC-III manual (the PO norms table) with the value of the SCAD Index (*not* sum of scaled scores) and read off the pertinent confidence interval.

Examiners are most likely to use Table 5.3 for children whose SCAD Indexes are low, but I've included the full range of Indexes from 50 to 150 in case examiners find other uses for the SCAD Index. Also, I have focused on comparisons between the PO and SCAD scores, as in Table 5.2, because the PO Index provides the best estimate of cognitive functioning for most children who are likely to be referred for evaluation. For some children, however, the VC Index is more appropriate; for example, children with moderate to severe visual-perceptual problems are not likely to demonstrate their intelligence validly on tasks such as Block Design and Picture Arrangement. Consult Prifitera and Dersh (1993, Table 5) for a table, analogous to Table 5.2, that compares a child's sum of scaled scores on the four VC subtests with the child's sum on the SCAD subtests. When comparing VC sum with SCAD sum, 8 and 11 points denote significance at the .05 and .01 levels, respectively. Among normal children, 22% have discrepancies of 8 or more points in favor of VC sum compared with 43% of the LD/ADHD sample.

When should examiners use Table 5.2 to compare the PO and SCAD sums of scaled scores and Table 5.3 to compute a SCAD Index? There are no clear-cut rules. Such comparisons might be made routinely for children referred for school-related problems or possible ADHD. The examiner's clinical perception is also a good cue. Any child who seems to evidence deficiencies in the processes measured by two or more SCAD subtests is a good candidate for the SCAD analysis. So is any child who scores significantly higher on VC than FD, or on PO than PS, in the seven-step method for WISC-III interpretation described in Chapter 3. See the case report, at the end of Chapter 6, for Tony G., an 11-year-old diagnosed with ADHD, for an application of Tables 5.2 and 5.3.

A word of caution, though. It is not a good idea to interpret the SCAD Index or sum of scaled scores if the child scored significantly differently on the FD and PS Indexes, regardless of direction. A difference of 16 points is required for significance at the .05 level (Wechsler, 1991, Table B.1), and a difference of 21 points is needed for $p < .01$. Significant differences will not be uncommon in view of the relatively low correlation between the FD and PS Indexes (they share only about 17% variance).

But when the child performs consistently poorly on the two Indexes, the result is important. The deficiency may be due to a single weak ability that is measured by both factors, to several weak abilities that are measured to different degrees by the four SCAD subtests, or to the effects of a pervasive behavior that affects both small factors such as low motivation or distractibility. The FD and PS factors measure short-term memory for auditory and visual stimuli, respectively. They both also demand good ability to manipulate numbers or abstract symbols and to encode information for further cognitive processing, and both are dependent on adequate auditory processing skills. The FD subtests require good auditory processing to interpret the stimuli for each item, whereas the PS subtests demand this ability to understand the spoken directions to each task.

Poor executive processing or planning ability may likewise affect performance on the SCAD subtests. Based on a factor analysis of WISC-R factor scores on VC, PO, and the FD triad along with various neuropsychological tests, Ownby and Matthews (1985) interpreted the factor on which FD loaded highest as an executive processing dimension. Stewart and Moely (1983) also provided evidence of the cognitive complexity of the FD triad. Wielkiewicz (1990) integrated all these findings with Kolligan and Sternberg's (1987) analysis of learning-disabled children's deficits from the perspective of Sternberg's triarchic theory.

Essentially, learning-disabled children may have deficiencies in the metacomponent (planning, monitoring, and evaluating) aspect of intelligent functioning, especially in a dysfunctional working memory that impairs problem solving—perhaps due to malfunctioning "peripheral systems that encode information from the environment into memory or decode the products of thinking into particular responses" (Lohman, 1989, p. 357). Working memory refers to a kind of middle ground between short-term and long-term memory. The information received (encoded) must be recoded and maintained in working memory long enough for the individual to recognize what type of problem must be solved and determine the best way to solve it; then the processes needed to solve the problem can be retrieved from long-term storage (Vernon & Jensen, 1984). Working memory has a small capacity and decays rapidly without rehearsal, yet effective problem solving depends on a certain amount of simultaneous retention and processing. Learning-disabled children with a dysfunctional working memory would be unable to coordinate the pertinent strategies after they encode the incoming stimuli. Problems with working memory are sometimes considered central to the diagnosis of dyslexia (Kerns & Decker, 1985; Spafford, 1989; Vargo, 1992), and many reading-disabled children seem to be deficient in the coding of phonological information into working memory (Byrne & Shea, 1979). All four SCAD subtests place heavy demands on the child's ability to encode information for subsequent mental processing.

Although Wielkiewicz (1990) was applying the Sternberg and Ownby-Matthews executive processing interpretation to the WISC-R distractibility triad, the "fit" is even better when Symbol Search joins the team. Even more so than the three WISC-R FD subtests, Symbol Search, which resembles tasks used in cognitive psychology research (Sternberg, 1993), is a measure of executive processing or planning ability. Symbol Search resembles the kinds of cognitive subtests that have defined planning factors in Naglieri and Das's (1988) research on the Luria-based PASS model, and that constitute the Planning scale in the Das-Naglieri Cognitive Assessment System (Das & Naglieri, in press). The PASS researchers, however, do not buy into these notions (Das, Naglieri, & Kirby, 1994); "we can only conclude that the interpretation of the WISC-R third factor as executive processing, which would be similar to the Planning component of the PASS model, is unsupported" (p. 123). Further, they do not interpret the WISC-III PS factor as a measure of planning ability, and believe that "speed of processing is not a unitary concept, and hence appears to be external to the PASS model, as will be processing speed scales from other IQ tests (Das et al., 1994, p. 117).

When the WISC-III FD and PS factors are evaluated separately, the FD dimension seems to be primarily a measure of Horn's SAR (Short-Term Acquisition and Retrieval), number ability, and sequential processing; PS appears to assess Horn's Gs or Broad Speediness, visual-motor coordination, and visual short-term memory. Research with children suffering from leukemia indicates that the cranial irradiation used in the medical treatment process has adverse effects on cognitive test performance, with specific deficits in visual processing speed, visual-motor integration, sequencing ability, and short-term memory (Cousens et al., 1990). Such deficits, apparently neurological in nature, would affect greatly a child's performance on both the FD and PS Indexes, and therefore produce a SCAD pattern due to a combination of deficits. Response speed and reaction time are especially known to be affected by neurological impairment to either hemisphere (Kaufman, 1990a, Chapter 11) and may be specifically related to lesions in the basal ganglia (Brouwers, Riccardi, Poplack, & Fedio, 1984; Price & Birdwell, 1978). Neurological and neuropsychological research has also identified great sensitivity to brain dysfunction for various deficits in visual-motor coordination (Cotman & McGaugh, 1980), sequencing ability (Gaddes, 1985), and short-term memory (Lezak, 1983; Reitan & Wolfson, 1992).

There are, therefore, some compelling reasons for the SCAD profile to be such a potent land mine for identifying children with neurological impairment or with exceptionalities that are believed to be associated with minimal brain dysfunction. The next sections deal separately with the two factors because for many children the FD and PS Indexes denote distinctly different abilities, one within the verbal domain and dependent on auditory memory and sequential processing, and the other within the nonverbal domain and dependent on visual memory and response speed. The first section concerns the FD factor, and the second section concerns the PS factor.

INTERPRETING THE FREEDOM FROM DISTRACTIBILITY FACTOR

Three topics are discussed in this section: *when* to interpret the FD factor, how to use clinical observations and clues from the WISC-III profile as aids to interpretation, and what additional measures should be administered to verify hypotheses regarding what ability a high or low FD Index reflects for a given child.

When to Interpret the FD Factor

The most sensible time to interpret the FD factor is when the following two conditions are met:

1. The child should have performed fairly consistently on Arithmetic and Digit Span. If the child's scaled scores are divergent, then a single Index that corresponds to the midpoint of these diverse abilities doesn't mean very much.
2. The child's FD Index should be at a different level, whether higher or lower, than other WISC-III scores. Thus the FD Index should correspond to a discrete, unitary ability or trait, and it should be a significant area of strength or weakness for the child.

Computing whether the FD Index is unitary is simple: Scaled scores on Arithmetic and Digit Span must differ by 4 points to be significant at the .05 level (Wechsler, 1991, Table B.4), and by 5 points to be significant at the .01 level. Examiners may choose either significance level, although 4 points is probably adequate. *Therefore, the FD Index is interpretable if its two component subtests have scaled scores that differ by less than 4 points.*

As part of Step 3 of the WISC-III Interpretive process (Chapter 3), examiners determine whether the VC and FD indexes differ significantly. If the answer is yes, then it is appropriate to try to interpret the relative strength or weakness on the FD factor. If the answer is no, then the examiner has other options. If the VC index is deemed a poor measure of the child's mental ability, for example, because of a learning disability or language disorder, then examiners should compare the FD Index with the PO index. For that comparison, 14 points is needed for significance at the .05 level (Wechsler, 1991, Table B.1); examiners who prefer the .01 level should use a difference of 18 points.

If neither the VC-FD nor the PO-FD comparison is significant, then the examiner should determine whether the two FD subtests emerge as a significant strength or weakness in Step 6 of the WISC-III interpretive process. As part of this process (see Chapter 3) the examiner selects which mean to use for comparison, either the mean of the 6 Verbal subtests or the mean of all 12 subtests. If either Arithmetic or Digit Span deviates significantly from the relevant mean, and the other scaled score is in the same direction (whether below or above the mean), then the Arithmetic-Digit Span combination denotes a relative strength or weakness for the child. In that case, the FD Index may be interpreted.

To interpret the FD Index, therefore, the two subtest scaled scores must be similar in magnitude, and there should be empirical evidence to indicate that the child performed relatively poorly or well on the two subtests that compose the FD factor.

Clinical Observations and the FD Factor

Once examiners have determined that it is sensible to interpret the FD factor, they still have the crucial task of deciding what the strength or weakness on the pair of subtests means. Does it reflect distractibility, anxiety, number facility, sequential processing, attention-concentration, auditory short-term memory, or another variable? Some examiners automatically interpret low scores on FD as evidence of distractibility by virtue of its unfortunate name, but such an interpretation is nonsensical for a child who attended closely to all tasks and concentrated on each item presented. Inferences about its meaning simply cannot be made without considering background information from referral sources, children's test-taking behaviors, the nature of their wrong responses to Arithmetic and Digit Span items, and their scores on other memory tests. In the case report of James C. in Chapter 7, for example, his low score on the FD Index is interpreted as poor auditory short-term memory based on observations of his good attention and concentration during the evaluation, his low scores on the WJ-R Short-Term Memory cluster, and referral information provided by his mother concerning his forgetting.

Distractibility and Anxiety

When children are obviously distracted during the testing session, as evidenced by inability to focus attention on the task at hand, overattentiveness to irrelevant stimuli in the environment, or loss of rapport following noises and distractions outside of the testing room, it is perfectly reasonable to infer that their relatively low score on the FD factor was due to distractibility. By the same token, a low FD Index may be attributed to anxiety if the examiner detects anxious behavior during the WISC-III examination, such as rigid posture, nervous mannerisms, overconcern with the stopwatch, pressing too hard on the pencil, or overreaction to failure. According to Lutey (1977, p. 222), the distractibility factor might easily be interpreted as "freedom from disruptive anxiety," the kind of anxiety that reflects a disturbed or uneasy *state*—perhaps specific to the testing situation—rather than the chronic anxiety associated with neuropsychiatric patients. Arithmetic and Digit Span, more than other Wechsler subtests including Coding, have consistently been found to be particularly related to measures of state anxiety.

Whenever a behavioral variable such as distractibility or anxiety is used as the explanation for poor performance on the FD factor, the examiner should keep two things firmly in mind. First, no suggestion should be made that the child is in any way deficient in his or her numerical problem-solving ability (Arithmetic) or short-term memory and sequential processing (Digit Span). Such deficiencies *may* exist, but cannot be inferred from the test administration since the low FD index is presumed to reflect the inhibiting effect of a behavioral variable rather than a cognitive deficiency. Second, the child's IQs and Indexes on the other factors may be underestimates of his or her current intellectual functioning; extreme distractibility or anxiety can easily have some impact on the child's score on any WISC-III subtest, not just the two associated with the FD factor.

Clear-cut observations of distractible or anxious test behavior force an examiner to be flexible when interpreting the FD factor. These behaviors may have been evident during Verbal subtests, but not during Performance tasks because of the interest value of the concrete materials. For such individuals, a behavioral explanation for poor performance on Digit Span and Arithmetic would be warranted, even if they evidenced a strength on the PS Index, whose component subtests are also generally vulnerable to anxiety and distractibility. Similarly, the number of specific subtests whose validity is questionable may be expanded to four or more for given children if, for example, they evidenced performance-inhibiting behaviors during the Block Design and Comprehension subtests.

The Guide to the Assessment of Test Session Behavior for the WISC-III and WIAT (GATSB; Glutting & Oakland, 1993), a standardized behavior-rating instrument that was mentioned in Chapter 1, can facilitate examiners' interpretations of children's test behaviors. Elevated standard scores on the Avoidance or Inattentiveness scales may suggest that anxiety or attentional problems affected the child's test scores.

Analysis of Wrong Responses and Style of Responding

The examiner would be wise to record incorrect responses for Arithmetic and Digit Span items, rather than merely marking them pass or fail. Some answers to Arithmetic problems will reflect poor mastery of computational skills, whereas other wrong responses can be used to infer selection of the wrong mathematical processes, forgetting the precise question, sequencing difficulties, thought disorders (if answers are "wild," such as getting back $100 change from a dollar), and so on. For example, a child whose wrong response is the right answer to step 1 of a two-step process may have difficulty sequencing the steps of a complex problem. In Digit Span, a sequencing problem may be evidenced by a child who consistently recalls the correct numbers spoken by the examiner but recites them in the wrong order. In contrast, a child with a deficient short-term memory might omit the last digit or one or two digits in the middle of an item; a distractible child may respond with numbers that bear no relationship to the digits in the item or may give no response at all.

Observations during Arithmetic and Digit Span also facilitate understanding the role of different behaviors on performance. During Arithmetic items, children may attempt to "write" with their fingers on the table, count on their fingers, repeat the item out loud to aid their recall of the exact wording, or ask for numerous repetitions of items (only one repetition is allowed). On Digit Span, mouthing the digits as they are spoken, auditory rehearsal, and covering up the eyes to block out the outside world are all fairly common behaviors. Each behavioral observation tells the examiner something different about the child and aids understanding of his or her test scores.

Integrating Multiple Data Sources

To interpret the FD factor effectively, it is apparent that subtest scores, behavioral observations, and the nature of wrong responses have to be integrated for each individual. Whether low scores on the FD Index are due to sequencing, distractibility, anxiety, or a number problem can often be inferred from behaviors and wrong responses. It is also useful to weigh additional information about the child to help deduce a working hypothesis. When sequencing is suspected as the difficulty, the examiner should check the child's Coding and Picture Arrangement scaled score; relatively poor performance on one or both of these visual sequencing tasks would be likely. Deficiencies in sequencing are sometimes blatant during Coding B when the child has to search actively for the 5 each time (for example), showing no awareness of its predictable placement in between the 4 and 6. In addition, a child with a sequencing problem is likely to manifest this deficiency in social situations and in academic achievement. Was one of the reasons for referral possibly associated with a sequencing lack—such as inability or refusal to follow directions? Is the child reported to have serious reading problems, especially in decoding words? Testing out the child's performance on subtests and scales that are construct-valid measures of sequential processing is essential before a sequential hypothesis can be accepted. Either the K-ABC Sequential Processing Scale or the Das-Naglieri Successive Processing Scale is a good choice.

If examiners believe that a behavioral variable accounted for a low FD Index, they should anticipate distractibility, anxiety, inability to concentrate, short attention span, and hyperactivity as likely reasons for referral. When the behaviors observed during a testing session corroborate referral problems, examiners have extra justification for reaching a conclusion regarding the meaning of low FD scores. However, they should not be intimidated if an apparently distractible or anxious child has been described as extremely attentive or relaxed in school. Test behaviors are sometimes quite different from behaviors in other circumstances; the examiner's task is to interpret scores in the context of behaviors observed during the testing session. Therefore, it would be inappropriate to consider a low FD Index as due to a behavioral variable if distractibility or anxiety was listed as a referral problem but was not at all evident during the WISC-III administration. Whenever distractibility or anxiety is believed to have contributed to depressed scores on the two subtests constituting the FD factor, the examiner should also anticipate relatively low scores on any other subtests during which these behaviors were definitely observed. In addition, an anxious child may well score relatively poorly on the Perceptual Organization, Processing Speed, and distractibility factors because of the vulnerability of highly speeded tasks such as Object Assembly or Symbol Search to the influence of anxiety.

Inadequate mastery of computational skills, compensatory behaviors such as finger counting or finger writing, the solving of oral arithmetic problems after the time limits expire, and a history of poor mathematical achievement all suggest that a child's low score on the FD factor reflects an inability to handle numerical symbols. A child with this deficiency is sometimes found to have an adequate forward digit span, which involves recall but no manipulation of numbers, coupled with almost a complete lack of ability to reverse digits. In general, however, Arithmetic and Code B are the best indicators of a child's numerical facility (or lack of it), with Digit Span merely serving as a check on a number-related hypothesis (Lutey, 1977). Nonetheless, the WISC-III manual includes tables that permit direct evaluation of the child's separate forward and backward spans, which has implications for interpreting the FD Index as primarily a measure of short-term memory versus number ability for certain children. The use of these tables is described later in the chapter.

Analysis of Number Items on the Information Subtest

Other important checks on a number hypothesis are the Information, Block Design, and Symbol Search subtests since a child with a severe symbolic problem may also fail most of the quantitative fact items (e.g., pennies in a nickel, days in a week), may experience considerable difficulty in copying two-dimensional abstract designs out of blocks, and may have problems rapidly identifying simple symbols from an array. As a rule, when an attentive and relaxed child with apparently normal sequencing ability performs poorly on the FD subtests, the examiner should suspect a symbolic difficulty even in the absence of corroborating behaviors. That hypothesis should be checked out, however, with measures of arithmetic ability, such as the Binet-4 Quantitative Reasoning Scale, or with tests of mathematics achievement.

The Information subtest is organized to facilitate comparison of a child's success with factual items that involve numbers versus those that do not. On the WISC-R, the number items were spread throughout the subtest, but on the WISC-III nearly all number items are included among the first dozen. In fact, half of the first 12 items require knowledge of number facts or concepts and half do not. Further, the sets of the 6 number items and the 6 nonnumber items are of approximately equal difficulty, as deduced by their item numbers (since items are sequenced by their approximate level of difficulty). These two-item sets are as follows:

Information Number Items	Information Nonnumber Items
2	1
3	4
6	5
8	7
10	9
11	12

One would hypothesize that children should perform about as well on the set of items involving numbers as on the set that is mostly number-free. Therefore, when they don't, the reason may be due to either strong or weak number ability. Whenever a low or high FD Index is believed to be a function of the child's number ability, compute the child's sum of item scores on each set of items. If the child is believed to have a weakness in number ability, a lower score on the "number" items would be a piece of corroborating evidence for that hypothesis. Similarly, a higher score on the number items would support a hypothesis of good number ability. A discrepancy of 2 or more points between the item sets is needed for corroboration. Because the items are relatively early in the 30-item Information subtest, this technique obviously won't be useful for supporting hypothesized number strengths in most older or brighter children. The method is also not useful for children ages 11 and above (except those suspected of intellectual deficiency) who start the Information subtest at Item 8 or 11. The method may be used for children ages 8 to 10 who begin with Item 5; just assume credit for Items 1–4.

High Scores on the Distractibility Factor

Except for the previous discussion of strengths as well as weaknesses in number ability, the preceding sections have focused on low FD scores, yet high scores are also encountered and require careful consideration. Despite the formal name given the factor, it is unlikely that a person will obtain a high factor score primarily because of Freedom from Distractibility. Similarly, even though Horn (1989) interprets the FD Index as measuring SAR, it is unlikely that children will earn high scores on Arithmetic merely because of a good auditory short-term memory. Good memory and attention-concentration can lead directly to high scores on Digit Span, but not on Arithmetic.

Attention, concentration, short-term memory, and freedom from anxiety or distractibility are necessary requisites for good performance on Arithmetic, but they cannot usually account for the high scores. More likely, these abilities and traits enable the child to exercise the skill or skills that underlie the tasks. In most instances, this skill is probably the Guilford-related ability to manipulate symbolic content and is closely associated with quantitative ability. Ordinarily, children must be able to compute, reason mathematically, and understand quantitative concepts to excel on the Arithmetic subtest. Supporting information for a number strength might come from good performance on Digits Backward (see next section); doing well on the set of "number" items on the information subtest; and from evidence of school achievement, where the child may excel in mathematics. In addition to performing well in arithmetic achievement, an adolescent may have made a relevant vocational choice such as becoming a mathematics teacher, accountant, or computer programmer.

Usually, high FD Indexes reflect either numerical ability or the ability to sequence information—what Bannatyne (1974) calls Sequential Ability and Kaufman and Kaufman (1983) refer to as Sequential Processing. In the illustrative case reports at the end of this chapter, Lourdes was shown to have an FD strength that reflected good number ability, a hypothesis verified by examination of her responses to Information and Digit Span, and by the results of supplementary subtests from the Binet-4 and Detroit-3; and Lucy had a strength in the sequential processing of information, a finding cross-validated by clinical observations and by her pattern of scores on the K-ABC.

Strengths on FD, however, may reflect other abilities. Examiners should utilize their own creativity in the interpretation of this factor. High scores may have a particular meaning for a given child based on observations and background information that are applicable only to the child tested; the same is true for low scores. Furthermore, an examiner from a specific orientation might have an entirely different interpretation of the third factor. For example, WISC-III examiners who feel comfortable with the Illinois Test of Psycholinguistic Abilities (ITPA) model (Kirk, McCarthy, & Kirk, 1968) may find it appropriate to interpret the third factor in terms of level of organization. Most WISC-III subtests are at the *representational* level of organization, which involves the mediation of complex activities requiring the meaning or significance of linguistic symbols. In contrast, Digits Forward is more closely associated with the *automatic* level of organization, which controls the retention of symbol sequences and the execution of over-learned, highly organized habits.

Even though Arithmetic is legitimately a representational task (Osgood & Miron, 1963), the subtest also involves mastery of computational facts; when these facts are learned at an automatic rote level, performance on Arithmetic will be elevated. In Guilford's terminology, the Arithmetic subtest requires Memory of Symbolic Implications, which Meeker (1975) defines as memory for well-practiced number operations. The latter skill is automatic, supporting the notion that a high or low FD index may reflect strong or weak automatic functioning for some individuals.

When searching for explanations of what the FD index means for a given child, it is wise to remember that an individual's high or low Index may not have a unitary explanation. More than one of the various interpretations given this factor may be reflected in an extreme FD Index. For example, as Lutey (1977, p. 223) aptly states: "The examiner should not overlook the possibility that [low FD scores] reflect *both* anxiety *and* poor numerical ability, since these logically may be related for many subjects."

The Stimulus Trace Hypothesis

One other label that has been given to the FD factor by investigators of mentally retarded individuals (Baumeister & Bartlett, 1962a, 1962b) is Stimulus Trace. These investigators interpret the factor from the perspective of Ellis's (1963) theory and consider it to reflect a child's ability to maintain the neural trace of a stimulus over brief intervals of time. This interpretation, which is also consistent with Hebb's (1949) theoretical framework and pertains to current cognitive psychology research on working memory (discussed previously), may well explain a low FD index for some mentally retarded or neurologically impaired children. The term "Stimulus Trace," as interpreted by Baumeister and Bartlett, is akin to short-term memory—a label that Cohen (1957) once believed was characteristic of the distractibility factor and that Horn (1989) interprets as the major ability assessed by the FD index.

The physiologically based Stimulus Trace or SAR (Short-Term Acquisition and Retrieval) factor, or working memory, is believed to relate to behavioral differences between normal and mentally retarded individuals and has typically included secondary loadings by Coding, Picture Arrangement, and Block Design to supplement the loadings by Arithmetic and Digit Span. Reaction time and inspection time research indicates significant differences between normal and retarded children, and significant correlations between these input and output measures and IQ (Jensen, Schafer, & Crinella, 1981; Nettlebeck & Young, 1989). These findings relate closely to the Stimulus Trace hypothesis, Ellis's theory, and the more recent pulse train theory associated with evoked potential research (Hendrickson & Hendrickson, 1980). These topics are beyond the scope of this book (see J. Kaufman, 1995, for a detailed discussion and research summary), but they may offer the best link between the FD and PS factors, and relate to the finding that both of these small WISC-III factors (and the WISC-R distractibility triad) tend to yield relatively low scores for a diversity of abnormal populations.

Forward and Backward Digit Span

Cognitive psychologists (Jensen & Figueroa, 1974) and neuropsychologists (Costa, 1975) have known for decades that Wechsler's Digits Forward and Digits Backward measure a different set of skills. Repeating digits in the same order as they are spoken is an automatic task that requires an immediate response with some mediation (chunking the numbers), and does not tax the individual's working memory. Reversing digits, in contrast, requires number manipulation and spatial visualization to recode the information in working memory; it requires representational thinking and is not an automatic task. Digits Forward is generally a poor measure of *g;* Digits Backward serves as a much better measure of general intelligence. Repeating digits in their reverse order is related to the visual-spatial ability of brain-damaged individuals and is impeded by right hemisphere damage, but repeating digits forward is not (Costa, 1975; Weinberg, Diller, Gerstman, & Schulman, 1972). Reversing digits seems to involve the formation of an internal visual representation of the information received auditorally (Gardner, 1981), and measures different abilities than repeating digits forward (Talley, 1986). Research suggests that Digits Forward assesses sequential or successive processing whereas Digits Backward measures both successive processing and planning ability (Schofield & Ashman, 1986).

Clinical psychologists of yesteryear tended to consider it irrational for people to have longer backward than forward spans and viewed such a finding as a sign of negativism, compulsive trends, or general mental disturbance (Kitzinger & Blumberg, 1951). Now, cognitive explanations seem more plausible. For example, some individuals have striking deficiencies in immediate rote recall of auditory information but are able to perform much better when the task demands virtually force them into "second gear" (to manipulate the stimuli actively in working memory instead of just receiving them passively). The examiner's instruction to repeat the digits backward sometimes serves as a wake-up call for a child who just flubbed the Digits Forward series.

Despite the well-known cognitive and neuropsychological distinction between the two halves of Digit Span, Wechsler's scales persist in providing a single scaled score based on their combination. Fortunately, however, the WISC-III manual offers tables that permit examiners to compare the child's forward and backward spans (Wechsler, 1991, Tables B.6 and B.7), a particular benefit for the interpretation of a child's high or low FD Index. To use these tables, examiners simply note the child's longest forward span and longest backward span. The child's longest span corresponds to the most digits the child was able to repeat correctly on each portion of the subtest. It makes no difference whether the child passes one trial or both trials for a given span; the only issue is the longest span that the child is able to repeat. These spans, therefore, do not correspond directly to the number of points that the child earns on each half of Digit Span.

Tables 5.4 and 5.5 were developed from one of the WISC-III tables (Table B.6). Table 5.4 shows the size of unusually *long* forward and backward spans for each age; Table 5.5 indicates spans that are unusually *short* for each age. Once again, "unusually" is defined statistically and corresponds to different percentages of the normal population; in this case, the extreme 15%, 5%, and 1% fit the distributions best.

Use Table 5.4 by entering with the child's longest forward and backward spans to determine whether either or both spans are unusually long for the child's age. For example, suppose that a 7-year-old had a forward span of 6

TABLE 5.4.   Unusually Long Forward and Backward Spans, by Age, Using Three Criteria of Unusualness

Percentage of Normal Population	Extreme 15%	Extreme 5%	Extreme 1%
Age 6			
Forward	—	7	8
Backward	4	—	5
Age 7			
Forward	—	7	8
Backward	—	5	6
Age 8			
Forward	7	8	9
Backward	5	6	7
Ages 9–10			
Forward	—	8	9
Backward	—	6	7
Ages 11–12			
Forward	8	9	—
Backward	6	7	8
Ages 13–14			
Forward	8	9	—
Backward	7	8	9
Ages 15–16			
Forward	9	—	—
Backward	7	8	9

Note: This table was developed from data presented in the WISC-III manual (Wechsler, 1991, Table B.6).

TABLE 5.5.   Unusually Short Forward and Backward Spans, by Age, Using Three Criteria of Unusualness

Percentage of Normal Population	Extreme 15%	Extreme 5%	Extreme 1%
Age 6			
Forward	—	3	2
Backward	0	—	—
Age 7			
Forward	—	3	2
Backward	—	0	—
Age 8			
Forward	—	—	3
Backward	2	—	0
Ages 9–16			
Forward	4	—	3
Backward	—	2	0

Note: This table was developed from data presented in the WISC-III manual (Wechsler, 1991, Table B.6).

and a backward span of 5. Entering Table 5.4 in the part that gives data for age 7 indicates that forward spans of 6 digits are not unusually large; a span of 7 digits is needed to be considered unusual for age 7. As indicated in the table, forward spans of 7 or more occurred in the Extreme 5% of 7-year-olds, and forward spans of 8 or more occurred in the Extreme 1%. The child's forward span of 6 is common, having occurred in more than 15% of children age 7; that's why it is excluded from Table 5.4. The child's backward span of 5, however, is unusually long for a 7-year-old. Entering the table in the appropriate portion indicates that backward spans of 5 or greater occurred in only 5% of children age 7. That unusually long backward span suggests that the child may have good facility with numbers. It would be inappropriate simply to infer good number ability from a long backward span, but an unusually long backward span would *support* a hypothesis of good number ability if the child's FD index was significantly high, and there were other bits of supportive information and data as well. And just as unusually long backward spans can enhance a hypothesized strength in number ability, an unusually long forward span suggests that excellent immediate auditory memory and sequential processing abilities may offer the best explanation of a relatively high FD Index. Again, additional behavioral, background, and test data are needed to accept either a memory or sequential hypothesis.

Use Table 5.5 in the same way as Table 5.4 to determine whether a child's forward or backward span is abnormally short. Suppose a child of 11 had a forward span of 3 and a backward span of 3. Entering Table 5.5 for Ages 9–16 years indicates that forward spans of 3 digits are unusually short, occurring in 1% of children ages 9 to 16 years. A comparable backward span of 3 is not abnormal for this age range, however. Spans of 3 digits occur in more than 15% of children ages 9–16; a backward span of 2 digits or less is needed to be unusual for a child of 11. An abnormally short forward span, if joined by additional data and information, can support poor short-term memory or sequential processing as an explanation of low FD; similarly, an unusually short backward span can provide a piece of the puzzle for hypothesizing poor number ability as the reason for a relatively low FD Index.

Of interest in the latter example is that the child had equal forward and backward spans of 3 digits. From Table B.7 in the WISC-III manual (Wechsler, 1991), it is apparent that it is unusual for children to have equal forward and backward spans, and very unusual to have longer backward than forward spans. The data on the differences between forward and backward spans indicate few meaningful fluctuations with age, so I'll only report data for the total standardization sample, ages 6 to 16 years. Approximately 85% of children have a forward span that is at least 1 digit longer than their backward spans. About 11% have no difference between their spans; 3% have backward spans that are 1 digit longer, and less than 1% have backward spans that are 2 or more digits longer than their forward spans. Therefore it is noteworthy, and requires interpretation, whenever a child's backward span either equals or exceeds his or her forward span. As mentioned earlier, one likely explanation is a deficient immediate auditory memory and perhaps a more generalized difficulty with automatic, as opposed to representational or complex, processing of information.

At the other end of the spectrum is unusually long forward spans relative to backward spans. The same table in the WISC-III manual indicates that it is quite common for children to have forward spans that exceed their backward spans by 3 digits; a difference of 4 or more digits, however, is unusual. Only 10% of children have forward spans that are 4 or more digits longer than their backward spans; 2% have backward spans that are 5 or more digits longer; and only 0.2% (2 out of 1,000 children) have backward spans that are 6 digits longer. When children have forward spans that are at least 4 digits longer than their backward spans, that result provides support for a weakness in number ability, presuming that other evidence also suggests a number deficiency.

Any hypothesis that depends, in part, on a child's forward span, backward span, or the difference between them should be cross-validated with alternate forms of each task. K-ABC Number Recall and WJ-R Digits Reversed are good analogs of Digits Forward and Digits Backward, respectively.

Fluctuations in the WISC-III Profile

It is always a good idea to follow up hypothesized strengths and weaknesses on the WISC-III by administering pertinent additional tests, scales, or subtests. But first, examiners should investigate the WISC-III profile thoroughly for additional interpretive clues regarding the meaning of a low or high FD Index.

If the child is believed to have a weak or strong short-term memory, examine the scaled score on *Information* to see if it is consistent with the FD Index (is it above or below the relevant mean used to determine the child's strong and weak areas on the WISC-III). From both Guilford's (1967) and Horn's (1985) theory, Information is a measure of retention. When a child's Information score is consistent with his or her scaled scores on the FD subtests, then the strong or weak area may extend to verbal memory, affecting both short-term and long-term storage capacities. Hypotheses of poor memory, as noted previously, require support from multiple sources such as referral information (the child is considered "forgetful") or observations of test behaviors (the child kept asking for verbal items to be repeated and had difficulty understanding the verbal directions to some nonverbal tasks such as Symbol Search and Picture Arrangement).

If the child's weakness or strength on FD is believed to be related to sequential processing, then check out the child's *Coding* scaled score. Coding is included in Bannatyne's Sequential category and had a meaningful factor loading on the Sequential Processing factor in the joint analysis of the WISC-R and K-ABC for a sample of 212 normal children (Kaufman & McLean, 1987). Also look at the child's scaled score on *Picture Arrange-*

ment, which involves visual sequencing. Picture Arrangement seems to require simultaneous problem solving for most children, so this subtest cannot be used to infer either a sequential processing deficit or asset. However, whenever Coding and Picture Arrangement are both consistent with the FD Index, that occurrence suggests that the child has a more pervasive sequential strength or weakness that affects the manipulation of both auditory and visual stimuli, extends to temporal and chronological sequences, and involves both vocal and motor output. Again, however, any inference of a sequential explanation of a high or low FD Index demands multifaceted corroboration. A proposed sequential deficit, for example, would be reinforced if difficulty in following directions was considered a problem area by a referral source or if the child repeated all the numbers correctly in the digit spans, but made errors by reversing some of the numbers.

Since Coding B involves the manipulation of numbers, and both Coding A and B involve symbols, it is especially important to consider multiple data sources to interpret the meaning of the Arithmetic-Digit Span-Coding triad when a child performs consistently on these subtests. A strength in number ability may be suggested for a child at least 8 years of age who performs well on the three subtests, with especially good performance on Arithmetic and Digits Backward, and who has consistently done well in math in school. Or a weakness in the manipulation of numbers and symbols may be indicated for a child who scores low on the FD subtests, and on Coding, Symbol Search, and Block Design, but evidenced no discernible anxiety, distractibility, reflectiveness, motivation problem, or visual-motor coordination difficulties.

Corroboration of Hypotheses with Other Tests

The best way to evaluate hypotheses derived from a blend of referral information, clinical observations of test-taking behaviors, detailed analysis of wrong responses, and fluctuations in the WISC-III subtest profile is to administer a judicious selection of subtests or scales from other test batteries. The tests listed in this section are particularly useful for following up hypotheses associated with the FD factor.

Short-Term Memory Hypotheses

If the child is suspected of having a problem with short-term memory, Horn's SAR, the examiner will want to verify this possibility with other tests of short-term memory (see the case of James in Chapter 7). Performance on immediate memory tests always requires verification because a child's low score may be due to situational factors rather than more pervasive memory deficits. Poor rapport, preoccupation, test-taking anxiety, distractibility due to a less-than-optimal testing environment, fatigue, and other test-specific factors are likely to affect immediate memory scores. Digit Span, by virtue of its administration at the end of the battery, is especially vulnerable. In addition, examiners who suspect an immediate memory problem will want to understand the parameters of the problem. Does the problem extend to visual-motor memory or to auditory memory that demands a motor instead of vocal response? Is the difficulty specific to numbers and number concepts, or does it generalize to words, sentences, stories, pictures, and designs? Is the deficit only in sequential memory or does it extend to simultaneous, visual-spatial recall? Incidentally, children who score high on the FD index, and seem to have good memories, also need follow-up to see if that apparent strength is both repeatable and generalizable.

Suggested subtests for following up a short-term memory hypothesis are listed here by input and output requirements:

Auditory Stimuli

Vocal Response	Motor Response
DAS Recall of Digits	K-ABC Word Order
K-ABC Number Recall	Detroit-3 Reversed Letters
Detroit-3 Sentence Imitation	
Detroit-3 Word Sequences	
KAIT Auditory Comprehension	
Das-Naglieri Word Series	
Das-Naglieri Sentence Repetition and Sentence Questions	
Binet-4 Memory for Sentences	
Binet-4 Memory for Digits	
WJ-R Memory for Sentences	
WJ-R Memory for Words	
WJ-R Numbers Reversed	
WJ-R Listening Comprehension	

Visual Stimuli

Vocal Response	Motor Response
DAS Recall of Objects	DAS Recall of Designs
	K-ABC Hand Movements
	K-ABC Spatial Memory
	Detroit-3 Design Sequences
	Detroit-3 Design Reproduction
	KAIT Memory for Block Designs
	Das-Naglieri Figure Memory
	Binet-4 Bead Memory
	Binet-4 Memory for Objects
	WJ-R Picture Recognition

Auditory and Visual Stimuli

Vocal Response

KAIT Rebus Learning
WJ-R Memory for Names
WJ-R Visual-Auditory Learning

Many of the suggested subtests measure simple rote recall, but a number of the tasks are complex. Detroit-3 Reversed Letters and WJ-R Numbers Reversed require the ability to recall stimuli in the reverse sequence, providing good follow-up for Digits Backward. Detroit-3 Design Sequences, Binet-4 Bead Memory, and K-ABC Hand Movements blend sequential memory with the simultaneous processing of visual stimuli. K-ABC Word Order requires the child to recall stimuli despite interference, and KAIT Auditory Comprehension assesses the ability to understand news stories and to make inferences about the information presented. WJ-R Listening Comprehension also assesses verbal comprehension, as does the "Sentence Questions" portion of the Das-Naglieri Sentence Repetition and Sentence Questions subtest. The two WJ-R and one KAIT task that demand the integration of visual and auditory stimuli (by learning the names associated with abstract symbols) are true learning tasks that invoke long-term as well as short-term memory processes; KAIT Rebus Learning also requires the examinee to apply rules and concepts, and KAIT Memory for Block Designs measures nonverbal concept formation as well as visual short-term memory.

If examiners are uncertain whether a low FD Index is due to attentional or memory problems, then they would be wise to administer the Das-Naglieri tests of attention. The Auditory Selective Attention subtest is particularly useful because it measures the kind of attentional skills needed to permit the child to respond appropriately to Arithmetic and Digit Span items. Administer the latter subtest even to individuals who are older than the designated range for the task; Naglieri (personal communication, 1993) indicated that Auditory Selective Attention would likely be a supplementary subtest, administered only to children ages 5 to 8 years.

When Information joins the FD subtests, suggesting a strength or weakness in verbal long-term as well as verbal short-term memory, the following measures are good for determining the generalizability of the child's performance on WISC-III Information: Detroit-3 Basic Information, K-ABC Faces & Places, and KAIT Famous Faces.

Sequential Hypotheses

When a child's Coding score is consistent with his or her FD index and a sequential explanation is hypothesized (as in the case of Lucy at the end of this chapter), examiners should consider administering any of the following complete scales: K-ABC Sequential Processing, Das-Naglieri Successive Scale, or WJ-R Short-Term Memory (Gsm) Scale. The two auditory-vocal memory subtests on both the Detroit-3 and Binet-4 also measure the sequential processing of information. The Das-Naglieri Successive Processing Scale is probably the most useful of these for distinguishing between sequential processing and memory because one task, as indicated previously, measures an aspect of verbal comprehension and another (Successive Speech Rate) does not measure memory at all.

If the child's Picture Arrangement score is consistent with the FD subtests and Coding, suggesting a deficit (or maybe an asset) in visual and auditory sequencing, the following subtests are good supplements to the WISC-III: Detroit-3 Story Sequences, Detroit-3 Design Sequences, Binet-4 Bead Memory, K-ABC Hand Movements, KAIT Rebus Learning, WJ-R Visual-Auditory Learning, Das-Naglieri Planned Codes (a Coding analog), and Das-Naglieri Planned Connections (a Trail Making analog).

If a child's auditory sequential deficit seems striking and pervasive, examiners may want to administer the WJ-R Sound Blending subtest to determine whether the child is able to sequence the syllables and phonemes that make up words.

Number Hypotheses

Examiners who believe that a high or low FD Index reflects a strength or weakness in number ability (see the case of Lourdes at the end of this chapter) have a diversity of subtests to choose from for supplementary testing. The various subtests can be grouped to parallel the role of numbers in the WISC-III tasks:

1. Some are like Digits Forward in that the numbers are not actively manipulated, but serve as semantic stimuli.
2. Some are like Coding B, in which the numbers are figural or symbolic stimuli but no computations are performed.
3. Some are like Digits Backward, as numbers are actively manipulated, transformed, or interpreted as being high or low, but no actual computations are necessary.
4. Some require the computational ability demanded by Arithmetic.
5. Some require the blend of computational skill, knowledge of quantitative concepts, and mathematical reasoning ability that are demanded by many Arithmetic items.
6. Some involve fluid problem solving with numbers, a skill that extends beyond the abilities measured by Arithmetic.

In addition to selecting supplementary subtests from cognitive batteries, I have also included subtests from three individual achievement tests: Kaufman Test of Educational Achievement—Comprehensive Form (K-TEA; Kaufman & Kaufman, 1985), WIAT, and WJ-R Achievement battery.

Numbers as Semantic Stimuli	Numbers as Visual (Figural or Symbolic) Stimuli
DAS Recall of Digits	Das-Naglieri Matching Numbers
K-ABC Number Recall	Das-Naglieri Visual Selective Attention
Binet-4 Memory for Digits	WJ-R Visual Matching

Manipulation and Interpretation of Numbers (but no Computations)	Computational Ability
DAS Speed of Information Processing Das-Naglieri Planned Connections WJ-R Numbers Reversed	DAS Basic Numerical Skills K-TEA Mathematics Computation WIAT Numerical Operations WJ-R Calculation

Fluid Problem Solving Using Numbers	Numerical Reasoning and Math Concepts
DAS Sequential and Quantitative Reasoning KAIT Logical Steps Binet-4 Number Series Binet-4 Equation Building K-SNAP Four-Letter Words	K-ABC Arithmetic Binet-4 Quantitative K-TEA Mathematics Applications WIAT Mathematics Reasoning WJ-R Applied Problems WJ-R Quantitative Concepts

Examiners should choose number-related subtests as supplements based on the specific asset or deficit to be cross-validated. Before any hypothesis of a number strength or weakness is inferred from scores on WISC-III subtests, however, it is essential to corroborate that finding with information about the child's classroom performance and by administration of at least one math subtest from an individual achievement battery. If a number problem is suspected, but memory or attentional problems cannot be ruled out as the reason for the low scores, then K-ABC Arithmetic is a good supplement; its zoo motif and colorful visual stimuli reduce the role of memory and often maintain the child's attention. If a child has an apparent strength in number ability, then a favorite task of mine is Binet-4 Equation Building. This clever subtest assesses both computational and reasoning skills in a challenging way and is not encumbered by either verbal comprehension or short-term memory.

INTERPRETING THE PROCESSING SPEED FACTOR

As with the discussion of the FD factor, three topics are discussed in this section: *when* to interpret the PS factor, how to aid understanding by integrating clinical observations and clues from the WISC-III profile, and what additional tests should be administered to verify hypotheses about high or low PS Indexes.

When to Interpret the PS Factor

The suggested guidelines for interpreting the PS factor are analogous to the rules for interpreting the FD factor: The child should have performed fairly consistently on Symbol Search and Coding, and the child's PS Index should be at a different level, whether higher or lower, than other WISC-III scores.

To compute whether the PS Index is unitary, compare the child's scaled scores on the two component subtests. Scaled scores on Symbol Search and Coding must differ by 4 points to be significant at the .05 level (Wechsler, 1991, Table B.4), and by 5 points to be significant at the .01 level. Like the results for the FD Index, *the PS Index is interpretable if its two component subtests have scaled scores that differ by less than 4 points.*

In Chapter 3, examiners determine whether the PO and PS indexes differ significantly. If the answer is yes, then it is appropriate to try to interpret the relative strength or weakness on the PS factor. If the answer is no, then the examiner should determine If the PO index is a poor measure of the child's mental ability; for example, a child with a moderate to severe visual-perceptual problem or fine-motor coordination difficulties cannot be assessed validly on the Performance Scale. In that instance, examiners should compare the PS Index with the VC index. For that comparison, 14 points is needed for significance at the .05 level (Wechsler, 1991, Table B.1), and 18 points is significant at $p < .01$. The PS index may be just as impaired as the PO Index by the child's visual-perceptual or fine motor problem. The VC versus PS contrast enables examiners to estimate the magnitude of that impairment.

If neither the PO-PS nor the VC-PS comparison is significant, then the examiner should apply Step 6 of the WISC-III interpretive process (Chapter 3) to determine whether the two PS subtests emerge as a significant strength or weakness. If either Symbol Search or Coding deviates significantly from the child's relevant mean, and the other scaled score deviates from the mean in the same direction, then the Symbol Search-Coding combination reflects a relative strength or weakness. In that event, the PS Index may be interpreted.

As was recommended for interpreting the FD Index, the two PS-subtest scaled scores must be similar in magnitude and should denote an area of significant strength or weakness, as prerequisites for interpretation of PS.

Clinical Observations and the PS Factor

The prior discussion in the FD section of the role of inferring distractibility and anxiety from the child's behaviors and referral information applies equally to the two PS subtests since both Symbol Search and Coding are extremely vulnerable to these behaviors. But, as noted, the PS Index is also very sensitive to low motivation, reflectiveness, compulsiveness, and poor fine-motor coordination, so examiners need to be vigilant to evidences of these aspects of behavior, personality, cognitive style, or neurological integrity. The GATSB Uncooperative Mood scale (Glutting & Oakland, 1993) may prove especially useful for inferring motivational problems during the WISC-III evaluation.

Symbol Search is mainly a measure of mental speed and Coding is mainly a test of psychomotor speed, so examiners often need to try to discern which of these two aspects of speed offers a better explanation of a low or high PS Index. Importantly, both mental speed and motor speed may be depressed in ADHD children relative to normal children (Mitchell, Chavez, Baker, Guzman, & Azen, 1990).

Observations during Symbol Search and Coding

Performance subtests in general provide wonderful stimuli for inferring behavioral or personality characteristics. Everything is external, fully within view of the observant examiner. The Symbol Search and Coding subtests are quite good at eliciting easily interpretable behaviors:

- They both require use of a pencil. Does the child hold the pencil awkwardly and labor over each item, or is the child's paper-and-pencil coordination fluid and smooth? Does the child break a pencil point or two because of too much pressure? Visual-motor coordination difficulties are easy to spot. In the case of Lourdes, whose report appears at the end of this chapter, her low PS Index was apparently due to poor paper-and-pencil coordination.

- They both provide permanent records of the child's test performance. If coordination problems weren't evident from how the child used a pencil (or if you forgot to look), what types of products are on the answer sheets? Are the Coding symbols poor replicas of the models or drawn with a shaky hand? Do the child's markings through the Symbol Search "Yes-No" boxes miss most of the appropriate box or otherwise look sloppy? Does the child make two or more errors on Coding, especially errors of reversal, rotation, or distortion of the stimulus? If so, the child may have a visual-perceptual or visual-motor integration problem.

- They both are "beat the clock" tests. Does the child lose interest during the tasks and slow down to a crawl? Does the child have difficulty sustaining attention and have to be reminded to continue? Is the child so unmotivated that even these reminders don't work? Is the child too immature to realize the importance of working at top speed, or too anxious to cope with the need to work very quickly? Does the child ask unimportant or irrelevant questions during either subtest? Is the child so reflective or insecure that he or she checks and rechecks each item to ensure its correctness? Is the child so compulsive or perfectionistic that each symbol copied during Coding must match the model with unnecessary precision? Or does the child understand the rules of the game and not look up until the examiner says "Stop"?

- Performance on both subtests can be enhanced by a good visual memory and handicapped by a weak visual memory. A child with an exceptional visual memory may memorize the symbol that is paired with each number on Coding B and thus not have to refer back very often to the key at the top of the page. Or, on Symbol Search, that same child may look once at the Target Group, scan the Search Group efficiently, and mark Yes or No correctly without having to look back at the Target stimuli. In contrast, children with poor visual memories may look two or three times at the key for Coding A or Coding B before writing the symbol, or waste time on Symbol Search by going back and forth between the Target Group and Search Group before making a Yes-No decision. Children with poor visual memories may display none of the aforementioned compensatory behaviors and therefore make numerous errors (unfortunately, there are no norms to quantify "numerous" on either subtest). Children believed to have a strength in visual memory would not be expected to mark any incorrect responses, or maybe one, on either subtest. The examiner's clinical acumen and judicious selection of follow-up tests are especially important for distinguishing among hypotheses of poor visual memory, insecurity, and visual-perceptual or visual-motor impairment.

- Both subtests may measure planning ability as it is defined within the Das-Naglieri PASS model. As such, the strategies the child uses to attack each PS subtest may reflect on that child's ability to plan, formulate, organize, and strategize. In Coding, for example, children have to "code the information distinguishing the symbol found, and carry this information in short-term memory long enough to reproduce the symbol in the proper answer box" (Estes, 1974, p. 745). Even more complex encoding functions are necessary to process two symbols during Symbol Search B while scanning the Search Group for "matches." There is some evidence that the ability to code the information in the symbols, probably by verbal mediation, is an important factor in success on Coding-Digit Symbol tasks (Estes, 1974; Royer, 1971), and for tasks such as Symbol Search. As such, a child's *strategy* is most likely a valuable determinant of performance. Sometimes poor strategies are quite evident. The examiner may notice, for example, that a left-handed child is blocking the key with his or her hand and thus not taking advantage of the second Coding Response Sheet that is provided. The test-taking approaches described in the previous paragraph, and interpreted in terms of visual memory assets or deficits, may actually be more indicative of the ability to plan and strategize than to remember visual stimuli. Coding also has aspects of successive processing from the vantage point of the PASS model, Bannatyne system, or K-ABC model, and that interpretation must also be considered. Again, observations and test scores from supplementary measures are essential for distinguishing among a variety of competing hypotheses.

When a child's high PS Index is apparently indicative of good planning ability, the Symbol Search score should be higher than the Coding score; conversely, the Symbol Search score should be lower for children believed to have a planning deficit. Symbol Search is a far better measure of g than Coding, and places more demands on the ability to plan effectively. Also, Symbol Search B requires children to process two stimuli at once, whereas both Coding A and B involve one stimulus at a time. A growing body of reaction time research indicates that the more complex the reaction time task and the more bits of information that have to be processed, the higher the relationship with intelligence (Jensen, 1985; Vernon, 1987). Similarly, an inverse relationship was found between reaction time and *g* loadings of WISC-R subtests (Hemmelgarn & Kehle, 1984).

Observations during Other Performance Subtests

The various hypotheses mentioned in the previous section as possibly explaining low or high PS Indexes may be easily checked out with observations made during the administration of PO subtests. Visual-perceptual difficulties noted during Coding (e.g., children who rotate or reverse symbols) may manifest themselves on other nonverbal tasks: on Block Design, when children have trouble with figure-ground distinctions, lose the square shape, don't recognize obvious errors in their productions, or rotate designs; on Object Assembly, when they construct most of a puzzle, yet have no clue about what object they are assembling, or when they have difficulty orienting a puzzle; on Picture Arrangement, when they misinterpret pictures, or solve at least one item from right to left; and on Picture Completion when they misperceive parts of the stimulus picture.

The immaturity that may be observed by not understanding the need to work very fast on the PS subtests is also likely to be seen on the PO tasks; these children may stack the pictures, puzzle pieces, or blocks instead of using them appropriately. Low motivation is discernible during timed problem-solving tasks that offer bonus points for speed, especially when the instructions tell the child to, "Try to work as quickly as you can." Children who dawdle, yet are testwise and mature enough to know better, are easy to spot on Block Design, Object Assembly, and Picture Arrangement. Anxiety, when a child is faced with a stopwatch and a clear mandate to solve the problems quickly, also requires little experience to detect, and the same is true for compulsive tendencies; some children labor over the task of constructing perfectly aligned squares on Block Design and precisely placed puzzle pieces on Object Assembly.

Reflectiveness is seen on all three subtests that offer time bonuses. Sometimes this reflective cognitive style is an asset, for example, when a child studies the array of blocks, puzzle pieces, or pictures before starting to manipulate the stimuli, or when the child spontaneously corrects mistakes when checking over the arrangement. The same trait, however, can be costly for children who check and recheck their picture arrangements before finally saying, "Done." The loss of bonus points due to the reflective style can substantially lower the subtest score, just as it can on Symbol Search for children who are reluctant to commit to a Yes or No.

Planning Ability

Some children, such as those who reflect before diving in to a problem, approach items on Block Design, Object Assembly, and Picture Arrangement with a plan or strategy in mind. They use insight, manipulate stimuli in their mind before touching them, and approach each solution in systematic fashion. Others, often the more impulsive or disorganized children, start moving blocks or pictures almost before the last word of the instructions is out of the examiner's mouth. They will put a pair of blocks together at random, rotate a block to see if that helps, and then start with another pair of blocks in an attempt to copy a different part of the design. Or they will assemble pairs of puzzle pieces or pairs of pictures, but be unable to integrate the separate pairs into a complete puzzle or picture arrangement. This type of trial-and-error problem solving reveals much about the child's thought processes and learning ability.

Whenever examiners believe that a low or high score on the PS index denotes poor or good planning ability, it is essential to corroborate that hypothesis with observations of the child's problem-solving approach on the PO subtests. Examiners can draw inferences from behavioral observations made during Symbol Search and Coding, but these are not true tests of problem solving in the sense that they do not seem to demand as high-level processes or strategies as the PO tasks. Before inferring that a child may have scored high on the PS Index because of well-developed planning ability, one should have observed insightful, organized problem solving on subtests such as Block Design and Picture Arrangement. If the child used trial-and-error methods of attack, then the PS strength does not likely reflect good planning ability. If good strategization was observed during the PO subtests, then the hypothesis requires further support from tasks that were specifically designed to measure planning ability and high-level, complex thinking such as the KAIT Fluid Scale of the WJ-R cluster of Fluid Reasoning subtests.

The interpretation of the PS Index as measuring planning ability seems warranted from the apparent similarity of the component subtests to the kinds of tasks used by Das and Naglieri to validate the Planning portion of the PASS model (although Das, Naglieri, & Kirby, 1994, do not seem to agree with that assertion). Planning represents Luria's Block 3 functions, and is defined as the ability to create intentions, plan and program actions, inspect performance, and regulate behavior (Naglieri & Das, 1990). Block 3 depends on the development of the prefrontal region of the frontal lobes; "the third functional unit is critical to complex human activity" and is "the last to develop" (Naglieri & Das, 1990, p. 310). According to Golden (1981), who is—like Das and Naglieri—a Luria researcher and theorist, the Block 3 Planning functions develop at about ages 11–12, on the average.

On the Das-Naglieri test of PASS processes, the Planning Scale is represented by four subtests, one that assesses speed of visual search (finding a target stimulus within a cluttered visual field), and three that assess visual-motor speed (underlining two identical numbers in the same row, translating letters to codes, connecting numbers or numbers and letters in sequence). All these subtests require very rapid performance to earn high scores and depend on visual-perceptual or visual-motor coordination for success. They are able to be administered to children as young as 5 years, and do not seem to require the kind of high-level, complex thinking that is supposed to emerge at about age 11 or 12, the age of onset for Piaget's formal operations. One of the subtests (Matching Numbers) is nearly identical to the WJ-R subtest Visual Matching, a marker for the Horn Gs or Processing Speed factor.

Therefore, it is possible that the factor labeled Planning in the PASS model—though unequivocally corresponding to an ability that is separate from the Attention, Simultaneous, and Successive factors—is in fact a measure of speed of information processing within the visual-motor modality. Das's original research on planning included complex problem-solving tests such as writing an essay and an analog of the game Master Mind (e.g., Das & Heemsbergen, 1983). Even though the more complex planning tasks tended to load on the same factors as the "simple" ones (Naglieri, 1989), only the simple ones made it into the final PASS battery.

Probably Das-Naglieri Planning, WJ-R Gs, and WISC-III PS are measures of *both* planning ability *and* visual processing speed. That is why it is so essential to observe carefully the child's problem-solving strategies during the PO subtests. Importantly, the Das-Naglieri test includes as a built-in part of the evaluation instructions to observe the child's strategies during planning tasks, and to ask the child specific questions to discover what strategies the child reports that he or she used to solve the problems.

Fluctuations in the WISC-III Profile

Observations of problem-solving strategies, visual-perceptual problems, and so forth do not necessarily translate to the level of a child's performance. Some children can earn high scores on Block Design, for example, despite a trial-and-error approach or orientation problems, while others may earn low scores on Picture Arrangement despite employing an insightful, organized approach to problem solving. Some hypotheses about the PS Index, however, demand corroboration based on the child's actual test scores:

- If the child is believed to have a good or poor short-term visual memory, check out the child's *Picture Completion* scaled score for consistency. Perhaps the memory strength or weakness generalizes to visual long-term memory. Also compare the child's *Digit Span* scaled score with the PS score to see if the asset or deficit is more pervasive and involves immediate memory, regardless of the nature of the stimuli. No memory hypothesis, however, is viable without supportive referral or observational data, and without cross-validation with other memory tests.
- If the child has visual-perceptual problems and has apparent difficulty with the abstract symbols and designs in the Symbol Search and Coding items, look for a low *Block Design* scaled score for corroboration; children who have problems with the visual stimuli on the PS subtests

should not be able to succeed with the complex abstract designs that must be constructed for Block Design. If the FD Index is low as well, the problem may be a more generalized difficulty in handling any type of abstract symbol, including numbers. One would anticipate relatively higher scores on *Picture Completion* and *Picture Arrangement,* both of which require the visual perception of meaningful (not abstract) stimuli. Whenever Symbol Search and Block Design covary together, however, be alert for hypotheses involving spatial visualization, an ability that has an important impact on a child's scores on both subtests and may affect Coding as well. Therefore, a deficit on this particular set of subtests may pertain to the integration and storage of information (visualization) rather than to the intake of abstract symbols.

- If an asset or deficit in planning ability is hypothesized, the *Picture Arrangement* scaled score should be consistent with the PS Index. That Wechsler subtest has long been considered to measure complex planning ability.

- If the high or low PS Index is thought to be related to mental processing speed (as opposed to psychomotor speed), then the *Object Assembly* scaled score should be at about the same level as the PS subtests. More than other PO subtests, Object Assembly is influenced by speed of problem solving, that is, by the number of bonus points that a child earns (see discussion of time bonus points in Chapter 4).

- If the child displays fine motor problems, a low PS Index is likely to be associated with low scores on *Object Assembly* and *Block Design,* each of which places heavy demands on visual-motor coordination. Higher scores would be expected on the two PO subtests that place less emphasis on coordination: *Picture Completion* and *Picture Arrangement.* The inferences from the WISC-III subtest profile concerning interpretations of the PS Index in terms of mental processing speed, visual-motor coordination, and visual perception of abstractions cannot be made without considerable supportive evidence. Scoring high on the two "Picture" subtests and low on Block Design, Coding, and Symbol Search, for example, might support a hypothesis of weak motor coordination, visual perceptual difficulties in processing abstract (as opposed to meaningful) stimuli, or the use of verbal mediation to enhance performance on Picture Completion and Picture Arrangement (see Verbal Compensation of Performance deficit in Chapter 3). Observations of the child's rate of responding, fine motor coordination, reflectiveness, verbal strategies, and so forth, are essential for interpreting the profile fluctuations, and a well-thought-out set of supplementary subtests is a must.

Corroboration of Hypotheses with Other Tests

Numerous subtests and scales from other test batteries serve as useful supplements for gaining insight into what the PS Index measures for a given child. To cross-validate the existence of a strength or weakness on the PS factor, before trying to interpret its meaning, examiners might select a few of the following highly similar subtests or scales: DAS Speed of information Processing, Das-Naglieri Planning Scale, and WJ-R Processing Speed Scale. Other tasks are organized by the various hypotheses that have been discussed.

Memory Hypotheses

To determine if the child has a strong or weak visual short-term memory, examiners might select from among numerous tests of this skill. The groupings shown distinguish between visual memory tests that require little or no fine motor coordination, and those that have a decided visual-motor component. This distinction is important for examiners to keep in mind to enable them to help distinguish between memory versus motor assets or deficits:

Visual Short-Term Memory (Requiring Little or No Coordination)	Visual Short-Term Memory (Requiring Visual-Motor Coordination)
DAS Recall of Objects	DAS Recall of Designs
K-ABC Spatial Memory	K-ABC Hand Movements
Detroit-3 Design Sequences	Detroit-3 Design Reproduction
Binet-4 Memory for Objects	KAIT Memory for Block Designs
WJ-R Picture Recognition	Das-Naglieri Figure Memory
	Binet-4 Bead Memory

To evaluate whether the asset or deficit generalizes to immediate auditory memory, or to memory of auditory and visual stimuli that are presented simultaneously, see the lists of subtests presented for following up memory hypotheses on the FD factor.

Hypotheses Concerning Processing of Abstract versus Meaningful Stimuli

To investigate whether the child differs in his or her ability to process different types of visual stimuli, administer tasks that measure similar processes, but that do it with abstract versus meaningful stimuli. Some of the tests of visual short-term memory can be organized by this distinction, as shown:

Visual Memory for Abstract Stimuli (Designs-Symbols)	Visual Memory for Meaningful Stimuli (People-Things)
DAS Recall of Designs	DAS Recall of Objects
Detroit-3 Design Sequences	K-ABC Spatial Memory
Detroit-3 Design Reproduction	Binet-4 Memory for Objects
KAIT Memory for Block Designs	WJ-R Picture Recognition
Das-Naglieri Figure Memory	

Binet-4 Copying is also useful for measuring the ability to handle abstract stimuli, and so are the Block Design analogs included in the Binet-4, DAS, and K-ABC. However, all these conceptual tasks require visual-motor coordination, making it difficult to separate motor ability from visual processing of abstractions, and most involve response speed as well. The best way to determine whether a child has difficulty handling abstract stimuli is to administer reasoning tasks that utilize abstract stimuli, but that reduce or eliminate the roles of both fine motor coordination and response speed. Raven's Progressive Matrices is ideal for that purpose, as are the various Raven clones such as the Matrix Analogies Test and similar subtests included in many test batteries (Binet-4, DAS, Das-Naglieri, Detroit-3, K-ABC, K-BIT, TONI). The WJ-R Concept Formation subtest also measures reasoning with abstract visual stimuli. As a contrast to the matrices tests, supplements are needed that assess reasoning with *meaningful* stimuli that are not contaminated with coordination or speed. The only task of that sort in contemporary tests is K-ABC Photo Series, so examiners may choose to resurrect the ITPA Visual Association subtest to administer along with Photo Series. Visual Association includes visual analogies that use meaningful, pictorial stimuli.

Examiners who wish to obtain information on Coding performance under conditions of reduced visual perceptual demands, along with data on a child's writing speed may wish to supplement the WISC-III with the measure of writing speed and the large print version of WISC-R Coding that Evans and Stroebel (1986) standardized on 283 children in grades 3 to 10.

Coordination and Speed

The fact that there are numerous reasoning tests that deemphasize coordination and speed is important for the assessment of any child whose coordination is suspect or who has difficulty working rapidly for any reason. Examiners may attribute low PS Indexes and poor performance on some PO subtests to a motor problem, reflectivity, or anxiety, and imply that the child would have scored higher with the speed and motor components removed. But why speculate when pertinent tests such as solving matrices or ordering the pictures in Photo Series can offer an objective answer? Other subtests that fill this role well are WJ-R Analysis-Synthesis, Binet-4 Paper Folding and Cutting, and WJ-R Spatial Relations. The latter two are especially valuable for following up hypotheses that are based, in part, on poor Block Design performance, because they are motor-free measures of spatial visualization.

Examiners who wish to follow up the hypothesis that the child's low or high PS Index is related to speed of mental processing should administer subtests that measure fluid reasoning ability under speeded conditions, but where the quickness is related to problem-solving speed, not psychomotor speed. Useful supplements include KAIT Mystery Codes, KAIT Logical Steps, Detroit-3 Story Sequences, and K-SNAP Four-Letter Words.

A Few Final Words

The PS factor is new and needs to be researched to better understand what it measures for different individuals. Though Symbol Search resembles tasks studied by cognitive psychologists (Lohman, 1989; Sternberg, 1993), measures the kinds of skills in which mentally retarded children (Jensen et al., 1981) and learning-disabled children (Kolligan & Sternberg, 1987) may be deficient, its specific nuances require systematic study of Symbol Search performance by normal children and by the kinds of children who are routinely referred for psychological evaluation.

Gender differences on Symbol Search and the PS Index must be understood. The test publisher provided no data on WISC-III gender differences in the manual, but they may loom especially important for the PS Index. Coding and its WAIS-R analog, Digit Symbol, are well known to yield significant and substantial differences of ½ standard deviation or more favoring females (Kaufman, 1990a, Chapter 6); these differences occur in normal and exceptional samples, and are seen worldwide in various adaptations of Wechsler's scales (Lynn & Mulhern, 1991; Moriarty & Ryan, 1987; Phelps & Ensor, 1987; Smith, Edmonds, & Smith, 1989). If Symbol Search produces similar gender differences, then the cumulative effect may be a striking female superiority on the PS Index. That possibility, and its diagnostic and interpretive implications, must be explored.

It is also important for psychologists to understand why the FD Index and PS Index, though they correlate only about .40, may covary together for a variety of exceptional samples. As mentioned earlier, deficiencies on both factors may pertain to the physiological variables that are associated with reaction time and evoked potential research and theory (Hendrickson & Hendrickson, 1980; Jensen, 1985; J. Kaufman, 1995; Lohman, 1989; Matarazzo, 1992; Vernon, 1987), and those variables have cognitive consequences pertaining to metacomponents and working memory. The specifics regarding the two small WISC-III factors can only be grasped by using the SCAD subtests in cognitive and neuropsychological research. Maybe the answer lies in quantum mechanics, as Weiss (1986) believes: "Multiplying memory span by mental speed, we obtain the entropy of short-term memory capacity, which is rate-limiting for performance in intelligence tests" (p. 737). Sounds good; I wish I understood it.

ILLUSTRATIVE CASE REPORTS

The two case reports that follow illustrate the important role one or both of the two "minor" WISC-III factors can play in test interpretation. Lourdes is an 8-year-old with Tourette's syndrome and emotional disturbance, and Lucy is a 7½-year-old with reading problems. WISC-III data are integrated with data from the Binet-4 and Detroit-3 in the case of Lourdes, and with the K-ABC and K-TEA in the case of Lucy. As with all the reports in this book, identifying features of each case have been altered.

Lourdes I., Age 8-1, Tourette's Syndrome, Obsessive Compulsive Disorder

WISC-III Profile

IQs		(90% conf.)	Factor Indexes		(90% conf.)
Verbal	73	(69–80)	Verbal Comprehension	70	(66–77)
Performance	78	(73–87)	Perceptual Organization	83	(78–92)
Full Scale	73	(69–79)	Freedom from Distractibility	96	(89–104)
V-IQ = P-IQ *(ns)*			Processing Speed	67	(64–80)

Verbal	Scaled Score	Performance	Scaled Score
Information	7	Picture Completion	8
Similarities	4	(Coding)	(3)
Arithmetic	8	Picture Arrangement	3
Vocabulary	5	Block Design	8
Comprehension	2-W	Object Assembly	9
(Digit Span)	(10)-S	*Symbol Search	4

* Symbol Search was used in IQ computations

Mean of 12 subtests = 6

Stanford-Binet—Fourth Edition (selected subtests)

Subtest	Standard Score (Mean = 50; SD = 8)	Percentile
Absurdities	32	1
Quantitative	48	39
Copying	29	<1
Bead Memory	37	5
Memory for Sentences	39	8
Memory for Objects	40	10

Detroit Tests of Learning Aptitude—Third Edition (selected subtests)

Subtest	Standard Score (Mean = 10; SD = 3)	Percentile
Word Opposites	9	37
Reversed Letters	5	5
Story Construction	4	2

Reason for Referral

Lourdes was referred for a psychological evaluation by her school because she is having emotional and behavioral problems at home and at school. The goal of this assessment is to better understand Lourdes's dynamics so that interventions can be made that will improve her functioning at home and at school. Lourdes was given a potential diagnosis of schizophrenia by a previous therapist, and it is essential to decide whether there is any evidence that points to Lourdes receiving this diagnosis. In addition, her increasingly frequent outbursts at home and at school are causing extreme concern, and reasons for these increased behaviors need to be explored.

Background Information

Lourdes is a Mexican-American girl who was born in Los Angeles. She speaks English almost exclusively although she hears Spanish spoken in her home on occasion, usually when her maternal grandmother comes to visit.

Several past case reports were reviewed that described Lourdes's neurological functioning, diagnosis of Tourette's syndrome, ADHD, and obsessive-compulsive disorder, and her pattern of intellectual strengths and weaknesses. She has also been diagnosed with learning disabilities, primarily in the areas of motor coordination, language, figure-ground problems, visual motor coordination, and the sequencing and organization of information. She was last evaluated almost 3 years ago, but no test data were available. On the Child Behavior Checklist, filled out by both parents prior to the present evaluation, Lourdes's profile reflected attention problems, thought problems, and problems in the social domain.

Lourdes lives with her 15-year-old sister, 3-year-old brother, mother, and father. She has been described as being "different" since birth and has been evaluated numerous times, beginning with a neurological evaluation at age 3. She has had delays in her development, including gross and fine motor delays, for which she has received occupational therapy.

Lourdes is currently participating in a school program for children with emotional disturbance and attends a regular classroom via this special program. She receives help from a special aide only one day per week, according to her father, and her classroom teacher is currently having many problems containing her behavior in the classroom. The teacher feels that her outbursts and her cursing are not due to the Tourette's and are more a product of impulse control. Her parents feel that these behaviors are out of Lourdes's control and are due to the Tourette's.

Aside from exhibiting these impulsive behaviors, Lourdes also has rapid mood swings. At times, Lourdes's mother says that Lourdes gets completely "out of control" by being verbally and physically abusive, destructive, and self-destructive. At school, Lourdes is generally observed to play alone. Lourdes is currently taking Haldol to control symptoms related to Tourette's, attentional problems, and obsessive-compulsive behaviors. In the past she has been on a variety of medications such as clonidine and Dexadrine.

Appearance and Test Behavior

Lourdes is a cute 8-year-old girl with straight, black hair. She was reluctant to leave the stuffed toys in the waiting area, and she brought five small animals into the testing room with her. During the first 30 minutes of testing, Lourdes complained that her stomach hurt, and she had to use the bathroom two times. The regularly used restroom has a small bathtub, mostly enclosed by a curtain, and that presented a problem; her mother reported that Lourdes has a phobia relating to showers in public places. During both trips to the bathroom, the examiner accompanied Lourdes into the restroom at the child's insistence. Lourdes was frightened by the bathtub despite being reassured that the shower did not work. She clapped her hands several times at the shower each time she entered the restroom. She continued the hand clapping at various points during the testing, usually when she also appeared anxious.

In general, Lourdes had a hard time accepting the constraints of a formal testing situation. She had trouble staying in her seat at any time that she did not have something to look at or to manipulate, and she was extremely impulsive. She would get up, pace about the room, and grab at things that caught her attention. During more motor-oriented tasks, Lourdes grabbed at the test materials, and would try to start the task immediately. When shown how to construct blocks into a design, Lourdes grabbed her blocks before the examiner could get the sample blocks placed so that she could copy them. Nonetheless, Lourdes was usually redirectable and seemed able to attend and concentrate adequately for the administration of most cognitive test items during the 2-hour testing session.

Lourdes needed constant encouragement on all tasks. When she was asked to draw a person, she started coloring different shades of green and naming each shade, until she was reminded twice that she needed to draw a picture of herself. She then looked up and said, "Can I draw me with breasts?" She did draw a picture of herself with breasts. On all paper-and-pencil tasks, she held the pencil awkwardly, occasionally used both hands at once, pressed too hard on the pencil (breaking the point twice), and demonstrated overall uncoordinated behavior. This lack of coordination was noticeable, but much less pronounced, on tests requiring manipulation of beads, blocks, and puzzle pieces. When asked oral questions, she sometimes answered only after the examiner repeated the question once, and sometimes three or four times. Occasionally, she would not answer at all, ignoring the examiner completely, but that behavior seemed to occur on the items that she did not know.

She had a particular lack of motivation during the last task administered, a personality task on which she was asked to look at inkblots and say what they might be. Lourdes put her head down, and only continued with much urging. She did complete the task, although when asked what in the blot made it look like what she named, she repeatedly said, "I don't know."

Although Lourdes had a flat affect during the testing procedure, she examined the examiner's face for a response when refusing to answer an item, grabbed an object she knew she shouldn't touch, and deliberately blew in the examiner's face. When the examiner commented that she didn't really like the latter behavior, Lourdes apologized quickly, and did not do it again. When Lourdes was anxious, she put her hands up to her face, or clapped her hands. There was no overt "anxious look" on her face.

After the testing session, when Lourdes came back for a visit with the consulting psychiatrist, she was anxious at first and did not seem able to focus on any activity. She smelled and tried to taste pieces of the board game that was out on the table. When she was allowed to explore the room on her own, she picked out a deck of Uno cards, and told the psychiatrist that she wished to play. She took the cards out and placed them in a pile. She turned up a "3" and said "tres." She was playing her own version of what she had deduced was a Spanish game. She was able to sit quietly and attend the rest of that session.

Tests Administered

WISC-III
Stanford-Binet-4 (six subtests)
Detroit-3 (three subtests)
Rorschach (Inkblot Test)
Human Figure Drawings

Tests Results and Interpretation

On the WISC-III, Lourdes achieved a Verbal IQ of 73, a Performance IQ of 78, and a Full Scale IQ of 73. These IQs are consistent within the Borderline range of intellectual functioning and rank her at about the 5th percentile when compared with other 8-year-olds. However, because of considerable scatter in her WISC-III profile, these IQs do not provide a meaningful picture of her cognitive abilities and should be ignored in favor of her profile of standard scores on the four Factor indexes that are also yielded by the WISC-III.

Within the Verbal Scale, she scored significantly and substantially higher on the Freedom from Distractibility (FD) Index (39th percentile) than on the Verbal Comprehension (VC) Index (2nd percentile) indicating much better functioning on tests that are sensitive to attention and concentration for success than on subtests that assess verbal conceptualization and expression. Her Performance profile also split in half; she earned a percentile rank of 13 on the Perceptual Organization (PO) Index, much higher than the 1st percentile that she achieved on the Processing Speed (PD) index. The best picture of her verbal versus nonverbal skills is provided by a comparison of her PO Index of 83 (Low Average function), which is significantly higher than her VC Index of 70 (Borderline functioning). The pattern of higher nonverbal than verbal intelligence is commonly found among children from Mexican-American and other Hispanic backgrounds even when, like Lourdes, English is the primary language spoken in the home. Her PO Index should be considered the best estimate of her intellectual functioning because linguistic or cultural factors affecting her verbal and global abilities may cause her intelligence to be underestimated.

Lourdes's Verbal subtest profile suggests that she performs best on tests that require a minimal amount of verbal output and that depend on memory rather than abstract reasoning for success. Her highest score was on an auditory short-term memory test (50th percentile) on which she repeated 4 numbers forward and also was able to reverse 4 digits. It is unusual for a child to have a backward span that equals or exceeds the forward span, occurring in about 15% of normal children. Because repeating digits backward requires number manipulation and reorganization, and repeating digits forward does not, children with good number ability sometimes perform unusually well on the task of reversing digits. In fact, good number ability probably explains why Lourdes performed so well on the FD factor, which includes a test of oral arithmetic in addition to the digit repetition subtest. Further evidence of a strength in number ability comes from an analysis of her responses to the WISC-III test of general information. The first 12 items include 6 that measure number facts and concepts (e.g., days in a week) and 6 that do not. She passed all 6 items involving number, but only 2 of the nonnumber items.

To help understand whether Lourdes's strength was primarily in number ability, short-term memory, or responding to verbal items requiring minimal verbalization, selected subtests were administered from the Stanford-Binet-4 and Detroit-3. Despite her relatively excellent performance on WISC-III Digit Span, she did not demonstrate an exceptional memory on the supplementary tasks when she was required to recall stimuli other than numbers. She performed poorly (5th to 10th percentile) on memory tests requiring her to repeat sentences, recognize pictures of objects, and repeat letters in the reverse order. Her relatively good performance (39th percentile) on the Binet-4 Quantitative subtest, which measures abilities such as counting, arithmetic reasoning, and number concepts, reinforces her strength in number ability.

The supplementary testing, coupled with her WISC-III scores, gave support for a weakness in the ability to express her ideas verbally. She scored at the 37th percentile on the Detroit-3 Word Opposites subtest, a vocabulary test requiring one-word responses, which is better than the 5th percentile she achieved on the WISC-III Vocabulary subtest (which requires children to explain the meanings of words). Her ability to provide one-word opposites is markedly better than her performance on three other subtests that demand much more verbal expression for success: a WISC-III test of social comprehension (less than 1st percentile), a Binet-4 test requiring children to find the absurdity in pictures (1st percentile), and a Detroit-3 test that presents a picture and requires children to construct a story about the picture (2nd percentile).

On WISC-III Vocabulary, Lourdes was able to sing the alphabet when asked to define it, but she responded that a donkey was a horse. On a task where Lourdes had to say how two items were alike, she answered many items in a concrete manner. She was able to say that both a cat and a mouse have tails, but she responded that an "apple is round and a banana looks like a smile" when asked how they were alike.

Lourdes had the greatest difficulty on tasks that measured her social knowledge and judgment and an understanding of social interactions, a finding that is consistent with observations of her test behavior and with the behaviors she is reported to display in school. She had a hard time answering common sense questions that relied on this type of knowledge. She was able to say what a person should do to take care of a cut finger ("wash it out and put a Band-Aid on it"), but when she was asked what people should do if they find a wallet or purse in a store, she responded, "play with it . . . get into it, get into the money." In response to a question asking why we need to wear seat belts, she did not answer and attempted to stick a bead into her eye. Lourdes also had great difficulty on two other tasks that measure social understanding, both of which utilize pictorial stimuli: a WISC-III subtest where she had to arrange mixed-up cards into a sequence so they told a story, and the Binet-4 task that required her to find absurdities in pictures such as boy trying to put his pants on upside down. Thus, Lourdes's problems with socially relevant items are not merely a function of her deficiencies in verbal expression.

Lourdes had considerable difficulty on a task where she was asked to quickly write symbols. She appeared to have a hard time working quickly with a pencil. Her developmentally immature figure drawings also indicate that Lourdes has trouble with pencil-and-paper tasks. Within the Performance Scale, she performed relatively well (Average range) on tests of spatial ability, achieving the 25th percentile on tests of assembling cut-up puzzles, copying abstract designs with blocks, and finding the missing parts of incomplete pictures. In contrast, her poor coordination with a pencil seems to explain her very poor Processing Speed Index of 67 (1st percentile).

Regarding personality functions, Lourdes tends to be an extremely slow processor of information. She is able to attend to and take in her environment, but her skills are variable. Sometimes, she can make a quick, accurate response, but other times she appears not to be attending and makes a very slow or no response. Many times, she will respond in an unusual or impulsive fashion, such as when she responded that a picture of an elephant missing a leg was missing a "penis." One hypothesis is that this impulsive style is due to her Tourette's disorder. Another hypothesis is that when she makes a slow or no response, she is concentrating on obsessional thoughts. There may be no way of knowing what is occupying her attention, but she seems pulled away into her own, inner world at these times. When Lourdes is pushed to respond, she demonstrates marked anxiety and even panic. These are the times when she may act out behaviorally or make responses to her environment that are not based on what is really present. Her overall behavior, however, does not warrant a diagnosis of schizophrenia.

Summary

Lourdes is an 8-year-old girl Mexican-American girl who has been diagnosed with Tourette's syndrome and obsessive compulsive disorder. She has been evaluated numerous times and is currently being followed by a neurologist. She has had many medication treatments in the past and is currently on Haldol to control her symptoms. Her behavior has gotten worse lately, and she has frequent behavioral outbursts. Lourdes was able to attend fairly well for the present cognitive evaluation, suggesting that the present tests results depict accurate estimates of her current level of functioning, but she was unmotivated when administered the Rorschach. During the cognitive evaluation, she frequently had a blank look on her face and sometimes was slow to respond to prompts; she was, however, redirectable.

Lourdes's range of intellectual functioning as measured by the WISC-III IQs suggests Borderline intellectual ability, but her IQs in the 70s do not adequately explain the range of her abilities as measured on the WISC-III and selected supplements from the Binet-4 and Detroit-3. She demonstrated Average spatial and number ability, but performed at an Intellectually Deficient level on tests of verbal expression, social judgment, and understanding, and paper-and-pencil coordination.

Lourdes has the capabilities to respond correctly to her environment and to connect socially with people when she feels able to. She does her best when she is not pushed for a response and when she can take the activity at her own pace. When she is made to respond, she appears to experience anxiety and panic. This may be due to a combination of obsessional thought interference and Tourette's disorder. Lourdes's reality testing was weakest when she was asked to do an unstructured task and appeared to be concentrating on inner activities. In response to the main referral question, she does not appear to be schizophrenic.

Recommendations

1. Her parents and teacher need to recognize when Lourdes needs to slow down. This might be especially apparent if she does not immediately make a verbal response, or if her face looks very distant. She will probably not be able to respond appropriately at these times. If it is possible, try to let Lourdes continue the activity at her own pace. This suggestion may be critical as a way of managing her behavior effectively, because behavioral tantrums are often the result of being interrupted.

2. Her parents should continue to obtain available information on obsessive compulsive disorder. The consulting psychiatrist has mailed them pertinent references.

3. Her parents should also continue to pursue and clarify neurological findings. There may be further information that her neurologist can provide.

4. Her parents should continue the work they have already begun to find the appropriate medication. This may take some persistence.

5. One or both parents should continue to work together with the consulting psychiatrist to clarify Lourdes's behavior patterns and to develop strategies to assist her with change.

6. Lourdes's parents and teacher should communicate regularly so that a better understanding of Lourdes's behaviors, and how to respond to them consistently, is reached. The consulting psychiatrist will meet with the parents and teacher to discuss these issues. Parents and teacher need to understand what to do when Lourdes acts out or needs to withdraw. A situation should be developed at school so that when Lourdes cannot respond she is allowed to just sit quietly and do her work at her own pace. Opportunities to work individually, or in small groups—especially when approaching new material—would be the most conducive to Lourdes's growth and academic progress.

7. Lourdes's strength in spatial ability suggests that she does well when solving problems in a simultaneous, gestalt-holistic manner, where she must integrate stimuli. She also seems to perform best when using visual stimuli. These assets can be used to enhance her functioning academically. A number of xeroxed pages from the K-ABC Interpretive manual have been mailed to Lourdes's parents and her teacher. These pages provide suggestions for teaching Lourdes various academic skills in reading, spelling, and arithmetic that take advantage of her good spatial/sequential abilities.

8. Lourdes's strength in number ability can also be put to good advantage to help improve her academic, social, and verbal expressive skills. With a little ingenuity, her teacher can develop lessons that incorporate number activities such as counting or dividing pictures or objects into equal groups. This approach should serve both as a motivational device and as a means of utilizing her strength to improve weak areas of functioning.

Examiner:
Alaina Lynn, MA

Lucy O., Age 7-7, Reading Problems

WISC-III Profile

IQs		(90% conf.)	Factor Indexes		(90% conf.)
Verbal	106	(100–111)	Verbal Comprehension	102	(96–108)
Performance	100	(93–107)	Perceptual Organization	99	(92–106)
Full Scale	104	(99–109)	Freedom from Distractibility	126	(115–130)
V-IQ = P-IQ *(ns)*			Processing Speed	114	(104–120)

Verbal	Scaled Score	Performance	Scaled Score
Information	8-W	Picture Completion	7-W
Similarities	12	(Coding)	(14)
Arithmetic	14-S	Picture Arrangement	12
Vocabulary	9	Block Design	10
Comprehension	12	Object Assembly	10
(Digit Span)	(15)-S	*Symbol Search	11

* Symbol Search was used in IQ computations

Mean of 12 subtests = 11

K-ABC Profile

Scale	Standard Score (± 90% conf.)	Mental Processing Subtests	Scaled Score
Sequential Processing	124 ± 9	Sequential	
Simultaneous Processing	105 ± 7	Hand Movements	13
Mental Processing Composite	114 ± 7	Number Recall	13
Achievement		Word Order	15-S
Faces & Places	89 ± 11	Simultaneous	
Riddles	96 ± 9	Gestalt Closure	10
(only subtests given)		Triangles	12
		Matrix Analogies	10
		Spatial Memory	9-W
SEQ > SIM (*p* < .01)		Photo Series	13

Kaufman Test of Educational Achievement—Comprehensive Form (K-TEA)

Subtest/Composite	Standard Score (±90% conf.)
Mathematics Composite	125 ± 5
Mathematics Computation	112 ± 7
Mathematics Applications	132 ± 7
Reading Composite	83 ± 3
Reading Decoding	84 ± 4
Reading Comprehension	83 ± 5
Spelling	96 ± 5
Battery Composite	98 ± 3

Referral and Background Information

Seven-year-old Lucy, a second grader, was referred for evaluation by her parents, who are concerned that Lucy is "dyslexic" and not learning to read. They have observed a particular set of problems that have caught their attention. These observations include writing words backwards, reversing "b's" and "d's," and "guessing" at words after recognition of the first and/or last letter. Lucy's second-grade teacher was interviewed as part of this evaluation and feels that Lucy's main area of difficulty is in reading and using word-attack skills. She also expressed concern that Lucy is behind in her spelling abilities, missing approximately 5 out of 15 weekly words.

Lucy lives in a middle-class home with her parents and her 4-year-old sister, Carly. Her development is reported to be normal, except for the presence of severe headaches every few months. No other significant illnesses or persistent medical complaints have been documented during Lucy's early childhood. Early developmental milestones occurred within normal time limits, with the exception of delayed speech, which began around age 2.

Lucy attended a private nursery school from age 3 to 4. This experience was reportedly positive and without difficulty. She has been enrolled at a public elementary school since she entered kindergarten at age 5. No problems were noted by her kindergarten or first-grade teachers.

Six months ago, Mrs. O's father, a school guidance counselor, alerted Mrs. O. to a possible reading problem after having spent some time with Lucy. In an effort to encourage growth in this area, Mr. O. has introduced educational computer games and dedicates his time to working with Lucy. Likewise, Mrs. O. frequently reads to Lucy and assists her with her daily homework.

Both Mr. and Mrs. O. describe their children as having been "liberally brought up." Mr. O. feels that Mrs. O. "spoils" Lucy, yet both subscribe to a permissive child-rearing style. Until recently, the children have occupied the same sleeping quarters as their parents. Although the children now sleep separately from their parents, Mrs. O. reads to Lucy at bedtime, sometimes for over an hour, because Lucy has difficulty falling asleep on her own.

Lucy is described by her parents as "unsure of herself" and experiencing "low self-esteem" in regard to her reading ability. According to Mr. O., she refuses to play with computer games if reading is required and verbalizes statements such as "I'm afraid" and "It's too hard." On the other hand, her parents feel that Lucy makes friends easily, is "bright" and has a good vocabulary, and does well because she's alert to "other cues." Lucy appears to have learned some compensatory behaviors, including eliciting from her sister the difference between left and right and manipulating her hands to help differentiate "b's" from "d's."

At school, Lucy was observed in her classroom setting and her behavior closely monitored. The BASC Student Observation System was used; it involves a 15-minute systematic sampling of 12 behavior categories, including assessment of both adaptive and maladaptive behaviors. Of the 9 problem categories, Lucy demonstrated behavior in only 1 category: Inappropriate Movement. While the children were at their desks writing sentences about a story they had just read, Lucy was unsure of herself and checked to see what the other children were writing, although she did not actually copy from their papers. All the other behaviors observed were in the adaptive behavior areas. Lucy responded appropriately to the teacher, interacted comfortably with her peers, attended to required tasks, and moved easily from one task to another.

Lucy was given the achievement portion of the Woodcock-Johnson Psycho-Educational Battery—Revised two weeks ago at school. Her scores on this comprehensive achievement test ranged from below average to average in the Broad Reading category (standard score = 89, 23rd percentile) to above average in the area of Broad Knowledge, where she earned a standard score of 115 and did better than 84 percent of children her age. On the individual subtests that comprise the achievement clusters, her worst performance was on Letter-Word Identification (standard score = 87, 20th percentile) and her best on Applied Problems, a math test, on which she earned a standard score of 122 and performed better than 93 percent of same age children. Furthermore, Lucy was given the Roswell-Chall Diagnostic Reading Test (also at school), which indicated that she was essentially a "nonreader." As a result of her test performance, Lucy was placed in a pull-out reading assistance program and is currently attending this program.

Appearance and Behavioral Characteristics

Lucy is a petite, pretty, white child with brown hair worn in a pony-tail halfway down her back. Her behavior during three testing sessions at the clinic reflected her pleasant, friendly demeanor and cooperative nature. As she grew more comfortable, she freely exchanged social conversation with the examiner. Using slow, methodical trail-and-error thought processes, Lucy was able to concentrate for long periods of time, revealing both a good, nondistractible attention span as well as high frustration tolerance. When faced with challenging tasks, Lucy was observed to use her hands as instructional aids. For example, when copying abstract designs, she used her hand (as one would a piece of paper) to cover previously recorded parts; when working with numbers, she frequently used her fingers to count. Other compensatory behaviors noted during the testing include projecting imaginary lines on visual stimuli to assist her in putting cut-up triangles together, relying on environmental clues such as the facial expression of the examiner, and calling on examples from her life experience when having difficulty expressing answers in words.

Lucy was reflective in her approach to problem solving and talked herself through most tasks, revealing a systematic, step-by-step approach. Although she responded positively to praise and was self-affirmative at times, she glanced up for approval or instruction when she was unsure of the adequacy of her performance and frequently scanned the examiner's face for indications of inaccuracy. Lucy appeared to be highly self-critical and was overly cognizant of failed items. It was not uncommon to hear her utter things like "That wasn't very good!," "I know I must have gotten that one wrong!," "I'm not that good at this!," "You dummy, what did you do that for!," and "I could have gotten it right if I had more time!"

There were several hints of auditory perceptual difficulty, such as when Lucy misinterpreted the examiner's carefully pronounced words (e.g., "games" was heard and responded to as "gangs"; "thief" was responded with "Is that the same as 'thief'?"). However, the problem was mild and does not seem to impair her cognitive or academic functioning. Her trial-and-error attempts indicated a poor interpretation of the picture-puzzle parts, suggesting a visual-perceptual problem. Whereas she was aware of a difficulty in this area, she was unable to find a solution.

Lucy experiences significant confusion regarding directionality. She copied symbols from right to left toward the end of a task requiring her to copy symbols from left to right. Initially, she was able to follow the instructions provided, but as she lost sight of the objective, she reverted to a more comfortable style of right to left. Although there was evidence of letter and number reversals, she was often able to "catch" these errors, erase them, and correct her mistakes. On several occasions, Lucy expressed that she could not read the words presented. Once, when asked to say the name of a person written on a stimulus card, she sheepishly remarked while looking down, "I hate it when you ask me these questions." On the other hand, when forced to apply word-attack skills, she can be successful. For example, she failed a reading comprehension problem by guessing on the basis of context clues. With some prompting from the examiner, she sounded out the word and got it correct.

The results of this evaluation are believed to reflect an accurate and valid portrayal of Lucy's current cognitive functioning.

Tests Administered

Wechsler Intelligence Scale for Children—Third Edition (WISC-III)

Kaufman Assessment Battery for Children (K-ABC)

Kaufman Test of Educational Achievement (K-TEA)
   Comprehensive Form

Bender-Gestalt Test of Visual-Motor Development (Bender-Gestalt)

Kinetic Family Drawing

House-Tree-Person

Sentence Completion Test for Children

Behavior Assessment System for Children (BASC): Student Observation
   System (results discussed in Background Information section)

Tests Results and Interpretation

Lucy scored in the Average range of intelligence on the WISC-III, earning a Verbal IQ of 106, a Performance IQ of 100, and a Full Scale of 104 ± 5. The 6-point discrepancy between her Verbal and Performance IQs is undoubtedly due to change, indicating that she performs about equally well whether solving verbal problems and expressing her ideas orally or solving nonverbal items via the manipulation of concrete materials. Her overall performance on the WISC-III surpassed approximately 61% of children her age. She scored at the High Average level on the K-ABC, achieving a Mental Processing Composite of 114 ± 7, comparable to the 82nd percentile.

Within the WISC-III Verbal Scale, she earned a significantly higher Index on the Freedom from Distractibility (FD) Factor (96th percentile) than on the Verbal Comprehension (VC) Factor (55th percentile) indicating much better functioning on tests that are dependent on attention and concentration for success than on tests of more conventional verbal intelligence. She had significant strengths on both subtests that compose the FD factor, solving oral arithmetic problems and auditory memory for digits. Lucy also performed well (91st percentile) on a nonverbal test that is often associated with the FD factor, Coding, which measures sequential ability and psychomotor speed. In contrast, she had a significant weakness on a Performance subtest requiring her to find the missing part in pictures (16 percentile), and on a Verbal test of Lucy's range of general factual knowledge (25th percentile). The latter weakness, coupled with a similar score on a test of oral vocabulary, denotes a limited fund of information, despite her enriched home environment and may be a consequence of her reading problem. The weakness in Picture Completion seems to pertain to a more pervasive problem with visual-spatial tasks that suggests difficulty solving problems using a simultaneous, gestalt-holistic approach.

She performed at the 39th percentile, overall, on Picture Completion and two other subtests that measure spatial/simultaneous ability, which is significantly lower than the 98th percentile that she achieved on three subtests that depend on step-by-step sequential processing for success: the two FD tasks plus Coding. On the K-ABC, which is organized around the sequential-simultaneous processing distinction, Lucy's separate standard scores reinforce her better skill at solving problems step-by-step (Sequential score = 124) than in a holistic, integrated fashion (Simultaneous score = 105). That difference is significant and noteworthy, and in complete agreement with the analysis of both her WISC-III subtest profile, and with the step-by-step problem-solving approach that was inferred from her verbalizations during several WISC-III and K-ABC tasks. She resorted to a more comfortable, sequential approach even when solving problems that would benefit most from a simultaneous strategy. Not coincidentally, Lucy's highest scores on the WISC-III Performance Scale and the K-ABC Simultaneous Scale were on three subtests that have visual-sequential components (the Coding subtest mentioned previously, along with two subtests that require the ordering of pictures).

Lucy was also administered two K-ABC Achievement subtests, a test of her ability to solve verbal riddles, and a measure of her general knowledge that demands naming pictures of famous people and places. Both tasks require a good fund of information plus good simultaneous processing for success, both of which seem to be her weak spots. Consistent with her WISC-III performance, Lucy averaged only the 31st percentile on these two K-ABC subtests.

Lucy's better global score on the K-ABC than WISC-III probably reflects the fact that her reading difficulties handicap her on some WISC-III Verbal subtests, thereby underestimating her intelligence on the WISC-III. She probably has High Average rather than Average intellectual ability when the indirect consequences of her reading problem are minimized, and she has Superior ability when solving problems via sequential processing.

The various compensatory mechanisms that Lucy employed when solving nonverbal items (e.g., blocking out parts of designs with her hand) and her problems in interpreting puzzle pieces during Object Assembly, coupled with her low Picture Completion score and a significant weakness on a K-ABC visual-spatial memory test, suggest that her visual-perceptual skills are not developed at an automatic level. Whereas her test scores on conceptual and reasoning tests that use visual stimuli indicate that she has adequate visual-perceptual abilities, she must concentrate to do well, especially when other demands such as reading are present. When encouraged, she is determined and willing to put forth the effort necessary to solve difficult problems, but she has a tendency to resist this kind of overwork. An example of this point is the loss of directionality observed on several tasks: Left to right is not automatic to Lucy and requires her to think. With feedback, however, she is able to learn and correct her mistakes. For example, Lucy seemed to benefit greatly from structured help by the examiner. After reversing blocks on WISC-III's Block Design, the examiner showed her the correct response (as required in the directions for administration). After this feedback, she assembled the next few items perfectly.

To explore Lucy's achievement in important school subjects, especially in the area of reading, the Comprehensive Form of the K-TEA was administered and an error analysis was performed. Whereas her overall Battery Composite standard score is 98 ± 3 and ranks her in the Average category, it does not reflect Lucy's true level of achievement. Of greater importance are her discrepant Reading Composite (83 ± 3, Below Average) and Mathematics Composite (125 ± 5, Well Above Average), which display a 42-point difference. Given her strong sequential preference and her Arithmetic strength on the WISC-III, it is not surprising to know that her best standard scores were on tests of mathematical skills. The difference in her cognitive processing capabilities is reflected in how she is learning in school and performing in the various subject areas. She scored significantly higher in math than in spelling or reading, and her spelling score was significantly higher than her reading score. Within math, Lucy's 20-point difference in favor of Mathematics Applications over Mathematics Computation is significant. Within reading, she performed equally poorly in the decoding of words (14th percentile) and in comprehension (13th percentile).

Because Lucy was referred as a result of her poor performance in reading, her error patterns on the reading and spelling subtests were analyzed to gain a better understanding of her weaknesses. When comparing the number of errors Lucy made in each subskill category with the average number of errors for children her age, Lucy evidenced weakness (she made more errors than 75% of second-grade children who attempted the same number of items) in the following areas for *both* Reading Decoding and Spelling: Closed Syllable (Short) Vowels and Vowel Digraphs and Diphthongs. On Reading Decoding, she also had difficulty with the category "Open Syllable (Long) and Final *e* Pattern Vowels." As is evident, and consistent with the results of the recent administration of the Woodcock-Johnson and with her parents' concerns, Lucy is not performing at the expected level in reading for children her age.

Lucy's drawings on the Bender-Gestalt earned her a Koppitz error score of 2, which is in the average range of performance for children her age. Of particular interest is the difficulty she had in copying a figure consisting of two overlapping hexagons. She became discouraged after attempting to approach the problem simultaneously (she tried to draw the perimeter of the whole), but after some prompting from the examiner she compensated by using a sequential means (she drew one hexagon at a time). The significance of this observation reminds us how pervasive this discrepant style enters into many things that she does and demonstrates that when encouraged she can improve and is fully remediable.

To explore personality and emotional characteristics, several projective measures were administered. These less formal tools included drawings and responding verbally to incomplete sentences. Based on inferences from these projectives, conversations with the examiner, clinical observations, background reports, and observations of Lucy in school, the following picture emerges. Lucy is a well-adjusted young girl who is well-liked by her family, teacher, and friends. She expressed a healthy interest in people, rock collecting, and in becoming an artist. She is aware of a variety of feelings and how to express them, and she is eager to please. Lucy sometimes demonstrated anxiety over not being perfect and showed concern regarding others' perceptions of her.

Diagnostic Impression

Based on Lucy's physical, developmental, behavioral, and scholastic history, and the results of this psychoeducational evaluation, a diagnosis of learning disabilities is made at the current time. This learning disability is best categorized by a DSM-III-R diagnosis of Developmental Reading Disorder, unspecified (#315.00). Lucy's reading difficulties are not viewed as a neurologically based problem but reflect a discrepancy in how she prefers to process information, resorting to a less efficient means at times. Reading is a complex act that requires both sequential and simultaneous processing.

Summary and Recommendations

Lucy is a delightful, 7½-year-old girl, who is friendly and cooperative. She displayed a sequential strength in her ability to solve problems but was less efficient when required to use simultaneous means of processing information. Her overall intelligence, as measured by the WISC-III and K-ABC, is Average to High Average, and she has a limited fund of information. Her greatest areas of academic difficulty are in reading, and she excels at solving math problems. Whereas her strength in mathematics has provided her with opportunities for scholastic success, her reading difficulties, along with her general lack of risk taking, have gotten her into a rut where she employs problem-solving strategies that are less efficient for the demands placed on her, both cognitively and in reading achievement. She is intrinsically aware of her greater ability to process information sequentially and continues to apply this mode even when it is not relevant. To help her acquire more success in reading, the following specific suggestions are made:

1. Assign Lucy individualized tutorial assistance to help strengthen different aspects of reading decoding and comprehension that rely primarily on her strength in sequential processing. Some of the tasks pair sequential with simultaneous techniques, which may help strengthen her ability to apply simultaneous strategies when necessary. Xeroxed portions of the K-ABC interpretive manual that contain information regarding pertinent remedial procedures have been mailed to Mr. and Mrs. O. and to Lucy's teacher. A variety of tasks and styles of introducing new information are provided in this handout.

If assistance is offered at the public school level, and a teacher can individualize instruction to meet Lucy's reading needs, then it would be beneficial for the school to use these guidelines. In Spelling, Lucy made an unusually high number of error on words that have vowel digraphs and diphthongs (she made 9 such errors, whereas the average child in her reference group made 1–4 errors). For example, she had difficulty with the "ea" in *reach* and the "ie" in *friend* (writing "rech" and "frend"). She had a weakness in this area in Reading Decoding as well. Suggestions for remediating this specific problem area for both reading and spelling have been included in the materials that were mailed. Several of the other weak areas in Spelling are also included in the remedial guidelines, although reading decoding and comprehension activities are stressed.

2. Implement the following "discrimination training" procedure to stop reversals of "b's" and "d's," and "p's" and "q's":

Discrimination Training as a Remedial Procedure

    a. Tutor constructs a deck of cards to include *one* of 2 confused stimuli (say "b") and several letters that are as far removed from "b" as possible: x v b s i w z.

    b. Cards are flashed to Lucy so that she learns to discriminate one—the "b"—and reject the others. Gradually, the deck of cards is expanded to include other letters that resemble "b" a little more: e a c f g j k l m n o r t u y.

    c. After Lucy learns to automatically tell whether a stimulus card is "b" or not, the most difficult distractors are added: h p q.

    d. Finally, the letter that caused maximum confusion—the "d"—is added. If done correctly, Lucy will be able to immediately decide if any given letter is a "b," and will therefore appropriately discriminate the "b" from the "d," which she will reject.

3. Lucy should be encouraged to use word-attack skills in lieu of guessing, whether she is reading in the classroom or in the home environment. Also, help her attend to the distinctive features of visual stimuli, which will build her reading recognition skills as well as allow her to take in more information from her surroundings.

4. A behavioral management program should be prepared to increase her level of motivation when faced with perceived difficult tasks such as reading. Consistent use of *positive,* gratifying experiences will work best considering Lucy's lack of confidence regarding her areas of weakness and her tendency to be hard on herself.

5. Monitor closely the difficulty level of new tasks, not only in an effort to avoid unnecessary frustration and discouragement, but to prevent her from learning a mistake. If she "learns" a mistake, she will repeat the error and it will be harder to correct later.

6. Facilitate Lucy's interest and participation in reading by creatively interacting with her. For example, have Lucy dictate a story of her own while another member of the family writes it down, eventually producing her own book.

7. Continued efforts to read to Lucy will be helpful, as well as offering her support and encouragement to grow in being able to read independently.

Examiners:

Ana Parente, MA; Patricia Petterson, MA

Supervisor:

Dr. Nadeen L. Kaufman

CHAPTER 6

Interpreting Subtest Profiles

Wechsler organized his subtests into a clinically useful dichotomy based on intuitive and rational considerations but recognized that "the abilities represented in the tests may also be meaningfully classified in other ways" (Wechsler, 1974, p. 9). Factor analysis yields a four-way division of the WISC-III, and other recategorizations based on the theoretical or practical approaches of Bannatyne, Guilford, or Horn also suggest that Wechsler's subtests require more than a simple two-way split to extract the most meaning from profile fluctuations. The clinical approach of Wechsler pioneers Rapaport, Gill, and Schaefer (1945–1946) also offers useful suggestions for organizing WISC-III subtests, such as in terms of input or output demands. For example, tasks may be grouped as a function of their sensitivity to attention and concentration (Arithmetic, Digit Span, Picture Completion, Coding, Symbol Search). Or they may be organized by their motor demands: visual organization (Picture Completion, Picture Arrangement), where motor coordination is of minimal importance, versus visual-motor coordination (Block Design, Object Assembly, Coding, Symbol Search), where motor ability can substantially affect test performance.

The variety of ways that psychologists have reorganized Wechsler's subtests, including the interpretation of small, exotic-sounding factors such as Contemporary Affairs or Maintenance of Contact (Lutey 1977; Saunders 1960), is almost endless. Virtually every technique has something to recommend it and is thus worthy of attention, if not necessarily respect. A diversity of methods contributed to the lists of shared abilities and "influences" enumerated for each subtest in Chapter 2; even one of the "exotic" factors (Freedom from Uncertainty) was included, as both Picture Completion and Object Assembly are believed to be influenced by the ability to respond when uncertain.

A comparison of the plethora of categorical systems reveals contradictions among them in the way different subtests are grouped. Picture Arrangement, for example, is included in Wechsler's Performance Scale and PO factor, and in Rapaport's Visual Organization group, but is considered by Meeker to measure *semantic* content from Guilford's theory.

Which system is correct? No one system is the correct one, but neither can any system be said to be wrong. Likewise, it is inappropriate to assume that one particular method is necessarily better than any other technique.

Each method has its special uniqueness and utility for different individuals. Bannatyne's Acquired Knowledge and Verbal Conceptualization categories may provide the key to the interpretation of a culturally disadvantaged or culturally different child's fluctuations within the Verbal Scale, whereas the factor structure may be more useful for understanding the profile of a highly distractible child who evidenced problems with visual memory. Similarly, the peaks and valleys in the Performance Scale profile of a child with obvious motor difficulties may be understood most sensibly by utilizing Rapaport's Visual Organization and Visual-Motor Coordination groups.

Poor scores on Coding, Symbol Search, and Picture Arrangement may reflect a deficiency in planning ability (Das-Naglieri PASS system), convergent production ability (Guilford), or in some other area such as integrated brain functioning or understanding complex oral directions. Uncovering the correct hypothesis depends on other test scores, clinical observation of test behaviors, the nature of incorrect responses, and pertinent background information.

No one system should be exclusively adhered to, but all should be learned well by examiners to permit the kind of flexibility of test interpretation that is so essential. In a sense, the examiner is trying to match the system to the individual, finding the approach that best explains the available data. Many clinicians utilize *personality* theories in this eclectic manner, selecting the one or two that best match an individual's presenting problems and personality dynamics rather than remaining unflinchingly loyal to Freud, Horney, Adler, Beck, Rogers, Sullivan, or Miller/Dollard. Yet these same clinicians are sometimes unwilling to employ this flexible approach in applying cognitive theories to an intelligence test profile.

Occasionally more than one model is required to explain scaled-score fluctuations satisfactorily. In the examples cited earlier, the profile of a culturally disadvantaged child with motor problems may require utilization of both Bannatyne's and Rapaport's recategorizations to interpret peaks and valleys within the Verbal and Performance Scales, respectively. In other instances, none of the popular systems may prove satisfactory, and examiners must call on alternative strategies to decipher the mysteries of a child's ability spectrum. These strategies may involve application of theories and research findings from areas such as developmental psychology, cognitive psychology, or neuropsychology; they may require interpretation of some of the less pervasive abilities that are shared by only two or three WISC-III subtests (e.g., learning ability, degree of abstract thinking); or they may stem from clinical analysis of the child's particular background and behaviors, thereby representing a novel and unique set of hypotheses that are not generalizable to other children.

How can a clinician examine complex interpretive issues in a systematic and direct way? The seven steps for interpreting WISC-III profiles, outlined and illustrated in Chapter 3, provide the system. Steps 1 to 6 lead the examiner through the interpretation of IQs and factor scores, and the determination of significant strengths and weaknesses within the subtest profile. Chapters 4 and 5 help examiners go beyond the empirical rules, providing in-depth understanding of the three IQs and four Factor Indexes.

Now we are up to Step 7, generating hypotheses to explain the subtest fluctuations. The goal of this chapter is to offer an organized method for identifying and validating hypotheses. The following section sets forth the philosophy and logic that underlie the kind of detective work needed for this process. Then several tables that provide the raw materials for profile inter-pretation are presented and explained. In the remainder of Chapter 6, a stepwise procedure is delineated and illustrated for solving the interpretive riddle of a child's WISC-III subtest fluctuations followed by a section on making meaningful recommendations and the presentation of two illustrative case reports.

A PHILOSOPHY OF PROFILE ATTACK

A WISC-III detective strives to use ingenuity, clinical sense, a thorough grounding in psychological theory and research, and a willingness to ad-minister supplementary cognitive tests to reveal the dynamics of a child's scaled-score profile. The need for detective work derives from one basic assumption: that the most valuable information about a child's mental abil-ities lies somewhere in between the global Full Scale IQ and the highly specific subtest scores. Whereas the overall IQ is too broad to provide in-sight into the child's strong and weak abilities, the separate scaled scores are far too narrow in their scope to be of much value for practical usage.

Previously, the Full Scale IQ was referred to as a target to be aimed at, and this metaphor reflects the guiding principle of a good detective. An in-dividual who is unduly concerned with the Full Scale IQ is saying implicitly that a child's intellectual abilities can be summarized by a single score. A detective ought to protest strenuously when confronted with this common allegation. Each new WISC-III profile should represent a challenge to prove emphatically that the child's abilities defy encapsulation in a single numeri-cal value or even in a range of values.

The first line of attack to be leveled against the Full Scale IQ comes from evaluation of Verbal-Performance IQ discrepancies, and the second line comes from the four Factor Indexes (see Chapters 4 and 5). The final artillery comes from subtest fluctuations. The discovery of significantly deviating scores within the two scales serves as the starting point for detec-tive work. The goal is to uncover hypotheses regarding abilities shared by two or more subtests or concerning influences that may have affected the test scores.

Too many examiners seem to fall into the rut of interpreting high and low subtest scores in isolation, reciting in their case reports cookbook prose about what each subtest purportedly measures. Mindless interpretation of this sort is a cop-out and does not usually provide information of any practical value. Some examiners explain a strong or weak ability by listing a string of skills supposedly measured by the subtest in question. For example, a low score on Block Design may be described as a weakness in "perceptual organization, analysis, and synthesis, visual-motor coordination, visual perception, and spatial visualization"—implying that the child has deficiencies in all the named areas! Apparently undaunted by the child's average or high scores in other tasks requiring good perceptual organization and visual-motor coordination, these examiners seem to sense no contradictions in their explication of the Block Design weakness. Or an examiner may credit a child with a strength in the "ability to distinguish essential from nonessential details" because of a high score in Picture Completion, totally overlooking the child's unimpressive performance on the other subtests that demand this same skill (Picture Arrangement, Similarities, and Symbol Search).

As a final illustration, an examiner may detect weaknesses in both Similarities and Comprehension, yet make no attempt to integrate the findings. Such a child may well be described as having poor "verbal concept formation" and possessing little "common sense, judgment, and practical information." These descriptive statements, apart from being based on meager evidence and not necessarily supported by the rest of the subtest profile, do not readily translate to meaningful recommendations. In contrast, by reporting that both Comprehension and Similarities measure abstract verbal reasoning and problem-solving skills, the examiner capitalizes on an ability that the two subtests share.

Hypotheses based on two subtests are more global and reliable than subtest-specific hypotheses and are generally more valuable because the child's skill transcends the specific stimuli, item content, and response style of any one task. In this instance, a significant weakness in verbal reasoning (compared with better performance on the other Verbal subtests, all of which require short-term or long-term memory) has implications for the kind of teaching style and materials that might be most effective for the child's educational program. For example, if the hypothesized weakness in verbal reasoning ability is supported by other test data and observations, the child would probably benefit from an approach that permitted the acquisition of factual knowledge and concepts without demanding much problem solving. At the same time, the weakness in verbal reasoning should be ameliorated to the fullest extent possible by utilizing any strengths that the child may have displayed during the testing session.

Thus the goals of psychoeducational detective work are to detect strong and weak areas in the profile that are *consistent* with all information contained in the profile, that are measured by *two or more* subtests, that are supported by clinical observations and background information, and that are cross-validated on supplementary cognitive measures. Pervasive hypotheses are far more likely than unique hypotheses to translate meaningfully to classroom activities. Only when the search for a global strength or weakness proves hopeless should an examiner settle for a subtest-specific hypothesis. When no Verbal or Performance subtests deviate significantly from the child's own mean scores, detectives are ordinarily not given the opportunity to exercise their interpretive skills.

However, even the absence of notable peaks and valleys in the WISC-III profile should not impel the examiner to yield to the Full Scale IQ as a final statement of the child's mental abilities. Good detectives seek clues by integrating all tests, subtests, and informal tasks that are administered to a child. A flat WISC-III profile should be a special motivation for the examiner to administer supplementary measures of intellectual skills that are not tapped well or at all by the WISC-III. For example, administer Fluid subtests from the KAIT, WJ-R, or DAS; attentional subtests from the Das-Naglieri; or short-term memory tasks from the Detroit-3, K-ABC, or Binet-4. Also give tests of creativity, adaptive behavior, and personality to enhance the assessment of intelligence within a broader context, and to provide the kinds of samples of behavior that increase the odds of detecting strengths and weaknesses in the child's ability spectrum.

TABLES TO AID IN WISC-III SUBTEST INTERPRETATION

To facilitate the examiner's job as detective, Tables 6.1 to 6.4 have been prepared. These tables represent a summative (although necessarily incomplete) overview of the material included in the subtest-by-subtest analysis in Chapter 2. They provide a thumbnail review of the abilities and noncognitive influences *shared* by at least two WISC-III subtests, and offer a graphic display of many combinations and groupings of these diverse tasks. (Unique abilities measured by each subtest and influences that affect performance primarily on a single WISC-III task are excluded from these tables.) In Tables 6.1 and 6.2, the abilities underlying test performance are segregated by scale, with Table 6.1 comprising verbal abilities and Table 6.2 being devoted exclusively to nonverbal performance skills. Table 6.3 includes abilities that specifically cut across the Verbal and Performance Scales, and Table 6.4 is restricted to the noncognitive influences that come into play, and sometimes loom quite large, for certain WISC-III subtests.

Tables of Shared Abilities

Tables 6.1 to 6.4 are not intended to be exhaustive, just as Chapters 4 and 5 are meant to illustrate the underlying abilities and variables that might explain IQ and Index differences, but not to exhaust the possibilities. Indeed, examiners who treat the preceding two chapters and the accompanying tables as finite and comprehensive will frequently find themselves stultified and frustrated when attempting to decode a child's profile. To serve best, the information presented here on subtest interpretation should constitute a

TABLE 6.1. Abilities Shared by Two or More WISC-III *Verbal* Subtests

Ability	Verbal Subtest						Reliability		Formula to Obtain Standard Score
	Infor- mation (I)	Simi- larities (S)	Arith- metic (A)	Vocab- ulary (V)	Compre- hension (C)	Digit Span (D)	Split- Half r_{xx}	Test- Retest r_{12}	
Input									
Understanding long questions					C		.90	.89	2.0x+40
Understanding words		S		V		D	.92	.90	2.1x+37
Auditory-vocal channel	I	S	A	V	C	D	.95	.94	1.1x+34
Integration/Storage									
Verbal conceptualization (Bannatyne)		S		V	C		.92	.92	1.9x+43
Acquired knowledge (Bannatyne)	I		A	V			.92	.92	1.9x+43
Memory (Guilford)	I		A			D	.91	.88	2.1x+37
Semantic cognition (Guilford)		S	A	V			.92	.91	2.0x+40
Culture-loaded knowledge	I				C		.88	.87	2.8x+44
Fund of information	I			V			.91	.92	2.7x+46
Handling abstract verbal concepts		S		V			.91	.91	2.7x+46
Long-term memory	I		A	V			.92	.92	1.9x+43
Verbal concept formation		S		V			.91	.91	2.7x+46
Verbal reasoning		S			C		.87	.86	2.8x+44
Output									
Much verbal expression	I	S		V	C		.92	.92	1.9x+43
Simple vocal response			A			D	.91	.88	2.1x+37

set of guidelines or parameters that define a framework from which to operate. However, the framework has to be an open one that permits limitless expansion both to accommodate the areas of expertise of each examiner and the individuality of each child tested and to promote the flexibility that is requisite for good detective work.

Even the development of Tables 6.1 to 6.4 was subjective. For example, Attention-concentration is included as an *ability* in Table 6.3 because of its roots in Rapaport's clinical theory, but "attention" and "concentration" are also listed as an influence affecting test performance in Table 6.4. In addition, cognitive style (field dependence-field independence) is classified as an "influence" in Table 6.4, even though Witkin and his associates often refer to "analytic ability," some researchers (Keogh & Hall, 1974) emphasize the importance of a skill called "analytic field approach," and McKenna (1990) insists that the so-called cognitive style is a cognitive ability and not a style at all. It is thus quite difficult to distinguish between cognitive abilities and noncognitive influences, much less present a complete and unambiguous method of profile interpretation.

All cognitive interpretations assigned to the specific quartets of subtests that compose the Verbal Comprehension (VC) and Perceptual Organization (PO) factors, and to the specific dyads of subtests that compose the Freedom from Distractibility (FD) and Processing Speed (PS) subtests, are excluded from Tables 6.1 to 6.3. These interpretations are discussed thoroughly in the preceding two chapters and need not clutter these already overloaded tables. The cognitive tables provide empirical information about each grouping of subtests: split-half reliability, test-retest reliability, and a formula for computing a standard score on each cluster of subtests. Like the IQs and Factor Indexes, these standard scores have a mean set at 100 and standard deviation set at 15. Reliabilities and formulas are excluded from Table 6.4 because these influences on test performance are intended as interpretive guides, not as specific clusters to be interpreted.

Reliability Coefficients and Standard Score Conversions

The split-half reliabilities and test-retest reliabilities for each cluster are based on the average values presented in the WISC-III manual (Wechsler, 1991, Tables 5.1 and 5.5). The formula for a composite was applied (Tellegen & Briggs, 1967), the same method used in the WISC-III manual to compute reliability of the IQ and Factor-based Scales. Separate values are provided for the test-retest coefficients for two reasons: (a) the test-retest values for 8 of the 12 subtests are lower than the split-half coefficients, with some discrepancies .10 or greater (Digit Span, Picture Arrangement, Block Design); and (b) the primary value of interpretive hypotheses is that they be repeatable, and the test-retest coefficient provides an index of each cluster's stability.

The formula for computing standard scores is provided to offer examiners a common, well-understood yardstick for comparing a child's performance

TABLE 6.2. Abilities Shared by Two or More WISC-III *Performance* Subtests

Ability	Picture Completion (PC)	Coding (Cd)	Picture Arrangement (PA)	Block Design (BD)	Object Assembly (OA)	Symbol Search (SS)	Reliability Split-Half r_{xx}	Reliability Test-Retest r_{12}	Formula to Obtain Standard Score
Input									
Complex verbal directions		Cd	PA	BD		SS	.90	.87	$1.7x+32$
Simple verbal directions	PC				OA		.82	.82	$2.9x+42$
Visual perception of abstract stimuli		Cd		BD		SS	.89	.87	$2.1x+37$
Visual perception of meaningful stimuli	PC		PA		OA		.86	.84	$2.1x+37$
Visual perception of *complete* meaningful stimuli	PC		PA		OA		.83	.80	$3.0x+40$
Visual-motor channel	PC	Cd	PA	BD	OA	SS	.92	.91	$1.2x+28$
Integration/Storage									
Visual processing (Gv) (Horn)	PC			BD	OA		.89	.88	$2.0x+40$
Spatial (Bannatyne)	PC			BD	OA		.89	.88	$2.0x+40$
Figural cognition (Guilford)	PC			BD	OA		.89	.88	$2.0x+40$
Convergent-production (Guilford)		Cd	PA			SS	.87	.84	$2.2x+34$
Figural evaluation (ages 6–7) (Guilford)	PC	Cd		BD	OA	SS	.90	.88	$1.4x+30$
Figural evaluation (ages 8+) (Guilford)	PC			BD	OA	SS	.90	.89	$1.6x+36$
Holistic (right-brain) processing	PC				OA		.82	.82	$2.9x+42$

276

	Cd	PC	PA	BD	OA	SS			
Integrated brain functioning	Cd		PA	BD		SS	.90	.87	1.7x+32
Nonverbal reasoning			PA		OA	SS	.80	.74	3.0x+40
Planning ability	Cd		PA				.82	.77	3.0x+40
Reproduction of models				BD			.87	.82	3.1x+38
Simultaneous processing		PC		BD	OA		.89	.88	2.0x+40
Spatial visualization				BD		SS	.87	.83	2.9x+42
Synthesis			PA	BD	OA		.88	.84	2.1x+37
Trial-and-error learning				BD	OA		.86	.82	2.8x+44
Visual memory	Cd	PC				SS	.87	.87	2.2x+34
Visual sequencing	Cd		PA				.82	.81	3.1x+38
Output									
Visual organization		PC	PA			SS	.83	.80	3.0x+40
Visual-motor coordination	Cd			BD	OA	SS	.90	.88	1.7x+32

Note: Mazes is eliminated from this table because examiners are advised not to administer it (see Chapter 2).

TABLE 6.3. Abilities Shared by Two or More WISC-III *Verbal* or *Performance* Subtests

Ability	Verbal								Performance				Reliability		Formula to Obtain Standard Score
	I	S	A	V	C	D	PC	Cd	PA	BD	OA	SS	Split-Half r_{xx}	Test-Retest r_{12}	
Input															
Attention-Concentration			A			D	PC	Cd				SS	.91	.90	1.5x+25
Distinguish essential from nonessential detail		S					PC		PA				.89	.88	1.7x+32
Encode information for processing			A			D		Cd				SS	.90	.88	1.7x+32
Integration/Storage															
Fluid ability (Gf) (Horn)		S	A						PA	BD	OA		.92	.90	1.3x+35
Crystallized ability (Gc) (Horn)	I	S		V	C				PA				.91	.90	1.3x+35
Achievement (Gc+Gq) (Horn)	I	S	A	V	C				PA				.92	.90	0.85x+49
Cognition (Guilford)		S	A	V	C		PC		PA	BD			.94	.94	1.1x+34
Evaluation (Guilford)		S	A	V	C		PC	Cd	PA	BD	OA		.93	.92	1.05x+27
Semantic content (Guilford)	I	S	A	V	C							SS	.95	.94	1.1x+34
Symbolic content (ages 8+) (Guilford)			A			D		Cd					.88	.84	2.3x+31
Sequential (Bannatyne)			A			D		Cd					.88	.84	2.3x+31
Common sense (cause-effect)					C				PA				.83	.77	3.0x+40
Concept formation		S		V						BD			.93	.92	2.0x+40
Facility with numbers (ages 8+)			A		C	D		Cd					.88	.84	2.3x+31
General ability	I	S	A	V	C							SS	.95	.95	1.05x+37
Learning ability			A	V				Cd		BD			.89	.89	2.2x+34
Reasoning		S	A		C				PA		OA		.91	.89	1.4x+30
Sequential processing			A			D							.88	.84	2.3x+31
Short-term memory (auditory or visual)			A			D		Cd				SS	.88	.85	2.2x+34
Social comprehension					C				PA				.83	.77	3.0x+40

Note: Mazes is eliminated from this table because examiners are advised not to administer it (see Chapter 2).

TABLE 6.4.   Influences Likely to Affect Scores on Two or More WISC-III *Verbal* or *Performance* Subtests

Influence	Verbal						Performance					
	I	S	A	V	C	D	PC	Cd	PA	BD	OA	SS
Ability to respond when uncertain							PC				OA	
Alertness to environment	I						PC					
Anxiety			A			D		Cd				SS
Attention span			A			D						SS
Cognitive style (field dependence-independence)							PC			BD	OA	
Concentration			A				PC	Cd				SS
Cultural opportunities	I			V	C				PA			
Distractibility			A			D		Cd				SS
Flexibility		S				D					OA	
Foreign language background	I			V								
Intellectual curiosity and striving	I			V								
Interests	I	S		V								
Learning disabilities/ ADHD			A			D		Cd				SS
Motivation level								Cd				SS
Negativism		S			C	D	PC					
Obsessive concern with accuracy and detail								Cd				SS
Outside reading	I	S		V								
Overly concrete thinking		S			C							
Persistence								Cd			OA	SS
Richness of early environment	I			V								
School learning	I		A	V								
Visual-perceptual problems								Cd		BD	OA	SS
Working under time pressure			A				PC	Cd	PA	BD	OA	SS

Note: Examiners should never infer a person's background or test behaviors from the pattern of subtest scores. Background information must be verified by reliable sources, and behaviors must be observed or inferred by the examiner during the testing session. The subtests listed in this table are the ones most likely affected by each influence (background or behavioral variable). However, it is unlikely that *all* subtests listed for a given influence will be affected, and it is conceivable that tasks not listed might be affected. For example, a person who lacks persistence may stop trying on numerous subtests, not just the ones that are most influenced by sustained effort (Coding, Object Assembly, Symbol Search).

on various clusters. The formulas, derived from techniques for linear equating outlined by Tellegen and Briggs (1967), are easy to use. In all formulas, *x* refers to the sum of scaled scores on the subtests composing the cluster. As an illustration, consider the Bannatyne category of Verbal Conceptualization (Table 6.1). Suppose the child earns scaled scores of 11 on Similarities, 12 on Vocabulary, and 14 on Comprehension. The sum of these three scaled scores is 37. The formula for Verbal Conceptualization is $1.9x + 43$. Multiplying 1.9 times 37 equals 70.3; adding the constant of 43 to that product equals 113.3, which rounds to 113.

The inclusion of the formulas is not intended as a mandate, or even a suggestion, that examiners routinely compute these standard scores. They are provided for those examiners who are statistically oriented and may find them useful. But even for "number" people, the formulas are not intended to be used indiscriminately or arbitrarily. The best times to use the formulas are (a) when the cluster emerges as a significant strength or weakness for a child and the computation of a standard score facilitates communication of that significant area of asset or deficit, and (b) when the examiner wants to compare the child's performance in two related areas that seem to be unequally developed (e.g., the ability to process abstract versus meaningful visual stimuli).

I do not ordinarily recommend including these standard scores in a case report, though, because there are already enough IQs and standard scores to report. Instead, translate the pertinent standard scores to percentiles. The value of 113 on Verbal Conceptualization, for example, converts to a percentile rank of 81. These conversions are readily available from many sources. In the WISC-III manual, they may be obtained from the conversion tables for each IQ Scale and Factor Index (Wechsler, 1991, Appendix A). Standard scores convert to a single percentile no matter what scale or cluster they denote; a score of 113 reflects the 81st percentile whether it is obtained on Bannatyne's Verbal Conceptualization cluster, Performance IQ, or the PS Index. Occasionally it makes sense to report the standard scores obtained for clusters of subtests. For example, standard scores on the Bannatyne categories are included in the illustrative case report for Tony at the end of this chapter because all four classifications provided meaningful information about his cognitive functioning, and neither his IQs nor Factor Indexes were particularly meaningful.

Additional Statistical Tables

Table 6.5 presents standard errors of measurement (SEm) and confidence intervals for the clusters in Tables 6.1 to 6.3, and Table 6.6 shows the size of the difference needed for significance when comparing standard scores on two clusters. To determine the size of the SEm or confidence interval for a given cluster, read its reliability (either split-half or test-retest, based on personal preference) from the table on which it appears, and enter the leftmost column of Table 6.5 with that value. Then read across to determine the bands of error. For example, Bannatyne's Verbal Conceptualization category has a split-half reliability coefficient of .92. Entering Table 6.5 with that value and reading across the row indicates that the SEm is 4 points, the 90% confidence interval is ±7 points, and the 95% confidence interval is ±8.5 points.

Since the test-retest coefficient for Verbal Conceptualization is the same as its split-half coefficient, the same values are yielded regardless of the choice of reliability. That's not always the case. For Guilford's category of

TABLE 6.5. Standard Errors of Measurement and Confidence Intervals for WISC-III Standard Scores Derived for Various Subtest Clusters Having Differing Degrees of Split-Half or Test-Retest Reliability

Reliability of Cluster	SEm	Confidence Interval 90%	95%
.74–.76	±7.5	±12.5	±14.5
.77–.79	±7.0	±11.5	±14.0
.80–.82	±6.5	±10.5	±13.0
.83–.85	±6.0	±10.0	±12.0
.86–.87	±5.5	± 9.0	±11.0
.88–.89	±5.0	± 8.5	±10.0
.90	±4.5	± 8.0	± 9.5
.91	±4.5	± 7.5	± 9.0
.92	±4.0	± 7.0	± 8.5
.93	±4.0	± 6.5	± 8.0
.94	±3.5	± 6.0	± 7.0
.95	±3.5	± 5.5	± 6.5

Note: SEm = Standard error of measurement. Values for SEm and confidence interval are rounded to the nearest half-point. The values in this table provide bands of error for a child's standard scores ($SD = 15$) on the "shared ability" subtest clusters presented in Tables 6.1, 6.2, and 6.3. Standard scores are derived for each cluster using the formulas indicated in these tables. The table is intended for use with split-half or test-retest coefficients, based on examiner preference.

convergent-production, for example, entering Table 6.5 with the split-half value (.87) produces a 90% confidence interval of ±9, whereas the test-retest value (.84) yields an interval of ±10. In general, using the test-retest values is a more conservative approach that produces wider confidence bands because most WISC-III subtests have lower stability (test-retest) than homogeneity (split-half).

Table 6.6 indicates the size of the difference between clusters required for statistical significance. Suppose the examiner wished to compare the child's Verbal Conceptualization standard score with his or her standard score on the Bannatyne Spatial category. From Table 6.2, we find out that the Spatial category has a split-half reliability coefficient of .89. First, we take the average of the two coefficients; the mean of .92 and .89 is .905, which rounds to .90 or .91, depending on the examiner's choice. Entering Table 6.6 with either .90 or .91, and reading across, we find that standard scores on those two categories must differ by between 13 and 16 points to be significant at the .05 level, and by 17 or more points to be significant at the .01 level. Examiners who prefer to use test-retest reliability coefficients would have computed an average value of .90 (the mean of .92 and .88) which yields the same significance values.

The values in Table 6.6 apply only when the clusters being compared do not have any subtests in common. The Verbal Conceptualization cluster,

TABLE 6.6. Size of Difference between Two WISC-III Subtest Clusters Required for Statistical Significance, Based on Their Average Split-Half or Test-Retest Reliability Coefficient

Average Reliability of Clusters	Number of Points between Standard Scores Needed for Statistical Significance	
	$p < .05$	$p < .01$
.76–.78	20–25	26+
.79–.81	19–24	24+
.82–.84	17–21	22+
.85–.87	16–19	20+
.88–.89	14–18	19+
.90–.91	13–16	17+
.92	12–14	15+
.93	11–13	14+
.94	10–12	13+
.95	9–11	12+

Note: Values needed for significance are rounded to the nearest point. The values in this table permit examiners to determine whether a child's standard scores on a given pair of "shared ability" subtest clusters differ significantly at the .05 or .01 level. The shared ability clusters are presented in Tables 6.1, 6.2, and 6.3, along with their reliability coefficients and formulas for computing standard scores. *This table may be used only when comparing two clusters that do not have one or more subtests in common.*

To use this table, compute the average reliability coefficient of the two clusters being compared. Then enter the row corresponding to the average coefficient, and determine if the standard-score difference between the two clusters is large enough to be statistically significant. The table is intended for use with split-half or test-retest coefficients, based on examiner preference.

therefore, could not be directly compared with Bannatyne's Acquired Knowledge cluster because both include the Vocabulary subtest. There are only two overlapping clusters, I believe, that examiners may commonly want to compare for a given child, so I've computed the average reliability for these specific contrasts:

1. *Verbal Conceptualization versus Acquired Knowledge* (Bannatyne, Table 6.1). When comparing these two clusters, the overlapping subtest (Vocabulary) must be removed from both clusters to compute the SEm of the difference. With Vocabulary removed, the average split-half reliability of these two clusters is .88. Enter Table 6.6 with that value.

2. *Fluid Ability (Gf) versus Crystallized Ability (Gc)* (Horn, Table 6.3). When comparing these two clusters, the overlapping subtests (Similarities and Picture Arrangement) must be removed from both clusters to compute the SEm of the difference. With the two subtests removed, the average split-half reliability of these two clusters is .90. Enter Table 6.6 with that value.

Are the Computations Necessary?

If you're not a number person, just ignore the formulas and the reliability coefficients in Tables 6.1 to 6.3, and make believe Tables 6.5 and 6.6 don't exist. The computation of empirical values for a diversity of subtest groupings turns profile interpretation into a *statistical* exercise. It is not. Effective detective work is a *logical* exercise that can become rigid, unimaginative, and confusing when operating out of a framework that demands computation and comparison of standard scores on overlapping clusters of subtests. Add the numbers to the process if they aid your own interpretive process and the communication of the test results. Otherwise, don't make life more difficult than necessary.

However, this is not to imply that statistics are to go by the wayside when investigating WISC-III profiles. Examiners should always determine the significance of each subtest's deviation from the child's own mean (using the table and guidelines in Chapter 3, Step 6) or risk interpreting mere chance fluctuations. Thus the first step in interpreting any WISC-III subtest profile is to make a series of simple statistical comparisons to decide whether the child has any area at all that is relatively strong or weak. If the answer is no, profile interpretation at the subtest level ordinarily stops immediately, and the child's IQs or Indexes (depending on the outcome of Steps 1 through 5 in the interpretive process) should be focused on since these global abilities are likely to account for any fluctuations in his or her WISC-III profile. If, however, there are a few significantly high or low scaled score, then examiners should exercise their license to carry out detective work.

The Logic of Detective Work

When a child is found to have a significant strength on the WISC-III, the examiner's task is to find out what ability led to the significantly high Verbal or Performance subtest score. Surely the child is not strong on all abilities that are associated with each separate subtest (see Chapter 2). Similarly, children who score significantly low on a WISC-III subtest cannot conceivably be weak in all the abilities presumably measured by that subtest. In both instances, examiners have to track down the specific area of strength or weakness by using the logical step-by-step approach of a detective.

When children have at least two strengths (or weaknesses) on the WISC-III, the examiner's challenge is to identify, if possible, the ability that is shared by the two or more significantly deviating subtests. Again, systematic detective work is necessary to isolate the child's integrity or deficiency. When many subtest scores deviate significantly from the child's mean, the Full Scale IQ and Verbal-Performance dichotomy provide a wholly unsatisfactory description of his or her abilities. The examiner's task, therefore, is to find a different model or category system that adequately and efficiently explains the obtained profile data.

The detective work necessary to explain the abilities underlying one, two, or several strengths and weaknesses in the WISC-III profile depends on (a) *internalization* of the shared and unique abilities, as well as the noncognitive influences that can markedly affect test performance, characterizing each of the 12 WISC-III subtests; (b) *anticipation* of the common patterns and groupings of subtests both within and across the Verbal and Performance Scales, based on an understanding of the various cognitive and neuropsychological groupings of Wechsler's subtests discussed in Chapters 2 through 5; and (c) *integration* of observed patterns of scores with background information about the child, clinical observation of his or her behaviors during the testing session, analysis of right and especially wrong responses to WISC-III items, and with scores that the child obtains on other scales, tests, and subtests that are administered or are available from the child's record.

THE INFORMATION-PROCESSING MODEL

Throughout this book, I have organized tasks and hypotheses in accordance with the information-processing model described in Chapter 1: Input-Integration-Storage-Output. Hypotheses in Tables 6.1 to 6.3 are likewise organized from this model. A few of the important contrasts from these tables are discussed in the following sections to provide a "simultaneous" overview of the interpretive process; then a "sequential" step-by-step method is provided and illustrated to identify hypotheses of specific areas of strength and weakness.

Input and Output

As discussed in Chapter 4 regarding interpretation of the WISC-III from a psycholinguistic model, Wechsler's subtests have traditionally been interpreted by researchers and clinicians in terms of the content of their items and the processes they are believed to assess. Picture Arrangement measures nonverbal reasoning and planning ability (processes) with regard to interpersonal situations (content), Arithmetic assesses reasoning as applied to numerical problems, and so on, in clinical text after text. Usually forgotten in these rational analyses is consideration of the nature of the input and output, apart from the specific content of the items. Does the individual have to respond to a long question or to a simple phrase on the Verbal Scale? Do the Performance subtests require children to perceive and process abstract stimuli or meaningful pictures of people and things? Does a correct verbal response require much spontaneous verbalization, or will a single word suffice; does a correct nonverbal response depend heavily on motor coordination?

Table 6.1 to 6.3 present several hypotheses that are grouped under the headings "Input" or "Output" to help examiners focus on variables that may not be in the forefront of their minds. The key notion in these categorizations is that some aspect of the properties of the stimulus or the response may affect children's performance on certain subtests *apart from the specific content or processes inherent in the tasks.* As elaborated in Chapter 4, the problem may be related to a deficiency in auditory reception or some other psycholinguistic process, although it may also pertain to factors such as memory, discrimination, and sequencing. The goal of the Input and Output categorizations is *not* to treat the WISC-III subtests as purely psycholinguistic tasks to be used as a basis for diagnosing or treating language difficulties. Rather, the aim is to generate hypotheses to explain fluctuations in WISC-III profiles from a different vantage point that may be especially valuable when the more conventional cognitive approaches lead to dead ends.

Verbal Input and Vocal Output

Stimuli for the Verbal subtests partition into two groupings, as presented in the Input section of Table 6.1:

Long Stimuli	Brief Stimuli
Information	Similarities
Arithmetic	Vocabulary
Comprehension	Digit Span

Each item in the three tasks with long stimuli requires the child to respond to a lengthy question. In contrast, Digit Span has very brief stimuli, and Vocabulary and Similarities have one- and two-word stimuli, respectively, once children understand the tasks. Even before children grasp the intent of the subtests, the Vocabulary and Similarities items include simple, repetitive questions unlike the more complex and varied questions included in the Information, Arithmetic, and Comprehension subtests. Children with an auditory reception deficit, who have difficulty in deriving meaning from spoken language, may experience more problems in understanding the long questions than the telegraphic stimuli of Similarities, Vocabulary, and Digit Span. Such individuals are also likely to have difficulty following the lengthy verbal directions to several Performance subtests, such as Picture Arrangement and Symbol Search. (Table 6.2, under Input, groups Performance subtests in two categories, those with simple verbal directions versus those with complex directions.)

Memory may play a dominant role in a child's success on the Verbal subtests with long questions or Performance subtests with complex directions. A child with a poor memory may recall lengthy stimuli incorrectly and respond to questions that are different from the ones actually asked by the examiner. Errors of this sort are difficult to distinguish from conventional wrong answers, especially for clinicians with limited experience. Examiners who sense that a child is remembering questions incorrectly should obviously repeat the items, even if they are not asked to do so by the child. (For Arithmetic only one, and for Digit Span no, repetition is permissible.) When children obtain low scores on Information, Arithmetic, and Comprehension because of a presumed inadequate short-term auditory memory, this hypothesized deficit requires much cross-validation, such as by a low scaled score in Digit Span, the need for much repetition of the instructions to some Performance subtests, and low scores on supplementary measures of immediate recall of auditory stimuli (see lists provided in Chapter 5 in the section on the FD factor).

The Verbal subtests with long versus brief stimuli differ in the degree to which context clues affect understanding of the items. Children with auditory discrimination deficiencies may be able to make sense out of the long questions by relying on the considerable context clues but have much difficulty with Similarities, Vocabulary, and Digit Span. The stimuli for the latter three subtests are not presented in a meaningful context, making the tasks potentially very difficult to comprehend for a child with a discrimination problem or with a mild hearing impairment.

More prevalent than a dichotomy in a child's ability to perform effectively with different kinds of stimuli is a division of the Verbal subtests in terms of the amount of vocal expression required for successful performance. Whereas some tasks require short (essentially one-word) responses, others demand a considerable degree of verbal expression skills. A division of the Verbal subtests along this output dimension is indicated in the Output section of Table 6.1 and summarized here:

Much Expression Required	Little Expression Required
Similarities	Information
Vocabulary	Arithmetic
Comprehension	Digit Span

Similarities merit inclusion with the two tasks that place a strong emphasis on spontaneous verbal expression, although it may occasionally group with the other triad. Some children with poor expressive but excellent conceptual skills can achieve much success on Similarities by responding with a single well-chosen word on each item, especially if that word corresponds to the pertinent abstract concept. On Vocabulary and Comprehension, however, it is difficult to compensate for deficient expressive ability, particularly in view of the large number of partially correct or incorrect responses that have to be queried by the examiner.

Before concluding that low scores on Vocabulary, Comprehension, and possibly Similarities are due to inadequate verbal expression, examiners need to review the child's responses and spontaneous verbalizations during the session. Verbal responses should consistently be terse, queries by the examiner should rarely lead to improved performance, and spontaneous comments are likely to be minimal and sparse of content. However, regardless of the amount of evidence that examiners can garner to support the hypothesis that low scores on some Verbal subtests reflect the child's inability to *communicate* knowledge (rather than the *absence* of the relevant knowledge), causality is difficult to infer.

Supplementary subtests that measure verbal conceptualization or reasoning, both with and without much verbal expression, will help clarify whether the child's problem is primarily conceptual or expressive. The following subtests are grouped by the amount of expression they require:

Much Expression Required	Little Expression Required
Binet-4 Vocabulary	DAS Similarities
Binet-4 Comprehension	Detroit-3 Word Opposites
Binet-4 Absurdities	K-ABC Riddles
Binet-4 Verbal Relations	KAIT Definitions
DAS Word Definitions	KAIT Double Meanings
Detroit-3 Story Construction	WJ-R Picture Vocabulary
KAIT Auditory Comprehension	WJ-R Oral Vocabulary
	WJ-R Verbal Analogies

Unlike other tests of oral vocabulary, the WJ-R subtest (called Antonyms and Synonyms in the WJ) requires one-word answers. The DAS Similarities subtest is included in the "little expression" cluster because the task of trying to relate *three* things usually invites a one-word response more so than relating *two* things in WISC-III Similarities. The Detroit-3 Story Construction and Binet-4 Absurdities subtests are good WISC-III supplements to assess verbal expressive abilities because they use visual stimuli, and therefore isolate expression from the reception or intake of verbal information. K-ABC Riddles, KAIT Double Meanings, and WJ-R Verbal Analogies are all excellent supplements because they assess verbal reasoning through one-word responses and are not just tests of word knowledge. Also, the five subtests mentioned in the preceding two sentences make ideal WISC-III supplements because each assesses skills that are not measured very well by the WISC-III Verbal subtests.

Three of the illustrative case reports involve children with either assets or deficits in verbal expression. Jennie L., a 16-year-old with autism and mental retardation, and Lourdes I., an 8-year-old with Tourette's syndrome, each had a weakness in verbal expression (their reports appear at the end of Chapter 4 and Chapter 5, respectively). Supplementary testing on the WJ-R and K-ABC (Jennie) and on the Binet-4 and Detroit-3 (Lourdes) verified the hypothesized weakness for both individuals, while indicating that Jennie had deficiencies in verbal conceptualization and reasoning as well as expression. James C., a 9-year-old whose report appears in Chapter 7, had a verbal expression strength that was supported by data from both the WISC-III and WJ-R. For all three children, clinical observations of their language behavior provided further support for the hypothesized weakness or strength in verbal expression.

Children (such as Lourdes) who are found to have adequate verbal conceptual and reasoning ability—but only on tasks that do not require more than a one-word response—may have a language disorder, such as a defect in the psycholinguistic process of expression within the auditory-vocal modality. Other plausible explanations are an expressive speech problem, extreme shyness, or fearfulness (where the limited expression represents withdrawal from an unpleasant situation). In addition, bilingual children may be unable to express themselves very well when English is their second language, and African-American children may be penalized because their slang words or jargon may not be understood by white examiners. Inexperienced examiners have to be alert to the warning in the WISC-III manual (Wechsler, 1991): "A child's score on a Verbal item should *never* be penalized because of improper grammar or poor pronunciation" (p. 47). Failure to heed this basic scoring rule will certainly artificially depress some children's scores on the three subtests demanding good expressive abilities.

Discovery of a potential speech or language disorder should yield a recommendation of a subsequent thorough evaluation by qualified professionals in these areas. When clinical observations suggest that shyness or fearfulness was responsible for depressed scores on verbal expressive subtests, retesting on the Verbal Scale is advised under more favorable and relaxed conditions. (As indicated in Chapter 3, practice effects are minimal for Verbal subtests.) Retesting in a different language and/or by an examiner whose cultural background matches the child's background is similarly advised when bilingualism or Black English seems responsible for depressed scores on some subtests.

In no case should the Verbal IQ or VC Index be considered a good estimate of a child's verbal intelligence when an inability to respond effectively leads to poor performance on the cognitive tasks requiring considerable verbal expression. A similar conclusion regarding Verbal IQ is usually warranted when the properties of the stimulus, rather than the content or process of the task, seem to materially affect a child's performance on several subtests. Likewise, discount the child's Performance IQ or PO and PS Indexes if the examiner suspects strongly that the child scored poorly on some subtests because he or she did not understand the verbal directions to the task. The use of practice items and permissible teaching for many WISC-III subtests, however, makes the latter occurrence unusual.

The discussion of stimuli and responses in this section is intended to broaden the scope of examiners' detective work and alert them to an alternate approach for interpreting fluctuations in WISC-III profiles. The same type of flexibility is needed when evaluating strengths and weaknesses on psycholinguistic test batteries. Although the ITPA (Illinois Test for Psycholinguistic Abilities) is not commonly used any more, its Auditory Reception subtest (sample items: "Do sausages frown?" "Do barometers congratulate?") illustrates this point nicely. This subtest is intended to measure a child's ability to derive meaning from auditory stimuli. The task can also be considered as an intellectual task that measures word knowledge, fund of information, and verbal concept formation and is subject to the influences of cultural opportunities at home, school learning, ability to respond when uncertain, and the Piaget notion of animism.

Visual Input and Motor Output

The stimuli used for the Performance subtests may be divided into the following categories, as indicated in Table 6.2:

Meaningful Stimuli	Abstract Stimuli
Picture Completion	Block Design
Picture Arrangement	Coding
Object Assembly	Symbol Search

The tasks with meaningful stimuli all involve manipulation of people or things, whereas Block Design, Coding, and Symbol Search require children to work with symbols and designs. Picture Completion and Object Assembly are spatial, "right-brained," simultaneous tasks, whereas Picture Arrangement demands temporal, visual sequencing. Yet they all undeniably include meaningful and concrete (as opposed to abstract) stimuli. Coding and Block Design are both extremely sensitive to brain dysfunction (Reitan & Wolfson, 1992); the abstractness of their respective stimuli may be the primary cause of depressed scores on these tasks for many brain-impaired children.

In Table 6.2, the category of visual perception of meaningful stimuli is presented both with and without Object Assembly. That is because the stimuli in Object Assembly are meaningful only for children who are able to identify the object to be assembled, and who can meaningfully interpret each separate part of the puzzle. For children with visual perceptual problems, the puzzle pieces may be as abstract as the cubes used for Block Design. The topic of the meaningfulness of visual stimuli is discussed in the portion of Chapter 5 devoted to the PS factor.

The type of response required by the various Performance subtests has also been used to partition the scale. Rapaport, Gill, and Schaefer (1945–1946) distinguished between nonverbal subtests demanding no essential motor coordination (visual organization group) and those heavily dependent on coordination (visual-motor coordination group). This dichotomy, modified slightly, appears in the Output section of Table 6.2 and is as follows:

Visual Organization	Visual-Motor Coordination
Picture Completion	Coding
Picture Arrangement	Block Design
	Object Assembly
	Symbol Search

The motor component of each Performance subtest was already discussed in Chapter 4. When examiners detect a clustering of children's Performance scaled scores into the two subdivisions in the preceding table, they must explore several possibilities before inferring any hypotheses. As noted in the earlier chapter, identical patterns may also relate to a child's verbal development, since Picture Completion and Picture Arrangement both have secondary loadings on the Verbal Comprehension factor. Hence high scores on the visual organization dyad may reflect verbal compensation for a performance deficit (see Chapter 3); relatively low scores may imply an inability to apply an age-appropriate amount of verbal mediation to nonverbal tasks. If the Object Assembly scaled score fails to cluster with the visual-motor coordination grouping and instead approaches the magnitude of the visual organization pair, the underlying skill may then be related to properties of the *stimulus* (meaningful vs. abstract) rather than the response.

In addition, it is feasible for Symbol Search to switch over to the visual organization subgroup for some uncoordinated children because it makes no difference how neatly or sloppily the child puts a mark through Yes or No. Clinical observations of children's motor coordination, evaluation of their responses, and consideration of their verbal ability and visual-perceptual skill are all essential activities for interpreting a discrepancy between visual organization and visual-motor coordination scores. Supplementary administration of additional perceptual and motor tasks, both cognitive and noncognitive, is also especially important for a child who obtains depressed scores on the WISC-III visual-motor subtests. Cognitive supplements are listed in Chapter 4; the best noncognitive supplements are included in neuropsychological test batteries.

A key distinction to make is whether a child's problem is more in the cognitive domain (visual-motor integration and nonverbal concept formation) or in the motor domain (fine-motor coordination). Confirmation of the latter hypothesis would render the Performance IQ and PO Index inadequate as estimates of the poorly coordinated child's nonverbal intelligence.

Integration and Storage

Most of the abilities measured by more than one WISC-III subtest that are included in Tables 6.1 to 6.3 concern the integration and storage of information. The next sections discuss two illustrative ways in which each scale can split in two: The Verbal Scale might divide into acquired knowledge and reasoning components, and the Performance Scale might divide on the basis of the type of mental process required for success.

Acquired Knowledge versus Reasoning

Potentially, the most valuable category for WISC-III interpretation in Bannatyne's (1971, 1974) scheme is Acquired Knowledge, comprising Information, Arithmetic, and Vocabulary. All these subtests are school related, are subject to the influence of home environment, and involve long-term memory. When a child's scaled scores on the Acquired Knowledge subtests cluster together and deviate from scores on the two tests of verbal reasoning (Similarities and Comprehension), the implications for test interpretation may be vital.

Consider the sample profiles of Verbal scores shown in the following tables for Sheila and Barbara, two 11-year-olds referred for evaluation to the same school psychologist. Both children are white, although they come from quite different backgrounds: Sheila lives under severe conditions of economic deprivation and is now in her fourth foster home; Barbara has upper middle-class parents who actively expose her to culturally enriching experiences and overtly encourage her academic success. Although the two girls achieved the same Verbal IQ of 98, their patterns of scores suggest that they differ substantially in their verbal skills and that the IQ provides an inadequate reflection of their respective verbal abilities. Their VC and FD Indexes also fail to paint a very different picture of the two girls. Both earned standard scores on the VC Index that differed trivially (2–3 points) from their standard scores on the FD Index, and all their Verbal scores (IQ and Indexes) were within the Average range of performance. Yet, they differed markedly in their verbal skills:

Sheila		**Barbara**	
Verbal Subtest	Scaled Score	Verbal Subtest	Scaled Score
Information	5	Information	11
Similarities	16	Similarities	7
Arithmetic	6	Arithmetic	11
Vocabulary	8	Vocabulary	13
Comprehension	13	Comprehension	6
(Digit Span)	(14)	(Digit Span)	(8)

Verbal IQ = 98
Verbal Comprehension Index = 103
Freedom from Distractibility Index = 101

Verbal IQ = 98
Verbal Comprehension Index = 96
Freedom from Distractibility Index = 98

Both profiles are interpretable from the vantage point of Bannatyne's Acquired Knowledge dimension and the verbal reasoning cluster. Using the formulas for computing standard scores provided in Table 6.1, Sheila had a standard score of 79 on the three Acquired Knowledge subtests (percentile rank equal to 8), strikingly lower than her standard score of 125 (95th percentile) on the two verbal reasoning subtests, both of which are less influenced by formal instruction. Sheila has remarkably intact verbal intelligence, indeed well above the average of other 11-year-olds, when faced with tasks that require her to figure out solutions to verbal problems. Her verbal ability is poor, however, when responding to problems or questions that are in large part contingent on the prior acquisition of concepts or facts.

Note that the two measures of verbal reasoning assess problem solving under different conditions. Similarities involves application of reasoning skills to a task that is not very meaningful, that is, discovering the common properties or abstract categories that unite two different concepts. In contrast, Comprehension requires a more practical and meaningful skill, the ability to interpret or explain real-life problem situations. Whereas some children may have considerable difficulty with Comprehension items because of limited exposure to given situations, the concepts used in Similarities items are familiar to virtually all children. Even the concepts that must be related in the more difficult Similarities items, such as salt, water, rubber, and paper, are known and used by young children. Thus Sheila can apply her intellect equally well whether responding within a meaningful context (Comprehension) or an abstract one (Similarities).

The impact of Sheila's environment is prominent in her performance on the Acquired Knowledge grouping and is also reflected to some extent in her school achievement. However, her success on the remaining Verbal subtests (particularly in the context of her deprived background) reveals outstanding intellectual strengths that, if channeled properly, portend well for future academic improvement. Note that she performed well on Digit Span (scaled score of 14, or 91st percentile), another test that is not school taught. Although Digit Span measures short-term memory, not reasoning, this ability is also an asset that will facilitate her learning ability.

Sheila was not even referred for learning problems because her teacher saw no inconsistency between her cultural background and academic performance. (Sheila was referred for a suspected *behavior* disorder.) However, her Verbal scaled-score profile indicates that much more can be expected of her than would be predicted from either her environment, her overall Verbal IQ, or her Factor Indexes. Sheila will function very well in some verbal situations and inadequately in others; her WISC-III Verbal IQ and VC Index offer no insight into this distinction and are really worthless.

Barbara performed at the 75th percentile on the Acquired Knowledge subtests (standard score of 110), compared with the 9th percentile on the two verbal reasoning subtests (standard score of 80). Although this discrepancy is not as dramatic as the difference observed for Sheila, the implications are still quite important. Barbara's home environment and parental push probably elevated her scores on the Acquired Knowledge tasks, a conclusion that is reinforced by her markedly lower performance on Similarities and Comprehension. Her Digit Span score was also relatively low (25th percentile). Her verbal intelligence is unimpressive whenever she cannot call on her store of verbal facts and concepts that have been acquired over the years. Barbara's fifth-grade teacher referred her for evaluation because of below-average achievement in some school subjects—learning difficulties that did not surface during the more fact-oriented primary grades. Based on cross-validation of the WISC-III Verbal profile with other test scores, clinical observations, and more objective background data, the psychologist concluded that Barbara's pattern of achievement in school subjects was entirely consistent with her varied verbal skills. Although some remedial steps were recommended, the main suggestion was counseling for both Barbara and her parents.

Which grouping of Verbal subtests, those in the Acquired Knowledge grouping, or the reasoning subtests that are generally less dependent on formal instruction, reflect a child's "true" verbal intelligence? For both Sheila and Barbara, the answer is neither. These children have two types of verbal intelligence and will appear bright or dull depending on the context. Consequently, both aspects of their verbal intelligence must be understood and respected to enable examiners to make optimally meaningful recommendations. As postulated in Chapter 1, *all* WISC-III subtests measure what an individual has learned. The fact that tasks such as Information and Arithmetic reflect formal learning should not minimize the incidental learning that is necessary for competence on subtests such as Similarities. One can easily realize the dynamic impact of the learning environment by imagining Sheila's Verbal IQ had she been raised in Barbara's upper-middle-class home, and vice versa.

In these examples, the Verbal subtests split neatly into two discrete groupings; unfortunately, profile interpretation is not usually so easy or straightforward. Examiners cannot be rigid when using a model such as Bannatyne's but need flexibility in their approach to detective work. One type of flexibility was just demonstrated: Bannatyne's Acquired Knowledge category was used to unravel the sample profiles, but his Verbal Conceptualization category was ignored because these two verbal groupings are *not* independent of content.

Other kinds of flexible interpretation might be necessary in other circumstances. For example, the interpretations given to the preceding sample profiles might have remained the same even without the clear-cut dichotomies that were observed. Sheila might easily have obtained a poor Comprehension score because this subtest, in addition to requiring social judgment and reasoning, is very influenced by cultural opportunities at home. A truly impoverished environment may make several of the questions meaningless to some children, preventing them from applying their good reasoning skills to the situations depicted in the items. Additionally, some subcultures may teach responses to some questions that are socially correct within that cultural group but are nevertheless scored zero by the WISC-III scoring system. An analysis of "wrong" Comprehension responses, coupled with an understanding of the values taught in the child's subculture, can support this hypothesis; such analyses are frequently necessary to interpret properly an African-American or Spanish-speaking child's Comprehension scaled score.

Barbara's Verbal scores also might easily have presented a more ambiguous picture to the examiner. Just as cultural factors could have depressed Sheila's Comprehension score, Barbara's enriched environment could have substantially improved her score on this subtest. Children who have poor reasoning skills but manage to perform adequately on Comprehension are usually easy to spot because they tend to parrot overlearned responses to numerous items without reflection or apparent understanding. Conversely, Vocabulary might have been depressed for Barbara (or inflated for Sheila) because it is still a conceptual task that has dual placement in Bannatyne's Verbal Conceptualization and Acquired Knowledge categories. And Barbara might have scored relatively low on Arithmetic, either because of its reasoning component, sequential aspect (it is included in Bannatyne's Sequencing group as well as Acquired Knowledge), or its sensitivity to behavioral influences such as distractibility and anxiety.

Arithmetic, like Comprehension, assesses reasoning in socially meaningful situations. However, the Arithmetic items do not provide an adequate measure of reasoning ability for children who have failed to master the essential computational skills. Barbara may have acquired the computational facts necessary for solving the Arithmetic items, yet may have failed numerous items anyway because of her reasoning deficiency. As discussed in Chapter 5, examination of wrong responses helps understand the reasons for a child's low Arithmetic score. For example, inadequate grounding in computational fact is suggested if a child subtracts 5 from 12 and concludes that the girl sold 8 newspapers; a reasoning difficulty is implied if the child adds 5 to 12 and replies that 17 newspapers were sold.

When children perform relatively well or poorly on reasoning tasks in the Verbal Scale, with both verbal and numerical stimuli, the examiners should immediately investigate whether the same level of ability was displayed on nonverbal problem-solving tasks, most notably Picture Arrangement and Object Assembly. They also should investigate the child's reasoning ability on supplementary measures of this skill, such as DAS Nonverbal Reasoning, KAIT Fluid Intelligence, and WJ-R Fluid Reasoning.

These illustrations should clarify both the need for flexibility and the necessity of integrating background information, behavioral observations, other test data, and the nature of wrong responses when attempting to interpret fluctuations within the Verbal scaled-score profile. One of the thorniest issues when evaluating children referred for school learning problems is to determine whether a low Acquired Knowledge standard score reflects a cognitive deficit (e.g., long-term memory) or an achievement deficit. That is to say, is the low score a cause or an effect of the learning problem in school? As discussed previously, ample research documentation supports the predictable notion that reading- and learning-disabled children earn relatively low scores on Bannatyne's Acquired Knowledge category (Kaufman, Harrison, & Ittenbach, 1990; Prifitera & Dersh, 1993; Nichols, Inglis, Lawson, & MacKay, 1988; Smith, Coleman, Dockecki, & Davis, 1977). However, memory deficits, both short-term and long-term, also characterize children with learning disabilities (Kolligan & Sternberg, 1987; Lohman, 1989). Consequently, examiners should administer pertinent supplementary measures to help infer whether low scores on Acquired Knowledge reflect a learning-disabled child's relative lack of school-related knowledge and skills, or deficiencies in basic memory processes necessary for performing well on cognitive tests and in the classroom.

The following steps are recommended for children who score significantly low on Bannatyne's Acquired Knowledge grouping as a means of better understanding the low score:

- Verify that the child has a documentable deficit in school achievement, based on standard scores obtained on instruments that were specifically developed for that purpose. Administer well-normed, comprehensive individual achievement tests such as the K-TEA Comprehensive Form, WIAT, or WJ-R Standard or Supplementary Achievement Battery.

- Determine the repeatability and generalizability of the Acquired Knowledge deficit. Administer subtests such as Detroit-3 Basic Information, K-ABC Faces & Places, and KAIT Famous Faces to find out if the child's range of factual knowledge is equally deficient when the questions are not as school-related as the WISC-III items, but focus on information acquired from alertness to the environment and everyday experiences; the latter two subtests also assess if the information deficit is evident when visual stimuli are used instead of verbal stimuli. Similarly, determine if the child's weak vocabulary is also observed when one-word answers are required, using either verbal stimuli (Detroit-3 Word Opposites, WJ-R Oral Vocabulary) or visual stimuli (WJ-R Picture Vocabulary). And identify the nature and extent of a low score in Arithmetic by choosing from among the various number tests listed in the FD section of Chapter 5. The greater the amount of evidence that can be accumulated in support of a hypothesis, the more reliable the hypothesis and the greater the likelihood that the strength or weakness will generalize beyond a specific content or item style.

- Determine whether the child has deficits in memory processes. Many short-term memory subtests are available, which serve as useful supplements, as listed in Chapter 5. Particularly useful for assessment of learning-disabled children are supplementary measures of long-term (secondary) memory. Acquired Knowledge assesses long-term (tertiary) memory, whereas memory subtests that push the memory span beyond 15 to 30 seconds, such as paired-associate learning tasks, measure secondary memory. Particularly valuable for this type of assessment are the WJ-R Memory for Names and Visual-Auditory Learning subtests, both of which are included on the Long-Term Retrieval Scale; KAIT Rebus Learning and Auditory Comprehension; and the Delayed Recall versions of these four subtests, which evaluate how much information is retained over a period of 30 to 45 minutes (KAIT) or several days (WJ-R). DAS Recall of Objects—Delayed measures long-term memory over a 15-to 20-minute interval, and is also useful. The two WJ-R subtests and KAIT Rebus Learning have the extra advantage of being true learning tasks.

If memory deficits are hypothesized for a learning-disabled child, examiners need to exercise considerable clinical acumen and understanding of the cognitive psychology literature to discern whether poor performance on Information, Arithmetic, and Vocabulary is due to the failure of the memory structures to be established, the inefficiency of encoding strategies needed for working memory, the inability to employ an appropriate strategy for retrieving stored knowledge, and so forth.

Children with school learning problems who have memory deficits but demonstrate good reasoning skills are likely to function best in a learning environment that allows for acquisition of facts and concepts through discovery, promotes intrinsic understanding of the subject matter to be learned, and deemphasizes rote memory. Children who have not learned efficiently in school and have the opposite profile (adequate memory but weak reasoning) may function best in an educational setting that shapes children's ability to figure things out, while actually providing them with frequent explanations of various facts and concepts, and that encourages rote learning techniques as a means of acquiring new information. Examiners who are able to understand the child's pattern of Verbal scores, and translate that pattern into its educational implications, should be able to make important suggestions regarding the selection of appropriate educational materials and teaching techniques and perhaps even the choice of the specific teacher or teachers whose styles are most likely to lead to the child's greatest chance for academic improvement.

If an overview of the WISC-III Verbal profile and data from supplementary testing lead examiners to conclude that performance on Information, Arithmetic, and Vocabulary reflect the consequences of the learning disability, then the Acquired Knowledge grouping cannot be considered to measure verbal intelligence. For that child, several Verbal subtests were no different than conventional achievement tests and their inclusion on an intelligence battery serve only to depress unfairly the child's Verbal IQ and VC index. Current diagnostic practices stipulate a minimum IQ and a sizable discrepancy between ability and achievement for children to be classified as learning disabled. If low scores on several WISC-III subtests can reasonably be attributed to poor school achievement rather than to limited cognitive or memory ability, the *consequences* of the suspected disorder will greatly affect identification of the disorder. Thus learning-disabled children might perform poorly in the Acquired Knowledge area *because* of their learning problem, thereby lowering their IQs and Indexes and decreasing the discrepancy between their ability and achievement—both of which diminish the likelihood of their proper diagnosis. In such cases, intelligence tests that minimize the role of acquired information and school-related skills on the assessment of intelligence, such as the Das-Naglieri and K-ABC, have obvious diagnostic advantages.

Both illustrative case reports at the end of this chapter concern Bannatyne's Acquired Knowledge grouping. Tony G., a high-functioning child, age 11, with ADHD, had a strength on the school-related subtests; Michael B., a 7-year-old referred for learning problems, had a weakness in Acquired Knowledge. Both profiles were consistent with pertinent background information and with the standard scores they earned on the WIAT.

Simultaneous Processing, Sequential Processing, and Planning

The WISC-III Performance Scale includes six subtests, but three of them consistently define the core of the scale: Picture Completion, Block Design, and Object Assembly. Factor analyses of Wechsler scales past and present indicate that these three subtests typically load highest on Perceptual Organization factors whether two, three, or more factors are interpreted (Kaufman, 1990a, Chapter 8; Wechsler, 1991). The group of subtests forms Bannatyne's Spatial category and Horn's Broad Visualization (Gv) cluster. It assesses a set of skills that was studied by Thurstone (1938) and included among his seven primary mental abilities under the name spatial relations; featured in Vernon's (1960) hierarchical theory of intelligence as one aspect of the major group factor that he termed Practical-Mechanical-Spatial; defined by Guilford (1967) as requiring the joint processes of figural cognition and figural evaluation; and investigated by Piaget and Inhelder (1967) in infants and children as a developmental progression from topological to projective to Euclidean space.

From a neuropsychological perspective, this triad of subtests measures the simultaneous processing of information, a synthetic, integrative ability associated with the right cerebral hemisphere from the vantage point of cerebral specialization researchers (Sperry, 1968; Springer & Deutsch, 1981); it denotes an aspect of the Block 2 coding functions from Luria's (1973, 1980) theory and research based on that theory (Naglieri & Das, 1990).

Various groups have performed relatively well on these three Wechsler Performance subtests, including children with reading and learning disabilities (Kaufman et al., 1990; Nichols et al., 1988; Prifitera & Dersh, 1993), ADHD (Prifitera & Dersh, 1993), autism (Lincoln, Allen, & Piacentini, in press), or mental retardation (Clarizio & Bernard, 1981; Kaufman & Van Hagen, 1977; Silverstein, 1968), and those who demonstrate the analytic field approach associated with the field-independent cognitive style (Goodenough & Karp, 1961).

Examiners need to be alert for a possible clustering of the Spatial-Simultaneous subtests within the Performance profile of all children tested. The triad may be higher than the other three nonverbal subtests, lower, or somewhere in between. Regardless of the patterning, the cohesiveness of children's subtest scores on Picture Completion, Block Design, and Object Assembly, in the face of divergent performance on other nonverbal tasks, indicates that the Performance IQ or PO index does not reflect a unitary trait and may give a misleading picture of their nonverbal intelligence.

Importantly, these subtests may provide the fairest assessment of the so-called true intellectual ability of children from disadvantaged environments and of children with reading or learning disabilities. Of all the WISC-III subtests, the Spatial-Simultaneous trio tend to be among the least dependent on specific cultural and educational opportunities. In contrast, the VC subtests reflect crystallized abilities, Picture Arrangement (which also has a Gc component) is dependent on cultural background and interpersonal experience, and Coding and Symbol Search are more dependent on speed of performance than on problem-solving ability for success. However, the Spatial-Simultaneous subtests would undoubtedly provide a poor estimate of intellectual functioning for individuals shown by comprehensive evaluation to have a field-dependent cognitive style, a learning disability with diagnosed visual-perceptual problems, or a known lesion in the right cerebral hemisphere.

Simultaneous versus Sequential Processing

In contrast to the spatial, simultaneous nature of the Picture Completion, Block Design, and Object Assembly subtests, Picture Arrangement and Coding both measure sequencing ability. Children who score at significantly different levels on the three simultaneous and two visual sequential subtests may be demonstrating a meaningful difference in their mental processing styles (i. e., right vs. left hemispheric functioning from cerebral specialization theory, or simultaneous versus successive coding from Luria theory). Examiners should investigate possible sequential assets or deficits by evaluating the child's level of performance on the FD Index, sometimes interpreted as a measure of sequential processing, and by administering supplementary subtests or scales (see Chapter 5). Examiners who believe that a child's pattern of WISC-III scaled scores is best explained by the sequential-simultaneous processing model should cross-validate that hypothesis by administering the pertinent scales from test batteries specifically developed from relevant neuropsychological theory, namely the Das-Naglieri or K-ABC. WJ-R Spatial Relations and Binet-4 Paper Folding and Cutting are also good supplements because they measure spatial-simultaneous ability with no motor demands.

Lucy O., a 7½-year-old whose case report appears at the end of Chapter 5, was referred because of reading problems. Her much higher FD than PO index suggested a high Sequential-low Simultaneous profile that was verified on the K-ABC. Tony G., whose report is at the end of this chapter, had a high Spatial-low Sequential WISC-III profile that was suggestive of a strength in simultaneous processing versus a weakness in sequential processing.

Patterns of high scores on Bannatyne's Spatial category and low scores on his Sequential category have been found to characterize many samples of reading- and learning-disabled children on the WISC (Rugel, 1974), WISC-R (Kaufman et al., 1990; Nichols et al., 1988), and now the WISC-III (Prifitera & Dersh, 1993). This group profile may suggest good simultaneous and poor sequential processing. Tittemore, Lawson, and Inglis (1985) like-wise have shown that a unitary unrotated factorial dimension derived from factor analysis of the WISC-R significantly distinguishes between groups of learning-disabled and normal children. Learning-disabled children earn higher scores than normal children on this so-called Learning Disabilities Index (LDI). Although the developers of the LDI interpret it as a continuous dimension of nonverbal and verbal abilities, it seems more parsimoniously interpreted as a simultaneous-sequential dimension: The subtests at one ex-treme of this Index are the simultaneous Picture Completion and Object Assembly, whereas the subtests at the other extreme are Digit Span, Arith-metic, and Coding (Lawson, Inglis, & Tittemore, 1987; Tittemore et al., 1985).

Bannatyne's groupings and the LDI suggest a high simultaneous-low se-quential patterning for groups of children diagnosed as learning disabled, and this pattern is identified for numerous other referred samples as well (see Chapter 5). Better than either approach for distinguishing between ex-ceptional and normal children on the WISC-III, however, is a comparison that includes Symbol Search and relies on analysis of the third and fourth factors; this topic is treated, with accompanying tables, in Chapter 5.

Simultaneous Processing versus Planning Ability

Sometimes Picture Arrangement and Coding are joined by Symbol Search, such that the child's Performance subtest profile splits in two. In that in-stance, the distinction may reflect a dichotomy between simultaneous proc-essing and planning ability, two of the components of the four-pronged Luria-based PASS model applied by Das and Naglieri (in press) to the field of test construction. The interpretation of the PS factor as a possible meas-ure of the ability to evaluate, organize, and plan was discussed in Chapter 5. From the PASS model, relatively high simultaneous processing ability and low planning ability have been identified for groups of reading-disabled and ADHD children, with planning deficiencies postulated for children with these disorders; for ADHD children, the poor planning ability seems intri-cately tied into concomitant attentional deficits (Naglieri & Das, 1990; Reardon & Naglieri, 1992).

The two-pronged division of the Performance Scale just described, how-ever, may have little to do with the Simultaneous-Planning distinction. Naglieri and Das (1990) interpret Picture Arrangement as a measure of simultaneous processing, not planning, and argue that Wechsler's scales do not provide effective measurement of planning ability. Also, from Guil-ford's theory, the Spatial-Simultaneous cluster measures the joint oper-ations of cognition and evaluation, in contrast to the combination of convergent-production and evaluation that seems to characterize Picture Arrangement, Coding, and Symbol Search. As reiterated throughout this book, and discussed specifically regarding planning ability elsewhere (see PS section of Chapter 5), interpretations of subtest groupings require multi-ple sources of data and observations to become viable hypotheses.

Holistic versus Integrated Cerebral Functioning

Block Design is the most likely to split apart from the Spatial-simultaneous triad of Performance subtests. When it does, and the child's score on Block Design is consistent with the other remaining three nonverbal subtests, the unifying theme may be related to the specialization of the two cerebral hemispheres. As discussed previously, the left hemisphere is specialized for a sequential, analytic, and logical mode of processing information, whereas the right hemisphere features a gestaltlike, holistic processing mode. The two subtests that best exemplify right-brain, holistic processing are Picture Completion and Object Assembly, whereas each of the remaining four Performance subtests incorporates task demands that require problem-solving input from both cerebral hemispheres. As such, success on those four subtests would seem to depend on the ability to integrate the processes associated with each hemisphere while solving each item. This distinction is shown here:

Right-Brain (Holistic) Processing	Integrated Brain Functioning
Picture Completion	Coding
Object Assembly	Picture Arrangement
	Block Design
	Symbol Search

The integrated subtests have two features that distinguish them from the right-brain tasks: (a) They require analytic or sequential processing, characteristic of the left hemisphere, in addition to the visual-spatial and nonverbal components that are more associated with the right hemisphere, and (b) they require considerable verbiage by the examiner during their administration. In contrast, Picture Completion and Object Assembly seem to require almost exclusively the holistic, synthetic right-brain cognitive style and are communicated simply by the examiner with a minimal amount of verbalization. Success on the integrated tasks seems, therefore, to depend on the processing style associated with the right hemisphere for interpreting the visual-spatial stimuli and performing the necessary gestaltlike syntheses, *and* on the left hemisphere processing style for comprehending the examiner's instructions and applying sequential or analytic processing, where appropriate. The problem-solving approach attributed to the right hemisphere seems capable of coping with the demands of the Picture Completion and Object Assembly subtests without much facilitation from its counterpart.

The role of the left hemisphere for some Performance subtests is not intended to minimize the importance of the right half of the brain for these tasks. Indeed, Reitan (1974, p. 45) believes that "Block Design is especially sensitive to posterior right hemisphere involvement and especially to right parietal and occipital damage whereas Picture Arrangement is more sensitive to anterior right temporal lesions." Nevertheless, Block Design requires analysis, a decidedly left-brain function, in addition to the subsequent holistic synthesis needed to assemble the blocks correctly; Reitan and Wolfson (1992) state, "Block Design is effective as a test of adequacy of right cerebral functions . . . in addition to having some validity as a general indicator of brain functions" (p. 124). Picture Arrangement requires children to size up a total situation (right hemisphere) but also demands good temporal or time-oriented sequencing skills (left hemisphere) for success; it "tends to be vulnerable to brain injury in general" (Lezak, 1983, p. 283). Coding is unquestionably a sequencing task, and Symbol Search depends on the ability to analyze the distinctive features of the target symbols before scanning a simultaneous array of options.

The fact that Block Design is not merely a right-hemisphere test, but depends heavily on the analytic left-brain processing style, is evident from Matarazzo's (1972, p. 212) statement: "Oddly enough, individuals who do best on the test are not necessarily those who see, or at least follow, the pattern as a whole, but more often those who are able to break it up into small portions." Spelberg (1987), in a study of 770 children and adolescents in The Netherlands, concluded that all subjects predominantly preferred an analytic to a synthetic strategy when constructing block designs. Furthermore, the need for integrated functioning on Block Design is evident in Lezak's (1983, pp. 56–58) description of the test performance of one patient with known damage to the right hemisphere and of another patient with damage to the visual-association area of the left hemisphere. The first patient had considerable difficulty with the items but had some success on the easier four-block designs by overtly instructing himself on what to do and by verbalizing the relationships among the blocks. The second patient performed quite well on Block Design until he stumbled over a nine-block item that is especially conducive to verbal analysis.

Discrepancies between children's scores on the holistic and integrated groupings of Performance subtests may well reflect a difference in the efficiency of their application of these two styles of problem solving. Performance on most Verbal subtests is commonly associated with left-hemisphere processing. When scores on the integrated tasks are comparable in magnitude to scores on the Verbal subtests, but different from scores on the holistic tasks, it is reasonable to hypothesize a discrepancy between the analytic—sequential and holistic—synthetic modes of processing information. In contrast, children may perform consistently on the holistic subtests (Picture Completion, Object Assembly) and so-called left hemisphere tasks (Verbal Scale) tasks but obtain either much higher or lower scores on the subtests requiring integrated functioning. In such instances, the individuals would seem to have equally developed processing styles but a decided strength or weakness in the ability to integrate the two processes.

All these hypotheses require follow-up with supplementary subtests. Children who are believed to be unusually strong or weak in holistic processing should be administered K-ABC Gestalt Closure, WJ-R Visual Closure, or

Detroit-3 Picture Fragments. (The K-SNAP Gestalt Closure subtest can be administered for children older than the K-ABC age range.) These tasks measures a skill that is a fairly pure measure of right-brain, holistic processing, and by requiring a vocal response they measure this ability within the visual-vocal channel. Tests used for neuropsychological assessment such as the Seashore Measures of Musical Talents (Seashore, Lewis, & Saetveit, 1960) also make good supplements; they permit assessment of nonverbal auditory perception, a right-hemispheric skill (Lezak, 1983) that is almost always ignored in favor of verbal measures of auditory perception. Good supplementary measures of integrated brain functioning include the various well-normed measures of matrix analogies that are readily available, DAS Sequential and Quantitative Reasoning, KAIT Logical Steps and Mystery Codes, and WJ-R Analysis-Synthesis and Concept Formation.

Integration demands a mutualism between the hemispheres. Stimuli need to be delegated to the appropriate system since handling stimuli through the inappropriate processing mode is not only inefficient but may interfere with processing in the preferred cognitive system. Sometimes one hemisphere must remain dormant to permit the other hemisphere to do what it does best. In addition, shifts from one mode to the other have to occur, often just to solve a single problem, depending on the specific demands of the task (Galin, 1976; Galin & Ornstein, 1974). Individual differences in hemispheric integration are to be anticipated and are likely to be evidenced on Picture Arrangement and Block Design; for maximally efficient performance, all children must integrate the processes of temporal sequencing and sizing up the whole story on the first subtest, and they all must first analyze and then synthesize on the second subtest.

Interestingly, the strength noted for a variety of exceptional samples on the Spatial-Simultaneous triad may be an artifact of the lumping of Block Design with the two so-called right-brain tasks. In a review of 18 WISC-R studies of learning-disabled children, consensus rankings showed the samples to perform best on Object Assembly and second-best on Picture Completion, but only fifth-best on Block Design (Kaufman et al., 1990, Table 7). Object Assembly ranked among the easiest three subtests for 14 of the samples, and Picture Completion was among the three easiest for 15 samples. In contrast, Block Design ranked among the top three for only three samples. A similar finding emerged for the WISC-III for 99 learning-disabled children (Prifitera & Dersh, 1993): They earned their highest score on Picture Completion (11.0), their second-highest on Object Assembly (10.5), and their fifth-highest on Block Design (9.7). Five samples of mentally retarded children tested on the WISC-R scored highest on the two Spatial-Simultaneous subtests that require holistic processing, with their mean scaled score on Block Design ranking a distant seventh (Kaufman et al., 1990, Table 9). These research findings are not necessarily a function of cerebral processing, but they do provide food for research thought.

In general, however, Block Design is probably the Performance subtest that is most likely to join the two so-called right-brain tasks for any given individual. Unlike Picture Arrangement, which is largely a temporal sequencing task with a Gc component, or the highly speeded Coding and Symbol Search, Block Design is heavily dependent on holistic processing for successful performance. Whereas the left-brain function of analysis is required to break up the designs into their component parts, the synthesis needed to construct the final products is quite similar to the requisite set of skills for Picture Completion and Object Assembly.

The right hemisphere seems to be more mature than the left at birth, both physiologically and functionally, and is also a more pervasive force in the very early stages of life (Bever, 1975; Carmon & Nachson, 1973; Seth, 1973). An infant perceives and learns nonverbally, sensorily, and spatially to a large extent during the first year of life (Hebb, 1949), styles of learning that are congruent with the processing mode of the right cerebral hemisphere. Although less mature than the right brain, the left brain is more adaptable at birth and has the capacity of subsuming complex and analytic functions (Bever, 1975). The greater adaptability of the left hemisphere may conceivably render it unusually vulnerable to the impact of cultural deprivation. Hence, disadvantaged children may have a right-brain leaning, at least in part, because of the resilience of the right hemisphere in the face of deprived environmental conditions. These hypotheses, however, have not been systematically tested with tasks included in intelligence tests or with analogous cognitive tasks.

Indirect support for the right-brain resilience hypothesis comes from Kagan and Klein's (1973) dramatic report of the cognitive development of the infants and children within two Indian cultures in Guatemala. Although the infants are startlingly deprived of stimulation during the first 15 months of life and seem to have the affect of Spitz and Wolf's (1946) orphans, by 11 years of age the children of these Indian cultures appear normal in every way. Incredibly, they even perform quite adequately on tests of "basic cognitive competencies," all of which seem to be predominantly right-brain in orientation, such as recall memory for familiar objects, recognition memory for pictures of objects and faces, perceptual analysis (embedded figures), and perceptual inference (Gestalt closure).

When children perform especially well on the WISC-III subtests that seem to be dependent on right-brain processing, and the results of subsequent assessment offer supportive evidence of a global strength in the holistic and nonverbal processing style of the right hemisphere, their Verbal subtest responses should be scrutinized carefully. A holistic cognitive style can actually be penalizing to a child on the Verbal Scale. According to some researchers (Kimura, 1966; Nebes, 1974), the key distinction between the two hemispheres concerns the organization of data on the principle of *conceptual* (left-brain) versus *structural* (right-brain) similarity. A cat and a mouse are alike to the left hemisphere because they are both animals (2-point response), but to the right hemisphere they both have four legs, fur, whiskers, and tails (1-point responses). Conceptual responses typically earn 2 points, whereas structural responses are more likely to be assigned no more than partial credit. Since the degree of abstractness in children's responses is rewarded for Vocabulary and some Comprehension items as well as for Similarities items, it is evident that a so-called right-brain processing style can substantially depress Verbal IQs. A left-hemisphere processing mode, in contrast, can have a negative effect on the Performance IQs, especially on the subtest scores that reflect the understanding of spatial relations. As Galin (1976, p. 18) states, "The tendency for the left hemisphere to note details in a form suitable for expression in words seems to interfere with the perception of the overall patterns."

The potential inhibiting effect of a particular processing mode on tasks best suited to the opposite mode bears again on the importance of integrated functioning. Individuals who perform relatively well on the nonverbal tasks that demand an integration of analytic and holistic processing may possess a very special and high-level intellectual strength that is conducive to school success (Witelson, 1976, 1977). Artists, mathematicians, and scientists, in discussing their own creative gifts, stress the integration of both processing modes as a key ingredient in their success (Galin, 1976). Low scores on the integrated functioning tasks may also have interpretive significance and may relate to the poor planning abilities of children with reading disabilities and ADHD (Naglieri & Das, 1990; Reardon & Naglieri, 1992), and to Denckla's (1974) hypothesis that developmental dyslexics may have faulty interhemispheric integration.

The preceding discussions of left-brain processing, right-brain processing, and integrated functioning should not be taken at neurological face value. More important than specific localization are the processing distinctions between the analytic, sequential, conceptual mode and the holistic, simultaneous, structural mode. These distinctions may not relate to the two cerebral hemispheres at all, and they fit in well with other neurological theories such as Luria's (1973, 1980). The key point for WISC-III interpretation, or for the interpretation of process-oriented tests such as the Das-Naglieri and K-ABC, is that children do, indeed, differ in problem-solving strategies. These strategies may be applied efficiently or inefficiently. The examiner's task is to identify the child's preferred strategies, determine whether these strategies are conducive to effective school learning, and apply this information to remedial suggestions.

A SYSTEMATIC METHOD FOR INTERPRETING SUBTEST FLUCTUATIONS

The technique described in this section is intended to generate *hypotheses* about children's functioning to better understand their strong and weak areas.

To the degree that ample evidence can be organized in support of a given hypothesis, examiners will be increasingly able to utilize the information to facilitate comprehension of the nature of a child's presenting problem and selection of any educational or psychological intervention that may be necessary. At no time, however, should examiners lose sight of the fact that the hypotheses, which are obtained by a post hoc analysis of profile data, are not facts and may indeed prove to be artifacts. When profile interpretation, accompanied by support from multiple data sources, leads to new insights about children, perhaps explaining why low scores do not reflect limited mental ability or showing that different educational materials or techniques are advisable, the recategorization of WISC-III subtests serves a useful function. When analysis of subtest fluctuations is used as a primary means of classifying, labeling, or placing children, or for other potentially harmful purposes, the practice should be immediately abandoned.

Examination of Tables 6.1 to 6.4 indicates that identical groupings of subtests can reflect different interpretations depending on the child's level of performance on other pertinent subtests. The guidelines outlined here, accompanied by examples, should help examiners distinguish among competing hypotheses. These guidelines are intended to operationalize Step 7 in the seven-step WISC-III interpretive approach in Chapter 3. The profile of Minerva C. will be used to illustrate the approach. Her WISC-III scores are as follows:

Minerva C.

IQs		Factor Indexes	
Verbal	98	Verbal Comprehension	95
Performance	98	Perceptual Organization	97
Full Scale	97	Freedom from Distractibility	96
		Processing Speed	99

Verbal	Scaled Score	Performance	Scaled Score
Information	7	Picture Completion	5-W
Similarities	13-S	(Coding)	(9)
Arithmetic	12-S	Picture Arrangement	13-S
Vocabulary	7	Block Design	12
Comprehension	9	Object Assembly	8
(Digit Span)	(6)	*Symbol Search	10

* Symbol Search was used in IQ computations

From Steps 1 to 5 of the Interpretive process, it is apparent that Minerva had minor, nonsignificant fluctuations in her IQs and Indexes. Her Verbal and Performance IQs are both interpretable based on the guidelines delineated in Chapter 3. (See Table 3.4 for an overview of the seven steps and the size of various discrepancies required for significance.) Neither the Verbal nor Performance Scale has an extensive amount of subtest scatter. The VC and FD Indexes do not differ significantly, and neither do the PO and PS Indexes. Pending analysis of her subtest profile, Minerva's Full Scale IQ of 97 seems to serve as an adequate summary of her cognitive abilities.

In Step 6 of the interpretive process, significant strengths and weaknesses are computed within the subtest profile. Since Minerva's V-P IQ discrepancy is smaller than 19 points, the mean of all 12 WISC-III subtests is used as a point of comparison for determining significant discrepancies. Her overall mean is 9.3, which rounds to 9. Based on the summative values for determining significant deviations reported in Table 3.4, Minerva has significant strengths in Similarities, Arithmetic, and Picture Arrangement, and a significant weakness in Picture Completion. These meaningful deviations are denoted in her profile with S or W. The deviations from her mean by Digit Span, Information, Vocabulary, and Block Design each fall one point short of significance. (If the more precise values given in Table 3.3 are used in conjunction with her exact mean of 9.3, then her strengths in Arithmetic and Picture Arrangement drop out.) Either statistical approach is acceptable, although I recommend the simpler one that uses rounded means and summary values.

In Minerva's case, both methods lead to the same conclusions regarding her hypothesized areas of strength and weakness.

Guidelines for Step 7 of the Interpretive Process (Generating Hypotheses)

The guidelines described here, and illustrated with Minerva's subtest profile, should be followed to identify potential areas of strength and weakness in children's WISC-III subtest profiles.

Guideline 1.   *Select a significant strength, and locate this subtest in Tables 6.1 to 6.4. Write down all shared abilities (and influences affecting performance) that involve this subtest.*

Example: Let us start with *Similarities,* the highest of Minerva's two Verbal strengths. From Tables 6.1, 6.3, and 6.4, all abilities or influences involving Similarities are listed (along with the other subtests associated with each skill):

Understanding words (as opposed to long questions)—S V D
Auditory-vocal channel—I S A V C D
Verbal Conceptualization (Bannatyne)—S V C
Semantic Cognition (Guilford)—S A V
Handling abstract verbal concepts—S V
Verbal concept formation—S V
Verbal reasoning—S C
Much verbal expression—S V C

Distinguishing essential from nonessential details—S PC PA SS
Fluid ability (Horn)—S A PA BD OA
Crystallized ability (Horn)—I S V C PA
Achievement (Horn)—I S A V C
Cognition (Guilford)—S A V PC BD OA
Semantic content (Guilford)—I S A V C PA
Concept formation—S V BD
General ability—I S A V C BD
Reasoning ability—S A C PA OA
Flexibility—S D OA
Interests—I S V
Negativism—S C D PC
Outside reading—I S V
Overly concrete thinking—S C

Guideline 2.   *One by one, consider each ability or influence affecting test performance and weigh the merits of each one by comparing scores on other pertinent subtests with the child's relevant mean.*
When determining the significance of a strength, scaled scores must exceed the child's mean score by the designated number of points or more. However, when tracking down hypotheses to explain the strength, less stringent criteria have to be applied. It is unreasonable to expect children to score significantly above the mean on *every* subtest that measures a particular ability. (For example, six different subtests assess the Guilford operation of cognition.) *It is reasonable to consider a shared ability as a strength if children score above their own mean scores on all pertinent subtests, with at least one discrepancy reaching statistical significance.* This rule, which should be interpreted as a guideline or rule of thumb rather than as a rigid principle, applies as well to weaknesses (for a weakness to be noteworthy, a child has to score *below* his or her mean scores on relevant subtests, with at least *one* discrepancy reaching significance). Two exceptions to the rule:

(a) *If three or four subtests constitute a shared ability, then it is acceptable to have one subtest that is equal to the mean.*

(b) *If five or more subtests constitute a shared ability, then it is acceptable to have one maverick subtest that is either equal to the mean or on the "wrong" side of the mean.* If the subtest is on the wrong side of the mean, however, it should not deviate significantly from the mean.

Example: Each ability (or influence affecting test performance) listed for Similarities should be systematically evaluated. The first ability on the list, understanding words (as opposed to long questions) in test directions, is rejected as a possible area of strength because Minerva's scores on Vocabulary and Digit Span are below her mean and thus are not consistent with her good score on Similarities. She does not have a strength in the entire auditory-vocal channel, the next ability listed, because of scores below her mean on half of the Verbal subtests. Her low Vocabulary score by itself is a sufficient reason to reject five of the next six hypotheses on the list as well: Verbal Conceptualization, Semantic Cognition, handling abstract verbal concepts, verbal concept formation, and much verbal expression. Verbal reasoning is rejected because Minerva's score on Comprehension equaled, but did not exceed, her mean.

The next ability on the list (distinguishing essential from nonessential details) looks promising since both Similarities *and* Picture Arrangement were significant strengths for Minerva, and Symbol Search was above her mean. However, she scored well below her Performance mean on Picture Completion, thereby rejecting this ability as a possible strength.

In contrast, there is considerable support in the profile to suggest a strength in the next ability on the list—*fluid ability*. Of the five subtests that measure this Horn ability, she had significant strengths in three and had a near-strength in Block Design. She scored just below her mean on Object Assembly, but because fluid ability is composed of five subtests, that lone exception to the pattern can be tolerated. Although Similarities is also included on Horn's crystallized ability cluster, that hypothesis is easily rejected because of her below-the-mean scores on Information and Vocabulary. For the same reason, the next hypothesis of strong Achievement (Horn's Gc plus Gq or quantitative ability) is rejected. So too are the next four hypotheses because of one or more subtests below Minerva's mean: Cognition, semantic content, concept formation, and general ability.

The cognitive hypothesis of *reasoning* ability, however, comes close to being an area of strength for Minerva. She had significant strengths on three of the subtests. However, she scored below her mean on Object Assembly and equal to her mean on Comprehension; only one maverick subtest is allowed, even for shared abilities that comprise five subtests. Fluid ability and reasoning ability are quite similar aspects of functioning. Both categories include her three significant strengths, and both involve problem solving. Fluid ability implies the ability to solve novel problems, whereas reasoning ability in general suggests the ability to solve any kind of problem, including the socially relevant questions in the Comprehension subtest.

The four remaining traits on the list are influences affecting test performance. "Interests" and "outside reading" can quickly be rejected because she scored below her Verbal mean on both Information and Vocabulary. The other two ("negativism" and "overly concrete thinking) are irrelevant for hypothesized strengths. Both traits are associated with low scores on the specific subtests, not high scores; also both depend on specific observations of test behavior, not just test performance.

Guideline 3. *Repeat Guidelines 1 and 2 for every other significant strength that has not been accounted for. Then follow analogous procedures for all significant weaknesses.*

Example: Regarding strengths, all three of Minerva's significant strong areas were accounted for by the hypothesis of well-developed fluid skills. Turning to weaknesses, only one subtest was significantly below her Verbal or Performance mean—Picture Completion. A list of abilities (and influences affecting performance), taken from Tables 6.2–6.4, is listed as follows for Picture Completion:

Simple verbal directions—PC OA
X Visual perception of meaningful stimuli—PC PA OA
X Visual perception of complete meaningful stimuli—PC PA
X Visual-motor channel
Visual processing (Horn)—PC BD OA
Spatial (Bannatyne)—PC BD OA
Figural Cognition (Guilford)—PC BD OA
X Figural Evaluation (Guilford)—PC BD OA SS
Holistic (right-brain) processing—PC OA
Simultaneous processing—PC BD OA
Visual memory—PC Cd SS
X Visual organization—PC PA
Attention-concentration—A D PC Cd SS
X Distinguishing essential from nonessential details—S PC PA
X Cognition—S A V PC BD OA
X Evaluation—C PC Cd PA BD OA SS
Ability to respond when uncertain—PC OA
Alertness to environment—I PC
Cognitive style (field dependence)—PC BD OA
Concentration—A PC Cd SS
Negativism—S C D PC
X Working under time pressure—A PC Cd PA BD OA SS

An "X" has been placed to the left of each ability involving any of Minerva's *strengths* (Similarities, Arithmetic, Picture Arrangement), indicating immediate rejection of these areas as possible *weaknesses*. Of the remaining hypotheses, Spatial ability (and the other interpretations of the Picture Completion-Block Design-Object Assembly triad) can be rejected as a possible weakness because Block Design is *above* Minerva's mean. *Holistic (right-brain) processing* may conceivably be her area of weakness since her Object Assembly score is below her mean. Visual memory is rejected as her weak ability because she scored at her mean on Coding and above her mean on Symbol Search.

The hypothesis "simple verbal directions" cannot be rejected on the basis of test scores, but this aspect of the intake of information is not likely to be a weakness for anyone. Rather, a child might perform relatively well on Picture Completion and Object Assembly because they are communicated so easily with simple verbal directions; in contrast, a child may score poorly on the other four subtests because they have complex verbal directions.

An "X" was not placed to the left of attention-concentration, negativism, or any hypothesis on the list that reflects an "influence" on test performance, even if Minerva had a significant strength on a subtest in the grouping. Such hypotheses are only meaningful if they have behavioral support from observations of the child's test-taking behaviors. If, for example, Minerva was observed to be negative during Picture Completion (by not complying with the directions), then that behavior might explain her low score even if she was not negative during other subtests. Similarly, based on the examination of her test scores, a possible explanation of her significant Picture Completion weakness pertains to Minerva's ability to respond when uncertain. But that hypothesis can only be supported if she was seen to be hesitant to respond or take a risk, especially when she was unsure of the response to a Picture Completion or Object Assembly item. More information is needed to clarify her low score on Picture Completion, which brings us directly to the next step in the procedure for performing detective work.

Guideline 4. *Integrate any apparent strengths or weaknesses in children's profiles with information about their backgrounds, observations of their test behaviors, and scores on other tests.*

Inferences about strong and weak areas of functioning, or about noncognitive influences that may have affected test performance, cannot be made out of context. For example, knowledge of children's home environments, school achievement, and interest patterns is essential before concluding that one of these factors accounted for peaks or valleys in their profiles. Observations of children's eye-hand coordination, method of holding a pencil, and technique of assembling blocks or puzzles must corroborate any assertion of a weakness or strength in visual-motor coordination. Analysis of children's spontaneous verbalizations, responses to WISC-III Verbal items, and performance on other verbal tasks is essential before accepting a hypothesis of well-developed or poorly developed verbal expression skills, and so forth.

Example: Minerva has been hypothesized to possess good fluid ability. Despite the support for this hypothesis from WISC-III subtest fluctuations, multiple evidence is needed from clinical observations and additional test data. Her thinking processes may have been revealed by any spontaneous verbalizations and problem-solving tactics during Picture Arrangement, her trial-and-error versus insightful approach during Object Assembly and Block Design, or the abstractness of her responses to Similarities and Comprehension items. These observations would have been likely to be congruent with a hypothesis of strong fluid reasoning ability; one would have expected a child with good fluid skills to demonstrate an organized, systematic approach to solving nonverbal problems and an adept application of abstract thinking when solving verbal items.

To quantify Minerva's strength in fluid thinking, number-oriented examiners may wish to use the formula provided in Table 6.3 to compute her standard score on the five fluid subtests. Her sum of scaled scores on these tasks is 58. Entering that value as x in the equation $(1.3x + 35)$ yields a fluid ability standard score of 110.4, which rounds to 110 and corresponds to the 75th percentile. Whenever examiners identify a strength or weakness for a child, it is often useful to compare the child's standard score on that ability to the child's standard score on an ability that comes closest to being the direct opposite (even if that other ability is not a significant strength or weakness). In this instance, crystallized ability offers an ideal contrast. Entering Minerva's sum of 49 in the formula for Gc (also $1.3x + 35$) equals 98.7 or 99 (47th percentile). Because the Gf and Gc groupings overlap by two subtests, the values for comparing clusters (Table 6.6) are not applicable. With the two subtests removed, the average split-half reliability of these two clusters is .90 (as indicated earlier in this chapter). Entering Table 6.6 with a value of .90 indicates 13 points is needed for significance at the .05 level; therefore, the 11-point difference in favor of Gf is not significant.

As discussed in Chapters 2 and 4, however, the WISC-III does not offer pure or unambiguous measures of fluid ability. If the observations of the child's problem-solving approach to nonverbal items suggest good organization and integration of stimuli, then those clinical observations, along with the emergence of fluid ability as a hypothesized strength from WISC-III profile analysis, keep the proposed Gf strength as a viable hypothesis that requires verification. The best supplements to administer are fluid reasoning tasks from other batteries that are construct-valid measures of Gf and that stress reasoning rather than visual-spatial ability. The DAS Nonverbal Reasoning Scale, two subtests from the KAIT Fluid Scale (Logical Steps and Mystery Codes), and two subtests from the WJ-R Fluid Reasoning cluster (Analysis-Synthesis and Concept Formation) are all excellent WISC-III supplements. It is unnecessary to supplement the WISC-III with additional measures of crystallized thinking because the VC Index provides an adequate estimate of Gc according to Horn (1989).

If the results of clinical observations of test behavior and/or supplementary testing do not support a strength in fluid ability, then other hypotheses should be entertained, perhaps some that were not even included on the original list. For example, Steps 1 and 2 could be repeated using lists of abilities associated with Picture Arrangement and Arithmetic (both significant strengths) if a hypothesis of good fluid ability is not supported.

Behavioral observations are especially important to determine the meaning of Minerva's low Picture Completion score. Did she evidence a hesitancy to respond when she was unsure of herself on that subtest, Object Assembly, or any other subtest? Does she seem to possess any of the personality characteristics associated with a field-dependent cognitive style (see Chapter 4)? Did she give any evidence of deficient skills in areas associated with the holistic processing style of the right hemisphere? (Does she have little success in school in music and art? Did she make little use of gestural and other nonverbal cues and have difficulty interpreting the examiner's nonverbal communication?) Was her low score a function of poor concentration, perhaps due to an inadequately established rapport on the first subtest administered in the battery?

Whereas the answers to these questions may help narrow the likely explanation of her low Picture Completion score, behavioral observations and background information do not usually suffice. Hypotheses generated from only two or three subtests are indeed tentative at best, particularly when only one subtest is significantly low. Additional testing is needed, using tasks that are believed to be good measures of so-called right-brain holistic processing. The various measures of Gestalt completion on the Detroit-3, WJ-R, K-ABC (or K-SNAP for children as old as Minerva) are suitable; so are design-copying tests such as Binet-4 Copying, and the various tests of visual recognition and recall listed in the PS section of Chapter 5.

What about the fact that Minerva obtained scaled scores of 6 or 7 on three subtests—Information, Vocabulary, and Digit Span? Can these scores be interpreted as weaknesses even though none is significantly below the Verbal mean of 8? The answer is no if there is no external support for a weakness, such as background information, clinical observations, or scores on other tests. The answer is also negative if the scores are interpreted separately as opposed to two at a time, or all three at a time. However, the answer is a cautious yes if the examiner can integrate behaviors and/or information pertaining to the child's background with the trio of relatively low scores. The particular subtests in question all involve recall, and the examiner may have supplementary information suggestive of a deficient memory (e.g., the parent or teacher may have checked "forgetful" or "does not retain" as a primary presenting problem). External support for a poorly developed memory, coupled with her below-average performance in several WISC-III tasks demanding good recall ability, would be enough to sustain a global-memory hypothesis.

Given Minerva's possible strength in fluid ability, her relatively low scores on Information and Vocabulary may denote a weakness in crystallized thinking, a possibility already discussed. Supplementary facts, observations, and data are essential. Information and Vocabulary are both subject to the influences of early environment; the examiner may know that the teenage girl in this illustration was raised in an impoverished environment.

All hypotheses generated from fluctuations in WISC-III profiles depend on external verification to remain truly viable. Such verification is especially crucial when the hypotheses are developed in the absence of at least one scaled score that deviates significantly from the child's mean. The administration of pertinent supplementary tests or subtests is almost a necessity in these instances, although examiners should get into the cross-validation habit for any hypothesis that may have diagnostic or remedial implications. Testing the limits is also an effective way to clarify the nature of ambiguous strengths and weaknesses, as discussed in Chapter 2 for several WISC-III subtests. This technique should ordinarily be conducted after the entire battery has been administered under standardized conditions. By improvising and administering the subtests under altered conditions, examiners may be able to decipher the specific cause of poor (or occasionally good) performance. Children may be asked to identify the picture of a word they could not define, arrange pictures to tell a story when less formal language is used than that required by the directions for administration, select a block design that matches a model that they were unable to construct, explain how they solved an arithmetic problem, and so on. Whereas children's responses during a testing-the-limits session cannot alter their obtained scores, examiners can gain insight into the dynamics of their integrities and deficits.

Guideline 5.   *If detective work fails to uncover hypotheses that "link" two or more subtests together, then interpret the unique abilities that are presumably measured by significantly high or low subtests.*

Every effort should be made to explain significant discrepancies from the child's mean score in terms of shared hypotheses that unite several subtests and are corroborated by behavioral observations and supplementary test data. When examiners fail to uncover reasonable hypothesized strengths and weaknesses after a flexible and eclectic analysis of profile fluctuations, they may resort to subtest-specific interpretations. These unique interpretations are listed in Table 6.7 for each subtest; these are the abilities listed with an asterisk in Chapter 2 to denote that the ability is measured primarily by only one WISC-III subtest. Table 6.7 also gives the percentage of reliable variance that is unique to each subtest, that is, the task's subtest specificity. Only Object Assembly has an inadequate amount of subtest specificity, indicating that the unique abilities associated with Object Assembly should ordinarily not be interpreted.

The fact that a subtest has an "ample" or "adequate" amount of specificity, however, does not mean that one *should* interpret the child's level of performance on these specific abilities. First, examiners should determine whether the child's scaled score on that subtest is significantly above or below his or her mean. Significant fluctuations are defined as scaled scores that deviate from the child's mean score by 3, 4, or 5 points, depending on the subtest (see Table 3.3 for precise values and Table 3.4 for "smoothed" values). I believe that a subtest's unique abilities should be interpreted for children only when their scaled score on that subtest deviates significantly from their average scaled score on the relevant scale. However, the mere fact of a significant fluctuation does not imply that the examiner should automatically interpret that subtest's uniqueness. As already stated, the examiner's

TABLE 6.7.   Specific Abilities Associated with Each WISC-III Subtest, and the Subtest Specificity of Each Subtest

WISC-III Subtest	Specific Abilities and Traits	Subtest Specificity* (Spec. Var.–Error Var.)
Verbal		
Information	Range of general factual knowledge	Adequate (25%–16%)
Similarities	Logical abstractive (categorical) thinking	Adequate (23%–19%)
Arithmetic	Computational skill	Adequate (30%–22%)
Vocabulary	Language development Word knowledge	Adequate (24%–13%)
Comprehension	Demonstration of practical information Evaluation and use of past experience Knowledge of conventional standards of behavior	Adequate (30%–23%)
Digit Span	Immediate rote recall	Ample (63%–15%)
Performance		
Picture Completion	Visual recognition and identification (long-term visual memory)	Ample (39%–23%)
Coding	Psychomotor speed	Ample (49%–23%)
Picture Arrangement	Anticipation of consequences Temporal sequencing and time concepts	Ample (48%–24%)
Block Design	Analysis of whole into component parts Nonverbal concept formation	Ample (34%–13%)
Object Assembly	Ability to benefit from sensory-motor feedback Anticipation of relationships among parts	Inadequate (26%–31%)
Symbol Search	Speed of visual search	Adequate (34%–26%)

Note: Spec. Var.–Error Var. = Specific Variance–Error Variance
* Subtest specificity or specific variance refers to the percentage of reliable variance that is unique to each subtest.

first line of investigation should be to conduct the thorough kind of detective work outlined in Guidelines 1 through 4 to try to discover what shared abilities might have been responsible for the significantly deviating score. Only when all hypotheses prove fruitless should an examiner acquiesce to an interpretation of a unique and highly specific strength or weakness. In such instances, examiners may wish to surround the specific scaled score with a band of error, using either the standard error of measurement values in the manual (Wechsler, 1991, Table 5.2) or the more accurate asymmetrical values computed by Kramer (1993).

Exceptions to this rule: Digit Span is a reliable subtest with a huge amount of specificity in measuring a skill (immediate auditory memory) that is not tapped very well by any other WISC-III subtest. Examiners should feel free to interpret a significantly high or low scaled score on Digit Span in terms of its specific abilities without first bending over backward to find a shared hypotheses. For Picture Arrangement and Coding, about *half* of each subtest's total variance is unique variance. It is also reasonable to interpret specific abilities on these subtests as strengths or weaknesses when shared abilities do not emerge or are not too convincing.

For the subtests with *ample* specificity, it is reasonable to interpret a unique ability for a subtest that deviates significantly from the child's mean (if more global hypotheses cannot be identified). For subtests with *adequate* specificity, however, more caution is needed: Add *one point* to the value required for significance in Table 3.4 before assigning a unique interpretation to a high or low subtest score. Object Assembly should not be given subtest-specific interpretations in usual circumstances. However, when an extraordinarily large deviation from a mean is observed (say, 6 or 7 points) and all hypotheses regarding shared abilities are rejected, it is reasonable for an examiner to speculate about a unique ability.

Example: In the sample profile of Minerva, all three significant strengths were united by the hypothesis of good fluid reasoning ability. Consequently, no specific or unique interpretations should be given to any of the three tasks; her elevated scores on all of these subtests are presumed to be a direct result of her well-developed Gf ability. Had it been impossible to find one or more hypotheses to explain the three high subtest scores, unique interpretations could have been used to account for the good performance on Picture Arrangement and Similarities, but not on Arithmetic. Picture Arrangement has *ample* specificity, so its uniqueness can be interpreted for any significant strength or weakness. Similarities and Arithmetic have *adequate* specificity, so unique abilities for these subtests should be interpreted if the deviation from the mean is an additional point more than the value required for significance. Both subtests require a 3-point deviation for significance; Minerva's scaled score of 13 on Similarities exceeds her mean of 9 by 4 points, but her score of 12 on arithmetic does not.

If supplementary observations or test scores impel the examiner to reject a hypothesized strength in fluid ability, then the examiner may identify a strong area that pairs up the two verbal strengths (Arithmetic and Similarities) but excludes Picture Arrangement. In that case, a subtest-specific explanation of the high score on Picture Arrangement would be defensible in view of its large amount of specific variance.

Picture Completion is the only subtest score that is significantly below the girl's Performance mean. Several hypotheses were raised (e.g., holistic processing, ability to respond when uncertain) that might subsequently be found to explain the deficit in Picture Completion. Should none of these fairly global explanations be given external support, it would be feasible to interpret Picture Completion's unique abilities. This subtest has ample specificity, and Minerva's profile almost invites a subtest-specific interpretation of Picture Completion: Her scaled score of 5 on that task is below her next-lowest Performance scaled score of 8, even after applying the appropriate asymmetrical band of error of 4.9 to 7.4 for Picture Completion, as determined from Kramer's (1993) table.

When interpreting specific abilities measured by WISC-III subtests, examiners should keep in mind that the list of unique abilities or traits extends well beyond the few abilities listed in Table 6.7. That table is confined to cognitive abilities but excludes traits or other influences that may pertain to only one subtest, or that may be characteristic of the particular child on the particular day of testing. Examiners may want to study the lists of influences for each subtest in Chapter 2. Some are excluded from Table 6.4 because they are associated primarily with a single subtest. Examples are "development of a conscience or moral sense" (Comprehension) and "exposure to comic strips" (Picture Arrangement). Also, a specific interpretation may pertain to idiosyncrasies about the subtest. Picture Completion and Information, for example, are the first two subtests administered; low scores may result from the child's lack of comfort and initial anxiety in the testing situation. Digit Span and Symbol Search are the last two administered, and low scores may result from boredom or fatigue.

Illustration—Nikki H., Age 12-7

Although an example was incorporated into the stepwise procedure for attacking WISC-III subtest profiles, an additional illustration will further clarify the approach.

Nikki was tested on the WISC-III as a part of a battery that was administered to determine her eligibility for a seventh-grade gifted program. Nikki's language arts teacher recommended her for the enrichment program because of her "exceptional scholastic achievement in reading and science, her keen interest in learning, and her wonderfully creative personality." Nikki comes from an upper-middle-class home that was described by her professional parents as providing much cultural and intellectual stimulation and fostering a love for learning. During the WISC-III evaluation, the examiner described Nikki as "a mature, attentive, alert, relaxed young lady with a realistic grasp of what she can and cannot do well." Also noted in the report were Nikki's "well coordinated motor activity," "trial-and-error approach to nonverbal tasks," "intense concentration and persistence," and "display of much creativity, particularly original thinking, in both her responses to test items and her spontaneous verbalizations." Nikki described herself as an avid reader. Her WISC-III scaled-score profile is as follows:

Nikki H.

IQs		Factor Indexes	
Verbal	140	Verbal Comprehension	139
Performance	116	Perceptual Organization	120
Full Scale	131	Freedom from Distractibility	124
V-IQ > P-IQ ($p < .01$)		Processing Speed	119

Verbal	Scaled Score	Performance	Scaled Score
Information	19-S	Picture Completion	13
Similarities	16	(Coding)	(18)-S
Arithmetic	17	Picture Arrangement	11
Vocabulary	18	Block Design	14
Comprehension	14	Object Assembly	15
(Digit Span)	(11)-W	*Symbol Search	9-W

* Symbol Search was used in IQ computations

Verbal mean = 16   Performance mean = 13

Summary of Steps 1 to 6 in the Interpretive Process

Steps 1 to 5 of the Interpretive process (see Chapter 3, especially the summary of the steps in Table 3.4) led to the following conclusions about Nikki's IQs and Factor Indexes:

1. The 24-point difference in favor of Verbal IQ is significant at the .01 level, and unusually large, occurring in the extreme 10% of normal children.
2. Her Full Scale IQ, therefore, is meaningless.
3. The amount of scatter among the five subtests used to compute Verbal IQ is *not* abnormal, and neither is the amount of scatter among the five subtests used to compute Performance IQ (Digit Span and Coding are excluded).
4. The 15-point difference between her VC Index of 139 and her FD Index of 124 is significant, although her PO and PS Indexes differ trivially.
5. The best summary of her verbal and nonverbal skills, therefore, is provided by her VC Index of 139 (99.5th percentile) and her PO Index of 120 (91st percentile), a difference that is both significant at the .01 level and unusually large (extreme 15%).
6. Her FD Index is not interpretable because of too much subtest variability (the 6-point difference between Arithmetic and Digit Span).
7. The PS Index also is not interpretable because of too much subtest variability (the 7-point difference between Symbol Search and Coding).

Significant strengths and weaknesses were computed within Nikki's subtest profile during Step 6 of the interpretive process. Since Nikki's V-P IQ discrepancy is larger than 19 points, the mean of the six Verbal subtests is used as a point of comparison for determining significant discrepancies for all Verbal subtests, and the mean of the six Performance subtests is used as a point of comparison for determining significant discrepancies for all Performance subtests

Her Verbal mean is 15.8, which rounds to 16. Her Performance mean is 13.3, which rounds to 13. Based on the summative values for determining significant deviations reported in Table 3.4, Nikki has one significant Verbal strength, Information, which is 3 points higher than her Verbal mean, and one significant Verbal weakness, Digit Span, which is 5 points below her Verbal mean. The Performance Scale also yields one significant strength and weakness relative to her Performance mean: Coding is 5 points above her mean and Symbol Search is 4 points below. All these meaningful deviations are denoted in her profile with S or W; note that three of the four are included on the two small WISC-III factors, suggesting that a reorganization of subtests is needed from a model other than the four-factor solution.

For reasons elaborated in Chapter 2, Symbol Search was used to compute Nikki's Performance and Full Scale IQs, even though she scored much higher on Coding than Symbol Search. Sometimes using Symbol Search yields higher IQs, and sometimes using Coding yields higher IQS; however, the decision of which subtest to use must be made before the WISC-III is administered. *It is wrong to switch after the fact because Coding is higher.*

Step 7 of the Interpretive Process: Generating Hypotheses

The guidelines described for hypothesis generation are now applied to Nikki's profile.

Interpreting the Strength on Information

The various hypotheses that might explain her significant strength on *Information,* obtained from Tables 6.1, 6.3, and 6.4, are listed as follows (variables that are associated with poor performance, such as understanding the words to long questions, are excluded):

Auditory-vocal channel—I S A V C D
Acquired Knowledge (Bannatyne)—I A V
Memory (Guilford)—I A D
Culture-loaded knowledge—I C
Fund of information—I V
Long-term memory—I A V
Simple vocal response—I A D
Crystallized ability (Horn)—I S V C PA
Achievement (Horn)—I S A V C
Semantic content (Guilford)—I S A V C PA

General ability—I S A V C BD
Alertness to environment—I PC
Cultural opportunities at home—I V C PA
Intellectual curiosity and striving—I V
Interests—I S V
Outside reading—I S V
Richness of early environment—I V
School learning—I A V

Most of the cognitive hypotheses are rejected either because of Nikki's significant weakness in Digit Span, her below-the-Verbal-mean score in Comprehension, or her equal-to-the-mean score in Similarities. For those hypotheses that include Performance subtests, the Performance scaled score is compared with Nikki's *Performance* mean, not the Verbal mean, even though a strength on a Verbal subtest is being investigated.

The following cognitive hypotheses are supported: Acquired Knowledge, fund of information, and long-term memory. All these abilities denote areas of strength. Her long-term (tertiary) memory is reflected in her ability to acquire so much knowledge and is undoubtedly responsible, in large part, for her success in the school-related skills of Information, Arithmetic, and Vocabulary. Her strength in "fund of information," though given clear-cut support by Nikki's profile of scores (based on the Information-Vocabulary dyad), is of lesser importance; examiners should always try to deduce the most *global* area of strength or weakness. In general, hypotheses based on three subtests are preferred to those based on two subtests, just as hypotheses based on four subtests are preferred to those based on three.

Using the formula in Table 6.1 for the Acquired Knowledge grouping yields a standard score of 146 (99.9th percentile), which is significantly higher than her standard score of 128 (97th percentile) on the two verbal reasoning subtests. She performed exceptionally well on both clusters of subtests, but the analysis of shared abilities provides a little more information about Nikki's abilities than is provided by her summary scores (V-IQ = 140; VC Index = 139).

Whereas some examiners might have focused on a unique interpretation of Information and lauded Nikki's exceptional range of general information, the single area of strength seems trivial in view of her consistently high performance (scaled scores of 17–19) on three subtests that compose the Acquired Knowledge/Long-term memory cluster. In view of our knowledge of Nikki and her home environment, several of the influences affecting test performance probably account, at least in part, for her strong Acquired Knowledge. Consequently, the extent of her outside reading, the richness of her early environment, her intellectual curiosity and striving, and her interests (in reading and in learning in general) are undoubtedly related to Nikki's outstanding verbal ability. (The fact that Similarities is in some of these clusters is irrelevant, since examiners must make qualitative, not quantitative, decisions about influences on test performance.) In addition, her high level of school achievement and the intellectual environment provided by her parents suggest that her Acquired Knowledge strength is also a function of Nikki's cultural opportunities at home and her school learning.

Interpreting the Weakness on Digit Span

Although typically it is sensible to interpret strengths before attacking weaknesses, the order of investigating significant discrepancies is really irrelevant. In this instance, the significant weakness in Digit Span is treated next, to complete the Verbal Scale before analyzing the Performance subtests. The various hypotheses involving *Digit Span*, listed in Tables 6.1, 6.3, and 6.4, are presented as follows (in addition, Digit Span and Arithmetic form the FD factor):

Understanding words (as opposed to long questions)—S V D
Auditory-vocal channel—I S A V C D
Memory (Guilford)—I A D
Simple vocal response—I A D
Attention-concentration—A D PC Cd SS
Encoding information for processing—A D Cd SS
Symbolic content (Guilford)—A D Cd
Sequencing (Bannatyne)—A D Cd
Anxiety—A D Cd SS
Attention span—A D SS
Distractibility—A D Cd SS
Flexibility—S D OA
Learning disabilities/ADHD—A D Cd SS
Negativism—S C D PC

In view of Nikki's high score on Information, all hypotheses involving that subtest, including Memory (from Guilford's perspective) can be rejected. The same is true for all hypotheses involving Coding on which Nikki earned a scaled score of 18, and all influences involving negative behaviors such as anxiety. As indicated by the examiner, this young girl was alert, aware, totally in tune with her environment, and decidedly *not* anxious, inattentive, or distractible during the evaluation. One additional hypothesis is suggested by Nikki's significant weakness in Symbol Search—the possibility that fatigue or boredom led to her depressed scores. (Digit Span and Symbol Search are the last two WISC-III subtests administered.) However, the examiner reported that Nikki was still eager, energetic, and highly interested in doing well at the end of the WISC-III session.

The only reasonable conclusion is that Nikki has a weakness in the unique ability measured by Digit Span—auditory short-term memory. Whether this apparent weakness is repeatable or generalizable to meaningful content could be checked out with supplementary measures. Following up of hypotheses with other measures was not necessary for Nikki, however, since the only question at issue was whether she qualified for the gifted program. She did.

Interpreting the Weakness on Symbol Search

Since fatigue cannot explain the significantly low score on Symbol Search, it is of interest to try to track down an explanation for this deviation. Hypotheses pertaining to *Symbol Search* are as follows (excluding the Symbol Search-Coding dyad that composes the PS factor):

Understanding complex verbal directions—Cd PA BD SS
Visual perception of abstract stimuli—Cd BD SS
Visual-motor channel—PC Cd PA BD OA SS
Convergent-production (Guilford)—Cd PA SS
Figural Evaluation (Guilford)—PC BD OA SS
Integrated brain functioning—Cd PA BD SS
Planning ability—PA SS
Spatial visualization—BD SS
Visual memory—PC Cd SS
Visual-motor coordination—BD OA Cd SS
Attention-concentration—A D PC Cd SS
Distinguishing essential from nonessential detail—S PC PA SS
Encoding information for processing—A D Cd SS
Evaluation (Guilford)—C PC Cd PA BD OA SS
Learning ability—V Cd SS
Anxiety—A D Cd SS
Attention span—A D SS
Concentration—A PC Cd SS
Distractibility—A D Cd SS
Learning disabilities/ADHD—A D Cd SS
Motivation level—Cd SS
Obsessive concern with detail—Cd SS
Persistence—Cd OA SS
Visual-perceptual problems—Cd BD OA SS
Working under time pressure—A PC PA BD OA Cd SS

Nearly all the cognitive hypotheses listed for Symbol Search can be rejected as weaknesses because of Nikki's significant strength on Coding and/or her above-the-Performance-mean scores on Block Design and Object Assembly. Distinguishing essential from nonessential details is rejected as an area of weakness because she scored exactly at her Verbal mean on Similarities and at her Performance mean on Picture Completion. And all the influences that are known to affect Symbol Search performance (the last 10 factors on the list) are rejected as explanations of Nikki's weakness in Symbol Search based on what we know about her background and the test behaviors reported by the examiner.

Planning ability is given support because her significant weakness in Symbol Search is joined by a below-average scaled score of 11 on Picture Arrangement. However, other explanations might account for her below-the-mean Picture Arrangement score, especially in view of its large amount of subtest-specific variance (see Table 6.7). Nikki is creative, as reported by her language-arts teacher, observed by the examiner, and also given empirical support by her high scores on the Torrance Tests of Creative Thinking (Torrance, 1974)—one of the instruments included in the battery administered to determine eligibility for the gifted program. Creativity can lower a child's score on a convergent task such as Picture Arrangement that rewards the one "best" story for each item. If Nikki's below-average (for her) performance on Picture Arrangement was due to the interference of her creative mind, it would be inappropriate to suggest that she has a relative weakness in planning ability; her weak area would simply be in the unique ability measured by Symbol Search.

Aware of this possibility, the examiner tested the limits on Picture Arrangement after the entire WISC-III was completed. One by one, Nikki's wrong arrangements were placed before her and she was asked to tell each story. Rather than revealing novel or defensible stories in her wrong arrangements, Nikki's verbalizations served to illustrate her difficulty in understanding the stories as integrated wholes. Consequently, her creativity did not seem to impede her performance on Picture Arrangement. Additional evidence that Nikki has relatively weak planning ability concerns the examiner's observation that she used a trial-and-error approach when solving nonverbal tasks. She did not use a planned or organized strategy when arranging pictures or constructing designs or puzzles. Instead, she started moving the concrete stimuli around as soon as the examiner finished the last instruction, putting pairs of puzzle pieces together, for example, then taking them apart and trying a different pair. During Symbol Search, she was unable to stick to a consistent strategy. First she looked briefly at the target stimuli and responded quickly; then when she caught two mistakes that she had made, she became flustered and switched to a deliberate strategy. This problem was not noted on Coding, which involves dealing with one stimulus at a time (Symbol Search requires two stimuli for children Nikki's age).

Her standard score on the two planning subtests computes to 100 using the formula in Table 6.2. Though still average for her age, the relative planning deficit stands in marked contrast to her areas of strength. Also, she performed lower on verbal reasoning than Acquired Knowledge subtests on the Verbal Scale, which is entirely consistent with the low scores on planning tests. Picture Arrangement, in addition, is probably the best measure of reasoning ability on the Performance Scale.

Interpreting the Strength on Coding

Turning to Nikki's significantly high score on *Coding,* a list of hypotheses involving this subtest is shown as follows (influences associated with poor performance on Coding are eliminated):

Understanding complex verbal directions—Cd PA BD SS
Visual perception of abstract stimuli—Cd BD SS
Visual-motor channel—PC Cd PA BD OA SS
Convergent-production (Guilford)—Cd PA SS
Integrated brain functioning—Cd PA BD SS
Reproduction of models—Cd BD
Visual memory—PC Cd SS
Visual sequencing—Cd PA
Visual-motor coordination—BD OA Cd SS
Attention-concentration—A D PC Cd SS
Encoding information for processing—A D Cd SS
Evaluation (Guilford)—C PC Cd PA BD OA SS
Symbolic content (Guilford)—A D Cd
Sequential (Bannatyne)—A D Cd
Facility with numbers—A D Cd
Sequential processing—A D Cd
Learning ability—V Cd SS
Concentration—A PC Cd SS
Persistence—Cd OA SS
Working under time pressure—A PC PA BD OA Cd SS

Nikki's significant weaknesses on Symbol Search and Digit Span and her relatively low score on Picture Arrangement lead to elimination of most of the hypothesized abilities. Empirical support is given to the hypothesis regarding reproduction of a model. However, Nikki's good ability on Object Assembly (scaled score = 15) indicates that she does not require a visual model for success. This hypothesized strength is thus *not* accepted. Observations during the psychomotor subtest seemed more supportive of a different hypothesized strength. She understood the task immediately and did not memorize any of the symbols; her most noteworthy behavior was the exceptionally quick and agile eye-hand coordination that she sustained for the duration of the subtest, as well as her dogged persistence. The examiner noted in the case report that Nikki was observed to have well-coordinated motor activity, and this ability was evident on *all* manipulative tasks. It is, therefore, sensible to hypothesize that Nikki's significant strength on Coding, along with above-average scaled scores on Object Assembly and Block Design, reflects well-developed visual-motor coordination. Does the significant weakness in Symbol Search (which is included in the visual-motor quartet of subtests) detract from this hypothesized area of strength? Not at all. Examiners have to be alert to the possible necessity of fragmenting global skills such as visual-motor coordination since the key to understanding a child's profile may depend on qualitative interpretation of each component subtest in a grouping. Nikki evidenced confusion and some frustration during Symbol Search because of an apparent weakness in her planning ability. It is unreasonable to expect excellent visual-motor coordination to compensate for this relative deficiency. Although coordination is more likely to emerge as an explanation for low rather than high scores for most children, in this instance it seems to best explain Nikki's high score on Coding and above-average scores on two other subtests that depend on agile motor ability for success.

Overview of Nikki's WISC-III Profile

Overall, Nikki is a creative girl with outstanding verbal intelligence and visual-motor coordination who demonstrated an exceptional long-term memory. Not surprisingly, she was selected for the gifted program. She has Very Superior Verbal Comprehension ability (99.6th percentile) and Superior Perceptual Organization ability (91st percentile) but was relatively weak in her planning ability (50th percentile) and in her auditory short-term memory (63rd percentile). These interpretations of Nikki's profile fluctuations are far more informative and meaningful and take into account more of her subtest scores than interpretations that focus either on the three global IQs or—at the opposite extreme—on the unique abilities presumably measured by the specific subtests.

HYPOTHESES AND RECOMMENDATIONS

The main aim of generating hypotheses from WISC-III profiles is *not* to diagnose an exceptionality or to plan methods for remediating a learning or behavioral disorder, but to help understand the children being evaluated—how they learn best, what they can do relatively well and relatively poorly, how their background and behavior interact with their cognitive functioning, and so forth. From this understanding comes diagnostic hypotheses and remedial suggestions, provided that the WISC-III is supplemented by additional instruments and that standardized testing, in general, is augmented by informal assessment, curriculum-based assessment, and evaluation in naturalistic settings. It is irrational to suppose that complex disorders such as mental retardation or learning disabilities can be diagnosed, based on 90 minutes or so of 1:1 contact between an unfamiliar examiner and apprehensive child. No matter how well rapport is established, the artificiality of the situation is constantly brought to the attention of the child by the stopwatch, the recording of virtually every word uttered by the child, and the examiner's dependence on a book to know precisely what to say. The fact that competent examiners with clinical experience and a thorough grounding in psychological theory can gain new insights into children's functioning based on administration of a single instrument such as the WISC-III is indeed impressive; expectations of an instant diagnosis or of automatic recommendations are unreasonable, as are the holding of intelligence tests for ransom until substantial evidence for treatment validity arrives (Witt & Gresham, 1985).

Hypotheses generated from WISC-III profiles, and profiles from the other comprehensive test batteries mentioned throughout this text, can aid greatly in understanding children, and this understanding can take many forms. Examiners may find out about well-developed or poorly developed *abilities,* such as memory, reasoning, spatial visualization, verbal concept formation, or convergent-production. Or they may uncover strong or weak *modes of processing* information, most notably analytic-sequential versus holistic-simultaneous, or planning-attention-successive-simultaneous. The nature of the *content* to be processed, that is, verbal-nonverbal or meaningful-abstract, may conceivably be isolated as the key distinction for some children. Or, the main finding of a WISC-III administration may be the examiner's awareness of how *nonintellective factors* interact with mental functioning. These nonintellective variables span a wide range from background variables (cultural opportunities at home, speaking Black English) and cognitive style (field dependence-field independence, reflective-impulsive) to characteristic or pervasive behaviors (anxiety, distractibility) and interests or hobbies (reading, solving jigsaw puzzles).

Many of these hypotheses have educational consequences, some of which have been alluded to throughout this book and are illustrated in the case reports. Certainly examiners would anticipate quite different teaching styles being effective for children with good reasoning and poor memory skills as opposed to those with good memory and poor reasoning. Different types of curricular materials are likely to be successful for children whose test performance varies directly with the content of the task, and different approaches to teaching reading or arithmetic should be recommended for children who show strengths in sequential versus simultaneous processing. Different learning environments might work best for children with divergent modes of problem solving: a structured, rule-governed, logical environment for analytic, "left-brained" individuals; and an unstructured, flexible, "discovery" environment for "right-brained" children. Similarly, learning environments may need to be adapted to children who are shown to have a specific cognitive style and to children whose intellectual functioning is impeded by extraneous variables such as inability to concentrate, anxiety, or emotional lability.

The translation of test hypotheses to recommendations will be an easier task for examiners who are thoroughly knowledgeable of theories of remediation and research on educational intervention, and who keep alert to available curricular materials and how to evaluate them. Crucial educational decisions are sometimes made on the basis of a psychological evaluation, and these decisions should be supported by ample evidence. As has been reiterated throughout this book, hypotheses suggested by a WISC-III profile should be verified by additional measures. In some instances, the best recommendations WISC-III examiners can make are the names of supplementary tests or tasks that must be administered, either by the examiners themselves or by other specialized professional personnel. Rarely should direct educational programming follow from an administration of the WISC-III in isolation. Additional data and criteria have to be considered before making suggestions derived from hypotheses that can only be considered as tentative.

Virtually never, in my opinion, should the WISC-III subtests form the specific content areas worthy of remediation. These areas are mere samples of behavior, intended to reflect an individual's abilities and modes of processing information, rather than a criterion-referenced set of topics that have to be mastered. Wechsler decidedly did not develop his scales with specific educational intervention in mind for improving the ability to tell how two things are alike or to construct abstract designs with blocks, just as Piaget never intended any parent or teacher to teach a child conservation of liquid.

What follows are some general suggestions for making meaningful recommendations based on the results of a thorough assessment (suggestions are courtesy of N. L. Kaufman, personal communication, 1993). Examiners who find the sequential-simultaneous model useful for making recommendations to improve a child's reading, arithmetic, and spelling skills should consult the lists of specific remedial suggestions in the *K-ABC Interpretive Manual* (Kaufman & Kaufman, 1983, Chapter 7). All the remedial suggestions in the K-ABC manual and in the following sections are based on the following assumptions about the remedial process: (a) The goal of remediation is twofold, to help the child advance to higher levels of academic and personal growth, and to close the gap between the child's strengths and weaknesses; (b) cognitive and behavioral strengths are the child's most potent raw materials for effecting change in the weak academic areas; and (c) any general list of remedial suggestions must be tailored and personalized for each child.

1. **The psychologist's job in writing recommendations in a case report is not to *be* the teacher, but to:**
   - Communicate what you have found out about the referred child's strengths and weaknesses.
   - Explain how you believe the teacher can best impart new information to the child.
   - Be aware of available curricular materials and be up to date on new materials (by browsing through exhibition halls at pertinent conventions), but recognize that it is the teacher's job to select the actual teaching materials once he or she understands your explanations of the child's functioning and needs.
   - Explain to the teacher basic principles of educational psychology and learning, if necessary, and not take for granted that he or she routinely applies basic principles that are axiomatic to you.

2. **For any child who is referred for school learning problems in one or more academic subjects and requires remediation:**
   - Individualize each area of instruction, so that the child is taught at his or her appropriate readiness level for each different skill.
   - Teach to the child's tolerance level and avoid pushing beyond. (For example, help the teacher pinpoint the child's threshold level and stay at it.)
   - Begin new tasks only when you know the child is not tired and is "ready" to learn.

3. **To improve a weakness in decoding information (input, or receptive processing of stimuli) for a child who has a meaningful difference in dealing with nonverbal versus stimuli or who differs in the processing of stimuli within a single channel (e.g., good visual perception of meaningful stimuli, but poor visual perception of abstract stimuli):**
   - Utilize the child's areas of strength by pairing new stimuli in a high-functioning domain with the same information presented through a deficit channel.
   - Ask the teacher to reinforce this paired association to make sure the child has a double opportunity to learn. Eventually, the teacher can gradually fade out dependency on the strength once new associations have been made. For example, if testing has revealed that the child has strengths in verbal ability, but weaknesses in visual-perceptual or nonverbal abilities, the child could be taught the letters of the alphabet by the teacher verbally describing what each letter looks like while showing the child picture cards of the letter. Once associations have been made, remove the verbal descriptions and the child can respond to the flash cards of the letters.

- Check out the child's ability to transfer input from one sensory channel to other sensory channels before proceeding with multi-sensory stimulation. For example, make sure child isn't being overloaded in the classroom by too many sources of incoming stimuli.
- For children with receptive language problems: (a) Be careful that language clarifies rather than disturbs learning, (b) check wording of directions to be sure all basic concepts are within the child's working vocabulary, (c) maintain visual contact with the learner, (d) use gestures to facilitate oral communication, (e) speak at a slower-than-usual tempo, and (f) touch the child before talking to him or her.

4. **To improve a weakness in the integration and storage of new learning:**

- Make use of all available feedback in the remedial setting, including the teacher's feedback when the child responds to a question or assignment; the child's feedback when the teacher confirms or corrects a response; and the internal and external feedback the child receives from his or her own actual and covert response behavior (vocal or motor); and self-corrections when using computerized instructional materials.
- Develop abilities functionally, in natural settings, and avoid contrived or artificial ones. For example, integrate new reading skills by having a variety of easy reading materials for the child to "practice" on instead of traditional drill or review with isolated words or phrases.
- Teach material that fulfills a practical need for the child before teaching material that is less relevant.
- For deficits in nonverbal problem solving, nonverbal concept formation, synthesis, simultaneous processing, or spatial ability (as long as child has at least some relative strength in a global or specific verbal or sequential area): (a) Try to enhance the meaning of visual stimuli (e.g., by pointing out what concrete object a figure most resembles); (b) capitalize on the child's verbal or sequential strengths when solving the nonverbal problems; and (c) encourage the child to use inner language when working out nonverbal problems. The latter suggestion is especially useful for deficits in time concepts (hours, days, weeks, seasons), direction, and relational concepts (e.g., fastest, halfway, half-full).

5. **To help slow learners, mentally retarded children, learning-disabled children, and so forth, generalize newly acquired information:**

- Provide set variations of initial learning bits and point out similarities or unity of information.

- Present the same information in many different ways to create adequate redundancy.
- Provide generous time allowances for remedial work. Sometimes the child does not succeed because he or she simply needed more time on an instructional task.
- Measure improvement graphically and show the record to the child to demonstrate that change is taking place.

6. **To help children with multiple areas of deficit (or moderate to severe deficits in one primary area):**
   - Remediate prerequisite deficits first. For example, remediate oral language before written language, and word recognition before reading comprehension.
   - Use task analysis to construct lessons within each skill area that progress from simple to more complex tasks.
   - Use minimal steps of increasing difficulty.
   - Encourage teachers to allow sufficient time to supervise new learning, and to monitor remedial work closely until it becomes a work habit.
   - Encourage teachers to join the child in cooperative effort to set and attain realistic goals.
   - Maintain a 90% success rate to avoid negative error learning and feelings of inadequacy.
   - Get some improvement each session. Don't keep trying the same approach if it is not successful.
   - Work on only one new skill at a time, presenting just a few new stimuli and limiting other variables to a bare minimum. This procedure avoids interference and overloading.

7. **To help children with memory problems, short-term, long-term, auditory, visual, and so forth:**
   - Use distributed review. Space out the demands for practice of new skills to avoid boredom and fatigue, and to provide for overlearning and the development of automatic skills. This suggestion is especially useful for math difficulties and word recognition skills. Suggest 10 three-minute sessions if a half-hour's work is necessary.
   - Provide the child with a written list of reminders. The child can check off each one that is completed as he or she progresses.
   - Follow a predictable routine so the child won't have to learn new formats for completing work successfully. This procedure will help preset expectations and reduce the memory load.
   - Don't accept the excuse of "I forgot" to allow the child to avoid assigned homework or chores. Have the child complete the assignment when reminded.

8. **To improve work habits, or to help children who have difficulty attending and concentrating, or who have low motivation:**
   - Use other pupils in cooperative remedial sessions, and in individual 1:1 tutoring. Peer tutors will serve as role models for appropriate study techniques and promote social support at the same time. A side benefit of peer tutors is the encouragement of a spirit of cooperation instead of competition.
   - Select instructional materials that are highly interesting to the child. For example, instead of a story in a basal reader, substitute reading the directions of a new game to be played later, an article about a star basketball player, or the instructions for assembling a model airplane.
   - Reinforce the student with tangible and intangible rewards when appropriate behavior is demonstrated. Gradually increase the requirements for the reinforcement. For example, classroom privileges, free time, and helping the teacher are tangibles; handshakes, smiles, praise are intangibles.
   - Write a contract with the child that lists expected behaviors and the reinforcements that will follow when the terms of contract are completed.
   - Structure the child's work environment in a way that promotes the reduction of distractions and intervening stimuli.
   - Highlight or circle important information on an assigned work paper, especially information that may otherwise be missed. For example, circle the directions to a task, the item numbers to be worked on in math, the main theme in an essay, and so forth.
   - Work on remedial activities when others are working on similar work projects, not during enjoyable activity time.
   - Use learning sets and advance organizers to enhance motivation for learning by relating previous abilities and knowledge to the present task.
   - For short attention spans, keep lessons very brief. Alternate quiet activities with active ones. Plan interruptions when longer lessons are given (e.g., have the child come to the teacher's table after a small task is completed, or get a necessary supply from the shelf when that part of an activity is reached).
   - Manipulate the child's sense of space within the learning environment. For example, use partitions, cubicles, screens, and quiet corners, and remove distracting stimuli.

ILLUSTRATIVE CASE REPORTS

The two case reports that follow show the importance both of subtest profile interpretation and personality assessment for a more complete understanding of children's overall functioning. Both the case of Tony, an 11-year-old with ADHD, and 7-year-old Michael, who has learning and emotional problems, utilize the WISC-III with the WIAT; some neuropsychological tests were also administered in the evaluation of Michael. Tony's profile is best understood using Bannatyne's four-category system in conjunction with the sequential-simultaneous model, and Michael's profile also seems most interpretable in terms of a portion of Bannatyne's approach. These reports have been fictionalized to some extent to protect anonymity of the clients and their families.

Tony G., Age 11-2, Attention-Deficit Hyperactivity Disorder, Behavior Problems, High Functioning

WISC-III Profile

IQs		(90% conf.)	Factor Indexes		(90% conf.)
Verbal	115	(109–119)	Verbal Comprehension	116	(109–121)
Performance	119	(111–124)	Perceptual Organization	117	(108–122)
Full Scale	119	(114–123)	Freedom from Distractibility	104	(96–111)
V-IQ = P-IQ *(ns)*			Processing Speed	104	(95–112)

Verbal	Scaled Score	Performance	Scaled Score
Information	17-S	Picture Completion	13
Similarities	9-W	(Coding)	(8)
Arithmetic	12	Picture Arrangement	9
Vocabulary	14	Block Design	15
Comprehension	11	Object Assembly	14
(Digit Span)	(9)	*Symbol Search	13

* Symbol Search was used in IQ computations
Mean of 12 subtests = 12

Wechsler Individual Achievement Test (WIAT)

Subtest/Composite	Standard Score (±90% conf.)
Mathematics Composite	115 ± 6
Mathematics Reasoning	107 ± 8
Numerical Operations	122 ± 9
Reading Composite	109 ± 6
Basic Reading	102 ± 7
Reading Comprehension	121 ± 8
Language Composite	109 ± 7
Listening Comprehension	111 ± 10
Oral Expression	105 ± 7
Writing Composite	112 ± 8
Spelling	102 ± 7
Written Expression	128 ± 12
Total Composite	113 ± 4

Referral and Background Information

Tony G. is an 11-year-old, African-American fifth-grade male who was referred by the psychiatrist he has been seeing for the past 4 months. The referring difficulties centered on Tony's teacher's concern that he was becoming violent at school. He reportedly attempted to choke another child on the playground. Other reported behaviors include engaging in "trancelike stares," being disruptive in the classroom, getting enraged easily, and evidencing tics. Interpersonal difficulties with peers were also observed during a school observation. He is sensitive to others' making fun of his glasses and gets upset easily, according to his teacher. At the time of the referral he had been placed on "minimum days" (half days) at school because of the teacher's reports of "uncontrollable, disruptive, aggressive behavior." These minimum days ended before lunch and he did not have recess with the rest of the class. His parents report that the other half day is spent doing schoolwork, playing sports, reading, or watching television.

Tony was diagnosed as suffering from Attention-Deficit Hyperactive Disorder by his current psychiatrist, and therapy began immediately, at which time the psychiatrist prescribed Ritalin. Since that time, Tony has had improved behavior both at home and at school. However, when his medication is not taken, or if he takes a smaller dose, his behavior can deteriorate.

Tony is the product of an uncomplicated full-term pregnancy. Forceps were used to aid in the delivery without side effects. His reported Apgar scores were both nine. His mother reported milestones were reached within the normal time frame with the exception of talking, which he accomplished early. Of note in his medical history is that he frequently suffered from ear infections from birth to age 2 years. He had one high fever at age 14 months, which required a 3-day hospitalization, and had the chicken pox at age two. He wears glasses to correct his vision but has normal hearing.

Tony is the only child of a home broken by divorce when he was 6 years old. His parents share physical custody and child-rearing responsibilities. Both parents have remarried and he has three half-siblings and three stepsiblings from these unions, all younger than Tony. Both natural parents and both stepparents attended the intake conference and provided information about Tony's childhood and background. Additional information was provided by his teacher and psychiatrist.

Behavioral difficulties began for Tony when he was in kindergarten. His mother described him as being restless, easily distracted, and needing a great deal of attention. These problems have been apparent both at home and at school. His third-grade teacher noted difficulties but responded by using behavioral techniques to which Tony responded well, per the parents' report. During his present fifth-grade year, he was placed in a gifted classroom, and the teacher reported much behavioral disturbance.

The BASC Student Observation System was used during a school visit by a staff member to provide accurate recording of Tony's behavior in the classroom. Use of the instrument involves a 15-minute systematic sampling of 12 behavior categories and includes assessment of both adaptive and maladaptive classroom behaviors. Tony was observed during a Reading-Social Studies lesson. The children read passages to themselves from their book and were then asked to respond to what they had read. Of the nine "Problem Behaviors" samples, Tony demonstrated behaviors in two of the categories: Inappropriate Movement and Inappropriate Vocalization. The movements consisted of frequently raising his hand vigorously in an attempt to get his teacher's attention, typically keeping his hand up as he resumed reading or the class discussion moved on. The vocalizations entailed frequent calling out of responses or observations without waiting to be called on, or calling out the teacher's name to get her attention if she didn't respond to his raised hand.

Tony also demonstrated behaviors in three "Adaptive Behaviors" categories that were applicable to the classroom activity taking place. Under "Response to Teacher-Lesson," he eagerly offered answers to several questions posed by the teacher and followed the lesson with obvious interest. Regarding "Peer Interaction," Tony worked cooperatively with the girl sitting next to him as they shared a book. He listened to her as she read quietly out loud, and helped her with the words when she hesitated in her reading. Under "Transition Movements," he readily put his desk in order and readied himself to be excused with the rest of the class for lunch. Throughout the 15-minute observation period, he was an eager participant and his problem behaviors seemed to result from his strong need to have his plentiful knowledge recognized by the teacher and students.

Appearance and Behavioral Characteristics

Tony presented as a thin, well-dressed, and well-groomed 11-year-old boy with glasses. He was pleasant throughout the testing sessions and often displayed a delightful sense of humor. All tasks asked of him were tackled with an air of wanting to do his best. He was motivated to complete the tasks and worked until told to stop. During the test sessions, he was on Ritalin; however, it appeared that he was more distractible and less able to focus during the afternoon session versus the morning testing session.

On structured tasks—ones with right or wrong answers, such as the intelligence and educational tests—he considered most questions and tasks carefully, taking his time when he was uncertain of the correct response. He was able to admit when he did not know the answers in an easygoing manner. On the projective tasks, however, he was more distractible and less able to attend to the task at hand. The latter response may be because of task requirements not having a right or wrong answer, or because of a differing level of Ritalin in his system at the time.

During the evaluation procedure, Tony displayed none of the behaviors described by the teacher in his gifted classroom. Many changes have been made in Tony's life since last fall when these incidents happened. Since last fall, he has been placed on Ritalin, removed from the gifted classroom, experienced an increase in structure at home and at school and experienced a reduction in the ambiguity in his life. All these changes have contributed to better behavioral control, happiness, and success for Tony.

Tests Administered

Wechsler Intelligence Scale for Children—Third Edition (WISC-III)
Wechsler Individual Achievement Test (WIAT)
Rorschach Inkblot Test (Rorschach)
Thematic Apperception Test (TAT)
Kinetic Family Drawing
House-Tree-Person Test
Behavior Assessment System for Children (BASC): Student Observation System (SOS) (results discussed in Background Information section)

Test Results and Interpretation

Intellectually, Tony is currently functioning in the High Average to Superior range on the WISC-III (Verbal IQ = 115, Performance IQ = 119, Full Scale IQ = 119) ranking at about the 90th percentile relative to other 11-year-olds. The chances are 9 out of 10 that his true Full Scale IQ is somewhere within the range of 114 to 123. The 4-point difference between his Verbal and Performance IQs is trivial, suggesting that he is functioning at about the same level on tasks that require him to understand verbal concepts and express his ideas verbally as on visual-motor tasks that assess nonverbal thinking. While these scores do not place him in the traditionally defined "gifted" range (Full Scale IQ of 130), the test results suggest many strengths and some relative weaknesses that may account for his previous placement in a gifted classroom as well as may explain some of his behavior.

He performed comparably on the two Factor Indexes that compose the Verbal Scale (Verbal Comprehension and Freedom from Distractibility) and also on the two Factor Indexes that compose the Performance Scale (Perceptual Organization and Processing Speed). Nonetheless, it is meaningful to group together the four subtests that comprise the FD and PS factors and compare them to the PO factor. Tony performed at the 87th percentile on the PO factor, significantly higher than the 58th percentile he achieved on the combination of the distractibility and speed factors. Such differences are common for children with ADHD or learning problems, because they typically have some difficulty with the four subtests on these small WISC-III factors. Differences at least as large as the one displayed by Tony occurred in 54% of the children in an ADHD/LD sample compared with only 16% of the normal children in a comparison group.

Tony's scores on the Verbal Scale exhibited too much scatter to permit meaningful interpretation of either his Verbal IQ or his Verbal Comprehension Index; he displayed a significant strength on a test of general factual information (99th percentile) and a significant weakness on a test requiring him to relate two verbal concepts (37th percentile). A better understanding of these significant deviations is provided by a recategorization of the WISC-III subtests by Bannatyne's system; this division gives more insight into Tony's strengths and weaknesses than is yielded by his IQs or Factor Indexes.

Standard scores have been computed for him on the four Bannatyne categories. Along with 90% confidence intervals and percentile ranks, these scores are as follows:

Bannatyne Categories

Verbal Conceptualization	108±4	70th %ile
Acquired Knowledge	125±4	95th %ile
Sequential	98±5	45th %ile
Spatial	124±5	95th %ile

Tony has a considerable amount of acquired verbal information, consistent with his good school achievement and with the behaviors he displayed during the school visit, but that Superior level is significantly better than the Average to High Average level he achieved on tests of verbal reasoning and conceptualization. He does better at acquiring factual knowledge than solving verbal problems. He also scored significantly higher in his performance on visual-spatial tasks (Superior) than on tests that require sequencing ability and the sequential processing of information (Average). Although the Picture Arrangement subtest (arranging pictures in the right order to tell a story) is excluded from Bannatyne's Sequential category, it is apparent that Tony's relative deficit in sequencing extends to his ability to solve these socially relevant nonverbal problems (37th percentile).

Tony's verbal-factual skills are well developed and visible, and he strives to increase his vocabulary and fund of information. He uses these skills to engage the world around him, which often consists of adults who, appropriately, reinforce his vocabulary and knowledge base. However, skills that are not as visible, such as sequencing ability, are not as well developed. These areas of functioning are still solidly in the Average to High Average range, which allowed him to function in his gifted class from an academic perspective. The high Spatial-low Sequential profile suggests that he processes information simultaneously rather than sequentially. That is, when asked to solve problems in a serial or temporal order rather than in a holistic, spatial manner, Tony does less well.

The results of the standardized achievement testing were quite consistent with the intellectual evaluation. His overall Total Composite on the WIAT was 113 (81st percentile), approximately equal to his WISC-III scores. He performed at the Average to High Average level in Mathematics, Reading, Language, and Writing. His lowest scores were on Spelling and Basic Reading (decoding), both at the 55th percentile. These achievement tasks are both dependent on sequential abilities, Tony's area of weakness. In contrast, his simultaneous strength may relate to his Superior scores on WIAT Reading Comprehension (92nd percentile) and Written Expression (97th percentile), since both tasks are facilitated by holistic abilities such as understanding the main point of a passage or organizing one's ideas. Within the Mathematics domain, Tony's better performance on Numerical Operations (93rd percentile) than Mathematics Reasoning (68th percentile) is entirely consistent with his better ability to acquire facts than to problem solve.

Tony showed adequate concentration and attention during all the testing, most likely as a result of his medication. Test results suggest that his level of mental functioning and academic achievement are greatly influenced by the kind of cognitive activity involved. He appears to have a good fund of factual information at his beck and call. He is curious and eager to learn and puts these assets to good use. He does well in memorizing facts and takes pride in being able to use these facts appropriately. When the tasks asked of him require this type of learning skill, he excels. When he is asked to put this information into an abstract, conceptual context, he is less effective.

Tony approached tasks with a slow, reflective style, which may be a result of his difficulty applying his knowledge to new situations. When he is faced with situations requiring rote answers, he does well because he can apply the rules he has learned about the situation directly. He has more difficulty when situations are ambiguous and require that he think about applying the rules. For example, he can apply the rules pertaining to vocabulary because there is a right or wrong answer. If he is asked to sound out or spell a word he does not know, it becomes more difficult for him.

Interpersonally, Tony has a similar style. He has difficulty when the rules are not steadfast and predictable. When he shares his knowledge of facts, he is on safe ground. He becomes shaky when confronted with new social situations or with ambiguity. Interpersonal relationships are not easily incorporated by Tony due to their unpredictable nature. They do not follow prescribed rules and he has a hard time understanding others as a result. He uses his intellect, humor, and imagination to "fill in the blanks" when he is uncomfortable in social settings. He is engaging and can often redirect the situation using these tools. When Tony cannot redirect social situations, he becomes less sure of himself and more frustrated. He sees himself generally as being smart and confident, and when he is not in control of the situation, he begins to doubt himself and perhaps even his worth. It appears that he is greatly identified with being "smart" and has built much of his self-esteem on this fact. Underlying this likelihood is a sense that Tony needs and seeks approval from others in order to feel good about himself. He sets high standards for himself, and these may not always be attainable. He equates success with getting good grades, not with the process of doing one's best.

Recommendations

1. It is clear from the assessment procedure that continued Ritalin treatment is essential for Tony to be able to interact appropriately with peers, teachers, siblings, and parents at this time. Consistent, evenly disbursed doses over the course of the day are preferable to the time-release regimen that he was under during the testing sessions. For example, if his dose is 30 mg per day, three 10-mg doses throughout the day would be preferable.

2. Tony could greatly profit from attending a social skills group comprised of others who share his difficulties. This setting would allow him to practice relating to others in a safe place, get valuable feedback about his behavior from peers in a positive manner, and teach him ways to manage his behavior.

3. Structured, predictable settings are preferable to Tony. He is more comfortable and is better able to perform with structured tasks. His best learning environment is one in which the rules are spelled out and nothing is ambiguous. Some situations in which he is involved are very structured situations. For example, he does well in and enjoys sports partly for this reason. Both the task itself, and the social interactions, are governed by the rules in sporting events.

4. Tony performed better on tests of acquired information than on tests of abstract reasoning. As information in school becomes increasingly abstract, he might have a more difficult time keeping up with peers in a gifted classroom. Nonetheless, his skill level in this area is certainly adequate for performing well in school, and he should be given another chance in the gifted program. His gifted teacher's main complaint was Tony's behavior rather than his ability or achievement, and his behavior has been greatly improved by the medication. The gifted teacher is reported to be quite structured in her approach, which fits into Tony's needs; also, in view of Tony's investment in being perceived as smart, a return to the gifted class will help his self-image.

5. Developing other means of gaining positive attention from parents and peers will be important for Tony. He knows that doing well in school and knowing facts gets him positive attention. Now it will be important to extend the praise to other areas of his life. Reinforcing his sports participation (even if he is not a star) and interacting with him, letting him know his humor is enjoyed, will begin to round out his perception of himself. Activities such as the Boy Scouts, Boys Club, or martial arts would again provide a structured setting, social interactions, and a model for Tony to follow.

6. Tony spoke lovingly and with concern about his half-siblings and stepsiblings. It would be beneficial to him to receive positive attention from his parents when he shows this love and concern. His "older brother" status will increase his self-esteem and help him develop responsibility toward others. This reinforcement should not be centered around "child care" activities, but at those times that he shares his toys and games, gives a spontaneous hug, or is just being gentle and kind.

7. Increasing Tony's one-on-one time with peers would be helpful at this stage in his life. Inviting a friend to come home with him after school for an hour would be a good start. These developing friendships might then evolve into sleep-overs at both houses. Putting aside one afternoon per week to just play will help Tony develop peer relations.

8. With regard to his school placement for next year, Tony should continue in the gifted program if the school and gifted teacher are willing to give him a second chance. If not, then he should be placed in a regular classroom with his current teacher, if possible (since his current regular class is a combined fifth-sixth grade). Establishing individual relationships with teachers and peers is extremely important at this time. If Tony will be in a different classroom next year, it would be helpful for him to be told of the class rules and the expectations of him before beginning the year. Increased support at home in the form of encouraging him to invite new classmates over to play will help ease the transition. If Tony has a different teacher next year, it is recommended that the parents wait a few weeks (3 to 4) and then make an appointment to introduce themselves to the teacher. This would set up a positive framework should any problems arise later.

9. During the school day Tony should be reinforced shortly after he displays positive or target behavior. Rewards should be given quickly and frequently to achieve the best results.

10. Because Tony has such a good store of information, he often wishes to share it with others. During class, this has caused problems in the past. Therefore, it is recommended that he be given a "Sharing Time" at the same time each day so that he can pass on the information he wishes to share. This procedure might alleviate his need to constantly raise his hand and shout out. Again, the consistency and predictability of such an arrangement would be helpful to Tony.

11. A new eye examination is recommended to ensure that his glasses prescription is still accurate.

Examiners:

Dr. Dana T. Grossman; Patricia Petterson, MA; Susan Glatz, MS

Supervisor to Ms. Petterson and Ms. Glatz:

Dr. Nadeen L. Kaufman

Michael B., Age 7-4, School Learning Problem, Emotional Difficulties

WISC-III Profile

IQs		(90% conf.)	Factor Indexes		(90% conf.)
Verbal	97	(92–102)	Verbal Comprehension	99	(93–105)
Performance	93	(87–100)	Perceptual Organization	94	(88–102)
Full Scale	94	(90–99)	Freedom from Distractibility	104	(96–111)
V-IQ = P-IQ (ns)			Processing Speed	104	(95–112)

Verbal	Scaled Score	Performance	Scaled Score
Information	7-W	Picture Completion	5-W
Similarities	12	(Coding)	(13)
Arithmetic	8	Picture Arrangement	10
Vocabulary	9	Block Design	10
Comprehension	11	Object Assembly	11
(Digit Span)	(13)	*Symbol Search	8

* Symbol Search was used in IQ computations
Mean of 12 subtests = 10

Wechsler Individual Achievement Test (WIAT)

Subtest/Composite	Standard Score (±90% conf.)
Mathematics Composite	88 ± 7
Mathematics Reasoning	94 ± 8
Numerical Operations	83 ± 10
Reading Composite	80 ± 4
Basic Reading	84 ± 6
Reading Comprehension	80 ± 7
Spelling	85 ± 7
Language Composite	92 ± 7
Listening Comprehension	88 ± 9
Oral Expression	99 ± 7
Total Composite	83 ± 4

Reason for Referral

Michael was referred by a social worker for a psychological evaluation to assess his current psychological functioning and to provide information that would help clarify the reasons for Michael's school-related difficulties.

Background Information

According to Michael's mother, Michael has had a rough time since pre-school. She noted that he has had mostly trouble with reading. Michael is now in the first grade and is in a Resource Specialist Program, receiving extra reading and spelling instruction 2 hours per week. He attends a public elementary school. Michael's mother reported that he is able to identify his upper and lower case letters, but he transposes letters and needs much repetition in order to learn. She was concerned that he might have a possible problem with memory.

Michael's mother described him as being somewhat of a loner. She indicated that he does play games well with other children but has extreme difficulty if he loses. She reports that he has a good sense of humor but is very hard on himself, gets easily frustrated, and is quick to anger. He does not have any significantly aggressive behavior toward either himself, property, or others.

Michael's mother reported that he was enuretic until last year. The bedwetting subsided when they introduced an alarm system, after approximately 6 weeks of trying. He has no other sleeping difficulties and has no eating problems. He had attended karate for a period of time last year, but currently is not in any specific group activities.

Michael is not taking any medications, and his mother reports that he has been in generally good physical health. He did have pressure equalization tubes in his ears between the ages of two and three, which needed to be revised on one occasion. His hearing has been felt to be good. He wears glasses, and this has been an ongoing issue. He apparently has an enlarged cornea and astigmatism. He wore an eye patch in kindergarten but that caused social problems for him.

Michael lives with his mother, father, and two older brothers ages 10 and 12. His parents have been married 19 years and his mother was 41 when Michael was born. She carried him to term and reported that she gained a lot of weight during the pregnancy; there were no problems associated with his birth. Michael was crawling by 8 months and walking between 18 months to 2 years of age. His mother felt he was normal. His use and development of single words appeared to develop at a normal rate according to her. When Michael was about 4 years of age, teachers claimed that he was disruptive in preschool but was learning at about the same rate as other children

Michael's mother reported that there are currently big homework battles. She described how Michael's father becomes very upset during these confrontations. Michael has particular difficulty reading and spelling. She also reports that the battles with Michael around home prompt her to get angry, resulting in occasional spankings. Both brothers are good students and have never presented behavioral problems. Aside from the assistance that Michael is receiving with a Resource Specialist, he is not receiving any other type of tutoring.

Results of testing during kindergarten, about 14 months ago, indicated the following: Peabody Picture Vocabulary Test—Revised (PPVT-R) standard score = 81; Test of Language Development Spoken Language Quotient = 100, Listening Quotient = 103, Speaking Quotient = 98, Semantics Quotient = 97, and Syntax Quotient = 102.

Appearance and Behavioral Characteristics

Michael is a handsome, 7-year 4-month-old boy. His speech was clear and generally easy to understand. He made good eye contact with the examiner and followed verbal directions reasonably well. He was not pleased with the idea of being tested and hoped that he would have more time to play with the examiner. He did understand why he was being evaluated and agreed that he was having problems in school. Michael complained to the examiner that he did not like homework or school. He complained about not having enough fun-time or recess, and about having to write his name on his papers. He said "I never liked school. . . . I'd rather be home." Michael also complained about his 10-year-old brother. He said, "Kevin always tries to steal my video games . . . my dad got me and it's special to me and I don't want to lose it."

During the testing, Michael generally seemed to put forth his best effort. However, he did fatigue easily and frequently would ask how much longer he would have to work. The testing was thus split into two sessions in order to complete all the tasks necessary. It was noted that Michael frequently protruded his tongue while writing. This behavior appeared to represent some kind of motor overflow. There was no evidence of any other atypical facial grimaces, tics, or unusual sounds. When tested with the Lateral Dominance Examination, he showed a clear pattern of mixed dominance. He is right-handed, right-eyed, and left-footed. His grip strength was noted to be stronger in his right hand than in his left hand, with a mean of 8 and 6 kgs respectively. However, his performance was about a year below age level with respect to his overall grip strength.

Tests Administered

Wechsler Intelligence Scale for Children—Third Edition (WISC-III)
Wechsler Individual Achievement Test (WIAT) (excluding Language Composite)
Developmental Test of Visual-Motor Integration
Gordon Diagnostic Examination
Lateral Dominance Examination
Kinetic Family Drawing Test
Thematic Apperception Test (TAT)
Rorschach Inkblot Test (Rorschach)
Child Behavior Check List

Test Results and Interpretation

On the WISC-III, Michael achieved a Verbal IQ of 97, Performance IQ of 93, and Full Scale IQ score of 94. He is currently functioning in the Average range of intelligence, at approximately the 34th percentile compared with other children almost 7½ years of age. The chances are 90 out of 100 that his true Full Scale IQ falls between 90 and 99. His intelligence is about equally well developed verbally and nonverbally, and the four separate Factor indexes are quite consistent with each other, ranging from 94 to 104, all well within the Average range of functioning.

As can be seen from his pattern of subtest scaled scores, there is some limited but noteworthy variability among the various subtests that comprise the WISC-III. This variability suggests that in spite of his even distribution between his Performance and Verbal IQs, and his consistent Factor indexes, there is some unevenness with respect to Michael's intellectual development. He demonstrated a significant weakness within the Verbal Scale, scoring at the 16th percentile on a test of general information, and he has a single significant weakness on the Performance Scale, achieving the 5th percentile in the subtest that required him to find the missing part of incomplete pictures.

His relatively poor performance on the general information test seems to reflect a more pervasive problem with tests that are heavily dependent on acquired, school-related information. Michael scored at the 23rd percentile on acquired knowledge subtests, namely the test of factual knowledge and tests of oral arithmetic and word definitions. This level of functioning is consistent with the standard score of 81 (10th percentile) that he earned last year on the PPVT-R, a measure of receptive vocabulary, and is likewise consistent with (and possibly a direct consequence of) his learning problems in school.

In contrast to this Low Average level on school-related test items, Michael scored at the High Average level (75th percentile) on verbal tasks that are not very dependent on formal schooling: two tests of verbal reasoning (solving socially relevant problems, telling how two concepts are alike), and a memory test requiring the repetition of digits spoken by the examiner, both forward and in the reverse sequence. Within the verbal sphere, Michael understands concrete words relatively well. For example, he was able to define the word thief as "someone who robs." However, he was not able to define words such as fable, precise, or absorb. He also showed some ability to think through verbal problems. However, he often yielded only partially correct answers and could not fully consider all the aspects of the problems at hand. At other times, Michael's difficulties with adequate self-control may have compromised his ability to think through a problem effectively. For example, when asked what he should do if a boy much smaller than him started to fight, he replied, "Say back off . . . if he doesn't back off, I'll kick his butt . . . I'll say that so he gets scared and runs away." It was also clear that there were times when Michael did not feel that he adequately could think through an answer. At those times, he would make a joke to cover his lack of knowledge or ability to form a solution. For example, when asked why it was important for cars to have license plates, he first responded, "To make them look dumb." However, with further prompting, he said, "To not lose track of the car."

One of the reasons that Michael may have difficulty adequately solving verbal problems is that his general fund of information, or knowledge of facts, limits his ability to make use of such knowledge for solving verbal problems. For example, when Michael was asked to tell the names of four seasons, he replied, "winter, summer, June, July." When asked how many things make a dozen, he replied, "One million." Although Michael seems fully capable of taking in environmental information, these responses provide some evidence that he is not doing so at a level that one would expect given his other general abilities. Michael's limited knowledge and fund of information, therefore, may be affecting his performance not only on the tests of acquired knowledge but also on the tests of verbal reasoning. His Verbal IQ of 97 and Verbal Comprehension Index of 99, therefore, may provide substantial underestimates of his true potential for intelligent functioning within the verbal domain.

On the Performance Scale, Michael demonstrated relatively average eye-hand coordination and visuomotor integration speed. He performed at an average range on both the Block Design and Object Assembly subtests of the WISC-III, which assess visuoconstructive abilities of abstractions and concrete objects, respectively. He also achieved a standard score of 108 (70th percentile) on the Developmental Test of Visual-Motor Integration, a paper-and-pencil design-copying test.

Michael's significant weakness on the WISC-III incomplete pictures test (Picture Completion) showed a relative weakness with respect to his ability to selectively attend to important visual information. He also performed below his own level of functioning on Symbol Search, which requires scanning of abstract stimuli and making rapid decisions about these stimuli. The latter task, like Picture Completion, is heavily influenced by visual selective attention.

A projective quality tended to intrude on some of his answers to the Picture Completion subtest, which may suggest that Michael has anxiety with respect to projected feelings of being damaged. For example, when he was shown a picture of a fox that had a missing ear and was to identify the missing part, he replied, "The ear . . . it got cut off." When asked to identify an elephant with a missing foot, he replied, "Foot . . . maybe it had surgery." At times he would identify missing elements from a kind of idiosyncratic perspective in which he assumed the part was missing from a viewpoint that could not possibly be seen given the stimulus materials. Thus, he would fail to attend to important missing elements and attribute the missing elements to something that could not be seen given the perspective of the picture. This unusual response style may suggest some weakness with respect to perceptual object constancy.

On the WIAT, Michael achieved a Total Composite of 83 which corresponds to a percentile rank of 13. He earned a Reading Composite standard score of 80 (9th percentile), Mathematics Composite standard score of 88 (21st percentile), and a Spelling standard score of 85 (16th percentile). His relatively low score in reading ability was evidenced both in basic decoding skills (14th percentile) and in comprehension (9th percentile). His highest WIAT standard score, 99 on the Oral Expression subtest, is consistent with the quotients of about 100 that he earned last year on the Test of Language Development.

Relative to Michael's Verbal IQ, his Reading Composite standard score is significantly discrepant from his general ability, and his spelling ability is also behind, but not to as significant a degree. Observations of Michael's responses on the WIAT indicated difficulties with letter reversals and inversions. He showed a significant difficulty phonetically approaching words. He would become frustrated and give up easily. These difficulties were seen in his spelling as well. It was also noteworthy that as he progressed in attempting to spell words, he lost more and more control over his fine motor response, which resulted in larger letters that were less well written.

On the Gordon Diagnostic Evaluation, Michael demonstrated particular difficulty with tasks of vigilance. This is a computer-based system that provides visual material to which a child attends and responds. On a delay task in which Michael was required to inhibit his responses an appropriate amount of time and then respond in order to receive points, he performed in a range typical of children his age. Thus, he did not show evidence of motor disinhibition, which is often associated with attentional difficulties. However, he had significant difficulty on tasks of vigilance. Michael had a great deal of difficulty maintaining his attention to a task and responding consistently over an extended period. As his attention fatigued, he began to make more errors of commission and also had fewer correct responses. Thus, Michael's attention would wane and this would result in his missing relevant information and attempting to compensate in a kind of random way that did not fit the task requirement. It was also clear, observing Michael during this task, that he would become extremely upset when he knew he made errors. Thus, a kind of cycle started that not only made him more self-critical when he noted his own errors but also created anxiety that in turn further compromised his attention and caused him to make more errors. These findings are consistent with the selective visual attention difficulties noted as a possible explanation of Michael's weak areas on the WISC-III Performance Scale.

The results of projective tests indicate that at this time Michael is experiencing some compromise with respect to the effectiveness and accuracy of his perceptions. Projected anger, coupled with fears of injury, lead to this compromise. The perceptual inaccuracies and fear of injury were also noted to a lesser degree in the more structured Picture Completion task on the WISC- III, discussed previously. On the Rorschach, for example, on Card 2, Michael sees, "A bug with blood growing out of it because it got bit—with a hole in the middle that was shaped like a heart." On Card 4 he sees, "A monster . . . it's going to destroy the whole universe!" And, on Card 5 he sees, "A bat that's angry and that's always angry." Thus, it is clear that Michael is having difficulty containing his affect and that the strength of his affect can distort the accuracy of his perceptions. At times, Michael will combine ideas into a whole in a way that violates the integrity of the object perceived.

The results of the Thematic Apperception Test (TAT) suggest that Michael may experience some subjective depression which he interprets as boredom. He may feel a sense of isolation and separateness from other peers and a feeling of exclusion. There is also some limited evidence suggesting that Michael feels that he is being perceived by others as abnormal. Although that perception may have some basis in reality, given the concerns about his current school performance and peer relationships, it is also likely that he is projecting this sense of damage.

Michael, in drawing a family picture, depicted his family as all doing separate activities and not really interacting. He placed himself at the greatest distance from his 10-year-old brother, Kevin, which may depict some of his conflict with respect to him. Again, Michael may not see himself as being integrated well with respect to his family and this feeling may add to his sense of separateness.

When Michael was asked to tell a little more about what he wished would happen with respect to school, he said, "I'd destroy all the school and all the kids that hate me . . . most do. I'd like to get a machine gun and blow their heads off!" When asked what he would want if he had three wishes, he answered, "A bazooka, a grenade, and a machine gun." When asked what kind of an animal he would want to be, he replied, "The most powerful animal in the whole world." Thus, Michael has a good deal of aggressive feelings and ideation, which likely add to the anxiety that he experiences; this anxiety in part dovetails with some relative focus on school, and children at school, as the targets of the anger, and may represent a displacement from anger directed at himself and anger related to phallic, narcissistic injury.

The results of the Child Behavior Check List indicate that Michael's mother is having the greatest concern with respect to his social difficulties and oppositional behavior. Overall, however, his scores are in an average range compared with other children his age with respect to both internalizing and externalizing behaviors. Given the other test findings, these results indicate that Michael is generally containing the overt manifestations of the intense anger and degree of frustration that he experiences.

Summary and Recommendations

Michael, a 7-year 4-month-old boy, is currently having some significant difficulties with school, particularly with respect to his reading, and is also troubled by problems with peer relationships and struggles in doing his homework. Multiple factors are contributing to the difficulties Michael is experiencing at this time. Michael is having some difficulty with respect to adequate attentional skills. This problem seems to be particularly true with visually based material that does not have high reward or intrinsic value for him. Michael, who scored in the Average range of intelligence on the WISC-III and demonstrated good ability on verbal tasks that are not overly dependent on school learning, is also showing difficulty reading and spelling. These achievement problems, in part, are due to his poor phonetic approach to words as well as difficulties with letter inversions and reversals. These academic problem areas will need to be worked on and monitored closely over the next year. He is developmentally at an age where some children show reversals and inversions, and it is not really abnormal. However, this relative weakness at this time, coupled with the attentional and perceptual difficulties, may be adding significantly to his struggle with reading and spelling as well as with written language.

Michael is having a fair degree of difficulty coping with the intense feelings of anger and frustration that he experiences. In school, and with respect to homework, it is likely that his frustration and anger lead to anxiety, which then compromises his attention, then disrupts his performance, and ultimately adds to his frustration. The examiner had the opportunity to observe this cycle of behavior with Michael in his office. The specificity and sources and reasons for the anger that Michael experiences will best be understood in the context of his psychotherapy. It is clear, however, that Michael harbors feelings that he is somehow damaged and that his anger can be absolute. Both such ideas can contribute significantly to his anxiety.

Overall, the examiner believes that, at this time, it is best to consider Michael's learning difficulties in reading and spelling as being due to relative weaknesses with respect to both visual attention and visual perception. These limitations, coupled with significant conflict and anxiety associated with academic performance in these areas, lead to inhibitions with respect to the development of these academic skills.

The examiner noted that Michael is also experiencing some feelings consistent with a level of depression. Michael feels isolated from other peers, not well integrated with respect to social activities; he is also self-critical and maintains a sense that he is damaged. His difficulties with school only represent a small part of the difficulty that he is having in general. Michael experiences significant jealousy of his 10-year-old brother, which may represent a displaced frustration with respect to unresolved Oedipal issues.

It is clear from the current evaluation that Michael needs intensive psychotherapy. This is the only way that he will be able to learn to cope better with the internal stresses that he experiences. Psychotherapy is also a primary avenue to help him work on his self-esteem and help better understand the reasons that he feels isolated and somehow damaged.

The examiner believes that Michael could benefit from an intensive educational tutoring program over the summer months. It is good that he is receiving Resource Specialist assistance with respect to reading and spelling. However, he could use such assistance to a greater degree when school is over in order to support the skills he has already obtained. The examiner will discuss with Michael's therapist and Michael's parents possible resources for such tutoring. Specifically, Michael needs a good deal of work on further development of a phonetic approach to reading. A supportive tutor who works closely with him at his developmental level might also help alleviate some of the anxiety that Michael is having with respect to academic performance.

Examiner:

Dr. Alan J. Lincoln

CHAPTER 7

Comprehensive Clinical and Psychoeducational Case Studies

This chapter includes the case studies of five children who were referred for evaluation to the psychoeducational clinic directed by my wife, Nadeen. She supervised these evaluations and the preparation of these comprehensive reports. The five children include three boys and two girls, who range in age from 6 to 15 years. Reasons for referral to the clinic always include a learning problem of some sort, although concomitant emotional problems (such as the encopresis displayed by James C.) are common.

These cases supplement the five cases already presented, one at the end of Chapter 4 and two each at the end of Chapters 5 and 6. Whereas those reports pertain primarily to the content covered in each specific chapter, the five reports in this chapter deal more generally with multiple topics treated throughout the entire book. Four of the children studied in this chapter were administered the WISC-III along with other comprehensive intelligence tests, including the WJ-R Tests of Cognitive Ability (James, age 9, and Ira, age 15), K-ABC (Nicole, age 6, and Dana Christine, age 8), and the KAIT (Ira, age 15). Greg was administered the WISC-III along with supplements from the WJ-R and DAS. All five children were administered individual achievement tests, plus assorted other measures such as the battery of projective tests administered to both James and Greg.

A key goal of the reports throughout this book, especially the ones in this chapter, is to demonstrate how to integrate test data from the WISC-III with data from other tests. Implicit in this goal are the notions of cross-validating hypotheses, integrating cognitive hypotheses with background information and clinical behaviors, effectively communicating the results of profile analysis, and translating the findings from these extensive evaluations to practical recommendations.

As is true for all reports in this book, names are changed and pertinent background information is either modified or deliberately vague. Also, the Test Results and Interpretation sections of all 10 reports have been modified by Nadeen and me to reflect as closely as possible the approach to WISC-III interpretation promoted in this book.

James C., Age 9-1, Learning Disability, Encopresis

WISC-III Profile

IQs		(90% conf.)	Factor Indexes		(90% conf.)
Verbal	112	(106–117)	Verbal Comprehension	120	(113–124)
Performance	89	(83–97)	Perceptual Organization	91	(85–99)
Full Scale	101	(96–106)	Freedom from Distractibility	87	(81–96)
V-IQ > P-IQ ($p < .01$)			Processing Speed	88	(82–98)

Verbal	Scaled Score	Performance	Scaled Score
Information	12	Picture Completion	10
Similarities	11	(Coding)	(8)
Arithmetic	6-W	Picture Arrangement	7
Vocabulary	15-S	Block Design	8
Comprehension	16-S	Object Assembly	9
(Digit Span)	(9)	*Symbol Search	7

* Symbol Search was used in IQ computations

Mean of 6 Verbal subtests = 12   Mean of 6 Performance subtests = 8

Woodcock-Johnson-Revised Cognitive Battery

Subtest	Standard Score ($\pm$ SEm)
1. Memory for Names	105 $\pm$ 4
2. Memory for Sentences	99 $\pm$ 6
3. Visual Matching	81 $\pm$ 7
4. Incomplete Words	99 $\pm$ 8
5. Visual Closure	115 $\pm$ 8
6. Picture Vocabulary	110 $\pm$ 6
7. Analysis-Synthesis	96 $\pm$ 5
8. Visual-Auditory Learning	95 $\pm$ 5
9. Memory for Words	70 $\pm$ 7
10. Cross Out	77 $\pm$ 8
11. Sound Blending	110 $\pm$ 5
12. Picture Recognition	131 $\pm$ 7
13. Oral Vocabulary	111 $\pm$ 6
14. Concept Formation	113 $\pm$ 4
Cluster	
15. Long-Term Retrieval (Tests 1 & 8)	100 $\pm$ 4
16. Short-Term Memory (Tests 2 & 9)	83 $\pm$ 5
17. Processing Speed (Tests 3 & 10)	78 $\pm$ 6
18. Auditory Processing (Tests 4 & 11)	107 $\pm$ 5
19. Visual Processing (Tests 5 & 12)	125 $\pm$ 7
20. Comprehension-Knowledge (Tests 6 & 13)	112 $\pm$ 4
21. Fluid Reasoning (Tests 7 & 14)	105 $\pm$ 3
Broad Cognitive Ability	**98 $\pm$ 3**

Woodcock-Johnson-Revised Achievement Battery

Subtest	Standard Score ($\pm$ SEm)
22. Letter-Word Identification	87 $\pm$ 4
23. Passage Comprehension	96 $\pm$ 5
24. Calculation	98 $\pm$ 5
25. Applied Problems	95 $\pm$ 5
26. Dictation	92 $\pm$ 5
27. Writing Samples	121 $\pm$ 3
28. Science	113 $\pm$ 6
29. Social Studies	117 $\pm$ 6
30. Humanities	117 $\pm$ 5
31. Word Attack	95 $\pm$ 4
32. Reading Vocabulary	103 $\pm$ 4
33. Quantitative Concepts	89 $\pm$ 6
34. Proofing	90 $\pm$ 5
35. Writing Fluency	97 $\pm$ 8
Cluster	
Basic Reading Skills (Tests 22 & 31)	91 $\pm$ 3
Reading Comprehension (Tests 23 & 32)	99 $\pm$ 3
Basic Math Skills (Tests 24 & 33)	93 $\pm$ 4
Basic Writing Skills (Tests 26 & 34)	90 $\pm$ 4
Written Expression (Tests 27 & 35)	108 $\pm$ 3
Broad Reading (Tests 22 & 23)	91 $\pm$ 3
Broad Mathematics (Tests 24 & 25)	96 $\pm$ 4
Broad Written Language (Tests 26 & 27)	103 $\pm$ 3
Broad Knowledge (Tests 28, 29, & 30)	118 $\pm$ 4

Woodcock-Johnson-Revised: Aptitude-Achievement Comparisons

Area	Aptitude	Achievement	SD Difference*
Basic Reading Skills	99	91	−0.82
Reading Comprehension	99	99	0.00
Basic Math Skills	100	93	+0.54
Basic Writing Skills	99	90	−0.84
Written Expression	99	108	+0.84
Broad Reading	99	91	−0.82
Broad Mathematics	100	96	−0.37
Broad Written Language	99	103	+0.37
Broad Knowledge	113	118	+0.84

* Computed by the software program *Compuscore for the WJ-R—3.0.*

Referral and Background Information

James is a 9-year-old Vietnamese boy who was adopted at birth by upper-middle-class white parents. James was referred to this clinic by a learning specialist at the private school he attends. Despite his age, James is currently in second grade at this school.

Mr. and Mrs. C. have recently become concerned regarding James's academic performance. Mrs. C. has observed that when James reads orally at home, he seems to have regressed from the level at which he was last year. She also feels that he has some difficulty with his memory; for example, when she helps him learn his spelling words, he often forgets them by the next day. She reported that, although she does not feel he is dyslexic, he does sometimes reverse letters and numbers. He also has difficulty following multiple-step directions. Previous hearing screenings have suggested a possible minor hearing deficit, and James's parents were interested in determining the role this may be playing in his learning difficulties. They planned to take James for a comprehensive audiological assessment but also wanted to obtain specific information about his intellectual functioning.

James is an only child who lives with his parents and a housekeeper in a single-family home in an exclusive neighborhood. Mr. C. is the CEO of a company that manufactures VCRs; Mrs. C. is a homemaker who is very active in James's school and the community. She does volunteer work 2 days a week in the geriatric wing of a local hospital.

James's birth mother reportedly experienced no serious health problems during her pregnancy, and James was carried to full term and delivered without complications. According to Mrs. C., his apgar score at birth was 10. Little else is known about his birth parents except that his birth mother was a 16-year-old unmarried high school student and his birth father was in his mid-30s and reportedly had a very bad temper. James's developmental milestones were timely relative to children his age. As an infant, James had difficulty keeping food down and frequently experienced projectile vomiting. He also had, and has continued to have, frequent ear infections.

James attended a private nursery school three times per week before beginning kindergarten at his current school at age 5 years. He reportedly demonstrated poor impulse control at school and was subsequently seen by a psychologist for counseling regarding this problem. The psychologist tested James's intellectual functioning on the WPPSI when he was exactly 6 years old. He earned a Full Scale IQ of 114 (Verbal IQ = 117; Performance IQ = 108), demonstrated short-term memory and sequencing difficulties, and was referred to a speech and language center for further evaluation. The speech pathologist found evidence of "auditory processing deficits characterized by discrimination and sequential-ordering problems that adversely affect his short-term memory and thought formulation skills." After several counseling sessions with the psychologist, it was felt that it would be beneficial to James to be held back in school for one year.

James's parents report that he is a very active, enthusiastic child. He has always been very agile and enjoys athletic activities. He has many friends and spends much of his time playing with them outdoors. He enjoys musical activities, such as listening to music, dancing, singing, and playing his keyboard. He also is a very good artist.

Mr. and Mrs. C. state that James is very sensitive to the actions of others and tends to remember every transgression against him. For example, if one of his friends says something negative to him, he may continue to hold a grudge and bring it up days later. He is apparently very "strong-willed," and his parents report difficulty coming up with a discipline technique to which he responds well. When James is tired or upset he still sucks his thumb. He also soils his pants approximately three or four times a month. The encopresis occurs when he is outdoors playing; he says that he becomes so involved in his playing that he does not want to take time out to go to the bathroom. Mr. and Mrs. C. state that, although James was essentially toilet-trained by the time he was 2½, he has never gone for an extended period of time without an encopretic incident. James's parents also report that he is often fearful of going into the bathroom or into his own room by himself. He has overheard talk regarding burglars breaking into houses in the neighborhood, and this has apparently fueled his fears.

Appearance and Behavioral Characteristics

James is a black-haired, small-statured, well-groomed Asian-American boy. During his first testing session, he was somewhat quiet and shy, although he responded quickly and confidently when queried about himself or about the test material. He demonstrated anxiety in this new situation by chewing on his fingers, his lip, and his shirtsleeve during the testing session. At the same time, he was very warm and cooperative in his interaction with the examiner, and he appeared to enjoy the testing procedure.

As he became more comfortable with the proceedings, his spontaneous conversation and oral asides to the test items increased. While working, he often softly hummed or quietly talked himself through a problem. For example, as he was putting together parts of a puzzle he commented, "It's a turtle! No, a pizza! Somehow these pieces have got to fit. Darn, this one's hard! Oh, good, I got it—it's a soccer ball! Is that the last one? I like these!" James enjoys competition, and during the testing he appeared challenged, rather than discouraged, by the more difficult items. For example, when he was working on written math and had clearly come to problems that were too difficult, he happily began to look at the more advanced problems to see if he could make a good guess at the answers. When he was shown pictures and asked to write a sentence for each of them, he said he liked the task and requested permission to write more than one sentence for some of the pictures. On other parts of the test, when he encountered questions he could not answer, he was not embarrassed or frustrated, but instead would make a comment like, "Oh, I haven't learned that yet." He demonstrated a mature level of social interaction with the examiner throughout the evaluation process.

Despite his sense of competition, James performed slowly on visual-motor tasks, evidencing much reflectivity and indecision even on tasks with minimal problem-solving demands. James is reportedly a good artist and athlete, and his fine-motor coordination was observed to be smooth and fluid.

His good verbal expressive abilities and creativity were evident throughout the evaluation. When he was asked to respond orally to a test item, his responses were often elaborate and comprehensive. For example, when he was asked what you should do if you lose a friend's ball, he stated, "First you try to find it, but if you can't after an hour, you might go to him and say 'sorry,' and then he might help to find it, but if you still can't find it and it means a lot to him, you should try to buy him another one." In explaining why it is good to have secret ballots, he said, "If you show everybody your vote, they will all say 'my side's better,' and fight; in secret ballots, they just count them, and people aren't so feisty." His responses also demonstrated a broad range of factual information.

James attended well to the tasks required of him. Although he would sometimes yawn and appear slightly restless after an extended period of testing, a short break always easily revived his interest and vigor. At no time did he show evidence of an attentional deficit. He paid close attention to the environment and was very curious about the things going on around him, including the materials used for one of the projective tests and the examiner's use of shorthand to record his responses. He tested the examiner's limits during the less structured projective assessment, attempting to take some control over the testing, but ultimately followed directions.

Tests Administered

Wechsler Intelligence Scale for Children—Third Edition (WISC-III)
Woodcock-Johnson Psycho-Educational Battery—Revised (WJ-R)
    Tests of Cognitive Ability: Extended Battery (Tests 1–14)
    Tests of Achievement: Standard and Supplemental Battery
Rorschach Inkblot Test (Rorschach)
Thematic Apperception Test (TAT)
Projective Drawings
Sentence Completion

Test Results and Interpretation

It should be initially noted that the global scores that are yielded from the standardized cognitive tests administered to James do not accurately portray his intellectual functioning. In James's case, examination of individual clusters of subtests on the WISC-III and WJ-R provides a clearer picture of his abilities and achievements.

On the WISC-III, James obtained a Full Scale IQ of 101, which falls within the Average range of intelligence and ranks James at the 53rd percentile, indicating that he performed better than 50% of those his approximate age in the reference group of children who were administered this test. He earned nearly the identical global score on the WJ-R, achieving a Broad Cognitive Ability standard score on the Extended (14-subtest) Battery of 98, also Average and comparable to the 45th percentile. But James is not average in his ability.

On the WISC-III, he earned a High Average Verbal IQ of 112, which is significantly higher than his Low Average Performance IQ of 89. However, extreme scatter within the Verbal scale makes his Verbal IQ uninterpretable: His verbal abilities ranged from the 9th percentile on an oral arithmetic test to the 98th percentile on a task requiring James to answer socially relevant questions. His poor score on solving oral arithmetic problems, along with a relatively weak score on a digit repetition subtest, reflect the difficulties with short-term memory that have been reported by his mother and were noted in his WPPSI profile 3 years ago. On the WJ-R, he also performed deficiently on the Short-Term Memory cluster, earning a standard score of 83 (12th percentile). He performed better on the WJ-R when the stimuli were meaningful (48th percentile when recalling sentences) than nonmeaningful (2nd percentile when recalling unconnected words). A common example of a task requiring auditory short-term memory of nonmeaningful stimuli is remembering an unfamiliar telephone number long enough to dial the number.

The deficit in auditory short-term memory accounts for a discrepancy between James's poor performance on the WISC-III Arithmetic subtest and his adequate scores on the WJ-R Mathematics achievement subtests. On the WJ-R, he was provided with a visual representation of the arithmetic task or was able to use paper and pencil to calculate. The WISC-III subtest, however, required that he listen to a word problem, remember its components, and calculate the answer without paper and pencil; his auditory short-term memory deficit interfered with his ability to work the problem. This deficit impacted his WISC-III Freedom from Distractibility Index (19th percentile), a score which for many children represents attentional difficulties. For James, who showed no evidence of attentional problems, his low score is related to his auditory short-term memory deficit.

Note, however, that James's deficit does not seem to be a function of the auditory processing difficulties that were noted 3 years ago by a speech pathologist. He scored in the Average range on the WJ-R Auditory Processing cluster (68th percentile). And whereas previous hearing examinations have suggested that James may have some type of mild hearing deficit, he demonstrated no behaviors that suggested that he was having difficulty hearing. Also, James's adequate performance on the WJ-R Auditory Processing subtests, such as Sound Blending, which require good hearing ability for success, implies that his auditory memory problem is not due to hearing loss.

His exceptional score on the socially relevant WISC-III Comprehension subtest, when coupled with the 95th percentile James achieved on a test of defining words presented orally and with his excellent ability to express his ideas with elaborate, spontaneous verbalizations, indicate an impressive strength in verbal expression. His verbal conceptual ability is good, but not quite as outstanding, when he must respond with a single word, or just a few well-chosen words. That is to say, he scored at the 80th percentile on the WJ-R Comprehension-Knowledge cluster, which is composed of two vocabulary tests, one requiring the naming of pictured objects, the other requiring James to give antonyms or synonyms. Also, on the WISC-III, he performed at the 69th percentile on verbal tests of general information and finding the commonality between two concepts.

The best description of the distinction between James's overall verbal and nonverbal abilities is probably provided by his Verbal Comprehension Index of 120 and his Perceptual Organization Index of 91. He demonstrated a Superior level (91st percentile) on tests requiring the ability to solve verbal problems and demonstrate factual acquisition, compared with an Average to Low Average level (27th percentile) on measures of nonverbal thinking and visual-motor coordination. The 29-point difference between these Indexes is both statistically significant and unusual, occurring in less than 5% of normal children and adolescents.

James's scores on the separate WISC-III Performance subtests were extremely consistent, offering little insight into the reason for his striking verbal-nonverbal discrepancy. However, the WJ-R clusters reveal that James has distinctly different levels of ability on the separate skills required for success on the WISC-III Performance Scale—visual perception, the ability to solve novel problems (fluid ability), and speed of visual-motor coordination. His ability to process visual stimuli in the absence of problem-solving and speed requirements was at the Superior level (95th percentile on WJ-R Visual Processing). For example, when James was required to recognize a previously presented picture within a set of distracting pictures, or when he was asked to identify an object that was distorted in some way, he performed very well. His fluid problem-solving ability and new learning was Average, as he scored at the 63rd percentile on the WJ-R Fluid Reasoning cluster and the 50th percentile on Long-Term Retrieval cluster. His speed of processing visual information, however, was at a Borderline to Low Average level (7th percentile on WJ-R Processing Speed cluster). Although James's scores on Visual Processing are very good, suggesting that he has the skills necessary to solve problems using visuospatial information, when the component of speed was added, his scores were extremely low. For example, when he was required to rapidly locate and circle two identical numbers in a row of six numbers, he performed very poorly.

James's relatively weak ability on the WISC-III nonverbal tasks, therefore, seems to be a function of his slowness when solving timed items, perhaps because of his reflective cognitive style and his need to use verbalizations during nonverbal problems. The fact that James performed as well on the WISC-III Processing Speed Index as on the Perceptual Organization Index suggests that his slowness depressed his scores on virtually all WISC-III Performance subtests. WJ-R results indicate that he has Average to Superior functioning within the visual-motor channel when the role of speed is reduced. This explanation is consistent with the fact that James's WPPSI Performance IQ at age 6 was 108, considerably higher than his present WISC-III Performance IQ of 87; the WPPSI Performance subtests place little emphasis on response speed.

On the WJ-R Tests of Achievement, James scored at the Average level on most reading, math, and writing subtests and clusters, with standard scores typically in the 90s. his written expression (70th percentile) was substantially better than his basic writing skills such as punctuation and capitalization (25th percentile). But even within the written comprehension arena, James evidenced his difficulties with visual-motor speed: He performed at a Superior level on the Writing Samples test (92nd percentile) but scored much lower when he had to formulate and write sentences as rapidly as possible (42nd percentile on Writing Fluency). His most consistently excellent performance was on tests of knowledge, performing at about the same High Average level (88th percentile) on tests of Science, Social Studies, and Humanities. The latter test results indicate that, in spite of James's specific learning difficulties, and problems with auditory short-term memory and visual processing speed, he has acquired a broad base of knowledge in many areas. And, as mentioned earlier, he demonstrates the ability to communicate this knowledge verbally.

His deficit areas impair his ability to achieve in academic subjects such as reading that depend on his weak skills. On the WJ-R, James demonstrated intact reasoning and new learning ability on a variety of tasks that demand the integration of auditory and visual stimuli. His impressive store of knowledge and good learning ability suggest that he has learned on his own to fully utilize his areas of strength to compensate for his areas of difficulty. This observation speaks well for his prognosis of becoming more successful if remediation suggestions are implemented.

On the WJ-R Tests of Achievement, James did better on the reading subtests that measure passage comprehension and reading vocabulary, both of which are presented in a meaningful context, than he did when he was required to identify isolated words and letters. In each of the scholastic achievement areas, he demonstrated a deficit in the underlying basic skills. This observation has been addressed in the Recommendations section of this report.

The WJ-R provides aptitude clusters that are predictive of specific areas of academic achievement. None of the discrepancies between James's achievement in a given area, and the aptitude score intended to predict that area, reached significance. However, James's Verbal IQ of 112, and, more specifically his Verbal Comprehension Index of 120, is significantly and substantially higher than his achievement scores in several areas.

An integration of the results of projective testing, clinical interviews with James, and clinical observations of his behavior presents the following picture of his personality functions. He is a creative, intellectually alert little boy who notices and becomes curious about the details of his environment, and who sometimes misses the big picture. James's problem solving and train of thought can become derailed by details, especially when he is dealing with unfamiliar or ambiguous stimuli. For example, James took a very long time to do the Sentence Completion test, partly because he analyzed each word of most sentence stems, often becoming distracted by the details of word choice, and then trying to come up with an answer that was both true and socially appropriate. This same variable probably relates to his slowness on novel nonverbal tasks.

Interestingly, although James is aware of social norms and values, he does not always choose to follow them. James's self-confidence sometimes leads him to ignore more conventional attitudes and conduct. While this can lead to creativity and may enhance his development as an individual, it can also lead to an attitude that rules do not apply to him. The tendency to think in this way is influenced by two other facets of James's personality: his use of denial as a psychological defense and the developmental issues with which he is currently struggling.

James's defensive style is primarily one of denial and avoidance of aggressive impulses, anger, and negative feelings and behavior. For instance, James denied being frightened of anything, ever seriously misbehaving, or getting into trouble. At times during the projective testing, James would become anxious and employ manipulative behavior in an attempt to refuse a task. In fact, at one point he claimed to have lost his voice even though that problem was not observed by the examiner. He also had great difficulty responding to sentence stems that pulled for negative feelings.

Another theme in this evaluation is James's striving for greater independence. He is moving away from emotional dependence on his parents and toward his friends. He is attempting to control his life and challenge authority; however, this developmental milestone causes conflicting feelings. By growing up, James risks emotionally losing his father, and this dynamic is even more conflictual because of his sense that the danger to his father is real. (James is quite aware that the men on his father's side of the family have died young of heart disease.) James therefore has difficulty expressing anger at his father, which creates the likelihood that James will express his anger indirectly, by oppositional and passive-aggressive acts. His encopresis and regressive thumb sucking may pertain to these conflicts.

James appears flooded with the demands of his environment and may not have the resources to cope with these demands. At times, he experiences situational anxiety and frustration, perhaps related to his conflicts and to his school learning problems. He uses both interpersonal interaction and his own intrapsychic resources to try to get what he wants and needs, but he is not very proficient at getting his needs met. That problem, coupled with the stress of struggling for independence and worrying about his father, makes him cope less effectively than he is capable of coping. This deficit appears to be situational and will probably disappear if he is able to regroup his defenses and refine his coping techniques.

Summary and Diagnostic Impression

James is a 9-year-old Vietnamese boy who was referred for an evaluation of possible learning difficulties. At the time of the initial interview with his parents, they expressed concern regarding his reading skills and his memory. He seemed to be regressing in his ability to read aloud, and he often had difficulty remembering his spelling words long enough to spell them correctly on tests. He also has a problem with soiling himself.

James was given the WISC-III, the WJ-R Tests of Cognitive Ability and Tests of Achievement, and projective tests. Although every global score on the cognitive measures showed James's performance to be Average, evaluation of profile fluctuations reveals abilities that range from Borderline to Very Superior. He is strongest in his verbal intelligence, especially verbal expression, but has substantial deficits in auditory short-term memory and visual processing speed that have hurt his academic achievement in reading and other skill areas. The consistency among the WISC-III and WJ-R scores indicates that the results obtained in this cognitive evaluation are not specific to one type of test or to noncognitive factors such as fatigue, boredom, or inattention. Despite the deficits, and some relatively low scores on achievement tests, James gave many indications that he has the ability to attend and to perform well academically. During the current evaluation, James showed no evidence of an attentional or motor deficit, and he gave no evidence of either the hearing or auditory processing problems that were identified by previous testings.

James's pattern of performance on cognitive and academic tests is consistent with a diagnosis of learning disability; this learning disability is best characterized by the DSM-III-R diagnosis of Developmental Reading Disorder (315.00). Regarding personality functions, his current overloaded state, developmental conflict, and coping deficit are not of sufficient severity to merit a diagnosis. However, his encopresis is. The fact that James soils diurnally at least monthly (and usually more frequently), and has done so since infancy, suggests that James suffers from Functional Encopresis, Primary Type (DSM-III-R: 307.70).

Recommendations

Pertaining to School Learning

1. James's deficit in auditory short-term memory suggests that he may have a difficult time responding appropriately when instructions are given orally. To ensure that he retains the information, it would benefit him to receive brief written instruction in addition to oral instruction whenever possible. For example, when the teacher orally gives an assignment to the class, she might provide James with a written note of the same information. Furthermore, James's teachers should be aware that James may often need to have instructions repeated, and James should be encouraged to ask for such repetition if he initially has difficulty understanding. In instances of

more elaborate instruction, allowing James to tape-record the information would permit relistening at a later time and would enhance his opportunity for learning the material.

2. To further minimize the impact of James's auditory short-term memory problem on his academic achievement, it should be kept in mind that, in general, the more meaningful and personalized the information is for James, the easier it will be for him to remember and assimilate it. Experiential learning, such as hands-on experiments, computer learning games, zoo and museum trips, or visits to historical sites, will provide more meaningful structure for acquiring information. James's wealth of facts in areas such as science indicate that he is able to assimilate information that has been made meaningful to him, and that once he has acquired it, he is able to retain it well.

3. According to the learning specialist who referred him, the school is aware that James is a visual learner; planning for his curriculum should continue to take this into consideration, as well as his exceptional verbal expressive and creative abilities. His strong visual processing ability suggests that for him learning will be aided by the presentation of concrete, visual representation of material whenever possible. It should be emphasized, however, that his poor performance on tests that entail visual processing *speed* indicates that when the component of time is added to visual tasks, James does poorly. Therefore, when a task involves visual processing, untimed procedures will provide more accurate assessment of James's abilities and will lead to more successful outcomes.

4. Organization will be important for James as school tasks become increasingly complex. It is important for James's study time, study materials, and the information that is to be learned to be meaningfully organized, which will reduce the number of things to be remembered. He should be encouraged to maintain a calendar for his assignments, to schedule daily study periods, to learn simple outlining techniques (which he could apply to a broad range of materials that he will be expected to learn), and to utilize mnemonic devices for organizing information that he must memorize. An example of a useful mnemonic device is arranging a list of facts so that the first letters of each fact form an easily remembered word; when that word is recalled, it will provide a cue for the facts themselves.

5. Another important means of organizing and simplifying material to be learned is to learn the basic rules of a skill well. For areas in which James has difficulty, such as spelling, knowing the rules and being able to recognize commonalities in words will reduce the instances in which he has to memorize new information. This procedure will also facilitate learning skills in areas such as math, reading, and written expression.

6. Individualized tutoring that takes into account James's learning deficits should be utilized to help James develop a solid base in the previously discussed rules. He performed poorly, relative to other students in his

class, on a recent set of criterion-referenced tests that were administered at school, suggesting that he has not picked up some of these basic facts through the usual classroom channels.

7. James's parents have made plans to have James's hearing evaluated by a pediatric audiologist. Although his current clinical evaluation yielded no indication of hearing difficulty, it is important that subtle hearing difficulties be ruled out.

8. The private school that he attends is a very competitive academic environment. Although the tests given to James at this clinic indicate that he is performing at grade level relative to national norms, the majority of children at his school perform above grade level. In a different school setting, James's academic performance would be largely within the normal range of the other students. In determining the optimal school setting for James, this observation must be balanced against the advantages of attending his current school, such as the small class size and the stimulating academic and social environment.

9. James has strong visuospatial skills, is creative, and enjoys artistic expression immensely. He is also physically agile and enjoys athletic activities and competition. These are important sources of self-esteem and should continue to be encouraged.

10. James is an exuberant, effervescent, and inquisitive child whose parents have obviously provided him with a wide range of opportunities to gain important experience and knowledge. They should be encouraged to continue this process, as it will be crucial in ensuring that James's strengths be utilized to help overcome his learning difficulties.

11. James's parents report that he is strong-willed and often does not respond readily to discipline measures such as "time-out." Many parents with bright, challenging children such as James find that a parenting class can provide easy and effective methods of setting limits and dealing with the resistance which is inevitable as the child moves toward adolescence. Either his current school or the local public school, should be able to provide specific recommendations for a parenting class in this area.

12. To ensure appropriate classroom placement for James next year, it is recommended that a copy of this report be sent to the learning specialist at his school.

13. It is recommended that James have a brief psychoeducational reevaluation in approximately one year to assess his progress and determine his continuing and emerging educational needs.

Pertaining to Encopresis and Emotional Needs

1. Because continued instances of encopresis are unusual for a child of James's age, he should be evaluated by a pediatric gastroenterologist to rule out a subtle physiological malfunction.

2. Assuming that there is no physiological basis for his problem, James should be encouraged to stop soiling to avoid peer ridicule and to stop an age-inappropriate behavior. A behavioral program, designed and implemented by a qualified professional, would help achieve this goal.

3. Until a systematic behavior management program is in place, certain general recommendations for dealing with James's encopresis should be instituted immediately: In order to take responsibility for his decision to remain outside playing, James should be made to clean himself and his underwear as soon as possible after he soils, *every time* he soils. Similarly, if James decides to stop playing and use the toilet, praise and/or other suitable rewards should follow quickly.

4. James's worry over his father's health might be alleviated by being allowed and encouraged to talk openly about his concerns. This talking could be done in the format of a family meeting where all family members are allowed and encouraged to share their thoughts and feelings in appropriate ways, or it can be done informally when the opportunity arises.

5. James's struggle for independence may take the form of oppositional, passive-aggressive, or controlling behavior. His family should carefully limit these self-defeating techniques and instead encourage open expression of feelings, especially anger, and pave the way for him to display positive, age-appropriate independent behaviors. He should be helped to learn how to be independent by being given control and responsibility for certain facets of his life, such as making all decisions about spending a finite amount of allowance money each week.

Examiners:
Patricia Petterson, MA; Susan Glatz, MS

Consultant for projective test interpretation:
Dr. Dana T. Grossman

Supervisor to Ms. Petterson and Ms. Glatz:
Dr. Nadeen L. Kaufman

Nicole A., Age 6-4, Juvenile Diabetes, Gifted with Possible Neurological Dysfunction

WISC-III Profile

IQs		(90% conf.)	Factor Indexes		(90% conf.)
Verbal	124	(118–128)	Verbal Comprehension	123	(116–127)
Performance	120	(111–125)	Perceptual Organization	116	(107–121)
Full Scale	124	(119–129)	Freedom from Distractibility	124	(113–129)
V-IQ = P-IQ *(ns)*			Processing Speed	111	(101–117)

Verbal	Scaled Score	Performance	Scaled Score
Information	16-S	Picture Completion	8-W
Similarities	12	(Coding)	(9)
Arithmetic	14	Picture Arrangement	12
Vocabulary	15	Block Design	17-S
Comprehension	13	Object Assembly	13
(Digit Span)	(14)	*Symbol Search	15

* Symbol Search was used in IQ computations
Mean of 12 subtests = 13

K-ABC Profile

Scale	Standard Score (± 90% conf.)	Mental Processing Subtests	Scaled Score
Sequential Processing	122 ± 7	Sequential	
Simultaneous Processing	109 ± 7	Hand Movements	14
Mental Processing Composite	116 ± 6	Number Recall	12
Achievement	122 ± 5	Word Order	14
Faces & Places	99 ± 11	Simultaneous	
Arithmetic	132 ± 10	Gestalt Closure	7-W
Riddles	120 ± 10	Triangles	16-S
Reading Decoding	121 ± 4	Matrix Analogies	11
		Spatial Memory	12
SEQ > SIM ($p < .05$)		Photo Series	11

Woodcock-Johnson-Revised Cognitive Battery (Selected Subtests)

Subtest/Cluster	Standard Score (± SEm)
1. Memory for Names	119±5
4. Incomplete Words	97±6
5. Visual Closure	85±8
8. Visual-Auditory Learning	142±5
14. Concept Formation	102±4
15. Delayed Recall: Memory for Names	83±6
16. Delayed Recall: Visual-Auditory Learning	90±6
19. Spatial Relations	129±7
Long-Term Retrieval (Tests 1 & 8)	138±4

Kaufman Test of Educational Achievement—Comprehensive Form (K-TEA)

Subtest/Composite	Standard Score (± 90% conf.)
Mathematics Composite	145±7
Mathematics Computation	141±10
Mathematics Applications	142±8
Reading Composite	149±4
Reading Decoding	144±5
Reading Comprehension	160±6
Spelling	146±9
Battery Composite	153±4

Referral and Background Information

Nicole, nearly 6½ years of age, was referred for evaluation by her parents who would like to gain some insight into her academic strengths and weaknesses. Their goal is to be able to best direct and assist her in future learning, by receiving guidance on how best to help Nicole work to her full potential. They also want to address placement issues in school. They are concerned as well about possible weaknesses for Nicole in memory and visual closure, which appeared as deficits on previous group testing with a Guilford-based instrument. Nicole also has had juvenile diabetes since she was 8 months old, which tends to cause hypoglycemic episodes. Such events have been linked to learning disabilities. Her parents would like to explore and rule out the possibility that Nicole might have any type of learning disability due to this factor that could cause future problems in her ability to succeed in school.

Nicole is in the first grade at a small private day school. Despite her parents' concern about the future, Nicole's mother reports that Nicole does well in school. In case they should decide to transfer her from the private school, they would like to know if she would qualify for the gifted program in public school.

Nicole lives in an upper middle-class home with her mother, father, and 3-year-old sister, Emily. Nicole's mother is a novelist who earned her Master of Fine Arts (MFA) degree in Creative Writing. She teaches a writer's workshop each semester at a local university while working on her third novel. Nicole's father is a high school basketball and football coach who teaches history and Spanish. Nicole has a close relationship with both her mother and father and gets along most of the time with her sister, with an occasional squabble or two. The family spends weekends together, just the four of them, or sometimes with other families doing recreational activities. Sometimes Nicole will pair off with her father to do things while mom takes care of the toddler.

Nicole's mother described her pregnancy and delivery of Nicole as normal. In her first month of life, Nicole developed mild jaundice that required monitoring but no treatment. When Nicole was approximately 6 months old, she became ill and began to lose weight; at approximately 8 months she lost 2 pounds over a period of 4 days, which led to a hospital stay and the subsequent diagnosis of juvenile diabetes. She has been receiving insulin injections three times a day since the diagnosis. As far as her mother knows, she has suffered only one seizure, which occurred at 18 months of age. Her mother also stated that Nicole had frequent earaches during her first 2 years of life. Her developmental milestones were all met at a normal pace once she started receiving the insulin shots. She walked at 13 months and started to talk at 16 months. Her mother described Nicole as always having been very verbal, more so than her peers.

Nicole attended preschool from age 2½ to 4 years old. She has been attending her current school since kindergarten, where she is "flourishing" with the individual attention that she receives there. She is able to read at what her mother would guess is above the first-grade level, sounding out words she doesn't know. She also knows how to count, add, and subtract, and "loves school."

Her first-grade teacher describes Nicole as "quite a model student" who is academically strong in math, reading, and social studies, and who is socially mature, creative, good at writing stories, and good at contributing appropriate material and ideas to the class. Her teacher perceives Nicole as a self-confident, polite, and energetic child who is not impulsive and does not "blab out." She also stated that Nicole deals with her diabetes very well and concluded: "All the children in the class seem to like her and she likes them. Nicole is the epitome of the perfect first grader."

At home, television doesn't interest her much, and if she's seen a program previously, she will go and do something else. Drawing and making things out of clay along with playing board games such as Monopoly Jr. are some of her hobbies. She loves to swim and took swimming lessons and attended a ceramics class this past summer. She also enjoys working in the yard with her dad, running errands, and going to ball games.

Nicole is described by her mother as being very outgoing and having high self-esteem. The hardest thing for Nicole is being different from other children due to her diabetes. When she was about 4 years old, she fought the insulin injections, but has now learned to cope in a variety of ways with her disease. She is able to talk about her diabetes with friends and goes with her family to fund-raisers where she meets other children who are also affected by juvenile diabetes. Nicole has a best friend named Max with whom she has grown up, and he appears to be very supportive of her and her special needs.

Appearance and Behavioral Characteristics

Nicole presented as an attractive white young girl, with light brown hair, blue eyes, and suntanned skin. She was dressed comfortably and appropriately for her age at each testing session, wearing her hair in a ponytail with occasional strands falling around her face and neck. Her voice was strong and clear, although she did speak with a slight lisp (her S's sometimes sounded like F's or X's), making some words hard to distinguish. She carried fruit and a glass of water to monitor her diabetes and willingly came to the testing room. She was a little nervous at the beginning of the first testing session, but seemed to relax after a few minutes of rapport building. Nicole became easily engaged in the tasks presented to her and remained attentive throughout the assessment. She appeared eager to please, often looking to the examiner for some reinforcement of her performance. She was very verbal during the testing, answering the test questions and sometimes elaborating to disclose more information than was requested. She remained motivated throughout the testing sessions and did not require a break in between any of the subtests. Nicole appeared to enjoy the testing situation and the attention she was receiving due to it, and stated that it was "fun."

Nicole's approach to the testing situation was that of earnest and sincere effort in her performance, with some parts of the assessment coming easily to her and others providing her with a challenge. At times, she was quick to process information and very spontaneous and eager with her responses, whereas at other times she was slower in her problem solving, taking the time to ponder her answers and very reluctant to admit when she did not know what the answer was. She verbalized her way through almost all the tasks presented to her, both verbal and nonverbal, whispering under her breath, either repeating the question asked by the examiner or working through the problem. Even when she didn't verbalize her thought processes, her mouth was often moving to form the shapes of words, although no sound was made. Nicole seemed to expel nervous energy, or anxiety she might have been experiencing, by motor movement. For example, she was almost constantly swinging of her legs under the testing table.

Nicole's apparent need for structure was illustrated in her ability to verbalize well when a specific question such as "do you like to eat pizza?" was asked of her; in contrast, an open-ended question such as "what did you do in school today?" made her flustered and left her unable to respond. She also showed some inflexibility in the strategies she employed during the testing, performing quickly and confidently on items for which the strategies were well-learned and familiar but taking a slow and cautious approach to more unfamiliar tasks. She showed some resistance to changing strategies once involved in a task, even though the task called for flexibility, preferring to stick with what she had learned and had worked well. This inflexibility was illustrated in her approach to the Woodcock-Johnson Revised subtest of Concept Formation, on which she kept returning to the problem-solving strategy of the previous item instead of being able to vary strategies as necessary. When Nicole was experiencing difficulties with items, she would often look down or look toward the examiner for some reinforcement, and then remain silent until prompted either to guess or move on to the next item. Even when Nicole was continually reminded that it was OK to just say "I don't know" if she didn't have an answer, rarely would she offer this response. Instead, she chose to remain silent or continue concentrating on the problem.

Nicole's perfectionist tendencies were displayed on many of the subtests, resulting in slower performance, which may have affected her scores on highly speeded tasks, such as a subtest that required her to rapidly copy abstract symbols paired with numbers. These tendencies were also illustrated on a subtest where she was required to put triangle pieces together to form a picture of a design. Here Nicole would put the pieces together correctly but then spend some extra time trying to line up them up perfectly. She maintained her concentration well and was very perceptive throughout the testing sessions. At one point, she explained to the examiner after a more difficult item on the triangles task just mentioned, "It was kind of confusing because there were no lines to separate the triangles" (all previous items had dividing lines on the picture to be copied). This observation also pertains to Nicole's need for, and use of, structure. She also reprimanded herself out loud if she caught, and self-corrected, a mistake. Surprisingly, on a K-ABC task that required her to put a series of photographs in the correct order of an event, Nicole knew she gave the pictures in the wrong order and stated so, but when asked if she would like to change them, she replied, "I don't care, no." This response seemed inconsistent with her previous behavior. Nicole was generally not shy about asking the examiner to read a question over if it was unclear or to explain what a word meant.

Interestingly, Nicole's projective drawings were unelaborated. She used stick figures for the people, allowing little detail in the drawings and only utilized the upper left-hand corner of the paper. When asked to draw a person with all its parts, she still produced a small stick figure but elaborated more on the arms and legs, actually using her own body as a model while drawing. She held her pencil in an awkward way, between her thumb and forefinger, and evidenced immature fine-motor coordination. Nonetheless, Nicole has nice handwriting for her age, which was unaffected by her awkward handling of the pencil. It is also noteworthy that during a math achievement subtest that permitted pencil and paper, she wrote the problem on the paper, but did the problem solving in her head or on her fingers, never actually using the paper.

Nicole's extreme persistence and patience were evident during the final part of the last testing session which went longer than expected due to her performance on a reading comprehension subtest. Although the paragraphs were long and difficult and took her a long time to get through, she never gave up. She phonetically sounded out words she didn't know and then continued on with the story.

Overall, Nicole had a positive attitude throughout the assessment, displaying the ability to maintain concentration and motivation for extended periods of time. Her performance fluctuated from working quickly and confidently when she was comfortable with a task, to a slower, more cautious yet persistent approach when she was unsure. Her apparent need for steady reinforcement when challenged was evidenced by her constant need for examiner approval, and she was reluctant to give up or admit she didn't know an answer; she was sometimes inflexible in her problem-solving strategies. Nicole was quite verbal throughout the testing, smiling and laughing with the examiner on occasion, never complaining even when it was obvious that she was tired. She appears to be a very pleasant little girl with a good sense of humor who is eager to please and enjoys doing school-related tasks.

Tests Administered

Wechsler Intelligence Scale for Children—Third Edition (WISC-III)

Kaufman Assessment Battery for Children (K-ABC)

Kaufman Test of Educational Achievement (K-TEA)
   Comprehensive Form

Woodcock-Johnson Psycho-Educational Battery—Revised (WJ-R)
   Tests of Cognitive Ability (Selected subtests)

McCarthy Scales Draw-A-Child

Informal projective drawings

Test Results and Interpretation

Nicole's WISC-III IQs (Verbal = 124, Performance = 120, Full Scale = 124) classify her intelligence as Superior and rank her at about the 95th percentile compared with other 6-year-olds. The four points favoring Verbal IQ is trivial, suggesting that she displays her intelligence about equally well whether responding to verbal questions or manipulating concrete materials to solve nonverbal problems. All her standard scores on the WISC-III Factor Indexes are reasonably consistent (111 to 124), although the scatter within her Performance subtest profile suggests that none of the measures of nonverbal functioning (Performance IQ, Perceptual Organization Index, Processing Speed Index) provide a meaningful picture of her abilities in that sphere.

On the Kaufman Assessment Battery for Children (K-ABC), Nicole earned a Sequential Processing Standard Score of 122±7, a Simultaneous Processing standard score of 109±7, a Mental Processing Composite standard score (IQ equivalent) of 116±6, and an Achievement standard score of 122±5. As on the WISC-III, these global scores classify her cognitive abilities at the High Average to Superior level of intelligence, ranking her at approximately the 90th percentile. The 13-point difference between her Sequential Processing (93rd percentile) and her Simultaneous Processing (73rd percentile) standard scores is statistically significant and suggests that she performs better when solving problems in a linear, step-by-step fashion than when integrating many stimuli at once. Nicole's good sequential processing was evidenced on the WISC-III as well by her Freedom from Distractibility Index of 124 (95th percentile). However, as she did on the WISC-III Performance Scale, Nicole exhibited scatter within her Simultaneous Processing profile, making her score of 109 of limited meaning. In fact, she does have a Simultaneous Processing weakness, but it is on the perceptual level, not the conceptual level. That is to say, she performed at only the 16th percentile on a perceptual test of Gestalt Closure, in contrast to the 98th percentile on a conceptual test of spatial visualization requiring her to copy abstract designs using triangular blocks. That finding was underscored by her significant weakness and strength on the WISC-III Performance Scale: She scored at the 25th percentile on a perceptual simultaneous task (finding the missing parts of pictures) and at the 99th percentile on Block Design. Her spatial visualization strength was supported by her good performance (95th percentile) on a speeded test requiring the rapid scanning of abstract symbols.

Her conceptual strength and perceptual weakness were each verified as well on the Woodcock-Johnson-Revised (WJ-R) Cognitive Battery. Nicole's excellent spatial visualization was displayed on the WJ-R Spatial Relations subtest (98th percentile), which requires mental visualization without motor involvement. And her perceptual difficulty was verified by her performance on the WJ-R Visual Closure task (15th percentile). Furthermore, this relative perceptual problem seems to extend to the auditory domain as well. She performed at the 43rd percentile (which is well below her level of intelligence) on an auditory analog of visual or Gestalt closure: a WJ-R subtest requiring her to identify a whole word when parts of it are missing.

The scatter displayed by Nicole on the WISC-III and K-ABC was evident throughout her performance on the various ability and achievement tasks administered to her. Sometimes this scatter was shown on tasks that measured very similar abilities. For example, when asked questions that tap general range of factual knowledge, she performed much better on WISC-III Information (98th percentile) than on K-ABC Faces & Places (47th percentile). The WISC III task utilizes auditory stimuli whereas the K-ABC subtest utilizes visual stimuli. On the WISC-III, her speed of processing information was better when the task was conceptual—the visualization task mentioned earlier—than when it was primarily psychomotor (37th percentile).

On the WJ-R, Nicole was administered four subtests that measure fluid intelligence (i.e., the ability to solve novel problems, with or without memory), including the Spatial Relations subtest mentioned previously. Her standard scores on these tasks ranged from 102±4 (56th percentile) on a test requiring her to demonstrate logical classification skills with abstract stimuli to 142±5 (99.8th percentile) on a task requiring her to associate words with symbols. The 40-point range on these similar tasks reflects, once more, an unusual degree of scatter. The symbol-association task, and a similar WJ-R fluid task also requiring memory (learning the names of space creatures), further illustrate the extreme variability in Nicole's cognitive spectrum. Overall, on the two fluid memory tasks, both of which assess the ability to learn new material, Nicole earned a standard score of 138±4 (99th percentile). Yet when she was given the delayed version of these two tasks 3 days later (to see how many symbols she still remembered), she obtained standard scores in the mid-80s (18th percentile). The huge difference in her initial and delayed learning ability (both of which are normed relative to other 6-year-olds) is more than 3 standard deviations in magnitude and, therefore, noteworthy.

One final example of her scatter is revealing. When asked with minimal structure to draw a picture of a girl, her drawing earned a developmental age of 5 years using the scoring system for the McCarthy Scales Draw-A-Child. But when Nicole was given specific structure ("Make a drawing of a whole girl. Put all of her parts in"), her subsequent drawing was evaluated at a 7½ year level.

Nicole's achievement on the Kaufman Test of Educational Achievement—Comprehensive Form (K-TEA) was astonishingly high. Her standard scores on the five separate subtests were all above the 99th percentile, ranging from 141±12 on Mathematics Computation to 160±7 on Reading Comprehension. Her Reading Composite of 149±5, Mathematics Composite of 145±8, Spelling score of 146±10, and K-TEA Battery Composite of 153±5 indicate broad-based, outstanding skills in diverse areas of school achievement.

Interestingly, her achievement scores are substantially higher than her scores on the WISC-III and K-ABC intelligence scales and even on the K-ABC Achievement Scale. Particularly of note is that she scored 144±6 on K-TEA Reading Decoding compared with 121±4 on the K-ABC subtest of the same name and format. This difference again reflects Nicole's scatter in her test performance. In this instance, she was observed to use a careful phonic strategy during the K-TEA (in a schoolworklike environment), but she abandoned a systematic phonic word-attack approach when K-ABC Reading Decoding was administered in the context of unfamiliar cognitive tasks.

Nicole's average standard score on the four WJ-R subtests that measure fluid ability is 123, which is similar to her global scores on the WISC-III and K-ABC. This consistency indicates a real discrepancy between her achievement and intelligence, in favor of the former, that is generalizable and not specific to a particular model of intelligence. Thus, Nicole demonstrates a generally Superior level of intellectual functioning, yet consistently performs at a substantially higher (Very Superior) level on school-based achievement.

Of great interest are the possible reasons for Nicole's extreme scatter in her test profile. She has the capacity for Very Superior functioning within the intellectual domain. Whereas her strongest verbal ability on the WISC-III Verbal Scale (98th percentile) was on tests of acquired knowledge (general information, word knowledge, oral arithmetic) and may simply reflect her exceptional school achievement, she also evidenced strengths that were unquestionably intellectual. She excelled on all three cognitive batteries on tests of spatial visualization, and she scored at the 99th percentile on the WJ-R tests of fluid memory. However, she is apparently unable to demonstrate her high level of conceptual development when her perceptual difficulties interfere. Her poorest scores on reasoning tasks were on solving concrete and abstract analogies, arranging photographs in chronological order, arranging pictures to tell a story, and logical classification with abstract shapes (all were at about the 60th to 65th percentile). Because of the heavy perceptual demands of these tasks, Nicole was hurt in her ability to solve the problems.

Nicole's style of work on novel conceptual tasks reflects a need for extreme structure. Her performance was frequently characterized by failure on easy items followed by success on much more difficult (but related) concepts. This pattern was illustrated previously by her vast improvement on the second drawing of a child. It was also demonstrated on other tasks. Even on her best performance on the K-ABC Mental Processing Scale (constructing designs with triangles), she solved the Sample item slowly and with much trial-and-error before catching on. On a test of nonverbal analogies, she failed an easy picture item, and the easiest abstract item, before learning to tackle more difficult items.

Her great concentration abilities, persistence, ability to benefit from feedback, and exceptional learning ability all contribute to this pattern. These variables, along with a nurturing and stimulating home and school environment, also relate to her outstanding achievement in school-related tasks. However, it is apparent that Nicole's success is accomplished in the face of specific perceptual deficits and a need for thinking time and structure. Her poor performance on the delayed recall of material learned just 3 days earlier is of mild concern. It may be that material that Nicole seems to have mastered will be forgotten without systematic review. Her inability to retain the paired associations of visual stimuli that she had learned at such a high level initially may be a function of her perceptual problem.

Summary and Diagnostic Impression

Nicole A. is a 6-year-old girl who was referred for an evaluation of her academic strengths and weaknesses and to explore the possibility of a learning disability due to her history of juvenile diabetes. During the evaluation, she was attentive, cooperative, persistent, and extremely verbal. The assessment shows Nicole to fall in the High Average to Superior range of intellectual functioning on several cognitive batteries, and to have Very Superior academic achievement. Her test performance was characterized by a large amount of scatter. In addition to exceptional achievement in all school areas assessed, she had strengths in spatial visualization, verbal concepts, and the ability to use her memory to learn new learning material. She had weaknesses in auditory and visual perception, response speed, and the retention of information that was previously learned at a high level. Nicole has an extreme need for structure.

Overall, Nicole is an intelligent, motivated, and delightful young girl who possesses strong concentration skills, persistence, learning ability, and the ability to benefit from feedback. She has been able to achieve at a very high level in school and on standardized measures of achievement, but she has done so despite apparent deficits. Her perceptual difficulties and huge scatter are consistent with possible mild neurological dysfunction associated with her medical history; but these results are in no way conclusive. The wide variability in performance may be merely a developmental phenomenon. In any case, Nicole's outstanding performance in every aspect of school achievement indicates that she has the capacity to compensate fully for any deficits that she now displays within the perceptual, memory, or cognitive domains.

Recommendations

1. Nicole is a bright child who is functioning at a very high level in school. It is recommended, if possible, that she remain in a small classroom environment similar to the one she is currently in. Although she is very motivated and has a high need for achievement, Nicole benefits tremendously from feedback and reinforcement that should be more readily available when there is a smaller student-teacher ratio in the classroom.

2. Nicole's needs will be best met in a learning setting where she is given considerable structure and reinforcement. She will excel in situations where there is little ambiguity present and sets of rules and strategies for problem solving are readily available to her.

3. In regard to placement as Nicole gets older, whether or not Nicole will qualify for the gifted program will depend on the criteria for the gifted program of the school in which she is enrolled. If the tests given are based heavily on school achievement, she should encounter no difficulties in qualifying. If the tests rely more on novel problem solving and tasks that call for perceptual processing, Nicole's weaknesses in these areas may become apparent. It is recommended that Nicole be tested in a very structured setting, one-on-one, with an examiner who is aware of her possible deficits. Regardless of the precise number she may earn on an intelligence test, Nicole is a gifted child who should be in accelerated classes.

4. Nicole's profile of strengths and weaknesses is suggestive of mild neurological impairment. Although this is a possibility, it has not affected her success and achievement in school. She is coping quite well with any deficits that may exist and therefore no special services are recommended.

5. Evident in Nicole's test-taking behavior is a fear of failure and subsequent refraining from risk-taking. It is recommended that she be encouraged to become more independent and to take more chances, and to realize it is OK to be wrong or make a mistake. This guidance should help her to become more comfortable with ambiguous situations and may speed up her mental processing, allowing her to make decisions faster because she will not be so constrained by the necessity to be correct.

Examiners:
   Jose Gonzalez, MA; Kristee Beres, MA; Paul Randolph, MA;
   Yossi Adir, MA; Danica Katz, BA

Supervisor:
   Dr. Nadeen L. Kaufman

Ira G., Age 15-0, Specific Learning Disability in Writing

WISC-III Profile

IQs		(90% conf.)	Factor Indexes		(90% conf.)
Verbal	106	(100–111)	Verbal Comprehension	104	(98–109)
Performance	108	(101–114)	Perceptual Organization	111	(103–117)
Full Scale	107	(102–111)	Freedom from Distractibility	109	(100–116)
V-IQ = P-IQ *(ns)*			Processing Speed	88	(82–98)

Verbal	Scaled Score		Performance	Scaled Score
Information	8-W		Picture Completion	7-W
Similarities	14-S		(Coding)	(6)-W
Arithmetic	12		Picture Arrangement	15-S
Vocabulary	11		Block Design	13
Comprehension	10		Object Assembly	12
(Digit Span)	(11)		*Symbol Search	9

* Symbol Search was used in IQ computations

Mean of 12 subtests = 11

KAIT Profile

IQs		(90% conf.)	Subtests	Standard Score
Crystallized	100	(95–105)	Crystallized	
Fluid	116	(111–121)	Definitions	9
Composite	109	(105–113)	Auditory Comprehension	10
			Double Meanings	12-S
Fluid > Crystallized (*p* < .01)			(Famous Faces)	(7)-W
			Fluid	
			Rebus Learning	12
			Logical Steps	10-W
			Mystery Codes	17-S
			(Memory for Block Designs)	(14)
			Delayed Recall	
			Auditory Delay	12
			Rebus Delay	13

Mean of 3 Core Crystallized subtests = 10

Mean of 3 Core Fluid subtests = 13

Woodcock-Johnson-Revised Cognitive Battery (Selected Subtests)

Subtest	Standard Score (± SEm)
2. Memory for Sentences	99±5
3. Visual Matching	88±7
4. Incomplete Words	88±9
5. Visual Closure	92±9
7. Analysis-Synthesis	129±6
8. Visual-Auditory Learning	106±4
10. Cross Out	94±7
11. Sound Blending	124±6
12. Picture Recognition	108±7
13. Oral Vocabulary	109±5
14. Concept Formation	140±4

Cluster

Processing Speed (Tests 3 & 10)	89±5
Auditory Processing (Tests 4 & 11)	107±6
Visual Processing (Tests 5 & 12)	97±7
Fluid Reasoning (Tests 7 & 14)	138±4

Woodcock-Johnson-Revised Achievement Battery

Subtest	Standard Score (± SEm)
22. Letter-Word Identification	133±4
23. Passage Comprehension	115±5
24. Calculation	111±4
25. Applied Problems	109±4
26. Dictation	80±5
27. Writing Samples	113±5
28. Science	101±6
29. Social Studies	110±5
30. Humanities	98±5
31. Word Attack	141±5
32. Reading Vocabulary	98±4
33. Quantitative Concepts	125±6
34. Proofing	94±4
35. Writing Fluency	97±8

Cluster

Basic Reading Skills (Tests 22 & 31)	140±3
Reading Comprehension (Tests 23 & 32)	107±3
Basic Math Skills (Tests 24 & 33)	121±4
Basic Writing Skills (Tests 26 & 34)	86±3
Written Expression (Tests 27 & 35)	104±5
Broad Reading (Tests 22 & 23)	128±3
Broad Mathematics (Tests 24 & 25)	112±4
Broad Written Language (Tests 26 & 27)	92±5
Broad Knowledge (Tests 28, 29, & 30)	103±3

Woodcock-Johnson-Revised: Aptitude-Achievement Comparisons

Area	Aptitude	Achievement	SD Difference*
Basic Reading Skills	104	140	+4.02
Reading Comprehension	104	107	+0.43
Basic Math Skills	116	121	+0.54
Basic Writing Skills	106	86	−1.96
Written Expression	106	104	−0.20
Broad Reading	103	128	+2.72
Broad Mathematics	116	112	−0.43
Broad Written Language	108	92	−1.37
Broad Knowledge	114	103	−1.03

*Computed by the software program *Compuscore for the WJ-R—3.0.*

Referral and Background Information

Ira is a 15-year-old white male who was referred to the clinic for evaluation by Ira's paternal grandfather, a psychologist. The reason for referral is to assess Ira's academic difficulties and evaluate the possibility of a learning disability. Ira lives with both his parents and a younger brother, Rob, age 13. Currently, both Rob and Ira attend private boarding schools and do not live at home during the school year. Ira performed well on the multiple-choice entrance exam to get into the school and is currently a sophomore.

Ira's father is a bank executive, and his mother is a receptionist in a doctor's office. Mrs. G. describes her pregnancy as normal, and Ira's developmental milestones were all met at a normal pace. Starting at age 2, Ira had frequent earaches but they subsided with time. Although Ira's speech is comprehensible, he mumbles and talks in a low tone of voice. Ira has seen an orthopedic surgeon for various broken bones that he has sustained while performing his favorite recreational activities, hiking, mountain climbing, and snowboarding.

At the age of 3, Ira began to attend preschool. He reportedly loved it, but when he attended kindergarten his feelings changed. During his elementary education, Ira was a B student and, according to Mrs. G., Ira's fourth-grade teacher was inspirational for him to enjoy writing. He won some poetry and writing awards, which were mainly judged on content rather than form. His sixth-grade year was inconsistent in that he had three teachers, all with very different teaching styles, and Ira had difficulty transitioning from one teacher to the next. In eighth grade, Ira missed a good portion of school between February and April because of mononucleosis. Since Ira began high school, according to Mrs. G., he has obtained irregular or inconsistent grades in school. Ira does well in oral expression and presentation of his ideas and in problem-solving skills, but he has difficulty with written assignments and exams. Ira is aware of his inconsistent performance in school and gets extra help from teachers; he also asks classmates for editing advice on written assignments.

Ira describes his academic performance in terms of having difficulty acclimating to a new term, and once he realizes he is behind, he finds that the work begins to get much harder. He also states that his writing is much better when he is able to write on topics that he enjoys. He has been having particular difficulty learning both geometry and French, and says that his main problem in French is that he knows the answer to questions but is unable to respond or retrieve the answer. He also adds that he has a difficult time writing in French, especially the spelling.

According to Mrs. G., Ira has average peer relationships with others his age and thinks that most adolescents his age are too boisterous and rowdy. Although he has friends at home, most of his friends are from school.

Appearance and Behavioral Characteristics

Ira, a tall, light-brown-haired adolescent with his hair in a ponytail, wore a t-shirt and wore sandals with no socks, on the days of the evaluation. He looks older than his age of 15. He appeared relaxed, yet he was quiet and sat far away from the examiner's table during the first testing session, but responded appropriately to the suggestion to move in closer. During testing, Ira was very cooperative. He demonstrated outstanding endurance on tasks and worked steadily throughout the two sessions. Although Ira listened carefully to the examiner's questions and performed suggested activities, test instructions to nonverbal items and questions to verbal items frequently had to be repeated. In addition, many times Ira guessed on items in which he was not sure of the question or answer, yet he usually guessed correctly. He did not offer much spontaneous conversation, and he mumbled or spoke in a low tone frequently. In addition to Ira's uncertainty, some of his responses were inconsistent. For example, he was able to define the word "nonsense" correctly, yet he did not understand the meaning of "nonsensical" as part of a question to a story he had heard.

In problem solving, Ira responded in a concrete fashion with a good analytic and sequential approach to tasks. He stated that he knew many of the categories or topics that he was asked but could not come up with the exact word or answer to the question. On tasks in which Ira had a conceptual understanding of what was expected of him, including complex problem-solving tasks, he performed fast and accurately. On the other hand, Ira performed much more slowly, and with some confusion, on apparently simple perceptual tasks, both visual and auditory. His rate of responding to visual-motor tasks also slowed down when the perceptual demands increased (e.g., when assembling puzzles). In addition, he rarely embellished or elaborated his responses, which were short and not always exact.

Overall, Ira did not express much affect during the testing session, or concern about his performance. Although he had some difficulties in encoding the visual and auditory stimuli presented, he rarely became distracted and attempted each task with effort. Therefore, the results of this evaluation are deemed fully valid and interpretable.

Tests Administered

Wechsler Intelligence Scale for Children—Third Edition (WISC-III)

Kaufman Adolescent and Adult Intelligence Test (KAIT)
Expanded Form

Woodcock-Johnson Psycho-Educational Battery—Revised (WJ-R)
Tests of Cognitive Ability: Selected Subtests
Tests of Achievement: Complete Battery

Test Results and Interpretation

Ira's WISC-III IQs (Verbal = 106, Performance = 108, Full Scale = 107) classify his intelligence as Average to High Average and rank him at about the 68th percentile compared with other 15-year-olds. Ira scored significantly higher on the Perceptual Organization (PO) Index (111) than on the Processing Speed (PS) Index (88), indicating that he performed better on tests of nonverbal reasoning than on tests of visual processing speed. However, he displayed marked subtest scatter within the PO factor, rendering the PO Index (like the P-IQ) inadequate as an estimate of Ira's nonverbal intelligence. Within the subtest profile, Ira evidenced strengths on tests of nonverbal reasoning and concept formation, notably on tasks that measure the ability to synthesize a whole from its parts (92nd percentile), and weaknesses on Verbal tests that depend on culture-loaded knowledge of facts and social conventions (34th percentile). More generally, however, Ira performed best on tests of fluid thinking, the ability to solve unfamiliar problems such as arranging pictures to tell a story, relating two verbal concepts, or matching abstract design with blocks (92nd percentile on five such tasks). In contrast, he performed less well on tests of crystallized thinking, which involve answering questions that are dependent on school learning and acculturation. The best estimate of his crystallized ability on the WISC-III is provided by his Verbal Comprehension Index of 104 (61st percentile).

Ira's apparent strength in fluid versus crystallized ability was verified by his scores on two test batteries that were specifically designed to measure those aspects of intelligence, the KAIT and Woodcock-Johnson—Revised (WJ-R). On the KAIT, he earned a Fluid IQ of 116±5, a Crystallized IQ of 100±5, and a Composite IQ of 109±4. The 16-point difference in favor of Fluid IQ is statistically significant, but it probably underestimates the degree of his superiority in fluid versus crystallized thinking. For one thing, he demonstrated a relative strength (75th percentile) on the one Crystallized subtest that also has a clear-cut fluid component (using clues to figure out words that have two entirely different meanings). In addition, Ira had a strength on the alternate Fluid subtest (Memory for Block Designs) and a weakness on the alternate Crystallized subtest (Famous Faces)—neither of which contributes to the KAIT IQs. Further evidence of a large fluid-crystallized difference comes from WJ-R test results: He earned an exceptional standard score of 138 (99th percentile) on the Fluid Reasoning Scale, compared with a standard score of 109 (73rd percentile) on a Crystallized vocabulary test (giving antonyms and synonyms).

Ira's three global estimates of intelligence are quite similar (WISC-III FS-IQ = 107, KAIT Composite IQ = 109; median score on 11 WJ-R cognitive subtests = 106), and all suggest overall average to above-average general intelligence. However, the key distinction in his ability profile involves his Superior fluid intelligence versus his Average crystallized intelligence. Across all three test batteries, Ira's strongest abilities (about 98th percentile) were on fluid subtests that demand planning ability, organizational skills, and verbal mediation (arranging pictures to tell a story, cracking complex codes, demonstrating logical classification skills, applying rules to solve logic problems). He also did well on fluid subtests requiring visualization, such as copying abstract designs both with and without a memory component. He demonstrated a weakness on one test of fluid thinking, scoring at the 25th percentile on the KAIT Logical Steps subtest, a measure of high-level reasoning ability that depends on verbal comprehension for success. Whereas all the fluid tests on which Ira excelled demand some level of verbal skill, only the latter subtest requires very good auditory processing to interpret complex questions spoken by the examiner, and that seems to represent one of Ira's problems.

On the WJ-R Auditory Processing Scale, he earned a standard score of 107±12 (68th percentile), which is Average, but that score is composed of two diverse abilities: He has an outstanding auditory skill (94th percentile) in his ability to connect spoken syllables and phonemes to form a word, but he is deficient (20th percentile) on the WJ-R subtest requiring him to identify incomplete words presented on cassette (e.g., identifying "table" from "tay-ul"). That type of auditory processing problem may mean that Ira has difficulty making efficient use of context clues and the redundancies of the English language; if so, he may have trouble understanding long or complex directions spoken by his teachers, just as he may have had difficulty with the KAIT Logical Steps subtest.

Interestingly, Ira had about a similar level of deficiency on analogous tests of visual closure, scoring at about the 20th–25th percentile when finding the missing parts of pictures or identifying pictures that are partially obscured. His difficulties with these tasks were also evident in his behavior; as noted, he seemed confused and responded slowly to these tasks. Ira's ability to integrate stimuli on the *perceptual* level (both auditory and visual) is below average for his age, in contrast to his very superior ability to integrate stimuli on the *conceptual* level (i.e., his fluid reasoning). His auditory and visual perceptual problems suggest that he may have difficulty fully understanding how similar topics are related to each other. These problem areas may pertain to his reported difficulties in "seeing the big picture" and in generalizing rules from one situation to another. This concreteness was evidenced during the KAIT Rebus Learning task when he responded in a rigid and concrete manner to the information he was taught, and had trouble integrating the new learning with prior knowledge of reading and grammar (e.g., when told that a symbol stood for "to or toward," he repeated "to or toward" every time he had to "read" that symbol).

Speed is also one of Ira's problem areas. He earned nearly identical standard scores (88–89, or 22nd percentile) on the WISC-III and WJ-R Processing Speed Scales, which measure the speed with which he can perform relatively low level visual-motor activities. Nonetheless, Ira's problems with speed of responding did not characterize his performance on complex problem-solving tasks. His strength on the KAIT code-cracking subtest and the WISC-III picture arranging task, for example, demand very rapid problem solving, and he was equal to the task.

Ira's achievement, as measured by the WJ-R, displayed as much scatter as his cognitive profile. He excelled at Basic Reading Skills (reading real words and sounding out nonsense words) earning a standard score of 140 ± 6 (99.6th percentile), but his Reading Comprehension was Average (107 ± 6; 67th percentile). His Written Expression, though Average (104 ± 10; 60th percentile), was far superior to his Basic Writing Skills (86 ± 6; 18th percentile). He also performed better in his Basic Math Skills (121 ± 8; 92nd percentile) than in Math Reasoning (109 ± 8; 73rd percentile).

Whereas Ira has an exceptional understanding of the rules of phonics, performing at the 99.7th percentile on a test of decoding nonsense words, he is relatively deficient in his knowledge of the rules of punctuation and capitalization (10th percentile) and grammar (33rd percentile on a measure of word usage). Problems in grammar and word usage were noted during the KAIT Rebus Learning subtest (which teaches examinees a new language), and undoubtedly relates to his difficulties in learning French.

The WJ-R provides aptitude scores in each area of achievement to determine whether an individual is achieving as well as would be predicted from his or her aptitude score. Ira's achievement in both reading and math are equal to or above his predicted scores. However, his achievement in knowledge of science, social studies, and humanities (58th percentile) is significantly below the score predicted for him. In addition, his scores on Broad Written Language (30th percentile) and Basic Writing Skills (18th percentile) are both significantly below his aptitude for writing. In the case of his basic writing skills, the discrepancy was quite large (nearly 2 standard deviations), suggesting a specific learning disability in writing.

Although Ira's reading ability is as good as one might predict for him in view of his reading aptitude, the 33-point discrepancy between his decoding and comprehension abilities is huge. It may, again, reflect his inability to grasp central concepts and generalize his knowledge. That lack was also seen in some of his concrete responses to questions about mock news stories that were played by cassette during the KAIT Auditory Comprehension subtest.

Ira has some outstanding strengths, especially in the ability to apply systematic rules in an organized fashion to solve complex novel problems. That particular strength suggests a great aptitude for school learning. On the KAIT, he also gave evidence that he retains information that he previously learned, performing relatively well (80th percentile) on two tests of delayed recall. He does have weaknesses in the speed with which he works and in the ability to process stimuli, both auditorally and visually. His visual processing and speed problems are of less general concern because of his ability to perform so well on complex visual-spatial and reasoning problems requiring rapid responding. His auditory problem, however, may cause him to misinterpret instructions spoken aloud in the classroom. His speed problem is most likely to hurt his school performance whenever he is forced to work quickly on tasks that are uninteresting or not challenging.

Ira certainly has the visualization and reasoning skills to succeed in geometry, which was reported to be a problem for him. Ironically, the one fluid task on which he performed poorly (KAIT Logical Steps) most resembles the kind of logic needed for geometric proofs. His possible difficulty in interpreting the complex verbal questions (stemming from his auditory processing problem), may have hampered his test performance. The same factor may hurt him in geometry.

He needs to improve his writing skills. Specific remediation on the rules of grammar, capitalization, and punctuation is essential; he will learn best if diagrams and other figures are used in the instruction process. He also needs to improve his general communication of ideas through writing. His performance on a test of Writing Fluency (43rd percentile), which assesses the ability to formulate sentences and write them down rapidly, suggests that he has difficulty conveying his ideas on tests in school; the measures of Processing Speed on the WISC-III and WJ-R also involve paper and pencil. He probably knows more than he is able to communicate. Also, his cognitive strength (solving novel problems) is not likely to be visible in school; in view of his articulation difficulties, he is probably not perceived as being as intelligent as he actually is.

Summary and Diagnostic Impressions

Ira G. is a 15-year-old white male who was referred to the clinic by his grandfather to gain more insight into Ira's academic difficulties and to evaluate the possibility of an existing learning disability. Ira is currently attending the 10th grade at a private boarding school, and he lives at home during the holidays and summer with both parents and a younger brother. Overall, Ira's attitude toward the examiner and the testing situation was very positive. He was cooperative, motivated, and approached tasks in a serious and effortful manner.

The evaluation took place on two consecutive days. Although Ira responded well to the examiners' questions, he retained a reluctance to express himself verbally. Ira's problem-solving skills seem to require a conceptual and analytic understanding before he can proceed. On difficult tasks that involved understanding perceptual information, Ira would slow down and guess or respond by saying he did not know the answer.

The WISC-III, KAIT, and WJ-R global scores classify Ira's cognitive ability at the Average to High Average level of intelligence. However, he performed considerably better when solving novel, abstract, and high level conceptual tasks than when solving school-related problems.

Ira displayed a degree of dichotomous performance on several of the WJ-R school achievement tests. On the one hand, he performed exceptionally well in basic reading, where he was able to pronounce words with great accuracy. Conversely, he demonstrated average ability in reading comprehension on passages. This discrepancy may reflect his inability to grasp main concepts and generalize findings. Even more discrepant was his written expression, at the average level, and his ability to apply basic writing skills, which was well below his ability or aptitude. This discrepancy was evident in Ira's poor usage of grammar rules. A discrepancy of this nature, along with the documented difficulties Ira has in written composition in school, are evidence of a Developmental Expressive Writing Disorder (DSM-III-R: 315.80).

Ira has the capacity to perform at a superior level of intellectual functioning, yet he is unable to demonstrate his conceptual development when his perceptual difficulties interfere. He performed poorly on perceptual tasks. Ira had difficulty with auditory processing of complex questions. He did not make efficient use of the redundancies in the English language, and as a result, he has difficulty understanding how similar topics are related. This problem occurred as well in the visual processing of stimuli. When tasks involved heavy perceptual processing, Ira's visual-motor performance began to slow. Both of these weaknesses affect his classroom performance. The auditory processing interferes with his understanding of what is expected, such as instructions. The visual-motor slowness affects his schoolwork when he is expected to work quickly on perceptual tasks.

Recommendations

1. In order to best utilize Ira's concrete, nonverbal, conceptual strengths, several general suggestions for academic accommodations are listed. (These are taken from a 1982 article by R. Sinatra, "Brain processing: Where learning styles begin," in volume 12 of *Early Years*, pages 49–51.)

   a. Provide a syllabus of lectures and materials. Analytic or sequential readers, as Ira is, often recall details but have difficulty understanding global ideas. Ira may learn more efficiently when information is presented in small, logical, sequential steps.

   b. Present illustrations or objects prior to, during, and after activities to tie in nonverbal experiences with the language-based materials.

The use of diagrams in the instruction process will aid Ira's conceptualization of main ideas and ability to generalize concepts.

c. Use drama, music, art, role playing, and group projects to develop reading and writing activities.

d. Supplement visual-auditory presentation with tactile cues and kinesthetic, hands-on experiences when possible. This suggestion includes lab activities, learning centers, and peer projects.

e. Involve the use of imagery and visual mnemonics to aid coding and recall.

f. Furnish a variety of assignments to facilitate and evaluate mastery of content (such as individual projects, videotaping, dramatization). Ira's comprehension difficulties will affect his performance based on how he is questioned. Therefore, the more diverse the presentation of materials, the better he will perform.

g. When possible, remove time limits from in-class assignments or allow completion outside the class. Also, provide extra time on tests, so that he is not hurried in responding.

h. Impart clear and consistent rules that are written out. Short-term goals, with positive feedback, will provide Ira with valuable information on monitoring his daily progress.

2. Another instructional strategy, Directed Reading Thinking Activity (DRTA), is to organize a before, during, and after reading plan. Before reading, have Ira predict what the story will be about based on main idea clues, such as title or accompanying illustrations. Then, record his predictions and make one purpose of reading be to verify the predictions he made. During the reading task, have him stop and check previous predictions, ruling out those that were incorrect. Have him make any additional predictions about what might take place in the story. Then, have Ira tie the story together by reviewing correct predictions. After reading, use mixed comprehension questions, starting with literal questions and proceeding to the inferential level. This method can also aid Ira's written expression by providing a structural format from which to write.

3. In addition, when Ira is asked to write, have him integrate present concepts with previously learned information or meaningful experiences with which Ira is familiar. Also, whenever possible, use reading materials related to content material being studied in other academic areas to provide reinforcement of language concepts and help incorporate and increase basic vocabulary. For example, if studying the Greek period in Western Civilization, read and write about Greek writings and have Ira bring in information from his Western Civilization class to his Social Studies class, and from both classes to his English Composition class.

4. Using the Write-Right Method, Ira will be able to free-write content of an assignment on a rough draft and edit corrections on the second draft.

First, provide Ira with procedures for generating ideas to write about. This procedural instruction will aid his organization and contextual skills. Encourage Ira to formulate the thoughts and sentences *orally.* Then, he needs to develop "story starters" by getting ideas from the teacher, the text, pictures, and peers. Have him generate an outline of the main points, which he can get by looking at his DRTA notes or the syllabus for that particular section. Next, Ira should free-write using the outline headings as main ideas (the first sentence); the subheadings and text-specific ideas as support statements and examples (the middle of the paragraph); and then he can develop a conclusion (the last sentence). Finally, have Ira use word processing programs to compensate for, or supplement, his poor mechanics and usage. Select programs, such as Grammatik 5, that can check proper grammar usage, punctuation, and spelling. Also use programs that can give Ira instant access to alternate words, such as synonyms, along with definitions, to increase and refine his written language expression (a program that does these things is Random House Webster's Electronic Dictionary and Thesaurus). Finally, have Ira reread his products for clarity and conciseness of expression. He may even have a peer give him feedback on these aspects of the writing.

As part of the process, Ira's teachers should check his performance and provide positive feedback for the correct skills he has mastered, and written suggestions for the weaknesses he needs to work on. Occasionally, he should be encouraged to change his paper and revise his mistakes, in order to develop an understanding of his errors.

For in-class essays, Ira should use an abbreviated version of this method along with the COPS procedure (Capitalization, Overall appearance, Punctuation, and Spelling) to check grammar usage (see *Learning Strategies Curriculum: The Error Monitoring Strategy,* a 1985 curriculum by J. B. Schumaker, D. M. Nolan, & D. D. Deshler, published by the University of Kansas, Lawrence, KS).

5. In mathematics, systematic and concrete approaches to math concepts will best accommodate Ira's learning style. Provide verbal rules to facilitate acquisition of the visual-spatial skills required for computation, so that he can connect the two. In addition, work on translating verbal problems into mathematical and visual-spatial analogs.

6. In reference to Ira's visual and auditory perceptual problems in note taking:

a. Have Ira question any directions, explanations, or instructions he does not understand.

b. Teach Ira how to paraphrase in deciding what information is worthy of writing down. At first, allow Ira to use a tape recorder for lectures and provide syllabi for topics. Next, encourage Ira to look for common patterns in the information that is provided, such as cause and effect, compare and contrast, sequential principles or laws followed by examples, descriptions, pro and con statements, flowchart style, and visual examples followed by possible variations. Once Ira notices the patterns, he should be able to enhance his listening and note-taking skills.

c. Use a variety of ways for Ira to obtain information without copying it (e.g., teachermade material or photocopies of the material).

7. Allow Ira to be tested orally, instead of by written examination.

8. In reference to Ira's visual and auditory perceptual problems in the quality of his assignments:

a. Provide Ira with clearly stated criteria for acceptable work.

b. Teach Ira procedures for improving the accuracy and quality of his work (listen to directions, make certain directions are understood, work at an acceptable pace, dedicate an allotted time for completion, check for errors, correct for completion and breadth).

c. Maintain a daily log of new terminology (as is done in his Biology class). This technique should increase his vocabulary and improve his word usage when writing.

d. Encourage Ira to distribute his study times in 10–15 minute periods across the day, instead of spending long periods of time trying to remember materials for an exam. Also, reviewing in the morning before an exam will benefit Ira's performance. Studying syllabi and main points every day will help him perform better on quizzes. In addition, reviewing terminology and studying his daily log will enhance his written expression.

9. Regarding his difficulty with French, it is suggested that Ira seek an alternate course—either an elective, computer course or a conversational French course, in which he does not have to be unduly penalized by his poor grammar and sequential skills. Frequently, courses on the country's culture will serve as good alternatives for students with Ira's difficulty learning foreign languages. If Ira cannot transfer out of French then an emphasis should be made on using the rules of the language.

10. A reevaluation is suggested for the end of his junior year or the very beginning of his senior year to determine his status concerning college placement.

Examiner:

Jose J. Gonzalez, MA

Supervisor:

Dr. Nadeen Kaufman

Dana Christine T., Age 8-6, Auditory Processing Difficulty, Language Disorder

WISC-III Profile

IQs		(90% conf.)	Factor Indexes		(90% conf.)
Verbal	122	(117–127)	Verbal Comprehension	125	(118–129)
Performance	125	(116–129)	Perceptual Organization	123	(114–128)
Full Scale	125	(119–129)	Freedom from Distractibility	121	(111–126)
V-IQ = P-IQ (ns)			Processing Speed	119	(108–124)

Verbal	Scaled Score	Performance	Scaled Score
Information	11-W	Picture Completion	12
Similarities	19-S	(Coding)	(14)
Arithmetic	10-W	Picture Arrangement	10-W
Vocabulary	12	Block Design	19-S
Comprehension	16	Object Assembly	14
(Digit Span)	(17)	*Symbol Search	13

* Symbol Search was used in IQ computations

Mean of 12 subtests = 14

K-ABC Profile

Scale	Standard Score (± 90% conf.)	Mental Processing Subtests	Scaled Score
Sequential Processing	112 ± 8	Sequential	
Simultaneous Processing	126 ± 7	Hand Movements	9-W
Mental Processing Composite	124 ± 6	Number Recall	15
Achievement		Word Order	12
Faces & Places	83 ± 9	Simultaneous	
Riddles	109 ± 9	Gestalt Closure	10-W
(only subtests given)		Triangles	15
		Matrix Analogies	18-S
SIM > SEQ (p < .05)		Spatial Memory	13
		Photo Series	12

Woodcock-Johnson-Revised Cognitive Battery (Selected Subtests)

Subtest/Cluster	Standard Score (± SEm)
4. Incomplete Words	93±8
6. Picture Vocabulary	104±6
11. Sound Blending	139±5
Auditory Processing (Tests 4 & 11)	123±5

Woodcock-Johnson-Revised Achievement Battery (Selected Subtests)

Subtest/Cluster	Standard Score (± SEm)
22. Letter-Word Identification	132±4
31. Word Attack	113±4
Basic Reading Skills (Tests 22 & 31)	124±3

Kaufman Test of Educational Achievement—Comprehensive Form (K-TEA)

Subtest/Composite	Standard Score (± 90% conf.)
Mathematics Composite	118±6
Mathematics Computation	125±7
Mathematics Applications	115±9
Reading Composite	126±4
Reading Decoding	116±5
Reading Comprehension	133±6
Spelling	98±6
Battery Composite	120±3

Referral and Background Information

Dana Christine was referred for evaluation by her parents after a teacher conference revealed she is having difficulties at school. Dana Christine is in third grade at a private school that has high admission standards, and her parents are concerned about whether this is the appropriate placement for her. It was reported that she is currently having difficulties with reading, writing, spelling, and with following complex directions. The purpose of the current evaluation is to define her cognitive strengths and weaknesses to determine the nature of her reported academic problems, and to determine what classroom modifications will assist her in working to her potential in the classroom.

At home, Dana Christine lives with her father, a biochemist who works for a large pharmaceutical company, her mother, a self-employed business consultant, and her two younger brothers, ages 6 and 3½. Mrs. T. reported that she is available for her children, making sure that her out-of-home consultation is limited to the hours that they are in school or preschool. In describing how Dana Christine responds to instruction at home, Mrs. T. said that she is easily sidetracked. For example, if she is engaged in a favorite activity, it gets in the way of her following through on requests from her parents.

Dana Christine's medical and developmental history appear to be within normal limits. Pregnancy was without difficulty, and her parents further report that she reached all developmental milestones on time. She experienced ear infections as a younger child, which were treated promptly, and have not caused further complications.

Dana Christine's academic history began with one year of nursery school, which was reportedly not a good experience. The school was unstructured, and she was not involved with the rest of the group, although she did spend time with one friend. Following nursery school, she entered a private school for kindergarten through second grade where she was very social and responded to the structure of the school. It was determined that she had a reading problem at the beginning of her second-grade school year. She currently receives remediation from a tutor to speed up her reading and to learn strategies for overcoming her confusion in following directions. She started her present school a few months ago at the beginning of third grade. Her parents report that they are unsure how she is currently doing in school, although they heard many negative comments and concerns at Dana Christine's recent teacher conference. Problems mentioned were her not finishing classroom tasks as instructed and having apparent confusion in following the teacher's instructions.

Dana Christine's parents see her as a "shy, reserved" girl who is currently losing confidence as was evident when she cried in class because she couldn't work out problems. She is described as a "careful worker," who takes time to plan before working. She is mechanically inclined and likes to put things together, although when she gets stuck, she has difficulty shifting mental sets.

During an observation of Dana Christine in her third-grade class, the students were reading sentences out loud from their spelling workbooks. While other children were volunteering to read sentences, Dana Christine was looking down at her lap as if to avoid eye contact with her teacher. The next exercise was a spelling assignment. Dana Christine worked diligently and appropriately on the assignment, asking no questions of her teacher (many children did ask questions). Afterward, the teacher asked questions about the exercise, but once again Dana Christine did not participate; she raised her hand once, but quickly pulled it down. Overall, she was quiet, attentive, and well behaved.

Dana Christine's teacher said, in an interview, that her "main concern with Dana Christine in the classroom is the speed at which she works." She describes Dana Christine as "a slow and cautious worker who gets overwhelmed by her work as it accumulates due to this slow work style." Dana Christine also has problems with Language Arts. She can "tackle reading but it takes her longer than it should, and she has difficulty with vocabulary, being unable to read some words, such as 'calm,' that other children in her class read easily." Dana Christine is so cautious and conscientious that it is hindering her performance. Her teacher noted that Dana Christine is good at math, "but any subject area that has complicated directions gives her trouble, whether the directions are written or given orally. If the directions call for a series of things to do, Dana Christine will become confused, and at the first sign of a problem she will go to the teacher for help. She also lacks in class participation." Her teacher believes that often "Dana Christine will know the right answer but will not share it if she is uncertain." Her peer relations are seen as normal, and her teacher described Dana Christine as "very sweet and a pleasure to have in the classroom."

Dana Christine's educational therapist, who has been working with her 1½ hours a week for the past 2 months, says: "Dana Christine is experiencing a processing problem, particularly in the area of auditory processing. Her writing is very slow, cautious, and careful. She may be feeling pressure at home not to make mistakes. Sometimes she will make perseverative behaviors like repetitive foot tapping, and her tongue sometimes goes back and forth in her mouth repetitively. Dana Christine is a doll to work with."

Appearance and Behavioral Characteristics

Dana Christine is an attractive, thin white girl with brown hair. She was neatly groomed and casually dressed, and appeared eager to attempt different tasks during the testing. She put forth much effort. At first, Dana Christine was soft spoken and shy, but shortly thereafter she became more open and interactive with the examiners. Even after several testing sessions, Dana Christine was on task, saying her responses with much emphasis, and had a jovial affect, laughing and smiling. Many times during the testing, Dana Christine had to have items repeated because she did not understand them, reflecting the auditory processing difficulties indicated by her educational therapist.

At times, she impulsively answered questions before she felt ready, and usually self-corrected her response with much reflectivity and indecisiveness. In general, Dana Christine was not spontaneous in her responses; she appeared to think through all alternatives before responding. Although described by her teacher as a nonrisk taker, Dana Christine would attempt every item presented to her and ventured a guess on all but the most difficult items for her, even if it took a relatively long time to respond. Although her tone of voice dropped when she was not sure of an item, she still continued to guess.

In addition, Dana Christine performed better and quicker when she used a gestalt or sense of what the entire task entailed, than when she used a trial-and-error approach. For example, when she understood a task such as phonetically sounding out words, she would begin to respond quickly and use sight vocabulary. On the other hand, when verbal tasks became more difficult Dana Christine would focus on parts of the answer in a trial-and-error fashion and not integrate the information holistically. In mathematics, Dana Christine applied an apparent holistic strategy to solve problems by regrouping numbers. She performed worst on items where she had to write out the problem and calculate the answer step-by-step as opposed to deriving the answer in her head, logically by deduction.

Throughout the testing, Dana Christine did not know or could not remember many names of objects or words that she wanted to use, which in turn caused her to speak using circumlocution. She had a difficult time labeling things, although she did demonstrate understanding of the object by explaining its use or purpose. On a task in which Dana Christine had to identify missing parts of pictures, she could not produce the label "hinge," but she pointed to it on the door of the examination room. Later in the testing session, another question arose regarding the word "hinge" and again she could not name it but explained its function. Another instance of this dysnomia was when she could not think of the word "stove," but described it as "something you cook on that is square and has four round things on it for pots."

In general, Dana Christine was very inquisitive and was able to concentrate for long periods. Her stamina and motivation to succeed on tasks were both assets for her during testing. Although she appeared inattentive at times, especially on first presentation of items that had to be repeated, she continued to persevere and undertake the task at hand. Dana Christine felt free to ask for clarification and structure when needed.

Tests Administered

Wechsler Intelligence Scale for Children—Third Edition (WISC-III)

Kaufman Assessment Battery for Children (K-ABC)

Kaufman Test of Educational Achievement (K-TEA)
   Comprehensive Form

Woodcock-Johnson Psycho-Educational Battery—Revised (WJ-R)
   Tests of Cognitive Ability (Selected subtests)
   Tests of Achievement (Selected subtests)

Test Results and Interpretation

On the WISC-III, Dana Christine earned a Verbal IQ of 122, a Performance IQ of 125, and a Full Scale IQ of 125, all of which classify her intelligence as Superior and rank her at approximately the 95th percentile when compared with other 8-year-olds. The chances are 9 out of 10 that her true Full Scale IQ is within the range from 119 to 129. The separate Indexes on the four WISC-III factors were likewise consistent, ranging from 119 on Processing Speed to 125 on Verbal Comprehension. Global scores on other tests also clustered in the 120s: K-ABC Mental Processing Composite (IQ equivalent) of 124, Woodcock-Johnson-Revised (WJ-R) Auditory Processing standard score of 123, WJ-R Basic Reading Skills standard score of 124, and Kaufman Test of Educational Achievement (K-TEA) Battery Composite of 120. All these scores have bands of error (90% confidence) of about ±3 to ±7 points.

Dana Christine's global scores suggest a child with consistently superior intellect and achievement; even the IQ of 119 reported for her on the group-administered Otis-Lennon School Ability Test agrees with the present results. Yet consistent functioning is precisely the opposite of what a more complete profile analysis reveals. Virtually every scale is replete with scatter, so much so that her global scores serve only to mask widely divergent skill areas. Both the Verbal and Performance Scales of the WISC-III yield IQs that cannot be meaningfully interpreted. Her Verbal subtest scores range from the 50th percentile on a test of oral arithmetic to the 99.9th percentile on a verbal reasoning task requiring her to tell how pairs of concepts are alike. That same percentile range (50 to 99.9) characterizes her Performance

profile. She was weakest in arranging pictures to tell a story, and most outstanding in copying abstract designs with blocks.

Extreme scatter was also seen on the K-ABC, WJ-R, and K-TEA. On the
K-ABC, she earned a significantly higher Simultaneous Processing than Sequential Processing standard score (126 vs. 112), suggesting that she performs better when solving problems using an integrated, holistic style than
when solving problems in a step-by-step manner. On the WJ-R, her Auditory Processing subtest scores spanned the huge range of 93 to 139 (33rd to
99.6th percentile), and her component scores on the tests of reading skills
were 113 on decoding nonsense words and 132 on identifying letters and
words. Her K-TEA global score included standard scores as diverse as 98 on
Spelling and 133 on Reading Comprehension.

Certain consistencies are evident in Dana Christine's peaks and valleys
on the various measures. She is astonishingly strong on tests of fluid thinking—the ability to solve novel problems—especially when these tasks involve abstract symbols, designs, or verbal concepts, and demand little verbal
mediation. She surpassed 999 out of 1,000 children her age on some fluid
tasks of this sort, such as two WISC-III subtests mentioned previously
(copying abstract designs and relating two verbal concepts). She also excelled on two K-ABC tests of "fluid" thinking, one similar to the design
copying task, and the other requiring Dana Christine to solve abstract analogies. In contrast to her Very Superior fluid ability with abstractions is her
Average ability when solving problems involving people and things. She performed at the 50th to 75th percentile on the WISC-III subtests of finding
the missing part in incomplete pictures and arranging pictures to tell a
story, and on two K-ABC subtests, one measuring visual closure, the other
requiring her to sequence photographs chronologically. Dana Christine was
also Average in her ability to solve problems assessing school-related skills,
scoring at the 63rd percentile on a combination of three subtests of acquired
knowledge (general information, oral arithmetic, oral vocabulary). This
relative weakness in "crystallized" thinking was also evident on a WJ-R test
of picture vocabulary (61st percentile), on a K-ABC subtest of solving verbal riddles (73rd percentile), and especially on a K-ABC task of general information requiring the identification of famous people and places (13th
percentile).

The dysnomia that Dana Christine evidenced throughout the evaluation
influenced her scores on the tests of acquired knowledge. Her inability to
retrieve common words undoubtedly lowered her scores on the tests of
factual information and vocabulary. Her store of facts and verbal concepts
is far greater than she is able to articulate. She also had difficulty using
language as a mediating process to solve problems, performing remarkably
better when she is able to rely on visual-spatial clues and relationships.
She was able to repeat 7 digits forward and 5 digits backward on the
WISC-III, unusually long spans that occur in only 15% of children age 8.
Repeating digits forward does not demand verbal mediation, and research
has shown that repeating digits backward depends on spatial visualization,

Dana Christine's strength. Also, she was observed to use her fingers as a mnemonic while repeating digits. In contrast to her excellent digit repetition (99th percentile on WISC-III and 99th percentile on the K-ABC), Dana Christine was weak when trying to copy a series of hand movements performed by the examiner on a K-ABC task (37th percentile). Though the latter task is facilitated by good visualization, it is also dependent on verbal mediation to code the movements. She was observed to move her lips in an attempt to code the movements as numbers, but she did not use this technique successfully.

Dana Christine evidenced her reported auditory processing problems during the evaluation, and this problem area was supported by a relatively weak score (33rd percentile) on the WJ-R subtest that required her to identify incomplete words presented on cassette (e.g., identifying "chicken" from "chih-en"). She has an outstanding auditory skill in her ability to connect spoken syllables and phonemes to form a word, but the auditory deficiency that she does have makes it difficult for her to understand long or complex directions spoken by her teacher. She had that difficulty during a sequential K-ABC subtest (Word Order), failing to comprehend a long set of instructions, and frequently asked questions or gave other indications that she did not understand verbal directions to tests. Just as Dana Christine had extreme difficulty with the test of incomplete words, she seems to have difficulty understanding a series of words; in both instances of auditory processing, she cannot take sufficient advantage of the redundancies of the English language.

Previously, it was indicated that Dana Christine performed better on the K-ABC Simultaneous than Sequential Processing Scale, and some problems were noted for her in step-by-step problem solving. However, her exceptional sequential memory for digits, and her high score on the WJ-R auditory subtest that required her to link phonemes presented sequentially, indicate no apparent deficit in sequential ability. Her relatively low Sequential Processing score is in part a function of her verbal mediation problem (Hand Movements) and her auditory processing difficulties (Word Order). Therefore, she does not seem to have a true sequential deficit.

The combination of her apparent dysnomia, auditory processing problem, and verbal mediation difficulty are likely to affect her school achievement in subtle ways and will not affect all areas equally. Consequently, she evidenced scatter in her pattern of achievement scores. Within the reading domain, Dana Christine displayed much better comprehension skills (standard score of 133 on K-TEA) than decoding abilities (116 on K-TEA decoding, 113 on WJ-R Word Attack). And, on the K-TEA, her spelling ability (45th percentile) is significantly lower than her overall mathematics skill (88th percentile) or reading ability (91st percentile).

Dana Christine's Processing Speed standard score of 119 (90th percentile) indicates that she is above average on measures of how quickly she can perform simple mental and motor operations. When the problems are complex, however, she performs at an extremely slow rate, reflecting carefully before giving her final response. The more complex the problem, such as when sequencing photographs on the K-ABC task, the more extreme her slow problem solving. Again, however, her slowness is most apparent when some verbal mediation is essential for success. As speed becomes a more important variable in school, this slowness is likely to become more of a problem. Her reflective style did not penalize her unduly on the WISC-III nonverbal tasks because at age 8 the emphasis is on getting the problems correct; at age 10 or 11, however, speed of responding assumes a much larger role on the WISC-III, and her scores would suffer in the future if she doesn't improve her problem-solving speed.

She was also very slow in answering items on the measures of academic achievement that were administered. Slow responding is not penalized on these individually administered achievement tests, but it is often not tolerated in the classroom. Her reading decoding scores of about 115 indicate above-average ability and her comprehension score of 133 reflects very superior skill; both denote reading ability that is above grade level, in contrast to the below-grade-level achievement that has been reported for her. As with her inability to communicate her knowledge base effectively, she has much better reading ability than she is able to demonstrate. Because Dana Christine's difficulties are very visible (auditory processing, verbal communication, slowness), and her areas of brilliance (visual-spatial problem solving) are not visible, Dana Christine will not appear to be nearly as bright as she is. Once her teachers get to know her better, as the school year progresses, they undoubtedly become more aware of her cognitive strengths as well as her behavioral assets such as perseverance and self-motivation.

With the exception of her scores on the K-ABC subtest of identifying famous people and places, and the one WJ-R auditory processing task, Dana Christine's weaknesses are still about average compared with other 8-year-olds, and are only weak relative to her own very high abilities. The fact that she is able to achieve so well in school is a tribute to her high intelligence and her ability to self-compensate for her weaknesses. But even with these positive attributes, her problem areas prevent her from communicating much of the information that she has learned, from comprehending some of the information taught in school (especially when it is presented orally without accompanying diagrams), when solving problems that depend on verbal mediation rather than visualization and nonverbal reasoning, and when required to work quickly.

Her specific weak areas that occurred both in spelling and reading decoding concerned prefixes and word beginnings, suffixes and word endings, closed syllable vowels, vowel digraphs and diphthongs, and consonant clusters and digraphs. She also had a notable reading decoding weakness in open syllable and final *e* pattern vowels. A guide to explain and illustrate these weak areas will be sent to her current teacher and educational therapist. Also to be sent are suggested teaching guidelines for spelling and reading decoding that will enable Dana Christine to capitalize on her strengths in visual- spatial, abstract problem solving.

Summary and Diagnostic Impressions

Dana Christine is an 8-year-old girl who was referred to the clinic for evaluation after school reports suggested that she is having specific difficulties with reading, writing, and spelling. She also has had difficulty finishing classroom tasks on time and has demonstrated some confusion in following her teacher's instructions. The purpose of the current evaluation is to determine the nature of her academic problems, to define her cognitive strengths and weaknesses, and to determine what classroom modifications will assist her in working to her potential academically.

Dana Christine presented initially as soft spoken and shy, but soon became more open and interactive with the examiners. She was very inquisitive and was able to concentrate for long periods. Her performance during testing indicated that she has a hard time understanding verbal directions as she asked for clarification on many test items. She also took a long time to answer questions when there were no time limits, although she often answered correctly on these occasions. Throughout testing, she demonstrated an expressive language difficulty, where she obviously had understanding of concepts, but was unable to name objects. She performed better when she was able to use a holistic approach to answer questions versus a trial-and-error strategy of problem solving.

Although Dana Christine's global scores suggest a child with consistently superior intellect and achievement, a complete profile analysis revealed much scatter in her performance and widely divergent skill areas. Significant scatter was found within her achievement scores. Within the reading domain, she displayed much better comprehension skills (superior range) than decoding skills (above-average range). Her average spelling ability was significantly lower than her above-average to superior mathematics and reading skills. She had difficulty using language as a mediating process to solve problems, performing significantly better when she was able to rely on visual clues and relationships. Her performance on tests of acquired knowledge was influenced by her dysnomia. She has difficulty retrieving common words, although her store of facts and verbal concepts is far greater than she is able to articulate.

Dana Christine displayed some outstanding auditory skills, while she also evidenced auditory processing problems during the evaluation. The auditory processing deficiency that she does have makes it difficult for her to understand long or complex directions spoken by her teacher or others. She performed better when she was able to ask questions to clarify instructions. She also worked extremely slowly on complex problems, with her slowness most apparent when some verbal mediation was essential for success.

The combination of her apparent dysnomia, auditory processing problem, and verbal mediation difficulty undoubtedly affect her school achievement. Hence, her display of strengths and weaknesses in different achievement areas. Her high achievement scores found in this evaluation speak to her high intelligence and her ability to compensate for her weaknesses. These abilities, along with her perseverance and self-motivation will help her overcome her current difficulties.

Recommendations

1. When Dana Christine uses phonics to sound out words, her reading appears to be at the same rate or faster than her regular schoolage peers, but she makes many sound substitution errors when reading. She performs better when she slows down her reading and relies on *whole word* sight vocabulary to pronounce words than when she uses sound cues from the *first letter* of the word, and then immediately says the whole word. What Dana Christine does is guess what the word sounds like. This approach may be more effective if an attempt is made to improve her reliability of guessing the correct word, by using context/visual cues to aid her. Furthermore, Dana Christine will probably benefit most from using and building her sight word vocabulary along with contextually based materials.

2. In order to augment Dana Christine's learning, she should be encouraged to be more independent by taking risks when she does not have all the information or know for sure when she is right or wrong. She can practice guessing when she is unsure but can make a reasonable attempt to figure out the answer. Another benefit is that she might increase the speed with which she works out problems mentally, becoming more time efficient.

3. Both Dana Christine's teacher and educational therapist may find themselves altering their specific methodology now that these subtle learning problems and their effects are documented. Both professionals have worked hard to individualize material to enhance Dana Christine's learning capacity. Viewed in light of this evaluation's findings, Dana Christine's need to look up words in the dictionary, for example, may no longer be seen as behavior of an overly conscientious or cautious child, but as a sign of her language difficulty. One thing, specifically, that can be instituted immediately in the classroom is for Dana Christine to be encouraged to participate in class by nonverbal means. Instead of raising her hand and being called on to explain verbally her thinking or observations, Dana Christine might have other means of communication creatively tried out. Tests of Dana Christine's acquired knowledge might also include more visual-spatial exercises or other nonverbal modes of assessment.

4. It is recommended that Dana Christine be taken to a Speech and Language facility where she can receive language therapy. Individual sessions that concentrate on verbal expression and verbal labeling, as well as auditory receptive language development, will help Dana Christine fill in some of the missing gaps and cut down on the inevitable frustration that a girl as bright as she undoubtedly experiences, especially in school.

Examiners: Jose Gonzalez, MA; Paul Randolph, MA

School Visit: Danica Katz, BA

Supervisor: Dr. Nadeen Kaufman

Greg T., Age 9-7, Behavior and Learning Problems

WISC-III Profile

IQs		(90% conf.)	Factor Indexes		(90% conf.)
Verbal	100	(95–105)	Verbal Comprehension	102	(96–108)
Performance	69	(65–79)	Perceptual Organization	65	(61–76)
Full Scale	83	(79–88)	Freedom from Distractibility	81	(76–91)
V-IQ > P-IQ ($p < .01$)			Processing Speed	86	(80–96)

Verbal	Scaled Score	Performance	Scaled Score
Information	11	Picture Completion	2
Similarities	9	(Coding)	(6)
Arithmetic	9	Picture Arrangement	7
Vocabulary	9	Block Design	5
Comprehension	12	Object Assembly	2
(Digit Span)	(4)-W	*Symbol Search	8

* Symbol Search was used in IQ computations

Mean of 6 Verbal subtests = 9   Mean of 6 Performance subtests = 5

Differential Ability Scales (Nonverbal Reasoning Scale)

Subtest	T Score ($\pm$ SEm) (mean = 50)	Percentile
Sequential & Quantitative Reasoning	53±4	62

Woodcock-Johnson Psycho-Educational Battery (Fluid Reasoning Subtests)

Subtest/Cluster	Standard Score ($\pm$ SEm)	Percentile
7. Analysis-Synthesis	99±5	47
14. Concept Formation	94±4	33
19. Spatial Relations	84±7	14
Fluid Reasoning (Tests 7 & 14)	96±4	40

Kaufman Test of Educational Achievement—Comprehensive Form (K-TEA)

Subtest/Composite	Standard Score ($\pm$ 90% conf.)	Grade Equiv.
Mathematics Composite	102±5	3-8
Mathematics Computation	121±6	4-9
Mathematics Applications	89±7	2-7
Reading Composite	82±4	2-2
Reading Decoding	81±4	2-1
Reading Comprehension	84±6	2-4
Spelling	105±5	4-4
Battery Composite	93±3	3-2

Referral and Background Information

Greg is a 9½-year-old white male who is tall for his age. He was referred for testing by his father following complaints by Greg's teacher that he was having difficulty in reading. Specifically, the teacher felt that Greg was having problems with reading comprehension because he did not seem to remember what he had read. However, Greg's father also described a number of other problems that Greg is having, which are troubling to him and to the school.

A fourth grader, Greg is described as being inattentive in school, staring off into space, being easily distracted, and fidgeting. His grades have declined steadily since the second grade to the point that he currently has a C average. He is also beginning to dislike school. At home, his father has noticed that Greg rushes through his schoolwork. His teacher agrees with Mr. T.'s observation, stating that Greg goes through his work quickly and with little attention to quality. Prior school records also describe Greg as being "impulsive." Two years ago, a school evaluation was performed on Greg which concluded that he becomes so anxious regarding math that he often just "tunes out and gives up on himself."

Greg is described by himself and his father as having few friends, being teased and beaten by peers, and feeling that other kids do not like him. At home he is described as being too aggressive with his three younger sisters and toddler brother, and as responding to discipline by repeating his bad behavior and not talking about his feelings. He is reported to scream at relatives and have tantrums when asked to do things or when he does not get what he wants. When Greg has a tantrum, he whines, hits objects, cries, stomps his feet, threatens to hit or kill his father, tells his father that he hates him, and insists that his father does not love him.

The product of an uncomplicated full-term pregnancy and delivery, Greg walked at 12 to 13 months, was toilet trained by 2½ years, and achieved most developmental milestones within normal limits. His speech was significantly delayed, and appeared at age 2½ only after he was engaged in speech therapy. He continues to have difficulty with the enunciation of S, K, and R, and remains in speech therapy twice weekly. His father reports that speech difficulties are found in both his and his wife's families. Greg's vision and hearing were tested shortly before the evaluation, and were found to be within normal limits. His father also reports that he feels Greg is clumsy. Greg has a congenital "nonessential hand tremor" for which he sees a neurologist. Greg takes 60 mg Inderal per day for this condition.

Greg is the oldest of five children born to his parents. He has twin sisters who are 8, a sister who is 5, and a brother who is almost 2. He lives with his parents and siblings. His mother is a nurse, who works from 11:00 P.M. to 7 A.M., and who sleeps during the daytime. A change from a conventional shift to a nighttime shift occurred 7 months ago and is likely to continue for at least 2 more years. Greg's father quit his semiskilled job in a factory to remain at home with the children. Greg is described as being closest to his mother, but as having good relationships with all family members. Greg and his twin sisters all have chores at home in addition to their schoolwork, but the sisters generally work slowly and Greg does most of the work for the three of them. In fact, his father reports that Greg does 99% of the housework. His chores include sweeping, picking things up, watching his siblings, and occasionally fixing a microwave dinner for them. Discipline techniques focus on sending Greg to his room or occasionally giving him spankings. He is rewarded by being given sweets, or by being allowed to ride his bike or play with his peers before doing chores.

Appearance and Behavioral Characteristics

Greg stands about 4 feet 10 inches tall and weighs about 100 pounds. He was disheveled and hastily dressed for the testing sessions. His forearms were bruised, which he claimed was from playing football. He appeared lethargic during all three testing sessions. His affect was blunted, and at times sad. He was cooperative during the testing procedures. His speech was marked by his inability to say the letter "R" and a slight hesitation before saying some words. These difficulties gave an air of immaturity to his speech. Despite his dull affect and lethargy, Greg was quite talkative during the testing sessions and appeared eager for adult attention.

Greg labeled some ambiguous items as familiar things in order to enable himself to respond more accurately to the item. For instance, he labeled a puzzle of a ball a "pizza" as a means of representing its roundness. He had great difficulty in putting puzzle pieces together but seemed to have no awareness of the poverty of his performance. In fact, he stated that he was "good at putting puzzle pieces together."

Greg seemed to enjoy putting blocks together to copy an abstract design but was again unable to put them together correctly. He evidenced numerous instances of visual-perceptual difficulties. When items became difficult, Greg seemed to stop analyzing them and consequently lost the 2×2 or 3×3 shape of several block designs. He completely lost the shape of a face puzzle. In essence, he was unable to make use of the concreteness of the things that the puzzles represented (e.g., a horse, a face). Instead of analyzing and reasoning, Greg used a haphazard trial-and-error approach that ultimately ended in frustration for Greg and failure on certain items that had time limits.

Greg's speed of working varied widely. When performing tasks he reported enjoying, he studied the task, reflected on his work, took his time, and showed active involvement. On a spelling test that he enjoyed, for example, Greg made up his own sentences, after listening to the examiner's sentences, even though that was not a requirement of the task. When working on other tasks that he seemed to know were more difficult for him, such as reading or solving verbal math problems, he worked more quickly and appeared not to be invested in his performance. This attempt to avoid failure by avoiding situations in which he might fail is Greg's style of handling problem areas. The lack of investment and effort appear to be Greg's characteristic way of handling repeated failure.

During an observation of Greg in school, a member of the clinic staff reported seeing Greg fidget, eat paper, and attempt to get attention from his peers through a variety of means. The staff member also noted that Greg's overtures toward his peers were rejected either by being ignored or by a verbal rebuff (e.g., "how gross"). Greg's teacher reported seeing Greg engage in a variety of inappropriate behaviors in the classroom, such as picking his nose. Greg frequently opts to stay in at lunchtime with his teacher, thereby avoiding peer contact. Greg's teacher has recently become so concerned by his isolation from his peers that he started a "friendship group" that included Greg and some of the children who tease him; the teacher's goal was to try and change the class's perception of Greg. Greg was observed during this group as they watched a film on self-esteem. After the film was over, Greg reported to the group that he has low self-esteem sometimes.

Tests Administered

Wechsler Intelligence Scale for Children—Third Edition (WISC-III)

Kaufman Test of Educational Achievement (K-TEA)
   Comprehensive Form

Differential Ability Scales (DAS) (Sequential & Quantitative Reasoning subtest)

Woodcock-Johnson Psycho-Educational Battery (3 Fluid Reasoning subtests)

Projective Drawings

Bender-Gestalt Test of Visual-Motor Development (Bender-Gestalt)

Thematic Apperception Test (TAT)

Rorschach Inkblot Test (Rorschach)

Sentence Completion

Test Results and Interpretation

On the WISC-III, Greg obtained a striking 31-point difference between his Average Verbal IQ of 100 and the Intellectually Deficient to Borderline level of functioning indicated by his Performance IQ of 69. These discrepant scores render his Low Average Full Scale IQ of 83 meaningless as an estimate of his ability, reflecting nothing more than a midpoint of several diverse skill areas. Greg's variable cognitive functioning was further revealed by his profile of Factor Indexes on the WISC-III. Within the Verbal domain, he performed significantly higher on the Verbal Comprehension (VC) Index (55th percentile) than on the Freedom from Distractibility Index (10th percentile). The latter score was primarily a function of very poor performance (9th percentile) on a supplementary test of digit repetition, resulting from either a weak auditory memory or from the concentration problems that occasionally surfaced during the evaluation. Otherwise, he performed with extreme consistency on the five subtests that contribute to the Verbal IQ, evidencing average ability in verbal concept formation, number ability, verbal reasoning, and long-term memory.

Within the Performance domain, Greg's Processing Speed index (18th percentile) was significantly higher than his Perceptual Organization (PO) Index (1st percentile). His speed of processing information, especially when faced with problems of minimal complexity, was far superior to his visual-spatial and visual-motor skills. The latter set of abilities revealed an Intellectually Deficient level of functioning on tasks that are presumed to measure the ability to reason with visual stimuli and solve nonverbal problems, and that depend on intact visual perception and coordination. His worst performance in this area was on tasks that require spatial ability for success, and he was especially weak (well below 1st percentile) on tests of holistic processing (assembling cut-up puzzles, finding the missing parts of pictures), a style of thinking associated with the right cerebral hemisphere.

Because of the scatter within both the Verbal and Performance Scales, the best estimates of his verbal and nonverbal abilities are provided by his VC Index of 102 and his PO Index of 65, respectively. That 37-point difference is quite unusual within the normal population, occurring in less than 1% of children and adolescents.

Greg's weaknesses were on tests that required answers based on his visual perceptions. Essentially, Greg is adept at verbal comprehension but has difficulty understanding and organizing his visual perceptions; he also has some difficulty in concentration, which would make it even more difficult for Greg to analyze what he perceives. Greg has learned to compensate for this problem to some extent by translating what he perceives in ways that are meaningful for him. For example, he called a triangular shape on the Bender-Gestalt a slice of pizza and a round puzzle on the WISC-III a pizza pie. He also does not process information as fast as most other children his age. Even though his Processing Speed Index was notably higher than his PO index, it was below average for 9-year-olds, and not commensurate with the Average level of ability that he displays on verbal tasks. Greg needs more time than most agemates to absorb and understand new information, which makes his rushing through his work even more problematic. He needs to spend time reviewing his work and the things he has recently learned.

Greg's problems in visual perception were evident while he was solving nonverbal items (e.g., he lost the "squareness" of the block designs he tried to copy) and were also revealed on other tests. On the Bender-Gestalt, a test of visual-motor development, Greg scored at the level expected of a 6–6½-year-old, based on the Koppitz scoring system. On the WISC-III Coding subtest, he referred to a symbol he had to copy as a "T," even though it was lying on its side; several rotations of other symbols were noted in Greg's attempts to copy the Coding symbols. Greg's perceptual problems account for some of the difficulties that his teacher and father have noticed, such as being clumsy and having problems in reading. Greg may find reading difficult in part because it requires perceptual distinctions.

Because the WISC-III Performance Scale is heavily dependent on visual perception, coordination, and speed, Greg's low P-IQ and PO Index were conceivably a result of his impairments and not indicative of poor nonverbal reasoning. To assess his nonverbal abilities more fairly, four additional subtests were administered that assess nonverbal reasoning and the ability to solve novel problems; none of these tasks places much emphasis on coordination or speed, and only one demands excellent visual-perceptual ability. He performed in the Average range on the WJ-R Fluid Reasoning Scale (standard score of 96, surpassing 40% of 9-year-olds) and scored about equally well on the two subtests that form the cluster: 47th percentile on the Analysis-Synthesis subtest, which measures the ability to apply logical rules, depicted pictorially, to new problems; and 33rd percentile on Concept Formation, which assesses the ability to categorize abstract shapes. On the DAS Sequential & Quantitative Reasoning subtest (which is included in the DAS Nonverbal Reasoning Composite and measures a child's understanding of number relationships), Greg also scored in the Average range (62nd percentile).

These supplementary test results indicate that Greg's nonverbal reasoning and thinking abilities were not adequately tapped by the WISC-III Performance Scale. His fluid and nonverbal reasoning skills are at an Average level, wholly consistent with his verbal abilities. The one additional reasoning test administered, WJ-R Spatial Relations, requires the child to visualize how abstract figures would look if they were combined. This task stresses visual-perceptual ability, but neither speed nor coordination is a factor. Greg performed worse on this subtest (14th percentile) than on the other reasoning tasks, but he performed much better on that visual-spatial subtest than he did on the WISC-III Performance subtests. It seems that Greg's greatest difficulty is solving spatial problems that require integration of visual perception, fine-motor coordination, and response speed.

The reading problem reported for Greg was documented by his score on the K-TEA Reading Composite (12th percentile), as he displayed about equal weakness in decoding words as in comprehension. Currently in the third month of fourth grade, Greg's reading corresponds to a grade equivalent of 2-2. In the Reading Comprehension subtest, he read the paragraphs aloud rather quickly and made errors. For instance, he would trip over words, skip words, and on one occasion added a word. Directly after reading a paragraph, he was asked to answer questions about it, and then proceed to the next paragraph. When he was uncertain of the answers, he did not appear to go back over the paragraph to find the answer. As the paragraphs became harder, he appeared to become so caught up in the chore of reading aloud that he did not pay attention to the content of what he was saying. The K-TEA error analysis indicated significant weakness in answering both literal and inferential questions. In the Reading Decoding subtest, weaknesses were observed in the following categories: suffixes and word endings, closed syllable (short) vowels, vowel digraphs and diphthongs, and single and double consonants.

On the mathematics portion of the K-TEA, Greg performed exceptionally well on Mathematics Computation (92nd percentile), much better than he performed on Mathematics Applications (23rd percentile). His grade equivalent in computation was 4-9 compared to 2-7 in his ability to apply the computations to verbal-numerical problems. He had special difficulty on math applications with elementary number concepts, and with problems requiring addition, subtraction, and multiplication. His low score in this area may not reflect a true deficit, however, because of the lack of motivation that was observed, perhaps due to anxiety or frustration. A similar "tuning out" in response to anxiety over math was reported in a school evaluation 2 years ago. His math ability is not seen as a learning problem, and Greg performed at an Average level on Spelling (63rd percentile, 4-4 grade equivalent).

Greg's responses on the personality assessment instruments bear out the results of the cognitive and academic evaluations, the clinical observations of his behavior, and the background information provided by his father and teacher. His Rorschach responses are typical of someone who is giving overly simplistic or economical answers. He appears reluctant to approach the complexities of his environment. Instead he preserves his resources. His approach to the world is affectively guarded and withdrawn. His simplistic approach pares down the amount of complexity and emotional responsiveness the environment evokes in him. This style of perceiving can often lead to difficulties, in that the perceiver will not notice things about his social environment that others would, and thus will fail to act appropriately. This perceptual style is the emotional equivalent of the visual difficulties noted on intellectual and academic testing, and may be physiologically based.

Two factors seem to relate to Greg's style of approaching the world. The first is Greg's trial-and-error approach to problem solving. He approaches each new situation or problem as totally new, and so does not profit from experience. He sees things differently from most people and will often have a difficult time of learning by watching others. He needs all his cognitive resources to cope with each new situation.

The second factor that relates to his simplistic responses is his need to defend himself against pain, as he does academically by rushing through work and by giving up. Some of Greg's responses tie in with this tendency, in that they represent a sense of frustration with interpersonal relationships, and of isolation from others. That is, when Greg becomes unhappy about his relationships or a social situation, he withdraws. Unfortunately, Greg often would prefer to get his needs met through interacting with others, so withdrawing only makes him more unhappy. Some of Greg's TAT stories and sentence completions had to do with relationships. He does not know how to get positive attention from peers, so he engages in odd or inappropriate behavior to interact with them.

Greg craves attention from both adults and peers. This dynamic was seen in his Rorschach response. Greg was resistant to doing the test, and attempted to refuse the first two cards. However, he ended up giving more than the normal number of responses, likely in an attempt to please the examiner. His staying in at lunchtime can be viewed similarly: Greg gets positive attention from his teacher and avoids rejection from his peers. He does not get all the attention he wants from his family either. Greg seems to feel that, in the absence of his mother, he and his twin sisters are the strong, capable family members. He sees his role as that of an adult, charged with cleaning, watching the children, and making certain things in the household run smoothly. He may become resentful of these chores and is overwhelmed by this role because of the responsibilities it imposes and because of the lack of time alone with his parents.

Greg is also depressed. The Rorschach and other projectives reveal that he has low self-esteem, has a poor image of his body, and is becoming introspective and likely dwelling on his perceived failures or faults. He appears to be very dissatisfied with himself and his life.

Greg tends to defend himself by avoiding, suppressing, and denying the things that bother him. He does these things because he does not know any other way to handle his feelings. He seems to believe that he has a choice between avoiding emotion and exploding with emotion. From time to time, however, his defenses against his feelings fail and Greg experiences intense emotions on which he acts. These emotional behaviors will tend to be impulsive and are likely to be related to anger, because Greg has problems controlling his anger.

At this time, Greg appears to have enough resources to cope with the stresses in his life. He has developed his own ways of handling long-term problems such as his mother being away and his speech difficulties. However, his coping ability would probably decrease with more stress, and he would become overwhelmed. It is important to note that even though Greg does have ways of handling his problems, his solutions are not working well enough for him. For instance, his method of dealing with his poor performance in reading is to not pay attention to reading lessons and tasks. Whereas that response helps him handle the anxiety and low self-esteem related to failure, it does not help him learn to read.

Diagnostic Impression

Greg is experiencing a long-term problem in speech of sufficient severity to warrant treatment, which the school is providing. He also has visual-perceptual problems and low scores on reading achievement. The latter scores are especially noteworthy when compared with his Verbal IQ or VC index. Thus, Greg seems to have learning disabilities in two areas, articulation and reading (DSM-III-R: 315.00 and 315.39).

Additionally, Greg is mildly depressed. He complains of low self-esteem, which is borne out by testing. His father reports that he is becoming more irritable; also, he was lethargic during testing and appears to have difficulty concentrating. These symptoms have apparently been present for some time since neither Greg, his father, or his teacher mentioned any recent changes in his mood or behavior. A diagnosis of Dysthymia (DSM-III-R: 300.40, early onset secondary type) best fits this collection of symptoms. His depression is likely secondary to his problems in school, relationship difficulties, and poor social skills. Recent stressors, such as his mother's change to a night shift, along with his increased responsibilities and decreased sense of support in the family, have probably made his depression worse.

Recommendations

1. Begin group psychotherapy to help Greg gain social skills, alleviate his depression, learn the subtle cues people use in interacting, change his maladaptive behaviors, and become more assertive with peers.

2. Involve Greg in a children's group at a local library to increase his interest in reading. This group should present reading as fun rather than as a task that may be failed.

3. Enroll Greg in a big brother program so that he can have some individual time with an adult male role model.

4. Advise his teacher of the severity of Greg's visual-perceptual and visual-motor problems, explaining how these difficulties will affect his academic performance as well as athletic success. A list of suggestions for teaching Greg primarily through auditory or tactile approaches rather than visual—to enable him to take in and understand more information—has been sent to his parents and teacher.

5. Give Greg consistent positive consequences for the quality of his work. That is, to help him take more time in his schoolwork and homework, reward Greg for paying attention to details and checking his work.

6. Advise Greg's parents to attend a parenting class in order to improve their ability to respond to Greg's tantrums and aggressive behavior.

7. When teaching Greg new information, especially abstract information, try to translate the concepts into meaningful, concrete terms. Make the tasks interesting to him. When he enjoys a task, he may display active and creative involvement in it (as when he devised his own original sentences during a spelling test).

8. Urge Greg to spend time reviewing his recent school notes and returned assignments, and reinforce him for doing so.

9. Similarly, use reinforcers to urge Greg to spend time reviewing his homework before handing it in to check for errors and messiness.

Examiners: Susan Glatz, MS; Patricia Petterson, MA
Consultant for projective test interpretation:
   Dr. Dana T. Grossman
Supervisor to Ms. Glatz and Ms. Petterson:
   Dr. Nadeen L. Kaufman

References

Abrahams, R. D. (1973). The advantages of Black English. In J. S. De Stephano (Ed.), *Language, society, and education: A profile of Black English*. Worthington, OH: Charles A. Jones.

Allen, M. H., Lincoln, A. J., & Kaufman, A. S. (1991). Sequential and simultaneous processing abilities of high-functioning autistic and language-impaired children. *Journal of Autism and Developmental Disorders, 21,* 483–502.

Allison, J., Blatt, S. J., & Zimet, C. N. (1968). *The interpretation of psychological tests*. New York: Harper & Row.

Anastasi, A. (1988). *Psychological testing* (6th ed.). New York: Macmillan.

Anderson, P. L., Cronin, M. E., & Kazmierski, S. (1989). WISC-R stability and re-evaluation of learning-disabled students. *Journal of Clinical Psychology, 45,* 941–944.

Anderson, S. W., Routh, D. K., & Ionasescu, V. V. (1988). Serial position memory of boys with Duchenne muscular dystrophy. *Developmental Medicine and Child Neurology, 30,* 328–333.

Andrew, J. M. (1974). Delinquency, the Wechsler P > V sign, and the I-level system. *Journal of Clinical Psychology, 30,* 331–335.

Andrews, T. J., & Naglieri, J. A. (1994). Aptitude treatment interactions (ATI) reconsidered. *Communique, 22* (6), 8–9.

Aram, D. M., & Ekelman, B. L. (1986). Cognitive profiles of children with early onset unilateral lesions. *Developmental Neuropsychology, 2,* 155–172.

Arter, J. A., & Jenkins, J. R. (1979). Differential diagnosis—prescriptive teaching: A critical appraisal. *Review of Educational Research, 49,* 517–555.

Arthur, G. (1947). *A point scale of performance: Revised form II: Manual for administering and scoring the tests*. San Antonio, TX: Psychological Corporation.

Asarnow, R. F., Tanguay, P. E., Bott, L., & Freeman, B. J. (1987). Patterns of intellectual functioning in non-retarded autism and schizophrenic children. *Journal of Child Psychology and Psychiatry, 28,* 273–280.

Asbury, C. A., Knuckle, E. P., & Adderly-Kelly, B. (1987). Effectiveness of selected neuropsychological and sociocultural measures for predicting WISC-R discrepancy group membership. *Educational and Psychological Research, 7,* 47–59.

Asbury, C. A., Stokes, A., Adderly-Kelly, B., & Knuckle, E. P. (1989). Effectiveness of selected neuropsychological, academic, and sociocultural measures for predicting Bannatyne categories in black Americans. *Journal of Negro Education, 58,* 177–188.

Ayres, R. R., & Cooley, E. J. (1986). Sequential versus simultaneous processing on the K-ABC: Validity in predicting learning success. *Journal of Psychoeducational Assessment, 4,* 211–220.

Bannatyne, A. (1971). Language, reading, and learning disabilities. Springfield, IL: Charles C. Thomas.

Bannatyne, A. (1974). Diagnosis: A note on recategorization of the WISC scaled scores. *Journal of Learning Disabilities, 7,* 272–274.

Baratz, J. C. (1970). Teaching reading in an urban Negro school system. In F. Williams (Ed.), *Language and poverty* (pp. 11–22). Chicago, IL: Markham.

Barkley, R. A., DuPaul, G. J., & McMurray, M. B. (1990). A comprehensive evaluation of attention deficit disorder with and without hyperactivity defined by research criteria. *Journal of Consulting and Clinical Psychology, 58,* 775–789.

Batsche, G. (1992, March). Scholl psychology and assessment: A future together? *Communique,* p. 2.

Bauman, R. (1971). An ethnographic framework for the investigation of communicative behaviors. *ASHA, 13,* 334–340.

Baumeister, A. A., & Bartlett, C. J. (1962a). A comparison of the factor structure of normals and retardates on the WISC. *American Journal of Mental Deficiency, 66,* 641–646.

Baumeister, A. A., & Bartlett, C. J. (1962b). Further factorial investigation of WISC performance of mental defectives. *American Journal of Mental Deficiency, 67,* 257–261.

Beck, B. L., & Spruill, J. (1987). External validation of the cognitive triad of the Personality Inventory for Children: Cautions on interpretation. *Journal of Consulting and Clinical Psychology, 55,* 441–443.

Berk, R. (1983). The value of WISC-R profile analysis for differential diagnosis of learning disabled children. *Journal of Clinical Psychology, 39,* 133–136.

Bever, T. G. (1975). Cerebral asymmetries in humans are due to the differentiation of two incompatible processes: Holistic and analytic. In D. Aaronson & R. Rieber (Eds.), *Developmental psycholinguistics and communication disorders.* New York: New York Academy of Sciences.

Bice, T. R., Halpin, G., & Halpin, G. (1986). A comparison of the cognitive styles of typical and mildly retarded children with educational recommendations. *Education and Training of the Mentally Retarded, 21,* 93–97.

Black, F. W. (1974). WISC Verbal—Performance discrepancies as indicators of neurological dysfunction in pediatric patients. *Journal of Clinical Psychology, 30,* 165–167.

Black, F. W. (1976). Cognitive, academic, and behavioral findings in children with suspected and documented neurological dysfunction. *Journal of Learning Disabilities, 9,* 182–187.

Bleker, E. G. (1983). Cognitive defense style and WISC-R V > P sign in juvenile recidivists. *Journal of Clinical Psychology, 39,* 1030–1032.

Bloom, A. S., Topinka, C. W., Goulet, M., Reese, A., & Podruch, P. E. (1986). Implications of large WISC/WISC-R verbal-performance IQ discrepancies. *Journal of Clinical Psychology, 42,* 353–357.

Bortner, M., Hertzig, M. E., & Birch, H. G. (1972). Neurological signs and intelligence in brain-damaged children. *Journal of Special Education, 6,* 325–333.

Boyd, T. A., & Hooper, S. R. (1987). Psychometric validity of proration and Digit Span substitution for estimating WISC-R Verbal and Full Scale IQs. *Perceptual and Motor Skills, 65,* 19–25.

Bracken, B. A., & McCallum, R. S. (Eds.). (1993a). *Journal of Psychoeducational Assessment monograph series, advances in psychoeducational assessment: Wechsler Intelligence Scale for Children—Third Edition.* Germantown, TN: Psychoeducational Corporation.

Bracken, B. A., & McCallum, R. S. (Eds.). (1993b). *Journal of Psychoeducational Assessment monograph series, advances in psychoeducational assessment: Woodcock-Johnson Psycho-Educational Battery—Revised.* Germantown, TN: Psychoeducational Corporation.

Bracken, B. A., McCallum, R. S., & Crain, M. (1993). WISC-III subtest composite reliabilities and specificities: Interpretive aids. In B. A. Bracken & R. S. McCallum (Eds.), *Journal of Psychoeducational Assessment monograph series, advances in psychoeducational assessment: Wechsler Intelligence Scale for Children—Third Edition* (pp. 22–34). Germantown, TN: Psychoeducational Corporation.

Braden, J. P. (1985). WISC-R deaf norms reconsidered. *Journal of School Psychology, 23,* 375–382.

Braden, J. P. (1992). The assessment of intelligence in deaf and hard-of-hearing people: A quantitative and qualitative research analysis. *School Psychology Review, 21,* 82–94.

Brandt, E. A. (1984). The cognitive functioning of American Indian children: A critique of McShane and Plas. *School Psychology Review, 13,* 74–82.

Brouwers, P., Riccardi, R., Poplack, D., & Fedio, P. (1984). Attentional deficits in long-term survivors of childhood acute lymphoblastic leukemia (ALL). *Journal of Clinical Neuropsychology, 6,* 325–336.

Brown, L., Sherbenou, R., & Johnsen, S. (1990). *Test of Nonverbal Intelligence—Second Edition.* Austin, TX: PRO-ED.

Brown, S. W., & Yakimowski, M. E. (1987). Intelligence scores of gifted students on the WISC-R. *Gifted Child Quarterly, 31,* 130–134.

Bruininks, R. H. (1978). *Bruininks-Oseretsky Test of Motor Proficiency.* Circle Pines, MN: American Guidance Service.

Budoff, M. (1987). The validity of learning potential assessment. In C. S. Lidz (Ed.), *Dynamic assessment: An interactional approach to evaluating learning potential.* New York: Guilford.

Burgess, A. (1991). Profile analysis of the Wechsler intelligence scales: A new index of subtest scatter. *British Journal of Clinical Psychology, 30,* 257–263.

Buriel, R. (1978). Relationship of three field-dependence measures to the reading and math achievement of Anglo American and Mexican American children. *Journal of Educational Psychology, 70,* 167–174.

Butler-Omololu, C., Doster, J. A., & Lahey, B. (1984). Some implications for intelligence test construction and administration with children of different racial groups. *Journal of Black Psychology, 10,* 63–75.

Byrne, B., & Shea, P. (1979). Semantic and phonetic memory codes in beginning readers. *Memory and Cognition, 7,* 333–338.

Campbell, B., & Wilson, B. J. (1986). An investigation of Kaufman's method for determining scatter on the WISC-R. *Journal of School Psychology, 24,* 373–380.

Carmon, A., & Nachson, I. (1973). Ear asymmetry in perception of emotional non-verbal stimuli. *Acta Psychologica, 37,* 351–357.

Carroll, J. B. (1993a). *Human cognitive abilities: A survey of factor analytic studies.* New York: Cambridge University Press.

Carroll, J. B. (1993b). What abilities are measured by the WISC-III? In B. A. Bracken & R. S. McCallum (Eds.), *Journal of Psychoeducational Assessment monograph series, advances in psychoeducational assessment: Wechsler Intelligence Scale for Children—Third Edition* (pp. 134–143). Germantown, TN: Psychoeducational Corporation.

Carter, C. (1977). Prospectus on black communications. *School Psychology Digest, 6,* 23–30.

Cattell, R. B., & Horn, J. L. (1978). A check on the theory of fluid and crystallized intelligence with description of new subtest designs. *Journal of Educational Measurement, 15,* 139–164.

Catron, D. W. (1978). Immediate test-retest changes in WAIS scores among college males. *Psychological Reports, 43,* 279–290.

Catron, D. W., & Thompson, C. C. (1979). Test-retest gains in WAIS scores after four retest intervals. *Journal of Clinical Psychology, 35,* 352–357.

Chevrie-Muller, C., Bouyer, J., le Normand, M. T., & Stirne, R. (1987). Language testing of preschool children in a bilingual population (Alsace, France). *School Psychology International, 8,* 117–125.

Clarizio, H., & Bernard, R. (1981). Recategorized WISC-R scores of LD children and differential diagnosis. *Psychology in the Schools, 18,* 5–12.

Clark, P., McCallum, R. S., Edwards, R. P., & Hildman, L. K. (1987). Use of the Slosson Intelligence Test in screening of gifted children. *Journal of School Psychology, 25,* 189–192.

Cleary, T. A., Humphreys, L. G., Kendrick, S. A., & Wesman, A. G. (1975). Educational uses of tests with disadvantaged students. *American Psychologist, 30,* 15–41.

Coates, S. (1975). Field independence and intellectual functioning in preschool children. *Perceptual and Motor Skills, 41,* 251–254.

Cohen, J. (1952). A factor-analytically based rationale for the Wechsler-Bellevue. *Journal of Consulting Psychology, 16,* 272–277.

Cohen, J. (1957). A factor-analytically based rationale for the Wechsler Adult Intelligence Scale. *Journal of Consulting Psychology, 21,* 451–457.

Cohen, J. (1959). The factorial structure of the WISC at ages 7-6, 10-6, and 13-6. *Journal of Consulting Psychology, 23,* 285–299.

Cohen, R. (1969). Conceptual styles: Cultural conflict and non-verbal tests of intelligence. *American Anthropologist, 71,* 825–856.

Cole, S., & Hunter, M. (1971). Pattern analysis of WISC scores achieved by culturally disadvantaged children. *Psychological Reports, 29,* 191–194.

Connelly, J. B. (1983). Recategorized WISC-R score patterns of older and younger referred Tlingit Indian children. *Psychology in the Schools, 20,* 271–275.

Cornell, D. G., & Wilson, L. A. (1992). The PIQ > VIQ discrepancy in violent and nonviolent delinquent boys. *Journal of Clinical Psychology, 48,* 256–261.

Costa, L. D. (1975). The relation of visuospatial dysfunction to digit span performance in patients with cerebral lesions. *Cortex, 11,* 31–36.

Cotman, C. W., & McGaugh, J. L. (1980). *Behavioral neuroscience.* New York: Academic Press.

Cousens, P., Ungerer, J. A., Crawford, J. A., & Stevens, M. M. (1991). Cognitive effects of childhood leukemia therapy: A case for four specific deficits. *Journal of Pediatric Psychology, 16,* 475–488.

Cronbach, L. J. (1977). *Educational psychology* (3rd ed.). New York: Harcourt Brace Jovanovich.

Crowl, T. K., & MacGinitie, W. H. (1974). The influence of students' speech characteristics on teachers' evaluations of oral answers. *Journal of Educational Psychology, 66,* 304–308.

Culbertson, F. M., Feral, C. H., & Gabby, S. (1989). Pattern analysis of the Wechsler Intelligence Scale for Children—Revised profiles of delinquent boys. *Journal of Clinical Psychology, 45,* 651–660.

Cummings, M. A., & Merrell, K. W. (1993). K-ABC score patterns of Sioux children: Mental processing styles, effects of school attendance, and relationship between raw scores and age. *Journal of Psychoeducational Assessment, 11,* 38–45.

Das, J. P., & Heemsbergen, D. B. (1983). Planning as a factor in the assessment of cognitive processes as a model for intelligence. *Journal of Psychoeducational Assessment, 1,* 1–16.

Das, J. P., & Naglieri, J. A. (in press). *Das-Naglieri Cognitive Assessment System.* Chicago, IL: Riverside.

Das, J. P., Naglieri, J. A., & Kirby, J. R. (1994). *Assessment of cognitive processes.* Boston, MA: Allyn & Bacon.

Davies, M. F. (1988). Individual differences in the reading process: Field independence and letter detection. *Perceptual and Motor Skills, 66,* 323–326.

Davis, F. B. (1959). Interpretation of differences among averages and individual test scores. *Journal of Educational Psychology, 50,* 162–170.

Decker, S. N., & Corley, R. P. (1984). Bannatyne's "genetic dyslexic" subtype: A validation study. *Psychology in the Schools, 21,* 300–304.

Denckla, M. B. (1974). Development of motor coordination in normal children. *Developmental Medicine and Child Neurology, 16,* 729–741.

Dennis, M. (1985a). Intelligence after early brain injury I.: Predicting IQ scores from medical variables. *Journal of Clinical and Experimental Neuropsychology, 7,* 526–554.

Dennis, M. (1985b). Intelligence after early brain injury II.: Predicting IQ scores from medical variables. *Journal of Clinical and Experimental Neuropsychology, 7,* 555–576.

Doll, B., & Boren, R. (1993). Performance of severely language-impaired students on the WISC-III, language scales, and academic achievement measures.

In B. A. Bracken & R. S. McCallum (Eds.), *Journal of Psychoeducational Assessment monograph series, advances in psychoeducational assessment: Wechsler Intelligence Scale for Children—Third Edition* (pp. 77–86). Germantown, TN: Psychoeducational Corporation.

Dollinger, S. J., Goh, D. S., & Cody, J. J. (1984). A note on the congruence of the WISC-R and the cognitive development scales of the Personality Inventory for Children. *Journal of Consulting and Clinical Psychology, 52,* 315–316.

Donders, J. (1992). Validity of the Kaufman Assessment Battery for Children when employed with children with traumatic brain injury. *Journal of Clinical Psychology, 48,* 225–230.

Dover, A., & Shore, B. M. (1991). Giftedness and flexibility on a mathematics set-breaking task. *Gifted Child Quarterly, 35,* 99–105.

Dumont, R., & Faro, C. (1993, May). The WISC-III: Almost two years old; proceeding with caution—practitioners' concerns. *NASP Communique, 21* (7), 12–15.

Dunn, L. M., & Dunn, L. (1981). *Manual for the Peabody Picture Vocabulary Test—Revised (PPVT-R).* Circle Pines, MN: American Guidance Service.

Eaves, R. C., & Cutchen, M. (1990). The construct validity of the Cognitive Levels Test and the Academic Levels Test when compared with the WISC-R and PIAT for a group of adjudicated delinquents. *Journal of Psychoeducational Assessment, 8,* 61–73.

Edwards, R., & Edwards, J. L. (1993). The WISC-III: A practitioner's perspective. In B. A. Bracken & R. S. McCallum (Eds.), *Journal of Psychoeducational Assessment monograph series, advances in psychoeducational assessment: Wechsler Intelligence Scale for Children—Third Edition* (pp. 144–150). Germantown, TN: Psychoeducational Corporation.

Elliott, C. D. (1990a). *Differential Ability Scales (DAS) administration and scoring manual.* San Antonio, TX: Psychological Corporation.

Elliott, C. D. (1990b). *Differential Ability Scales: Introductory and technical handbook.* San Antonio, TX: Psychological Corporation.

Ellis, N. R. (1963). The stimulus trace and behavioral inadequacy. In N. R. Ellis (Ed.), *Handbook of mental deficiency.* New York: McGraw-Hill.

Estes, W. K. (1974). Learning theory and intelligence. *American Psychologist, 29,* 740–749.

Evans, J. R., & Stroebel, S. (1986). A standardization of two measures that supplement WISC-R Coding subtest results. *Journal of Clinical Psychology, 42,* 654–657.

Fagan, T., & Bracken, B. A. (1993). Reaction to Naglieri's "role of intelligence assessment." *The School Psychologist, 47*(3), 6–7.

Feuerstein, R. (1979). *The dynamic assessment of retarded performers.* Baltimore, MD: University Park Press.

Fischer, W. E., Wenck, L. S., Schurr, K. T., & Ellen, A. S. (1985). The moderating influence of gender, intelligence, and specific achievement deficiencies on the Bannatyne categorization. *Journal of Psychoeducational Assessment, 3,* 245–255.

Flaugher, R. L. (1978). The many definitions of test bias. *American Psychologist, 33,* 671–679.

Flynn, J. R. (1984). The mean IQ of Americans: Massive gains 1932 to 1978. *Psychological Bulletin, 95,* 29–51.

Flynn, J. R. (1987). Massive gains in 14 nations: What IQ tests really measure. *Psychological Bulletin, 101,* 171–191.

Forceville, E. M. J., Dekker, M. J. A., Aldenkamp, A. P., Alpherts, W. C. J., & Schelvis, A. J. (1992). Subtest profiles of the WISC-R and WAIS in mentally retarded patients with epilepsy. *Journal of Intellectual Disability Research, 36,* 45–59.

Frank, G. (1983). *The Wechsler enterprise: An assessment of the development, structure, and use of the Wechsler tests of intelligence.* New York: Pergamon.

Freeman, B. J., Lucas, J. C., Forness, S. R., & Ritvo, E. R. (1985). Cognitive processing of high-functioning autistic children: Comparing the K-ABC and WISC-R. *Journal of Psychoeducational Assessment, 3,* 357–362.

Galin, D. (1976). Educating both halves of the brain. *Childhood Education, 53,* 17–20.

Galin, D., & Ornstein, R. (1974). Individual differences in cognitive style I: Reflective eye movements. *Neuropsychologia, 12,* 367–376.

Gardner, H. (1983). *Frames of mind: The theory of multiple intelligences.* New York: Basic Books.

Gardner, R. (1981). Digits Forward and Digits Backward as two separate tests: Normative data on 1567 school children. *Journal of Clinical Child Psychology, 10,* 131–135.

Garner, T., & Rubin, D. L. (1986). Middle class blacks' perception of dialect and style shifting: The case of southern attorneys. *Journal of Language and Social Psychology, 5,* 33–48.

Gilger, J. W., & Geary, D. C. (1985). Performance on the Luria-Nebraska Neuropsychological Test Battery—Children's Revision: A comparison of children with and without significant WISC-R VIQ-PIQ discrepancies. *Journal of Clinical Psychology, 41,* 806–811.

Glasser, A. J., & Zimmerman, I. L. (1967). *Clinical interpretation of the WISC.* New York: Grune & Stratton.

Glutting, J. J., McDermott, P. A., Prifitera, A., & McGrath, E. A. (in press). Core profile types for the WISC-III and WIAT: Development and their application in identifying multivariate IQ-achievement discrepancies.

Glutting, J. J., McGrath, E. A., Kamphaus, R. W., & McDermott, P. A. (1992). Taxonomy and validity of subtest profiles on the Kaufman Assessment Battery for Children. *Journal of Special Education, 26,* 85–115.

Glutting, J. J., & Oakland, T. (1993). *GATSB: Guide to the Assessment of Test Session Behavior for the WISC-III and the WIAT.* San Antonio, TX: Psychological Corporation.

Glutting, J. J., Oakland, T., & McDermott, P. A. (1989). Observing child behavior during testing: Constructs, validity, and situational generality. *Journal of School Psychology, 27,* 155–164.

Golden, C. J. (1981). The Luria-Nebraska Children's Battery: Theory and formulation. In G. W. Hynd & J. E. Obrzut (Eds.), *Neuropsychological assessment and the school-age child: Issues and procedures* (pp. 277–302). New York: Grune & Stratton.

Good, R. H., III, Vollmer, M., Creek, R. J., Katz, L., & Chowdhri, S. (1993). Treatment utility of the Kaufman Assessment Battery for Children: Effects of matching instruction and student processing strength. *School Psychology Review, 22,* 8–26.

Goodenough, D. R., & Karp, S. A. (1961). Field dependence and intellectual functioning. *Journal of Abnormal and Social Psychology, 63,* 241–246.

Grace, W. C. (1986). Equivalence of the WISC-R and WAIS-R in delinquent males. *Journal of Psychoeducational Assessment, 4,* 257–262.

Grace, W. C., & Sweeney, M. E. (1986). Comparisons of the P > V sign on the WISC-R and WAIS-R in delinquent males. *Journal of Clinical Psychology, 42,* 173–176.

Granier, M. J., & O'Donnell, L. (1991, August). Children's WISC-III scores: Impact of parent education and home environment. Paper presented at the meeting of the American Psychological Association, San Francisco, CA.

Greenblatt, E., Mattis, S., & Trad, P. V. (1991). The ACID pattern and the freedom from distractibility factor in a child psychiatric population. *Developmental Neuropsychology, 7,* 121–130.

Grossman, F. M., & Galvin, G. A. (1989). Referred children's cognitive patterns on the WISC-R. *Perceptual and Motor Skills, 68,* 1307–1311.

Guilford, J. P. (1967). *The nature of human intelligence.* New York: McGraw-Hill.

Guilford, J. P. (1977). *Way beyond the IQ: Guide to improving intelligence and creativity.* Buffalo, NY: Barely Limited.

Guilford, J. P. (1988). Some changes in the structure-of-intellect model. *Educational and Psychological Measurement, 48,* 1–4.

Haddad, F. A., Juliano, J. M., & Vaughan, D. (1994). Long-term stability of individual WISC-R IQs of learning disabled children. *Perceptual and Motor Skills, 74,* 15–18.

Hakuta, K., & Garcia, E. E. (1989). Bilingualism and education. *American Psychologist, 44,* 374–379.

Hambleton, R. K. (1990). Criterion-referenced testing methods and practices. In T. B. Gutkin & C. R. Reynolds (Eds.), *The handbook of school psychology* (2nd ed., pp. 388–415). New York: Wiley.

Hammill, D. D. (1991). *Detroit Tests of Learning Aptitude—Third Edition: Examiner's manual.* Austin, TX: Pro-Ed.

Hardy, J. B., Welcher, D. W., Mellits, E. D., & Kagan, J. (1976). Pitfalls in the measurement of intelligence: Are standard intelligence tests valid instruments for measuring the intellectual potential of urban children? *Journal of Psychology, 94,* 43–51.

Harrison, P. L., Kaufman, A. S., Hickman, J. A., & Kaufman, N. L. (1988). A survey of tests used for adult assessment. *Journal of Psychoeducational Assessment, 6,* 188–198.

Hausman, R. M. (1988). The use of Budoff's learning potential assessment techniques with a Mexican American, moderately handicapped student. In R. L. Jones (Ed.), *Psychoeducational assessment of minority group children: A casebook* (pp. 65–75). Berkely, CA: Cobb & Henry.

Haynes, J. P., & Bensch, M. (1983). Female delinquent recidivism and the P > V sign on the WISC-R. *Journal of Clinical Psychology, 39,* 141–144.

Haywood, H. C. (1988). Dynamic assessment: The Learning Potential Assessment Device. In R. L. Jones (Ed.), *Psychoeducational assessment of minority group children: A casebook* (pp. 39–63). Berkely, CA: Cobb & Henry.

Heath, S. B. (1989). Oral and literate traditions among black Americans living in poverty. *American Psychologist, 44,* 367–373.

Hebb, D. O. (1949). *The organization of behavior.* New York: Wiley.

Hemmelgarn, T. E., & Kehle, T. J. (1984). The relationship between reaction time and intelligence in children. *School Psychology International, 5,* 77–84.

Hendrickson, D. E., & Hendrickson, A. E. (1980). The biological basis of individual differences in intelligence. *Personality and Individual Differences, 1,* 3–33.

Herring, S., & Reitan, R. M. (1986). Sex similarities in Verbal and Performance IQ deficits following unilateral cerebral lesions. *Journal of Consulting and Clinical Psychology, 54,* 537–541.

Hirshoren, A., & Kavale, K. (1976). Profile analysis of the WISC-R: A continuing malpractice. *The Exceptional Child, 23,* 83–87.

Hishinuma, E. S., & Yamakawa, E. S. (1993). Construct and criterion-related validity of the WISC-III for exceptional students and those who are "at risk." In B. A. Bracken & R. S. McCallum (Eds.), *Journal of Psychoeducational Assessment monograph series, advances in psychoeducational assessment: Wechsler Intelligence Scale for Children—Third Edition* (pp. 94–104). Germantown, TN: Psychoeducational Corporation.

Hodges, K., Horwitz, E., Kline, J., & Brandt, D. (1982). Comparison of various WISC-R summary scores for a psychiatric sample. *Journal of Clinical Psychology, 38,* 830–837.

Holcomb, W. R., Hardesty, R. A., Adams, N. A., & Ponder, H. M. (1987). WISC-R types of learning disabilities: A profile analysis with cross-validation. *Journal of Learning Disabilities, 20,* 369–373.

Holroyd, J., & Wright, F. (1965). Neurological implications of WISC Verbal-Performance discrepancies in a psychiatric setting. *Journal of Consulting Psychology, 29,* 206–212.

Hoover, M. R. (1990). A vindicationist perspective on the role of Ebonics (Black language) and other aspects of ethnic studies in the university. *American Behavioral Scientist, 34,* 251–262.

Horn, J. L. (1968). Organization of abilities and the development of intelligence. *Psychological Review, 75,* 242–259.

Horn, J. L. (1970). Organization of data on life-span development of human abilities. In L. R. Goulet & P. B. Baltes (Eds.), *Life-span developmental psychology* (pp. 423–466). New York: Academic Press.

Horn, J. L. (1985). Remodeling old models of intelligence. In B. B. Wolman (Ed.), *Handbook of intelligence: Theories, measurements, and applications* (pp. 267–300). New York: Wiley.

Horn, J. L. (1989). Cognitive diversity: A framework of learning. In P. L. Ackerman, R. J. Sternberg, & R. Glaser (Eds.), *Learning and individual differences* (pp. 61–116). New York: Freeman.

Horn, J. L. (1991). Measurement of intellectual capabilities: A review of theory. In K. S. McGrew, J. K. Werder, & R. W. Woodcock (Eds.), *Woodcock-Johnson Technical manual: A reference on theory and current research* (pp. 197–246). Allen, TX: DLM Teaching Resources.

Horn, J. L., & Cattell, R. B. (1966). Refinement and test of the theory of fluid and crystallized intelligence. *Journal of Educational Psychology, 57,* 253–270.

Horn, J. L., & Cattell, R. B. (1967). Age differences in fluid and crystallized intelligence. *Acta Psychologica, 26,* 107–129.

Horn, J. L., & Hofer, S. M. (1992). Major abilities and development in the adult period. In R. J. Sternberg & C. A. Berg (Eds.), *Intellectual development* (pp. 44–99). Boston, MA: Cambridge University Press.

Horn, J. L., & McArdle, J. J. (1980). Perspectives on mathematical/statistical model building (MASMOB) in research on aging. In L. W. Poon (Ed.), *Aging in the 1980s: Psychological issues* (pp. 503–541). Washington DC: American Psychological Association.

Horn, J. L., & Stankov, L. (1982). Auditory and visual factors of intelligence. *Intelligence, 6,* 165–185.

Hubble, L. M., & Groff, M. G. (1982). WISC-R Verbal Performance IQ discrepancies among Quay-classified adolescent male delinquents. *Journal of Youth and Adolescence, 11,* 503–508.

Humphreys, L. G. (1967). Critique of Cattell's "Theory of fluid and crystallized intelligence: A critical experiment." *Journal of Educational Psychology, 58,* 120–136.

Imm, P. S., Foster, K. Y., Belter, R. W., & Finch, A. J. (1991). Assessment of short-term visual memory in child and adolescent psychiatric inpatients. *Journal of Clinical Psychology, 47,* 440–443.

Ittenbach, R. F. (1989). *Race, gender and maternal education differences on three measures of the Early Screening Profiles.* Unpublished doctoral dissertation, University of Alabama.

Jensen, A. R. (1985). Methodological and statistical techniques for the chronometric study of mental abilities. In C. R. Reynolds & V. L. Willson (Eds.), *Methodological and statistical advances in the study of individual differences* (pp. 51–116). New York: Plenum.

Jensen, A. R., & Reynolds, C. R. (1982). Race, social class and ability patterns on the WISC-R. *Personality and Individual Differences, 3,* 423–438.

Jensen, A. R., & Reynolds, C. R. (1983). Sex differences on the WISC-R. *Personality and Individual Differences, 4,* 223–226.

Jensen, A. R., Schafer, E. W. P., & Crinella, F. M. (1981). Reaction time, evoked brain potentials, and psychometric g in the severely retarded. *Intelligence, 5,* 179–197.

Jones, R. L. (Ed.). (1988). *Psychoeducational assessment of minority group children: A casebook.* Berkeley, CA: Cobb & Henry.

Joschko, M., & Rourke, B. P. (1985). Neuropsychological subtypes of learning-disabled children who exhibit the ACID pattern on the WISC. In B. P. Rourke (Ed.), *Neuropsychology of learning disabilities: Essentials of subtype analysis* (pp. 65–88). New York: Guilford.

Kagan, J. (1966). Reflection—impulsivity: The generality and dynamics of conceptual tempo. *Journal of Abnormal Psychology, 71,* 17–24.

Kagan, J., & Klein, R. E. (1973). Cross-cultural perspectives on early development. *American Psychologist, 28,* 947–961.

Kagan, S., & Zahn, G. L. (1975). Field dependence and the school achievement gap between Anglo American and Mexican American children. *Journal of Educational Psychology, 67,* 643–650.

Kamphaus, R. W. (1993). *Clinical assessment of children's intelligence.* Boston, MA: Allyn & Bacon.

Kamphaus, R. W., & Platt, L. O. (1992). Subtest specificities for the WISC-III. *Psychological Reports, 70,* 899–902.

Kaplan, G. J., Fleshman, J. K., & Bender, J. R. (1973). Long-term effects of otitis media: A ten-year cohort study of Alaskan Eskimo children. *Pediatrics, 52,* 577–585.

Karnes, F. A., Whorton, J. E., Currie, B. B., & Cantrall, S. W. (1986). Correlations of scores on the WISC-R, Stanford-Binet, the Slosson Intelligence Test, and the Developing Cognitive Abilities Test for intellectually gifted youth. *Psychological Reports, 58,* 887–889.

Karp, S. A. (1963). Field dependence and overcoming embeddedness. *Journal of Consulting Psychology, 27,* 294–302.

Katz, J. (1978). The effects of conductive hearing loss on auditory function. *ASHA, 10,* 879–886.

Kaufman, A. S. (1975). Factor analysis of the WISC-R at eleven age levels between 6-½ and 16-½ years. *Journal of Consulting and Clinical Psychology, 43,* 135–147.

Kaufman, A. S. (1976a). A new approach to the interpretation of test scatter on the WISC-R. *Journal of Learning Disabilities, 9,* 160–168.

Kaufman, A. S. (1976b). Verbal-Performance IQ discrepancies on the WISC-R, *Journal of Consulting and Clinical Psychology, 44,* 739–744.

Kaufman, A. S. (1979a). Cerebral specialization and intelligence testing. *Journal of Research and Development in Education, 12,* 96–107.

Kaufman, A. S. (1979b). *Intelligent testing with the WISC-R.* New York: Wiley.

Kaufman, A. S. (1979c). The role of speed on WISC-R performance across the age range. *Journal of Consulting and Clinical Psychology, 47,* 595–597.

Kaufman, A. S. (1982). The impact of WISC-R research for school psychologists. In C. R. Reynolds & T. B. Gutkin (Eds.), *The handbook of school psychology* (pp. 156–177). New York: Wiley.

Kaufman, A. S. (1990a). *Assessing adolescent and adult intelligence.* Boston, MA: Allyn & Bacon.

Kaufman, A. S. (1990b). The WPPSI-R: You can't judge a test by its colors. *Journal of School Psychology, 28,* 387–394.

Kaufman, A. S. (1992). Evaluation of the WISC-III and WPPSI-R for gifted children. *Roeper Review, 14,* 154–158.

Kaufman, A. S. (1993a). Joint exploratory factor analysis of the Kaufman Assessment Battery for Children and the Kaufman Adolescent and Adult Intelligence Test for 11- and 12-year-olds. *Journal of Clinical Child Psychology, 22,* 355–364.

Kaufman, A. S. (1993b). King WISC the Third assumes the throne. *Journal of School Psychology, 31,* 345–354.

Kaufman, A. S. (in press-a). A reply to Macmann and Barnett: Lessons from the blind men and the elephant. *School Psychology Quarterly.*

Kaufman, A. S. (in press-b). Practice effects. In R. J. Sternberg (Ed.), *Encyclopedia of intelligence.* New York: Macmillan.

Kaufman, A. S., Harrison, P. L., & Ittenbach, R. F. (1990). Intelligence testing in the schools. In T. B. Gutkin & C. R. Reynolds (Eds.), *The handbook of school psychology* (2nd ed., pp. 289–327). New York: Wiley.

Kaufman, A. S., & Horn, J. L. (1994). Age changes on tests of fluid and crystallized ability for females and males on the Kaufman Adolescent and Adult Intelligence Test (KAIT) at ages 17 to 94 years. Manuscript submitted for publication.

Kaufman, A. S., & Kamphaus, R. W. (1984). Factor analysis of the Kaufman Assessment Battery for Children (K-ABC) for ages 2-½ through 12-½. *Journal of Educational Psychology, 76,* 623–637.

Kaufman, A. S., & Kaufman, N. L. (1983). *Interpretive manual for the Kaufman Assessment Battery for Children (K-ABC).* Circle Pines, MN: American Guidance Service.

Kaufman, A. S., & Kaufman, N. L. (1985). *Manual for the Kaufman Test of Educational Achievement—Comprehensive Form (K-TEA).* Circle Pines, MN: American Guidance Service.

Kaufman, A. S., & Kaufman, N. L. (1991). *Manual for the Kaufman Brief Intelligence Test (K-BIT).* Circle Pines, MN: American Guidance Service.

Kaufman, A. S., & Kaufman, N. L. (1993). *Manual for the Kaufman Adolescent and Adult Intelligence Test (KAIT).* Circle Pines, MN: American Guidance Service.

Kaufman, A. S., Kaufman, N. L., Dougherty, E. H., & Tuttle, K. S. C. (1994a). *Kaufman WISC-III Integrated Interpretive System.* Odessa, FL: Psychological Assessment Resources.

Kaufman, A. S., Kaufman, N. L., Dougherty, E. H., & Tuttle, K. S. C. (1994b). *Kaufman WISC-III Integrated Interpretive System Checklist for Behaviors Observed During Administration of WISC-III Subtests.* Odessa, FL: Psychological Assessment Resources.

Kaufman, A. S., & McLean, J. E. (1986). K-ABC/WISC-R factor analysis for a learning disabled population. *Journal of Learning Disabilities, 19,* 145–153.

Kaufman, A. S., & McLean, J. E. (1987). Joint factor analysis of the K-ABC and WISC-R with normal children. *Journal of School Psychology, 25,* 105–118.

Kaufman, A. S., & Van Hagen, J. (1977). Investigation of the WISC-R for use with retarded children: Correlation with the 1972 Stanford-Binet and comparison of WISC and WISC-R profiles. *Psychology in the Schools, 14,* 10–14.

Kaufman, A. S., & Wang, J. (1992). Gender, race, and education differences on the K-BIT at ages 4 to 90 years. *Journal of Psychoeducational Assessment, 10,* 219–229.

Kaufman, J. L. (1995). *Visual and auditory evoked brain potentials, the Hendricksons' pulse train hypothesis, and the fluid and crystallized theory of intelligence.* Unpublished doctoral dissertation, California School of Professional Psychology, San Diego, CA.

Kavale, K. (1990). Effectiveness of special education. In T. B. Gutkin & C. R. Reynolds (Eds.), *The handbook of school psychology* (2nd ed., pp. 870–900). New York: Wiley.

Kavale, K. A., & Forness, S. R. (1984). A meta-analysis of the validity of Wechsler scale profiles and recategorizations: Patterns or parodies? *Learning Disabilities Quarterly, 7,* 136–156.

Keith, T. Z. (1990). Confirmatory and hierarchical confirmatory analysis of the Differential Ability Scales. *Journal of Psychoeducational Assessment, 8,* 391–405.

Keith, T. Z., & Novak, C. G. (1987). Joint factor structure of the WISC-R and K-ABC for referred school children. *Journal of Psychoeducational Assessment, 5,* 370–386.

Kellerman, J., Moss, H. A., & Siegel, S. E. (1982). Verbal/Performance discrepancy in children with cancer: A statistical quirk. *Journal of Pediatric Psychology, 7,* 263–266.

Kender, J. P., Greenwood, S., & Conrad, E. (1985). WAIS-R performance patterns of 565 incarcerated adults characterized as underachieving readers and adequate readers. *Journal of Learning Disabilities, 18,* 379–383.

Keogh, B. K., & Hall, R. J. (1974). WISC subtest patterns of educationally handicapped and educable mentally retarded pupils. *Psychology in the Schools, 11,* 296–300.

Kerns, K., & Decker, S. N. (1985). Multifactorial assessment of reading disability: Identifying the best predictors. *Perceptual and Motor Skills, 60,* 747–753.

Kimura, D. (1966). Dual function asymmetry of the brain in visual perception. *Neuropsychologia, 4,* 275–285.

Kirk, S. A., & Kirk, W. D. (1971). *Psycholinguistic learning disabilities.* Urbana, IL: Illinois University Press.

Kirk, S. A., McCarthy, J. J., & Kirk, W. D. (1968). *Examiner's manual: Illinois Test of Psycholinguistic Abilities.* Urbana, IL: Illinois University Press.

Kitzinger, H., & Blumberg, E. (1951). Supplementary guide for administering and scoring the Wechsler-Bellevue Intelligence Scale (Form I), *Psychological Monographs, 65,* 1–20.

Kline, R. B., Snyder, J., Guilmette, S., & Castellanos, M. (1992). Relative usefulness of elevation, variability, and shape information from WISC-R, K-ABC, and Fourth Edition Stanford-Binet profiles in predicting achievement. *Psychological Assessment, 4,* 426–432.

Kolligan, J., Jr., & Sternberg, R. J. (1987). Intelligence, information processing, and specific learning disabilities: A triarchic synthesis. *Journal of Learning Disabilities, 20,* 8–17.

Kramer, J. H. (1993). Interpretation of individual subtest scores on the WISC-III. *Psychological Assessment, 5,* 193–196.

Kramer, J. J., Ullman, D. P., & Schellenberg, R. P. (1987). The viability of scatter analysis on the WISC-R and the SBIS: Examining a vestige. *Journal of Psychoeducational Assessment, 5,* 37–47.

Krauskopf, C. J. (1991). Pattern analysis and statistical power. *Psychological Assessment, 3,* 261–264.

Labov, W. (1970). The logic of Nonstandard English. In F. Williams (Ed.), *Language and poverty* (pp. 153–189). Chicago, IL: Markham.

Lajoie, S. P., & Shore, B. M. (1986). Intelligence: The speed and accuracy trade-off in high aptitude individuals. *Journal for the Education of the Gifted, 9,* 85–104.

Lawson, J. S., Inglis, J., & Tittemore, J. A. (1987). Factorially defined Verbal and Performance IQs derived from the WISC-R: Patterns of cognitive ability in normal and learning disabled children. *Personality and Individual Differences, 8,* 331–341.

Levinson, E. M., & Folino, L. (1994). Correlations of scores on the Gifted Evaluation Scale with those on the WISC-III and Kaufman Brief Intelligence Test for students referred for gifted evaluation. *Psychological Reports, 74,* 419–424.

Levy, J., & Trevarthen, C. (1976). Metacontrol of hemisphere function in human and split-brain patients. *Journal of Experimental Psychology: Human Perception and Performance, 2,* 299–312.

Lewandowski, L. J., & DeRienzo, P. J. (1985). WISC-R and K-ABC performance of hemiplegic children. *Journal of Psychoeducational Assessment, 3,* 215–221.

Lewnau, E. B. (1986, December). Pragmatic aspects of the language of speakers of Black American English. *ASHA Reports Series: American Speech Language Hearing Association, No. 16,* 11–116.

Lezak, M. D. (1983). *Neuropsychological assessment* (2nd ed.). New York: Oxford University Press.

Lezak, M. D. (1988). IQ: R. I. P. *Journal of Clinical and Experimental Neuropsychology, 10,* 351–361.

Lincoln, A., Allen, M. H., & Piacentini (in press). The assessment and interpretation of intellectual abilities in people with autism. In E. Schopler & G. Mesibov (Eds.), *Learning and cognition in autism.* New York: Plenum.

Lincoln, A., Kaufman, J. L., & Kaufman, A. S. (in press). The application of intelligence tests in clinical and psychoeducational assessment. In M. Hersen & R. T. Ammerman (Eds.), *Advanced abnormal child psychology.* Hillsdale, NJ: Erlbaum.

Lipsitz, J. D., Dworkin, R. H., & Erlenmeyer-Kimling, L. (1993). Wechsler Comprehension and Picture Arrangement subtests and social adjustment. *Psychological Assessment, 5,* 430–437.

Little, S. G. (1992). The WISC-III: Everything old is new again. *School Psychology Quarterly, 7,* 148–154.

Lohman, D. F. (1989). Human intelligence: An introduction to advances in theory and research. *Review of Educational Research, 59,* 333–373.

Lohman, D. F. (1993). Teaching and testing to develop fluid abilities. *Educational Researcher, 22,* 12–23.

Lowe, J. D., Jr., Anderson, H. N., Williams, A., & Currie, B. B. (1987). Long-term predictive validity of the WPPSI and the WISC-R with black school children. *Personality and Individual Differences, 7,* 551–559.

Lueger, R. J., Albott, W. L., Hilgendorf, W. A., & Gill, K. J. (1985). Neuropsychological and academic achievement correlates of abnormal WISC-R verbal-performance discrepancies. *Journal of Clinical Psychology, 41,* 801–805.

Lufi, D., & Cohen, A. (1985). Using the WISC-R to identify attention deficit disorder. *Psychology in the Schools, 22,* 40–42.

Lufi, D., Cohen, A., & Parish-Plass, J. (1990). Identifying attention deficit hyperactive disorder with the WISC-R and the Stroop Color and Word Test. *Psychology in the Schools, 27,* 28–34.

Luria, A. R. (1966). *Human brain and psychological processes.* New York: Harper & Row.

Luria, A. R. (1973). *The working brain: An introduction to neuropsychology.* New York: Basic Books.

Luria, A. R. (1980). *Higher cortical functions in man* (2nd ed.). New York: Basic Books.

Lutey, C. (1977). *Individual intelligence testing: A manual and sourcebook* (2nd and enlarged ed.). Greeley, CO: Carol L. Lutey Publishing.

Lynn, R. (1990). The role of nutrition in secular increases in intelligence. *Personality and Individual Differences, 11,* 273–285.

Lynn, R., & Mulhern, G. (1991). A comparison of sex differences on the Scottish and American standardization samples of the WISC-R. *Personality and Individual Differences, 12,* 1179–1182.

Macmann, G. M., & Barnett, D. W. (in press). Structural analysis of correlated factors: Lessons from the Verbal-Performance dichotomy of the Wechsler scales. *School Psychology Quarterly.*

Macmann, G. M., Plasket, C. M., Barnett, D. W., & Siler, R. F. (1991). Factor structure of the WISC-R for children of superior intelligence. *Journal of School Psychology, 29,* 19–36.

Maller, S. J., & Braden, J. P. (1993). The construct and criterion-related validity of the WISC-III with deaf adolescents. In B. A. Bracken & R. S. McCallum (Eds.), *Journal of Psychoeducational Assessment monograph series, advances in psychoeducational assessment: Wechsler Intelligence Scale for Children—Third Edition* (pp. 105–113). Germantown, TN: Psychoeducational Corporation.

Marr, D. B., & Sternberg, R. J. (1987). The role of mental speed in intelligence: A triarchic perspective. In P. A. Vernon (Ed.), *Speed of information-processing and intelligence* (pp. 271–294). Norwood, NJ: Ablex.

Marwit, S. J., Marwit, K. L., & Boswell, J. J. (1972). Negro children's use of nonstandard grammar. *Journal of Educational Psychology, 63,* 218–224.

Marwit, S. J., & Neumann, G. (1974). Black and white children's comprehension of standard and nonstandard English passages. *Journal of Educational Psychology, 66,* 329–332.

Matarazzo, J. D. (1972). *Wechsler's measurement and appraisal of adult intelligence* (5th ed.). Baltimore, MD: Williams & Wilkins.

Matarazzo, J. D. (1992). Psychological testing and assessment in the 21st century. *American Psychologist, 47,* 1007–1018.

Matarazzo, J. D., Daniel, M. H., Prifitera, A., & Herman, D. O. (1988). Inter-subtest scatter in the WAIS-R standardization sample. *Journal of Clinical Psychology, 44,* 940–950.

Matheson, D. W., Mueller, H. M., & Short, R. H. (1984). The validity of Bannatyne's acquired knowledge category as a separate construct. *Journal of Psychoeducational Assessment, 2,* 279–291.

Matson, D. E., & Fischer, M. (1991). A comparison of internalizers, externalizers, and normals using the WISC-R and Wisconsin Card Sorting Test. *Journal of Psychoeducational Assessment, 9,* 140–151.

Mayman, M., Schafer, R., & Rapaport, D. (1951). Interpretation of the WAIS in personality appraisal. In H. H. Anderson & G. L. Anderson (Eds.), *An introduction to projective techniques* (pp. 541–580). New York: Prentice-Hall.

McArdle, J. J. (1988). Dynamic but structural equation modeling of repeated measures data. In J. R. Nesselroade & R. B. Cattell (Eds.), *Handbook of multivariate experimental psychology* (2nd ed.). New York: Plenum.

McCullough, D. A., Walker, J. L., & Diessner, R. (1985). The use of Wechsler scales in the assessment of Native Americans of the Columbia River Basin. *Psychology in the Schools, 22,* 23–28.

McDermott, P. A., Fantuzzo, J. W., & Glutting, J. J. (1990). Just say no to subtest analysis: A critique on Wechsler theory and practice. *Journal of Psychoeducational Assessment, 8,* 290–302.

McDermott, P. A., Fantuzzo, J. W., Glutting, J. J., Watkins, M. W., & Baggaley, A. R. (1992). Illusions of meaning in the ipsative assessment of children's ability. *Journal of Special Education, 25,* 504–526.

McDermott, P. A., Glutting, J. J., Jones, J. N., Watkins, M. W., & Kush, J. (1989). Core profile types in the WISC-R national sample: Structure, membership, and application. *Psychological Assessment, 1,* 292–299.

McGhee, R. (1993). Fluid and crystallized intelligence: Confirmatory factor analysis of the Differential Ability Scales, Detroit Tests of Learning Aptitude-3, and Woodcock-Johnson Psycho-Educational Battery—Revised. In B. A. Bracken & R. S. McCallum (Eds.), *Journal of Psychoeducational Assessment monograph series, advances in psychoeducational assessment: Woodcock-Johnson Psycho-Educational Battery—Revised* (pp. 39–53). Germantown, TN: Psychoeducational Corporation.

McKenna, F. P. (1990). Learning implications of field dependence-independence: Cognitive style versus cognitive ability. *Applied Cognitive Psychology, 4,* 427–437.

McShane, D. A., & Berry, J. W. (1989). Native North American Indians: Indians and intuitive abilities. In S. H. LeVine & J. W. Berry (Eds.), *Cultural context of human abilities* (pp. 385–426). New York: Wiley.

McShane, D., & Cook, V. (1985). Transcultural intellectual assessment: Performance by Hispanics on the Wechsler scales. In B. B. Wolman (Ed.), *Handbook of intelligence* (pp. 737–785). New York: Wiley.

McShane, D. A., & Plas, J. M. (1984a). The cognitive functioning of American Indian children: Moving from the WISC to the WISC-R. *School Psychology Review, 13,* 61–73.

McShane, D. A., & Plas, J. M. (1984b). Response to a critique of the McShane and Plas review. *School Psychology Review, 13,* 83–88.

Meeker, M. N. (1969). *The structure of intellect.* Columbus, OH: Charles E. Merrill.

Meeker, M. N. (1975). *Glossary for SOI factor definitions: WISC-R Analysis.* Available from SOI Institute, 214 Main St., El Segundo, CA.

Meinhardt, M., Hibbett, C., Koller, J., & Busch, R. (1993). Comparison of the Woodcock-Johnson Psycho-Educational Battery—Revised and the Wechsler Intelligence Scale for Children—Revised with incarcerated adolescents. In B. A. Bracken & R. S. McCallum (Eds.), *Journal of Psychoeducational Assessment monograph series, advances in psychoeducational assessment: Woodcock-Johnson Psycho-Educational Battery—Revised* (pp. 64–70). Germantown, TN: Psychoeducational Corporation.

Messer, S. B. (1976). Reflection-impulsivity: A review. *Psychological Bulletin, 83*, 1026–1052.

Minton, H. L., & Schneider, F. W. (1980). *Differential psychology.* Prospects Heights, IL: Waveland Press.

Mitchell, W. G., Chavez, J. M., Baker, S. A., Guzman, B. L., & Azen, S. P. (1990). Reaction time, impulsivity, and attention in hyperactive children and controls. A video game technique. *Journal of Child Neurology, 5*, 195–204.

Moffitt, T. E., & Silva, P. A. (1987). WISC-R Verbal and Performance IQ discrepancy in an unselected cohort: Clinical significance and longitudinal stability. *Journal of Consulting and Clinical Psychology, 55*, 768–774.

Montessori, M. (1964). *The Montessori method.* New York: Shocken.

Moriarty, A., & Ryan, G. (1987). WISC-R patterns and correlates in an Irish clinic sample. *Irish Journal of Psychology, 8*, 127–137.

Morris, J. M., & Bigler, E. D. (1987). Hemispheric functioning and the Kaufman Assessment Battery for Children: Results in the neurologically impaired. *Developmental Neuropsychology, 3*, 67–79.

Naglieri, J. A. (1979). *A comparison of McCarthy GCI and WISC-R IQ scores for educable mentally retarded, learning disabled, and normal children.* Unpublished doctoral dissertation, University of Georgia.

Naglieri, J. A. (1985). *Matrix Analogies Test—Expanded Form.* San Antonio, TX: Psychological Corporation.

Naglieri, J. A. (1989). A cognitive processing theory for the measurement of intelligence. *Educational Psychologist, 24*, 185–206.

Naglieri, J. A. (1992). Two roads diverged in a wood: Choosing g or PASS cognitive processes. *Advances in Cognition and Educational Practice, 1A*, 112–144.

Naglieri, J. A. (1993a). Pairwise and ipsative comparisons of WISC-III IQ and Index scores. *Psychological Assessment, 5* (1), 113–116.

Naglieri, J. A. (1993b). The role of intelligence assessment in school psychology. *The School Psychologist, 47* (2), 9, 14–15, 17.

Naglieri, J. A., & Das, J. P. (1988). Planning-Arousal-Simultaneous-Successive (PASS): A model for assessment. *Journal of School Psychology, 26*, 35–48.

Naglieri, J. A., & Das, J. P. (1990). Planning, Attention, Simultaneous, and Successive (PASS) cognitive processes as a model for intelligence. *Journal of Psychoeducational Assessment, 8*, 303–337.

Naglieri, J. A., Das, J. P., Stevens, J. S., & Ledbetter, M. F. (1991). Confirmatory factor analysis of planning, attention, simultaneous, and successive cognitive processing tasks. *Journal of School Psychology, 29*, 1–17.

Naglieri, J. A., & Jensen, A. R. (1987). Comparison of black-white differences on the WISC-R and the K-ABC: Spearmen's hypothesis. *Intelligence, 11,* 21–43.

Nebes, R. D. (1974). Hemispheric specialization in commisurotomized man. *Psychological Bulletin, 81,* 1–14.

Nettlebeck, T., & Young, R. (1989). Inspection time and intelligence in 6-year-old children. *Personality and Individual Differences, 10,* 605–614.

Newby, R. F., Recht, D. R., Caldwell, J., & Schaefer, J. (1993). Comparison of WISC-III and WISC-R IQ changes over a 2-year time span in a sample of children with dyslexia. In B. A. Bracken & R. S. McCallum (Eds.), *Journal of Psychoeducational Assessment monograph series, advances in psychoeducational assessment: Wechsler Intelligence Scale for Children—Third Edition* (pp. 87–93). Germantown, TN: Psychoeducational Corporation.

Nichols, E. G., Inglis, J., Lawson, J. S., & MacKay, I. (1988). A cross-validation study of patterns of cognitive ability in children with learning difficulties, as described by factorially defined WISC-R Verbal and Performance IQs. *Journal of Learning Disabilities, 21,* 504–508.

Oakland, T. (1983). Concurrent and predictive validity estimates for the WISC-R IQs and ELPs by racial-ethnic and SES groups. *School Psychology Review, 12,* 57–61.

Oakland, T., De Mesquita, P., & Buckley, K. (1988). Psychological, linguistic and sociocultural correlates of reading among Mexican American elementary students. *School Psychology International, 9,* 219–228.

Oakland, T., & Glutting, J. J. (1990). Examiner observations of children's WISC-R test-related behaviors: Possible socioeconomic status, race, and gender effects. *Psychological Assessment, 2,* 86–90.

O'Grady, K. E. (1983). A confirmatory maximum likelihood factor analysis of the WAIS-R. *Journal of Consulting and Clinical Psychology, 51,* 826–831.

Ortiz, V., & Volloff, W. (1987). Identification of gifted and accelerated Hispanic students. *Journal for the Education of the Gifted, 11,* 45–55.

Osgood, C. E., & Miron, M. S. (Eds.). (1963). *Approaches to the study of aphasia.* Urbana, IL: Illinois University Press.

Ownby, R. L., & Matthews, C. G. (1985). On the meaning of the WISC-R third factor: Relations to selected neuropsychological measures. *Journal of Consulting and Clinical Psychology, 53,* 531–534.

Paget, K. D. (1982). Intellectual patterns of conduct problem children on the WISC-R. *Psychology in the Schools, 19,* 439–445.

Phelps, L. (1989). Comparison of scores for intellectually gifted students on the WISC-R and the Fourth Edition of the Stanford-Binet. *Psychology in the Schools, 26,* 125–129.

Phelps, L., & Ensor, A. (1987). The comparison of performance by sex of deaf children on the WISC-R. *Psychology in the Schools, 24,* 209–214.

Phelps, L., Leguori, S., Nisewaner, K., & Parker, M. (1993). Practical interpretations of the WISC-III with language-disordered children. In B. A. Bracken & R. S. McCallum (Eds.), *Journal of Psychoeducational Assessment monograph series, advances in psychoeducational assessment: Wechsler Intelligence Scale for Children—Third Edition* (pp. 71–76). Germantown, TN: Psychoeducational Corporation.

Piaget, J., & Inhelder, B. (1967). The child's conception of space. New York: Norton.

Piedmont, R. L., Sokolve, R. L., & Fleming, M. Z. (1989). An examination of some diagnostic strategies involving the Wechsler intelligence scales. *Psychological Assessment, 1,* 181–185.

Plake, B. S., Reynolds, C. R., & Gutkin, T. B. (1981). A technique for the comparison of the profile variability between independent groups. *Journal of Clinical Psychology, 37,* 142–146.

Post, K. R. (1992). *A comparison of WISC-R and WISC-III scores on urban special education students.* Unpublished educational specialists thesis, James Madison University, Harrisonburg, VA.

Post, K. R., & Mitchell, H. R. (1993). The WISC-III: A reality check. *Journal of School Psychology, 31,* 541–545.

Price, R. A., & Birdwell, D. A. (1978). The central nervous system in childhood leukemia. III. Mineralizing microangiopathy and dystrophic calcification. *Cancer, 42,* 717–728.

Prifitera, A., & Dersh, J. (1993). Base rates of WISC-III diagnostic subtest patterns among normal, learning-disabled, and ADHD samples. In B. A. Bracken & R. S. McCallum (Eds.), *Journal of Psychoeducational Assessment monograph series, advances in psychoeducational assessment: Wechsler Intelligence Scale for Children—Third Edition* (pp. 43–55). Germantown, TN: Psychoeducational Corporation.

Psychological Corporation. (1992). *Manual for the Wechsler Individual Achievement Test (WIAT).* San Antonio, TX: Psychological Corporation.

Quay, H. C. (1987). Intelligence. In H. C. Quay (Ed.), *Handbook of juvenile delinquency* (pp. 106–117). New York: Wiley.

Quay, L. C. (1971). Language, dialect, reinforcement, and the intelligence test performance of Negro children. *Child Development, 42,* 5–15.

Quay, L. C. (1972). Negro dialect and Binet performance in severely disadvantaged black four-year-olds. *Child Development, 43,* 245–250.

Ramirez, M. (1972). *Current educational research: The basis for a new philosophy for educating Mexican Americans.* Teacher Corps Assistance Project, Center for Communication Research, University of Texas, School of Communication, Austin, TX.

Ramirez, M., & Price-Williams, D. R. (1974). Cognitive styles of three ethnic groups in the United States. *Journal of Cross-Cultural Psychology, 5,* 212–219.

Rapaport, D., Gill, M. M., & Schafer, R. (1945–46). *Diagnostic psychological testing.* Chicago, IL: Year Book Publishers.

Rattan, G. (1992). Speed of information processing: A third factor of the WISC-R. *Journal of School Psychology, 30,* 83–90.

Raven, J. C., Court, J. H., & Raven, J. (1983). *Manual for Raven's Progressive Matrices and Vocabulary Scales (Section 3)—Standard Progressive Matrices.* London: Lewis.

Reams, R., Chamrad, D., & Robinson, N. M. (1990). The race is not necessarily to the swift: Validity of WISC-R bonus points for speed. *Gifted Child Quarterly, 34,* 108–110.

Reardon, S. H., & Naglieri, J. A. (1992). PASS cognitive processing characteristics of normal and ADHD males. *Journal of School Psychology, 30*, 151–163.

Reed, H. B. C. (1976). Pediatric neuropsychology. *Journal of Pediatric Psychology, 1*, 5–7.

Reitan, R. M. (1955). Certain differential effects of left and right cerebral lesions in human adults. *Journal of Comparative and Physiological Psychology, 48*, 474–477.

Reitan, R. M. (1959). The comparative effects of brain damage on the Halstead Impairment Index and the Wechsler-Bellevue Scale. *Journal of Clinical Psychology, 15*, 281–285.

Reitan, R. M. (1966). Diagnostic inferences of brain lesions on psychological test results. *Canadian Psychologist, 7*, 386–392.

Reitan, R. M. (1974). *Methodological problems in clinical neuropsychology* (pp. 19–46). In R. M. Reitan & L. A. Davison (Eds.), *Clinical neuropsychology: Current status and applications*. New York: Wiley.

Reitan, R. M. (1988). Integration of neuropsychological theory, assessment, and application. *The Clinical Neuropsychologist, 2*, 331–349.

Reitan, R. M., & Wolfson, D. (1985). *The Halstead-Reitan Neuropsychological Battery: Theory and clinical interpretation*. South Tucson, AZ: Neuropsychology Press.

Reitan, R. M., & Wolfson, D. (1992). *Neuropsychological evaluation of older children*. South Tucson, AZ: Neuropsychology Press.

Reschly, D. J. (1988). Special education reform: School psychology revolution. *School Psychology Review, 17*, 459–475.

Reschly, D. J. (1993, Winter). From testing to interventions: The last 25 years in school psychology. *The School Psychologist, 47*(1), 1, 10–11.

Reschly, D. J., & Tilly, W. D. (1993, September). The WHY of system reform. *Communique*, pp. 1, 4–6.

Reynolds, C. R., & Ford, L. (in press). Comparative three-factor solutions of the WISC-III and WISC-R at 11 age levels between 6-½ and 16-½ years. *Journal of School Psychology.*

Reynolds, C. R., & Kaiser, S. M. (1990). Test bias in psychological assessment. In T. B. Gutkin & C. R. Reynolds (Eds.), *The handbook of school psychology* (2nd ed., pp. 487–525). New York: Wiley.

Reynolds, C. R., & Kamphaus, R. W. (1992). *BASC: Behavior Assessment System for Children manual*. Circle Pines, MN: American Guidance Service.

Ribner, S., & Kahn, P. (1981). Scatter on the WISC as an indicator of intellectual potential. *Psychology in the Schools, 18*, 39–42.

Robinson, E. L., & Nagle, R. J. (1992). The comparability of the Test of Cognitive Skills with the Wechsler Intelligence Scale for Children—Revised and the Stanford-Binet: Fourth Edition with gifted children. *Psychology in the Schools, 29*, 107–112.

Roid, G. H., Prifitera, A., & Weiss, L. G. (1993). Replication of the WISC-III factor structure in an independent sample. In B. A. Bracken & R. S. McCallum (Eds.), *Journal of Psychoeducational Assessment monograph series, advances in psychoeducational assessment: Wechsler Intelligence Scale for Children—Third Edition* (pp. 6–21). Germantown, TN: Psychoeducational Corporation.

Rosso, M., Falasco, S. L., & Koller, J. R. (1984). Investigations into the relationship of the PPVT-R and the WISC-R with incarcerated delinquents. *Journal of Clinical Psychology, 40,* 588–591.

Royer, F. L. (1971). Information processing of visual figures in the digit symbol substitution test. *Journal of Experimental Psychology, 87,* 335–342.

Rugel, R. P. (1974). WISC subtest scores of disabled readers: A review with respect to Bannatyne's recategorization. *Journal of Learning Disabilities, 7,* 48–55.

Saccuzzo, D. P., Johnson, N. E., & Russell, G. (1992). Verbal versus Performance IQs for gifted African American, Caucasian, Filipino, and Hispanic children. *Psychological Assessment, 4,* 239–244.

Said, J. A., Waters, B. G. H., Cousens, P., & Stevens, M. M. (1989). Neuropsychological sequelae of central nervous system prophylaxis in survivors of childhood acute lymphoblastic leukemia. *Journal of Consulting and Clinical Psychology, 57,* 251–256.

Sapp, G. L., Chissom, B., & Graham, E. (1985). Factor analysis of the WISC-R for gifted students: A replication and comparison. *Psychological Reports, 57,* 947–951.

Sattler, J. M. (1974). *Assessment of children's intelligence* (rev. ed.). Philadelphia: Saunders.

Sattler, J. M. (1988). *Assessment of children* (3rd ed.) San Diego, CA: Author.

Sattler, J. M. (1992). *Assessment of children: WISC-III and WPPSI-R supplement.* San Diego, CA: Author.

Saunders, D. R. (1960). A factor analysis of the information and Arithmetic items of the WAIS. *Psychological Reports, 6,* 367–383.

Scarbaugh, M. E. (1983, September). Working up, writing up. *School Psychology in Illinois, 5,* 8.

Scarbaugh, M. E. (1992, May/June). PRO and CONtroversy. *School Psychology in Illinois, 13,* 11–12.

Schiff, M. M., Kaufman, A. S., & Kaufman, N. L. (1981). Scatter analysis of WISC-R profiles for learning disabled children with superior intelligence. *Journal of Learning Disabilities, 14,* 400–404.

Schofield, N. J., & Ashman, A. F. (1986). The relationship between Digit Span and cognitive processing across ability groups. *Intelligence, 10,* 59–73.

Schuerger, J. M., & Witt, A. C. (1989). The temporal stability of individually tested intelligence. *Journal of Clinical Psychology, 45,* 294–302.

Schwean, V. L., Saklofske, D. H., Yackulic, R. A., & Quinn, D. (1993). WISC-III performance of ADHD children. In B. A. Bracken & R. S. McCallum (Eds.), *Journal of Psychoeducational Assessment monograph series, advances in psychoeducational assessment: Wechsler Intelligence Scale for Children—Third Edition* (pp. 56–70). Germantown, TN: Psychoeducational Corporation.

Seashore, C. E., Lewis, D., & Saetveit, J. G. (1960). *Seashore Measures of Musical Talents.* New York: Psychological Corporation.

Seashore, H. G. (1951). Differences between verbal and performance IQs on the WISC. *Journal of Consulting Psychology, 15,* 62–67.

Seth, G. (1973). Eye-hand coordination and handedness: A developmental study of visuo-motor behavior in infancy. *British Journal of Educational Psychology, 43,* 35–49.

Shapiro, E. G., & Dotan, N. (1986). The Kaufman Assessment Battery for Children and neurologic findings. *Developmental Neuropsychology, 2,* 51–64.

Shapiro, E. S., & Derr, T. F. (1990). Curriculum-based assessment. In T. B. Gutkin & C. R. Reynolds (Eds.), *The handbook of school psychology* (2nd ed., pp. 365–387). New York: Wiley.

Schaw, S. R., Swerdlik, M. E., & Laurent, J. (1993). Review of the WISC-III. In B. A. Bracken & R. S. McCallum (Eds.), *Journal of Psychoeducational Assessment monograph series, advances in psychoeducational assessment: Wechsler Intelligence Scale for Children—Third Edition* (pp. 151–160). Germantown, TN: Psychoeducational Corporation.

Shellenberger, S. (1977). *A cross-cultural investigation of the Spanish version of the McCarthy Scales of Children's Abilities for Puerto Rican children.* Unpublished doctoral dissertation, University of Georgia.

Shellenberger, S., & Lachterman, T. (1979). Cognitive and motor functioning on the McCarthy Scales by Spanish-speaking children. *Perceptual and Motor Skills, 49,* 863–866.

Siegler, R. S. (1989). Strategy diversity and cognitive assessment. *Educational Researcher, 18,* 15–20.

Silver, C. H., & Tipps, K. L. (1993). Memory abilities of reading-disabled children with VIQ-PIQ differences. *Journal of Psychoeducational Assessment, 11,* 270–277.

Silver, L. B. (1993). Introduction and overview to the clinical concepts of learning disabilities. *Child and Adolescent Psychiatric Clinics of North America: Learning Disabilities, 2,* 181–192.

Silver, S. J., & Clampit, M. K. (1988). Demographic distribution of third factor deficits in the standardization sample of the Wechsler Intelligence Scale for Children—Revised. *Journal of Psychoeducational Assessment, 6,* 309–314.

Silverstein, A. B. (1968). WISC subtest patterns of retardates, *Psychological Reports, 23,* 1061–1062.

Silverstein, A. B. (1969). An alternative factor analytic solution for Wechsler's scales. *Educational and Psychological Measurement, 29,* 763–776.

Silverstein, A. B. (1982). Pattern analysis as simultaneous statistical inference. *Journal of Consulting and Clinical Psychology, 50,* 234–240.

Silverstein, A. B. (1989). On the use of the WISC-R supplementary subtests as alternates. *Psychological Reports, 64,* 580–582.

Silverstein, A. B. (1993). Type I, Type II, and other types of errors in pattern analysis. *Psychological Assessment, 5,* 72–74.

Simensen, R. J., & Sutherland, J. (1974). Psychological assessment of brain damage: The Wechsler scales. *Academic Therapy, 10,* 69–81.

Sininger, Y. S., Klatzky, R. L., & Kirchner, D. M. (1989). Memory scanning speed in language-disordered children. *Journal of Speech and Hearing Research, 32,* 289–297.

Slate, J. R., & Chick, D. (1989). WISC-R examiner errors: Cause for concern. *Psychology in the Schools, 26,* 78–84.

Slate, J. R., & Hunnicutt, L. C. (1988). Examining errors on the Wechsler scales. *Journal of Psychoeducational Assessment, 6,* 280–288.

Slate, J. R., & Jones, C. H. (1990). Student error in administering the WISC-R: Identifying problem areas. *Measurement and Evaluation in Counseling and Development, 23,* 137–140.

Slate, J. R., Jones, C. H., Coulter, C., & Covert, T. L. (1992). Practitioners' administration and scoring errors of the WISC-R: Evidence that we do err. *Journal of School Psychology, 30,* 77–82.

Slate, J. R., Jones, C. H., Graham, L. S., & Bower, J. (in press). Correlations of WISC-III, WRAT-R, KM-R, and PPVT-R scores in students with specific learning disabilities. *Learning Disabilities Research and Practice.*

Smith, A. (1983). Overview or "underview"? Comment on Satz and Fletcher's "Emergent trends in neuropsychology: An overview." *Journal of Consulting and Clinical Psychology, 51,* 768–775.

Smith, M. D., Coleman, J. M., Dokecki, P. R., & Davis, E. E. (1977). Recategorized WISC-R scores of learning disabled children. *Journal of Learning Disabilities, 10,* 444–449.

Smith, T., Edmonds, J. E., & Smith, B. (1989). The role of sex differences in the referral process as measured by the Peabody Picture Vocabulary Test—Revised and the Wechsler Intelligence Scale for Children—Revised. *Psychology in the Schools, 26,* 354–358.

Snow, R. E., & Farr, M. J. (Eds.). (1987). *Aptitude, learning, and instruction: Vol. 3, conative and affective process analyses.* Hillsdale, NJ: Erlbaum.

Spafford, C. (1989). Wechsler Digit Span subtest: Diagnostic usefulness with dyslexic children. *Perceptual and Motor Skills, 69,* 115–125.

Sparrow, S. S., Balla, D. A., & Cicchetti, D. V. (1984). *Survey form manual (interview edition) of the Vineland Adaptive Behavior Scales.* Circle Pines, MN: American Guidance Services.

Spelberg, H. C. (1987). Problem-solving strategies on the block-design task. *Perceptual and Motor Skills, 65,* 99–104.

Sperry, R. W. (1968). Hemisphere deconnection and unity in conscious awareness. *American Psychologist, 23,* 723–733.

Spitz, H. H. (1989). Variations in Wechsler interscale IQ disparities at different levels of IQ. *Intelligence, 13,* 157–167.

Spitz, R. A., & Wolf, K. M. (1946). *Anaclitic depression: An inquiry into the genesis of psychiatric conditions in early childhood, II.* (pp. 313–342). In A. Freud et al. (Eds.), *The psychoanalytic study of the child, Vol. II.* New York: International Universities Press.

Springer, S. P., & Deutsch, G. (1981). *Left brain right brain.* San Francisco, CA: Freeman.

Stanley, J. C., George, W. C., & Salano, C. H. (Eds.). (1977). The gifted and the creative: A fifty year perspective. Baltimore, MD: Johns Hopkins University Press.

Sternberg, R. J. (1977). *Intelligence, information processing, and analogical reasoning: The componential analysis of human abilities.* Hillsdale, NJ: Erlbaum.

Sternberg, R. J. (1982). Lies we live by: Misapplications of tests in identifying the gifted. *Gifted Child Quarterly, 26,* 157–161.

Sternberg, R. J. (1985). *Beyond IQ: A triarchic theory of human intelligence.* New York: Cambridge University Press.

Sternberg, R. J. (1987). Synopsis of a triarchic theory of human intelligence. In S. H. Irvine & S. E. Newstead (Eds.), *Intelligence and cognition: Contemporary frames of reference* (pp. 141–175). Boston, MA: Martinus Nijhoff.

Sternberg, R. J. (1993). Rocky's back again: A review of the WISC-III. In B. A. Bracken & R. S. McCallum (Eds.), *Journal of Psychoeducational Assessment monograph series, advances in psychoeducational assessment: Wechsler Intelligence Scale for Children—Third Edition* (pp. 161–164). Germantown, TN: Psychoeducational Corporation.

Stewart, K. J., & Moely, B. E. (1983). The WISC-R third factor: What does it mean? *Journal of Consulting and Clinical Psychology, 51,* 940–941.

Stone, B. J. (1992a). Joint confirmatory factor analyses of the DAS and WISC-R. *Journal of School Psychology, 30,* 185–195.

Stone, B. J. (1992b). Prediction of achievement by Asian American and white children. *Journal of School Psychology, 30,* 91–99.

Stone, B. J., Gridley, B. E., & Gyurke, J. S. (1991). Confirmatory factor analysis of the WPPSI-R at the extreme end of the age range. *Journal of Psychoeducational Assessment, 8,* 263–270.

Stoner, S. B., & Glynn, M. A. (1987). Cognitive styles of school-age children showing attention deficit disorders with hyperactivity. *Psychological Reports, 61,* 119–125.

Strom, D. A., Mason, E. M., Williams, D. L., Dean, R. S., & Fischer, W. E. (1988). Relationship of auditory discrimination ability to WISC-R subtest performance in learning-disabled children. *Developmental Neuropsychology, 4,* 275–282.

Sullivan, P. M., & Schulte, L. E. (1992). Factor analysis of WISC-R with deaf and hard-of-hearing children. *Psychological Assessment, 4,* 537–540.

Sutter, E., Bishop, P., & Battin, R. R. (1987). Psychometric screening for attention deficit disorder in a clinical setting. *Journal of Psychoeducational Assessment, 3,* 227–235.

Swyter, L. J., & Michael, W. B. (1982). The interrelationships of four measures hypothesized to represent the field dependence-field independence construct. *Educational and Psychological Measurement, 42,* 877–888.

Talley, J. L. (1986). Memory in learning disabled children: Digit span and the Rey Auditory Verbal Learning Test. *Archives of Clinical Neuropsychology, 1,* 315–322.

Tanner-Halverson, P., Burden, T., & Sabers, D. (1993). WISC-III normative data for Tohono O'oodham Native American children. In B. A. Bracken & R. S. McCallum (Eds.), *Journal of Psychoeducational Assessment monograph series, advances in psychoeducational assessment: Wechsler Intelligence Scale for Children—Third Edition* (pp. 125–133). Germantown, TN: Psychoeducational Corporation.

Taylor, R. L., Ziegler, E. W., & Partenio, I. (1984). An investigation of WISC-R Verbal-Performance differences as a function of ethnic status. *Psychology in the Schools, 21,* 437–441.

Teeter, A., Moore, C. L., & Petersen, J. D. (1982). WISC-R verbal and performance of Native American students referred for school learning problems. *Psychology in the Schools, 19,* 39–44.

Teeter, P. A., & Smith, P. L. (1993). WISC-III and WJ-R: Predictive and discriminant validity for students with severe emotional disturbance. In B. A. Bracken & R. S. McCallum (Eds.), *Journal of Psychoeducational Assessment monograph series, advances in psychoeducational assessment: Wechsler Intelligence Scale for Children—Third Edition* (pp. 114–124). Germantown, TN: Psychoeducational Corporation.

Tellegen, A., & Briggs, P. F. (1967). Old wine in new skins: Grouping Wechsler subtests into new scales. *Journal of Consulting Psychology, 31,* 499–506.

Thorndike, E. L. (1926). *Measurement of intelligence.* New York: Teacher's College, Columbia University.

Thorndike, R. L. (1971). Concepts of culture-fairness. *Journal of Educational Measurement, 8,* 63–70.

Thorndike, R. L., Hagen, E. P., & Sattler, J. M. (1986). *Technical manual for the Stanford-Binet Intelligence Scale—Fourth Edition.* Chicago, IL: Riverside.

Thorndike, R. M. (1990). Would the real factors of the Stanford-Binet—Fourth Edition please come forward? *Journal of Psychoeducational Assessment, 8,* 412–435.

Thorndike, R. M. (1992, March). *Intelligence tests: What we have and what we should have.* Paper presented at the meeting of the National Association of School Psychologists, Nashville, TN.

Thurstone, L. L. (1938). Primary mental abilities. *Psychometric Monographs,* (1).

Tittemore, J. A., Lawson, J. S., & Inglis, J. (1985). Validation of a learning disabilities index (LDI) derived from a principal components analysis of the WISC-R. *Journal of Learning Disabilities, 18,* 449–454.

Torrance, E. P. (1974). *Torrance Tests of Creative Thinking: Directions manual and scoring guide.* Lexington, MA: Ginn & Company.

Torrance, E. P. (1977). *Discovery and nurturance of giftedness in the culturally different.* Reston, VA: Council for Exceptional Children.

Torrance, E. P. (1982). Identifying and capitalizing on the strengths of culturally different children. In C. R. Reynolds & T. B. Gutkin (Eds.), *The handbook of school psychology* (pp. 481–500). New York: Wiley.

Truscutt, S. D., Narrett, C. M., & Smith, S. E. (1994). WISC-R subtest reliability over time: Implications for practice and research. *Perceptual and Motor Skills, 74,* 147–156.

Turkheimer, E., & Farace, E. (1992). A reanalysis of gender differences in IQ scores following unilateral brain lesions. *Psychological Assessment, 4,* 498–501.

Van Hagen, J., & Kaufman, A. S. (1975). Factor analysis of the WISC-R for a group of mentally retarded children and adolescents. *Journal of Consulting and Clinical Psychology, 43,* 661–667.

Vargo, F. E. (1992). *Wechsler subtest profiles: Diagnostic usefulness with dyslexic children.* Unpublished doctoral dissertation, American International college, Springfield, MA.

Vernon, P. A. (1987). New developments in reaction time research. In P. A. Vernon (Ed.), *Speed of information-processing and intelligence* (pp. 1–20). Norwood, NJ: Ablex.

Vernon, P. A., & Jensen, A. R. (1984). Individual and group differences in intelligence and speed of information processing. *Personality and Individual Differences, 5,* 411–423.

Vernon, P. E. (1960). *The structure of human abilities* (rev. ed.), London: Methuen.

Wadsworth, B. J. (1978). *Piaget for the classroom teacher.* New York: Longman.

Walker, N. W. (1985). Interactional effects of socioeconomic status and cognitive tempo on WISC-R performance. *Measurement and Evaluation in Counseling and Development, 18,* 58–63.

Washington, V. M., & Miller-Jones, D. (1989). Teacher interactions with nonstandard English speakers during reading instruction. *Contemporary Educational Psychology, 14,* 280–312.

Watson, B. L. (1969). *Field dependence and early reading achievement.* Doctoral dissertation, University of California, Los Angeles (University Microfilms No. 70-14, 335, Ann Arbor, MI)

Wechsler, D. (1939). *Measurement of adult intelligence.* Baltimore, MD: Williams & Wilkins.

Wechsler, D. (1974). *Manual for the Wechsler Intelligence Scale for Children— Revised (WISC-R).* San Antonio, TX: Psychological Corporation.

Wechsler, D. (1989). *Manual for the Wechsler Preschool and Primary Scale of Intelligence—Revised (WPPSI-R).* San Antonio, TX: Psychological Corporation.

Wechsler, D. (1991). *Manual for the Wechsler Intelligence Scale for Children— Third Edition (WISC-III).* San Antonio, TX: Psychological Corporation.

Weinberg, J., Diller, L., Gerstman, L., & Schulman, P. (1972). Digit span in right and left hemiplegics. *Journal of Clinical Psychology, 28,* 361.

Weiss, L. G., Prifitera, A., & Roid, G. H. (1993). The WISC-III and the fairness of predicting achievement across ethnic and gender groups. In B. A. Bracken & R. S. McCallum (Eds.), *Journal of Psychoeducational Assessment monograph series, advances in psychoeducational assessment: Wechsler Intelligence Scale for Children—Third Edition* (pp. 35–42). Germantown, TN: Psychoeducational Corporation.

Weiss, V. (1986). From memory span and mental speed toward the quantum mechanics of intelligence. *Personality and Individual Differences, 7,* 737–749.

Weltner-Brunton, S. L., Serafica, F. C., & Friedt, G. R. (1988). Is earlier better? Reading achievement and WISC-R stability in earlier vs. later identified students with learning disabilities. *Learning Disabilities Quarterly, 11,* 71–79.

Wender, P. H. (1971). Minimal brain dysfunction in children. New York: Wiley.

Wesman, A. G. (1968). Intelligent testing. *American Psychologist, 23,* 267–274.

Wielkiewicz, R. M. (1990). Interpreting low scores on the WISC-R third factor: It's more than distractibility. *Psychological Assessment, 2,* 91–97.

Wielkiewicz, R. M., & Daood, C. J. (1993). Correlations between WISC-R subtests and scales of the Personality Inventory for Children. *Psychological Reports, 73,* 1343–1346.

Williams, F. (Ed.). (1970). *Language and poverty.* Chicago, IL: Markham.

Witelson, S. F. (1976). Sex and the single hemisphere: Specialization of the right hemisphere for spatial processing. *Science, 193,* 425–427.

Witelson, S. F. (1977). Development dyslexia: Two right hemispheres and none left. *Science, 195,* 309–311.

Witkin, H. A., Dyk, R. B., Faterson, H. G., Goodenough, D. R., & Karp, S. A. (1974). *Psychological differentiation.* Potomac, MD: Erlbaum.

Witkin, H. A., & Goodenough, D. R. (1977). Field dependence and interpersonal behavior. *Psychological Bulletin, 84,* 661–689.

Witkin, H. A., Moore, C. A., Goodenough, D. R., & Cox, P. W. (1977). Field-dependent and field-independent cognitive styles and their educational implications. *Review of Educational Research, 47,* 1–64.

Witkin, H. A., Oltman, P. K., Raskin, E., & Karp, S. A. (1971). *Manual for the Embedded Figures Tests.* Palo Alto, CA: Consulting Psychologists Press.

Witt, J. C., & Gresham, F. M. (1985). Review of the Wechsler Intelligence Scale for Children—Revised. In J. V. Mitchell (Ed.), *Ninth mental measurements yearbook* (pp. 1716–1719). Lincoln, NE: University of Nebraska Press.

Woodcock, R. W. (1990). Theoretical foundations of the WJ-R measures of cognitive ability. *Journal of Psychoeducational Assessment, 8,* 231–258.

Woodcock, R. W., & Johnson, M. B. (1989). *Woodcock-Johnson Tests of Cognitive Ability: Standard and supplemental batteries.* Allen, TX: DLM/Teaching Resources.

Woo-Sam, J., & Zimmerman, I. L. (1972). Speed as a variable on three WISC Performance subtests. *Perceptual and Motor Skills, 34,* 451–455.

Zimmerman, I. L., & Woo-Sam, J. M. (1973). *Clinical interpretation of the Wechsler Adult Intelligence Scale.* New York: Grune & Stratton.

Zimmerman, I. L., & Woo-Sam, J. M. (1985). Clinical applications. In B. B. Wolman (Ed.), *Handbook of intelligence: Theories, measurements, and applications* (pp. 873–898). New York: Wiley.

Author Index

Abrahams, R. D., 12
Adams, N. A., 209
Adderly-Kelly, B., 21, 56
Albott, W. L., 149
Aldenkamp, A. P., 213
Allen, M. H., 155–156, 213, 297
Allison, J., 58, 144
Alpherts, W. C. J., 213
Anastasi, A., 194
Anderson, H. N., 163
Anderson, P. L., 182
Anderson, S. W., 213
Andrew, J. M., 146
Andrews, T. J., 35, 36
Aram, D. M., 145, 213
Arter, J. A., 33
Arthur, G., 139
Asarnow, R. F., 155, 213
Asbury, C. A., 21, 56
Ashman, A. F., 233
Ayres, R. R., 33
Azen, S. P., 243

Baggaley, A. R., 2, 4, 30, 213
Baker, S. A., 243
Balla, D. A., 99
Bannatyne, A., 15, 27, 49, 55, 186, 231, 290
Baratz, J. C., 162–163
Barkley, R. A., 213
Barnett, D. W., 2, 28–29, 197
Bartlett, C. J., 232
Batsche, G., 4
Battin, R. R., 212
Bauman, R., 162

Baumeister, A. A., 232
Beck, B. L., 209
Belter, R. W., 85
Bender, J. R., 160
Bensch, M., 146
Berk, R., 56, 213
Bernard, R., 56, 297
Berry, J. W., 158, 160
Bever, T. G., 48, 303
Bice, T. R., 186
Bigler, E. D., 145
Birch, H. G., 145
Birdwell, D. A., 224
Bishop, P., 212
Black, F. W., 116
Blatt, S. J., 58, 144
Bleker, E. G., 146
Bloom, A. S., 149
Blumberg, E., 233
Boren, R., 38–89, 155, 215
Bortner, M., 145
Boswell, J. J., 162
Bott, L., 155, 213
Bouyer, J., 160
Bower, J., 181
Boyd, T. A., 60, 62
Bracken, B. A., 7, 18, 36, 44, 175, 195, 214
Braden, J. P., 152
Brandt, D., 213
Brandt, E. A., 160
Briggs, P. F., 221–222, 275, 279
Brouwers, P., 224
Brown, L., 139
Brown, S. W., 197

Bruininks, R. H., 189
Buckley, K., 186–187
Budoff, M., 36
Burden, T., 159–160
Burgess, A., 107
Buriel, R., 187
Busch, R., 146, 178
Butler-Omololu, C., 21
Byrne, B., 223

Caldwell, J., 38, 215
Campbell, B., 127
Cantrall, S. W., 197
Carmon, A., 303
Carroll, J. B., 3, 43
Carter, C., 12, 162
Castellanos, M., 107
Catron, D. W., 143
Cattell, R. B., 19, 49–50, 151, 167–168, 180
Chamrad, D., 196–197
Chavez, J. M., 243
Chevrie-Muller, C., 160
Chick, D., 127
Chissom, B., 197
Chowdhri, S., 33
Cicchetti, D. V., 99
Clampit, M. K., 213
Clarizio, H., 56, 297
Clark, P., 197
Cleary, T. A., 22
Coates, S., 185
Cody, J. J., 209
Cohen, A., 209, 212
Cohen, J., 48, 104, 212, 232
Cohen, R., 187
Cole, S., 163
Connelly, J. B., 56
Conrad, E., 147
Cook, V., 21, 29, 56, 158–161
Cooley, E. J., 33
Corley, R. P., 182
Cornell, D. G., 146–147
Costa, L. D., 232–233
Cotman, C. W., 224
Coulter, C., 127
Court, J. H., 139
Cousens, P., 212, 224
Covert, T. L., 127

Cox, P. W., 185–187
Crain, M., 44, 214
Crawford, J. A., 212, 224
Creek, R. J., 33
Crinella, F. M., 232, 251
Cronbach, L. J., 167
Cronin, M. E., 182
Crowl, T. K., 163
Culbertson, F. M., 146
Cummings, M. A., 159
Currie, B. B., 163, 197
Cutchen, M., 146

Daniel, M. H., 107
Daood, C. J., 213
Das, J. P., 14, 17, 36, 60, 224, 246–247, 297–299, 304
Davies, M. F., 187
Davis, F. B., 27, 125
Dean, R. S., 182
Decker, S. N., 182, 223
Dekker, M. J. A., 213
De Mesquita, P., 186–187
Denckla, M. B., 304
Dennis, M., 145
DeRienzo, P. J., 145
Derr, T. F., 36
Dersh, J., 55, 181–183, 186, 217–220, 222, 297–298, 302
Deutsch, G., 48, 57, 146, 297
Diessner, R., 159
Diller, L., 233
Doll, B., 38, 89, 155, 215
Dollinger, S. J., 209
Donders, J., 145
Doster, J. A., 21
Dotan, N., 145–146
Dougherty, E. H., 9, 14, 26, 158
Dover, A., 196
Dumont, R., 38, 100
Dunn, L., 179
DuPaul, G. J., 213
Dworkin, R. H., 58, 75, 87
Dyk, R. B., 185, 186, 275

Eaves, R. C., 146
Edmonds, J. E., 251
Edwards, J. L., 4
Edwards, R., 4

Edwards, R. P., 197
Ekelman, B. L., 145, 213
Ellen, A. S., 182
Elliott, C. D., 14, 170
Ellis, N. R., 232
Ensor, A., 251
Erlenmeyer-Kimling, L., 58, 75, 87
Estes, W. K., 17, 244
Evans, J. R., 250

Fagan, T., 36
Falasco, S. L., 146
Fantuzzo, J. W., 2, 4, 30, 213, 230
Farace, E., 179
Faro, C., 38, 100
Farr, M. J., 58
Faterson, H. G., 185–186, 275
Fedio, P., 224
Feral, C. H., 146
Feuerstein, R., 8, 36
Finch, A. J., 85
Fischer, M., 213
Fischer, W. E., 182
Flaugher, R. L., 6
Fleming, M. Z., 58
Fleshman, J. K., 160
Flynn, J. R., 37
Folino, L., 197
Forceville, E. M. J., 213
Ford, L., 57, 217
Forness, S. R., 56, 213, 216
Foster, K. Y., 85
Frank, G., 3
Freeman, B. J., 155, 213
Friedt, G. R., 182

Gabby, S., 146
Galin, D., 302, 304
Galvin, G. A., 213
Garcia, E. E., 21
Gardner, H., 19, 25
Gardner, R., 233
Garner, T., 21, 162
Geary, D. C., 149
George, W. C., 184
Gerstman, L., 233
Gilger, J. W., 149
Gill, K. J., 149
Gill, M. M., 48, 269, 289

Glasser, A. J., 48
Glutting, J. J., 2, 4, 9–10, 21, 30, 32–33, 213, 227, 230, 242
Glynn, M. A., 186
Goh, D. S., 209
Golden, C. J., 246
Good, R. H., 33
Goodenough, D. R., 185–187, 275, 297
Goulet, M., 149
Grace, W. C., 146–147
Graham, E., 197
Graham, L. S., 181
Granier, M. J., 118, 147, 183
Greenblatt, E., 213, 216
Greenwood, S., 147
Gresham, F. M., 4, 17, 33
Gridley, B. E., 212
Groff, M. G., 146
Grossman, F. M., 213
Guilford, J. P., 49, 52–54, 184, 236, 297
Guilmette, S., 107
Gutkin, T. B., 107
Guzman, B. L., 243
Gyurke, J. S., 212

Haddad, F. A., 182
Hagen, E. P., 14, 27, 173
Hakuta, K., 21
Hall, R. J., 107, 186, 275
Halpin, G., 186
Hambleton, R. K., 13
Hammill, D. D., 13, 166
Hardesty, R. A., 209
Hardy, J. B., 8
Harrison, P. L., 37, 55, 104, 117, 148, 181–182, 184, 186, 212, 302
Hausman, R. M., 36
Haynes, J. P., 146
Haywood, H. C., 36
Heath, S. B., 21, 162
Hebb, D. O., 167, 303
Heemsbergen, D. B., 247
Hemmelgarn, T. E., 245
Hendrickson, A. E., 232, 251
Hendrickson, D. E., 232, 251
Herman, D. O. 107
Herring, S., 37
Hertzig, M. E., 145
Hibbett, C., 146, 178

Hickman, J. A., 37
Hildman, L. K., 197
Hilgendorf, W. A., 149
Hirshoren, A., 26
Hishinuma, E. S., 89, 103, 166, 215, 217–218
Hodges, K., 213
Hofer, S. M., 18, 51–52, 169, 179
Holcomb, W. R., 209
Holroyd, J., 145
Hooper, S. R., 60, 62
Hoover, M. R., 21, 162
Horn, J. L., 15, 17–19, 29, 49–52, 70, 151, 167–169, 171, 173–176, 179–180, 182, 230, 232, 236
Horwitz, E., 213
Hubble, L. M., 146
Humphreys, L. G., 22, 169
Hunnicutt, L. C., 127
Hunter, M., 163
Imm, P. S., 85
Inglis, J., 182, 186, 212, 297–299
Inhelder, B., 297
Ionasescu, V. V., 213
Ittenbach, R. F., 55, 99, 104, 117, 148, 181–182, 184, 186, 212, 302

Jenkins, J. R., 33
Jensen, A. R., 11–12, 163, 174, 196, 199, 223, 232, 245, 251
Johnsen, S., 139
Johnson, M. B., 13, 176–177
Johnson, N. E., 197
Jones, C. H., 127, 181
Jones, J. N., 30, 32
Jones, R. L., 36
Joschko, M., 212–213
Juliano, J. M., 182

Kagan, J., 8, 193, 303
Kagan, S., 187
Kahn, P., 107
Kaiser, S. M., 22
Kamphaus, R. W., 9, 32, 42, 44, 49, 58, 61, 123, 166, 172, 199
Kaplan, G. J., 160
Karnes, F. A., 197
Karp, S. A., 185–186, 275, 297
Katz, J., 160

Katz, L., 33
Kaufman, A. S., 5, 9, 12, 14, 17–18, 22, 25–26, 28–29, 32–33, 37–40, 48, 50–51, 55, 58, 99, 104, 116–118, 125, 139–140, 143, 145, 147–148, 155–156, 158–159, 165–166, 168, 171–172, 174–175, 179–184, 186, 190–191, 194–197, 199–200, 211–213, 217, 224, 231, 236, 239–240, 251, 297–298, 302
Kaufman, J. L., 155, 232, 251
Kaufman, N. L., 9, 12, 14, 18, 22, 25–26, 33, 37, 50, 99, 139, 148, 158–159, 171–172, 174–175, 179, 231, 240
Kavale, K., 26, 33, 35, 56, 213, 216
Kazmierski, S., 182
Kehle, T. J., 245
Keith, T. Z., 169, 174
Kellerman, J., 147
Kender, J. P., 147
Kendrick, S. A., 22
Keogh, B. K., 107, 186, 275
Kerns, K., 223
Kimura, D., 303
Kirby, J. R., 36, 224, 246, 299
Kirchner, D. M., 155, 195
Kirk, S. A., 27, 33, 152, 231
Kirk, W. D., 27, 33, 152, 231
Kitzinger, H., 233
Klatzky, R. L., 155, 195
Klein, R. E., 303
Kline, J., 213
Kline, R. B., 107
Knuckle, E. P., 21, 56
Koller, J., 146, 178
Kolligan, J., Jr., 11, 223, 251
Kramer, J. H., 107
Kramer, J. J., 107
Krauskopf, C. J., 109, 115, 125
Kush, J., 30, 32

Labov, W., 163
Lachterman, T., 159
Lahey, B., 21
Lajoie, S. P., 196–197
Laurent, J., 4
Lawson, J. S., 182, 186, 212, 297–299
Ledbetter, M. F., 17
Leguori, S., 154–155, 195, 215

le Normand, M. T., 160
Levinson, E. M., 197
Levy, J., 48
Lewandowski, L. J., 145
Lewis, D., 302
Lewnau, E. B., 21
Lezak, M. D., 3, 224, 301–302
Lincoln, A., 155, 156, 213, 297
Lipsitz, J. D., 58, 75, 87
Little, S. G., 18
Lohman, D. F., 12, 17, 50, 223, 251
Lowe, J. D., Jr., 163
Lucas, J. C., 213
Lueger, R. J., 149
Lufi, D., 209, 212
Luria, A. R., 20, 48, 57, 297, 304
Lutey, C., 209, 226, 229, 269
Lynn, R., 38, 251

MacGinitie, W. H., 163
MacKay, I., 182, 186, 212, 297–298
Macmann, G. M., 2, 28–29, 197
Maller, S. J., 152
Marr, D. B., 196
Marwit, K. L., 162
Marwit, S. J., 162–163
Mason, E. M., 182
Matarazzo, J. D., 36, 48, 50, 107, 168, 251, 301
Matheson, D. W., 56
Matson, D. E., 213
Matthews, C. G.
Mattis, S., 213, 216
Mayman, M., 48
McArdle, J. J., 169
McCallum, R. S., 7, 18, 44, 175, 195, 197, 214
McCarthy, J. J., 33, 231
McCullough, D. A., 159
McDermott, P. A., 2, 4, 9, 30, 32–33, 213, 230
McGaugh, J. L., 224
McGhee, R., 166, 170
McGrath, E. A., 32–33
McKenna, F. P., 187, 275
McLean, J. E., 174–175, 199, 236
McMurray, M. B., 213
McShane, D., 21, 29, 56, 158–161
Meeker, M. N., 15, 19, 52, 231

Meinhardt, M., 146, 178
Mellits, E. D., 8
Merrell, K. W., 159
Michael, W. B., 185–187
Miller-Jones, D., 21, 163
Minton, H. L., 12
Miron, M. S., 47, 79, 152, 231
Mitchell, H. R., 38
Mitchell, W. G., 243
Moely, B. E., 212, 223
Moffitt, T. E., 118, 143, 149
Montessori, M., 184
Moore, C. A., 185–187
Moore, C. L., 159
Moriarty, A., 251
Morris, J. M., 145
Moss, H. A., 147
Mueller, H. M., 56
Mulhern, G., 251

Nachson, I., 303
Nagle, R. J., 197
Naglieri, J. A., 4, 14, 12, 17, 35–36, 60, 101, 109, 115, 139, 148, 163, 174, 189, 199, 224, 246–247, 297–299, 304
Narrett, C. M., 182
Nebes, R. D., 303
Nettlebeck, T., 232
Neumann, G., 163
Newby, R. F., 38, 215
Nichols, E. G., 182, 186, 212, 297–298
Nisewaner, K., 154–155, 195, 215
Novak, C. G., 174

O'Donnell, L., 118, 147, 183
O'Grady, K. E., 29
Oakland, T., 9–10, 12, 21, 186–187, 227, 242
Oltman, P. K., 185
Ornstein, R., 302
Ortiz, V., 159
Osgood, C. E., 47, 79, 152, 231

Paget, K. D., 213
Parish-Plass, J., 212
Parker, M., 154–155, 195, 215
Partenio, I., 158
Petersen, J. D., 159

Phelps, L., 154–155, 195, 197, 215, 251
Piacentini, 155–156, 297
Piaget, J., 297
Piedmont, R. L., 58
Plake, B. S., 107
Plas, J. M., 21, 29, 158, 160
Plasket, C. M., 197
Platt, L. O., 44
Podruch, P. E., 149
Ponder, H. M., 209
Poplack, D., 224
Post, K. R., 38
Price, R. A., 224
Price-Williams, D. R., 186–187
Prifitera, A., 7, 22, 32–33, 42–43, 46, 55,
    103–104, 107, 161, 165, 181–183,
    186, 217–220, 222, 297–298, 302

Quay, H. C., 147
Quay, L. C., 163
Quinn, D., 215, 217–218

Ramirez, M., 186–187
Rapaport, D., 48, 269, 289
Raskin, E., 185
Rattan, G., 194
Raven, J. C., 139
Reams, R., 196–197
Reardon, S. H., 299, 304
Recht, D. R., 38, 215
Reed, H. B. C., 145
Reese, A., 149
Reitan, R. M., 37, 58, 82, 84, 91, 164,
    224, 289, 300–301
Reschly, D. J., 4, 26, 33, 35
Reynolds, C. R., 9, 12, 22, 57, 107, 217,
    232
Ribner, S., 107
Riccardi, R., 224
Ritvo, E. R., 213
Robinson, E. L., 197
Robinson, N. M., 196–197
Roid, G. H., 7, 22, 42–43, 46, 103–104,
    161, 165
Rosso, M., 146
Rourke, B. P., 212–213
Routh, D. K., 213
Royer, F. L., 244

Rubin, D. L., 21, 162
Rugel, R. P., 56, 181, 186, 298
Russell, G., 197
Ryan, G., 251

Sabers, D., 159–160
Saccuzzo, D. P., 197
Saetveit, J. G., 302
Said, J. A., 212
Saklofske, D. H., 215, 217–218
Salano, C. H., 184
Sapp, G. L., 197
Sattler, J. M., 14, 27, 49, 58, 104, 125,
    173
Saunders, D. R., 269
Scarbaugh, M. E., 38, 87
Schaefer, J., 38, 215
Schafer, E. W. P., 232, 251
Schafer, R., 48, 269, 289
Schaw, S. R., 4
Schellenberg, R. P., 107
Schelvis, A. J., 213
Schiff, M. M., 148
Schneider, F. W., 12
Schofield, N. J., 233
Schuerger, J. M., 143
Schulman, P., 233
Schulte, L. E., 152
Schurr, K. T., 182
Schwean, V. L., 215, 217–218
Seashore, C. E., 302
Seashore, H. G., 116, 183
Serafica, F. C., 182
Seth, G., 303
Shapiro, E. G., 145–146
Shapiro, E. S., 36
Shea, P., 223
Shellenberger, S., 159–160
Sherbenou, R., 139
Shore, B. M., 196–197
Short, R. H., 56
Siegel, S. E., 147
Siegler, R. S., 196
Siler, R. F., 197
Silva, P. A., 118, 143, 149
Silver, C. H., 182
Silver, L. B., 10, 15, 47, 147, 152
Silver, S. J., 213

Silverstein, A. B., 60, 62, 109, 115, 125–126, 186, 297
Simensen, R. J., 145
Sininger, Y. S., 155, 195
Slate, J. R., 127, 181
Smith, A., 145
Smith, B., 251
Smith, P. L., 177, 215
Smith, S. E., 182
Smith, T., 251
Snow, R. E., 58
Snyder, J., 107
Sokolve, R. L., 58
Spafford, C., 223
Sparrow, S. S., 99
Spelberg, H. C., 301
Sperry, R. W., 20, 48, 146, 164, 297
Spitz, H. H., 38
Spitz, R. A., 303
Springer, S. P., 48, 57, 146, 297
Spruill, J., 209
Stankov, L., 169, 182
Stanley, J. C., 184
Sternberg, R. J., 3, 8, 11, 19, 25, 167, 196, 223–224, 251
Stevens, J. S., 17
Stevens, M. M., 212, 224
Stewart, K. J., 212, 223
Stirne, R., 160
Stokes, A., 21, 56
Stone, B. J., 18, 170–171, 179, 212
Stoner, S. B., 186
Stroebel, S., 250
Strom, D. A., 182
Sullivan, P. M., 152
Sutherland, J., 145
Sutter, E., 212
Sweeney, M. E., 146
Swerdlik, M. E., 4
Swyter, L. J., 185–187

Talley, J. L., 233
Tanguay, P. E., 155, 213
Tanner-Halverson, P., 159–160
Taylor, R. L., 158
Teeter, A., 159
Teeter, P. A., 177, 215
Tellegen, A., 221–222, 275, 279

Thompson, C. C., 143
Thorndike, E. L., 17
Thorndike, R. L., 14, 22, 27, 173
Thorndike, R. M., 104, 172–173
Thurstone, L. L., 297
Tilly, W. D., 4, 26, 33, 35
Tipps, K. L., 182
Tittemore, J. A., 299
Topinka, C. W., 149
Torrance, E. P., 12, 99, 184
Trad, P. V., 213, 216
Trevarthen, C., 48
Truscutt, S. D., 182
Turkheimer, E., 179
Tuttle, K. S. C., 9, 14, 26, 158

Ullman, D. P., 107
Ungerer, J. A., 212, 224

Van Hagen, J., 186, 297
Vargo, F. E., 223
Vaughan, D., 182
Vernon, P. A., 11, 196, 223, 245, 251, 297
Vollmer, M., 33
Volloff, W., 159

Wadsworth, B. J., 184
Walker, J. L., 159
Walker, N. W., 73
Wang, J., 159
Washington, V. M., 21, 163
Waters, B. G. H., 212
Watkins, M. W., 2, 4, 30, 32, 213
Watson, B. L., 187
Wechsler, D., 2, 6–7, 14, 16, 27, 29, 31, 38, 42, 46–48, 58, 61–62, 79, 89, 98–99, 101, 103, 108–109, 111, 116, 118, 125–127, 129, 131–132, 136–137, 140, 147, 165, 170, 190, 195–197, 201, 212, 215–217, 221, 225, 233–235, 242, 269, 275, 280, 288, 297
Weinberg, J., 233
Weiss, L. G., 7, 22, 42–43, 46, 103–104, 161, 165
Weiss, V., 251
Welcher, D. W., 8
Weltner-Brunton, S. L., 182

Wenck, L. S., 182
Wesman, A. G., 6, 22, 27
Whorton, J. E., 197
Wielkiewicz, R. M., 209, 211–213, 223
Williams, A., 163
Williams, D. L., 182
Williams, F., 21
Wilson, B. J., 127
Wilson, L. A., 146–147
Witelson, S. F., 304
Witkin, H. A., 185–187, 275
Witt, A. C., 143
Witt, J. C., 4, 17, 33
Wolf, K. M., 303
Wolfson, D., 58, 82, 84, 91, 164, 224, 289, 301

Woo-Sam, J. M., 49, 58, 140, 146, 192
Woodcock, R. W., 13, 18, 50–51, 166, 168–169, 173–174, 176–177, 179
Wright, F., 145

Yackulic, R. A., 215, 217–218
Yakimowski, M. E., 197
Yamakawa, E. S., 89, 103, 166, 215, 217–218
Young, R., 232
Zahn, G. L., 187
Ziegler, E. W., 158
Zimet, C. N., 58, 144
Zimmerman, I. L., 48–49, 58, 140, 146, 192

Subject Index

Abilities:
Bannatyne's recategorization system, 55–58
changes in, 32. *See also* Practice effect
development of, 328
by input–integration/storage–output (tables), 276–277, 278, 279. *See also* Information-processing model
measured by WISC-III, 41–96
for each subtest (table), 314
performance, 276–277
verbal, 274
verbal and performance scales, 150, 278
not measured by WISC-III, 52
shared with other subtests, 47–58
Arithmetic subtest, 69
Block Design subtest, 90
Coding subtest, 83
Comprehension subtest, 74
Digit Span subtest, 78
Information subtest, 64
Object Assembly subtest, 92–93
Picture Arrangement subtest, 86
Picture Completion subtest, 80–81
Similarities subtest, 66
Symbol Search subtest, 95
Vocabulary subtest, 71–72
understanding, 325
Abstract thinking, 11, 44, 50, 73, 77. *See also* Clinical considerations
Absurdities, *see* Stanford-Binet—Fourth Edition (Binet-4)
Achievement tests/testing, 6–7
ACID profile, 182–183, 216–219

Acquired knowledge (Bannatyne), 55, 57, 147, 181
reasoning *vs.*, 290–297
recategorization system and, 57
Adaptive behavior, 8, 68, 70, 75
ADHD, *see* Attention-Deficit Hyperactivity Disorder (ADHD)
Adir, Yossi, 370
African-Americans, 7, 9, 21, 56, 136, 146, 161–163. *See also* Black English; Case studies/sample profiles, Nathan S.
and Full Scale IQ, 22
K-ABC and, 12
nonverbal communication, 12
Age trends, 29, 42, 44
Alsace, France (study), 160
Alternatives *vs.* supplements, 36
American Indians, 56, 151, 158–161. *See also* Native Americans
Animal House, subtest, 17
Anti-profile researchers, 128, 130. *See also* Critics
Antisocial behavior indicators, 39
Antisocial children, 88
Anti-testing, *see* Opponents of IQ testing
Anxiety, 9, 70
assessment of, 70
impact of, 33, 49, 69, 78–79, 83, 91, 93, 95–96
Aphasia, 149
Arithmetic–Digit Span–Coding triad, 54, 211–214
Arithmetic subtest, 68–71. *See also* Subtests overviews
associated factors, 47

Arithmetic subtest *(Continued)*
  behavioral observations, 71
  Block Design subtest and, 89
  bonus points, 70
  classification of, 43, 51
  clinical considerations, 69–71
  comparison with other subtests, 69
  correlates of, 45
  Digit Span subtest and, 49, 77
  distractibility factor, 213
  empirical analysis, 68
  g factor, 52
  look for reason for error, 69–70
  memory assessment, 50, 53
  number ability, 13
  processing speed, assessment of, 150
  proportion of variance, 68
  reasoning, 150
  and retarded children, 70
  specificity, 45, 68
  summary of analysis, 68–71
  tasks, 11
  test the limits, 70
  things not measured, 70
Army Beta, 181
Arthur's Stencil Design, 139
Artificial intelligence, 16
Asian Americans, 160
Attention-Deficit Hyperactivity Disorder
    (ADHD), 69, 214–222
  case study, 331–338
  Coding subtest and, 83
  Digit Span subtest and, 78
  distractibility triad and, 212
  field dependence/field independence
      and, 186
  planning ability and, 299, 304
  Symbol Search subtest and, 95
Attention problems, detection of, 96,
    210–211
Attention span, 69, 78–79
Auditory difficulty, 178
  case study, 383–392
  influence of, 10–11, 73
Auditory Intelligence (Ga), 50–52, 178.
    See also Horn and Cattell's
    fluid-crystallized theory
Austria, IQ gains in, 37

Autism:
  case study, 201–208
  distractibility factor and, 213
  linguistic problems, 155–156
  verbal problems, 151

Background information, significance of,
    310, 312
Bannatyne's recategorization system, 50,
    55–58
  Acquired Knowledge grouping, 147
BASC, *see* Behavior Assessment System
    for Children (BASC)
Beer and wine item, 39
Behavior, sample of *vs.* exhaustive, 7–8
Behavioral (B) content, 53–55
Behavioral observations, 9, 49, 310,
    312–313
  objective aids to categorize, 9
  significance of, 9, 49, 310, 312–313
Behavior Assessment System for Children
    (BASC):
  Student Observation Form/Scale, 9
    in case report for Lucy O., 260–268
    in case report for Tony G., 331–338
Behavior problems:
  case studies, 331–338, 393–401
Belgium, IQ gains in, 37
Bender-Gestalt Test of Visual-Motor
    Development, 85
    in case report for Greg T., 331–338
    in case report for Lucy O., 260–268
Beres, Kristee, 153–154, 370
Bias, test, 21–23, 26
Bilingualism, 21, 22, 23, 28, 158–160,
    161
Binet-4, *see* Stanford-Binet—Fourth
    Edition (Binet-4)
Black English:
  impact of, 15
  as nonintellective factor, 325
  rules of, 21, 162
  verbal-nonverbal discrepancies and,
      146, 161–163
Block Design subtest, 89–91. *See also*
    Subtests overviews
  abstraction and, 11
  autistic children and, 155

bonus points, 210
brain functions and, 300, 302
classification of, 43, 51
clinical considerations, 90–91
comparison with other subtests, 90
concept formation assessment, 150
coordination and, 13, 200
empirical analysis, 89–90
and Gv factor, 176
holistic processing and, 303
Object Assembly subtest and, 92
Performance deficit and, 138
Picture Arrangement subtest and, 85
Picture Completion subtest and, 80
proportion of variance, 89–90
specificity, 45, 89
speed and, 192–194
summary of analysis, 89–91
Symbol Search subtest and, 94
Bodily-kinesthetic intelligence, 19
Body-Adjustment test, 185, 186
Bonferroni correction, 101, 109, 115, 125
Bonus points, 34, 70, 89, 93, 151, 192, 210
Boredom, 84, 96
Brain damage, 29, 36, 82, 91, 144,
    145–146, 212
    drug therapy, 212
Brain hemispheres, 18, 47–48, 160, 164,
    179, 300–304
Broad Speediness (Gs), 50–52, 139, 168.
    See also Horn and Cattell's
    fluid-crystallized theory
Broad Visualization (Gv), 50–52,
    168–169, 172–173, 176–177,
    179–180, 297. See also Horn and
    Cattell's fluid-crystallized theory
    and Wechsler performance scale
    (overview), 179
Bruininks-Oseretsky Test of Motor
    Proficiency, 189

Case studies/sample profiles:
    case reports:
        Dana Christine T. (auditory
            processing difficulty, language
            disorder), 383–392
        Greg T. (behavior and learning
            problems), 393–401

    Ira G. (specific learning disability in
        writing), 371–382
    James C. (learning disability,
        encopresis), 348–360
    Jennie L. (autism, mental
        retardation), 201–208
    Lourdes I. (Tourette's syndrome,
        obsessive compulsive disorder),
        252–259
    Lucy O. (reading problems), 260–268
    Michael B. (school learning problem,
        emotional difficulties), 339–346
    Nicole A., (juvenile diabetes, gifted
        with possible neurological
        dysfunction), 361–370
    Tony G. (ADHD/behavior problems,
        high functioning), 331–338
sample profiles:
    Aliza G. (verbal compensation),
        138–139
    Harvey A. (V-P IQ difference
        uninterpretable), 112–113, 130,
        132–133
    Melinda B. (V-P IQ difference
        uninterpretable), 113–114
    Nathan S. (large V-P IQ discrepancy,
        plus subtest scatter), 120–121,
        131–133
    Nikki H., 316–324
Cerebral damage, see Brain damage
Cerebral functioning, integrated,
    300–304. See also Brain hemispheres
Cerebral specialization theory, 20, 48,
    145–146, 174. See also Brain
    hemispheres
Child Behavior Check List:
    in case report for Michael B., 339–346
Children's Embedded Figures Test, 185,
    186
Clang associations, 72
Clinical considerations, 15–16, 42, 58
    Arithmetic subtest, 69–71
    Block Design subtest, 90–91
    Coding subtest, 84–85
    Comprehension subtest, 75–77
    Digit Span subtest, 79–80
    Information subtest, 64–65
    Object Assembly subtest, 93–94

Clinical considerations *(Continued)*
  Picture Arrangement subtest, 87–89
  Picture Completion subtest, 81–82
  Similarities subtest, 67–68
  Symbol Search subtest, 96
  Vocabulary subtest, 72–73
Clinically rich items, deletion of, 38–39
Coding subtest, 58, 59–61, 82–85. *See
    also* Subtests overviews
  abstractions and, 11
  Arithmetic subtest and, 68
  associated factors, 47
  Block Design subtest and, 89
  classification of, 43
  clinical considerations, 84–85
  comparison with other subtests, 83–84
  Comprehension subtest and, 74
  coordination and, 13
  as correlate, 45
  Digit Span subtest and, 77
  distractibility factor, 213
  empirical analysis, 82–83
  g factor, 52
  Information subtest and, 63
  memory assessment and, 150
  Object Assembly subtest and, 92
  performance deficits and, 138
  Picture Arrangement subtest and, 85
  Picture Completion subtest and, 80
  proportion of variance, 82–83
  psycholinguistic deficiency and, 156–157
  reliability, 61
  sequencing ability and, 298–299
  Similarities subtest and, 66
  specificity, 45, 82
  substitution for (by Symbol Search), 58,
    59–61
  summary of analysis, 82–85
  Symbol Search *vs.,* 59–61, 94–95
  tasks, 17
  visual-motor coordination, 139
  Vocabulary subtest and, 71
Cognition (C) operation, 53–55
Cognitive styles:
  field dependence/field independence,
    81, 90, 93, 185–187
  impulsive-reflective, 87, 91, 93, 96,
    193
Cohen, Jacob, 212

Communication model/theory (Osgood),
    79, 152, 156. *See also*
    Information-processing model
Componential analysis, 8
Comprehension subtest, 73–77. *See also*
    Subtests overviews
  autistic children and, 155
  classification of, 43, 51
  clinical considerations, 75–77
  comparison with other subtests, 74–75
  empirical analysis, 73–74
  influences on, 316
  proportion of variance, 74
  psycholinguistic deficiency and, 157
  semantic evaluation, 55
  social understanding assessment, 150
  specificity, 45, 73
  summary of analysis, 73–77
  tasks, 10–11
Concentration, 69, 81, 91, 93
Concept Formation, 50, 150
Concrete thinking, 67, 73. *See also*
    Abstract thinking
Conscience, development of, 74
Contents dimension (Guilford SOI model),
    19, 53
Contracts, 330
Convergent production (N) operation, 53
Cookbook interpretation, 23
Coordination hypothesis, 13
Coordination problems, 93, 96, 188–190
Core profile approach, 32
Creativity, 68, 86
Cree Indians, 159
Criterion-referenced tests, 36
Critics, 2–5
  McDermott-Glutting (profile
    "malpractice"), 29–33, 36
  Macmann and Barnett ("only *g*"),
    28–29, 36
  Witt-Gresham (treatment validity),
    33–37
Critics, response to:
  generally, 25
  left-brained scientific view, 28–37
  right-brained intuitive view, 25–28
Crystallized Intelligence (Gc), 50–52,
    167, 168. *See also* Horn and Cattell's
    fluid-crystallized theory

defined, 19, 50, 179
measurement of, 167–168, 172–175, 179
and Wechsler verbal scale (overview), 179
Culture, influence of, 21, 49, 65, 72, 74, 86, 88
Culture loaded, 6, 12, 159
  vs. culture biased, 6
Curiosity, influence of, 64, 72
Curriculum-based assessment, 36
Cybernetics, 10

DAS, *see* Differential Abilities Scales (DAS)
Das-Naglieri Cognitive Assessment System, 14, 36
  Auditory Selective Attention, 158
  core subtests, 51
  Figure Memory, 199
  Matching Numbers, 14
  Matrices, 189
  Planned Codes, 139, 199
  Planned Connections, 14, 139, 199
  Planned Search, 17, 184
  Simultaneous Verbal, 158, 178
  theories behind, 17
  and treatment validity, 34
Davis, Fred, 27
Decision-making, 16
Decisions, educational, 22
Deficits, multiple, 329
Delinquents, 146, 147, 178
Detroit Tests of Learning Aptitude—Third Edition (Detroit 3), 14, 139
  Basic Information, 167
  in case report for Lourdes I., 252–259
  Design Reproduction, 13, 199
  Design Sequences, 139
  and Horn analysis, 52
  joint factor analysis, 169
  Picture Fragments, 158, 166, 176, 302
  Reversed Letters, 158
  Story Construction, 153, 158, 167, 179
  Symbolic Relations, 189
  theories behind, 51
  verbal/nonverbal grouping, 166
  Word Opposites, 166, 179

Developmental receptive language disorder, 213
Developmental Test of Visual-Motor Integration:
  in case report for Michael B., 339–346
Differential Abilities Scales (DAS), 14, 24, 139, 175
  in case report for Greg T., 393–401
  in case report for Jennie L., 201–208
  correlation with WISC-III/WISC-R, 169–171
  and *g,* 43
  and Horn-Cattell, 52, 151, 169
  joint analyses, 179
  Matrices, 170, 189
  Nonverbal Reasoning, 169, 171, 311
  Pattern Construction, 166, 170
  psychometric properties, 141
  Recall of Designs, 139, 170
  Sequential & Quantitative Reasoning, 14, 17, 154, 170, 180
  Spatial scale, 169
  Special Nonverbal Scale, 142
  Speed of Information Processing, 139
  theories behind, 51
  Verbal Ability, 142, 169
  verbal-nonverbal discrepancies, 169–171
Digit Span subtest, 58–61, 62–63, 77–80.
    See also Subtests overviews
  Arithmetic subtest and, 49
  associated factors, 47, 60, 62
  Backward subtest, 79, 232, 235–236
  Block Design subtest and, 89
  classification of, 43
  clinical considerations, 79–80
  comparisons with other subtests, 78
  Comprehension subtest and, 74
  distractibility factor, 213
  empirical analysis, 77–78
  Forward subtest, 79, 232, 235–236
  g factor, 52
  influences on, 316
  Information subtest and, 63
  memory assessment, 53, 150
  number ability, 13, 79
  Object Assembly subtest and, 92
  Picture Arrangement subtest and, 85
  Picture Completion subtest and, 80
  proportion of variance, 78

Digit Span subtest *(Continued)*
  psycholinguistic deficiency and, 157
  Similarities subtest and, 66
  specificity, 45, 77, 315
  summary of analysis, 77–80
  Symbol Search subtest and, 94
  tasks, 11, 17
  validity and, 211
  Vocabulary subtest and, 71
Distractibility, *see* Freedom from
    Distractibility (FD) factor
  assessment of, 70
  influence of, 69–70, 78–79, 83, 85, 91,
      93, 95–96
  triad, 104, 212
Divergent production (D) operation, 53
Doppelt, Jerome, 27
Duchenne muscular dystrophy, 213
Dyslexic children, 49, 55

Early environment, influence of, 64, 72
Ebonics, 162
Elephant story analogy, 28
Ellipsis, 73
Embedded Figures Test, 185, 186–187
Emotional disturbance/difficulties, 20–21,
    75, 213
  case study, 339–346
Emotional responses, 77
Empirical analysis methods, 42–47
  g loading, 41, 42–44
  intercorrelations, 41, 45
  proportions of variance associated with
      different factors, 41–42, 45–47
  reliability (split-half and test-retest), 41
  subtest specificity, 41, 44–45
Empirical analysis results:
  Arithmetic subtest, 68
  Block Design subtest, 89–90
  Coding subtest, 82–83
  Comprehension subtest, 73–74
  Digit Span subtest, 77–78
  Information subtest, 63
  Object Assembly subtest, 92
  Picture Arrangement subtest, 85–86
  Picture Completion subtest, 80
  Similarities subtest, 65–66
  Symbol Search subtest, 94–95
  Vocabulary subtest, 71

Encopresis (case study), 348–360
Epilepsy, 213
Evaluation (E) operation, 53–55
Examiner's role/responsibility, 15, 23–25,
    35
Exceptions to rules, 133–143
  prorated IQs, need for, 136–137
  retesting effects, 140–143
  verbal compensation of performance
      deficit, 137–140
Expression, 105
Externalizers, 213
Extremists, 27

Factors indexes, 97, 103–106. *See also*
    Freedom from Distractibility (FD)
    factor; Perceptual Organization
    (PO) factor; Processing Speed (PS)
    factor; Verbal Comprehension (VC)
    factor
  analysis, 103–105, 170
  defined, 103–105
  exceptional samples, 214, 216
  and Horn-Cattell, 52
  and information processing model,
      11–12. *See also* Information-
      processing model
  interpretation and, 100–101
  and model, 11–12
  Naglieri's alternate approach, 115
  pairing up, 105–106
Fatigue, 84, 96
FD, *see* Freedom from Distractibility (FD)
    factor
Feedback:
  benefits of, 91, 93
  utilizing, 67, 328
Fetal alcohol syndrome, 160
Field-dependence/field independence, 81,
    90, 93, 179, 185–187, 325
Fight item (deleted in WISC-III), 38, 39,
    87
Figural (F) content, 53–55
Flaws, 31
Fleischner, Jeannette, 28
Flexibility, 66, 68, 78, 93
Fluid Intelligence (Gf), 50–52, 167–170,
    176–180. *See also* Horn and Cattell's
    fluid-crystallized theory

vs. Crystallized Intelligence, *see* Horn and Cattell's fluid-crystallized theory
measurement of, 179
and Wechsler performance scale, 179–180
Follow-up questioning, 77
Foreign language background, influence of, 64, 72. *See also* Bilingualism
France, Alsace, 160
France, IQ gains in, 37
Freedom from Distractibility (FD) factor, 34, 57. *See also* Distractibility
Arithmetic subtest and, 47, 68, 103
associated subtests and, 47
Block Design subtest and, 90
case reports, 251–268
Coding subtest and, 83
Comprehension subtest and, 74
Digit Span subtest and, 78, 103
distractibility triad, 211–214
and factor pairing, 105–106
and Horn-Cattell theory, 168
Information subtest and, 63
interpretation of:
Backward Digit Span, 232, 235–236
clinical observations, 226–232
factor analysis, 103–105
Forward Digit Span, 232, 235–236
hypotheses corroboration, 237–241
profile fluctuations, 236–237
Object Assembly subtest and, 92
Picture Arrangement subtest and, 86
Picture Completion subtest and, 80
research analyses of, 212
and school learning problems, 182
Similarities subtest and, 66
Symbol Search subtest and, 94
timing of, 225–226
as validity scale, 210–211
Vocabulary subtest and, 71
Full Scale IQ, 7, 43, 98–99, 123, 143
and bilingual/bicultural children, 161
Hispanics, 161
interpretation of, 7, 98–99
and Macmann/Barnett, 28
meaningless statistic, 189
as a predictor, 22

retesting and, 140–141
Functional thinking, 73

g (general intelligence):
discrepancy and, 44
factor loading, 42–44, 123
orientation, 28–29
overvaluation of, 43
Ga, *see* Auditory Intelligence (Ga)
Gardner, Howard, 25
GATSB (Guide to the Assessment of Test Session Behavior), 9–10
Gc, *see* Crystallized Intelligence (Gc)
Gender, 9
Gender, significance of, 9
General ability, scoring and, 123
Geometric Design, 166
Germany, IQ gains in, 37
Gf, *see* Fluid Intelligence (Gf)
Gf-Gc theory, *see* Horn and Cattell's fluid-crystallized theory
Gifted children, 39
case study, 361–370
Hispanics, 159
identification of, 7
learning disabilities sample, 148
and speed, 196–198
Glatz, Susan, 338, 360, 401
Global scores, interpretation of, 122–132
Gonzalez, Jose, 370, 382, 392
Gordon Diagnostic Examination:
in case report for Michael B., 339–346
Gq, *see* Quantitative Thinking (Gq)
Grossman, Dana T., 338, 360, 401
Gs, *see* Broad Speediness (Gs)
Gsm, *see* Short-Term Acquisition and Retrieval (SAR or Gsm)
Guide to the Assessment of Test Session Behavior (GATSB), 9–10
Guilford's Structure of Intellect Model (SOI), 19, 50, 52–55
Gv, *see* Broad Visualization (Gv)

Handicaps, physical, 20, 200–201
Hearing-impaired, 20, 73, 151, 152. *See also* Auditory difficulty
Helping agent, 7
Heredity *vs.* environment, 6

Hispanics, 7, 9, 21, 56, 151, 158–161
  and Full Scale IQ, 22
  verbal-nonverbal discrepancies in, 29,
    158–161
Holistic processing, 300–304, 309
Holistic-simultaneous *vs.* linear sequential,
  164
Home environment, influence of, 43. *See
  also* Culture, influence of
Horn and Cattell's fluid-crystallized
    theory, 18, 19, 50–52, 167–184
  Binet-4 and, 172–174
  Comprehension factor, 19
  crystallized ability, 308
  DAS and, 169–171
  defined, 179
  fluid ability, 308, 311, 315
  Gc measurement, 167–168, 179
  Gf measurement, 167, 179–180
  Gv measurement, 179–180
  K-ABC and, 174–175
  KAIT and, 171–172
  learning disabilities and, 180–183
  socioeconomic influences, 183–184
  WJ-R and, 175–178
House-Tree-Person Test:
  in case report for Lucy O., 260–268
  in case report for Tony G., 331–338
Human Figure Drawings:
  in case report for Lourdes I., 252–259
Hypotheses:
  corroboration of, 237–241, 248–251
  generation of, 13–14, 15, 132–133, 304,
    306–316, 324
  goal of, 324
  guidelines for, 306–316

IEP (individualized education program), 35
Illinois Test of Psycholinguistic Abilities
    (ITPA), 33
Imagery, visual, 68
Impulsivity, 80–81, 87, 93
Individualized education program (IEP), 35
Individual uniqueness, 26, 32
Influences on subtest performance, 42
  Arithmetic subtest, 69
  Block Design subtest, 90
  Coding subtest, 83–84
  Comprehension subtest, 74–75

Digit Span subtest, 78
  Information subtest, 64
  Object Assembly subtest, 93
  Picture Arrangement subtest, 86
  Picture Completion subtest, 81
  Similarities subtest, 66–67
  Symbol Search subtest, 95
  Vocabulary subtest, 72
Information-processing model, 42,
    147–148, 151. *See also* Input;
    Integration/storage; Output
  components, 10–13
    input, 152–163, 284–290
    integration and storage, 163–187,
      290–297
    output, 188–201, 284–290
  planning, 299–304
  sequential processing, 297–299
  simultaneous processing, 297–304
  and treatment validity, 35
  and usefulness of WISC-III, 10–13
  utilization of, 10–13
  and verbal-nonverbal differences,
    147–148, 166
  verbal-nonverbal discrepancies,
    147–148, 166
Information subtest, 63–65. *See also*
    Subtests overviews
  Arithmetic subtest and, 68
  classification of, 43, 51
  clinical considerations, 64–65
  Coding subtest and, 82
  comparison with other subtests, 64
  Comprehension subtest and, 74
  correlates, 45
  Digit Span subtest and, 77
  empirical analysis, 63
  memory assessment, 53, 150
  Picture Arrangement subtest and, 85
  proportion of variance, 63
  Similarities subtest and, 66
  specificity, 45, 63
  summary of analysis, 63–65
  tasks, 10–11
  Vocabulary subtest and, 71
Input, 10, 12, 152–163, 284–290. *See also*
    Information-processing model
  Arithmetic subtest, 69
  Block Design subtest, 90

Coding subtest, 83
Comprehension subtest, 74
Digit Span subtest, 78
Information subtest, 64
Object Assembly subtest, 92
Picture Arrangement subtest, 86
Picture Completion subtest, 80
Similarities subtest, 66
Symbol Search subtest, 95
Vocabulary subtest, 71
Insecurity, 94
Integrated interpretive System Checklist
    for Behaviors Observed During
    Administration of WISC-III subtests,
    9
Integration and storage, 10, 47, 163–187,
    290–297. *See also* Information-
    processing model
    Arithmetic subtest, 69
    Block Design subtest, 90
    Coding subtest, 83
    Comprehension subtest, 74
    Digit Span subtest, 78
    and fluid *vs.* crystallized intelligence,
        167–184
    and Guilford's operation of evaluation,
        184–187
    Information subtest, 64
    Object Assembly subtest, 92–93
    Picture Arrangement subtest, 86
    Picture Completion subtest, 81
    Similarities subtest, 66
    Symbol Search subtest, 95
    verbal-nonverbal discrepancies and,
        163–187
    Vocabulary subtest, 72
Intelligence, hierarchical theory of, 297
"Intelligent" testing, 1–40
    basic tenets, 6–14
    clinical considerations, 15–16
    cultural considerations, 20–21
    effortful interpretation, 23–25
    integration of basic tenets, 14–25
    practical considerations, 20–21
    psychometric considerations, 15–16
    test bias, 21–23
    theoretical considerations, 16–20
Internalizers, 213
Interpersonal intelligence, 19

Interpreting WISC-III profile (7-step
    system), 97–143
    exceptions, *see* Exceptions to rules
    Full Scale IQ, 98–99
    hypothesis generation, *see* Hypotheses
    illustration of, 316–324
    steps summarized (table), 134–135
    strengths, *see* Strengths, interpreting
    validity factors ("small factors" FD and
        PS), 122, 209–268
    verbal/nonverbal dimensions, 122,
        144–208
    verbal-performance IQ discrepancy:
        abnormal size of, 115–122
        interpretability of, 102–115
        statistical significance, 99–102
    weaknesses, *see* Weaknesses,
        interpreting
Ipsative assessment/procedure, 5, 29–30,
    129
    profile interpretation, critics of, 32
IQs, prorated, 136–137
IQs, time trends in, 37–38
IQ-testing opponents, *see* Critics; Critics,
    response to
ITPA, *see* Illinois Test of Psycholinguistic
    Abilities (ITPA)
ITPA Auditory Reception, 178

Japan, IQ gains in, 37
Japanese language, 21
Juvenile diabetes (case study), 361–370

K-ABC, *see* Kaufman Assessment Battery
    for Children (K-ABC)
KAIT, *see* Kaufman Adolescent and Adult
    Intelligence Test (KAIT)
Katz, Danica, 370, 392
Kaufman, Nadeen, 268, 338, 360, 370,
    382, 392, 401
Kaufman Adolescent and Adult Intelligence
    Test (KAIT), 14, 17, 24, 176
    Auditory Comprehensions, 172
    in case report for Ira G., 371–382
    correlation with WISC-III, 171–172
    Crystallized IQ, 142
    Definitions, 179
    Double Meanings, 172, 179
    Famous Faces, 172, 179

Kaufman Adolescent and Adult Intelligence
Test (KAIT) *(Continued)*
Fluid IQ, 142
and Horn analysis, 52, 151, 169, 171–172
joint analyses, 179
joint factor analysis, 171–172
Logical Steps, 14, 172, 180, 184, 302,
304, 311
Memory for Block Designs, 199
Mystery Codes, 17, 139, 172, 180, 302,
311
psychometric properties, 141
Rebus Learning, 17, 172, 180
theories behind, 17, 50
and verbal-nonverbal discrepancies,
171–172
Kaufman Assessment Battery for Children
(K-ABC), 14, 17, 139, 176
Achievement Scale, 12, 142, 174–175
and autism, 156
and brain studies, 145–146
in case report for Dana Christine T.,
383–392
in case report for Jennie L., 201–208
in case report for Lucy O, 260–268
in case report for Nicole A., 361–370
and cerebral damage study, 145–146
correlations with WISC-III, 174–175
Faces & Places, 12, 22, 158, 175, 179
and *g*, 43
and Gc factor, 175
Gestalt Closure, 158, 176, 301
Hand Movements, 13, 156, 199
and Horn-Cattell, 52, 151, 169, 174
joint analyses, 176
and language disorders, 155
Matrix Analogies, 174
Mental Processing, 156
Photo Series, 139, 174, 189, 199
psychometric properties, 141
Reading Understanding, 12
Riddles, 175, 179
Sequential Processing Scale, 33
Simultaneous Processing Scale, 142,
155, 174–175
Spatial Memory, 176
theories behind, 17, 51
and treatment validity, lack of, 33–34
Triangles, 156, 176, 199

verbal-nonverbal discrepancies, 174–175
Word Order, 158
Kaufman Brief Intelligence Test (K-BIT),
139, 202, 250
Definitions, 179
Matrices, 139, 154, 189, 205
Kaufman Short Neurological Assessment
Procedure (K-SNAP):
Four Letter Words, 241, 250
Gestalt Closure, 158, 302, 312
Kaufman Test of Educational
Achievement—Comprehensive Form
(K-TEA), 240
in case report for Dana Christine T.,
383–392
in case report for Greg T., 393–401
in case report for Lucy O., 251,
260–268
in case report for Nicole A., 361–370
Mathematics Applications, 241
Mathematics Computation, 241
K-BIT, *see* Kaufman Brief Intelligence
Test (K-BIT)
Kinetic Family Drawing:
in case report for Lucy O., 260–268
in case report for Michael B., 339–346
in case report for Tony G., 331–338
K-SNAP, *see* Kaufman Short Neurological
Assessment Procedure (K-SNAP)
K-TEA, *see* Kaufman Test of Educational
Achievement (K-TEA)

Language disorders, 154–155
case study, 383–392
Larry P. case, 2, 26
Lateral Dominance Examination:
in case report for Michael B., 339–346
Learning-disabilities/problems, 56
Arithmetic subtest and, 69, 70
case studies, 339–346, 348–360,
371–382, 393–401
Coding subtest and, 83, 85
communication abilities and, 152
diagnosis of, 325
Digit Span subtest and, 78
distractibility triad, 212
Gf-Gc theory and, 180–183
"gifted" sample, 148
information-processing model and, 10

recategorization system and, 56
recommendations for, 328–329
strengths and, 302
Symbol Search subtest and, 95–96
Learning Disability Index (LDI), 299
Learning environments, 325–326
"Learning" tasks, 17
Limitations, awareness of, 24
Limits, see Testing-the-limits
Lincoln, Alan J., 346
Linear sequential vs.
    holistic-simultaneous, 164
Luria's neuropsychological model, 17, 60
Lynn, Alaina, 259

McCarthy, Dorothea, 1, 28
McCarthy Draw-A-Child:
    in case report for Nicole A., 361–370
McDermott-Glutting, see Critics
Macmann and Barnett, see Critics
Mandatory reevaluation, 143
Manipulation, 88
Matrix Analogies Test, 139, 189
Mazes, 43, 45, 58, 59, 60, 61–62, 123
Memory (M) operation, 53–55
Memory:
    assessment of, 53, 70
    long-term, 150
    recommendations for problems, 329
    rote, 79
    short-term, 84, 96, 99, 150, 157
    working memory, 11, 19, 48, 54, 223,
        232, 233, 251
Mental retardation, 7, 75, 186, 213, 325,
    328–329
    Arithmetic subtest and, 70
    case study, 201–208
Methode clinique, 8
Mexican-Americans, 187
Milk and water vs. beer and wine, 39
Minority groups, 2, 7, 22, 36, 56, 146. See
    also African-Americans; Hispanics
Modality groups, 33
Modality training studies, 35
Models:
    information-processing model, see
        Information-processing model
    fluid-crystallized theory, see Horn and
        Cattell's fluid crystallized theory

recategorization system, see Bannatyne's
    recategorization system
structure of intellect (SOI), see
    Guilford's structure of intellect
    model (SOI)
Moral sense, development of, 74
Motivational problems:
    Coding subtest and, 84–85
    detection of, 210–211
    Digit Span subtest and, 79
    recommendations for, 330
    Symbol Search subtest and, 95–96
Multiple intelligence theory, 19
Multiple sources, importance of, 13–14,
    157

Naglieri's alternate approach, 115
Naglieri's Matrix Analogies Test, 139,
    189. See also Das-Naglieri Cognitive
    Assessment System
Native Americans, 21, 28, 36, 56, 148,
    151, 158–161
    and verbal vs. performance, 29
Navajos, 29, 148, 159
Negativism, 67, 75, 78–79, 81
Netherlands, IQ gains in, 37
Neurological theory, 17
Neuropsychological batteries, 7, 302
New Zealand sample, 149
Noncognitive explanations, 43
Nonintellective factors, 325
Nonverbal problem solving:
    Perceptual Organization (PO) Index
        and, 210
    speed of, see Speed of performance
Nonverbal thinking, 105
Normative interpretation, 30
Number ability, 13, 79, 105

Object Assembly subtest, 92–94. See also
    Subtests overview
    autistic children and, 155
    Block Design subtest and, 89
    bonus points, 93
    classification of, 43, 51
    clinical considerations, 93–94
    comparison with other subtests, 92–93
    coordination and, 13, 200
    development of, 39

Object Assembly subtest *(Continued)*
  empirical analysis, 92
  g factor, 52
  and Gv factor, 176
  obsessiveness during, 9
  performance deficits and, 138
  Picture Completion subtest and, 80
  proportion of variance, 92
  reasoning, assessment of, 150
  specificity, 9, 45, 92, 315
  speed factor, 192, 210
  summary of analysis, 92–94
  tasks, 11
Observations, significance of, 9, 49, 310,
    312–313
Obsessive compulsive disorder (case
    study), 252–259
Obsessiveness, 67, 73, 76, 82, 84, 90, 93, 95
Ojibwa Indians, 160
Operations dimension (Guilford SOI
    model), 53
Opponents of IQ testing, *see* Critics
Orthopedic handicaps, 200–201
Otitis media, 160
Output, 10, 12, 47, 188–201. *See also*
    Information-processing model
  Arithmetic subtest, 69
  Block Design subtest, 90
  Coding subtest, 83
  Comprehension subtest, 74–75
  coordination problems, 188–190
  Digit Span subtest, 78
  Information subtest, 64
  Object Assembly subtest, 93
  Picture Arrangement subtest, 86
  Picture Completion subtest, 80
  Similarities subtest, 66–67
  speed of nonverbal problem solving,
    191–201
  Symbol Search subtest, 95
  verbal-nonverbal discrepancies and,
    188–201
  Vocabulary subtest, 72
Overelaboration, 73
Overinclusiveness, 73

Parental education, 183
Parente, Ana, 268

Passivity, 78
PASS (Planning-Attention-Simultaneous-
    Successive) model, 4, 17, 20, 36, 299.
    See also Das-Naglieri
Perceptual Organization (PO) factor, 34,
    46, 57–58, 102–106
  Arithmetic subtest and, 68
  Block Design subtest and, 46, 103
  Coding subtest and, 82
  Comprehension subtest, 74
  Digit Span subtest, 78
  factor pairing, 105–106
  and Horn-Cattell theory, 168
  Information subtest and, 63
  Object Assembly subtest and, 46, 92,
    103
  Picture Arrangement subtest and, 46,
    85, 103
  Picture Completion subtest and, 46, 80,
    103
  Similarities subtest and, 66
  Symbol Search subtest and, 94
  Vocabulary subtest and, 71
Performance ability, scoring and, 124
Performance deficit, verbal compensation
    for, 137–140
Performance IQ, *see* Verbal-performance
    IQ discrepancy
Performance Scale, 29, 32. *See also*
    specific subtests
Perseveration, 73, 82, 85, 91, 93
Persistence, 84, 91, 93, 95
Person-relative metrics, 30
Petterson, Patricia, 268, 338, 360, 401
Piaget, Jean, 8, 17, 19, 326
Piaget-based methods/curriculums, 184
Picture Arrangement subtest, 85–89, 180.
    See also Subtests overviews
  Arithmetic subtest and, 68
  associated factors, 47
  bonus points, 210
  brain functioning and, 300–301
  classification of, 43, 51
  clinical considerations, 87–89
  clinical information source, 15
  comparison with other subtests, 86
  Comprehension subtest and, 87
  correlates, 45

difference from WISC-R, 38
Digit Span subtest and, 77
factor pattern, mild exception to, 103
influences on, 316
and practice effect, 31
proportion of variance, 85–86
psycholinguistic deficiency and, 156–157
semantic evaluation, 55
sequencing ability of, 298–299
social understanding, assessment of, 150
specificity, 45, 85
speed and, 89, 192–194
summary of analysis, 85–89
tasks, 11
verbal mediation assessment, 150
Picture Completion subtest, 80–82, 180.
    See also Subtests overviews
Block Design subtest and, 89
classification of, 43
clinical considerations, 81–82
Coding subtest and, 82
comparison with other subtests, 80–81
difference from WISC-R, 38
empirical analysis, 80
memory assessment, 150
Object Assembly subtest and, 92
psycholinguistic deficiency and, 157
specificity, 45, 80
summary of analysis, 80–82
Symbol Search subtest and, 94
tasks, 11
Planning-Attention-Simultaneous-
    Successive, see PASS model
PO, see Perceptual Organization (PO)
    factor
PPVT-R, 179
Practice effect, 31–33, 149
Primary Mental Abilities IQ (PMA IQ),
    196
Problem-solving:
Block Design subtest and, 91
nonverbal, see Nonverbal problem-solving
Object Assembly subtest and, 93
Picture Arrangement subtest and, 87
Procedures, standardized:
benefits of, 27
need for, 8–10
Process groups, 33

Processing Speed (PS) factor:
Arithmetic subtest and, 68
Block Design subtest and, 90
case reports, 251–268
Coding subtest and, 47, 60, 83, 103
Comprehension subtest and, 74
Digit Span subtest and, 78
factor pairing, 105–106
Information subtest and, 63
interpreting, 103–105
    clinical observations, 242–247
    hypotheses corroboration, 248–251
    overview, 103–105
    profile fluctuations, 247–248
    timing of, 241–242
low, 210
Object Assembly subtest and, 92
Picture Arrangement subtest and, 86
Picture Completion subtest and, 80
Similarities subtest and, 66
Symbol Search subtest and, 95, 103
validity scale, as, 210–211
Vocabulary subtest and, 71
Products dimension (Guilford SOI model),
    53
Profile interpretation, see Interpreting
    WISC-III profile (7-step system)
value of, 26
Profile malpractice, 29–33
Projective Drawings:
in case report for Greg T., 393–401
in case report for James C., 348–370
in case report for Nicole A., 361–370
Proportion of variance (attributed to
    factors), see Empirical analysis
    methods; Empirical analysis results;
    specific subtests
Prorated IQs, 136–137
PS, see Processing Speed (PS) factor
Psycholinguistic deficiency, 152–154, 178
autistic children, 155–156
clues of, 156–158
overview, 152–154
profile interpretation and, 156–158
severe language disorder, 154–155
verbal-nonverbal discrepancies,
    generally, 152–154
Psychologist, role of, 100, 327

Psychometric tree, 2–3
"Pure" factors, 100, 110
Puzzles, manipulation of, 93–94

Q methodology, 32
Quantitative reasoning, 302
Quantitative Thinking (Gq), 50–52, 70.
    See also Horn and Cattell's
    fluid-crystallized theory

Randolph, Paul, 370, 392
Raven-like tests/skill, 180, 189
Raven's Matrices Test, 139
Reading, influence of, 64, 67
Reading disabled children, 56, 212, 299,
    304
    case study, 260–268
Reasoning:
    ability, 308
    acquired knowledge and, 290–297
    verbal and performance scales, 150
Recategorization system, 55–58
Recommendations, suggestions for,
    327–330
Record form, 97, 99–100
Reflectivity, 90, 93, 193
Reliability, *see* Empirical analysis
        methods; Empirical analysis results
Remediation, suggestions for, 326–327
Repression, 72
Reschly-Tilly approach, 35
Response, *see specific subtests*
    speed, measurement of, 105. *See also*
        Speed of performance
Retesting effect, *see* Practice effect
Rigidity, 68, 91, 93
Rod-and-Frame test, 185, 186
Rorschach Inkblot Test, 186
    in case report for Greg T., 393–401
    in case report for James C., 348–360
    in case report for Lourdes I., 252–259
    in case report for Michael B., 339–346
    in case report for Tony G., 331–338
Rote memory, 79
Russian language, 21

Same/alike concepts, 68
SAR, *see* Short-Term Acquisition and
    Retrieval (SAR or Gsm)

SCAD profile, 219–227
Scatter, subtest (illustration), 120–121,
    133
Schizophrenia, 136, 213
School learning:
    influence of, 64, 69, 72
    deficit areas, 182
    distractibility triad and, 213
    problems (case report), 339–346
    recommendations for, 327
Seashore Measures of Musical Talents, 302
Self-concept, 91, 93
Self-references, 73
Semantic (M) content, 53–55
Sentence Completion Test:
    in case report for Greg T., 393–401
    in case report for James C., 348–360
    in case report for Lucy O., 260–268
Sequencing Ability (Bannatyne), 55
Sequential category, 57
Sequential processing, 105, 298–299
Sequential reasoning, 302
Sequential/simultaneous, 174–175
Shared abilities, 273, 275, 307. *See also*
    Abilities
Shepherd, Margaret Jo, 28
Short-Term Acquisition and Retrieval
    (SAR or Gsm), 50–52, 139, 168. *See*
    also Horn and Cattell's
    fluid-crystallized theory
Significance, calculating, 101–102
Similarities subtest, 65–68. *See also*
    Subtests overviews
    abstract *vs.* concrete responses, 67
    Arithmetic subtest and, 68
    classification of, 43, 51
    clinical considerations, 67–68
    Coding subtest and, 82
    comparison with other subtests, 66–67
    Comprehension subtest and, 74
    correlates, 45
    and creativity, 68
    Digit Span subtest and, 77
    and ellipsis, 69
    empirical analysis, 65–66
    and feedback, 67
    fluid component, 67
    Information subtest and, 63
    obsessive responses, 67

and overelaboration, 69
overinclusive responses, 67
overlearned associations, 67
performance scale and, 166
psycholinguistic deficiency and, 156
rigidity *vs.* flexibility, 68
sample item, 68
and self-references, 69
specificity, 45, 65
summary of analysis, 65–68
tasks, 10–11
verbal mediation assessment, 150
Vocabulary subtest and, 71
Simultaneous/sequential, 174–175,
298–299
Sioux, 159
Slow learners, recommendations for,
328–329
Small factors, 122
Social intelligence, 70
Social sensitivity, 87
Social understanding, 150
Socioeconomic status, 9
and Gf-Gc theory, 183–184
Software, interactive, 14, 26
SOI, *see* Guilford's Structure of Intellect
Model (SOI)
Sontag, Marvin, 27
Spatial Ability (Bannatyne), 55
Spatial-Simultaneous subtest, 297–298
Spatial subtest, 57, 297
Special education, reevaluations and, 143
Specificity, 315. *See also specific subtests*
Speed of performance, 30, 190–201
ability level and, 193–195
behavioral variables and, 195–196
chronological age and, 191–193
giftedness and, 196–198
orthopedic handicaps and, 200–201
supplementary testing for, 198–200
understanding of impact of time, 198
Stability, 31, 32
Standardized procedures, *see* Procedures,
standardized
Stanford-Binet—Fourth Edition (Binet-4),
17, 50, 139, 142, 151, 158, 169,
172–180, 229, 231, 238–241, 249,
251, 273, 287, 298, 312
Abstract/Visual Reasoning Scale, 142

Absurdities, 153, 158, 173, 174, 179
analogs to WISC-III and K-ABC, 142
Bead Memory, 173
in case report for Jennie L., 201–208
in case report for Lourdes I., 252–259
Copying, 139, 173, 176
correlation WISC-R/WISC-III, 173
Equation Building, 14, 174, 180
and *g*, 43
Gc factor, 172–174
Gv factor, 172–173
and Horn-Cattell model, 52, 151, 169,
172–174
joint analyses, 176
Matrices, 173, 174
Memory for Sentences, 173
Number Series, 173, 174, 180
Paper Folding and Cutting, 139, 158,
174, 176, 189, 199
Pattern Analysis, 173, 176
quantitative tests, 173
theories behind, 17, 50
verbal-nonverbal discrepancies,
172–174
Verbal Reasoning Scale, 142
Stencil Design, 139
Steps (7) in interpreting WISC-III profile,
97–143. *See also* Interpreting
WISC-III profile
table summary, 134–135
Sternberg, Robert, 25
Storage, *see* Information-processing model
Story Construction subtest, 166
Strengths:
ability comparisons, 307–309
determination of, 122–123
integration of, 310–313
selection of, 306–307
Structure of intellect model, *see* Guilford's
Structure of Intellect Model (SOI)
Subtest analysis methods, 41–63. *See*
specific subtest
abilities shared with other subtests, 41,
47–58
as behavior samples, 7–8
clinical considerations, 42, 58
deviant scores, 136–137
empirical, 41–47
fluctuations, 132–133, 304–324

Subtest analysis methods *(Continued)*
  g loading, 41, 42–44
  influences (background/behavioral),
    42, 49
  intercorrelations, 41, 45
  measurement of, 6–7
  model (input–integration–
    storage–output), 42. *See also*
    Information-processing model
  profile interpretation, 269–271,
    283–284
  proportions of variance associated with
    different factors, 41–42, 45–47
  reliability (split-half and test-retest), 41
  specificity, 44, 45. *See specific subtests*
  subtest specificity, 41, 44–45
Subtest profiles:
  hypotheses generation, 132–133
  interpreting strengths/weaknesses,
    122–132
  pairwise comparisons, 129–130
    empirical method, 125–130
    V-P IQ discrepancies of 0–18 points,
      123–124
    V-P IQ discrepancies of 19 or more
      points, 124
Subtests overviews (tables/lists with all):
  abilities (illustrative) both
    verbal/performance, 150
  Bannatyne categories (classification as),
    55
  differences required for significance,
    126, 127
  factor loadings (VC, PO, FD, PS), 103
  factor loadings (verbal/performance),
    165
  g measurement assessment
    (good/fair/poor), 43
  Guilford's SOI model (classification
    according to), 54
  Horn factors (Gc, Gf, Gv, SAR, Gs),
    51–52
  proportion of variance, 46, 48
  specificity (ample/adequate/inadequate),
    45
Subtest summaries, 63–96. *For
    breakdown, see specific subtest*
  Arithmetic subtest, 68–71
  Block Design subtest, 89–91

Coding subtest, 82–85
Comprehension subtest, 73–77
Digit Span subtest, 77–80
Information subtest, 63–65
Object Assembly, 92–94
Picture Arrangement subtest, 85–89
Picture Completion subtest, 80–82
Similarities subtest, 65–68
Symbol Search, 94–96
Vocabulary subtest, 71–73
Supplementary testing, 7–8, 18, 198–200,
    313
  for auditory-motor problems, 158
  for children with auditory stimuli
    problems, 153
  for performance deficit, 139
  for practice effect, 141
  for visual/vocal problems, 158
Symbolic (S) content, 53–55
Symbol Search subtest, 94–96. *See also*
    Subtests overviews
  abstractions, 11
  addition of, 209
  classification of, 43
  clinical considerations, 96
  Coding *vs.*, 59–61, 82
  comparison with other subtests, 95
  coordination and, 13, 200
  empirical analysis, 94–95
  g factor, 52
  influences on, 316
  Information subtest and, 63
  performance deficit and, 138
  performance profile, 299
  processing speed, assessment of, 150
  psycholinguistic deficiency and, 157
  scoring caution, 96
  Similarities subtest and, 66
  specificity, 45, 94
  substitute for Coding subtest, 58, 59–61
  summary of analysis, 53–55
  tasks, 17
  validity and, 211
  visual-motor coordination, 139
  Vocabulary subtest and, 71

Tagalog, 21
TAT, *see* Thematic Apperception Test
    (TAT)

Test abuse, 7
Test bias, 21–23. *See also* Bias, test
Testing environment, 79
Testing-the-limits, 39, 79
  Arithmetic subtest, 70
  Block Design subtest, 91, 139
  Coding subtest, 85
  Comprehension subtest, 75
  Information subtest, 65
  nonverbal items, 139
  Picture Arrangement subtest, 88
  procedures for, 8
  Symbol Search subtest, 96
Test of Nonverbal Intelligence (TONI), 139
Test-retest, 31
Test-teach-test dynamic, 8
Test-train-retest paradigm, 36
Thematic Apperception Test (TAT):
  in case report for Greg T., 393–401
  in case report for James C., 348–360
  in case report for Michael B., 339–346
  in case report for Tony G., 331–338
Thorndike, Robert L., 27
Thought disorders, 88
Time pressure, 69, 81, 84, 86, 90, 93, 95
Tlingit, 159
Tohono O'odham Indians, 159, 160
TONI, *see* Test of Nonverbal Intelligence
  (TONI)
"Top Ten Reasons Why . . . ," 59
Tourette's syndrome (case study),
  252–259
Treatment validity, 33–37
Trends (over time) in IQs, 37–38
Triarchic theory, 19

Unilateral lesions, 213. *See also* Brain
  damage
Uniqueness, individual, 26, 32

VC, *see* Verbal Comprehension (VC) factor
VC-PO discrepancy, *see* Verbal-nonverbal
  discrepancies
Verbal compensation of performance
  deficit, 137–140
  sample profile (Aliza G.), 138
Verbal Comprehension (VC) factor, 34,
  102, 103–106
  Arithmetic subtest and, 47, 68

Block Design subtest and, 47, 89
Coding subtest and, 82
Comprehension subtest, 74, 103
Digit Span subtest and, 78
Factor Indexes, pairing of, 105–106
Information subtest, 63, 103
interpretation of, 103–105
Object Assembly subtest and, 47, 92
Picture Arrangement subtest and, 85
Picture Completion subtest and, 46, 80
Similarities subtest, 66, 103
Symbol Search subtest and, 94
variance, 46
Vocabulary subtest, 71, 103
Verbal Conceptualization Ability
  (Bannatyne), 55, 105
Verbal intelligence, nonverbal vs., 164–167
Verbal IQ, performance *vs.*, *see*
  Verbal-Performance IQ discrepancy
Verbal Mediation, 150
Verbal-nonverbal discrepancies, 144–208.
  See also Interpreting WISC-III profile
  meaning of large discrepancies, 148–150
  overview of, 144–150
    children with unilateral brain lesions,
      145–146
    and the information-processing model
      (input–integration–storage–
      output), 147–148
    search for characteristic profiles,
      146–147
    what WISC-III discrepancies measure,
      140–152
Verbal-performance IQ discrepancy, 29,
  99–102, 115–122, 122–124
  determining abnormality, 115–122
  determining interpretability, 102–115
  questions (4) to ask, 108
  determining statistical significance,
    101–102
  empirical and historical considerations,
    100
  exceptions to the rules, 133
  illustrative profile, 120–121
Verbal Scale, *see specific subtests*
Verbal subtests, character of, 10. *See*
  specific subtests
Verbal visual-spatial stimuli,
  interpretation of, 164, 166

Vietnamese language, 21
Visual acuity, 88
Visual impairment, 84, 96
Visual-motor coordination, 105, 139
Visual perception, 88
Visual-perceptual/visual-motor problems:
   case sample, 153–154
Visual processing problems, 154
Vocabulary subtest, 71–73. *See also*
      Subtests overviews
   Arithmetic subtest and, 68
   autistic children and, 155
   clang associations, 72
   classification of, 43, 51
   clinical considerations, 72–73
   comparison with other subtests, 71–72
   Comprehension subtest and, 74
   concept formation assessment, 150
   conflict-laden items, 72
   correlates, 45
   Digit Span subtest and, 77
   empirical analysis, 71
   and hearing difficulties, 73
   Information subtest and, 63
   obsessive children, 73
   overelaboration/overinclusiveness,
         ellipsis, self-references, 73
   perseveration, 73
   Picture Arrangement subtest and, 85
   proportion of variance, 71
   psycholinguistic deficiency and,
         156–157
   recurring themes in responses, 72
   Similarities subtest and, 66
   specificity, 45, 71
   summary of analysis, 71–73
   tasks, 10–11
V-P IQ discrepancies:
   and treatment validity, 34
V-P IQ discrepancy, *see* Verbal-nonverbal
      discrepancies

WAIS, *see* Wechsler Adult Intelligence
      Scale (WAIS)
WAIS-R, *see* Wechsler Adult Intelligence
      Scale—Revised (WAIS-R)
Weaknesses:
   comparison of, 309–310
   determination of, 122–123

improvement of, 327–328
integration of, 310–313
Wechsler, David, ix–xv, 27–28, 209
   view of intelligence, 16
Wechsler Adult Intelligence Scale (WAIS):
   and delinquents, 147
   and gains in IQs, 38
   and retesting, 143
   and right-hemisphere damage, 179
   and testing of delinquents, 147
Wechsler Adult Intelligence
      Scale—Revised (WAIS-R), 39
   and autism, 155
   and bonus points on Arithmetic, 70
   and delinquents, 147
   discrepancies in, 29
   factor analysis, 107
   and gains in IQs, 38
   joint analyses, 175, 179
   and life span changes, 29
   Picture Arrangement, 89, 104
   Picture Completion, 176
   retesting, 140
   and right-hemisphere damage, 179
   two-factor solution for, 165
   verbal-nonverbal discrepancies, 171
   verbal/performance correlations,
         165
   vs. WISC-III, 40
Wechsler-Bellevue, 18, 37, 100, 105
Wechsler Individual Achievement Test
      (WIAT):
   in case report for Michael B., 297,
         339–346
   in case report for Tony G., 297,
         331–338
   and cross-validation sample, 43, 103
   GATSB for, 227
   for low score on Bannatyne's Acquired
         Knowledge grouping, 295
   Numerical Operations, 241
   Mathematics Reasoning, 241
Wechsler Intelligence Scale for
      Children—Revised (WISC-R), 2
   and African-Americans, 12
   Arithmetic (no bonus points), 70
   and Bannatyne categories, 57
   behavior during, 9, 21
   black and white pictures, 38

and brain-damaged children, 145–146
clinical items eliminated from
    WISC-III, 87
and Coding or Mazes, 59
correlations with Binet-4, 173
correlations with DAS, 170
correlations with K-ABC, 174–175
correlations with WJ-R (table), 177
and delinquents, 146
factor structure, 104, 171–172
and FD factors, 57
and gains in IQs, 38
and hearing-impaired children, 152
joint factor analysis, 171–172
large V-P IQ discrepancies, 149
and learning disabilities, 182
and Mazes, 61
and practice effects, 31
and retesting, 140
same name factors, 140
Similarities (no sample item), 68
supplementary subtests, 60
and treatment validity, 33
verbal-performance discrepancy,
    116–118
vs. WISC-III, 37–39
WISC-III differences, 88–89, 104
Wechsler Intelligence Scale for
    Children—Third Edition
    (WISC-III):
and Horn's theory, 19
and learning tasks, 17
Performance Scale, 18
and practice effect, 31
record form, 97, 99–100
and reevaluating children (caution), 143
Verbal Scale, 18
vs. WAIS-R, 40
vs. WISC-R, 37–39
vs. WPPSI-R, 39–40
Wechsler Preschool and Primary Scale of
    Intelligence (WPPSI), 100
Hispanics and American Indians, 159,
    160
verbal vs. nonverbal intelligence, 165,
    166
Wechsler Preschool and Primary Scale of
    Intelligence—Revised (WPPSI-R),
    100

distractibility factor, 212
and retesting, 140
speed, emphasis on, 39
two-factor solution for, 165
vs. WISC-III, 37, 39–40
Wesman, Alexander, 27
WIAT, see Wechsler Individual
    Achievement Test (WIAT)
WISC, see Wechsler Intelligence Scale for
    Children (WISC)
WISC-R, see Wechsler Intelligence Scale
    for Children—Revised (WISC-R)
WISC-III, see Wechsler Intelligence Scale
    for Children—Third Edition
    (WISC-III)
Witt-Gresham, 33–38. See also Opponents
    of IQ testing
WJ-R, see Woodcock-Johnson
    Psycho-Educational
    Battery—Revised (WJ-R)
Woodcock-Johnson Psycho-Educational
    Battery—Revised (WJ-R), 14, 17, 24
academic achievement, 355
Achievement:
    in case report for Dana Christine T.,
        383–392
    in case report for Ira G., 371–382
    in case report for James C., 348–360
Analysis-Synthesis, 17, 180, 184, 302,
    311
Cognitive:
    in case report for Dana Christine T.,
        383–392
    in case report for Greg T., 393–401
    in case report for Ira G., 371–382
    in case report for James C., 348–360
    in case report for Jennie L., 201–208
    in case report for Nicole A., 361–370
Cognitive Ability, 175, 178
Concept Formation, 158, 180, 302, 311
correlations with WISC-R, 177
correlations with WISC-III, 175–178
Cross Out, 13
Fluid Reasoning Scale, 154
four factors, 178
G factors, 175–176
Gv factor, 166, 176
and Horn-Cattell, 52, 151, 175–178
and information-processing model, 178

Woodcock-Johnson Psycho-Educational
    Battery—Revised (WJ-R)
    (Continued)
  joint analyses, 169, 176
  Memory for Names, 17
  Oral Vocabulary, 179
  Picture Recognition, 176
  Picture Vocabulary, 158, 179
  PS factor tests, 139
  psychometric properties, 141
  Spatial Relations, 139, 189
  theories behind, 17, 51
  Verbal Analogies, 179

  verbal-nonverbal discrepancies,
      175–178
  Visual Closure, 158, 176, 301–302
Work habits, 91, 93, 330
Working memory, 11, 19, 48, 54, 223,
    232, 233, 251
WPPSI-R, *see* Wechsler Preschool and
    Primary Scale of
    Intelligence—Revised (WPPSI-R)
WRAT-R, 26
Wrong responses, 65

Zimmerman, Irla Lee, 212